HARD LOOKS™

I'VE SPENT MY LIFE BATTLING THE BEAST,

from places people shouldn't go to places that shouldn't exist. The beast is child abuse, and this is what I've learned: behavior is the truth. Evil exists. Predators stalk among us, giggling at our fascination, sneering at our naive belief in their "rehabilitation." Darwin is recoiling in his grave, gasping at how our species has failed to master evolution, fearing our fate. I turned to "fiction" because I wanted a bigger jury than I'd ever find in a courtroom. I don't promise to entertain you. But I do promise you some truth-revealing behavior of my own.

This collection originated as prose, in a great number of forums. When Dark Horse proposed doing these stories in "graphic novel" format, I was skeptical. That is, until I heard I'd be working with magnificent writers like Joe Lansdale and James Colbert and Chet Williamson and Charles de Lint. And when I saw the incredible artwork of Geof Darrow and Gary Gianni and James O'Barr and David Lloyd and Harry Morris, I was hooked. Good thing I was — the writers didn't just "adapt" any more than the artists just "illustrated." My religion is that of the guerilla fighter: gestalt. I believe the whole is greater than the sum of its parts. Presenting my work in this format has been the difference between a newly mined rock and a fully faceted diamond . . . dimensionally realized beyond my individual ability to do so.

The straightest way to characterize what you're about to read is mini-movies. And not silent ones.

If this stuff hits you, if it makes you angry, if it moves you to <u>do</u> something, I have my reward. If you don't like the material, I'll take the weight. But if you do, put the credit where it belongs . . . on the writers and artists who collaborated so beautifully. And on Dark Horse for taking the risk.

Andrew Vachss has been a federal investigator in sexually transmitted diseases, a social caseworker, a community organizer, and has directed a maximum-security prison for "aggressive-violent" youthful offenders. Now a lawyer in private practice, he represents children and youth exclusively. Vachss is the author of several novels in the "Burke" series, as well as Shella, Batman: The Ultimate Evil, and Cross: Genesis. Special projects include Another Chance to Get It Right, a "children's book for adults," from Dark Horse, and the forthcoming La Curazon del Niñez. His non-fiction work has appeared in Parade, Antæus, The New York Times, and numerous other forums. His books have been translated into twenty languages and have won The Grand Prix de Littérature Policiére (France), The Falcon Award (Japan), and The Deutschen Krimi Preis (Germany). The stories contained in this collection appear, along with others, in prose form in Born Bad (Vintage), and his latest novel, False Allegations, will be published by Knopf next month. Vachss was born in New York City, lived and worked in numerous locations from Chicago to Biafra (Nigeria, during the 1968-69 civil war), and lectured all over the world. Vachss now lives, reluctantly and temporarily, in the city of his birth.

ANDREW VACHSS

HARD LOOKS

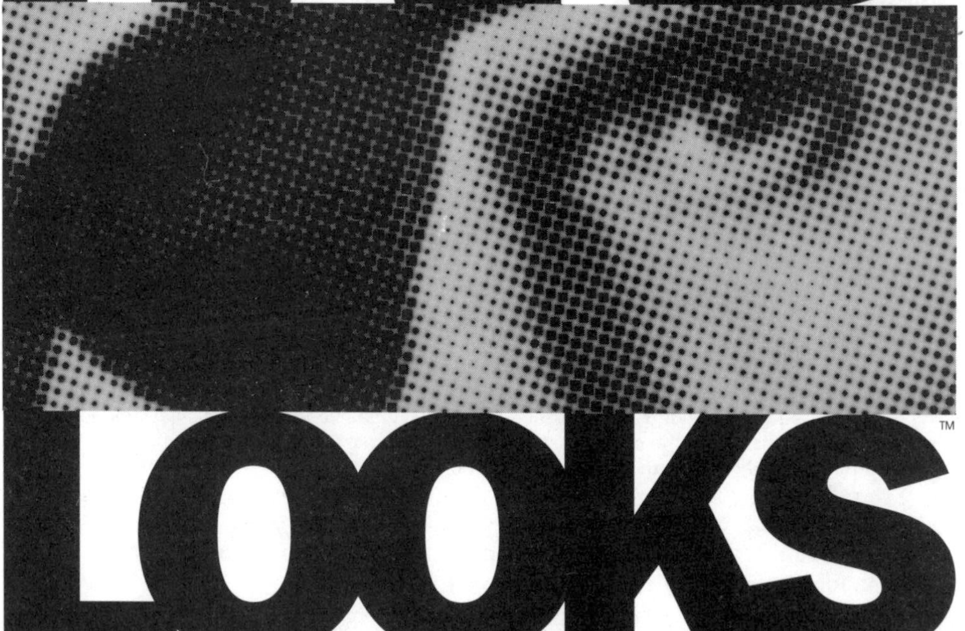

ADAPTED STORIES

DARK HORSE COMICS®

collection designer MARK COX
collection design manager BRIAN GOGOLIN
film coordinator RICH POWERS
publisher MIKE RICHARDSON

Published by
Dark Horse Comics, Inc.
10956 SE Main Street
Milwaukie, OR 97222

First edition: September 1996
ISBN: 1-56971-209-3

10 9 8 7 6 5 4 3 2 1
Printed in Canada

This book features twenty stories from the Dark Horse comic-book series *Hard Looks*™. Seven of these stories were published in the first-edition collection; the remaining thirteen are collected here for the first time.

executive vice president NEIL HANKERSON
vice president of publishing DAVID SCROGGY
vice president of sales & marketing LOU BANK
vice president of finance ANDY KARABATSOS
general counsel MARK ANDERSON
director of editorial adm. MELONEY C. CHADWICK
creative director RANDY STRADLEY
director of production & design CINDY MARKS
art director MARK COX
computer graphics director SEAN TIERNEY
director of sales MICHAEL MARTENS
director of licensing TOD BORLESKE
director of operations MARK ELLINGTON
director of m.i.s. DALE LAFOUNTAIN

Lettering for: "Dumping Ground" by DAVE GIBBONS; "Unwritten Law" and
"Hostage" PAT BROSSEAU; "Lynch Law" and "Stone Magic" WARREN PLEECE; "Family
Resemblance" ELLIE DE VILLE; "Anytime I Want" and "Joy Ride" JAMES O'BARR;
"Warlord," "Drive By," "Man to Man," "White Alligator," "Exit," "Born Bad," "Cain," and
"Replay" CLEM ROBINS; "Treatment" KEN HOLEWCZYNSKI; "Dead Game" JOHN
BERGIN; "A Flash of White" ELITTA FELL; and "Placebo" MICHAEL HEISLER.

TABLE OF CONTENTS

for Eric . . .

the air down here was too toxic for you, kid
I miss you,
but I'll see you soon enough

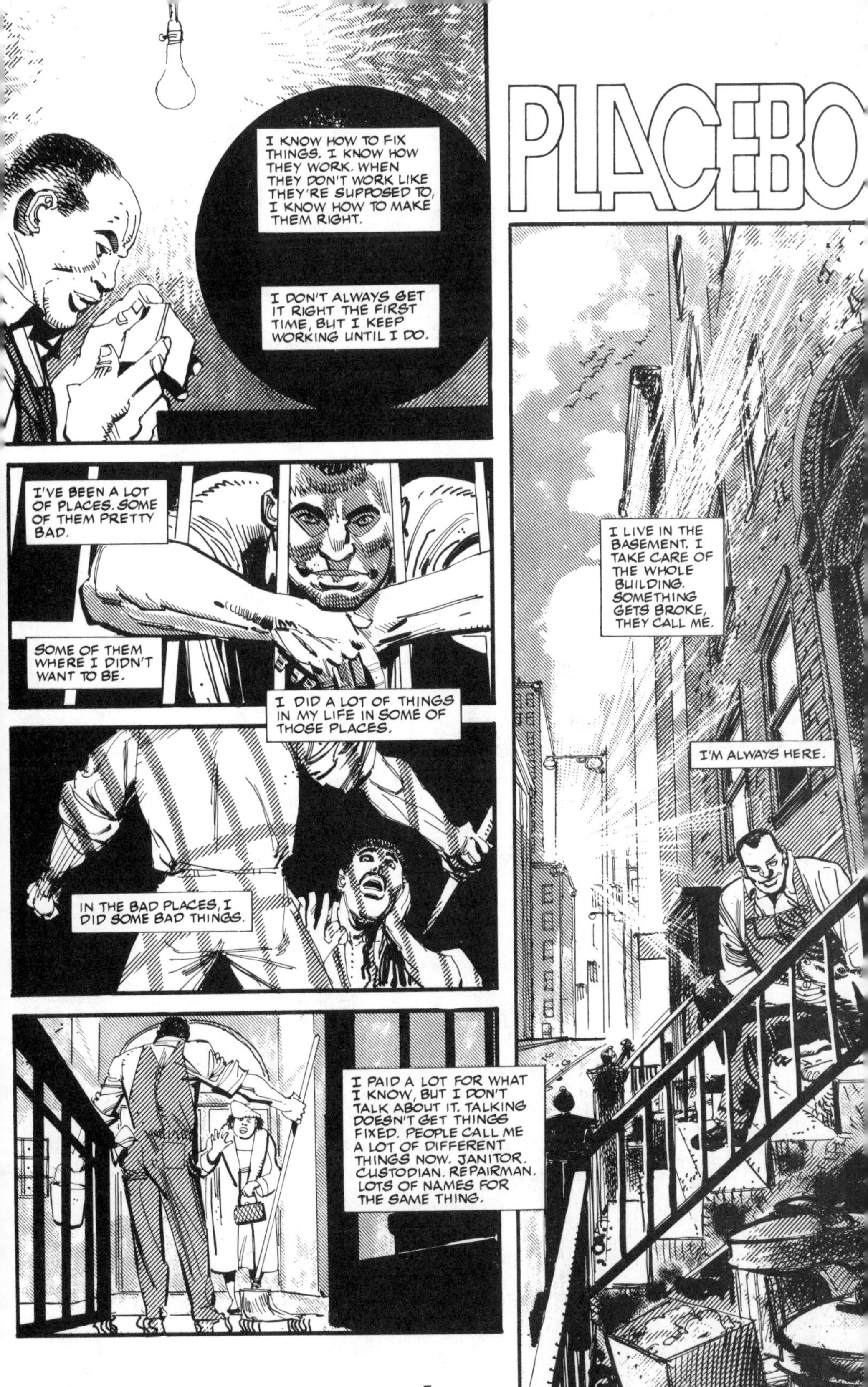

PLACEBO
I KNOW HOW TO FIX THINGS. I KNOW HOW THEY WORK. WHEN THEY DON'T WORK LIKE THEY'RE SUPPOSED TO, I KNOW HOW TO MAKE THEM RIGHT.
I DON'T ALWAYS GET IT RIGHT THE FIRST TIME, BUT I KEEP WORKING UNTIL I DO.
I'VE BEEN A LOT OF PLACES. SOME OF THEM PRETTY BAD.
SOME OF THEM WHERE I DIDN'T WANT TO BE.
I DID A LOT OF THINGS IN MY LIFE IN SOME OF THOSE PLACES.
IN THE BAD PLACES, I DID SOME BAD THINGS.
I PAID A LOT FOR WHAT I KNOW, BUT I DON'T TALK ABOUT IT. TALKING DOESN'T GET THINGS FIXED. PEOPLE CALL ME A LOT OF DIFFERENT THINGS NOW. JANITOR. CUSTODIAN. REPAIRMAN. LOTS OF NAMES FOR THE SAME THING.
I LIVE IN THE BASEMENT. I TAKE CARE OF THE WHOLE BUILDING. SOMETHING GETS BROKE, THEY CALL ME.
I'M ALWAYS HERE.

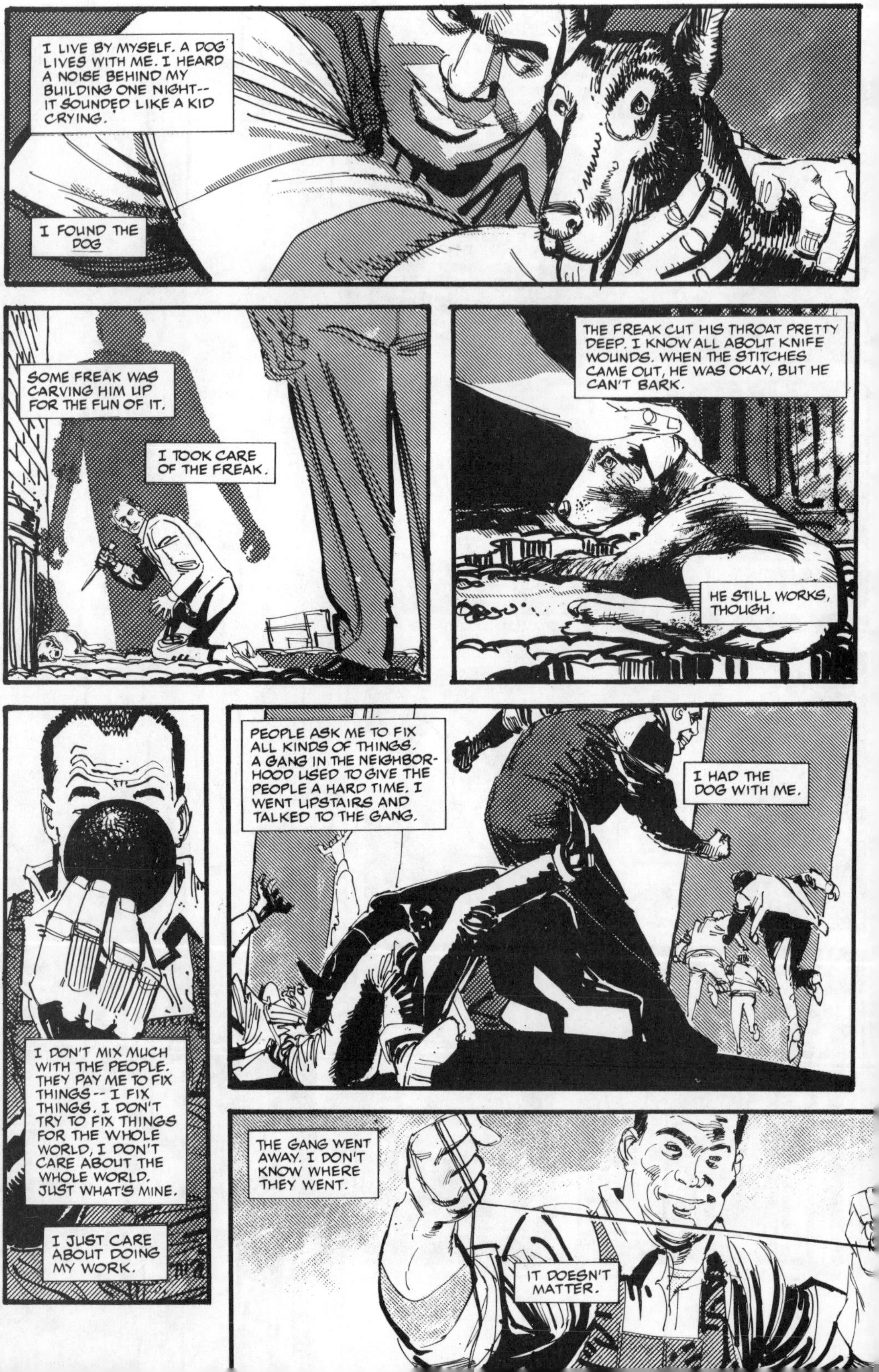
I LIVE BY MYSELF. A DOG LIVES WITH ME. I HEARD A NOISE BEHIND MY BUILDING ONE NIGHT-- IT SOUNDED LIKE A KID CRYING.
I FOUND THE DOG
SOME FREAK WAS CARVING HIM UP FOR THE FUN OF IT.
I TOOK CARE OF THE FREAK.
THE FREAK CUT HIS THROAT PRETTY DEEP. I KNOW ALL ABOUT KNIFE WOUNDS. WHEN THE STITCHES CAME OUT, HE WAS OKAY, BUT HE CAN'T BARK.
HE STILL WORKS, THOUGH.
I DON'T MIX MUCH WITH THE PEOPLE. THEY PAY ME TO FIX THINGS-- I FIX THINGS. I DON'T TRY TO FIX THINGS FOR THE WHOLE WORLD, I DON'T CARE ABOUT THE WHOLE WORLD. JUST WHAT'S MINE.
I JUST CARE ABOUT DOING MY WORK.
PEOPLE ASK ME TO FIX ALL KINDS OF THINGS. A GANG IN THE NEIGHBORHOOD USED TO GIVE THE PEOPLE A HARD TIME. I WENT UPSTAIRS AND TALKED TO THE GANG.
I HAD THE DOG WITH ME.
THE GANG WENT AWAY. I DON'T KNOW WHERE THEY WENT.
IT DOESN'T MATTER.

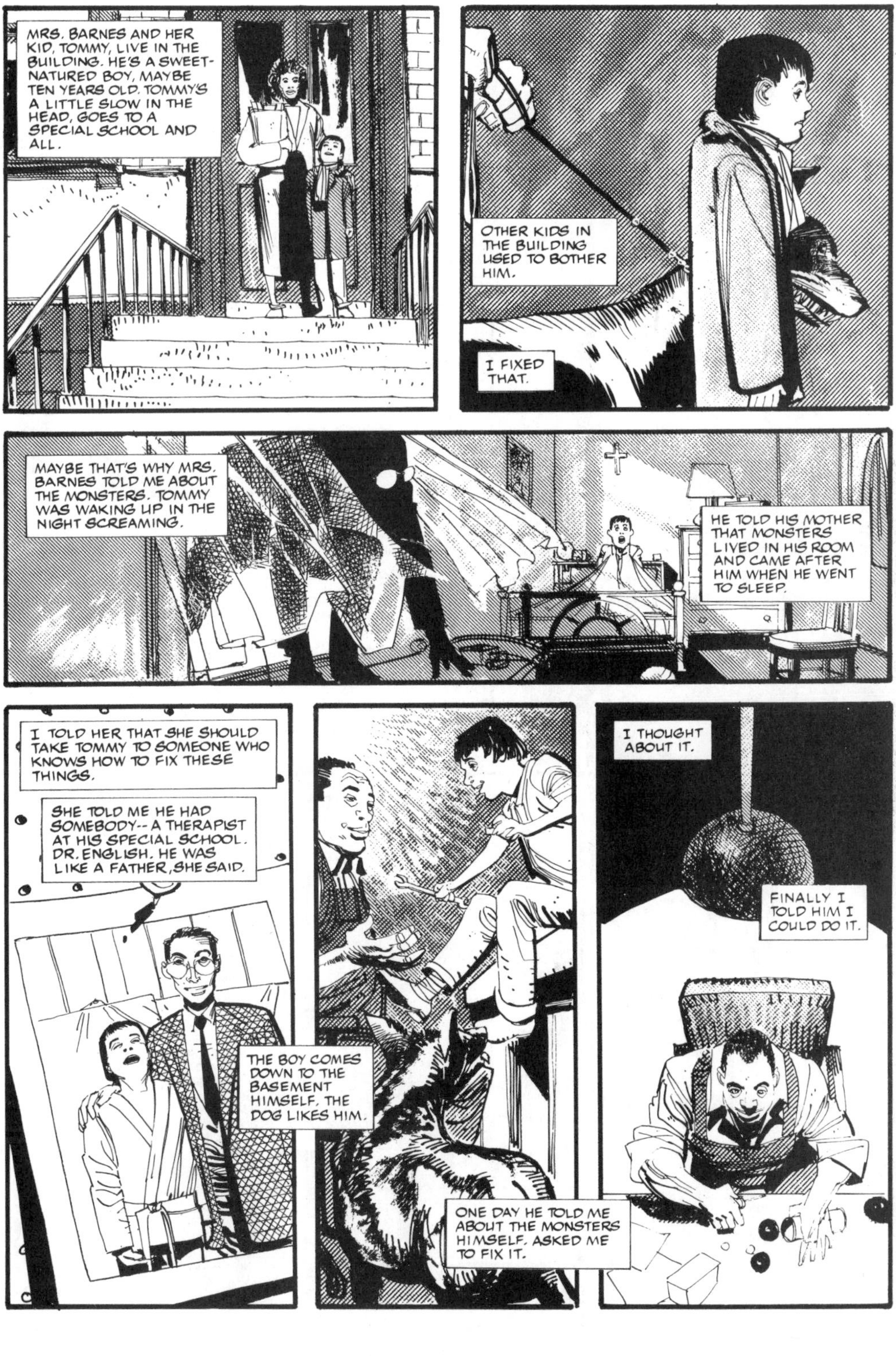
MRS. BARNES AND HER KID, TOMMY, LIVE IN THE BUILDING. HE'S A SWEET-NATURED BOY, MAYBE TEN YEARS OLD. TOMMY'S A LITTLE SLOW IN THE HEAD, GOES TO A SPECIAL SCHOOL AND ALL.
OTHER KIDS IN THE BUILDING USED TO BOTHER HIM.
I FIXED THAT.
MAYBE THAT'S WHY MRS. BARNES TOLD ME ABOUT THE MONSTERS. TOMMY WAS WAKING UP IN THE NIGHT SCREAMING.
HE TOLD HIS MOTHER THAT MONSTERS LIVED IN HIS ROOM AND CAME AFTER HIM WHEN HE WENT TO SLEEP.
I TOLD HER THAT SHE SHOULD TAKE TOMMY TO SOMEONE WHO KNOWS HOW TO FIX THESE THINGS.
SHE TOLD ME HE HAD SOMEBODY-- A THERAPIST AT HIS SPECIAL SCHOOL. DR. ENGLISH. HE WAS LIKE A FATHER, SHE SAID.
THE BOY COMES DOWN TO THE BASEMENT HIMSELF. THE DOG LIKES HIM.
ONE DAY HE TOLD ME ABOUT THE MONSTERS HIMSELF. ASKED ME TO FIX IT.
I THOUGHT ABOUT IT.
FINALLY I TOLD HIM I COULD DO IT.

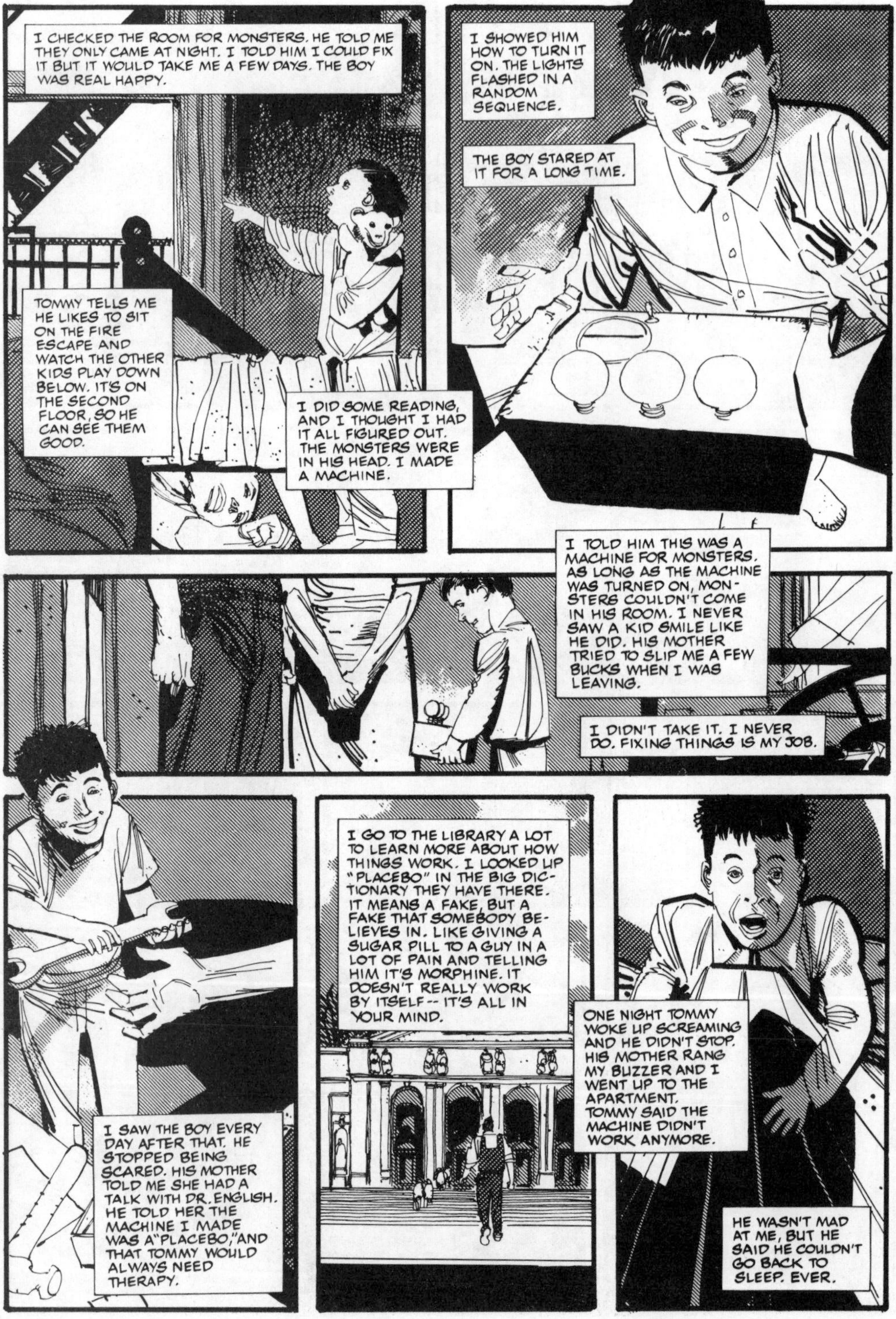
I CHECKED THE ROOM FOR MONSTERS. HE TOLD ME THEY ONLY CAME AT NIGHT. I TOLD HIM I COULD FIX IT BUT IT WOULD TAKE ME A FEW DAYS. THE BOY WAS REAL HAPPY.
TOMMY TELLS ME HE LIKES TO SIT ON THE FIRE ESCAPE AND WATCH THE OTHER KIDS PLAY DOWN BELOW. IT'S ON THE SECOND FLOOR, SO HE CAN SEE THEM GOOD.
I DID SOME READING, AND I THOUGHT I HAD IT ALL FIGURED OUT. THE MONSTERS WERE IN HIS HEAD. I MADE A MACHINE.
I SHOWED HIM HOW TO TURN IT ON. THE LIGHTS FLASHED IN A RANDOM SEQUENCE.
THE BOY STARED AT IT FOR A LONG TIME.
I TOLD HIM THIS WAS A MACHINE FOR MONSTERS. AS LONG AS THE MACHINE WAS TURNED ON, MONSTERS COULDN'T COME IN HIS ROOM. I NEVER SAW A KID SMILE LIKE HE DID. HIS MOTHER TRIED TO SLIP ME A FEW BUCKS WHEN I WAS LEAVING.
I DIDN'T TAKE IT. I NEVER DO. FIXING THINGS IS MY JOB.
I SAW THE BOY EVERY DAY AFTER THAT. HE STOPPED BEING SCARED. HIS MOTHER TOLD ME SHE HAD A TALK WITH DR. ENGLISH. HE TOLD HER THE MACHINE I MADE WAS A "PLACEBO," AND THAT TOMMY WOULD ALWAYS NEED THERAPY.
I GO TO THE LIBRARY A LOT TO LEARN MORE ABOUT HOW THINGS WORK. I LOOKED UP "PLACEBO" IN THE BIG DICTIONARY THEY HAVE THERE. IT MEANS A FAKE, BUT A FAKE THAT SOMEBODY BELIEVES IN. LIKE GIVING A SUGAR PILL TO A GUY IN A LOT OF PAIN AND TELLING HIM IT'S MORPHINE. IT DOESN'T REALLY WORK BY ITSELF -- IT'S ALL IN YOUR MIND.
ONE NIGHT TOMMY WOKE UP SCREAMING AND HE DIDN'T STOP. HIS MOTHER RANG MY BUZZER AND I WENT UP TO THE APARTMENT. TOMMY SAID THE MACHINE DIDN'T WORK ANYMORE.
HE WASN'T MAD AT ME, BUT HE SAID HE COULDN'T GO BACK TO SLEEP. EVER.

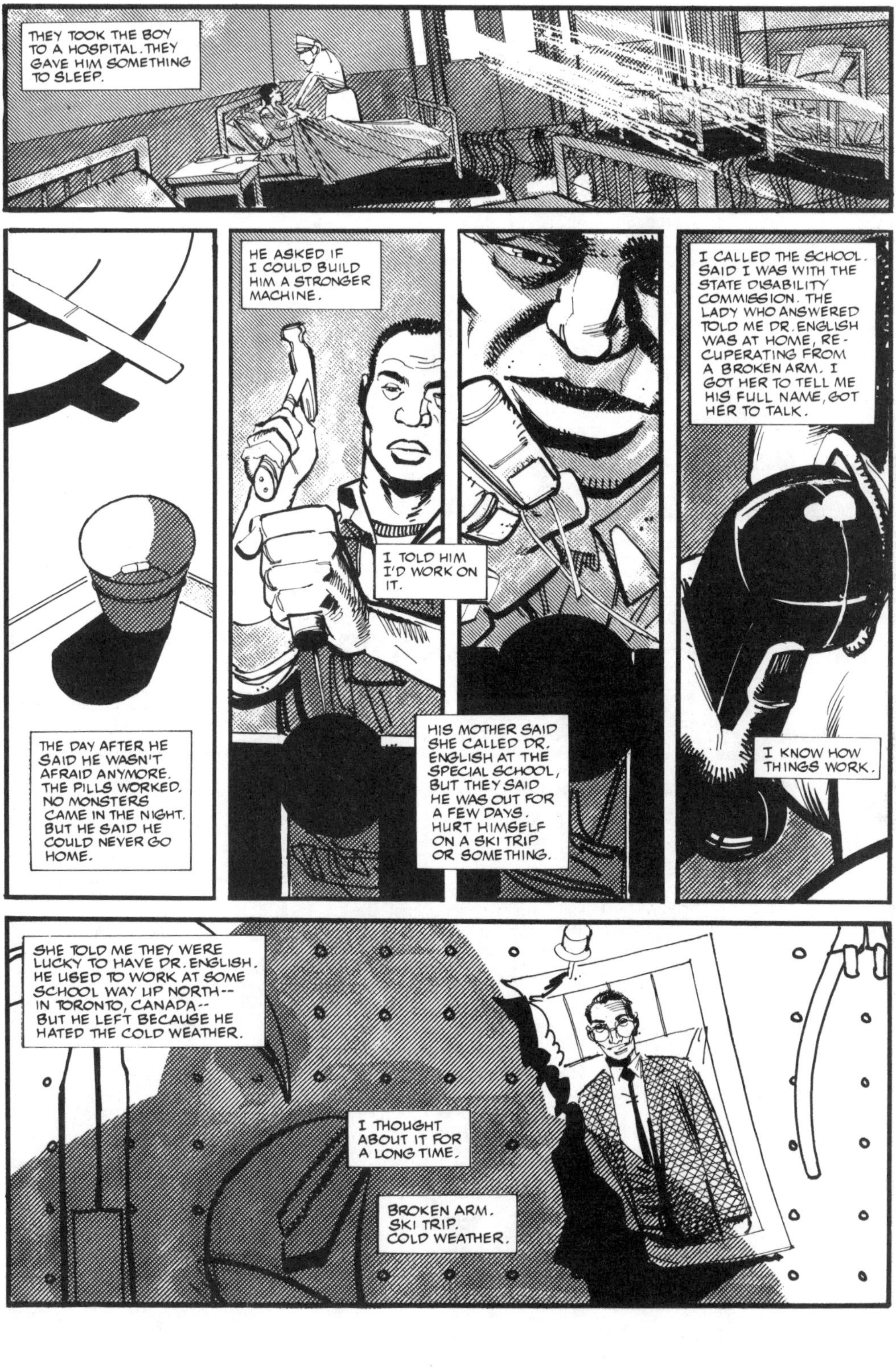
THEY TOOK THE BOY TO A HOSPITAL. THEY GAVE HIM SOMETHING TO SLEEP.
THE DAY AFTER HE SAID HE WASN'T AFRAID ANYMORE. THE PILLS WORKED. NO MONSTERS CAME IN THE NIGHT. BUT HE SAID HE COULD NEVER GO HOME.
HE ASKED IF I COULD BUILD HIM A STRONGER MACHINE.
I TOLD HIM I'D WORK ON IT.
HIS MOTHER SAID SHE CALLED DR. ENGLISH AT THE SPECIAL SCHOOL, BUT THEY SAID HE WAS OUT FOR A FEW DAYS. HURT HIMSELF ON A SKI TRIP OR SOMETHING.
I CALLED THE SCHOOL. SAID I WAS WITH THE STATE DISABILITY COMMISSION. THE LADY WHO ANSWERED TOLD ME DR. ENGLISH WAS AT HOME, RE-CUPERATING FROM A BROKEN ARM. I GOT HER TO TELL ME HIS FULL NAME, GOT HER TO TALK.
I KNOW HOW THINGS WORK.
SHE TOLD ME THEY WERE LUCKY TO HAVE DR. ENGLISH. HE USED TO WORK AT SOME SCHOOL WAY UP NORTH-- IN TORONTO, CANADA-- BUT HE LEFT BECAUSE HE HATED THE COLD WEATHER.
I THOUGHT ABOUT IT FOR A LONG TIME.
BROKEN ARM. SKI TRIP. COLD WEATHER.

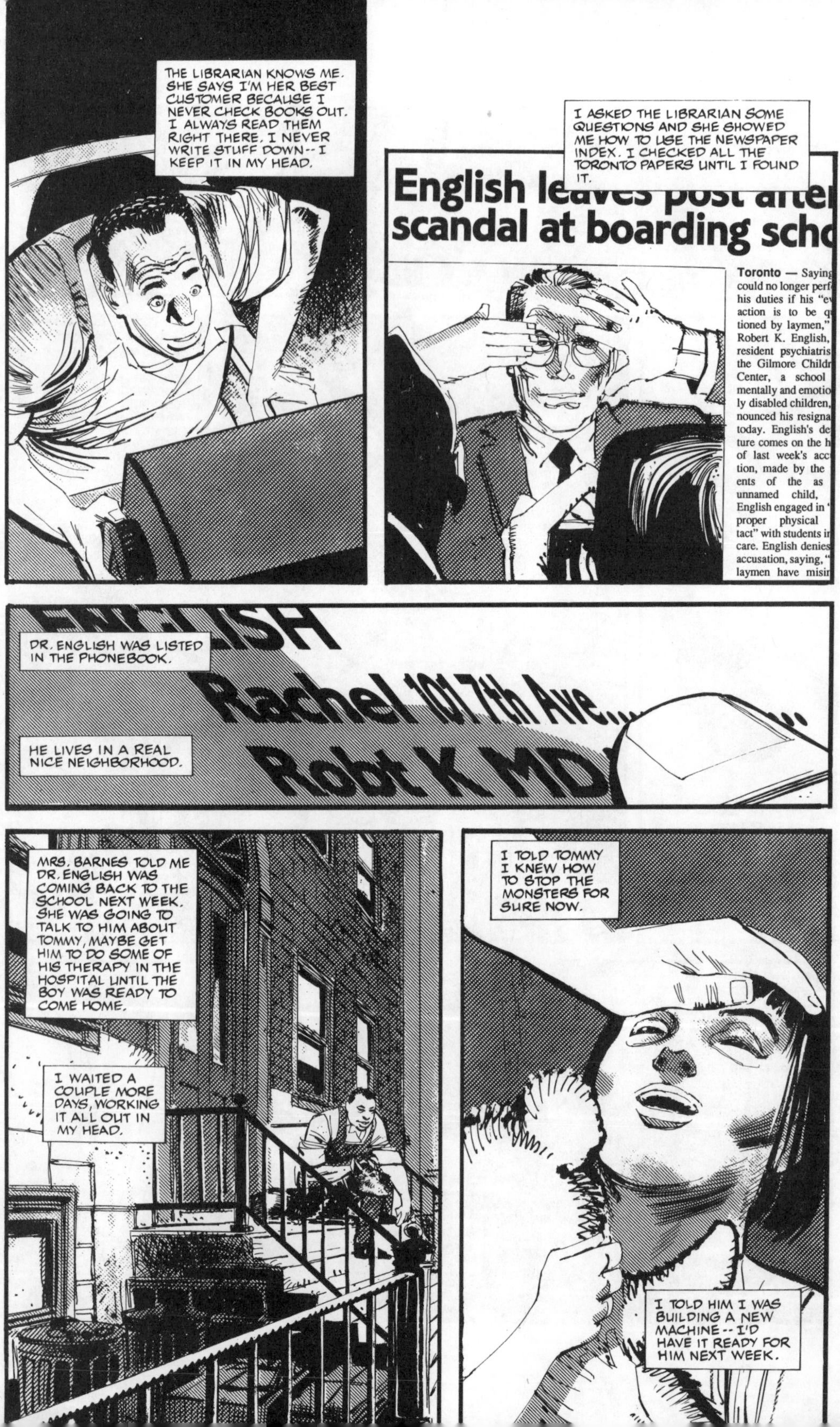
THE LIBRARIAN KNOWS ME. SHE SAYS I'M HER BEST CUSTOMER BECAUSE I NEVER CHECK BOOKS OUT. I ALWAYS READ THEM RIGHT THERE. I NEVER WRITE STUFF DOWN-- I KEEP IT IN MY HEAD.
I ASKED THE LIBRARIAN SOME QUESTIONS AND SHE SHOWED ME HOW TO USE THE NEWSPAPER INDEX. I CHECKED ALL THE TORONTO PAPERS UNTIL I FOUND IT.
English leaves post after
scandal at boarding scho
Toronto — Saying could no longer perf his duties if his "e action is to be q tioned by laymen," Robert K. English, resident psychiatris the Gilmore Childr Center, a school mentally and emotio ly disabled children, nounced his resigna today. English's de ture comes on the h of last week's acc tion, made by the ents of the as unnamed child, English engaged in " proper physical tact" with students i care. English denies accusation, saying, " laymen have misin
ENGLISH
DR. ENGLISH WAS LISTED IN THE PHONEBOOK.
Rachel 10 7th Ave...
Robt K MD
HE LIVES IN A REAL NICE NEIGHBORHOOD.
MRS. BARNES TOLD ME DR. ENGLISH WAS COMING BACK TO THE SCHOOL NEXT WEEK. SHE WAS GOING TO TALK TO HIM ABOUT TOMMY, MAYBE GET HIM TO DO SOME OF HIS THERAPY IN THE HOSPITAL UNTIL THE BOY WAS READY TO COME HOME.
I WAITED A COUPLE MORE DAYS, WORKING IT ALL OUT IN MY HEAD.
I TOLD TOMMY I KNEW HOW TO STOP THE MONSTERS FOR SURE NOW.
I TOLD HIM I WAS BUILDING A NEW MACHINE-- I'D HAVE IT READY FOR HIM NEXT WEEK.

I TOLD HIM WHEN HE GOT HOME I WANT HIM TO WALK THE DOG FOR ME. OUT IN THE BACK WHERE THE OTHER KIDS PLAYED. I TOLD HIM I'D TEACH HIM HOW. HE REALLY LIKED THAT. HE SAID HE'D TRY AND COME HOME IF I WAS SURE THE NEW MACHINE WOULD WORK.
I GAVE HIM MY WORD.
I'M WORKING ON THE NEW MACHINE IN MY BASEMENT NOW.
I KNOW HOW TO FIX THINGS.
WHEN IT GETS DARK TONIGHT...

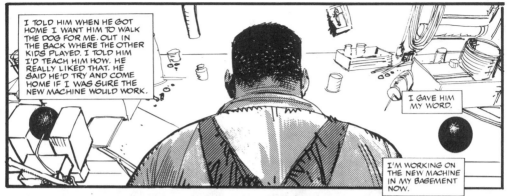

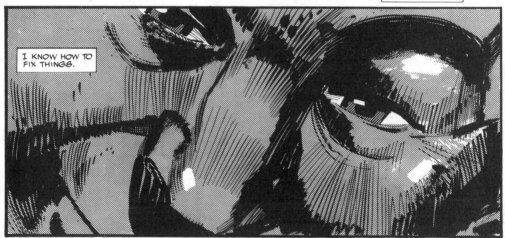

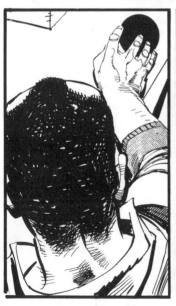

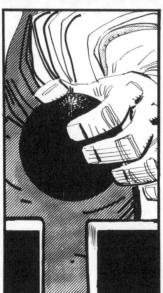

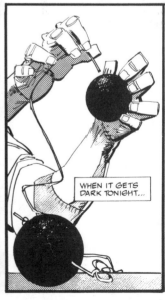

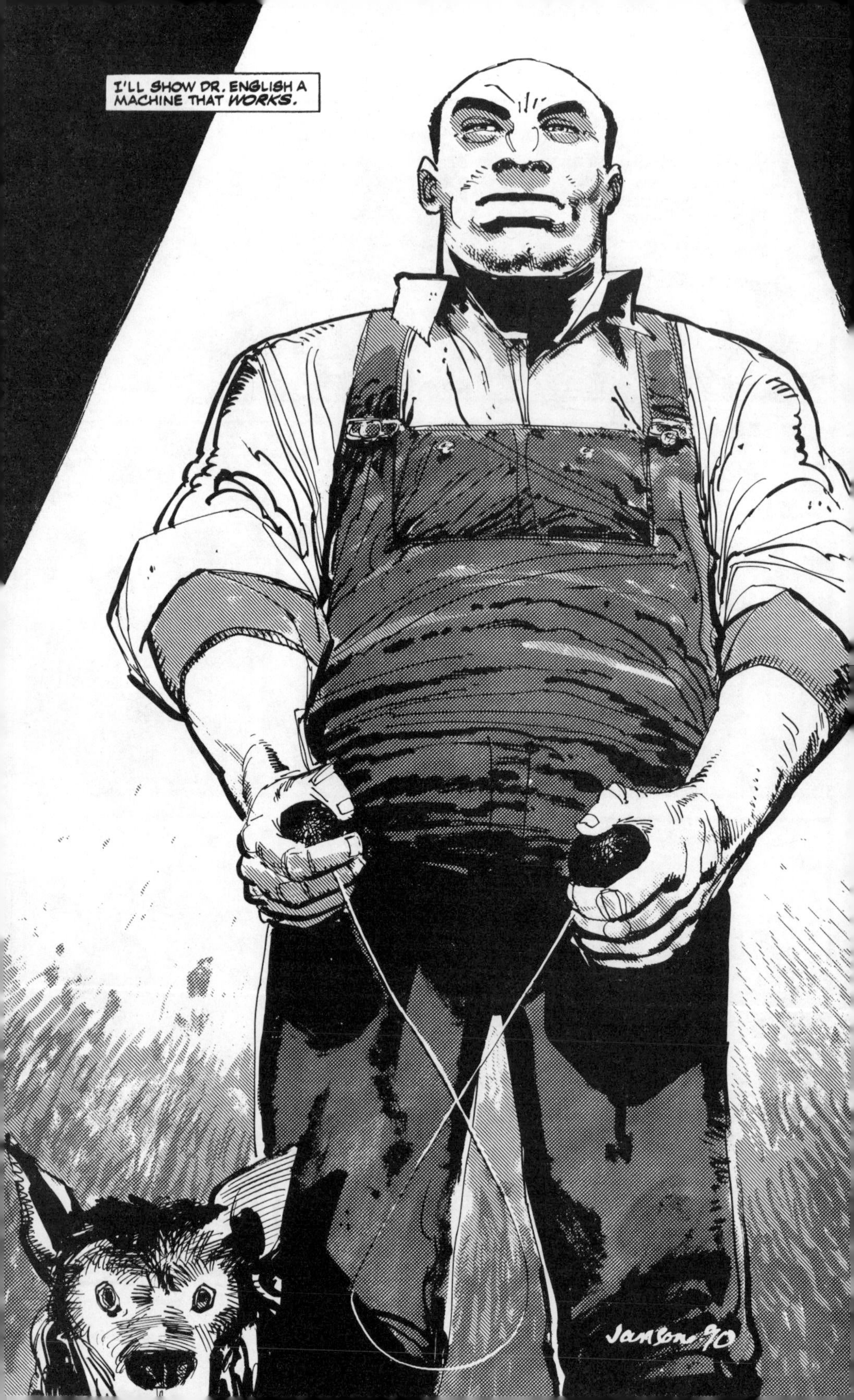
I'LL SHOW DR. ENGLISH A MACHINE THAT WORKS.
Janson '90

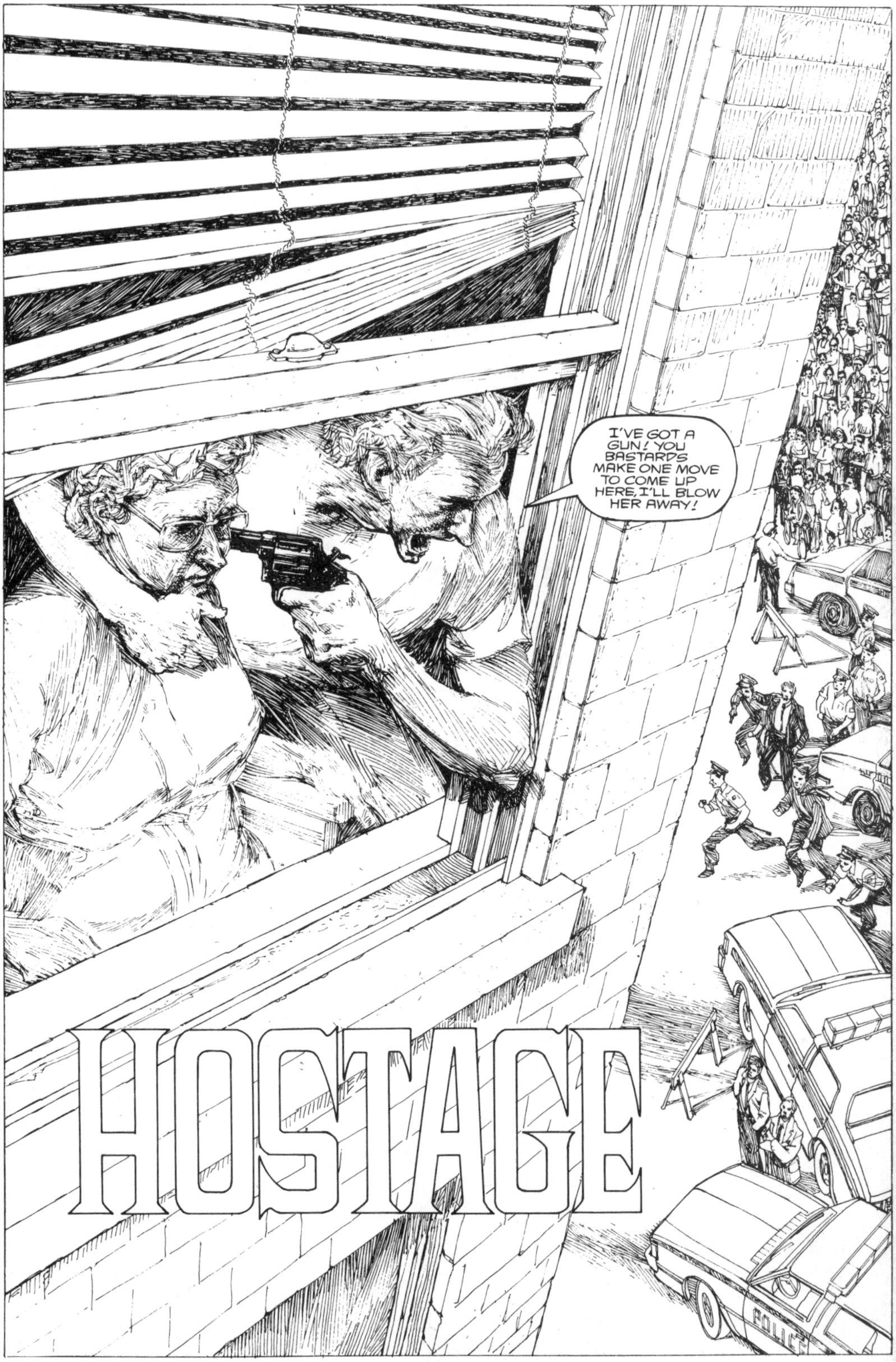
I'VE GOT A GUN! YOU BASTARDS MAKE ONE MOVE TO COME UP HERE, I'LL BLOW HER AWAY!
HOSTAGE
POLICE

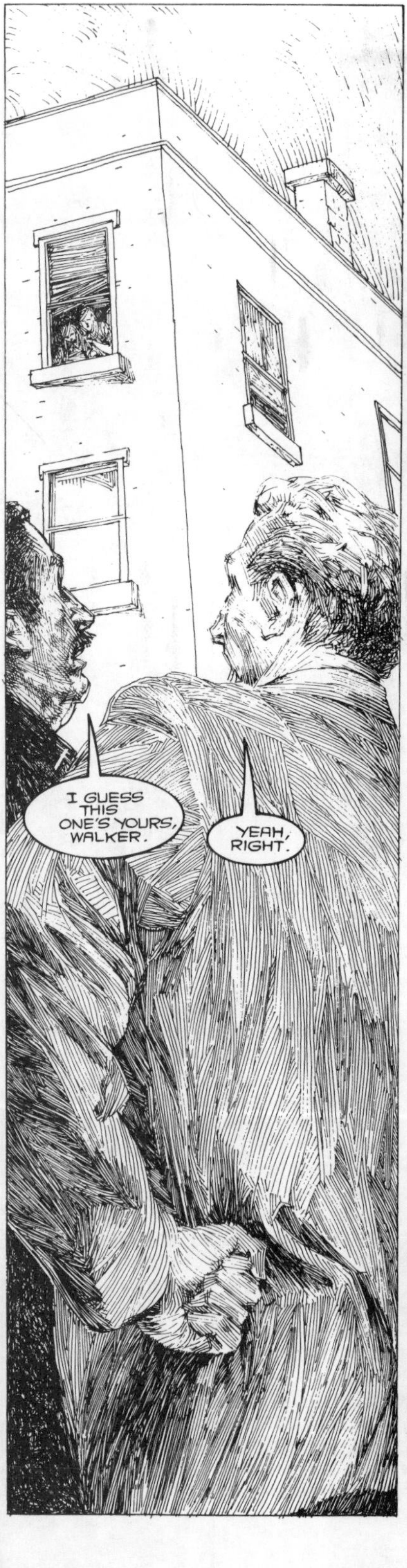
I GUESS THIS ONE'S YOURS, WALKER.
YEAH, RIGHT.

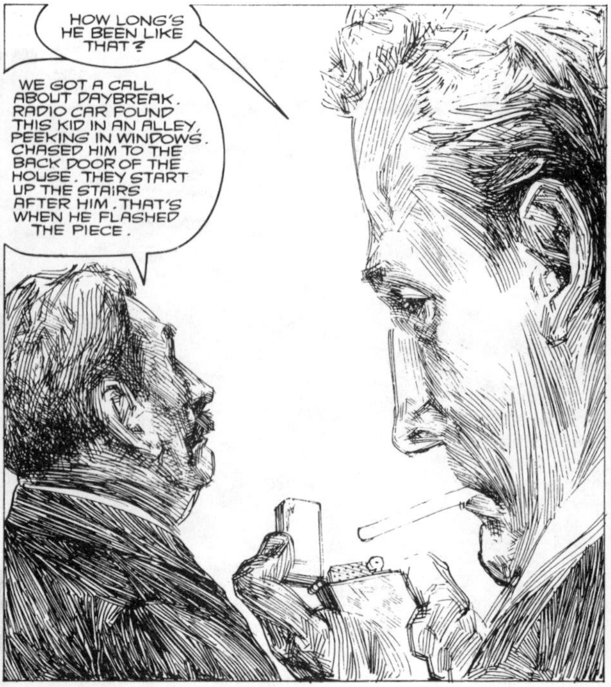
HOW LONG'S HE BEEN LIKE THAT?
WE GOT A CALL ABOUT DAYBREAK. RADIO CAR FOUND THIS KID IN AN ALLEY, PEEKING IN WINDOWS. CHASED HIM TO THE BACK DOOR OF THE HOUSE. THEY START UP THE STAIRS AFTER HIM. THAT'S WHEN HE FLASHED THE PIECE.

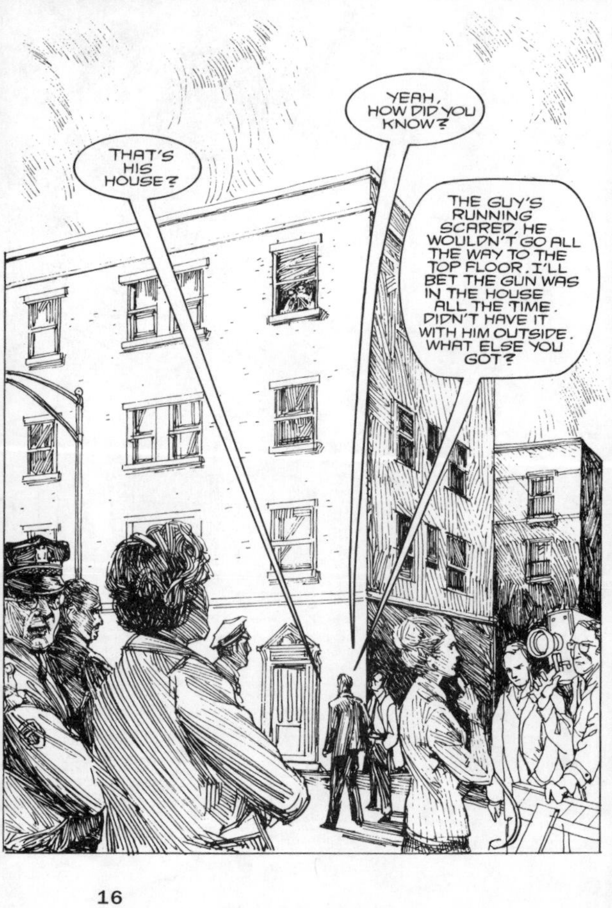
THAT'S HIS HOUSE?
YEAH, HOW DID YOU KNOW?
THE GUY'S RUNNING SCARED, HE WOULDN'T GO ALL THE WAY TO THE TOP FLOOR. I'LL BET THE GUN WAS IN THE HOUSE ALL THE TIME. DIDN'T HAVE IT WITH HIM OUTSIDE. WHAT ELSE YOU GOT?

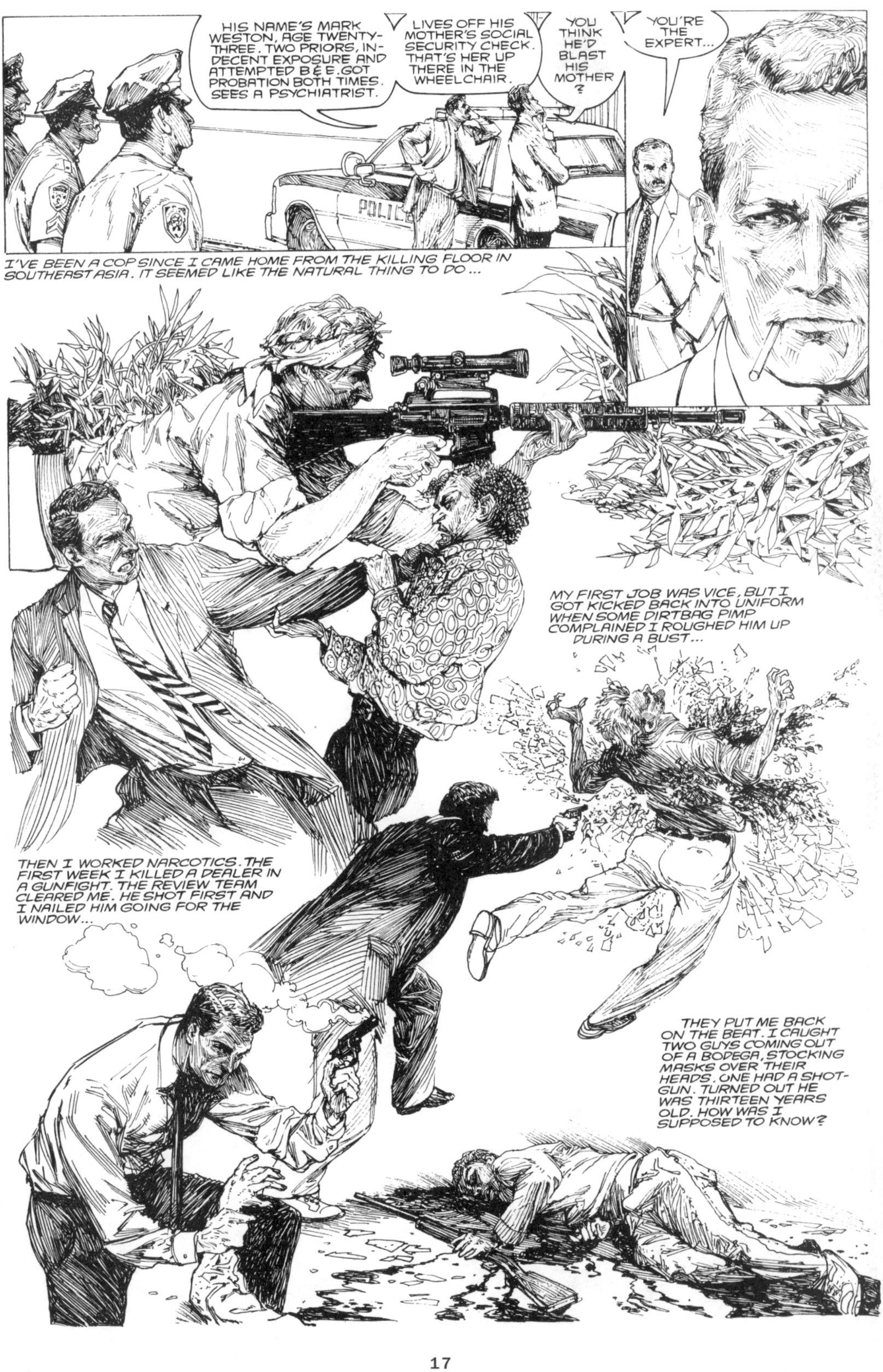
HIS NAME'S MARK WESTON, AGE TWENTY-THREE. TWO PRIORS, INDECENT EXPOSURE AND ATTEMPTED B & E. GOT PROBATION BOTH TIMES. SEES A PSYCHIATRIST.
LIVES OFF HIS MOTHER'S SOCIAL SECURITY CHECK. THAT'S HER UP THERE IN THE WHEELCHAIR.
YOU THINK HE'D BLAST HIS MOTHER?
YOU'RE THE EXPERT...
POLICE
I'VE BEEN A COP SINCE I CAME HOME FROM THE KILLING FLOOR IN SOUTHEAST ASIA. IT SEEMED LIKE THE NATURAL THING TO DO...
MY FIRST JOB WAS VICE, BUT I GOT KICKED BACK INTO UNIFORM WHEN SOME DIRTBAG PIMP COMPLAINED I ROUGHED HIM UP DURING A BUST...
THEN I WORKED NARCOTICS. THE FIRST WEEK I KILLED A DEALER IN A GUNFIGHT. THE REVIEW TEAM CLEARED ME. HE SHOT FIRST AND I NAILED HIM GOING FOR THE WINDOW...
THEY PUT ME BACK ON THE BEAT. I CAUGHT TWO GUYS COMING OUT OF A BODEGA, STOCKING MASKS OVER THEIR HEADS. ONE HAD A SHOTGUN. TURNED OUT HE WAS THIRTEEN YEARS OLD. HOW WAS I SUPPOSED TO KNOW?

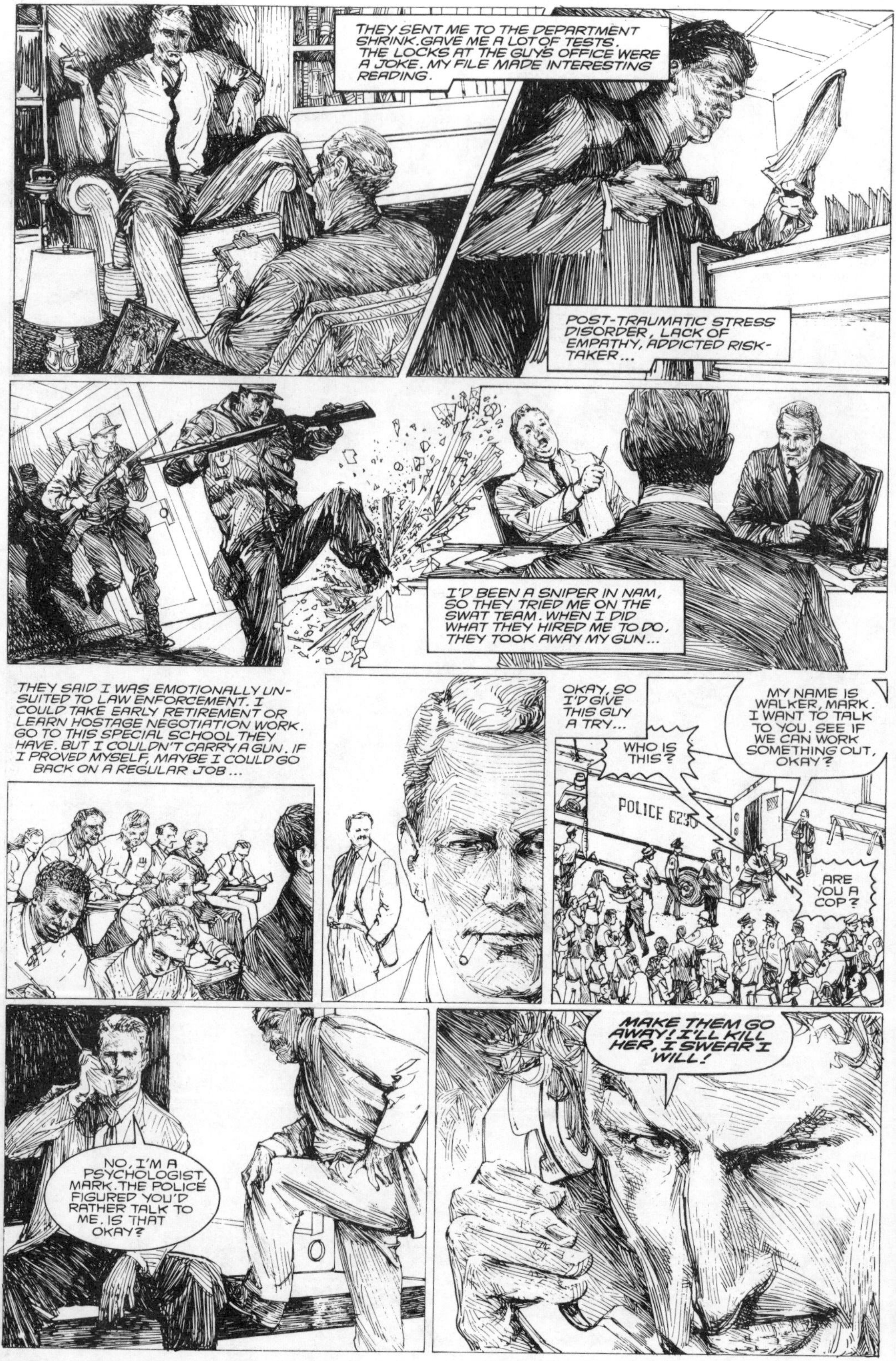
THEY SENT ME TO THE DEPARTMENT SHRINK. GAVE ME A LOT OF TESTS. THE LOCKS AT THE GUY'S OFFICE WERE A JOKE. MY FILE MADE INTERESTING READING.
POST-TRAUMATIC STRESS DISORDER, LACK OF EMPATHY, ADDICTED RISK-TAKER...
I'D BEEN A SNIPER IN NAM, SO THEY TRIED ME ON THE SWAT TEAM. WHEN I DID WHAT THEY HIRED ME TO DO, THEY TOOK AWAY MY GUN...
THEY SAID I WAS EMOTIONALLY UNSUITED TO LAW ENFORCEMENT. I COULD TAKE EARLY RETIREMENT OR LEARN HOSTAGE NEGOTIATION WORK. GO TO THIS SPECIAL SCHOOL THEY HAVE. BUT I COULDN'T CARRY A GUN. IF I PROVED MYSELF, MAYBE I COULD GO BACK ON A REGULAR JOB...
OKAY, SO I'D GIVE THIS GUY A TRY...
MY NAME IS WALKER, MARK. I WANT TO TALK TO YOU. SEE IF WE CAN WORK SOMETHING OUT, OKAY?
WHO IS THIS?
POLICE 6230
ARE YOU A COP?
NO, I'M A PSYCHOLOGIST, MARK. THE POLICE FIGURED YOU'D RATHER TALK TO ME. IS THAT OKAY?
MAKE THEM GO AWAY! I'LL KILL HER, I SWEAR I WILL!

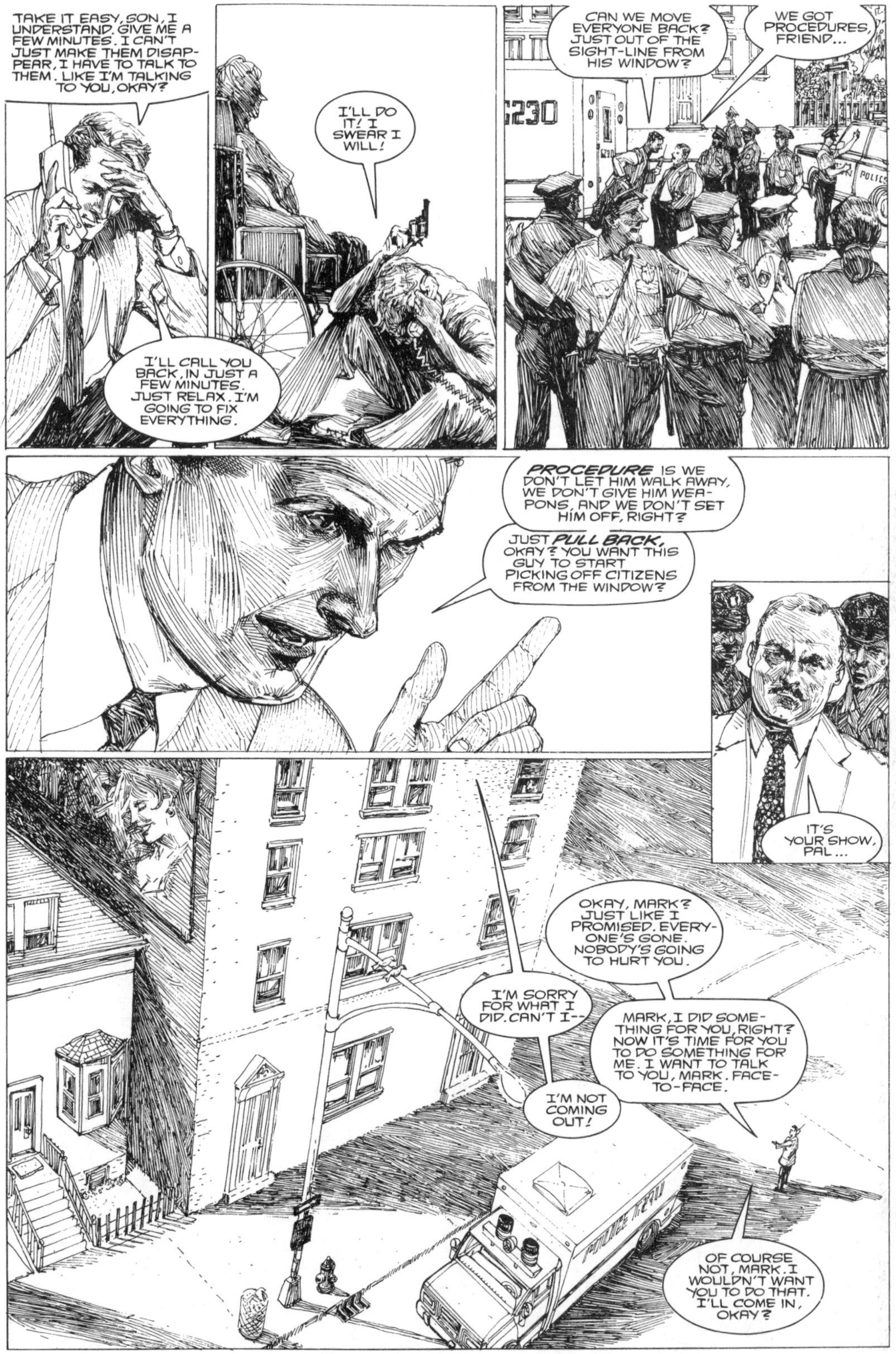
TAKE IT EASY, SON, I UNDERSTAND. GIVE ME A FEW MINUTES. I CAN'T JUST MAKE THEM DISAPPEAR, I HAVE TO TALK TO THEM. LIKE I'M TALKING TO YOU, OKAY?
I'LL CALL YOU BACK, IN JUST A FEW MINUTES. JUST RELAX. I'M GOING TO FIX EVERYTHING.
I'LL DO IT! I SWEAR I WILL!
CAN WE MOVE EVERYONE BACK? JUST OUT OF THE SIGHT-LINE FROM HIS WINDOW?
WE GOT PROCEDURES, FRIEND...
PROCEDURE IS WE DON'T LET HIM WALK AWAY, WE DON'T GIVE HIM WEAPONS, AND WE DON'T SET HIM OFF, RIGHT?
JUST PULL BACK, OKAY? YOU WANT THIS GUY TO START PICKING OFF CITIZENS FROM THE WINDOW?
IT'S YOUR SHOW, PAL...
OKAY, MARK? JUST LIKE I PROMISED. EVERYONE'S GONE. NOBODY'S GOING TO HURT YOU.
I'M SORRY FOR WHAT I DID. CAN'T I--
MARK, I DID SOMETHING FOR YOU, RIGHT? NOW IT'S TIME FOR YOU TO DO SOMETHING FOR ME. I WANT TO TALK TO YOU, MARK. FACE-TO-FACE.
I'M NOT COMING OUT!
OF COURSE NOT, MARK. I WOULDN'T WANT YOU TO DO THAT. I'LL COME IN, OKAY?

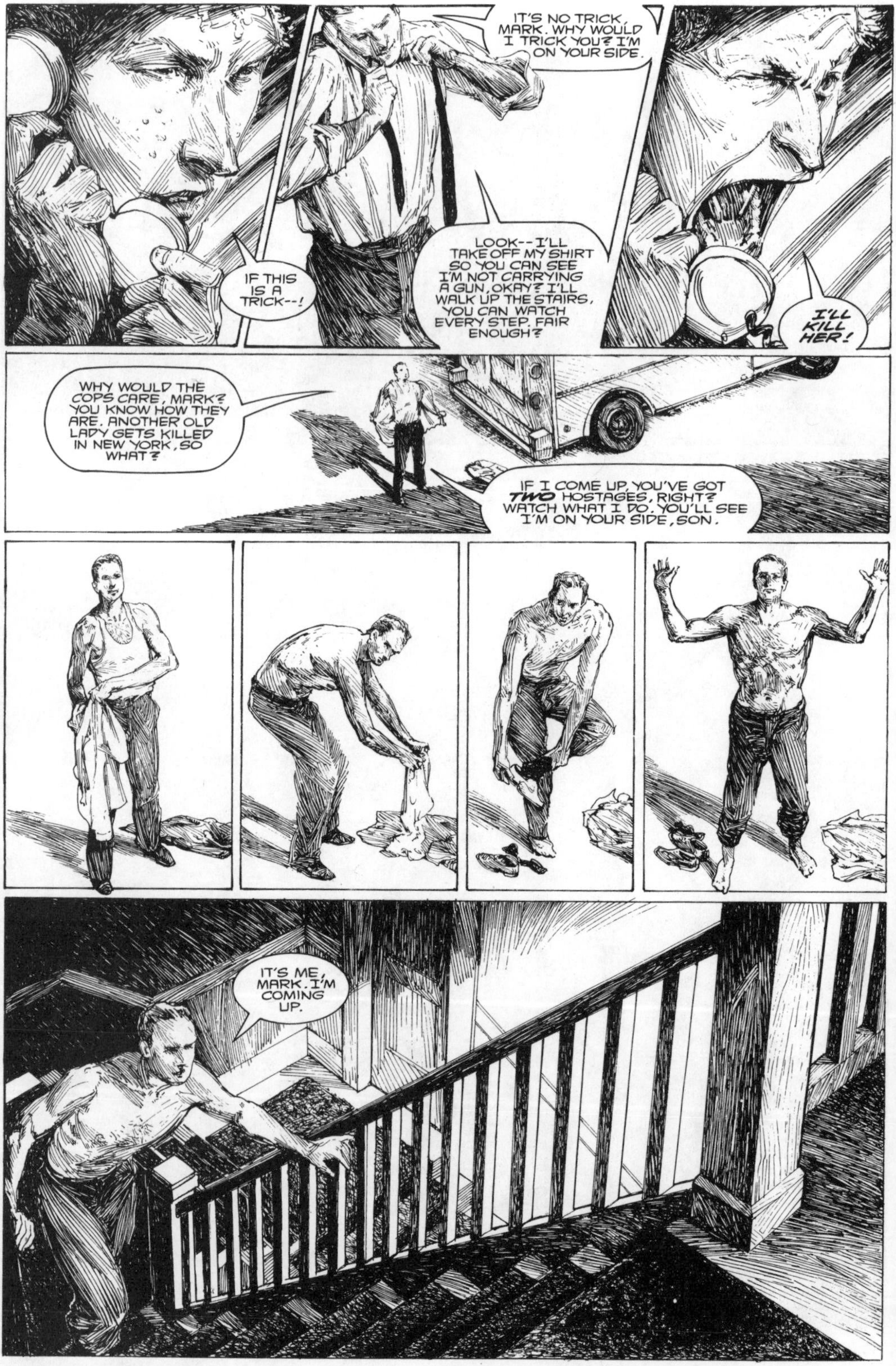
IT'S NO TRICK, MARK. WHY WOULD I TRICK YOU? I'M ON YOUR SIDE.
IF THIS IS A TRICK--!
LOOK--I'LL TAKE OFF MY SHIRT SO YOU CAN SEE I'M NOT CARRYING A GUN, OKAY? I'LL WALK UP THE STAIRS, YOU CAN WATCH EVERY STEP. FAIR ENOUGH?
I'LL KILL HER!
WHY WOULD THE COPS CARE, MARK? YOU KNOW HOW THEY ARE. ANOTHER OLD LADY GETS KILLED IN NEW YORK, SO WHAT?
IF I COME UP, YOU'VE GOT TWO HOSTAGES, RIGHT? WATCH WHAT I DO. YOU'LL SEE I'M ON YOUR SIDE, SON.
IT'S ME, MARK. I'M COMING UP.

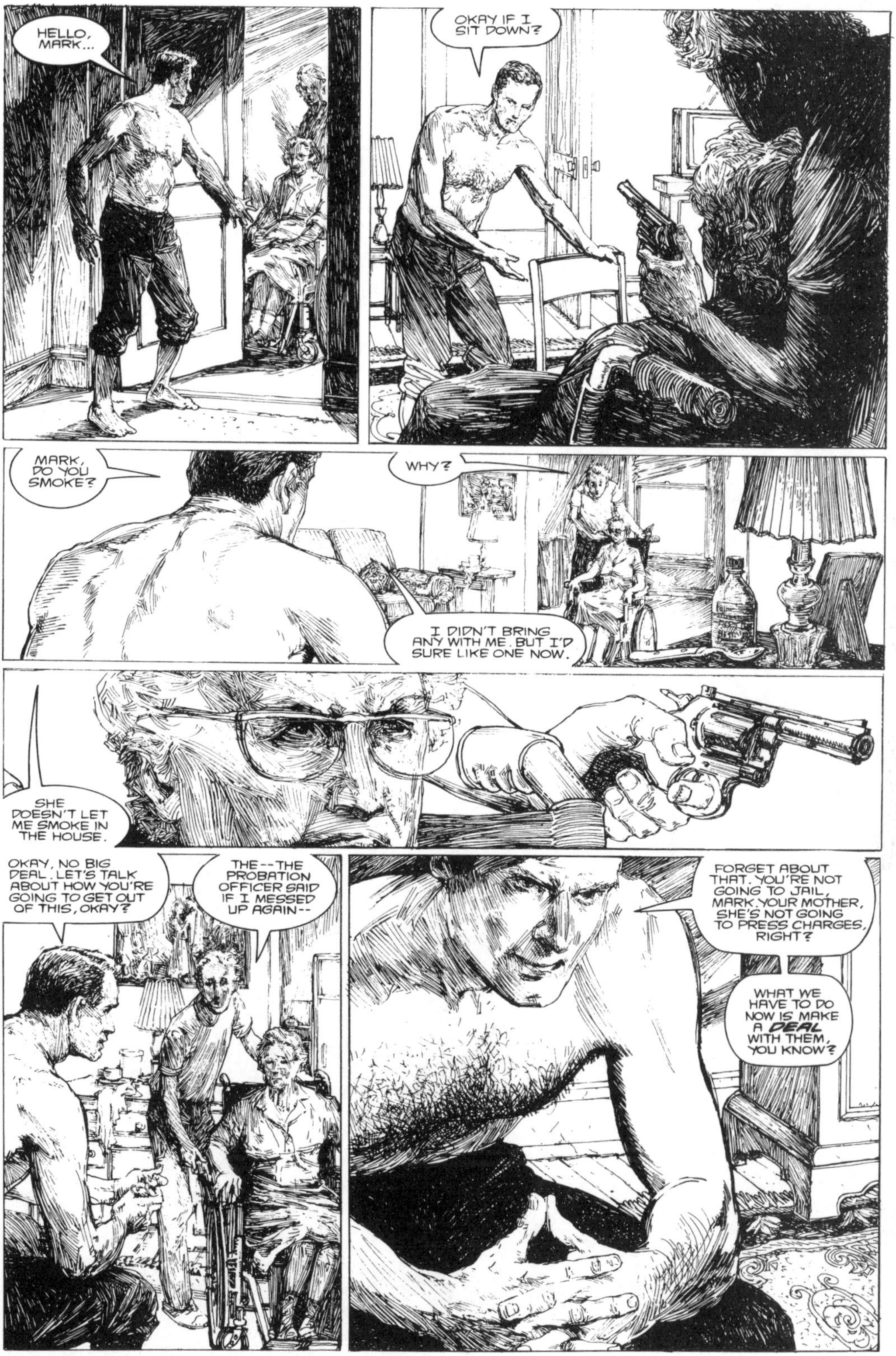
HELLO, MARK...
OKAY IF I SIT DOWN?
MARK, DO YOU SMOKE?
WHY?
I DIDN'T BRING ANY WITH ME. BUT I'D SURE LIKE ONE NOW.
SHE DOESN'T LET ME SMOKE IN THE HOUSE.
OKAY, NO BIG DEAL. LET'S TALK ABOUT HOW YOU'RE GOING TO GET OUT OF THIS, OKAY?
THE--THE PROBATION OFFICER SAID IF I MESSED UP AGAIN--
FORGET ABOUT THAT. YOU'RE NOT GOING TO JAIL, MARK. YOUR MOTHER, SHE'S NOT GOING TO PRESS CHARGES, RIGHT?
WHAT WE HAVE TO DO NOW IS MAKE A *DEAL* WITH THEM, YOU KNOW?

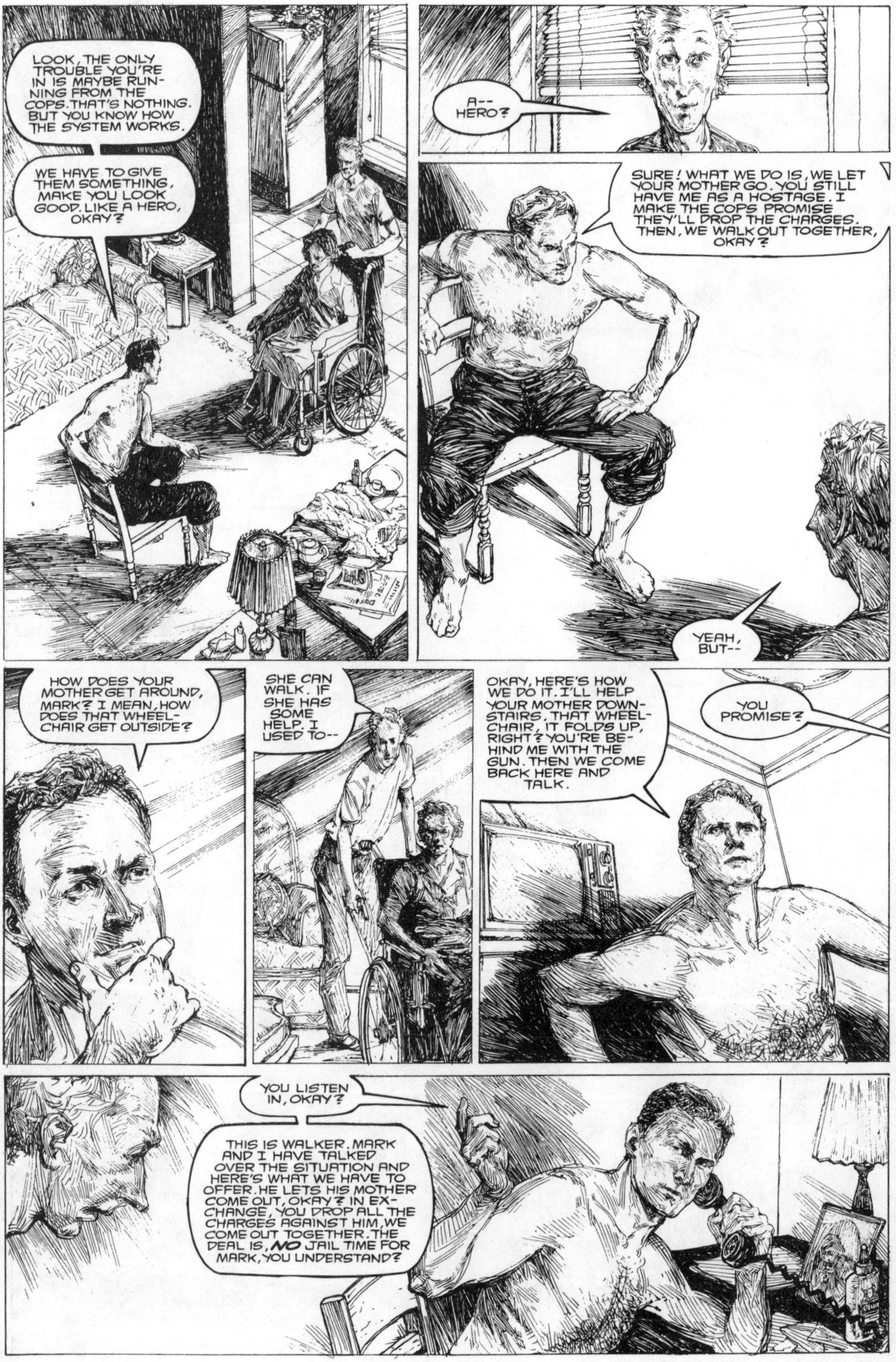

LOOK, THE ONLY TROUBLE YOU'RE IN IS MAYBE RUNNING FROM THE COPS. THAT'S NOTHING. BUT YOU KNOW HOW THE SYSTEM WORKS.
WE HAVE TO GIVE THEM SOMETHING, MAKE YOU LOOK GOOD. LIKE A HERO, OKAY?
A-- HERO?
SURE! WHAT WE DO IS, WE LET YOUR MOTHER GO. YOU STILL HAVE ME AS A HOSTAGE. I MAKE THE COPS PROMISE THEY'LL DROP THE CHARGES. THEN, WE WALK OUT TOGETHER, OKAY?
YEAH, BUT--
HOW DOES YOUR MOTHER GET AROUND, MARK? I MEAN, HOW DOES THAT WHEEL-CHAIR GET OUTSIDE?
SHE CAN WALK. IF SHE HAS SOME HELP. I USED TO--
OKAY, HERE'S HOW WE DO IT. I'LL HELP YOUR MOTHER DOWN-STAIRS. THAT WHEEL-CHAIR, IT FOLDS UP, RIGHT? YOU'RE BE-HIND ME WITH THE GUN. THEN WE COME BACK HERE AND TALK.
YOU PROMISE?
YOU LISTEN IN, OKAY?
THIS IS WALKER. MARK AND I HAVE TALKED OVER THE SITUATION AND HERE'S WHAT WE HAVE TO OFFER. HE LETS HIS MOTHER COME OUT, OKAY? IN EX-CHANGE, YOU DROP ALL THE CHARGES AGAINST HIM, WE COME OUT TOGETHER. THE DEAL IS, NO JAIL TIME FOR MARK, YOU UNDERSTAND?

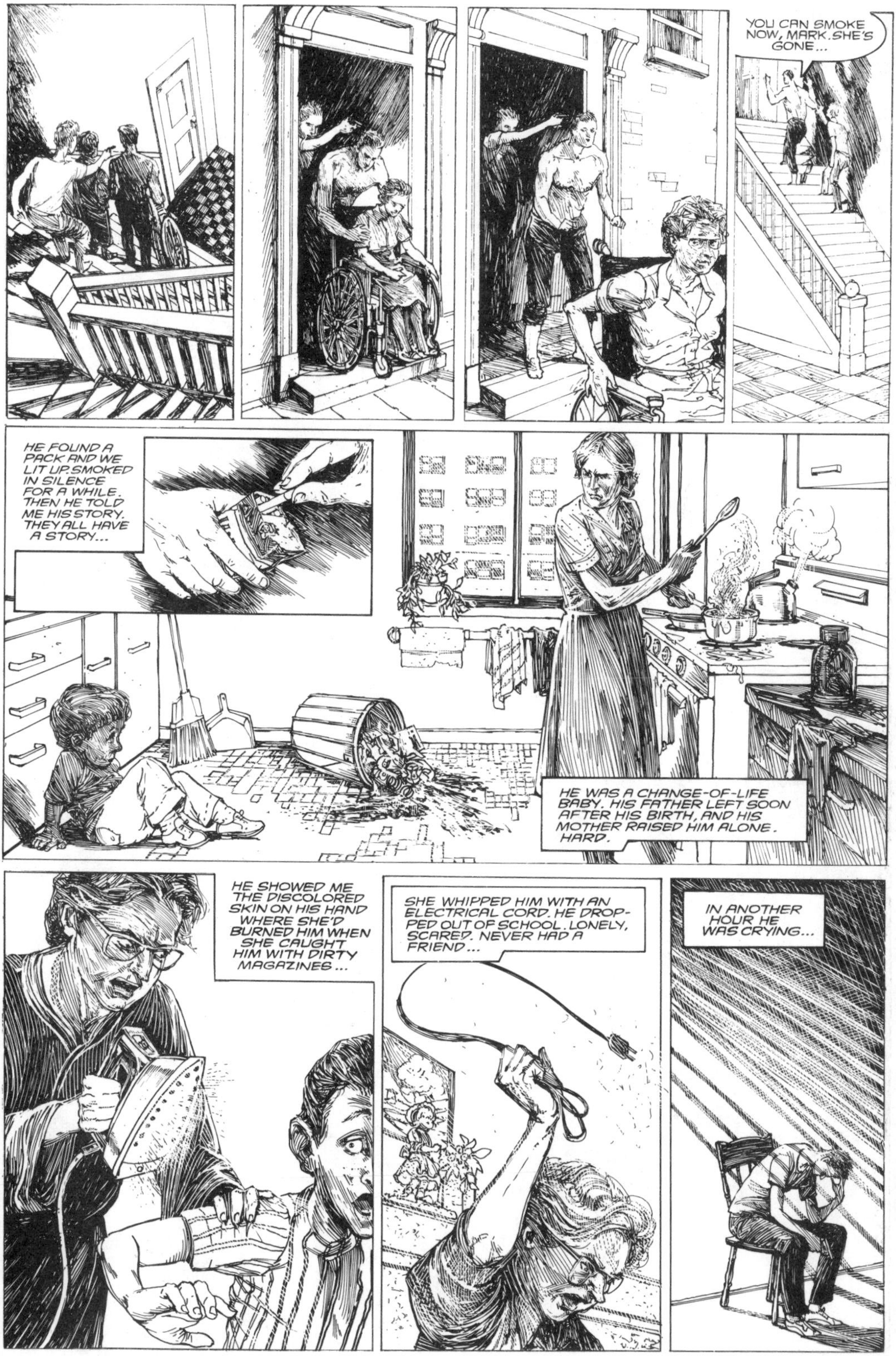
YOU CAN SMOKE NOW, MARK. SHE'S GONE...
HE FOUND A PACK AND WE LIT UP. SMOKED IN SILENCE FOR A WHILE. THEN HE TOLD ME HIS STORY. THEY ALL HAVE A STORY...
HE WAS A CHANGE-OF-LIFE BABY. HIS FATHER LEFT SOON AFTER HIS BIRTH, AND HIS MOTHER RAISED HIM ALONE. HARD.
HE SHOWED ME THE DISCOLORED SKIN ON HIS HAND WHERE SHE'D BURNED HIM WHEN SHE CAUGHT HIM WITH DIRTY MAGAZINES...
SHE WHIPPED HIM WITH AN ELECTRICAL CORD. HE DROPPED OUT OF SCHOOL. LONELY, SCARED. NEVER HAD A FRIEND...
IN ANOTHER HOUR HE WAS CRYING...

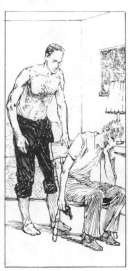

I TALKED TO HIM. TOLD HIM HE WAS GOING TO A BETTER PLACE.

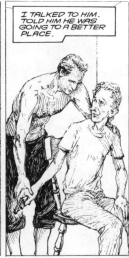

WHERE NO-BODY COULD EVER HURT HIM AGAIN...

BLAM!
BLAM!

SELF-DEFENSE. MAYBE NOW THEY'LL GIVE ME MY GUN BACK...

24

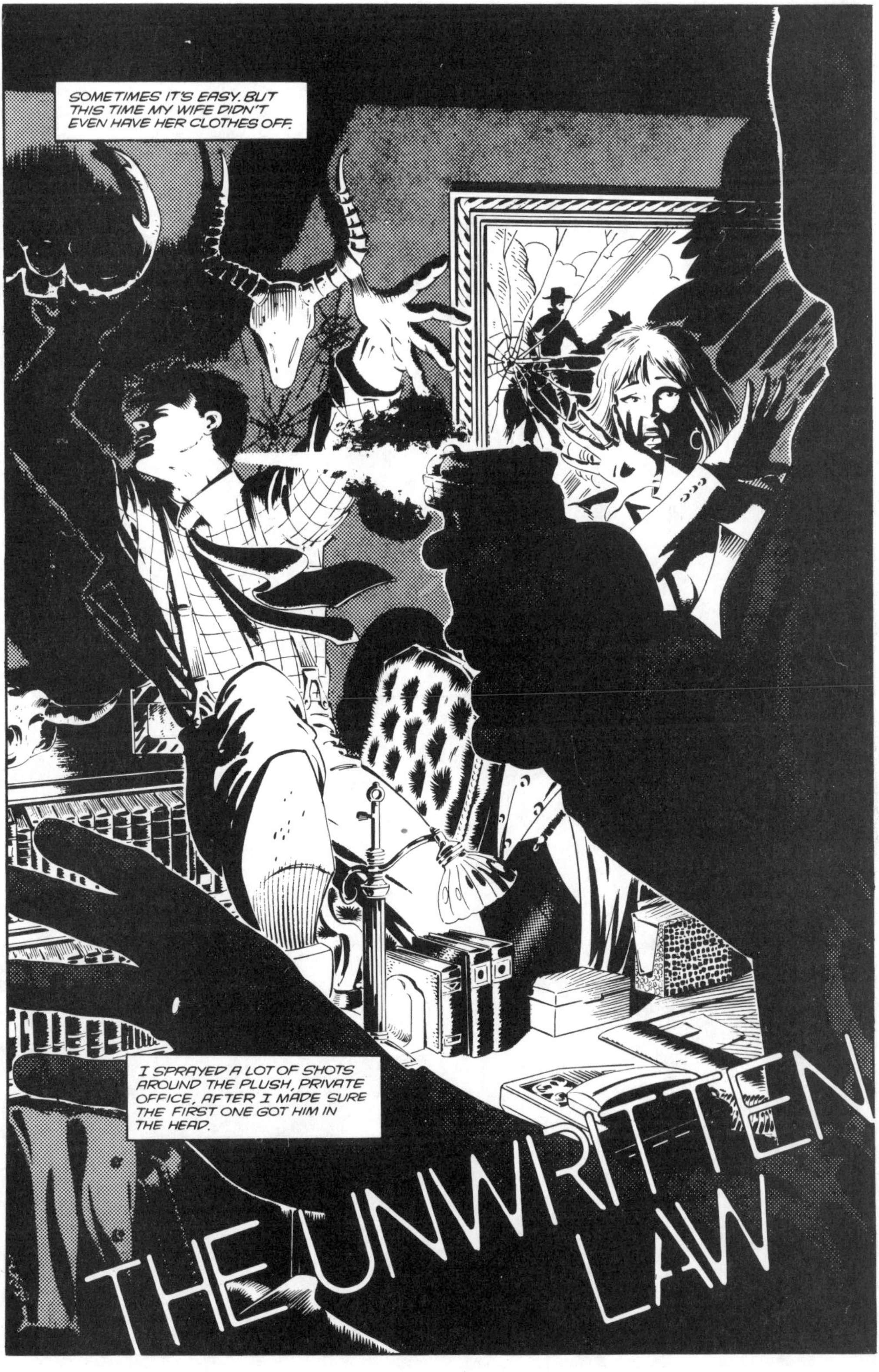
SOMETIMES IT'S EASY. BUT THIS TIME MY WIFE DIDN'T EVEN HAVE HER CLOTHES OFF.
I SPRAYED A LOT OF SHOTS AROUND THE PLUSH, PRIVATE OFFICE, AFTER I MADE SURE THE FIRST ONE GOT HIM IN THE HEAD.
THE UNWRITTEN LAW

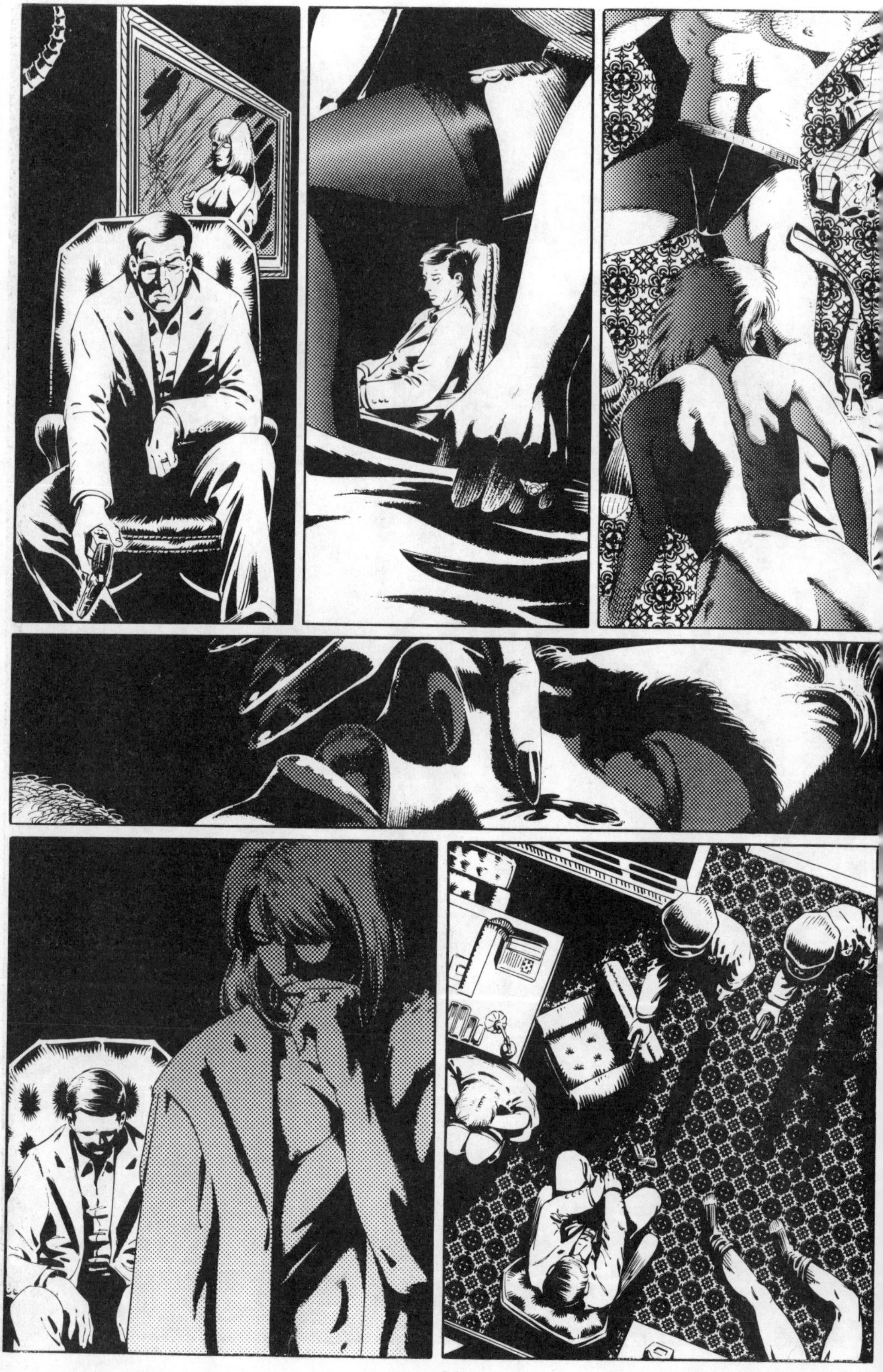

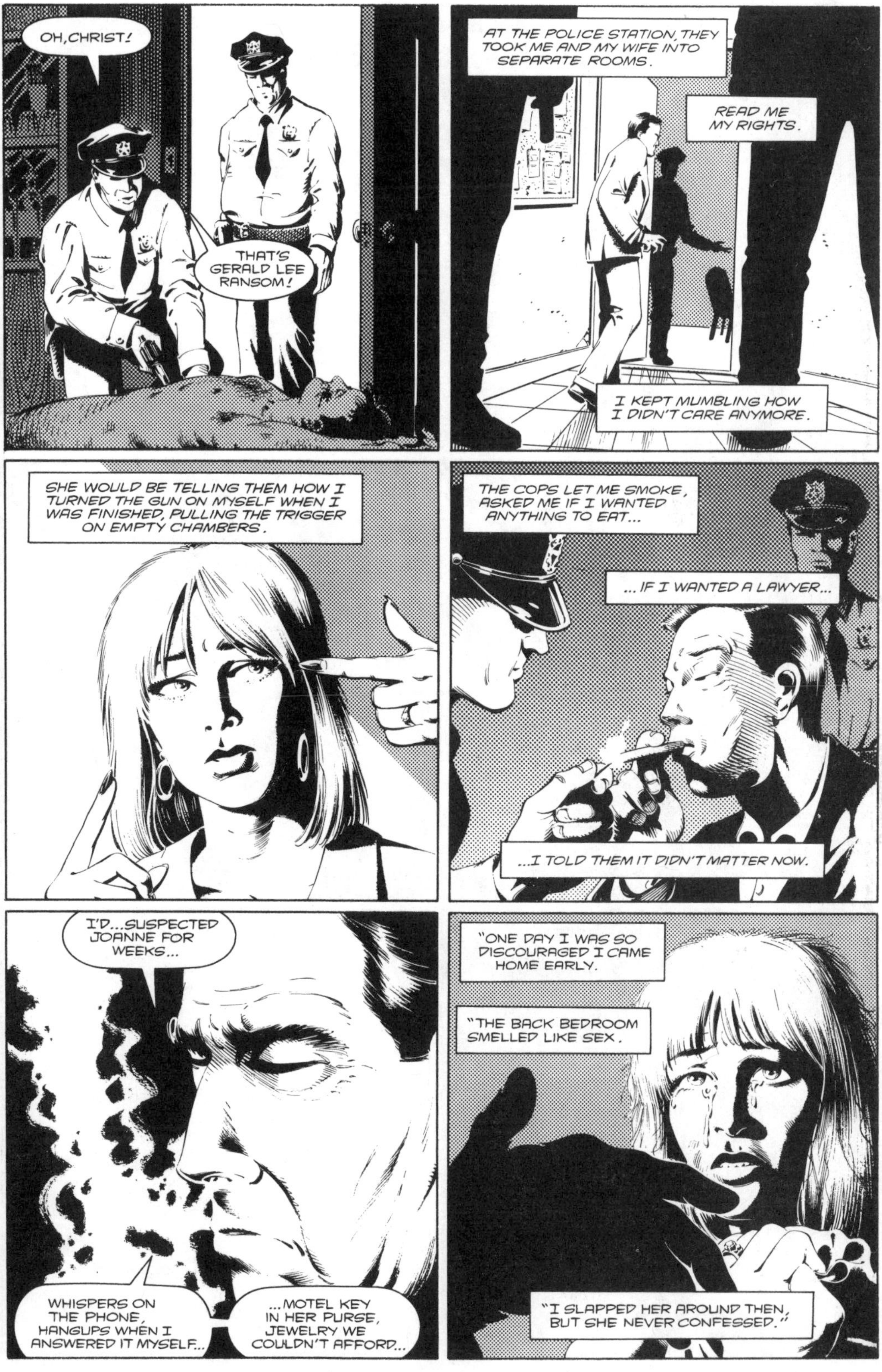
OH, CHRIST!
THAT'S GERALD LEE RANSOM!
AT THE POLICE STATION, THEY TOOK ME AND MY WIFE INTO SEPARATE ROOMS.
READ ME MY RIGHTS.
I KEPT MUMBLING HOW I DIDN'T CARE ANYMORE.
SHE WOULD BE TELLING THEM HOW I TURNED THE GUN ON MYSELF WHEN I WAS FINISHED, PULLING THE TRIGGER ON EMPTY CHAMBERS.
THE COPS LET ME SMOKE, ASKED ME IF I WANTED ANYTHING TO EAT...
... IF I WANTED A LAWYER...
...I TOLD THEM IT DIDN'T MATTER NOW.
I'D...SUSPECTED JOANNE FOR WEEKS...
WHISPERS ON THE PHONE, HANGUPS WHEN I ANSWERED IT MYSELF...
...MOTEL KEY IN HER PURSE, JEWELRY WE COULDN'T AFFORD...
"ONE DAY I WAS SO DISCOURAGED I CAME HOME EARLY.
"THE BACK BEDROOM SMELLED LIKE SEX.
"I SLAPPED HER AROUND THEN, BUT SHE NEVER CONFESSED."

THAT NIGHT...I TOLD HER I HAD TO GO TO A SALES MEETING.

IT WASN'T TRUE...

"I KNEW WHERE SHE WAS GOING.

"I'D HEARD HER TALK ABOUT *GERRY* BEFORE.

"HOW SHE WAS GOING TO RE-DO HIS WHOLE OFFICE, GIVE HIM A BIG *DISCOUNT*...

"...GET HIM TO TALK ABOUT HER WORK TO ALL HIS BIG BUSINESS PALS...

"I KNEW IT WAS A LIE."

WERE YOU GOING TO KILL HER TOO?

I DIDN'T KNOW *WHAT* I WAS GOING TO DO...

...MAYBE JUST THROW A SCARE INTO HIM, TELL HIM TO STAY AWAY FROM MY WIFE.

"BUT WHEN I SAW THEM TOGETHER...

"...HER BENT OVER HIS BIG DESK, BUTT IN THE AIR LIKE THAT...

"...HIM PUSHING INTO HER FROM BEHIND LIKE A DOG..."

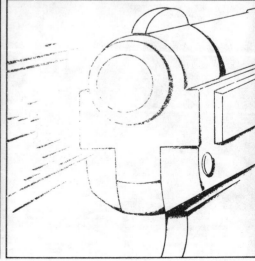

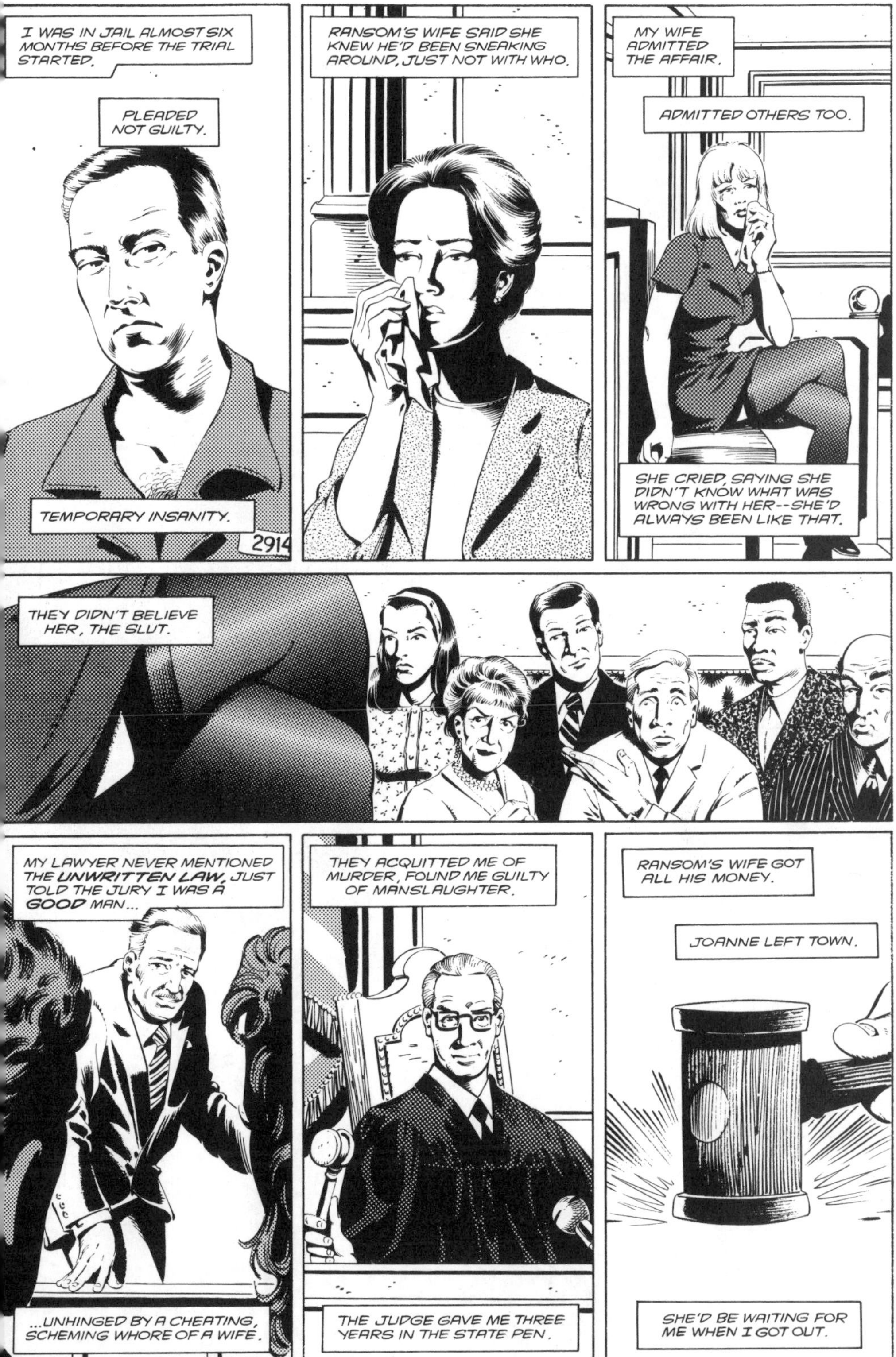
I WAS IN JAIL ALMOST SIX MONTHS BEFORE THE TRIAL STARTED.
PLEADED NOT GUILTY.
TEMPORARY INSANITY.
2914
RANSOM'S WIFE SAID SHE KNEW HE'D BEEN SNEAKING AROUND, JUST NOT WITH WHO.
MY WIFE ADMITTED THE AFFAIR.
ADMITTED OTHERS TOO.
SHE CRIED, SAYING SHE DIDN'T KNOW WHAT WAS WRONG WITH HER--SHE'D ALWAYS BEEN LIKE THAT.
THEY DIDN'T BELIEVE HER, THE SLUT.
MY LAWYER NEVER MENTIONED THE UNWRITTEN LAW, JUST TOLD THE JURY I WAS A GOOD MAN...
...UNHINGED BY A CHEATING, SCHEMING WHORE OF A WIFE.
THEY ACQUITTED ME OF MURDER, FOUND ME GUILTY OF MANSLAUGHTER.
THE JUDGE GAVE ME THREE YEARS IN THE STATE PEN.
RANSOM'S WIFE GOT ALL HIS MONEY.
JOANNE LEFT TOWN.
SHE'D BE WAITING FOR ME WHEN I GOT OUT.

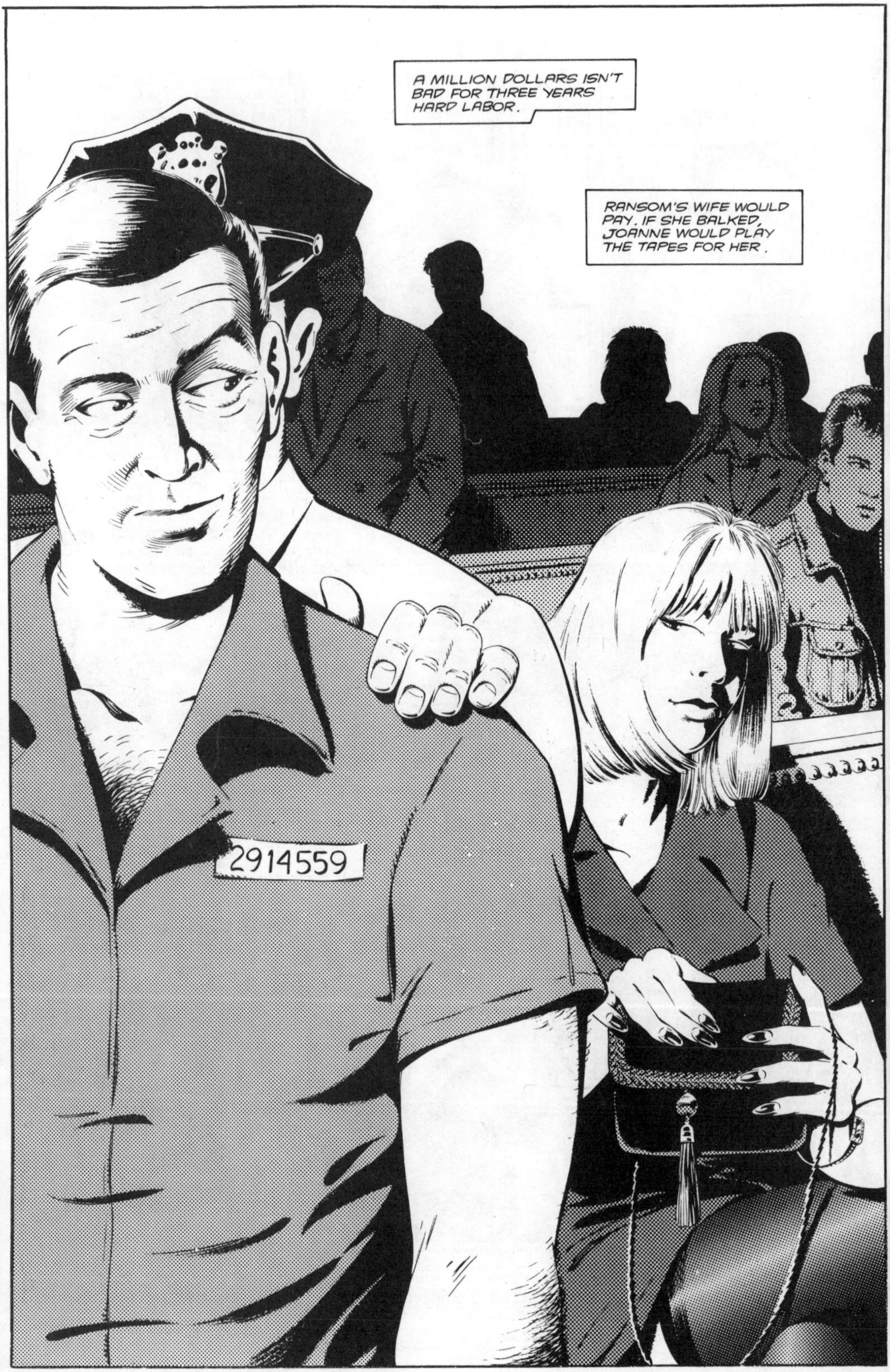
A MILLION DOLLARS ISN'T BAD FOR THREE YEARS HARD LABOR.
RANSOM'S WIFE WOULD PAY. IF SHE BALKED, JOANNE WOULD PLAY THE TAPES FOR HER.
2914559

FAMILY RESEMBLANCE

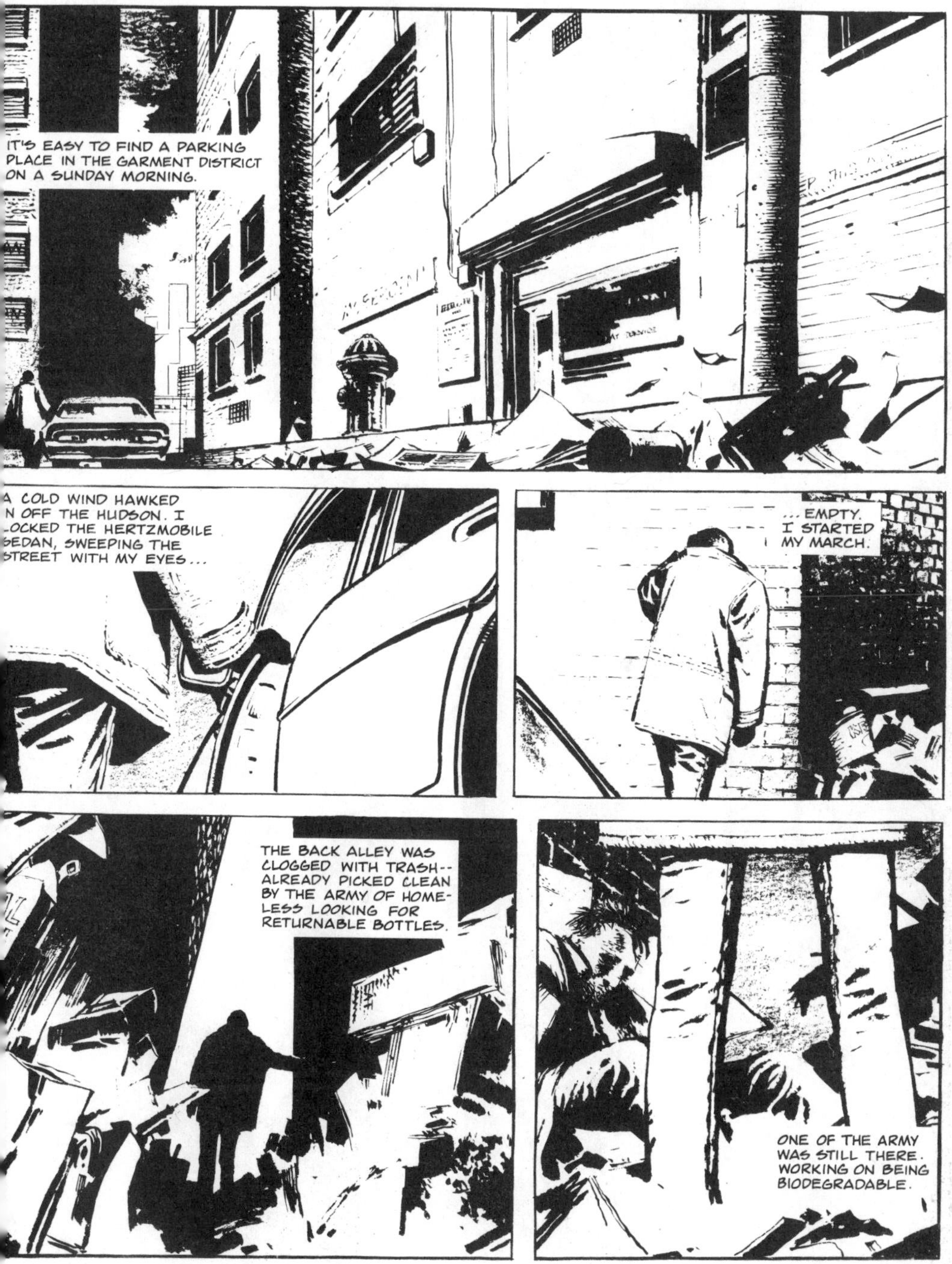
IT'S EASY TO FIND A PARKING PLACE IN THE GARMENT DISTRICT ON A SUNDAY MORNING.
A COLD WIND HAWKED N OFF THE HUDSON. I OCKED THE HERTZMOBILE SEDAN, SWEEPING THE STREET WITH MY EYES...
...EMPTY. I STARTED MY MARCH.
THE BACK ALLEY WAS CLOGGED WITH TRASH-- ALREADY PICKED CLEAN BY THE ARMY OF HOME-LESS LOOKING FOR RETURNABLE BOTTLES.
ONE OF THE ARMY WAS STILL THERE. WORKING ON BEING BIODEGRADABLE.

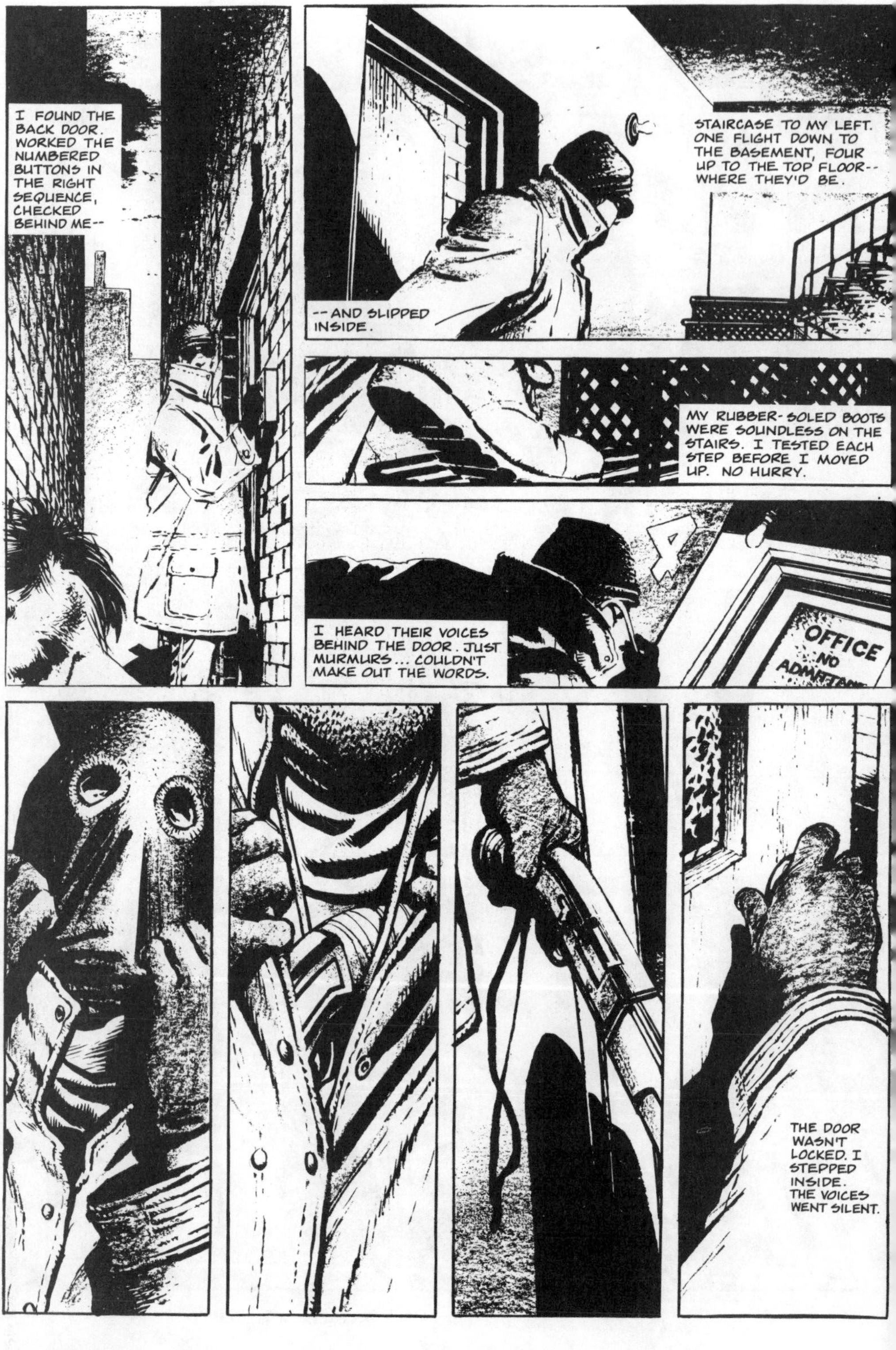
I FOUND THE BACK DOOR. WORKED THE NUMBERED BUTTONS IN THE RIGHT SEQUENCE, CHECKED BEHIND ME--
--AND SLIPPED INSIDE.
STAIRCASE TO MY LEFT. ONE FLIGHT DOWN TO THE BASEMENT, FOUR UP TO THE TOP FLOOR--WHERE THEY'D BE.
MY RUBBER-SOLED BOOTS WERE SOUNDLESS ON THE STAIRS. I TESTED EACH STEP BEFORE I MOVED UP. NO HURRY.
I HEARD THEIR VOICES BEHIND THE DOOR. JUST MURMURS... COULDN'T MAKE OUT THE WORDS.
4
OFFICE
NO
THE DOOR WASN'T LOCKED. I STEPPED INSIDE. THE VOICES WENT SILENT.

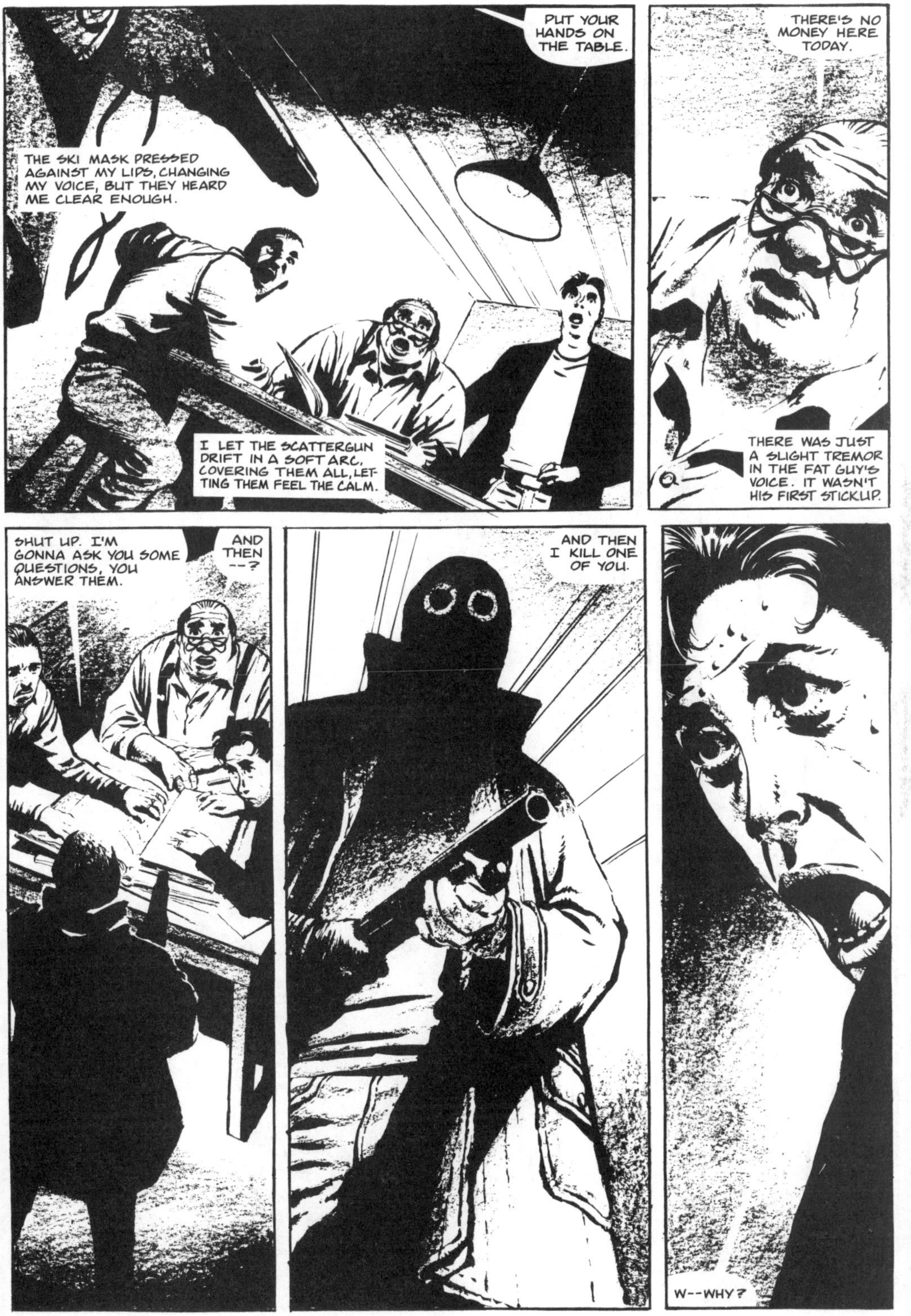
PUT YOUR HANDS ON THE TABLE.
THE SKI MASK PRESSED AGAINST MY LIPS, CHANGING MY VOICE, BUT THEY HEARD ME CLEAR ENOUGH.
I LET THE SCATTERGUN DRIFT IN A SOFT ARC, COVERING THEM ALL, LETTING THEM FEEL THE CALM.
THERE'S NO MONEY HERE TODAY.
THERE WAS JUST A SLIGHT TREMOR IN THE FAT GUY'S VOICE. IT WASN'T HIS FIRST STICKUP.
SHUT UP. I'M GONNA ASK YOU SOME QUESTIONS, YOU ANSWER THEM.
AND THEN --?
AND THEN I KILL ONE OF YOU.
W--WHY?

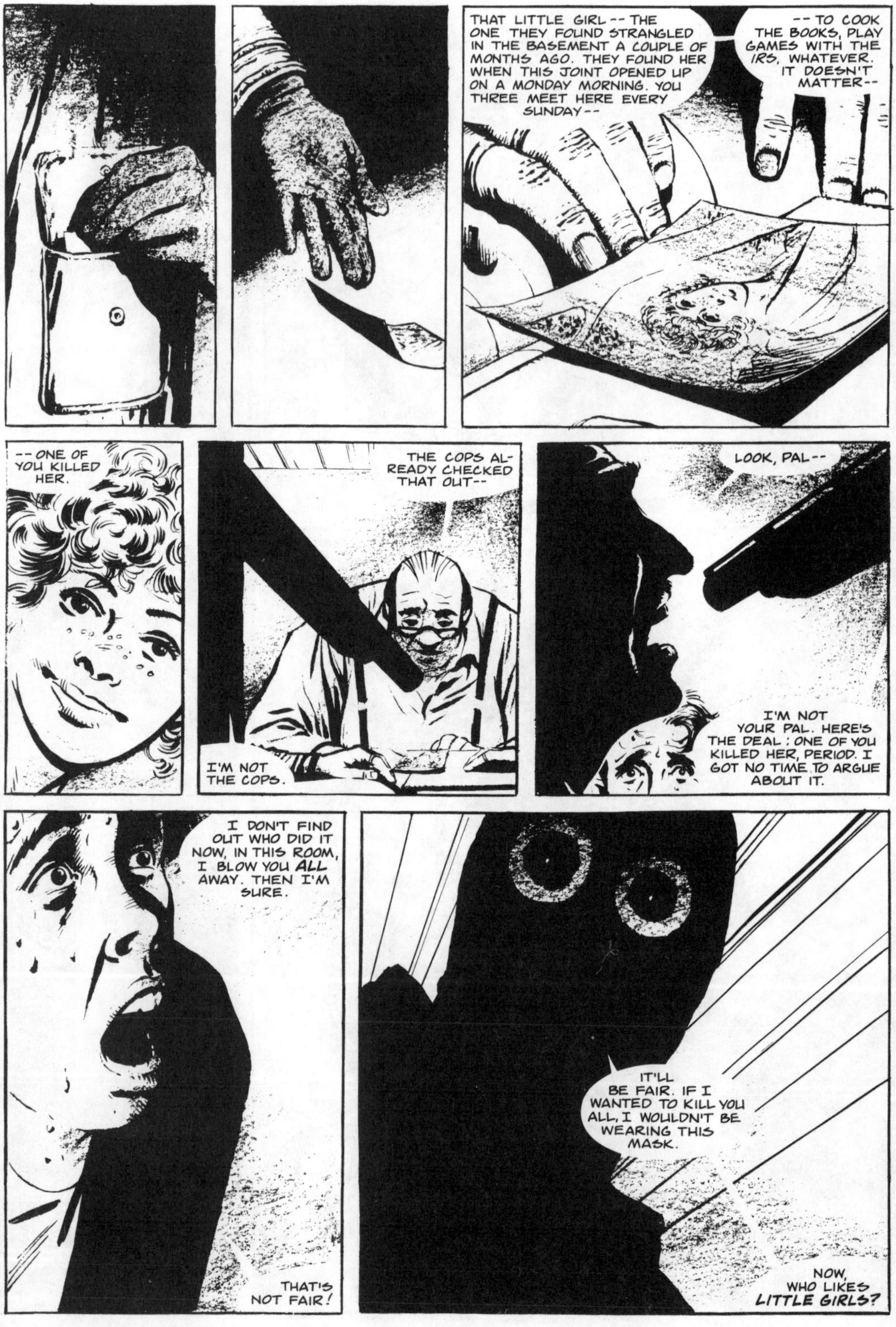
THAT LITTLE GIRL -- THE ONE THEY FOUND STRANGLED IN THE BASEMENT A COUPLE OF MONTHS AGO. THEY FOUND HER WHEN THIS JOINT OPENED UP ON A MONDAY MORNING. YOU THREE MEET HERE EVERY SUNDAY --
-- TO COOK THE BOOKS, PLAY GAMES WITH THE IRS, WHATEVER. IT DOESN'T MATTER --
-- ONE OF YOU KILLED HER.
THE COPS ALREADY CHECKED THAT OUT --
I'M NOT THE COPS.
LOOK, PAL --
I'M NOT YOUR PAL. HERE'S THE DEAL: ONE OF YOU KILLED HER, PERIOD. I GOT NO TIME TO ARGUE ABOUT IT.
I DON'T FIND OUT WHO DID IT NOW, IN THIS ROOM, I BLOW YOU ALL AWAY. THEN I'M SURE.
THAT'S NOT FAIR!
IT'LL BE FAIR. IF I WANTED TO KILL YOU ALL, I WOULDN'T BE WEARING THIS MASK.
NOW, WHO LIKES LITTLE GIRLS?

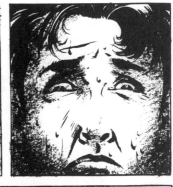

LAST CHANCE.

YOU KEEP MAGAZINES IN A DESK DRAWER?

IT'S NOT WHAT YOU THINK! I'M STRAIGHT-- YOU ASK ANYONE!

IT'S NOT ME! ASK MARKIE--ASK HIM ABOUT WHERE HE WAS A COUPLE A YEARS AGO!

THAT WASN'T FOR ANYTHING VIOLENT! I-- I JUST LIKED TO LOOK!

IN WINDOWS?

I WAS-- SICK. BUT I'M OKAY NOW. I SEE A THERAPIST AND EVERYTHING--

-- RIGHT, UNCLE MANNY? TELL HIM!

YEAH, MARKIE WOULDN'T HURT ANYONE.

35

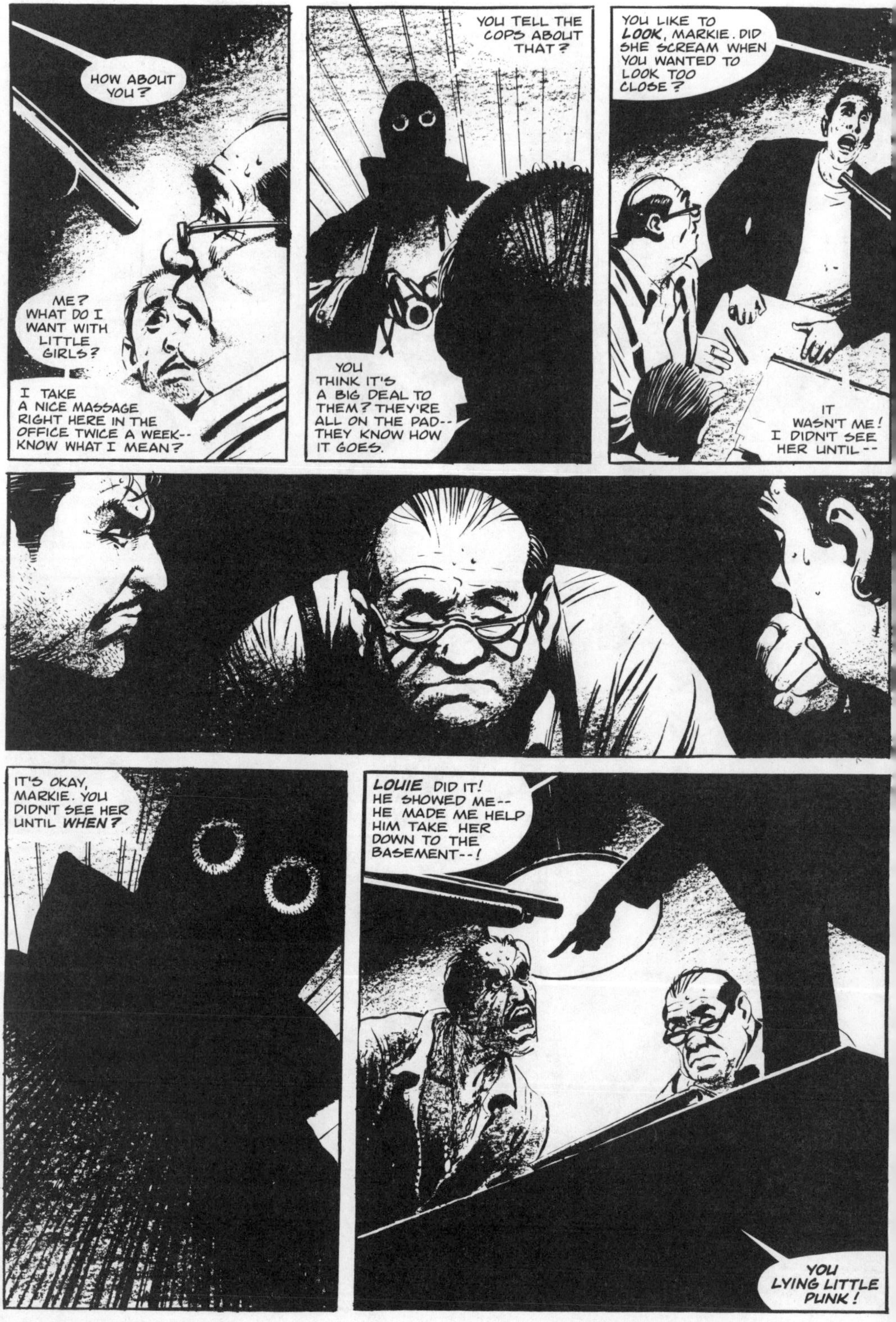
HOW ABOUT YOU?
ME? WHAT DO I WANT WITH LITTLE GIRLS?
I TAKE A NICE MASSAGE RIGHT HERE IN THE OFFICE TWICE A WEEK-- KNOW WHAT I MEAN?
YOU TELL THE COPS ABOUT THAT?
YOU THINK IT'S A BIG DEAL TO THEM? THEY'RE ALL ON THE PAD-- THEY KNOW HOW IT GOES.
YOU LIKE TO LOOK, MARKIE. DID SHE SCREAM WHEN YOU WANTED TO LOOK TOO CLOSE?
IT WASN'T ME! I DIDN'T SEE HER UNTIL--
IT'S OKAY, MARKIE. YOU DIDN'T SEE HER UNTIL WHEN?
LOUIE DID IT! HE SHOWED ME-- HE MADE ME HELP HIM TAKE HER DOWN TO THE BASEMENT--!
YOU LYING LITTLE PUNK!

HE *ALWAYS* WANTED ME OUTA HERE -- NEVER WANTED A PARTNER --

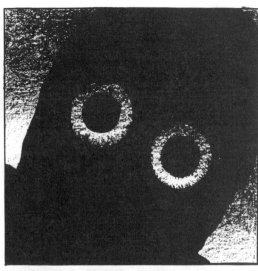

YEAH... OKAY, I TOOK HER DOWN-STAIRS --

-- BUT *AFTER* THIS FREAK FINISHED WITH HER. IT WASN'T ME. THE COPS KNOW-- MANNY PAYS THEM REGULAR!

HE SAID SHE CAME HERE LOOK-ING FOR A JOB!

I GUESS SHE NEEDED MONEY AND--

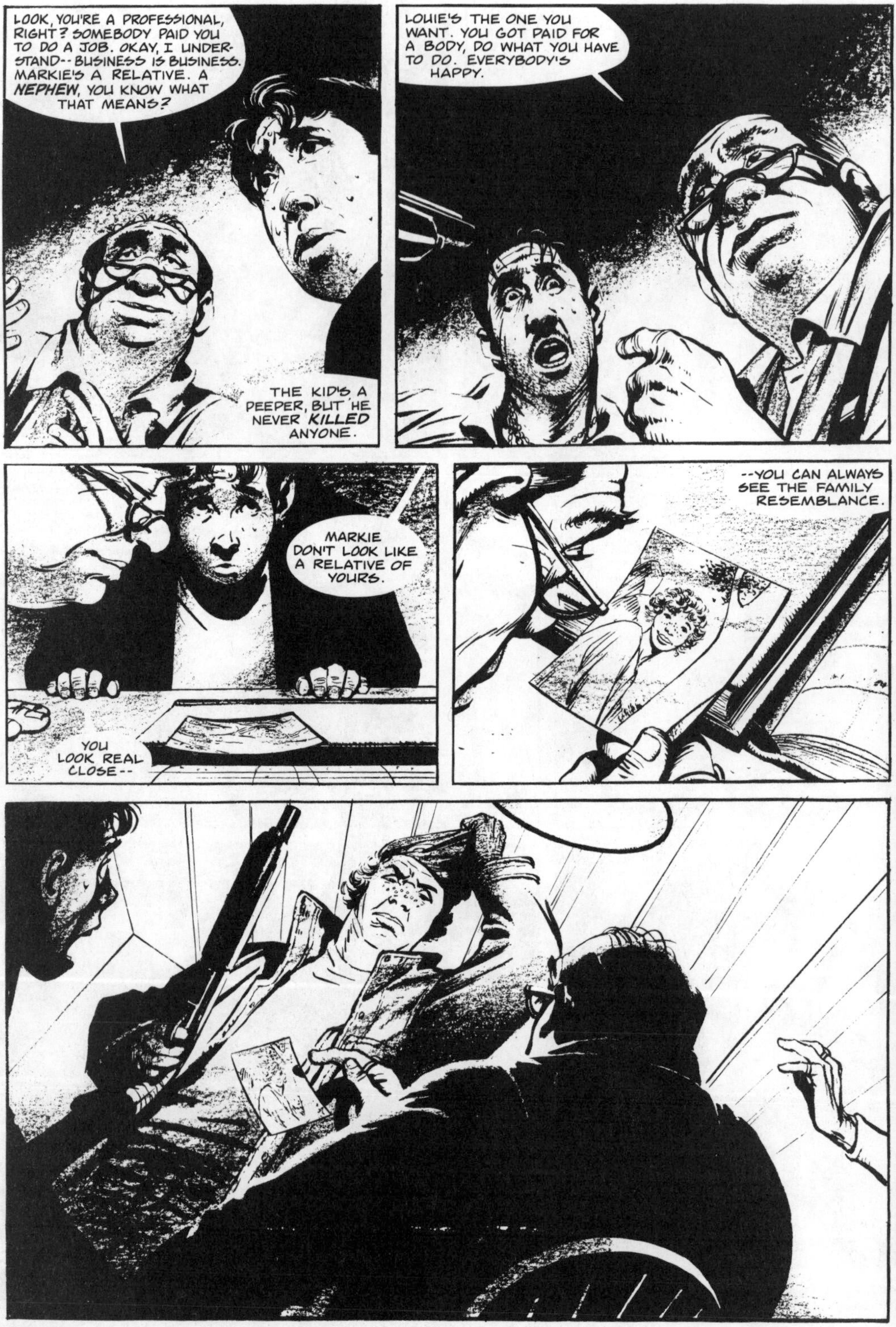
LOOK, YOU'RE A PROFESSIONAL, RIGHT? SOMEBODY PAID YOU TO DO A JOB. OKAY, I UNDERSTAND--BUSINESS IS BUSINESS. MARKIE'S A RELATIVE. A NEPHEW, YOU KNOW WHAT THAT MEANS?
THE KID'S A PEEPER, BUT HE NEVER KILLED ANYONE.
LOUIE'S THE ONE YOU WANT. YOU GOT PAID FOR A BODY, DO WHAT YOU HAVE TO DO. EVERYBODY'S HAPPY.
MARKIE DON'T LOOK LIKE A RELATIVE OF YOURS.
YOU LOOK REAL CLOSE--
--YOU CAN ALWAYS SEE THE FAMILY RESEMBLANCE.

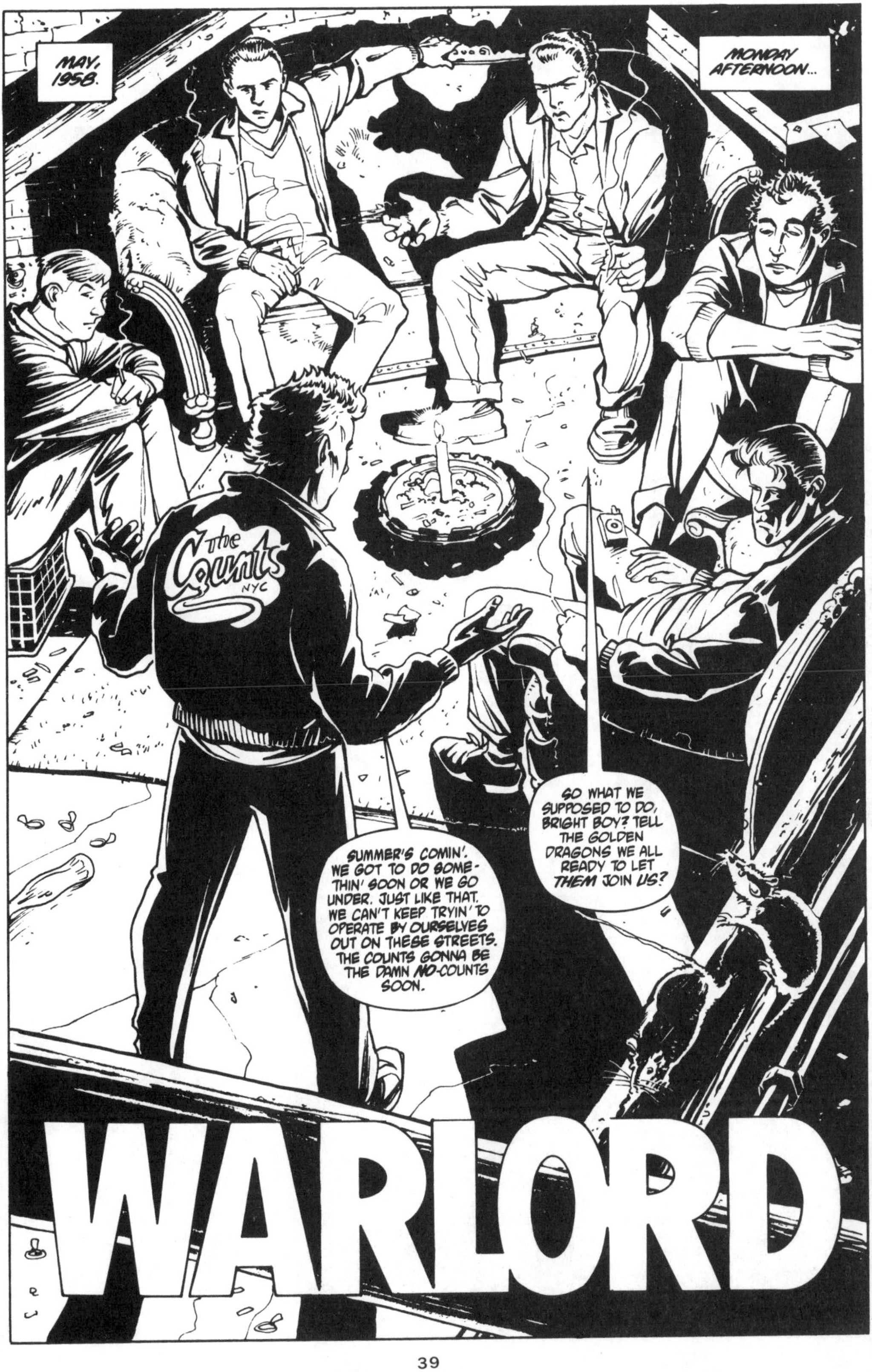
MAY, 1958.
MONDAY AFTERNOON...
the Counts NYC
SUMMER'S COMIN'. WE GOT TO DO SOME-THIN' SOON OR WE GO UNDER. JUST LIKE THAT. WE CAN'T KEEP TRYIN' TO OPERATE BY OURSELVES OUT ON THESE STREETS. THE COUNTS GONNA BE THE DAMN NO-COUNTS SOON.
SO WHAT WE SUPPOSED TO DO, BRIGHT BOY? TELL THE GOLDEN DRAGONS WE ALL READY TO LET THEM JOIN US?
WARLORD

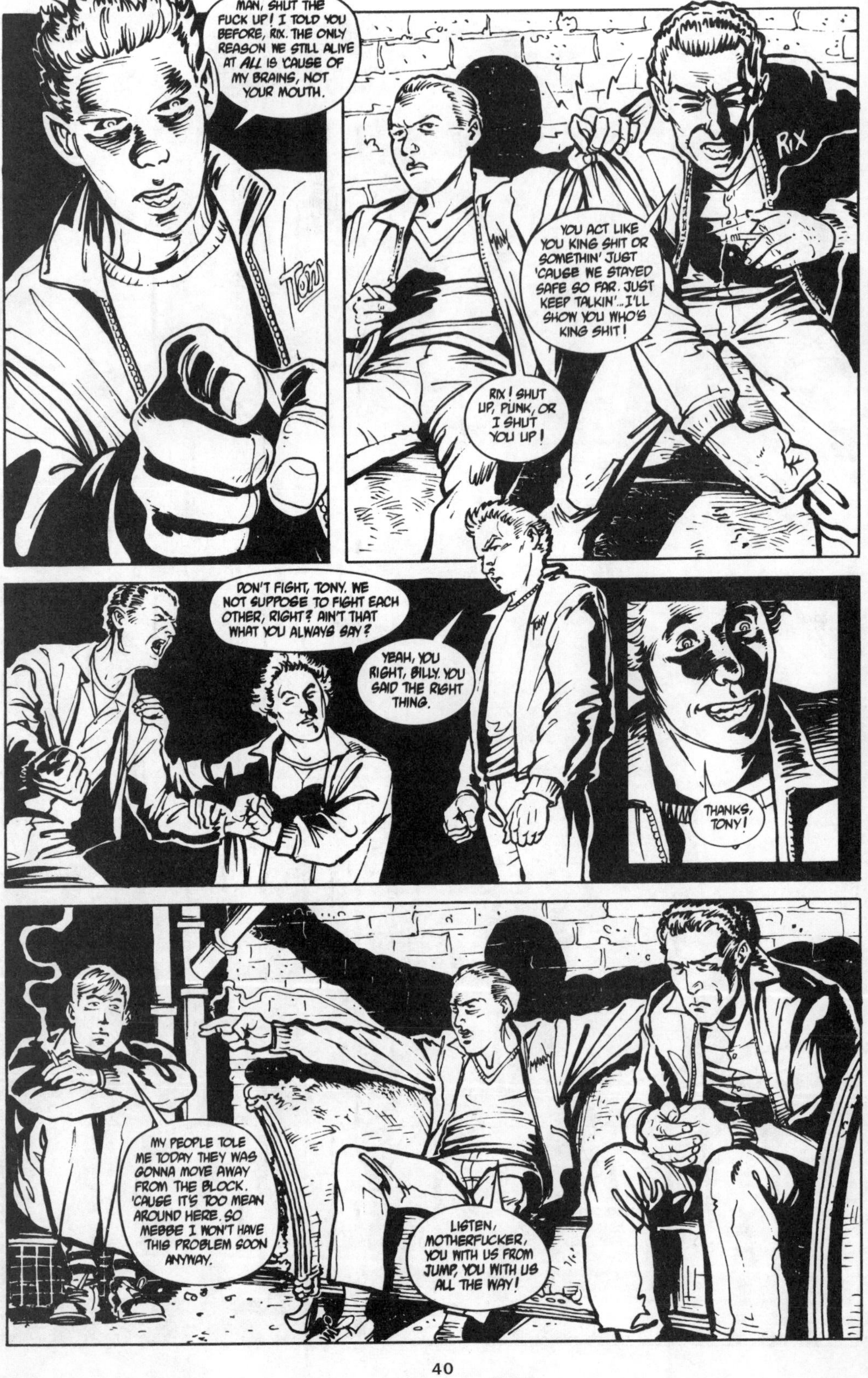

MAN, SHUT THE FUCK UP! I TOLD YOU BEFORE, RIX. THE ONLY REASON WE STILL ALIVE AT ALL IS 'CAUSE OF MY BRAINS, NOT YOUR MOUTH.
RIX
YOU ACT LIKE YOU KING SHIT OR SOMETHIN' JUST 'CAUSE WE STAYED SAFE SO FAR. JUST KEEP TALKIN'...I'LL SHOW YOU WHO'S KING SHIT!
RIX! SHUT UP, PUNK, OR I SHUT YOU UP!
DON'T FIGHT, TONY. WE NOT SUPPOSE TO FIGHT EACH OTHER, RIGHT? AIN'T THAT WHAT YOU ALWAYS SAY?
YEAH, YOU RIGHT, BILLY. YOU SAID THE RIGHT THING.
TONY
THANKS, TONY!
MY PEOPLE TOLE ME TODAY THEY WAS GONNA MOVE AWAY FROM THE BLOCK. 'CAUSE IT'S TOO MEAN AROUND HERE. SO MEBBE I WON'T HAVE THIS PROBLEM SOON ANYWAY.
LISTEN, MOTHERFUCKER, YOU WITH US FROM JUMP, YOU WITH US ALL THE WAY!

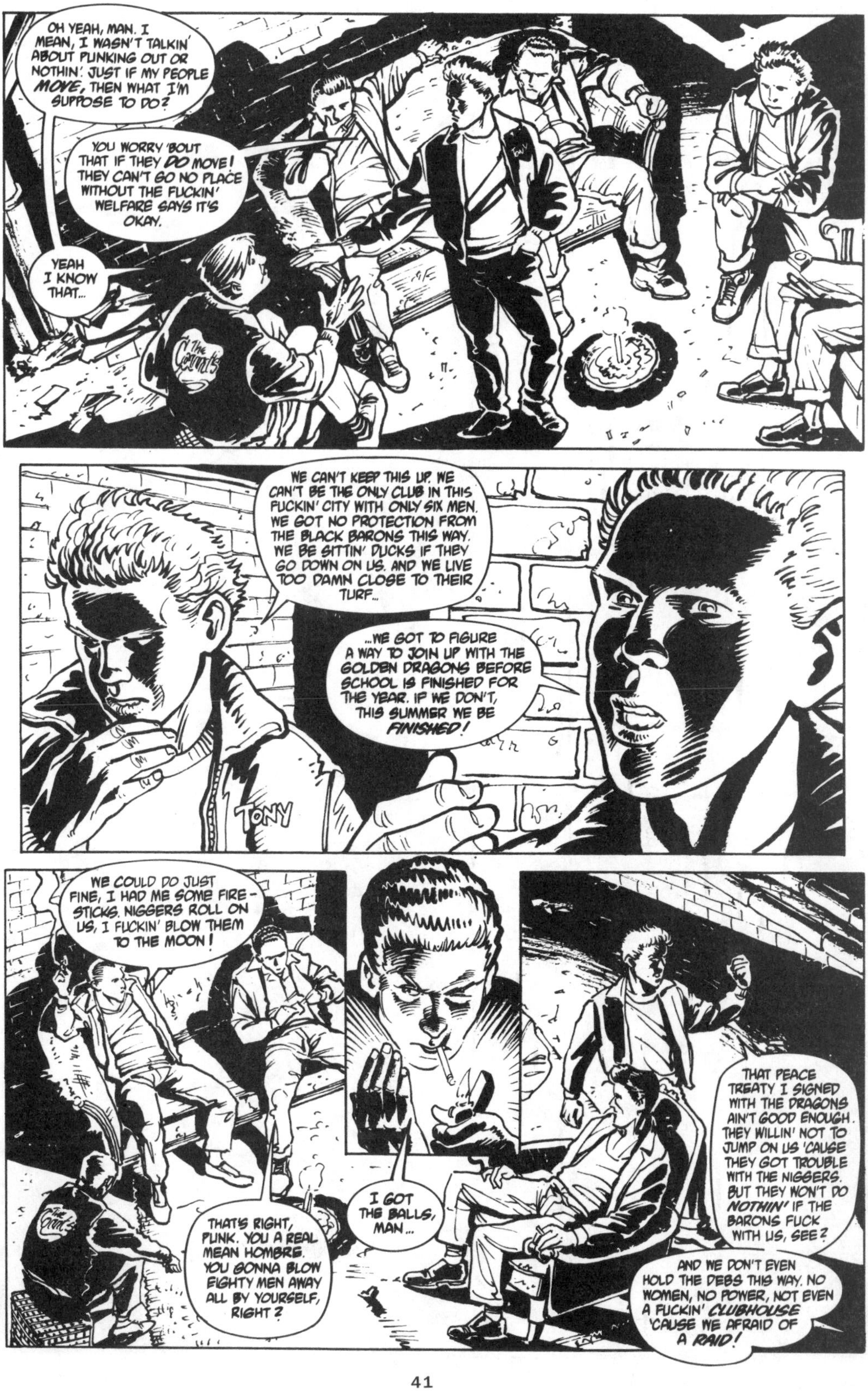
OH YEAH, MAN. I MEAN, I WASN'T TALKIN' ABOUT PUNKING OUT OR NOTHIN'. JUST IF MY PEOPLE MOVE, THEN WHAT I'M SUPPOSE TO DO?
YOU WORRY 'BOUT THAT IF THEY DO MOVE! THEY CAN'T GO NO PLACE WITHOUT THE FUCKIN' WELFARE SAYS IT'S OKAY.
YEAH I KNOW THAT...
WE CAN'T KEEP THIS UP. WE CAN'T BE THE ONLY CLUB IN THIS FUCKIN' CITY WITH ONLY SIX MEN. WE GOT NO PROTECTION FROM THE BLACK BARONS THIS WAY. WE BE SITTIN' DUCKS IF THEY GO DOWN ON US. AND WE LIVE TOO DAMN CLOSE TO THEIR TURF...
...WE GOT TO FIGURE A WAY TO JOIN UP WITH THE GOLDEN DRAGONS BEFORE SCHOOL IS FINISHED FOR THE YEAR. IF WE DON'T, THIS SUMMER WE BE FINISHED!
WE COULD DO JUST FINE, I HAD ME SOME FIRE-STICKS. NIGGERS ROLL ON US, I FUCKIN' BLOW THEM TO THE MOON!
THAT'S RIGHT, PUNK. YOU A REAL MEAN HOMBRE. YOU GONNA BLOW EIGHTY MEN AWAY ALL BY YOURSELF, RIGHT?
I GOT THE BALLS, MAN...
THAT PEACE TREATY I SIGNED WITH THE DRAGONS AIN'T GOOD ENOUGH. THEY WILLIN' NOT TO JUMP ON US 'CAUSE THEY GOT TROUBLE WITH THE NIGGERS. BUT THEY WON'T DO NOTHIN' IF THE BARONS FUCK WITH US, SEE?
AND WE DON'T EVEN HOLD THE DEBS THIS WAY. NO WOMEN, NO POWER, NOT EVEN A FUCKIN' CLUBHOUSE 'CAUSE WE AFRAID OF A RAID!

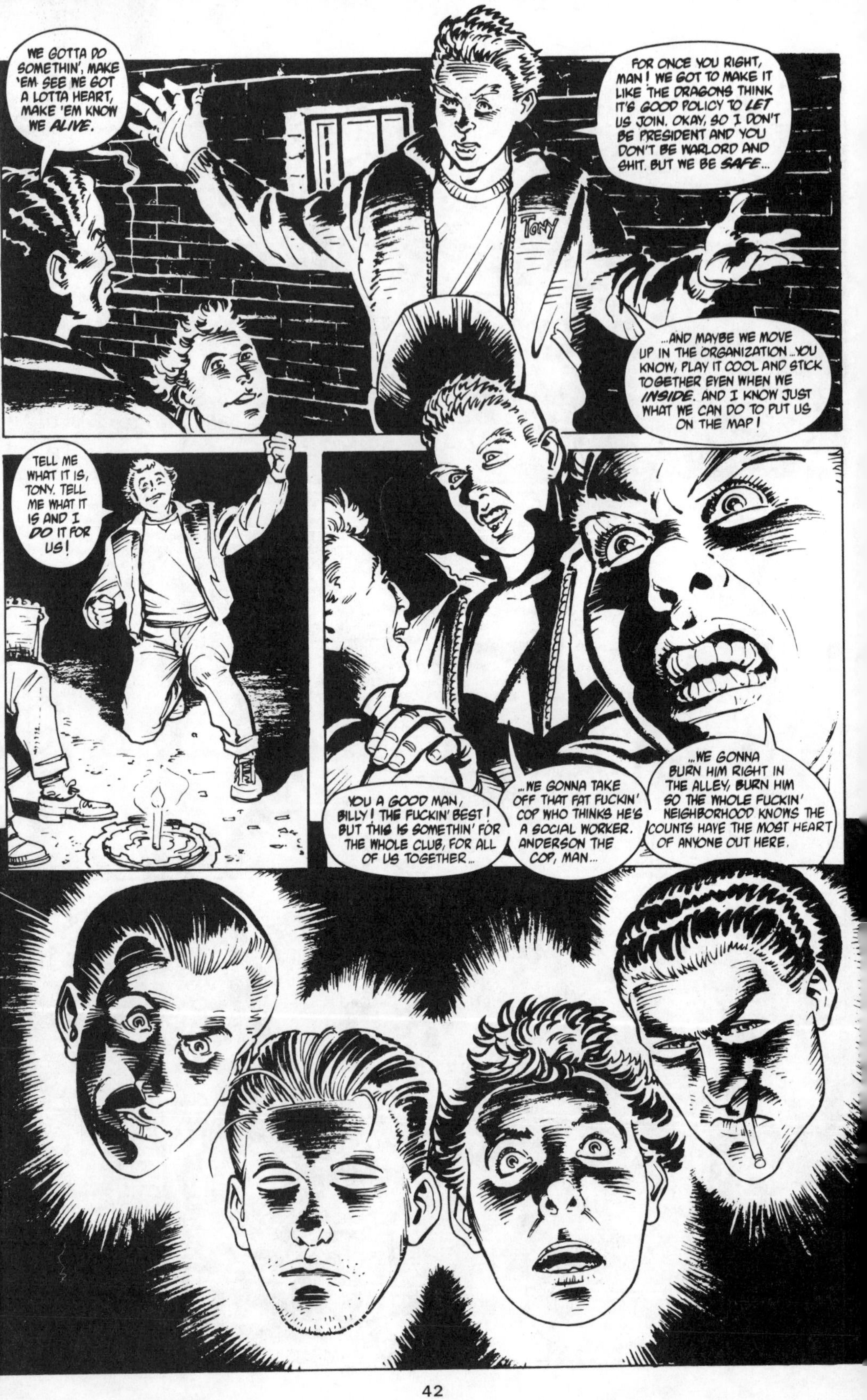
WE GOTTA DO SOMETHIN', MAKE 'EM SEE WE GOT A LOTTA HEART, MAKE 'EM KNOW WE ALIVE.
FOR ONCE YOU RIGHT, MAN! WE GOT TO MAKE IT LIKE THE DRAGONS THINK IT'S GOOD POLICY TO LET US JOIN. OKAY, SO I DON'T BE PRESIDENT AND YOU DON'T BE WARLORD AND SHIT. BUT WE BE SAFE...
TONY
...AND MAYBE WE MOVE UP IN THE ORGANIZATION...YOU KNOW, PLAY IT COOL AND STICK TOGETHER EVEN WHEN WE INSIDE. AND I KNOW JUST WHAT WE CAN DO TO PUT US ON THE MAP!
TELL ME WHAT IT IS, TONY. TELL ME WHAT IT IS AND I DO IT FOR US!
YOU A GOOD MAN, BILLY! THE FUCKIN' BEST! BUT THIS IS SOMETHIN' FOR THE WHOLE CLUB, FOR ALL OF US TOGETHER...
...WE GONNA TAKE OFF THAT FAT FUCKIN' COP WHO THINKS HE'S A SOCIAL WORKER. ANDERSON THE COP, MAN...
...WE GONNA BURN HIM RIGHT IN THE ALLEY, BURN HIM SO THE WHOLE FUCKIN' NEIGHBORHOOD KNOWS THE COUNTS HAVE THE MOST HEART OF ANYONE OUT HERE.

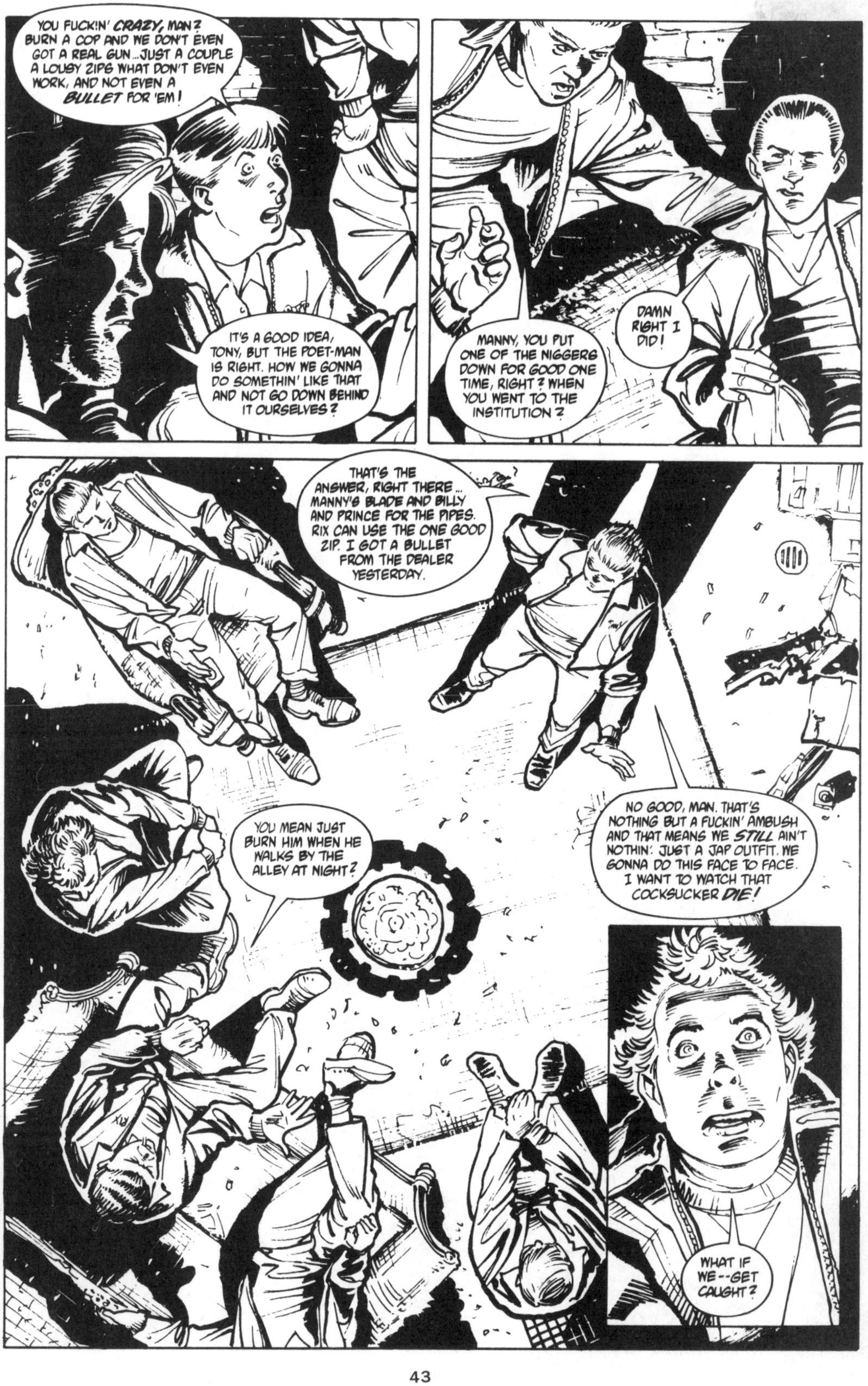
YOU FUCK!N' *CRAZY*, MAN? BURN A COP AND WE DON'T EVEN GOT A REAL GUN...JUST A COUPLE A LOUSY ZIPS WHAT DON'T EVEN WORK, AND NOT EVEN A *BULLET* FOR 'EM!
IT'S A GOOD IDEA, TONY, BUT THE POET-MAN IS RIGHT. HOW WE GONNA DO SOMETHIN' LIKE THAT AND NOT GO DOWN BEHIND IT OURSELVES?
MANNY, YOU PUT ONE OF THE NIGGERS DOWN FOR GOOD ONE TIME, RIGHT? WHEN YOU WENT TO THE INSTITUTION?
DAMN RIGHT I DID!
THAT'S THE ANSWER, RIGHT THERE... MANNY'S BLADE AND BILLY AND PRINCE FOR THE PIPES. RIX CAN USE THE ONE GOOD ZIP. I GOT A BULLET FROM THE DEALER YESTERDAY.
YOU MEAN JUST BURN HIM WHEN HE WALKS BY THE ALLEY AT NIGHT?
NO GOOD, MAN. THAT'S NOTHING BUT A FUCKIN' AMBUSH AND THAT MEANS WE *STILL* AIN'T NOTHIN'. JUST A JAP OUTFIT. WE GONNA DO THIS FACE TO FACE. I WANT TO WATCH THAT COCKSUCKER *DIE*!
WHAT IF WE--GET CAUGHT?

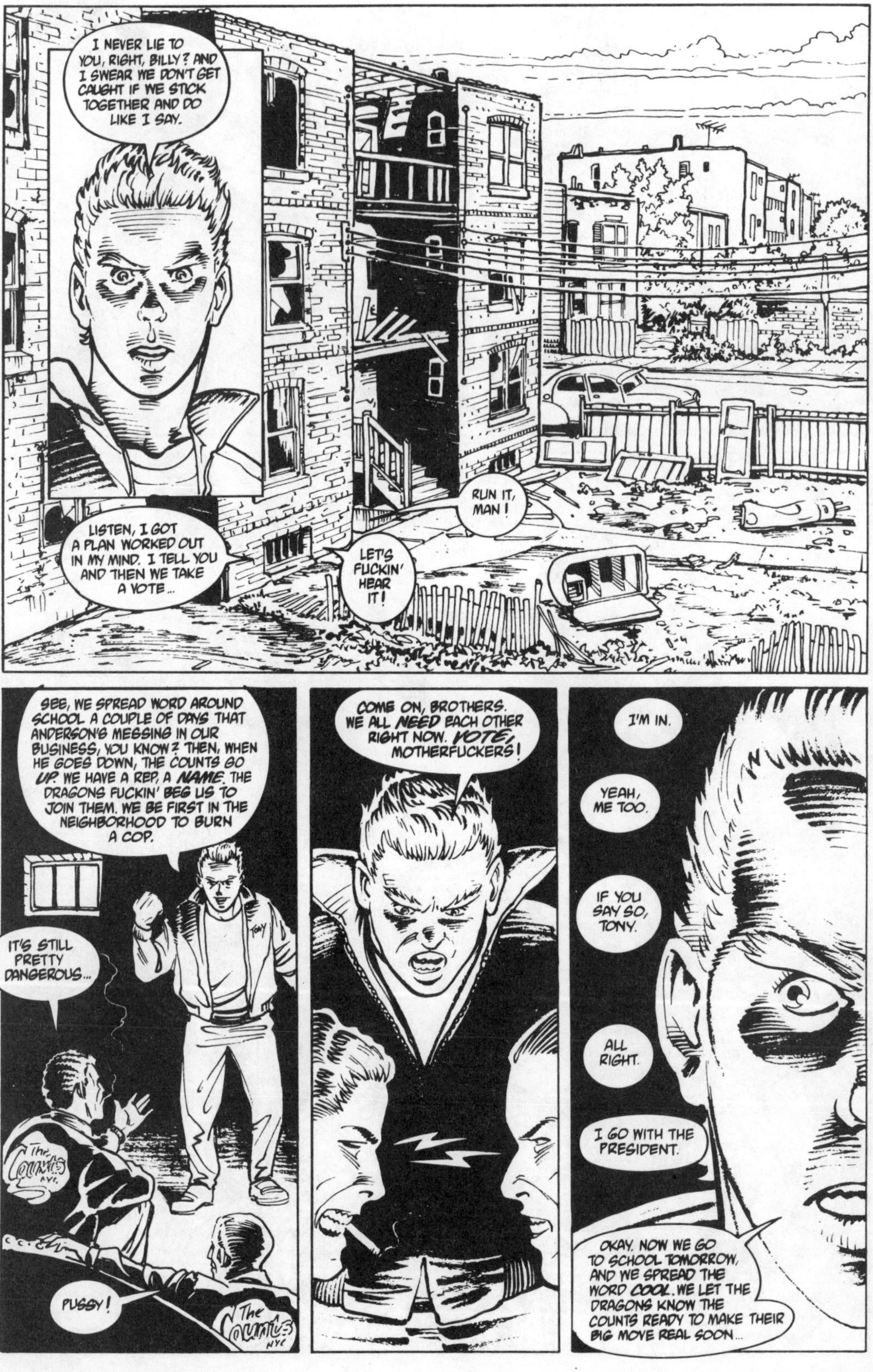
I NEVER LIE TO YOU, RIGHT, BILLY? AND I SWEAR WE DON'T GET CAUGHT IF WE STICK TOGETHER AND DO LIKE I SAY.
LISTEN, I GOT A PLAN WORKED OUT IN MY MIND. I TELL YOU AND THEN WE TAKE A VOTE...
LET'S FUCKIN' HEAR IT!
RUN IT, MAN!
SEE, WE SPREAD WORD AROUND SCHOOL A COUPLE OF DAYS THAT ANDERSON'S MESSING IN OUR BUSINESS, YOU KNOW? THEN, WHEN HE GOES DOWN, THE COUNTS GO UP. WE HAVE A REP, A NAME. THE DRAGONS FUCKIN' BEG US TO JOIN THEM. WE BE FIRST IN THE NEIGHBORHOOD TO BURN A COP.
IT'S STILL PRETTY DANGEROUS...
PUSSY!
COME ON, BROTHERS. WE ALL NEED EACH OTHER RIGHT NOW. VOTE, MOTHERFUCKERS!
I'M IN.
YEAH, ME TOO.
IF YOU SAY SO, TONY.
ALL RIGHT.
I GO WITH THE PRESIDENT.
OKAY. NOW WE GO TO SCHOOL TOMORROW, AND WE SPREAD THE WORD COOL. WE LET THE DRAGONS KNOW THE COUNTS READY TO MAKE THEIR BIG MOVE REAL SOON...

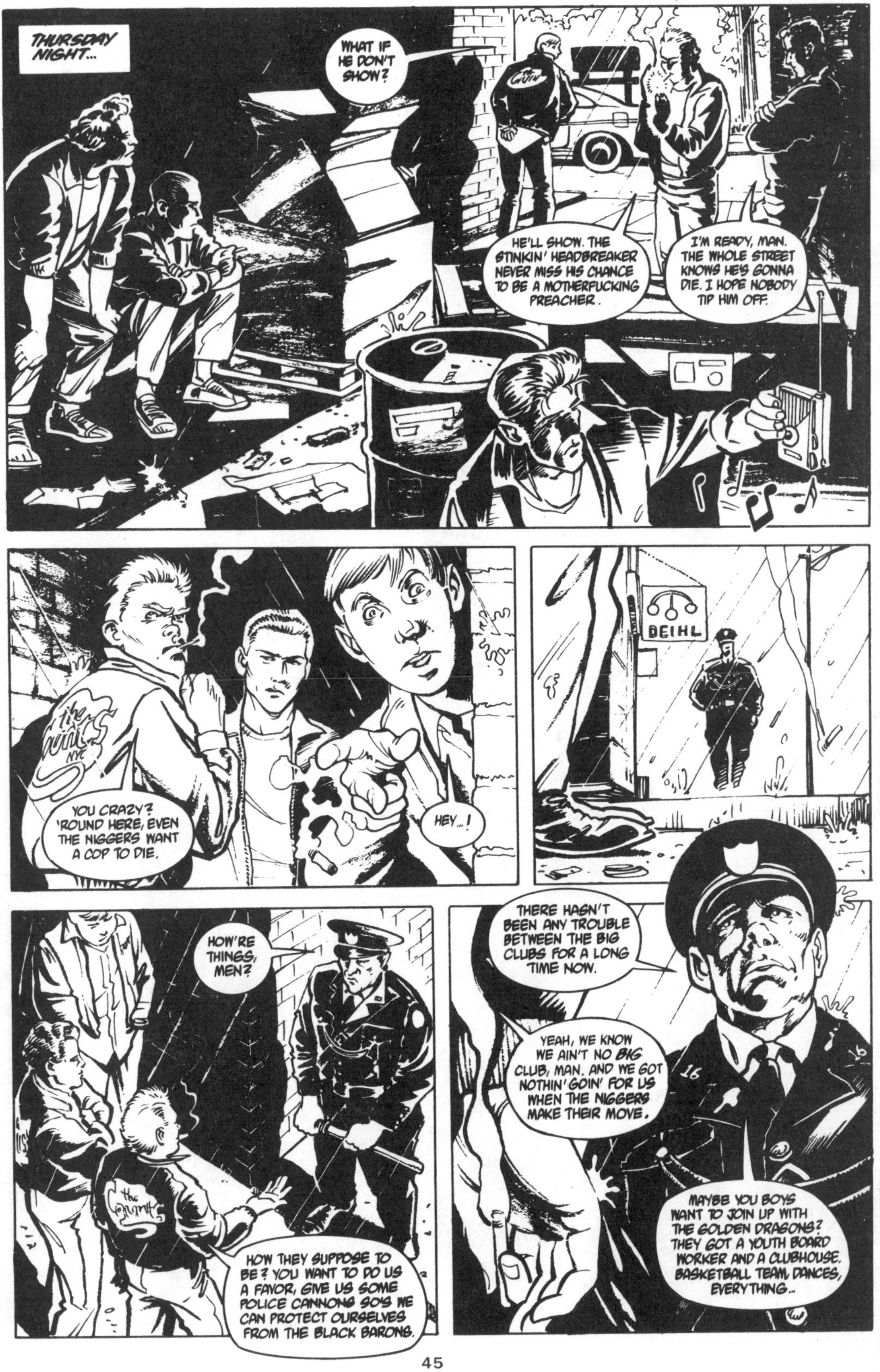
THURSDAY NIGHT...
WHAT IF HE DON'T SHOW?
HE'LL SHOW. THE STINKIN' HEADBREAKER NEVER MISS HIS CHANCE TO BE A MOTHERFUCKING PREACHER.
I'M READY, MAN. THE WHOLE STREET KNOWS HE'S GONNA DIE. I HOPE NOBODY TIP HIM OFF.
YOU CRAZY? 'ROUND HERE, EVEN THE NIGGERS WANT A COP TO DIE.
HEY...!
DEIHL
HOW'RE THINGS, MEN?
HOW THEY SUPPOSE TO BE? YOU WANT TO DO US A FAVOR, GIVE US SOME POLICE CANNONS SO'S WE CAN PROTECT OURSELVES FROM THE BLACK BARONS.
THERE HASN'T BEEN ANY TROUBLE BETWEEN THE BIG CLUBS FOR A LONG TIME NOW.
YEAH, WE KNOW WE AIN'T NO BIG CLUB, MAN, AND WE GOT NOTHIN' GOIN' FOR US WHEN THE NIGGERS MAKE THEIR MOVE.
MAYBE YOU BOYS WANT TO JOIN UP WITH THE GOLDEN DRAGONS? THEY GOT A YOUTH BOARD WORKER AND A CLUBHOUSE. BASKETBALL TEAM, DANCES, EVERYTHING...

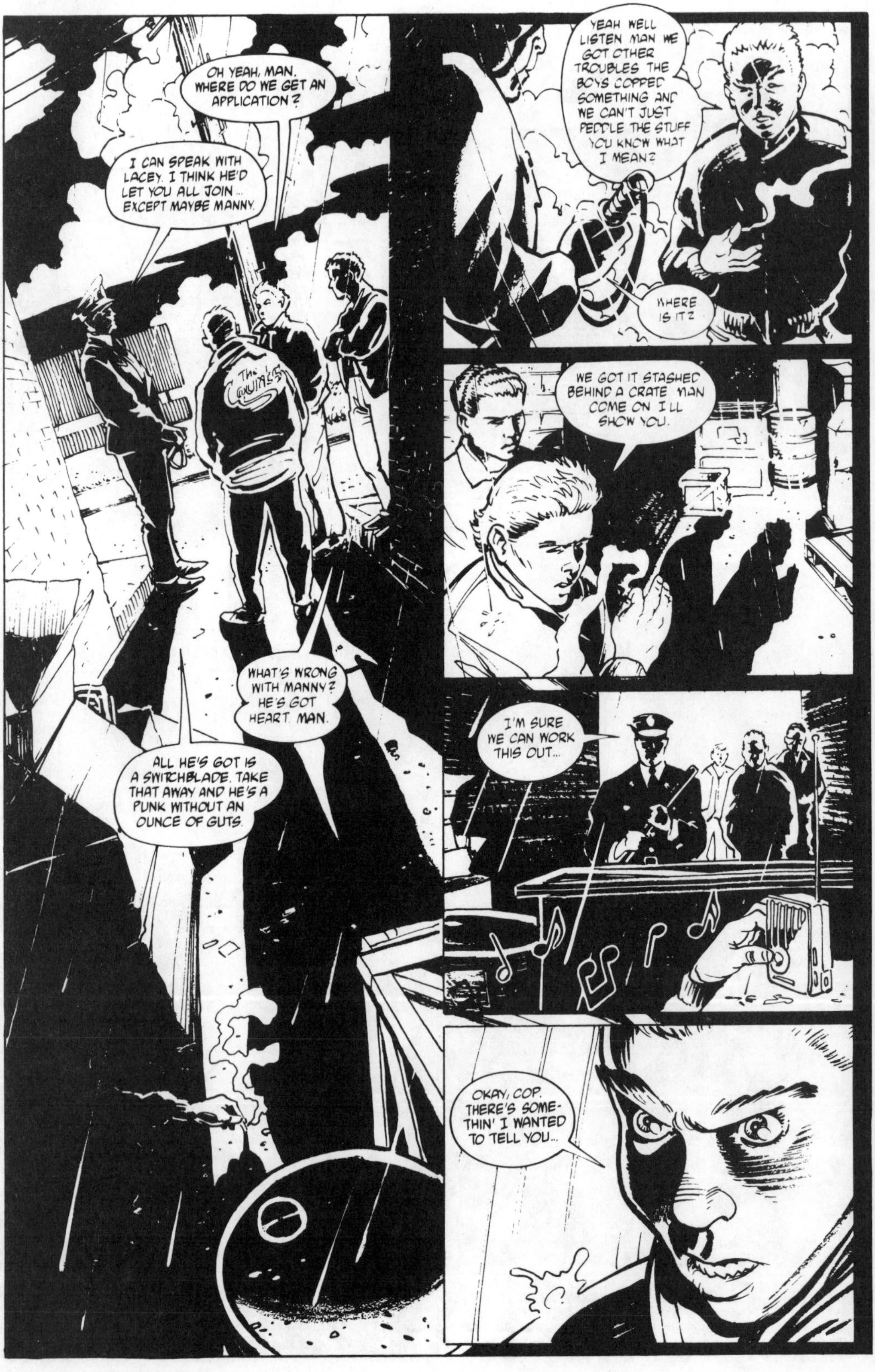
OH YEAH, MAN. WHERE DO WE GET AN APPLICATION?
I CAN SPEAK WITH LACEY. I THINK HE'D LET YOU ALL JOIN... EXCEPT MAYBE MANNY.
WHAT'S WRONG WITH MANNY? HE'S GOT HEART, MAN.
ALL HE'S GOT IS A SWITCHBLADE. TAKE THAT AWAY AND HE'S A PUNK WITHOUT AN OUNCE OF GUTS.
YEAH WELL LISTEN MAN WE GOT OTHER TROUBLES THE BOYS COPPED SOMETHING AND WE CAN'T JUST PEDDLE THE STUFF YOU KNOW WHAT I MEAN?
WHERE IS IT?
WE GOT IT STASHED BEHIND A CRATE MAN COME ON I'LL SHOW YOU.
I'M SURE WE CAN WORK THIS OUT...
OKAY, COP. THERE'S SOME-THIN' I WANTED TO TELL YOU...

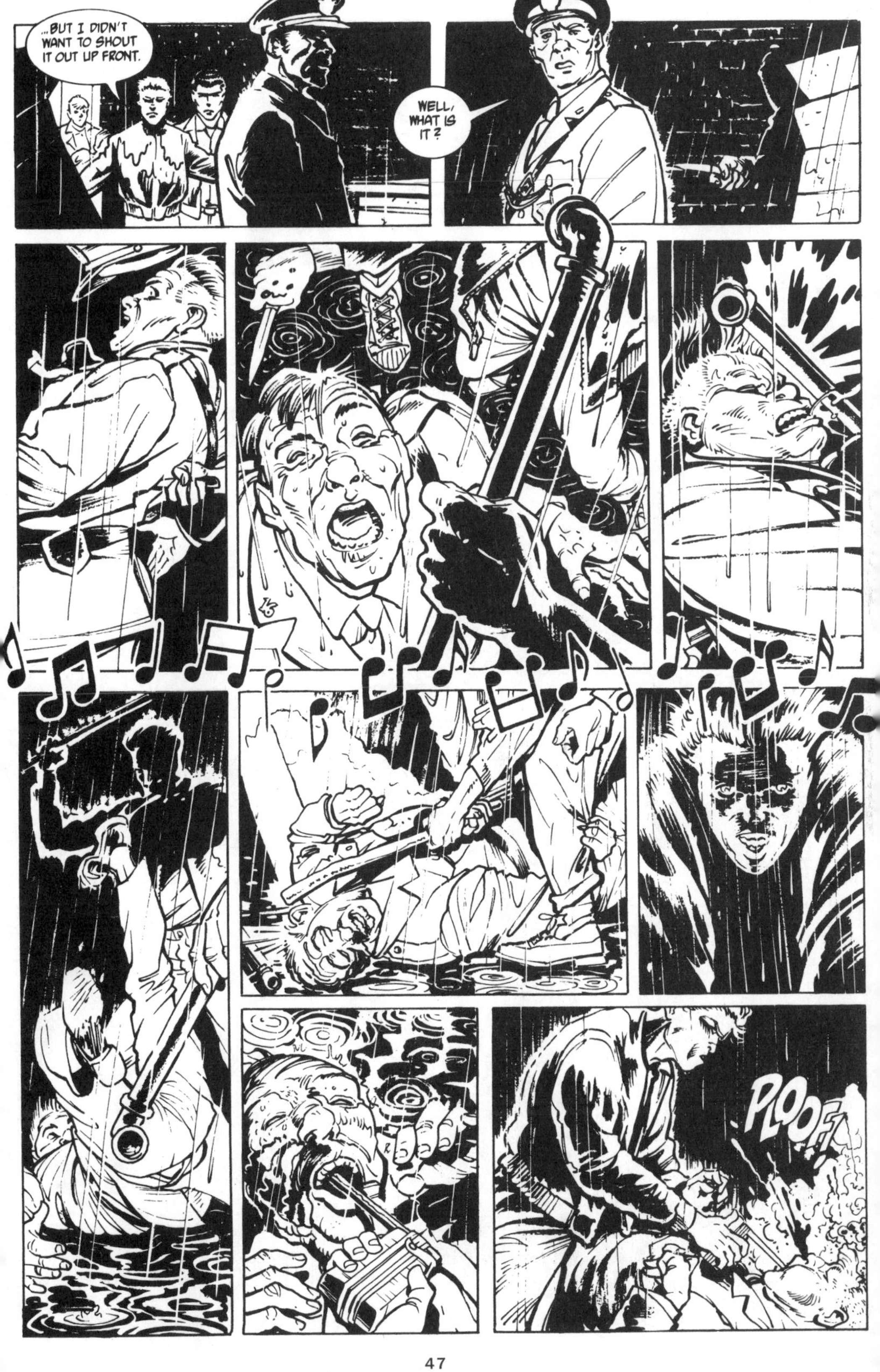
...BUT I DIDN'T WANT TO SHOUT IT OUT UP FRONT.
WELL, WHAT IS IT?
PLOOF!

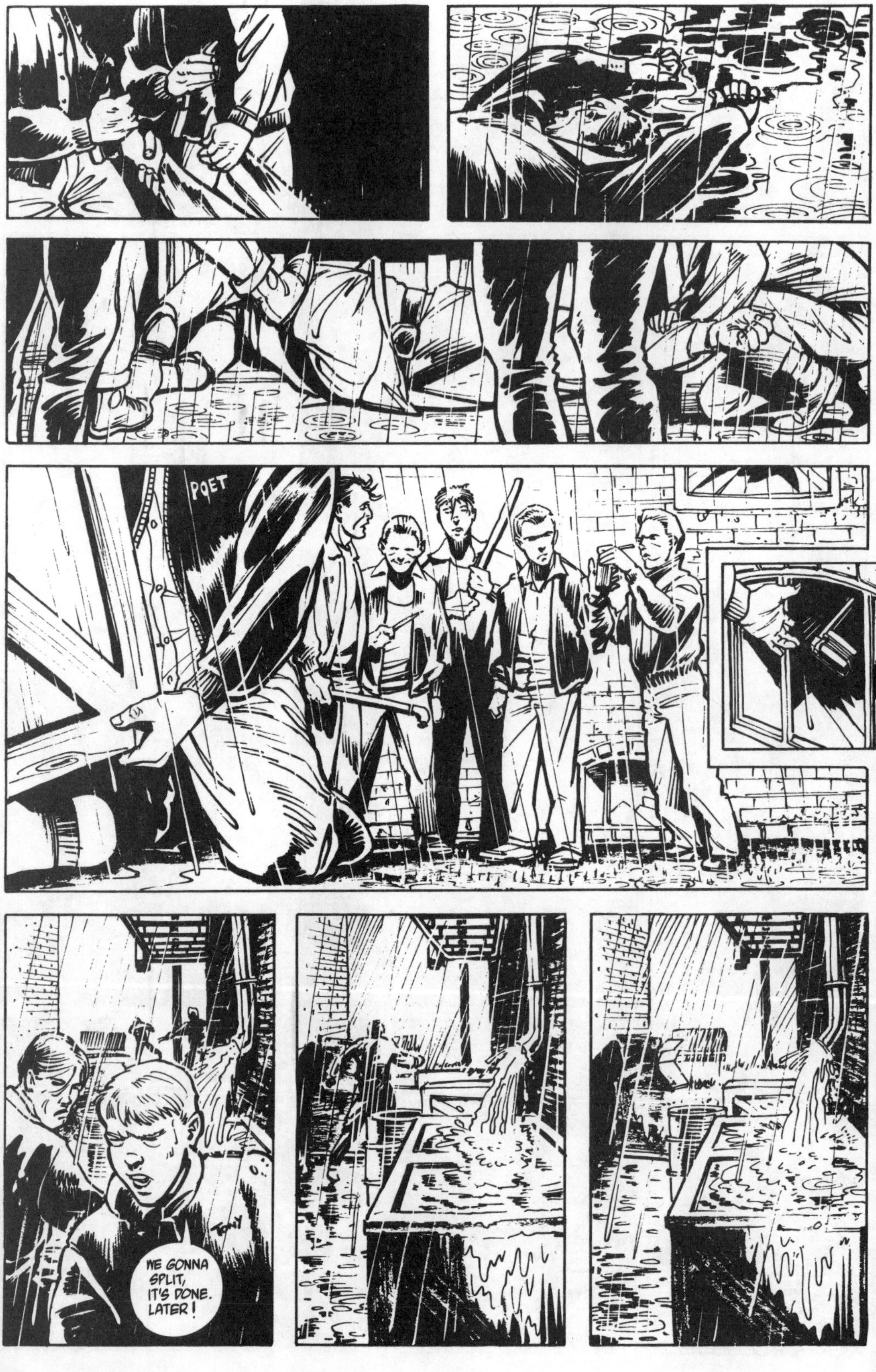
POET
TONY
WE GONNA SPLIT, IT'S DONE. LATER!

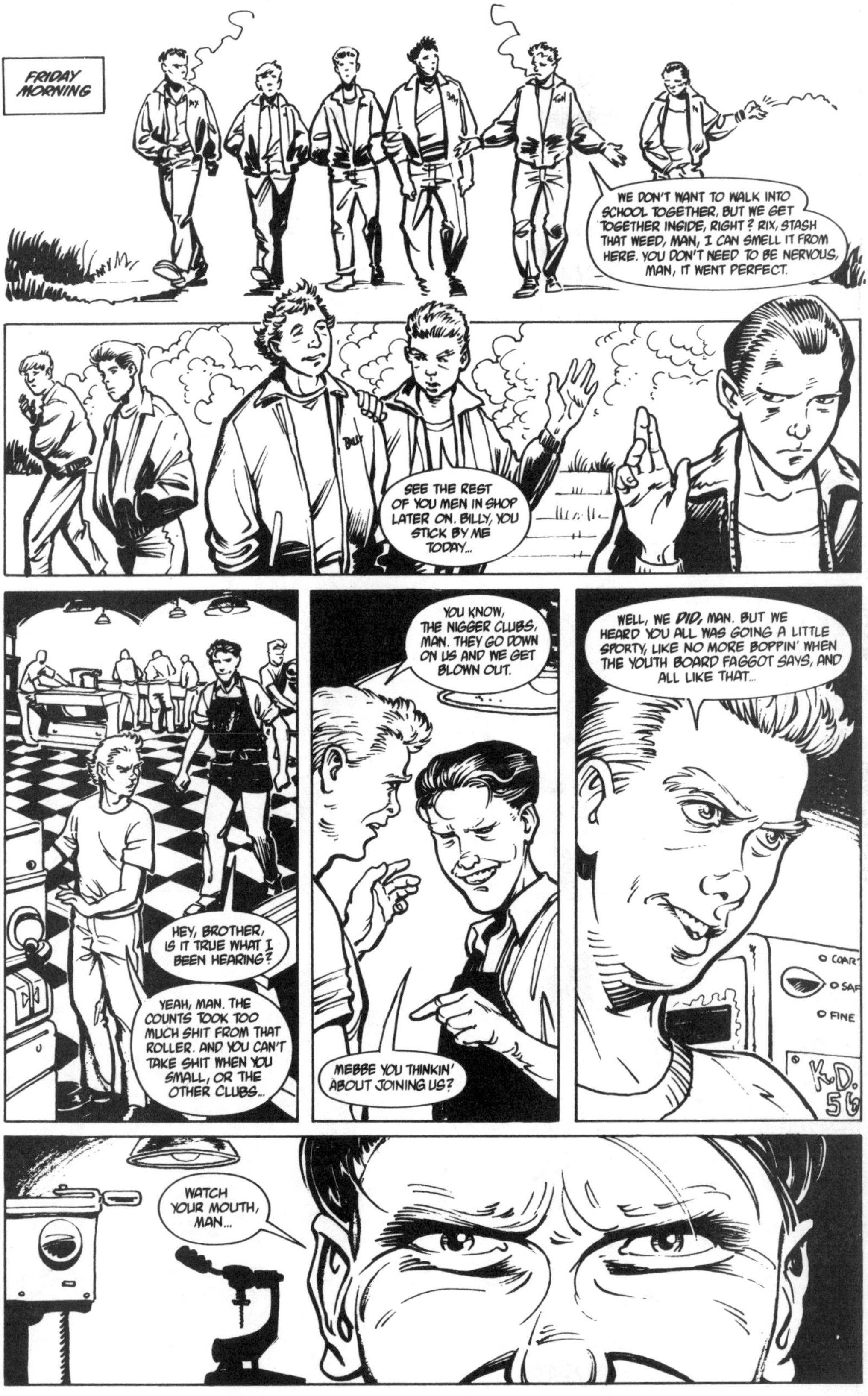
FRIDAY MORNING
WE DON'T WANT TO WALK INTO SCHOOL TOGETHER, BUT WE GET TOGETHER INSIDE, RIGHT? RIX, STASH THAT WEED, MAN, I CAN SMELL IT FROM HERE. YOU DON'T NEED TO BE NERVOUS, MAN, IT WENT PERFECT.
SEE THE REST OF YOU MEN IN SHOP LATER ON. BILLY, YOU STICK BY ME TODAY...
HEY, BROTHER, IS IT TRUE WHAT I BEEN HEARING?
YEAH, MAN. THE COUNTS TOOK TOO MUCH SHIT FROM THAT ROLLER. AND YOU CAN'T TAKE SHIT WHEN YOU SMALL, OR THE OTHER CLUBS...
YOU KNOW, THE NIGGER CLUBS, MAN. THEY GO DOWN ON US AND WE GET BLOWN OUT.
MEBBE YOU THINKIN' ABOUT JOINING US?
WELL, WE *DID*, MAN. BUT WE HEARD YOU ALL WAS GOING A LITTLE SPORTY, LIKE NO MORE BOPPIN' WHEN THE YOUTH BOARD FAGGOT SAYS, AND ALL LIKE THAT...
FINE
K.D. 56
WATCH YOUR MOUTH, MAN...

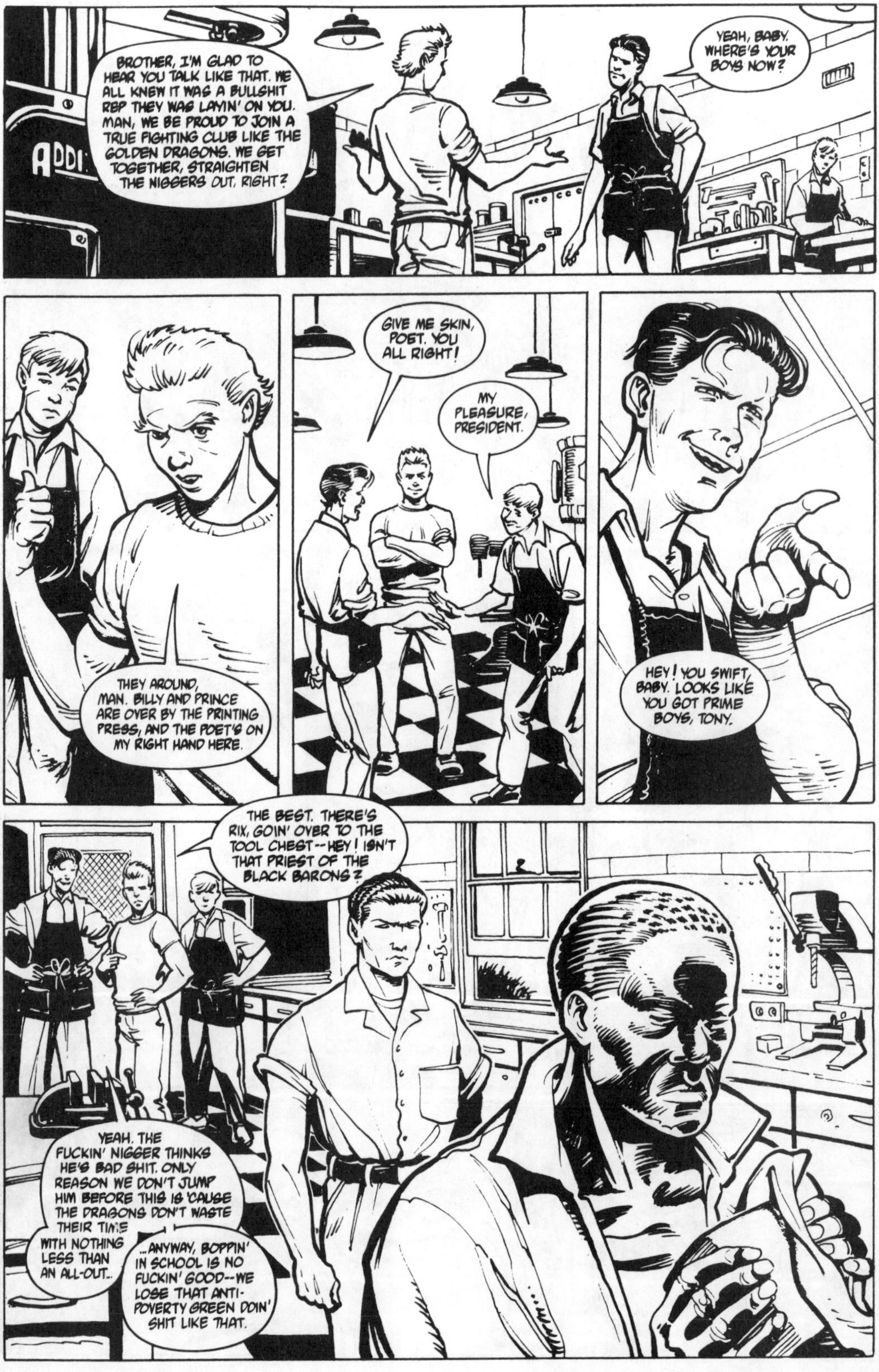
BROTHER, I'M GLAD TO HEAR YOU TALK LIKE THAT. WE ALL KNEW IT WAS A BULLSHIT REP THEY WAS LAYIN' ON YOU. MAN, WE BE PROUD TO JOIN A TRUE FIGHTING CLUB LIKE THE GOLDEN DRAGONS. WE GET TOGETHER, STRAIGHTEN THE NIGGERS OUT, RIGHT?
YEAH, BABY. WHERE'S YOUR BOYS NOW?
ADDI
THEY AROUND, MAN. BILLY AND PRINCE ARE OVER BY THE PRINTING PRESS, AND THE POET'S ON MY RIGHT HAND HERE.
GIVE ME SKIN, POET. YOU ALL RIGHT!
MY PLEASURE, PRESIDENT.
HEY! YOU SWIFT, BABY. LOOKS LIKE YOU GOT PRIME BOYS, TONY.
THE BEST. THERE'S RIX, GOIN' OVER TO THE TOOL CHEST--HEY! ISN'T THAT PRIEST OF THE BLACK BARONS?
YEAH. THE FUCKIN' NIGGER THINKS HE'S BAD SHIT. ONLY REASON WE DON'T JUMP HIM BEFORE THIS IS 'CAUSE THE DRAGONS DON'T WASTE THEIR TIME
WITH NOTHING LESS THAN AN ALL-OUT..
...ANYWAY, BOPPIN' IN SCHOOL IS NO FUCKIN' GOOD--WE LOSE THAT ANTI-POVERTY GREEN DOIN' SHIT LIKE THAT.

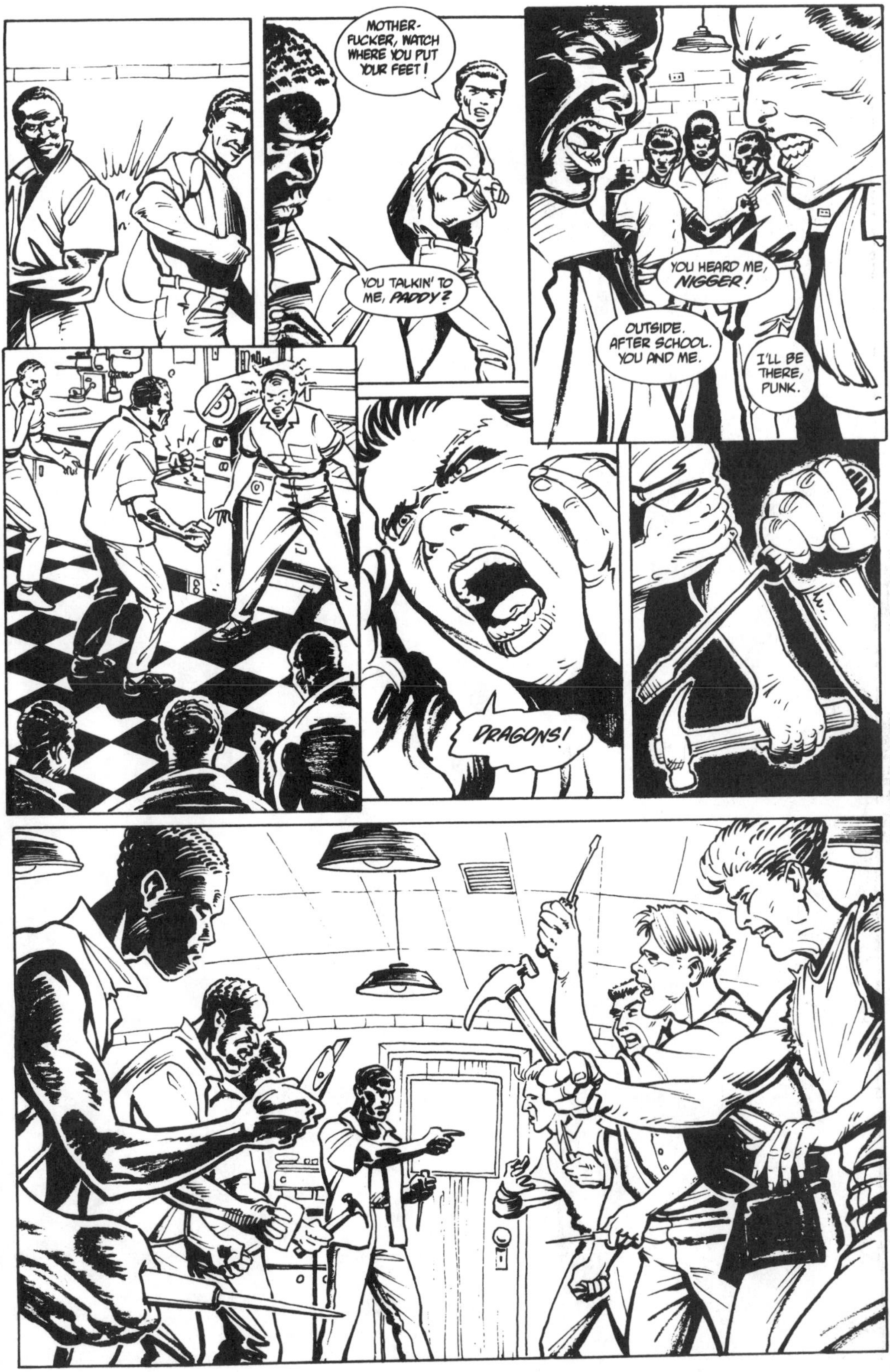
MOTHER-FUCKER, WATCH WHERE YOU PUT YOUR FEET!
YOU TALKIN' TO ME, PADDY?
YOU HEARD ME, NIGGER!
OUTSIDE. AFTER SCHOOL. YOU AND ME.
I'LL BE THERE, PUNK.
DRAGONS!

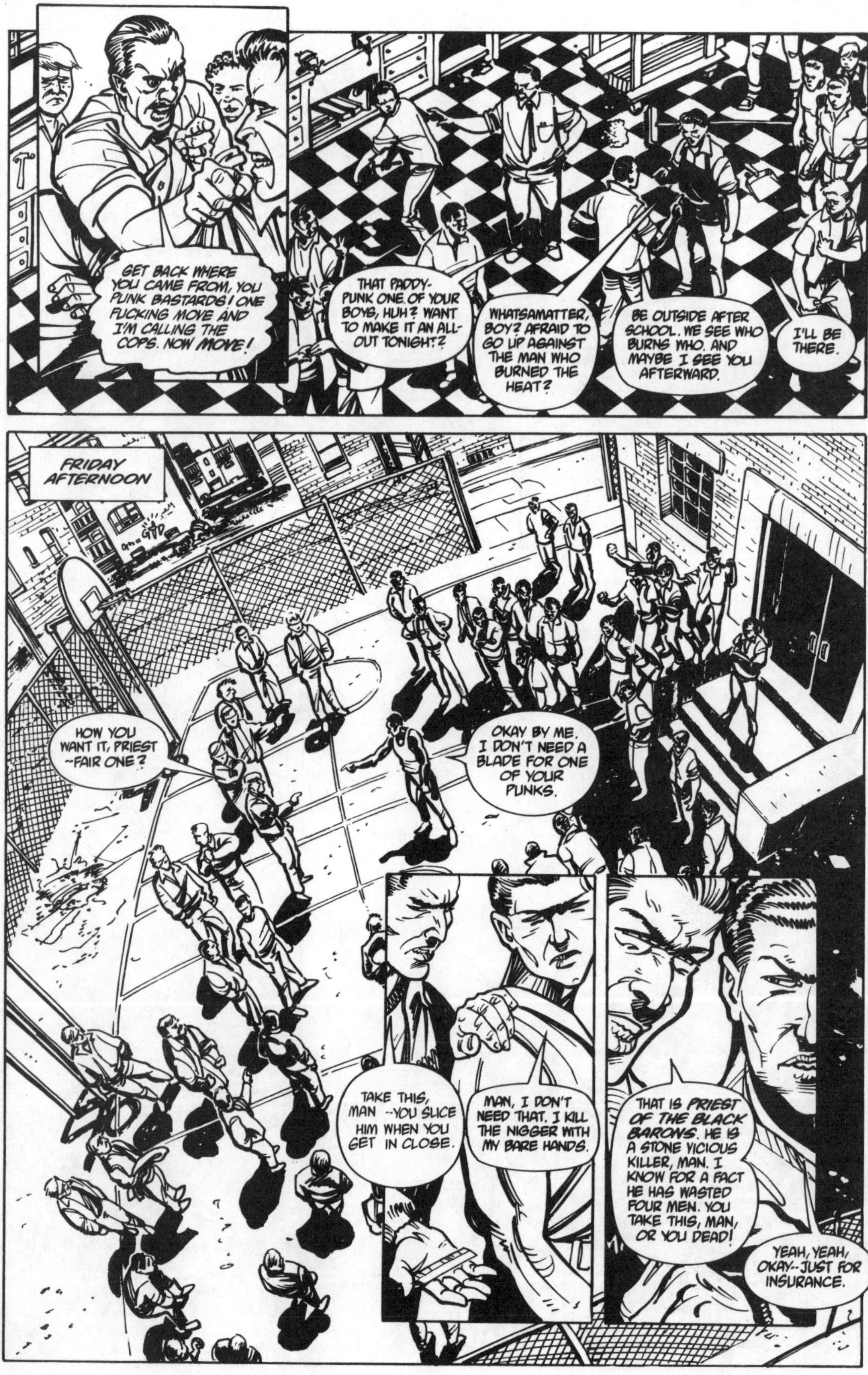
GET BACK WHERE YOU CAME FROM, YOU PUNK BASTARDS! ONE FUCKING MOVE AND I'M CALLING THE COPS. NOW MOVE!
THAT PADDY-PUNK ONE OF YOUR BOYS, HUH? WANT TO MAKE IT AN ALL-OUT TONIGHT?
WHATSAMATTER, BOY? AFRAID TO GO UP AGAINST THE MAN WHO BURNED THE HEAT?
BE OUTSIDE AFTER SCHOOL. WE SEE WHO BURNS WHO. AND MAYBE I SEE YOU AFTERWARD.
I'LL BE THERE.
FRIDAY AFTERNOON
HOW YOU WANT IT, PRIEST --FAIR ONE?
OKAY BY ME. I DON'T NEED A BLADE FOR ONE OF YOUR PUNKS.
TAKE THIS, MAN --YOU SLICE HIM WHEN YOU GET IN CLOSE.
MAN, I DON'T NEED THAT. I KILL THE NIGGER WITH MY BARE HANDS.
THAT IS PRIEST OF THE BLACK BARONS. HE IS A STONE VICIOUS KILLER, MAN. I KNOW FOR A FACT HE HAS WASTED FOUR MEN. YOU TAKE THIS, MAN, OR YOU DEAD!
YEAH, YEAH, OKAY--JUST FOR INSURANCE.

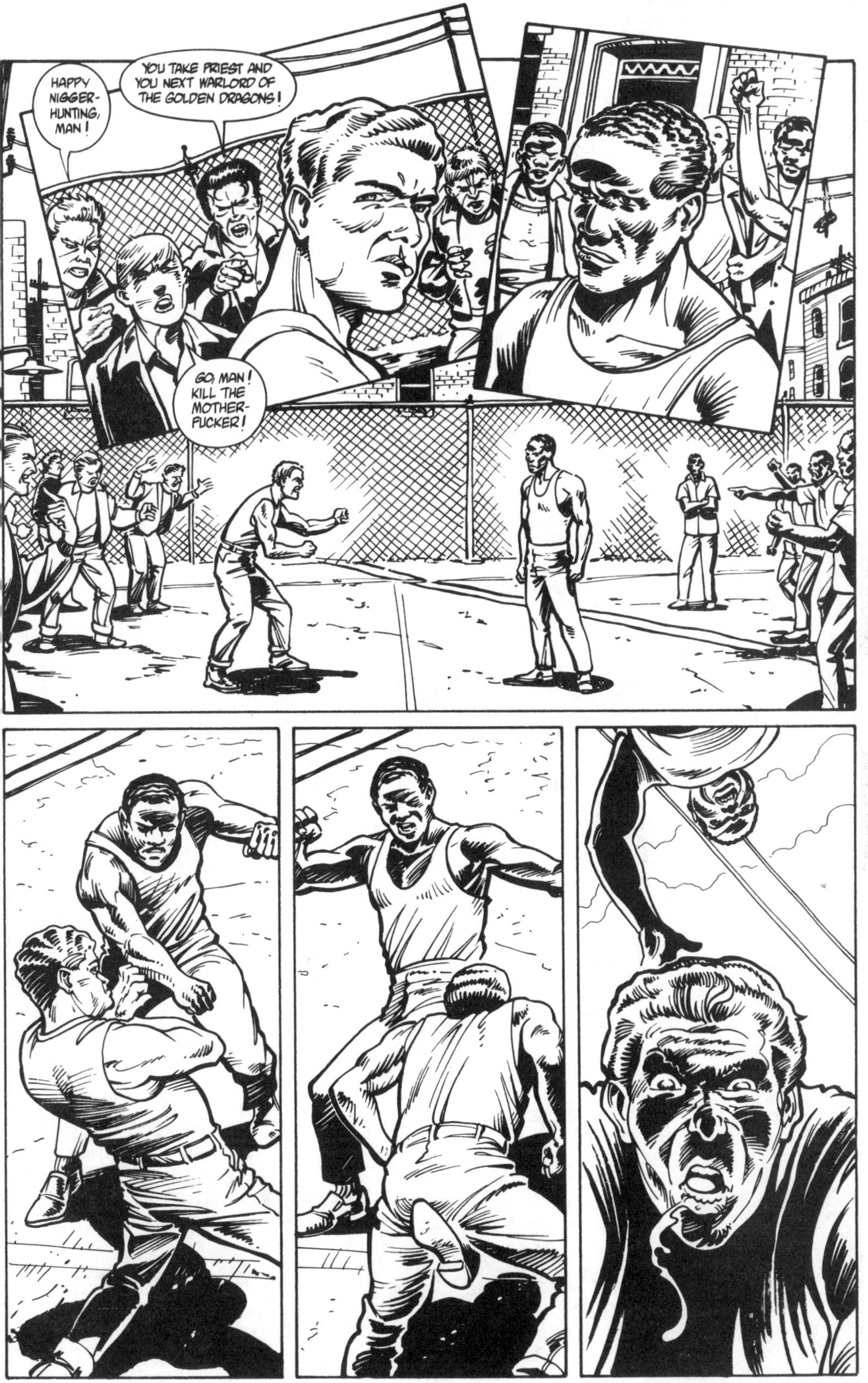
HAPPY NIGGER-HUNTING, MAN!
YOU TAKE PRIEST AND YOU NEXT WARLORD OF THE GOLDEN DRAGONS!
GO, MAN! KILL THE MOTHER-FUCKER!

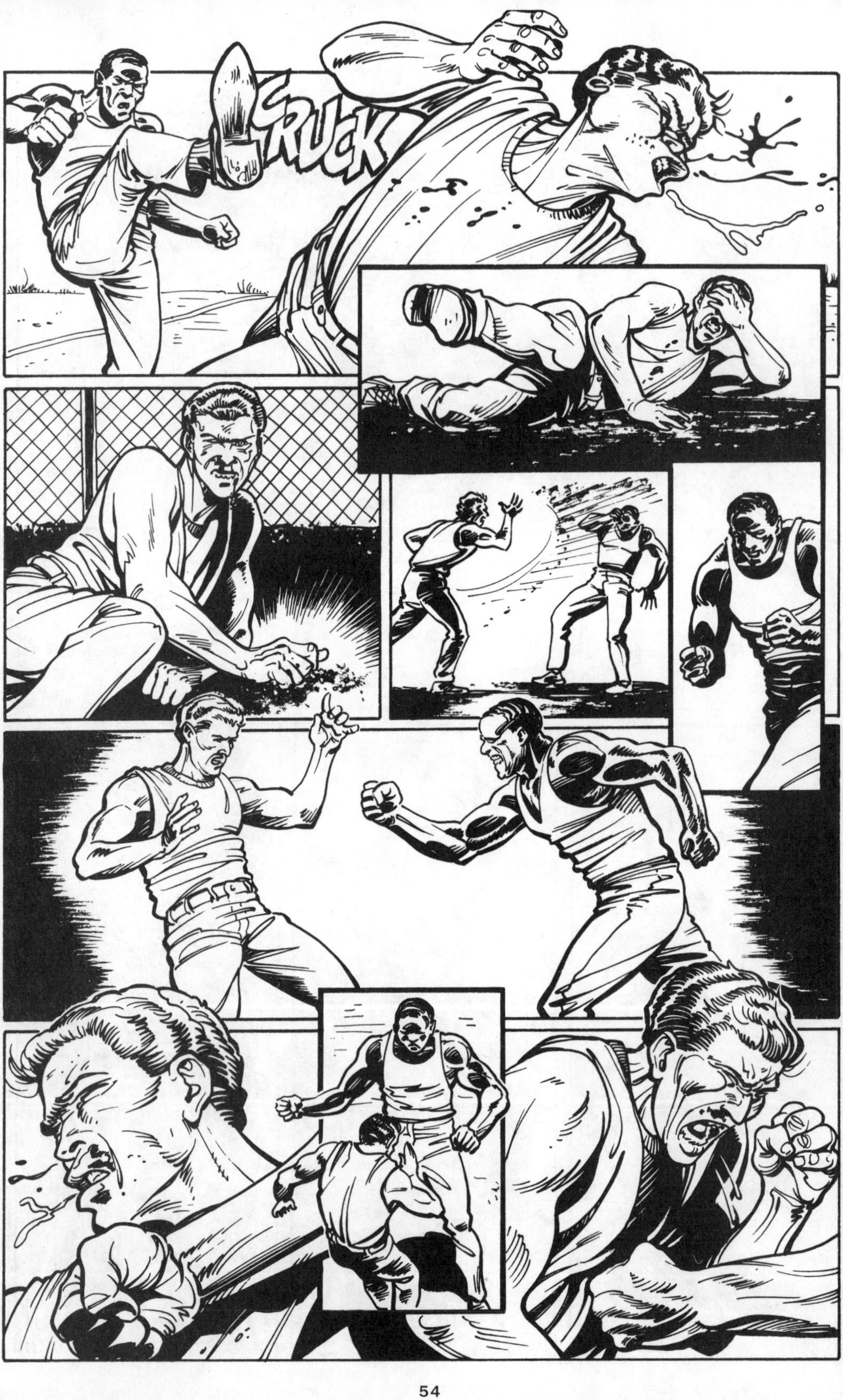
CRUCK

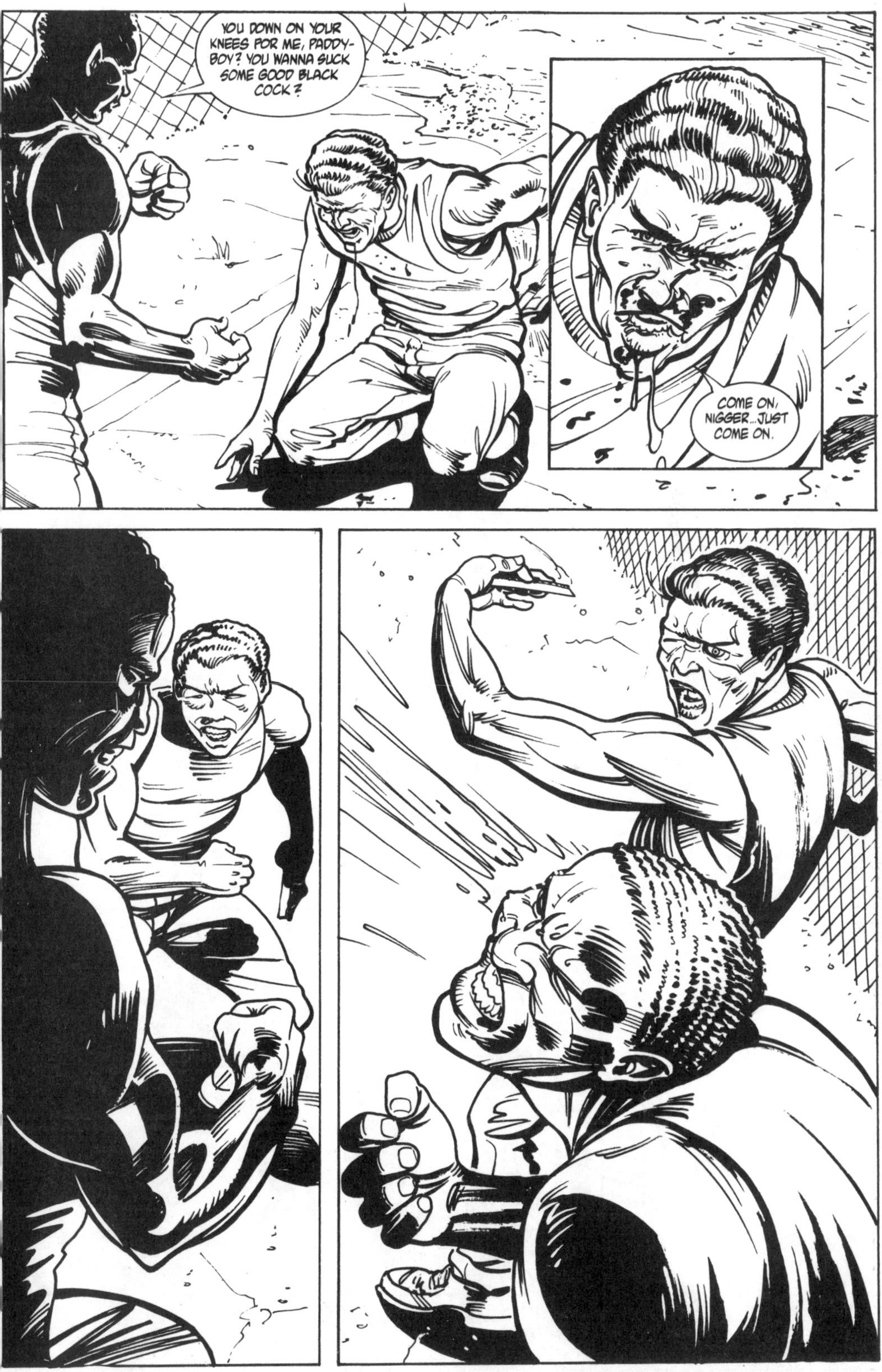
YOU DOWN ON YOUR KNEES FOR ME, PADDY-BOY? YOU WANNA SUCK SOME GOOD BLACK COCK?
COME ON, NIGGER...JUST COME ON.

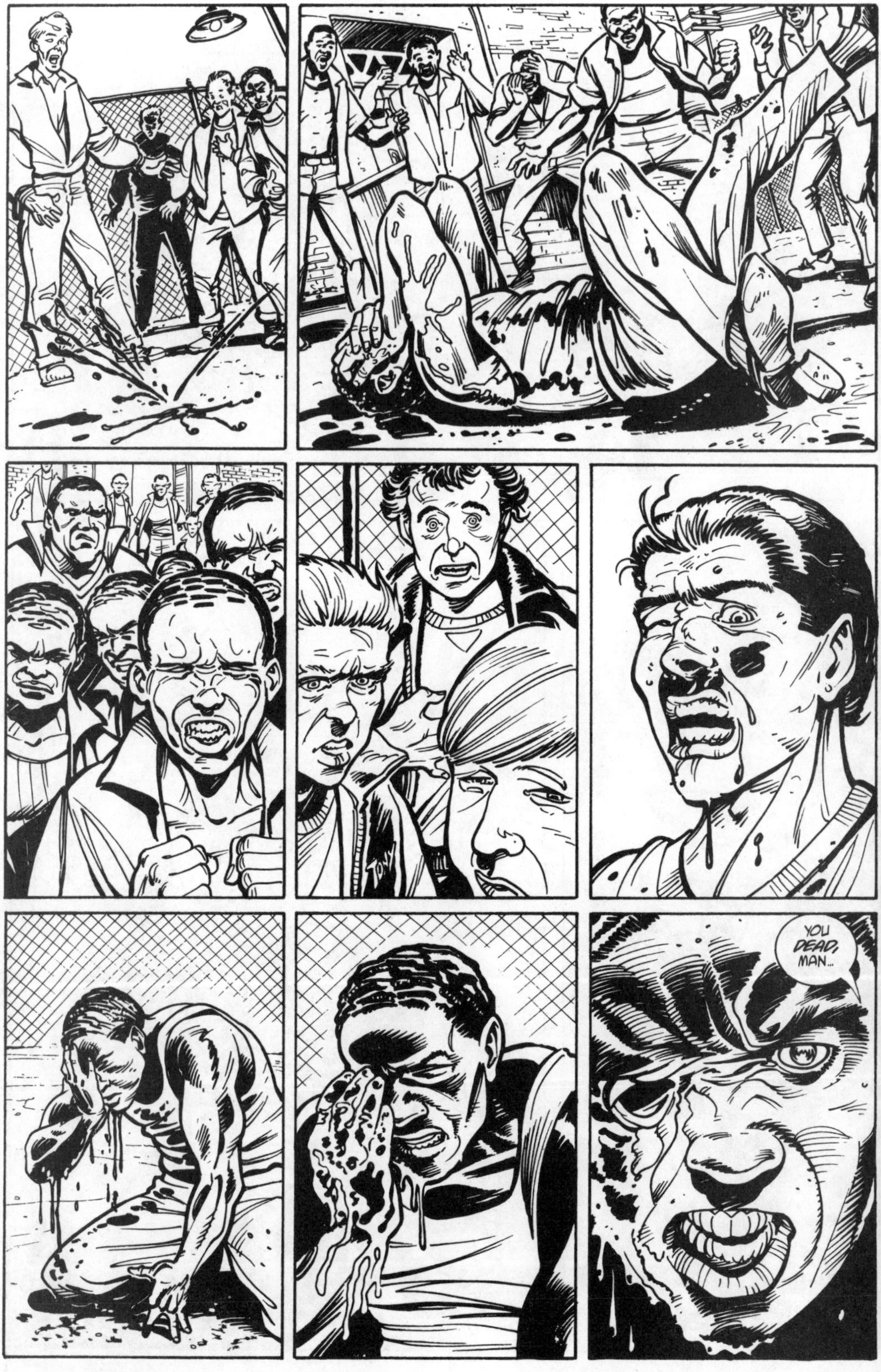
YOU DEAD, MAN...

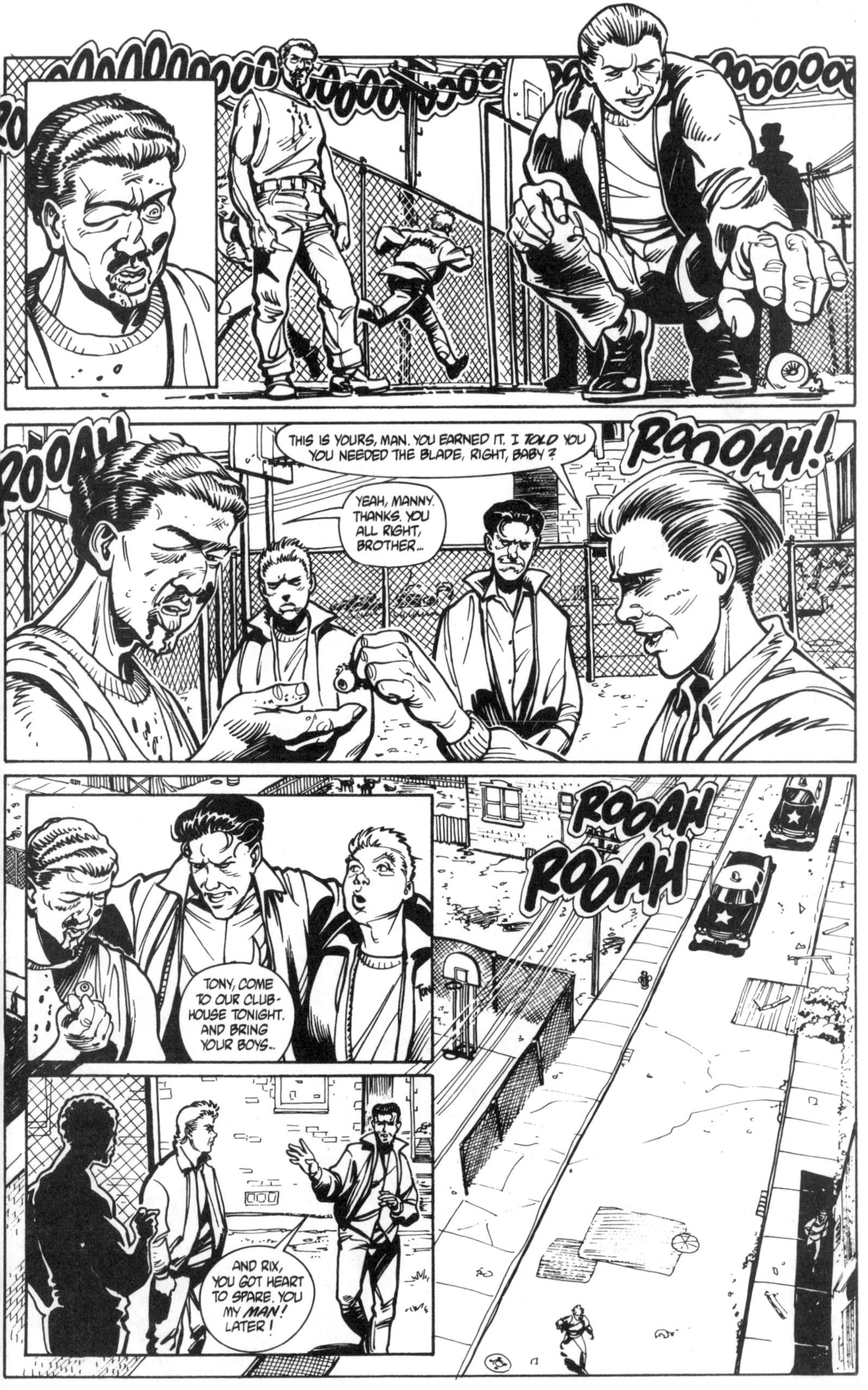

ROOOOOOOOOOOOOOOOOOOOOOOOOOOOOOOOOOOO
ROOAH
THIS IS YOURS, MAN. YOU EARNED IT. I *TOLD* YOU YOU NEEDED THE BLADE, RIGHT, BABY?
ROOOAH!
YEAH, MANNY. THANKS. YOU ALL RIGHT, BROTHER...
ROOAH
ROOAH
TONY, COME TO OUR CLUB-HOUSE TONIGHT. AND BRING YOUR BOYS..
AND RIX, YOU GOT HEART TO SPARE. YOU MY *MAN*! LATER!

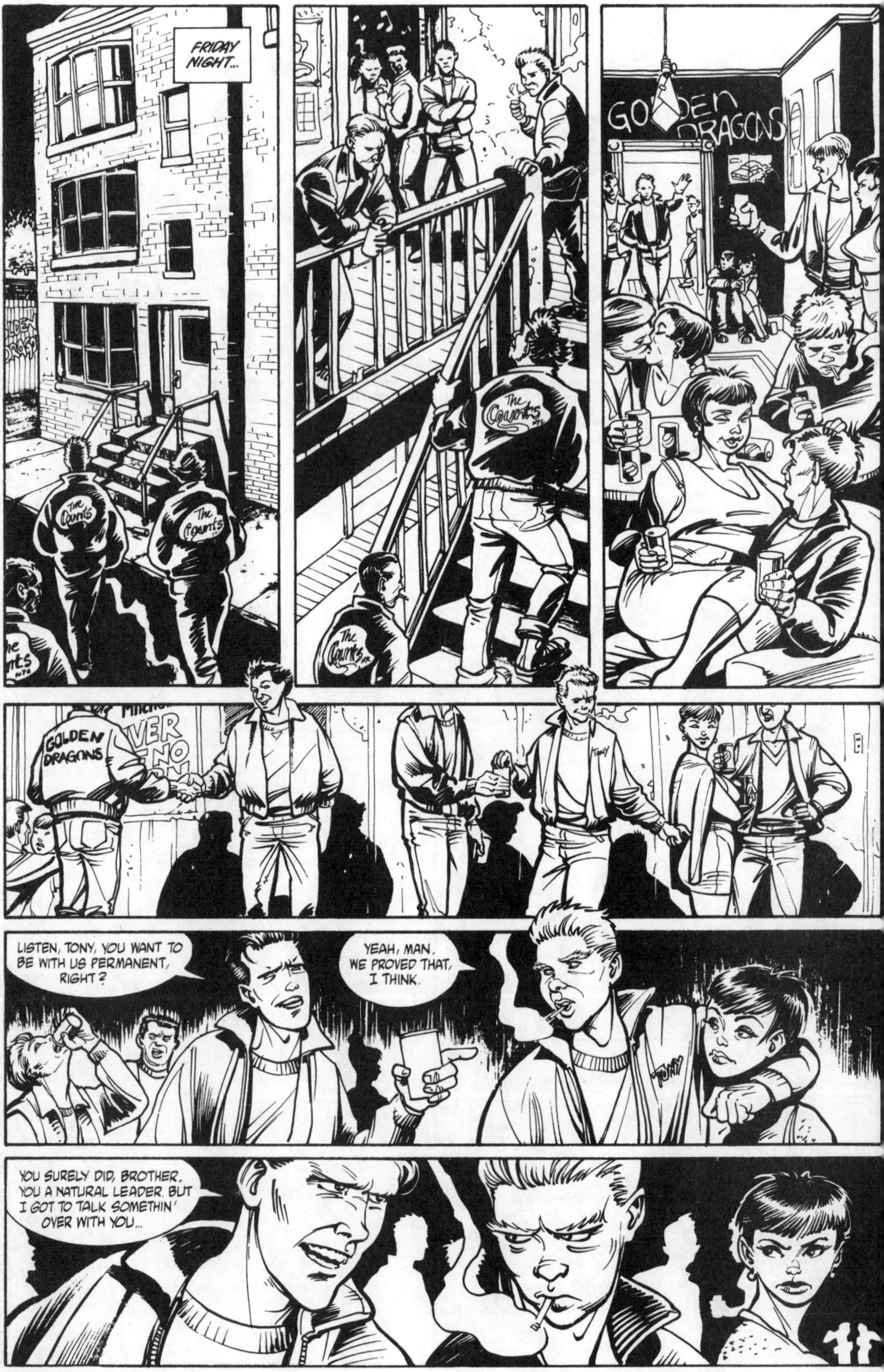
FRIDAY NIGHT...
THE COUNTS
GOLDEN DRAGONS
LISTEN, TONY, YOU WANT TO BE WITH US PERMANENT, RIGHT?
YEAH, MAN. WE PROVED THAT, I THINK.
YOU SURELY DID, BROTHER. YOU A NATURAL LEADER. BUT I GOT TO TALK SOMETHIN' OVER WITH YOU...

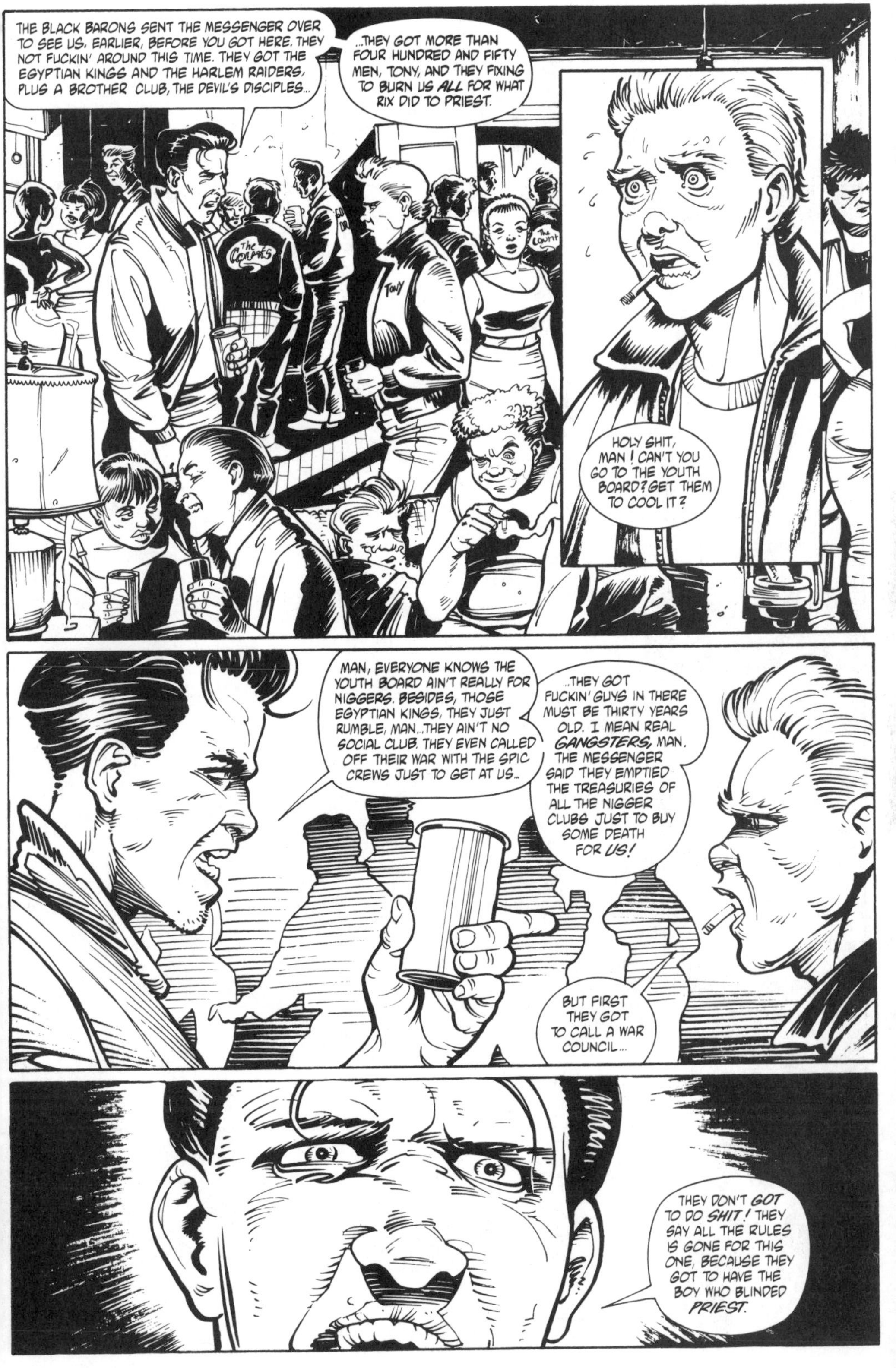
THE BLACK BARONS SENT THE MESSENGER OVER TO SEE US. EARLIER, BEFORE YOU GOT HERE. THEY NOT FUCKIN' AROUND THIS TIME. THEY GOT THE EGYPTIAN KINGS AND THE HARLEM RAIDERS, PLUS A BROTHER CLUB, THE DEVIL'S DISCIPLES...
...THEY GOT MORE THAN FOUR HUNDRED AND FIFTY MEN, TONY, AND THEY FIXING TO BURN US ALL FOR WHAT RIX DID TO PRIEST.
HOLY SHIT, MAN! CAN'T YOU GO TO THE YOUTH BOARD? GET THEM TO COOL IT?
MAN, EVERYONE KNOWS THE YOUTH BOARD AIN'T REALLY FOR NIGGERS. BESIDES, THOSE EGYPTIAN KINGS, THEY JUST RUMBLE, MAN...THEY AIN'T NO SOCIAL CLUB. THEY EVEN CALLED OFF THEIR WAR WITH THE SPIC CREWS JUST TO GET AT US...
...THEY GOT FUCKIN' GUYS IN THERE MUST BE THIRTY YEARS OLD. I MEAN REAL GANGSTERS, MAN. THE MESSENGER SAID THEY EMPTIED THE TREASURIES OF ALL THE NIGGER CLUBS JUST TO BUY SOME DEATH FOR US!
BUT FIRST THEY GOT TO CALL A WAR COUNCIL...
THEY DON'T GOT TO DO SHIT! THEY SAY ALL THE RULES IS GONE FOR THIS ONE, BECAUSE THEY GOT TO HAVE THE BOY WHO BLINDED PRIEST.

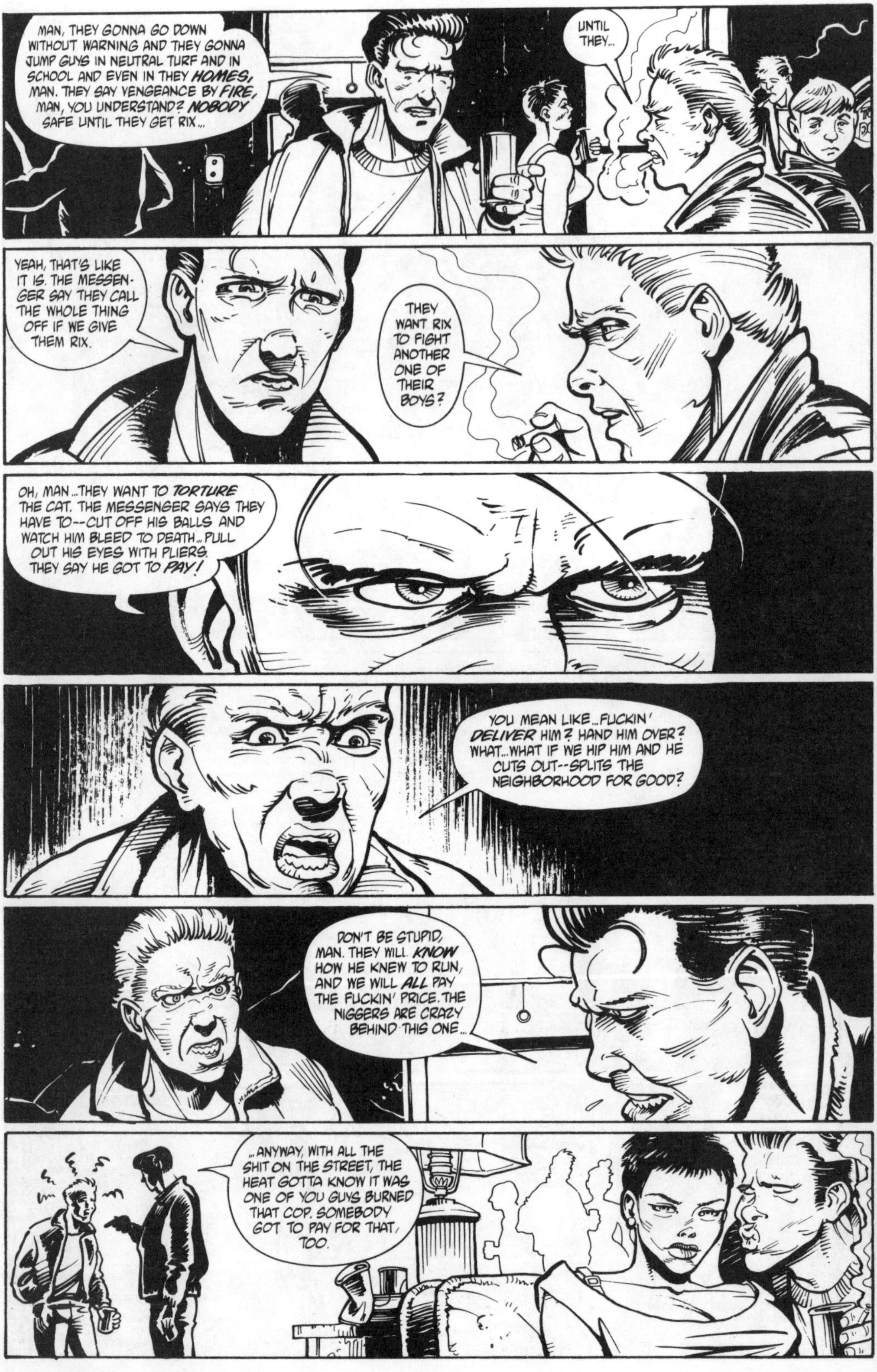

MAN, THEY GONNA GO DOWN WITHOUT WARNING AND THEY GONNA JUMP GUYS IN NEUTRAL TURF AND IN SCHOOL AND EVEN IN THEY HOMES, MAN. THEY SAY VENGEANCE BY FIRE, MAN, YOU UNDERSTAND? NOBODY SAFE UNTIL THEY GET RIX...
UNTIL THEY...
YEAH, THAT'S LIKE IT IS. THE MESSENGER SAY THEY CALL THE WHOLE THING OFF IF WE GIVE THEM RIX.
THEY WANT RIX TO FIGHT ANOTHER ONE OF THEIR BOYS?
OH, MAN...THEY WANT TO TORTURE THE CAT. THE MESSENGER SAYS THEY HAVE TO--CUT OFF HIS BALLS AND WATCH HIM BLEED TO DEATH...PULL OUT HIS EYES WITH PLIERS. THEY SAY HE GOT TO PAY!
YOU MEAN LIKE...FUCKIN' DELIVER HIM? HAND HIM OVER? WHAT...WHAT IF WE HIP HIM AND HE CUTS OUT--SPLITS THE NEIGHBORHOOD FOR GOOD?
DON'T BE STUPID, MAN. THEY WILL KNOW HOW HE KNEW TO RUN, AND WE WILL ALL PAY THE FUCKIN' PRICE. THE NIGGERS ARE CRAZY BEHIND THIS ONE...
...ANYWAY, WITH ALL THE SHIT ON THE STREET, THE HEAT GOTTA KNOW IT WAS ONE OF YOU GUYS BURNED THAT COP. SOMEBODY GOT TO PAY FOR THAT, TOO.

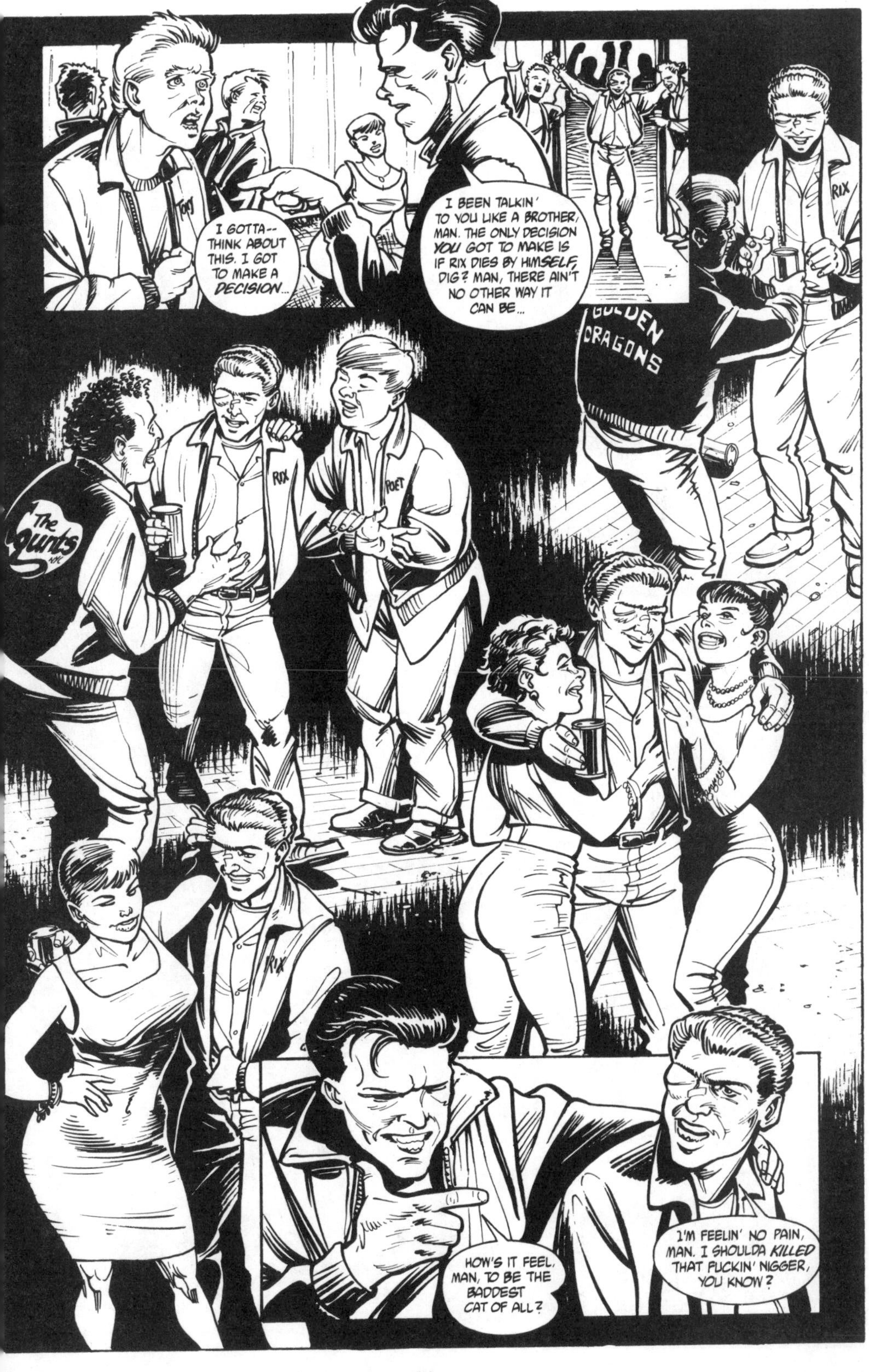
I GOTTA-- THINK ABOUT THIS. I GOT TO MAKE A *DECISION*...
I BEEN TALKIN' TO YOU LIKE A BROTHER, MAN. THE ONLY DECISION *YOU* GOT TO MAKE IS IF RIX DIES BY HIM*SELF*, DIG? MAN, THERE AIN'T NO OTHER WAY IT CAN BE...
RIX
GOLDEN DRAGONS
RIX
POET
RIX
HOW'S IT FEEL, MAN, TO BE THE BADDEST CAT OF ALL?
I'M FEELIN' NO PAIN, MAN. I SHOULDA *KILLED* THAT FUCKIN' NIGGER, YOU KNOW?

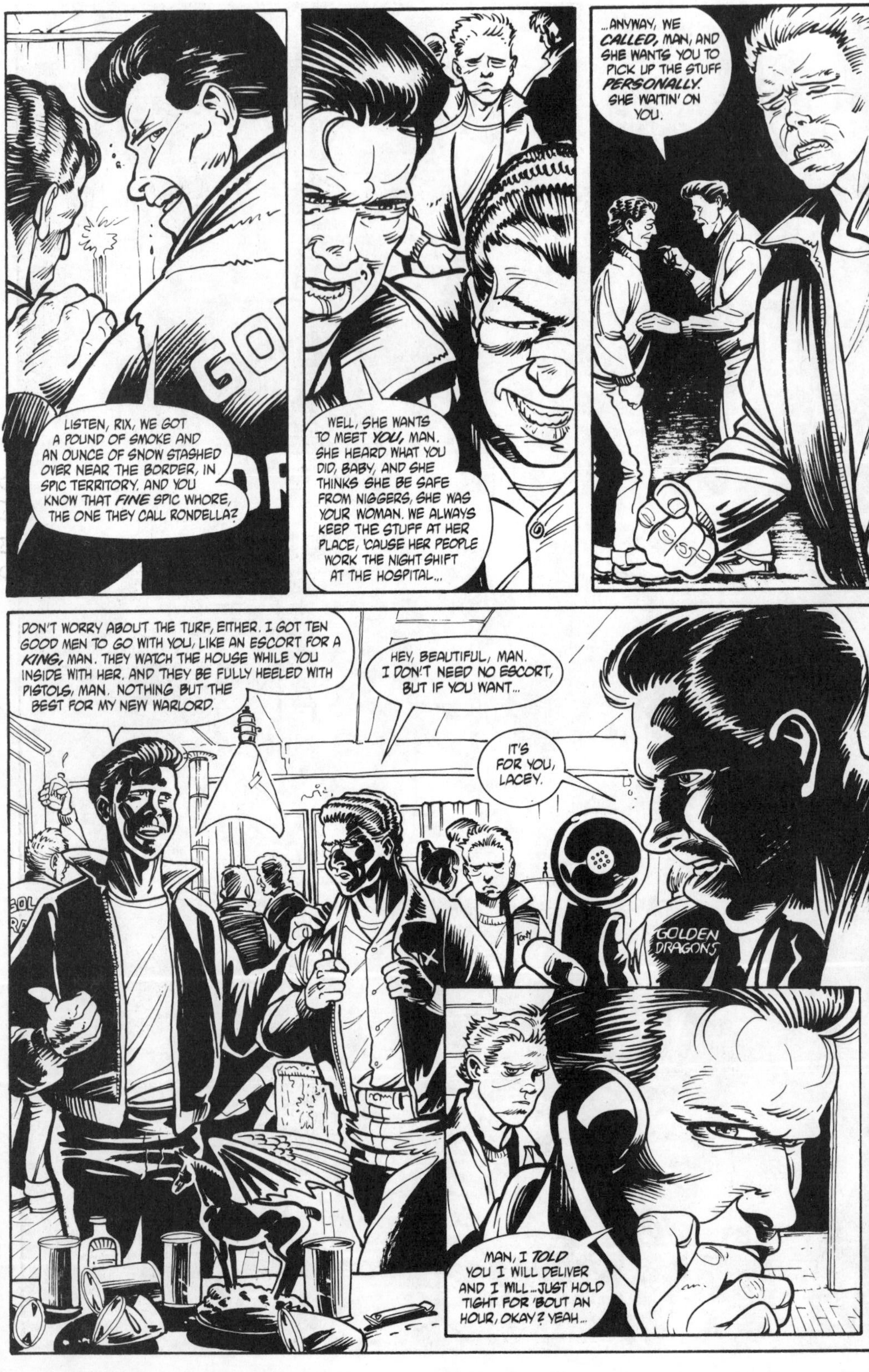
LISTEN, RIX, WE GOT A POUND OF SMOKE AND AN OUNCE OF SNOW STASHED OVER NEAR THE BORDER, IN SPIC TERRITORY. AND YOU KNOW THAT *FINE* SPIC WHORE, THE ONE THEY CALL RONDELLA?
WELL, SHE WANTS TO MEET *YOU,* MAN. SHE HEARD WHAT YOU DID, BABY, AND SHE THINKS SHE BE SAFE FROM NIGGERS, SHE WAS YOUR WOMAN. WE ALWAYS KEEP THE STUFF AT HER PLACE, 'CAUSE HER PEOPLE WORK THE NIGHT SHIFT AT THE HOSPITAL...
...ANYWAY, WE *CALLED,* MAN, AND SHE WANTS YOU TO PICK UP THE STUFF *PERSONALLY.* SHE WAITIN' ON YOU.
DON'T WORRY ABOUT THE TURF, EITHER. I GOT TEN GOOD MEN TO GO WITH YOU, LIKE AN ESCORT FOR A *KING,* MAN. THEY WATCH THE HOUSE WHILE YOU INSIDE WITH HER. AND THEY BE FULLY HEELED WITH PISTOLS, MAN. NOTHING BUT THE BEST FOR MY NEW WARLORD.
HEY, BEAUTIFUL, MAN. I DON'T NEED NO ESCORT, BUT IF YOU WANT...
IT'S FOR YOU, LACEY.
GOLDEN DRAGONS
MAN, I *TOLD* YOU I WILL DELIVER AND I WILL...JUST HOLD TIGHT FOR 'BOUT AN HOUR, OKAY? YEAH...

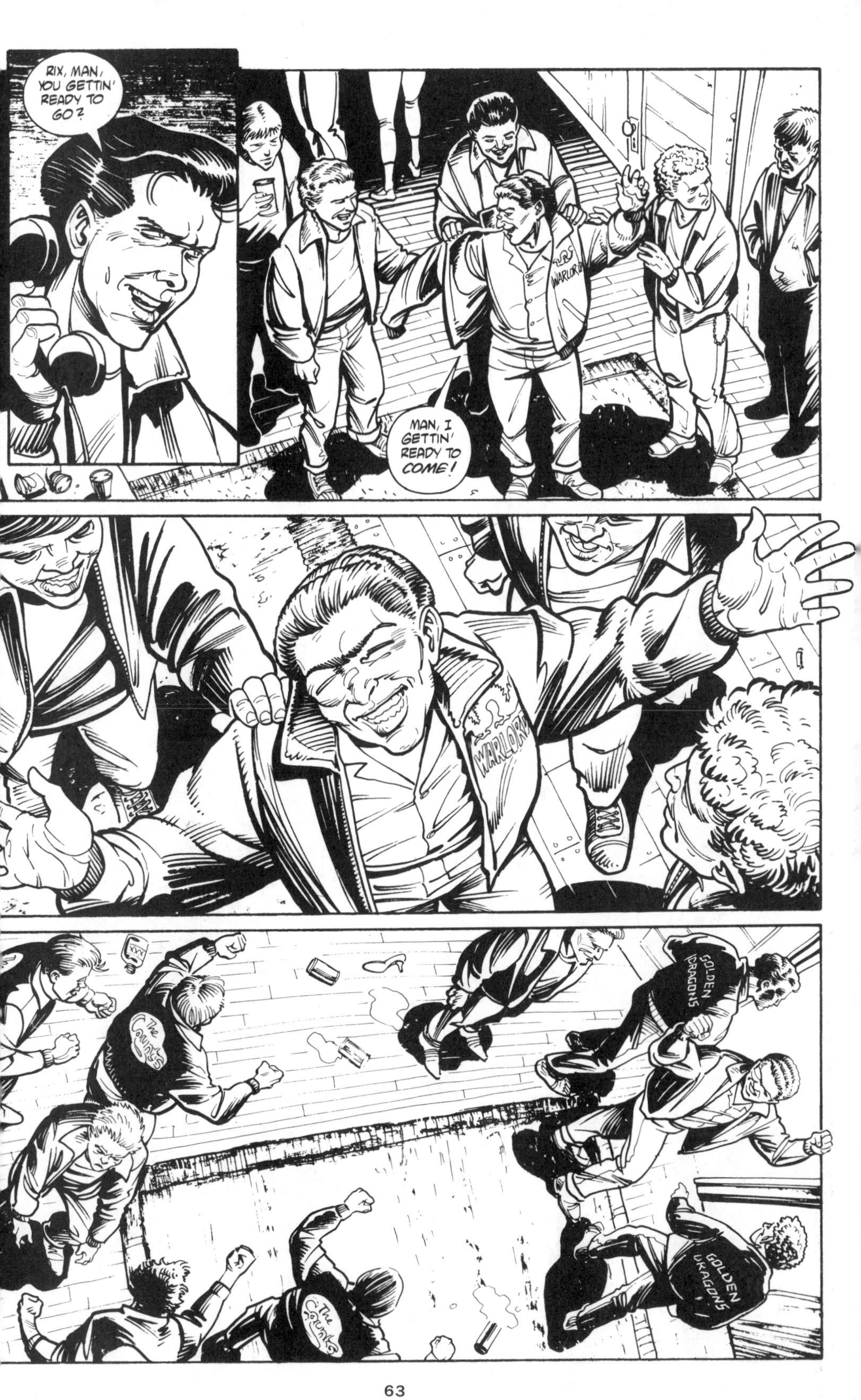
RIX, MAN, YOU GETTIN' READY TO GO?
MAN, I GETTIN' READY TO COME!
WARLORD
WARLORD
The Counts
GOLDEN DRAGONS
GOLDEN DRAGONS
The Counts

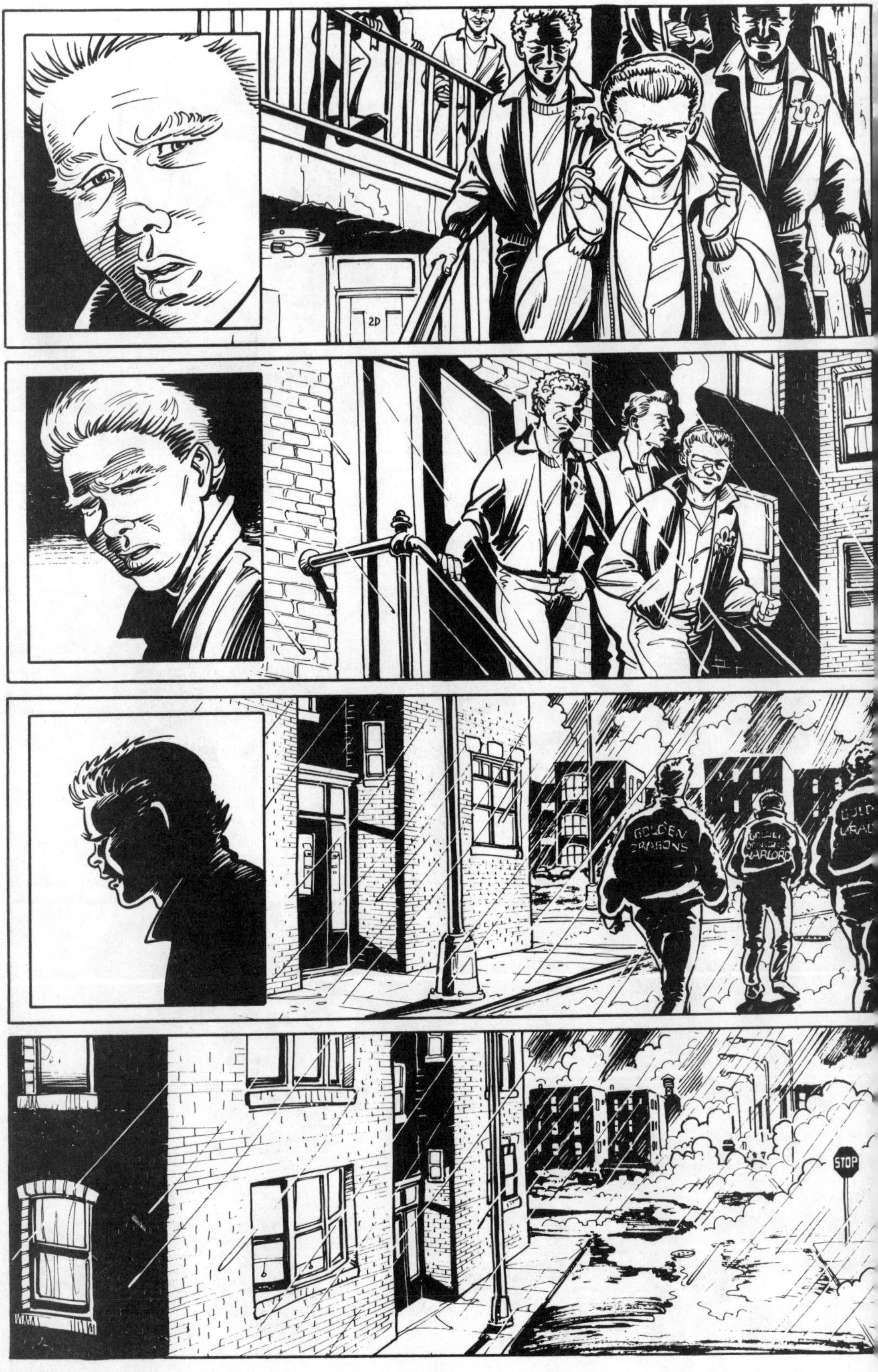
2D
GOLDEN DRAGONS
WARLORD
STOP

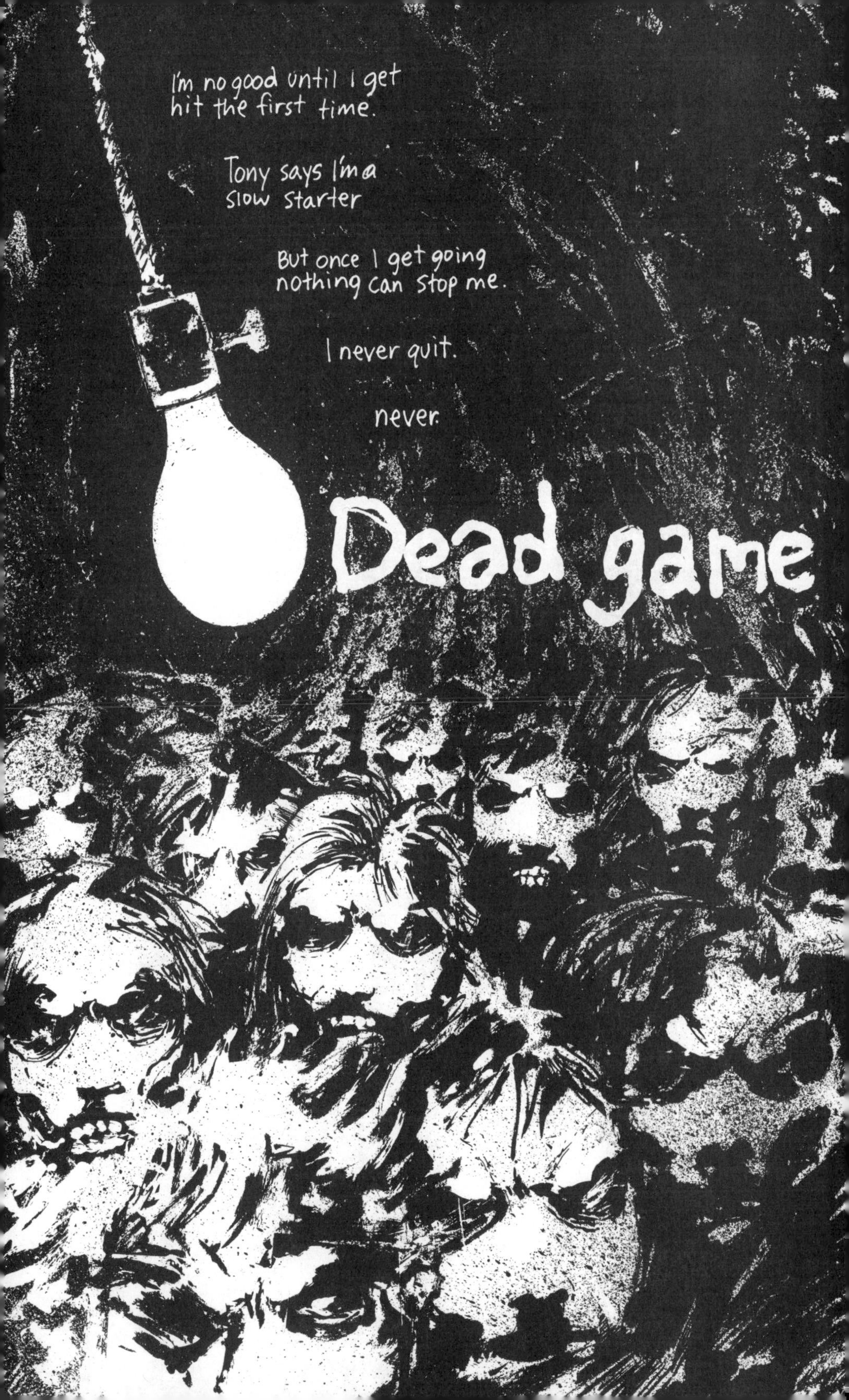
I'm no good until I get hit the first time.
Tony says I'm a slow starter
But once I get going nothing can stop me.
I never quit.
never.
Dead game

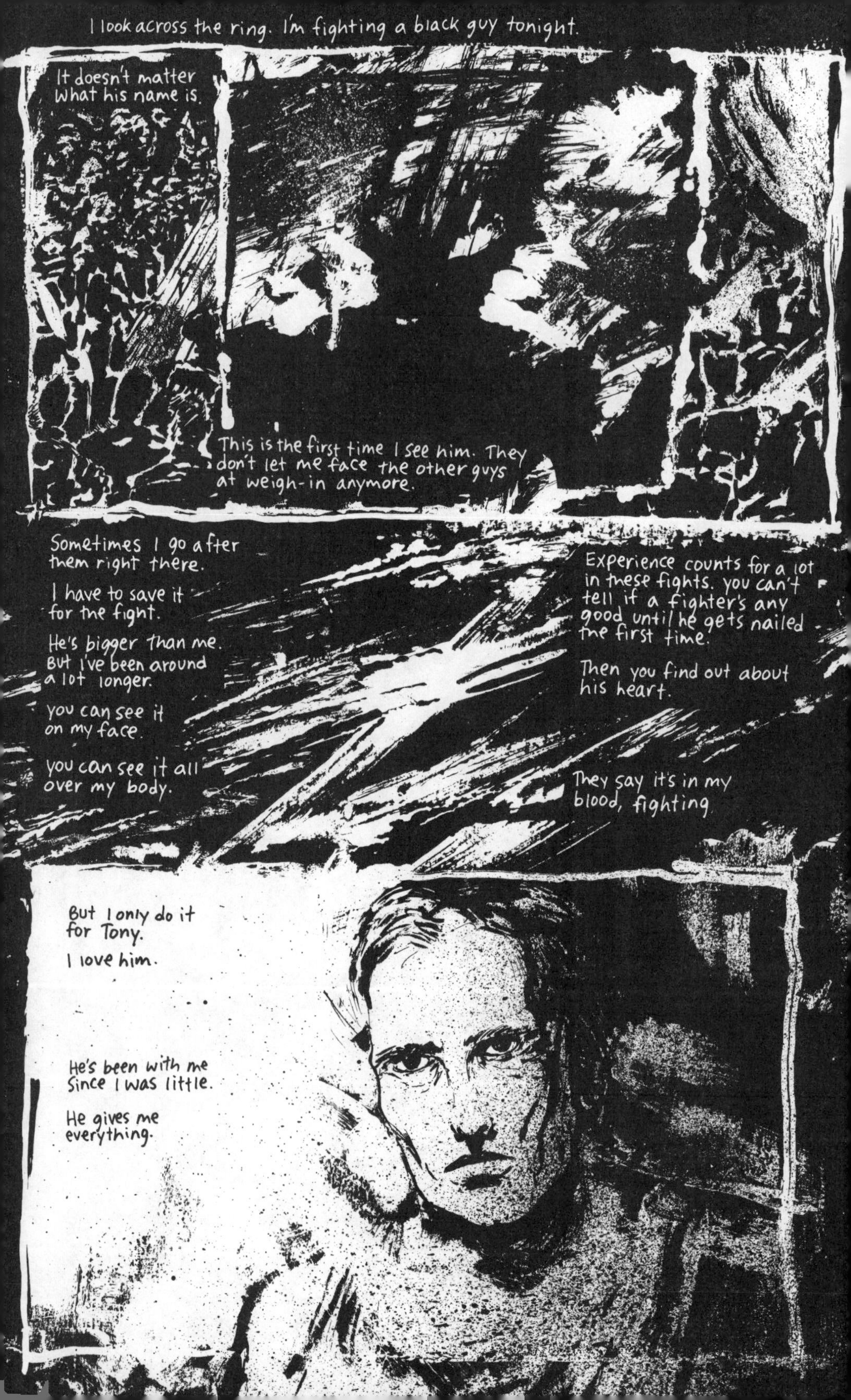
I look across the ring. I'm fighting a black guy tonight.
It doesn't matter what his name is.
This is the first time I see him. They don't let me face the other guys at weigh-in anymore.
Sometimes I go after them right there.
I have to save it for the fight.
He's bigger than me. But I've been around a lot longer.
you can see it on my face.
you can see it all over my body.
Experience counts for a lot in these fights. you can't tell if a fighter's any good until he gets nailed the first time.
Then you find out about his heart.
They say it's in my blood, fighting.
But I only do it for Tony.
I love him.
He's been with me since I was little.
He gives me everything.

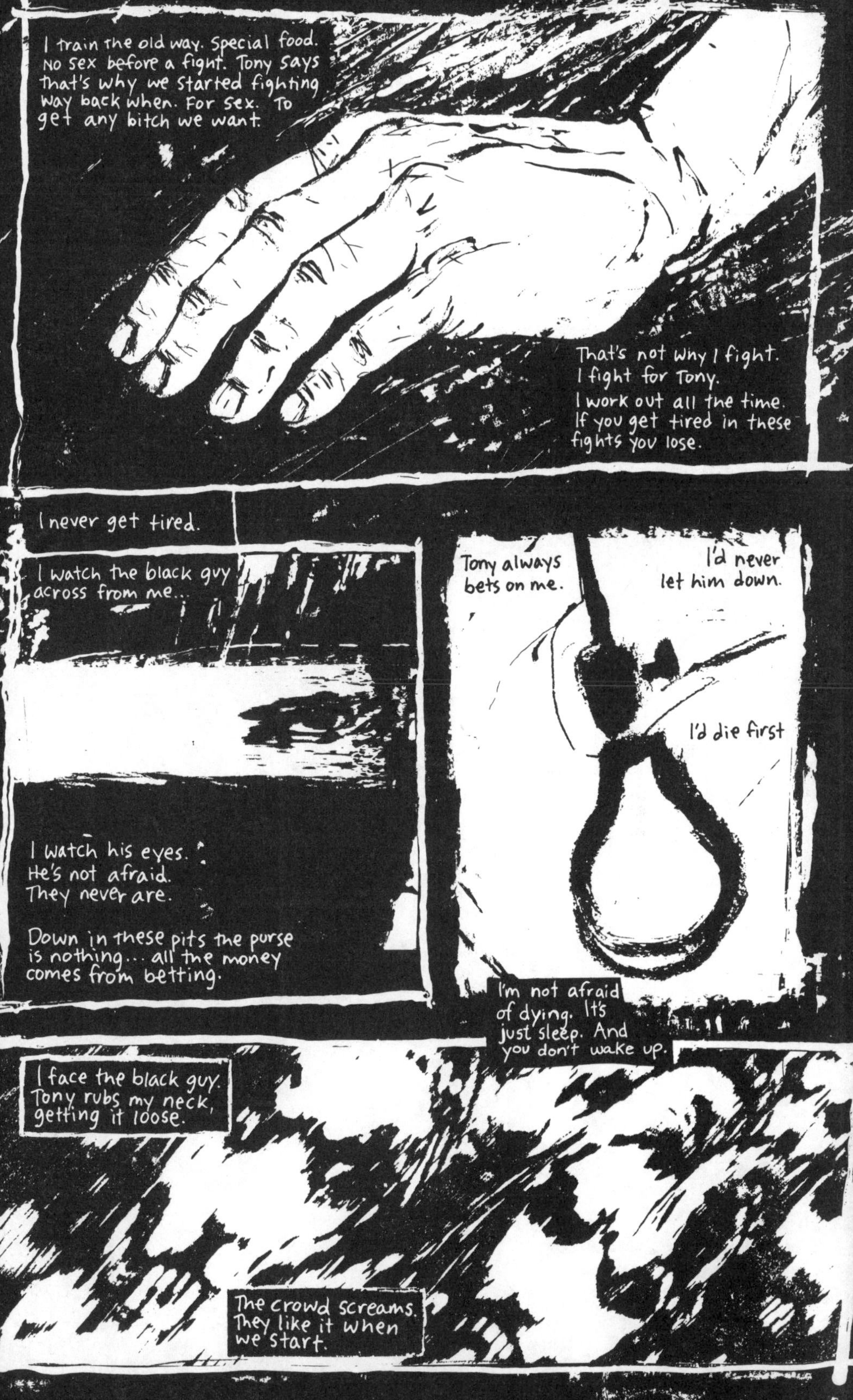

I train the old way. Special food. No sex before a fight. Tony says that's why we started fighting way back when. For sex. To get any bitch we want.
That's not why I fight. I fight for Tony.
I work out all the time. If you get tired in these fights you lose.
I never get tired.
I watch the black guy across from me...
I watch his eyes. He's not afraid. They never are.
Down in these pits the purse is nothing... all the money comes from betting.
Tony always bets on me.
I'd never let him down.
I'd die first
I'm not afraid of dying. It's just sleep. And you don't wake up.
I face the black guy. Tony rubs my neck, getting it loose.
The crowd screams. They like it when we start.

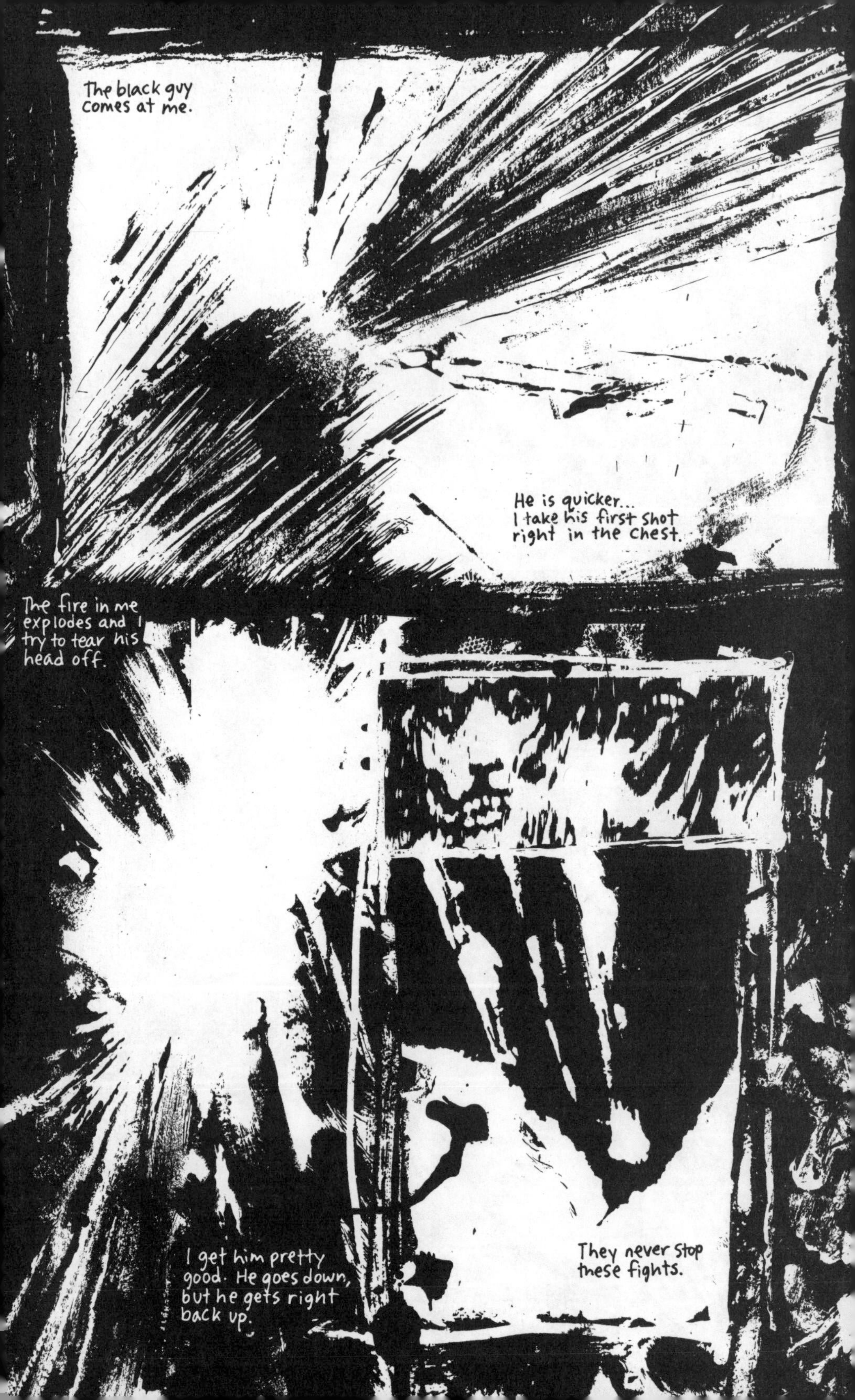
The black guy comes at me.
He is quicker... I take his first shot right in the chest.
The fire in me explodes and I try to tear his head off.
I get him pretty good. He goes down, but he gets right back up.
They never stop these fights.

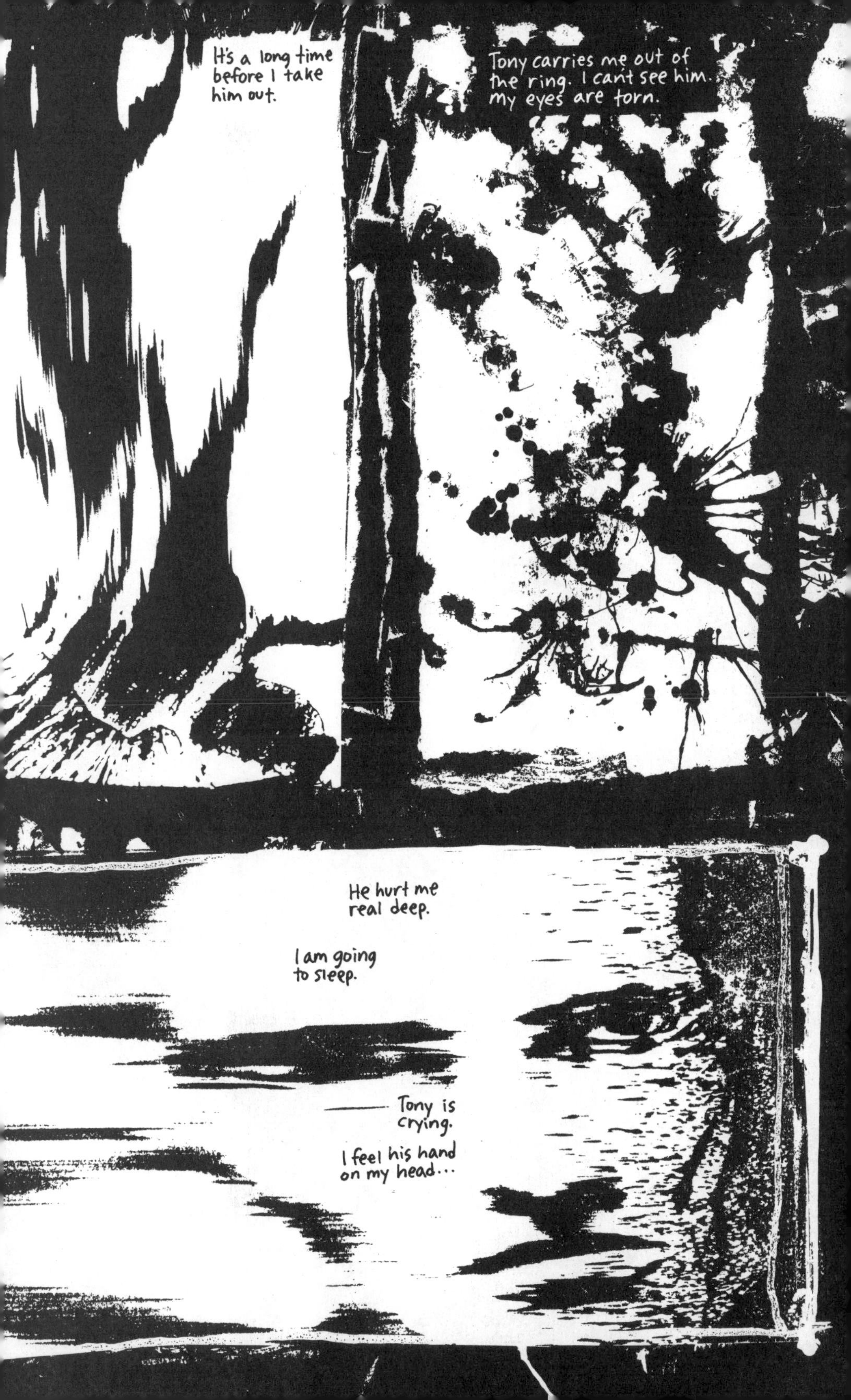
It's a long time before I take him out.
Tony carries me out of the ring. I can't see him. my eyes are torn.
He hurt me real deep.
I am going to sleep.
Tony is crying.
I feel his hand on my head...

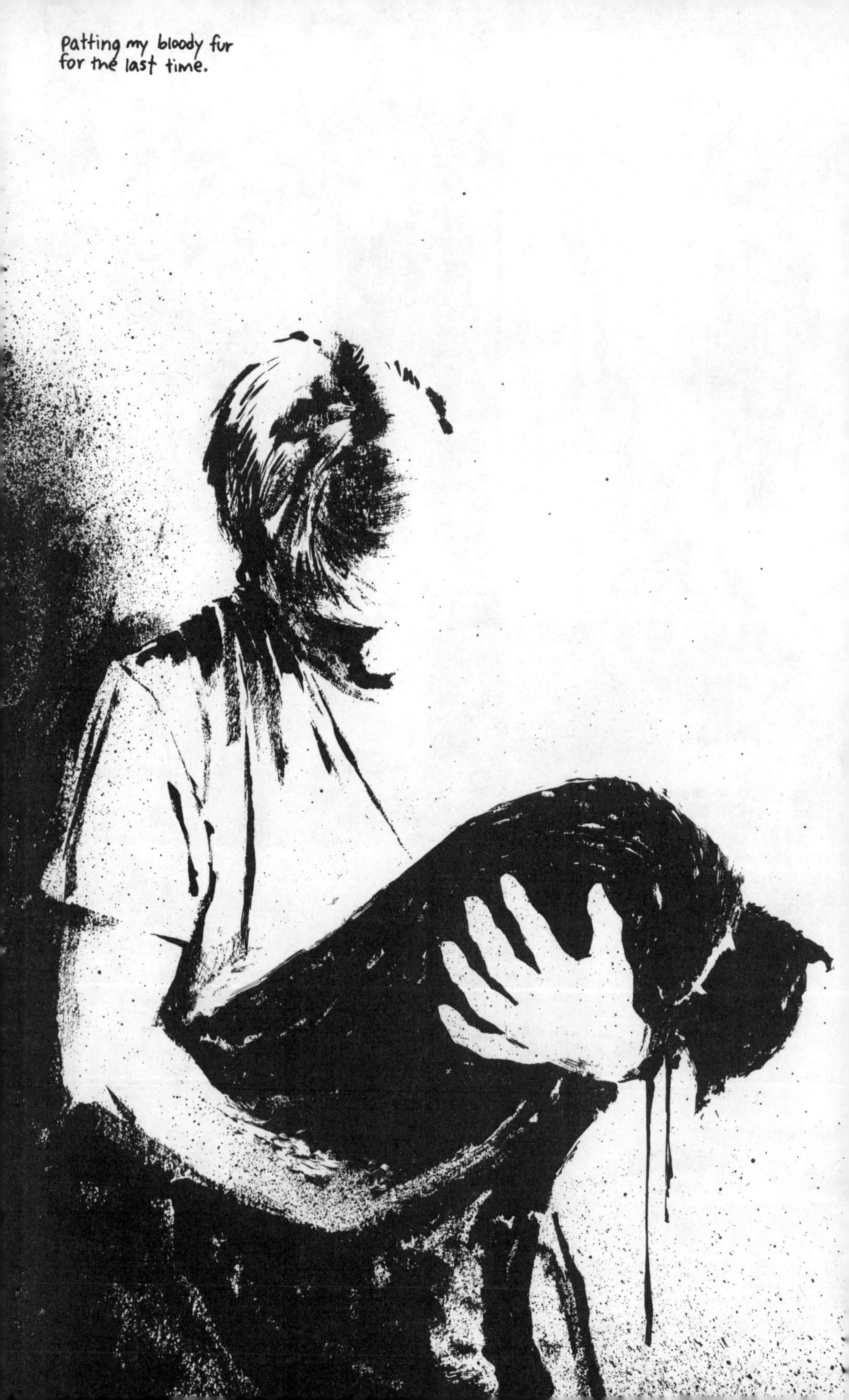
patting my bloody fur
for the last time.

A FLASH OF WHITE

THE HIGHRISE ACROSS THE STREET HAS A LOT OF WINDOWS. THEY'VE GOT ALL DIFFERENT COVERINGS: CURTAINS, DRAPES, LEVELOR BLINDS.

THE BITCH IN 24-G HAS CURTAINS, BUT SHE NEVER DRAWS THEM.

SHE PARADES AROUND IN FRONT OF HER BEDROOM WINDOW IN HER UNDERWEAR, TRYING ON DIFFERENT OUTFITS.

SOMETIMES SHE LOOKS RIGHT OUT THE WINDOW.

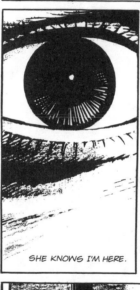

SHE KNOWS I'M HERE.

I MADE THE DIAGRAM OF THE BUILDING MYSELF. I'M IN AND OUT ALL THE TIME, MAKING DELIVERIES FOR A FLORIST.

THEY GOT ME THAT JOB WHEN THEY LET ME OUT.

I DON'T REALLY NEED THE JOB, I HAVE THE MONEY MY MOTHER LEFT ME. BUT THE BITCH AT PROBATION, SHE SAID I GOT TO HAVE EMPLOYMENT.

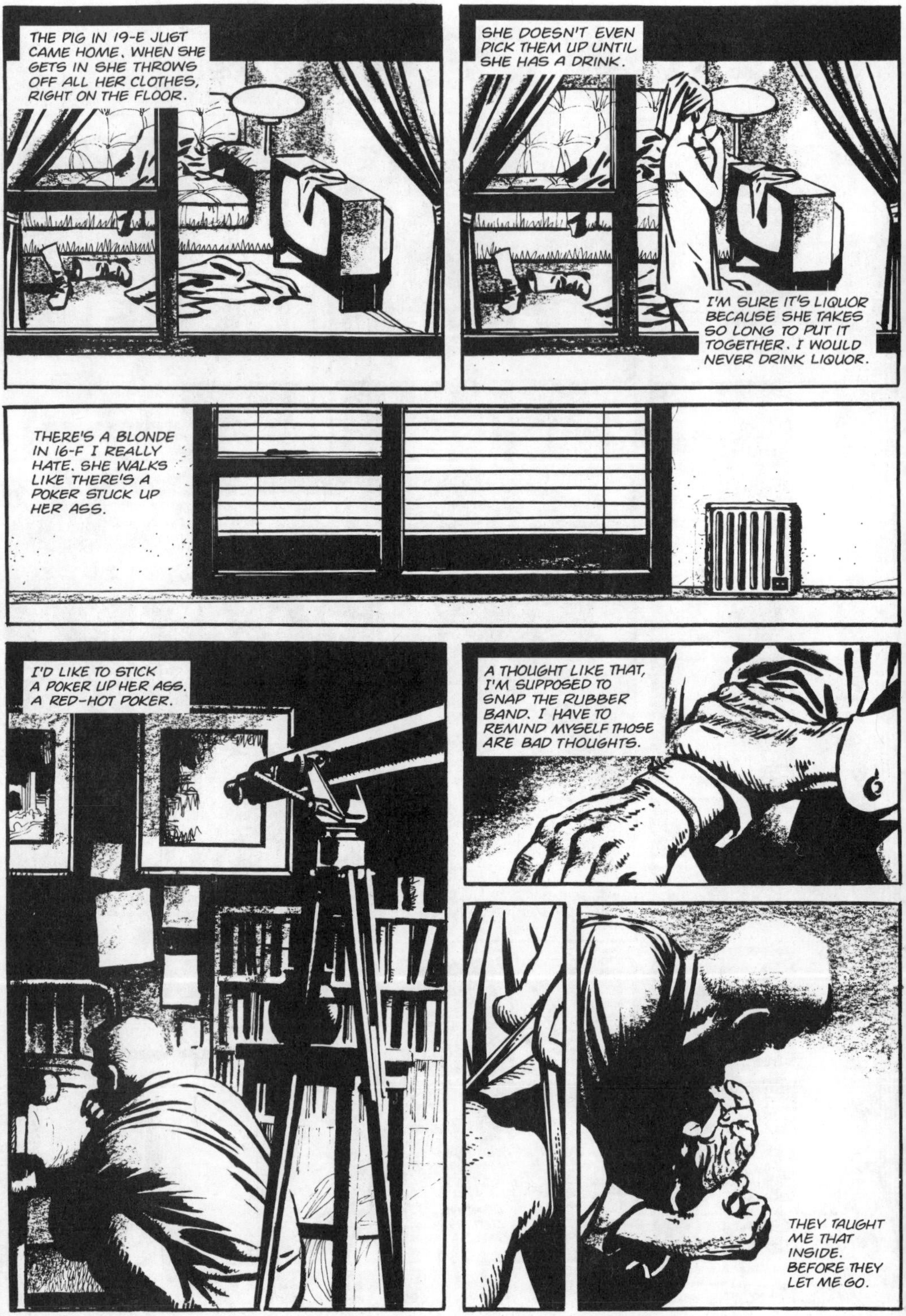
THE PIG IN 19-E JUST CAME HOME. WHEN SHE GETS IN SHE THROWS OFF ALL HER CLOTHES, RIGHT ON THE FLOOR.
SHE DOESN'T EVEN PICK THEM UP UNTIL SHE HAS A DRINK.
I'M SURE IT'S LIQUOR BECAUSE SHE TAKES SO LONG TO PUT IT TOGETHER. I WOULD NEVER DRINK LIQUOR.
THERE'S A BLONDE IN 16-F I REALLY HATE. SHE WALKS LIKE THERE'S A POKER STUCK UP HER ASS.
I'D LIKE TO STICK A POKER UP HER ASS. A RED-HOT POKER.
A THOUGHT LIKE THAT, I'M SUPPOSED TO SNAP THE RUBBER BAND. I HAVE TO REMIND MYSELF THOSE ARE BAD THOUGHTS.
THEY TAUGHT ME THAT INSIDE. BEFORE THEY LET ME GO.

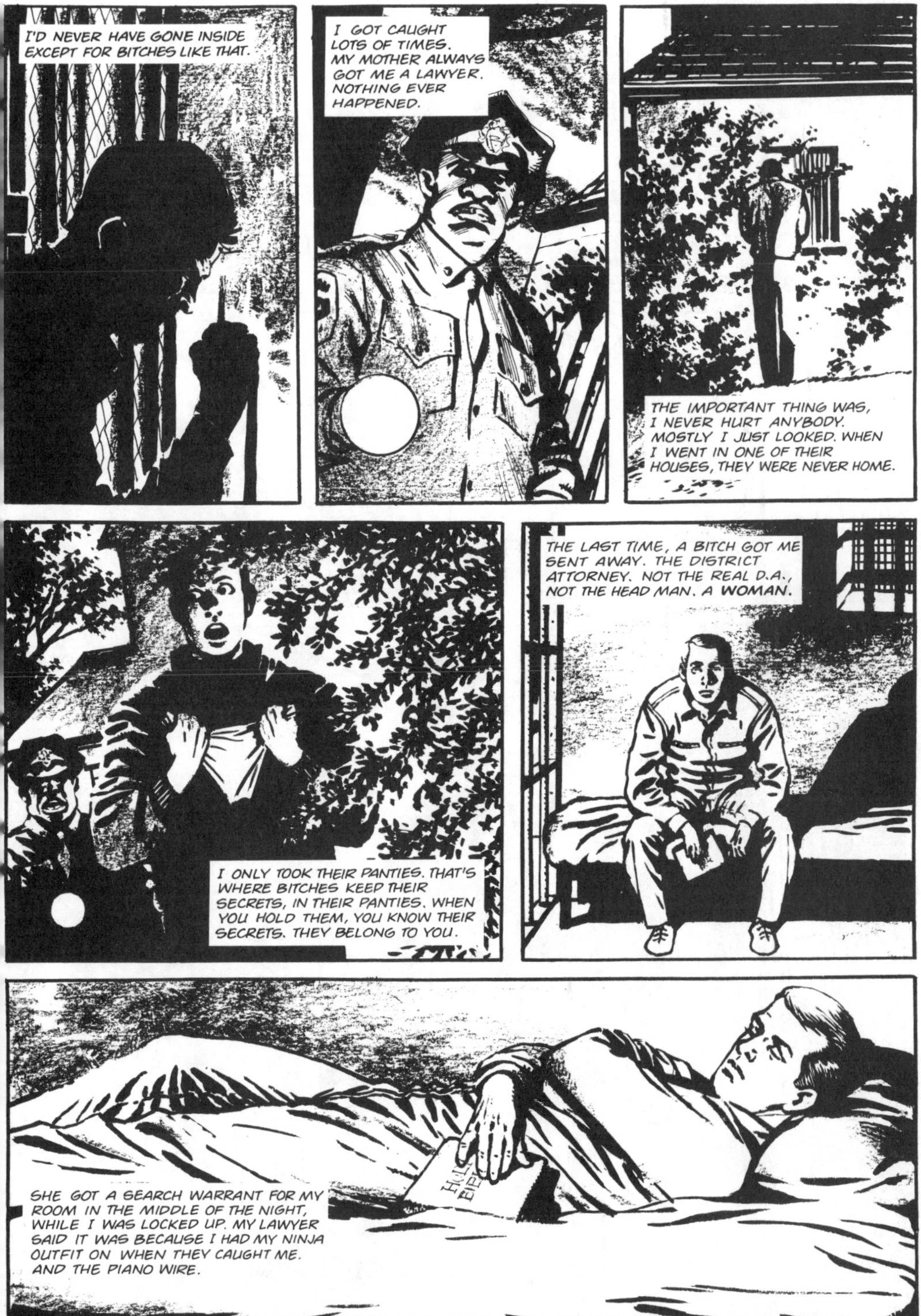
I'D NEVER HAVE GONE INSIDE EXCEPT FOR BITCHES LIKE THAT.
I GOT CAUGHT LOTS OF TIMES. MY MOTHER ALWAYS GOT ME A LAWYER. NOTHING EVER HAPPENED.
THE IMPORTANT THING WAS, I NEVER HURT ANYBODY. MOSTLY I JUST LOOKED. WHEN I WENT IN ONE OF THEIR HOUSES, THEY WERE NEVER HOME.
I ONLY TOOK THEIR PANTIES. THAT'S WHERE BITCHES KEEP THEIR SECRETS, IN THEIR PANTIES. WHEN YOU HOLD THEM, YOU KNOW THEIR SECRETS. THEY BELONG TO YOU.
THE LAST TIME, A BITCH GOT ME SENT AWAY. THE DISTRICT ATTORNEY. NOT THE REAL D.A., NOT THE HEAD MAN. A **WOMAN**.
SHE GOT A SEARCH WARRANT FOR MY ROOM IN THE MIDDLE OF THE NIGHT, WHILE I WAS LOCKED UP. MY LAWYER SAID IT WAS BECAUSE I HAD MY NINJA OUTFIT ON WHEN THEY CAUGHT ME. AND THE PIANO WIRE.

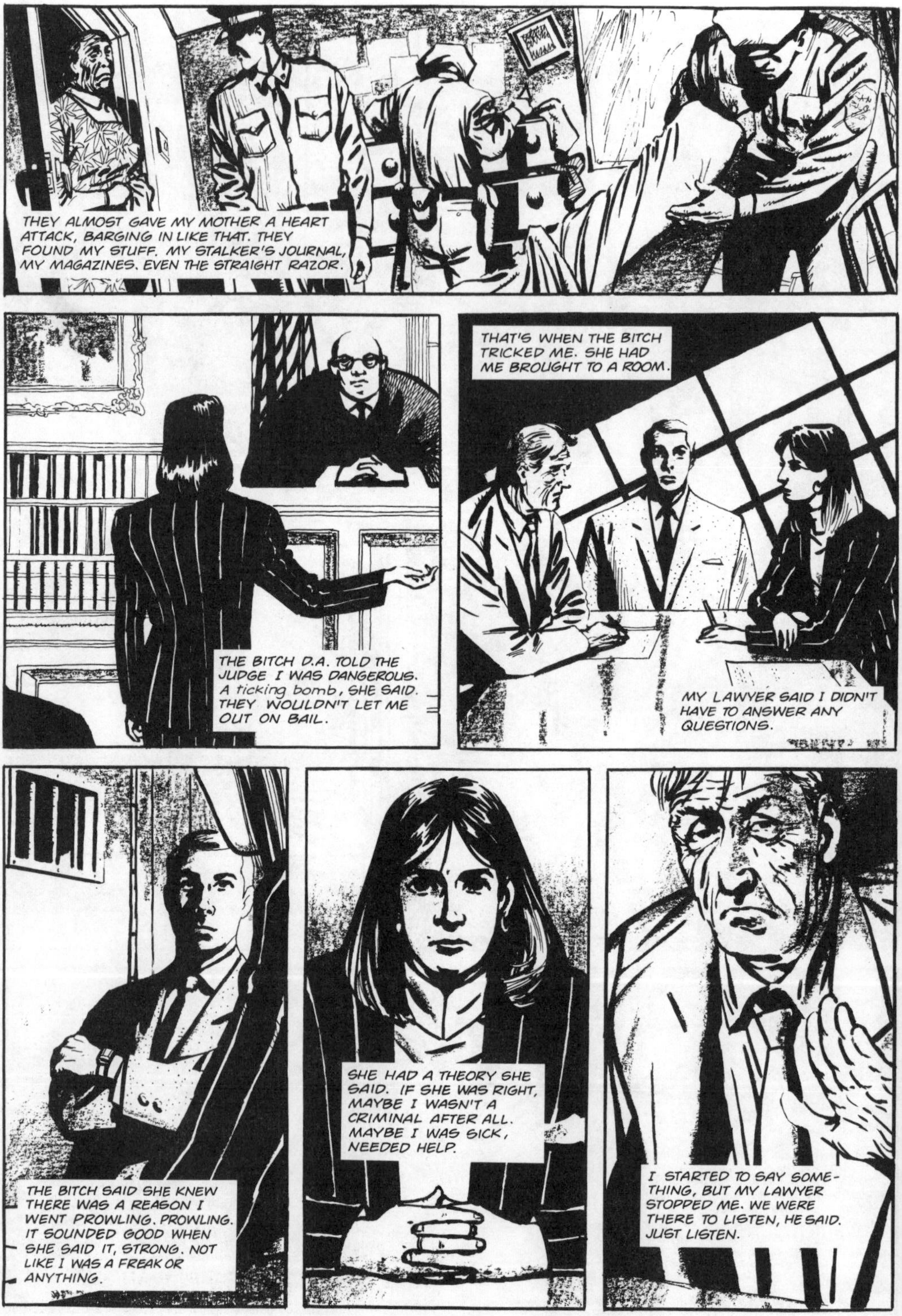
THEY ALMOST GAVE MY MOTHER A HEART ATTACK, BARGING IN LIKE THAT. THEY FOUND MY STUFF. MY STALKER'S JOURNAL, MY MAGAZINES. EVEN THE STRAIGHT RAZOR.
THE BITCH D.A. TOLD THE JUDGE I WAS DANGEROUS. A ticking bomb, SHE SAID. THEY WOULDN'T LET ME OUT ON BAIL.
THAT'S WHEN THE BITCH TRICKED ME. SHE HAD ME BROUGHT TO A ROOM.
MY LAWYER SAID I DIDN'T HAVE TO ANSWER ANY QUESTIONS.
THE BITCH SAID SHE KNEW THERE WAS A REASON I WENT PROWLING. PROWLING. IT SOUNDED GOOD WHEN SHE SAID IT, STRONG. NOT LIKE I WAS A FREAK OR ANYTHING.
SHE HAD A THEORY SHE SAID. IF SHE WAS RIGHT, MAYBE I WASN'T A CRIMINAL AFTER ALL. MAYBE I WAS SICK, NEEDED HELP.
I STARTED TO SAY SOMETHING, BUT MY LAWYER STOPPED ME. WE WERE THERE TO LISTEN, HE SAID. JUST LISTEN.

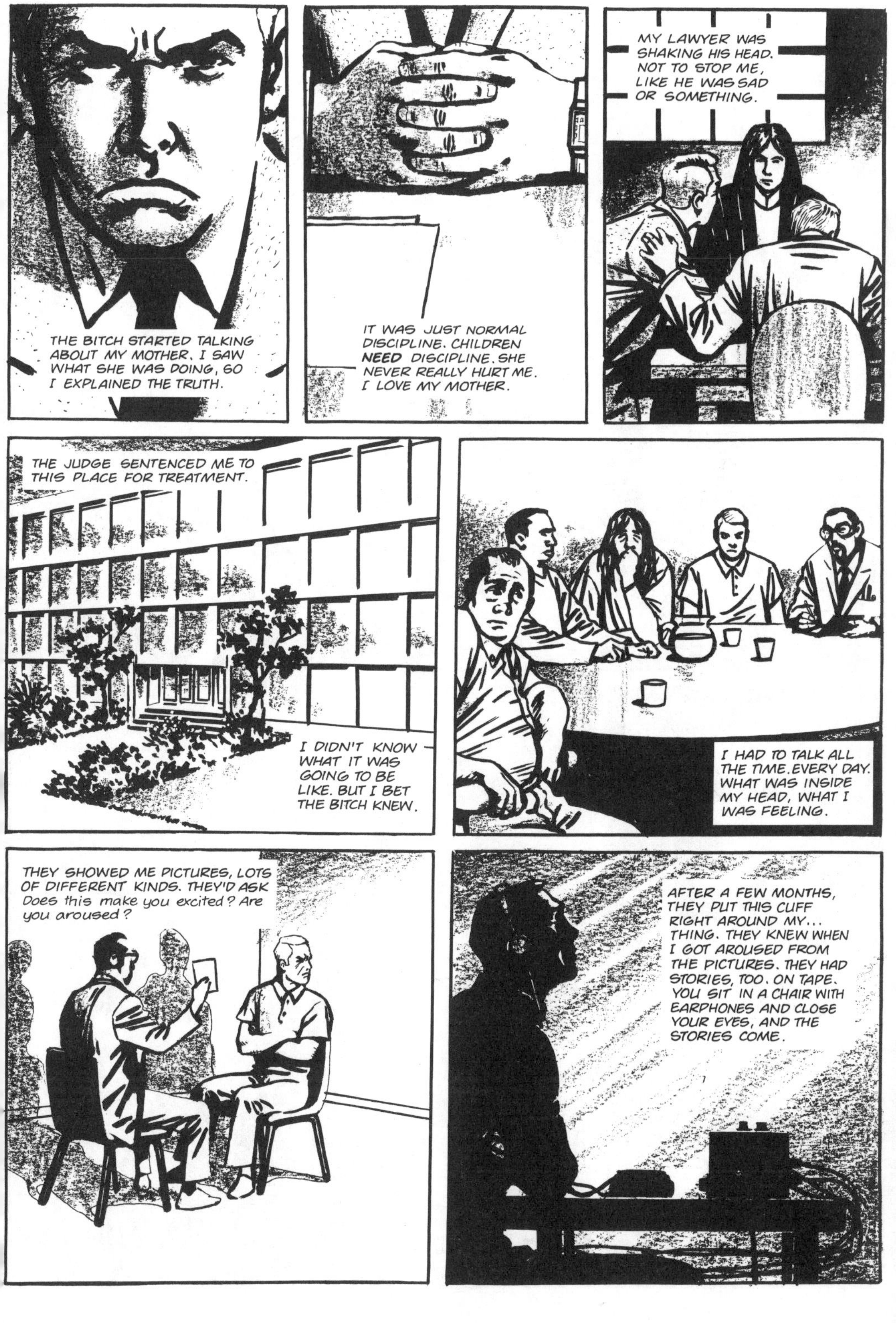
THE BITCH STARTED TALKING ABOUT MY MOTHER. I SAW WHAT SHE WAS DOING, SO I EXPLAINED THE TRUTH.
IT WAS JUST NORMAL DISCIPLINE. CHILDREN **NEED** DISCIPLINE. SHE NEVER REALLY HURT ME. I LOVE MY MOTHER.
MY LAWYER WAS SHAKING HIS HEAD. NOT TO STOP ME, LIKE HE WAS SAD OR SOMETHING.
THE JUDGE SENTENCED ME TO THIS PLACE FOR TREATMENT.
I DIDN'T KNOW WHAT IT WAS GOING TO BE LIKE. BUT I BET THE BITCH KNEW.
I HAD TO TALK ALL THE TIME. EVERY DAY. WHAT WAS INSIDE MY HEAD, WHAT I WAS FEELING.
THEY SHOWED ME PICTURES, LOTS OF DIFFERENT KINDS. THEY'D ASK *Does this make you excited? Are you aroused?*
AFTER A FEW MONTHS, THEY PUT THIS CUFF RIGHT AROUND MY... THING. THEY KNEW WHEN I GOT AROUSED FROM THE PICTURES. THEY HAD STORIES, TOO. ON TAPE. YOU SIT IN A CHAIR WITH EARPHONES AND CLOSE YOUR EYES, AND THE STORIES COME.

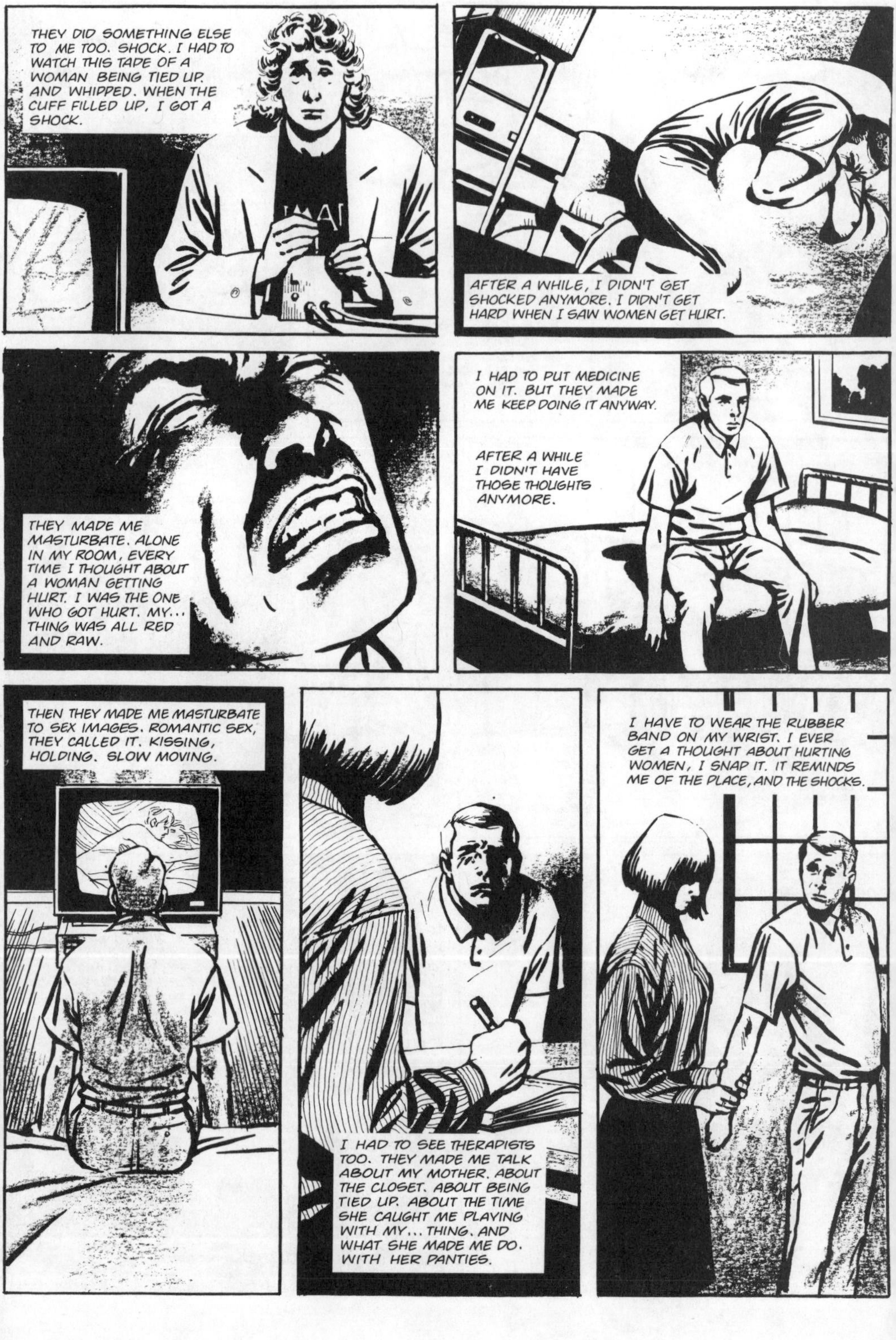

THEY DID SOMETHING ELSE TO ME TOO. SHOCK. I HAD TO WATCH THIS TAPE OF A WOMAN BEING TIED UP. AND WHIPPED. WHEN THE CUFF FILLED UP, I GOT A SHOCK.
AFTER A WHILE, I DIDN'T GET SHOCKED ANYMORE. I DIDN'T GET HARD WHEN I SAW WOMEN GET HURT.
THEY MADE ME MASTURBATE. ALONE IN MY ROOM, EVERY TIME I THOUGHT ABOUT A WOMAN GETTING HURT. I WAS THE ONE WHO GOT HURT. MY... THING WAS ALL RED AND RAW.
I HAD TO PUT MEDICINE ON IT. BUT THEY MADE ME KEEP DOING IT ANYWAY.
AFTER A WHILE I DIDN'T HAVE THOSE THOUGHTS ANYMORE.
THEN THEY MADE ME MASTURBATE TO SEX IMAGES. ROMANTIC SEX, THEY CALLED IT. KISSING, HOLDING. SLOW MOVING.
I HAD TO SEE THERAPISTS TOO. THEY MADE ME TALK ABOUT MY MOTHER. ABOUT THE CLOSET. ABOUT BEING TIED UP. ABOUT THE TIME SHE CAUGHT ME PLAYING WITH MY... THING. AND WHAT SHE MADE ME DO. WITH HER PANTIES.
I HAVE TO WEAR THE RUBBER BAND ON MY WRIST. I EVER GET A THOUGHT ABOUT HURTING WOMEN, I SNAP IT. IT REMINDS ME OF THE PLACE, AND THE SHOCKS.

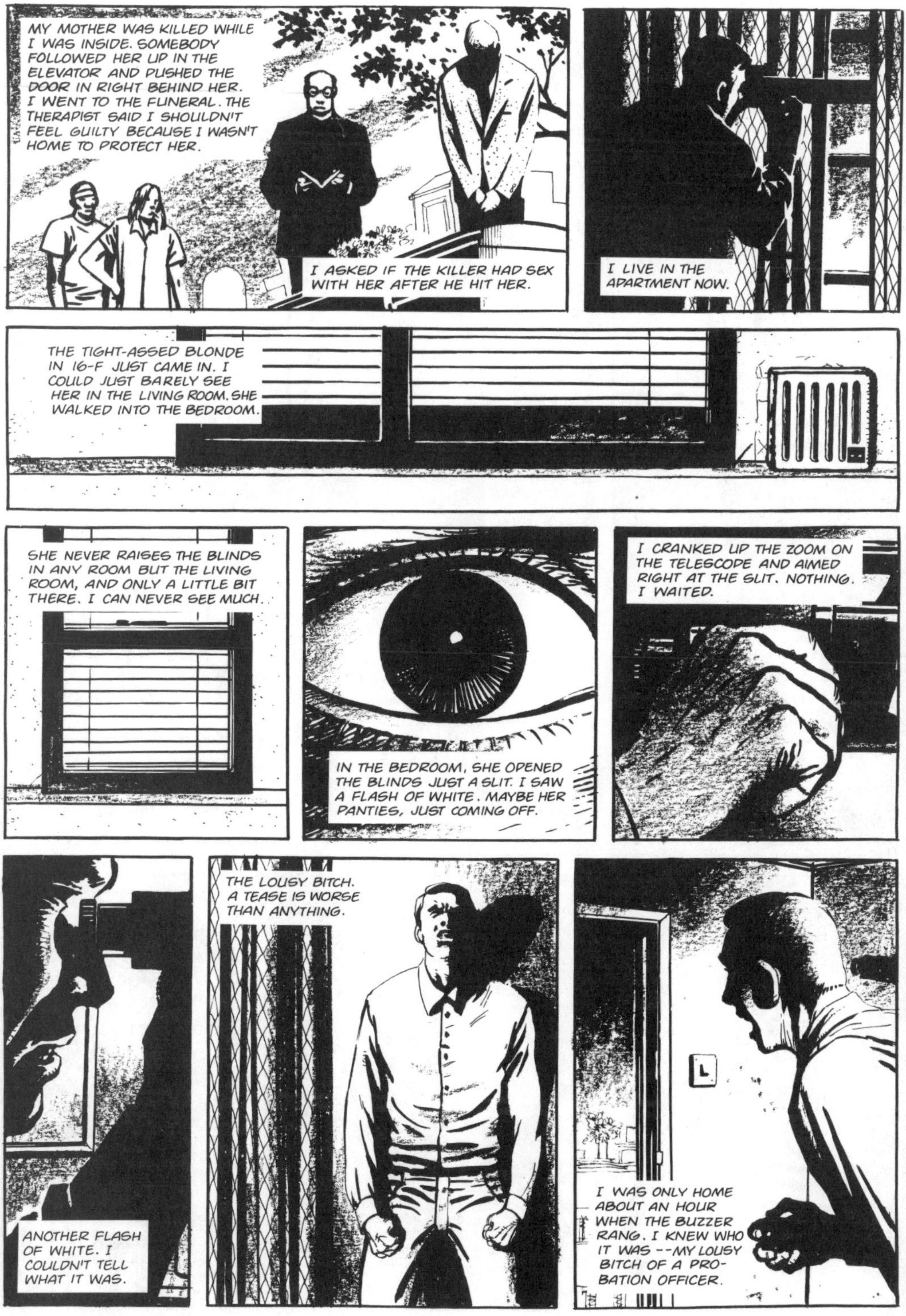
MY MOTHER WAS KILLED WHILE I WAS INSIDE. SOMEBODY FOLLOWED HER UP IN THE ELEVATOR AND PUSHED THE DOOR IN RIGHT BEHIND HER. I WENT TO THE FUNERAL. THE THERAPIST SAID I SHOULDN'T FEEL GUILTY BECAUSE I WASN'T HOME TO PROTECT HER.
I ASKED IF THE KILLER HAD SEX WITH HER AFTER HE HIT HER.
I LIVE IN THE APARTMENT NOW.
THE TIGHT-ASSED BLONDE IN 16-F JUST CAME IN. I COULD JUST BARELY SEE HER IN THE LIVING ROOM. SHE WALKED INTO THE BEDROOM.
SHE NEVER RAISES THE BLINDS IN ANY ROOM BUT THE LIVING ROOM, AND ONLY A LITTLE BIT THERE. I CAN NEVER SEE MUCH.
IN THE BEDROOM, SHE OPENED THE BLINDS JUST A SLIT. I SAW A FLASH OF WHITE. MAYBE HER PANTIES, JUST COMING OFF.
I CRANKED UP THE ZOOM ON THE TELESCOPE AND AIMED RIGHT AT THE SLIT. NOTHING. I WAITED.
ANOTHER FLASH OF WHITE. I COULDN'T TELL WHAT IT WAS.
THE LOUSY BITCH. A TEASE IS WORSE THAN ANYTHING.
I WAS ONLY HOME ABOUT AN HOUR WHEN THE BUZZER RANG. I KNEW WHO IT WAS --MY LOUSY BITCH OF A PRO- BATION OFFICER.

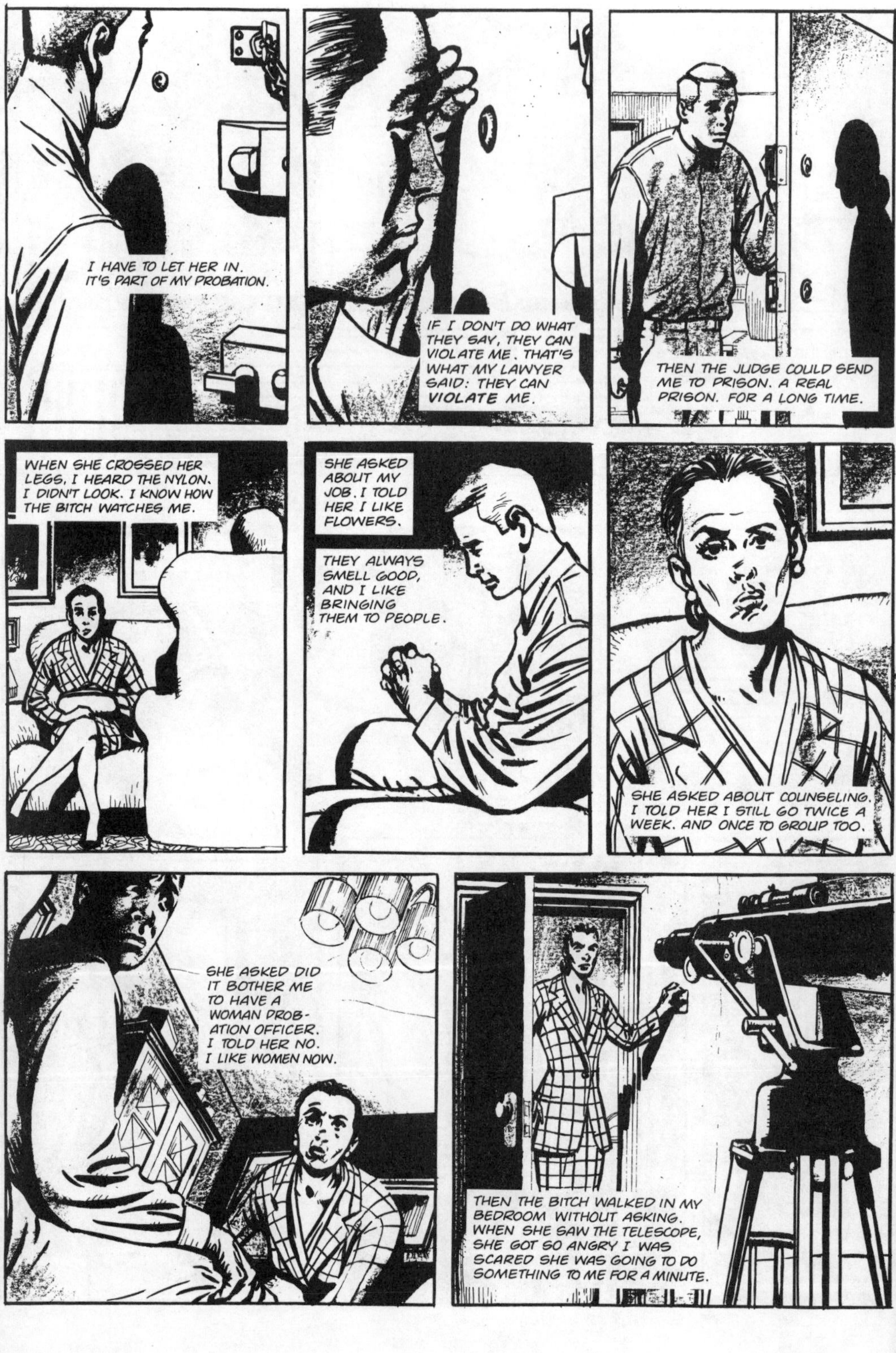
I HAVE TO LET HER IN. IT'S PART OF MY PROBATION.
IF I DON'T DO WHAT THEY SAY, THEY CAN VIOLATE ME. THAT'S WHAT MY LAWYER SAID: THEY CAN VIOLATE ME.
THEN THE JUDGE COULD SEND ME TO PRISON. A REAL PRISON. FOR A LONG TIME.
WHEN SHE CROSSED HER LEGS, I HEARD THE NYLON. I DIDN'T LOOK. I KNOW HOW THE BITCH WATCHES ME.
SHE ASKED ABOUT MY JOB. I TOLD HER I LIKE FLOWERS.
THEY ALWAYS SMELL GOOD, AND I LIKE BRINGING THEM TO PEOPLE.
SHE ASKED ABOUT COUNSELING. I TOLD HER I STILL GO TWICE A WEEK. AND ONCE TO GROUP TOO.
SHE ASKED DID IT BOTHER ME TO HAVE A WOMAN PROB-ATION OFFICER. I TOLD HER NO. I LIKE WOMEN NOW.
THEN THE BITCH WALKED IN MY BEDROOM WITHOUT ASKING. WHEN SHE SAW THE TELESCOPE, SHE GOT SO ANGRY I WAS SCARED SHE WAS GOING TO DO SOMETHING TO ME FOR A MINUTE.

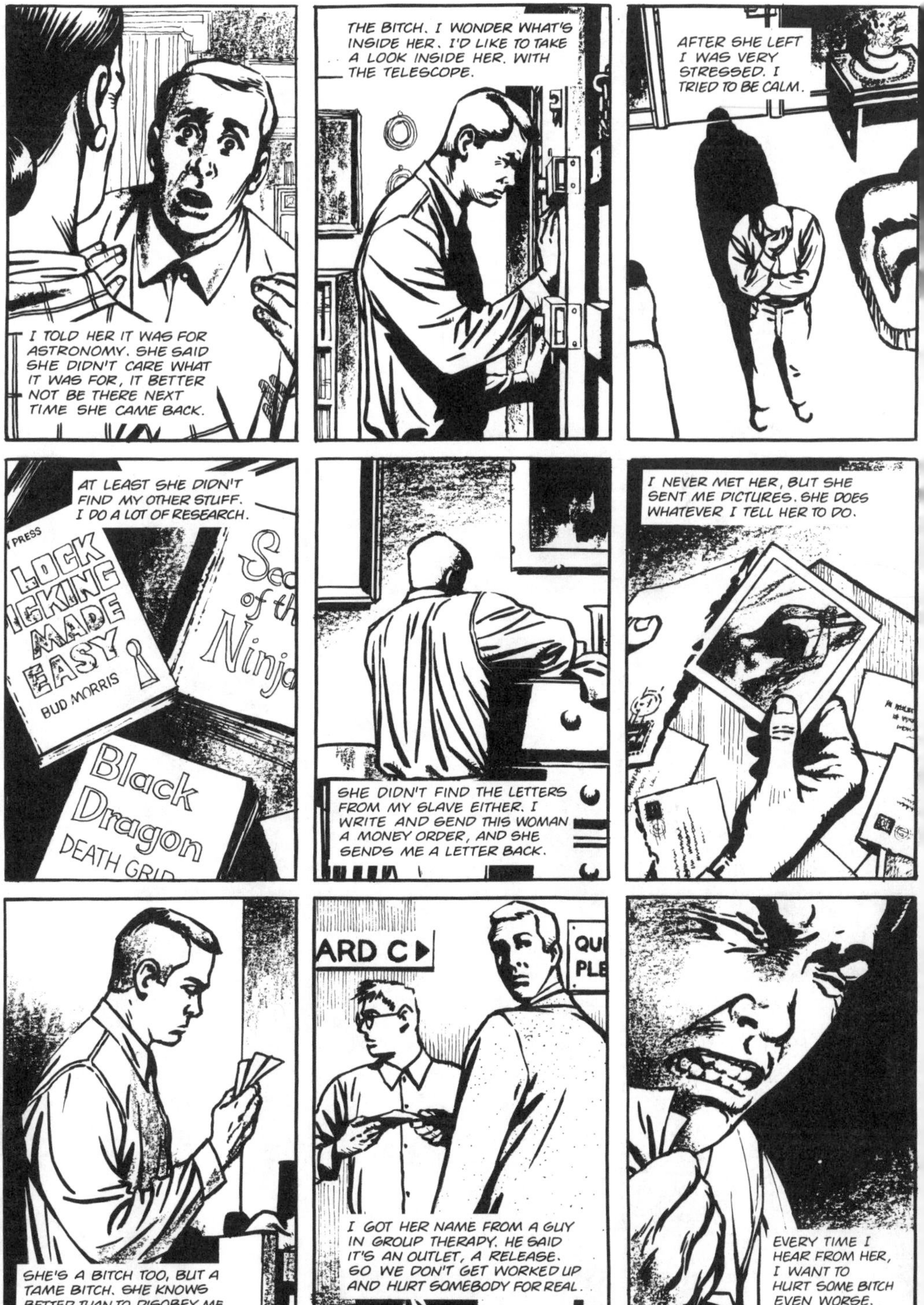
I TOLD HER IT WAS FOR ASTRONOMY. SHE SAID SHE DIDN'T CARE WHAT IT WAS FOR, IT BETTER NOT BE THERE NEXT TIME SHE CAME BACK.
THE BITCH. I WONDER WHAT'S INSIDE HER. I'D LIKE TO TAKE A LOOK INSIDE HER. WITH THE TELESCOPE.
AFTER SHE LEFT I WAS VERY STRESSED. I TRIED TO BE CALM.
AT LEAST SHE DIDN'T FIND MY OTHER STUFF. I DO A LOT OF RESEARCH.
PRESS
LOCK
ICKING
MADE
EASY
BUD MORRIS
Sec
of th
Ninja
Black
Dragon
DEATH GRIP
SHE DIDN'T FIND THE LETTERS FROM MY SLAVE EITHER. I WRITE AND SEND THIS WOMAN A MONEY ORDER, AND SHE SENDS ME A LETTER BACK.
I NEVER MET HER, BUT SHE SENT ME PICTURES. SHE DOES WHATEVER I TELL HER TO DO.
SHE'S A BITCH TOO, BUT A TAME BITCH. SHE KNOWS BETTER THAN TO DISOBEY ME.
ARD C
QU
PLE
I GOT HER NAME FROM A GUY IN GROUP THERAPY. HE SAID IT'S AN OUTLET, A RELEASE. SO WE DON'T GET WORKED UP AND HURT SOMEBODY FOR REAL.
EVERY TIME I HEAR FROM HER, I WANT TO HURT SOME BITCH EVEN WORSE.

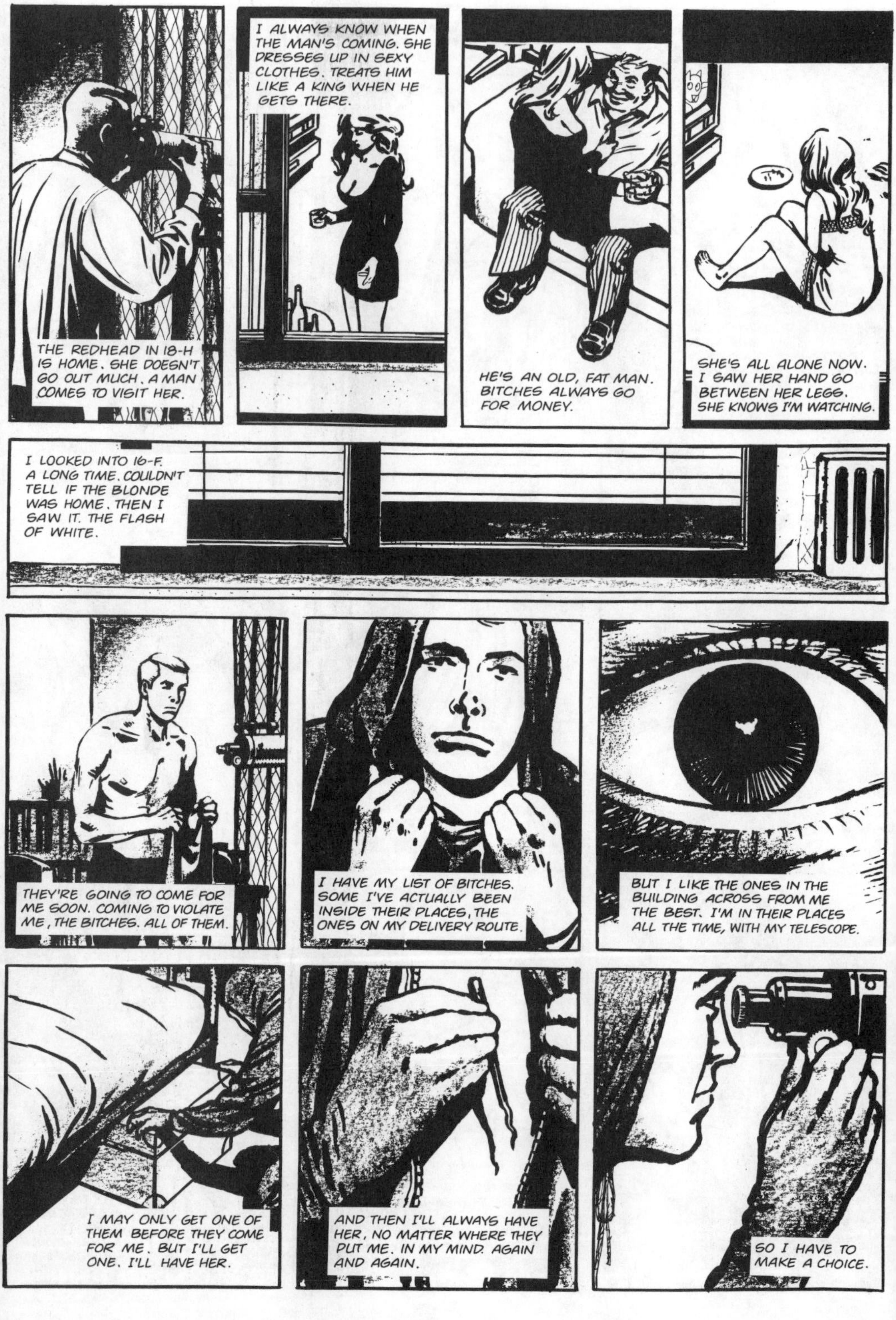
THE REDHEAD IN 18-H IS HOME. SHE DOESN'T GO OUT MUCH. A MAN COMES TO VISIT HER.
I ALWAYS KNOW WHEN THE MAN'S COMING. SHE DRESSES UP IN SEXY CLOTHES. TREATS HIM LIKE A KING WHEN HE GETS THERE.
HE'S AN OLD, FAT MAN. BITCHES ALWAYS GO FOR MONEY.
SHE'S ALL ALONE NOW. I SAW HER HAND GO BETWEEN HER LEGS. SHE KNOWS I'M WATCHING.
I LOOKED INTO 16-F. A LONG TIME. COULDN'T TELL IF THE BLONDE WAS HOME. THEN I SAW IT. THE FLASH OF WHITE.
THEY'RE GOING TO COME FOR ME SOON. COMING TO VIOLATE ME, THE BITCHES. ALL OF THEM.
I HAVE MY LIST OF BITCHES. SOME I'VE ACTUALLY BEEN INSIDE THEIR PLACES, THE ONES ON MY DELIVERY ROUTE.
BUT I LIKE THE ONES IN THE BUILDING ACROSS FROM ME THE BEST. I'M IN THEIR PLACES ALL THE TIME, WITH MY TELESCOPE.
I MAY ONLY GET ONE OF THEM BEFORE THEY COME FOR ME. BUT I'LL GET ONE. I'LL HAVE HER.
AND THEN I'LL ALWAYS HAVE HER, NO MATTER WHERE THEY PUT ME. IN MY MIND. AGAIN AND AGAIN.
SO I HAVE TO MAKE A CHOICE.

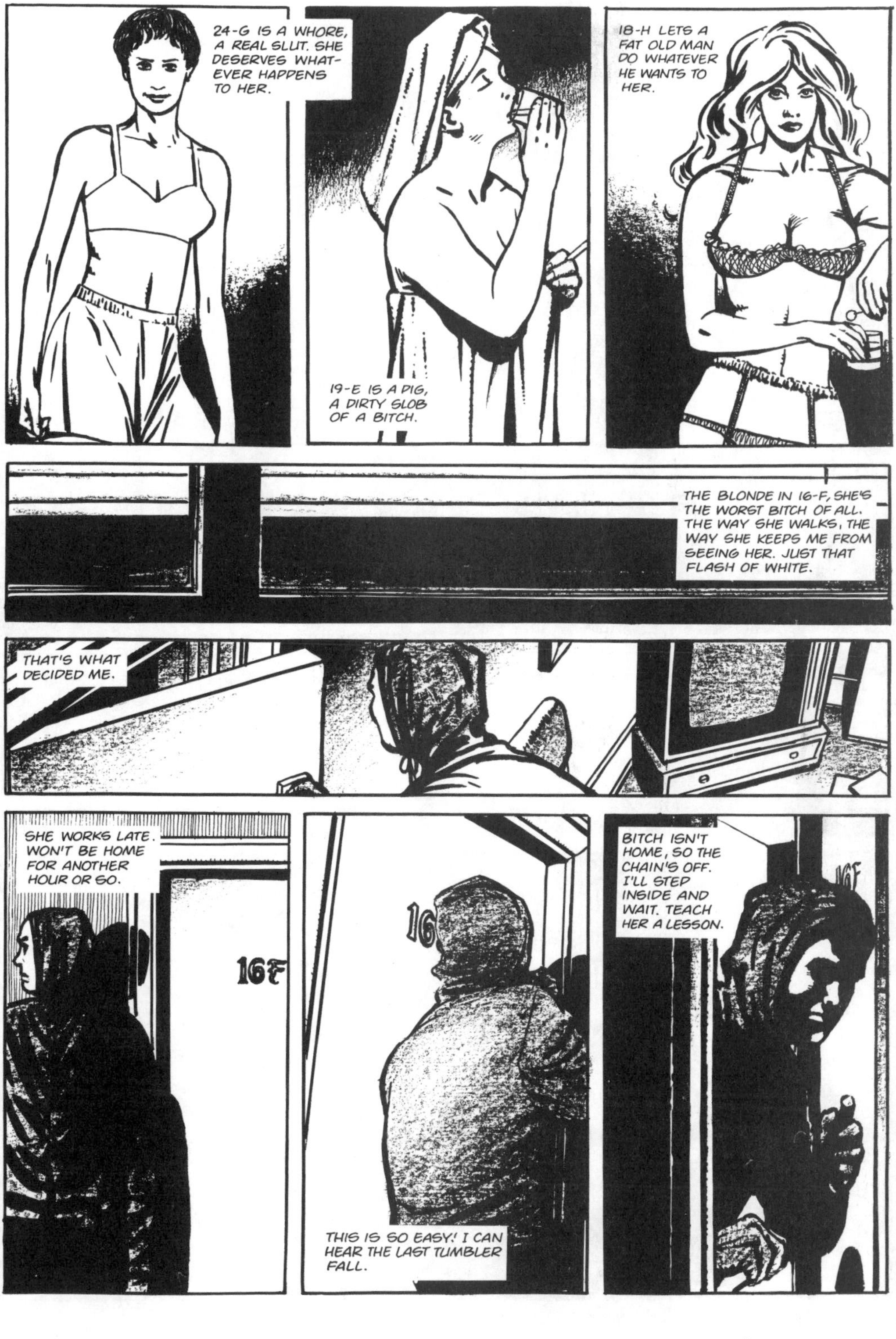
24-G IS A WHORE, A REAL SLUT. SHE DESERVES WHATEVER HAPPENS TO HER.
19-E IS A PIG, A DIRTY SLOB OF A BITCH.
18-H LETS A FAT OLD MAN DO WHATEVER HE WANTS TO HER.
THE BLONDE IN 16-F, SHE'S THE WORST BITCH OF ALL. THE WAY SHE WALKS, THE WAY SHE KEEPS ME FROM SEEING HER. JUST THAT FLASH OF WHITE.
THAT'S WHAT DECIDED ME.
SHE WORKS LATE. WON'T BE HOME FOR ANOTHER HOUR OR SO.
16F
16
THIS IS SO EASY! I CAN HEAR THE LAST TUMBLER FALL.
BITCH ISN'T HOME, SO THE CHAIN'S OFF. I'LL STEP INSIDE AND WAIT. TEACH HER A LESSON.
16F

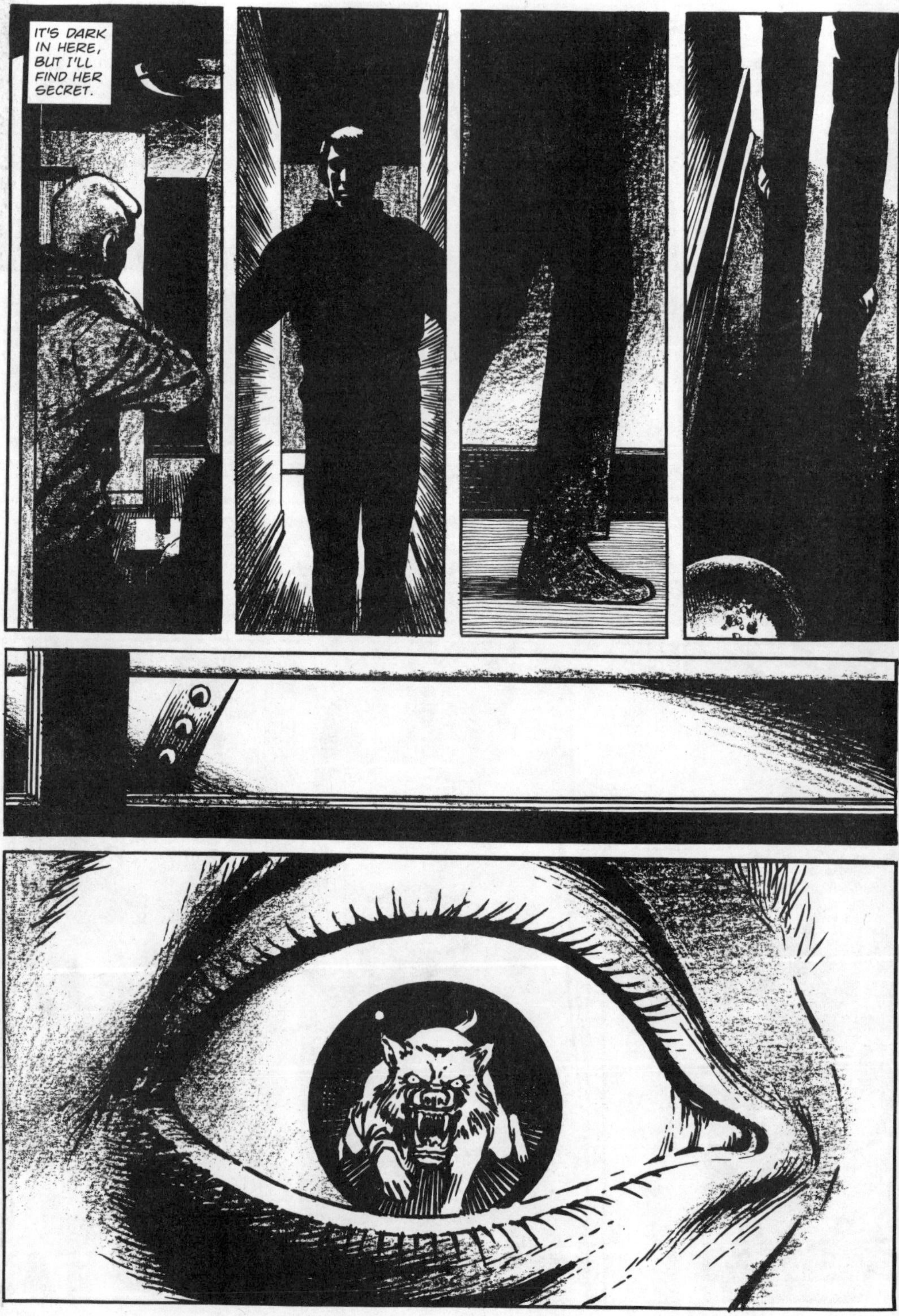
IT'S DARK IN HERE, BUT I'LL FIND HER SECRET.

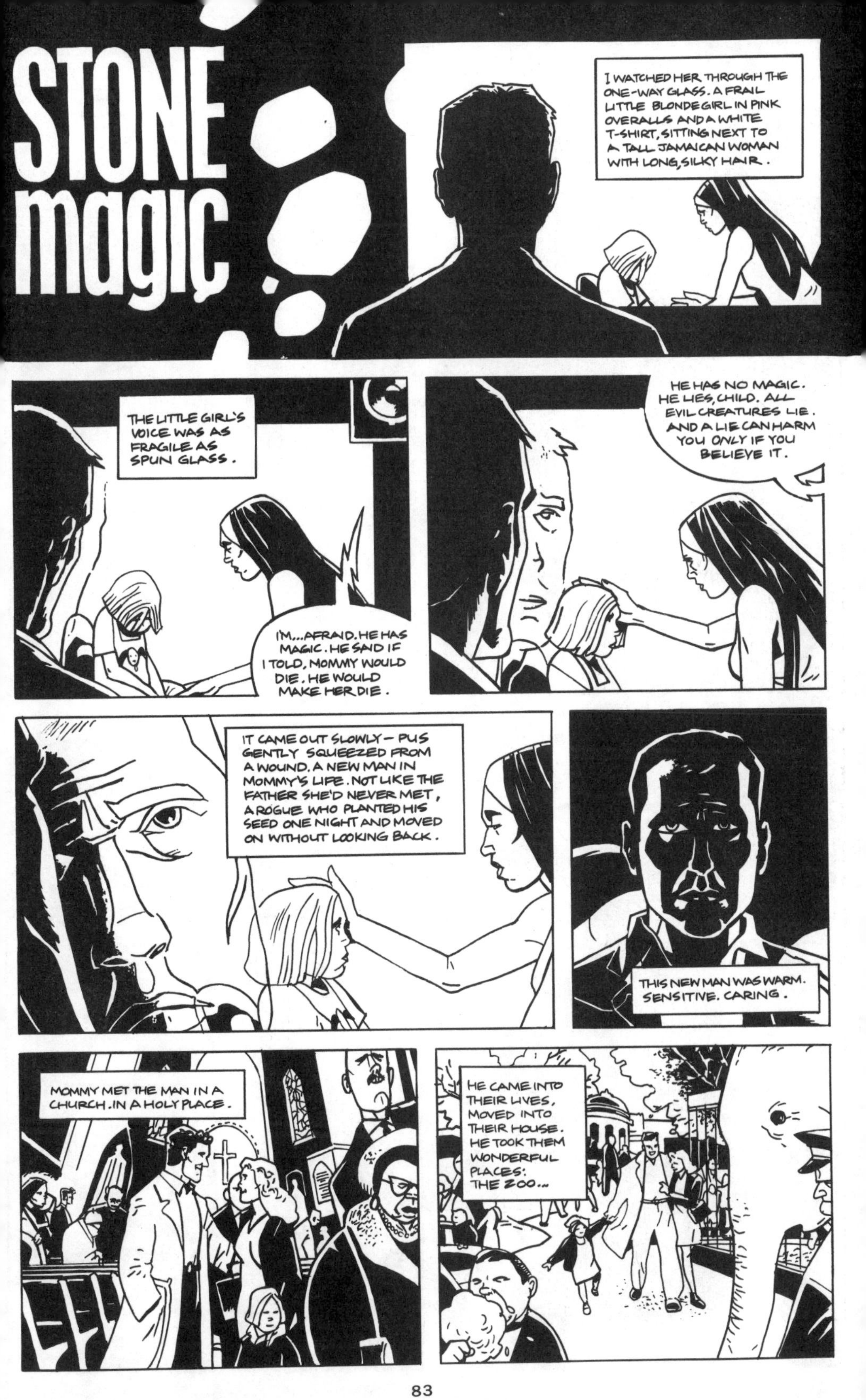
STONE magic
I WATCHED HER THROUGH THE ONE-WAY GLASS. A FRAIL LITTLE BLONDE GIRL IN PINK OVERALLS AND A WHITE T-SHIRT, SITTING NEXT TO A TALL JAMAICAN WOMAN WITH LONG, SILKY HAIR.
THE LITTLE GIRL'S VOICE WAS AS FRAGILE AS SPUN GLASS.
I'M...AFRAID. HE HAS MAGIC. HE SAID IF I TOLD, MOMMY WOULD DIE. HE WOULD MAKE HER DIE.
HE HAS NO MAGIC. HE LIES, CHILD. ALL EVIL CREATURES LIE. AND A LIE CAN HARM YOU ONLY IF YOU BELIEVE IT.
IT CAME OUT SLOWLY — PUS GENTLY SQUEEZED FROM A WOUND. A NEW MAN IN MOMMY'S LIFE. NOT LIKE THE FATHER SHE'D NEVER MET, A ROGUE WHO PLANTED HIS SEED ONE NIGHT AND MOVED ON WITHOUT LOOKING BACK.
THIS NEW MAN WAS WARM. SENSITIVE. CARING.
MOMMY MET THE MAN IN A CHURCH. IN A HOLY PLACE.
HE CAME INTO THEIR LIVES, MOVED INTO THEIR HOUSE. HE TOOK THEM WONDERFUL PLACES: THE ZOO...

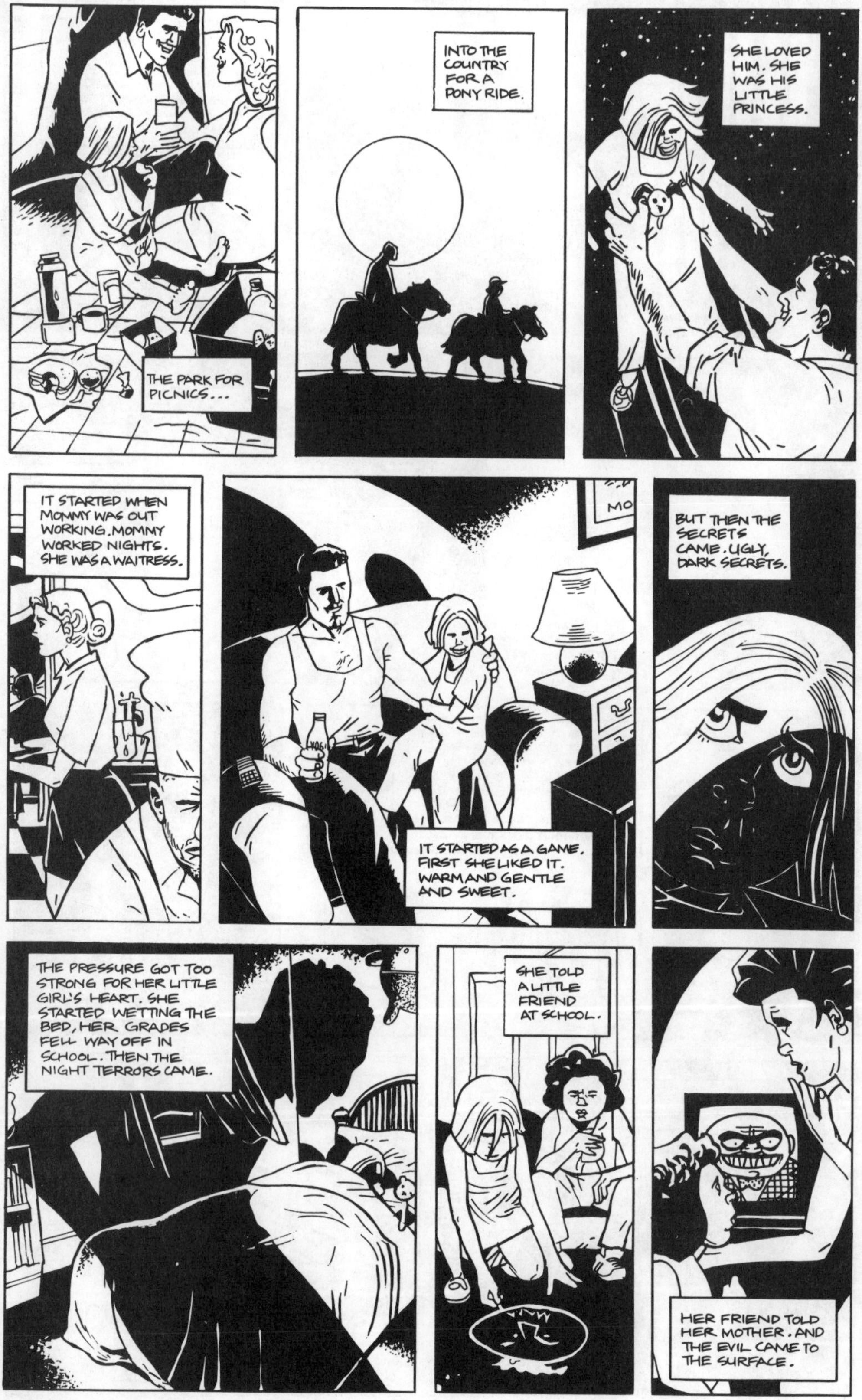
THE PARK FOR PICNICS...
INTO THE COUNTRY FOR A PONY RIDE.
SHE LOVED HIM. SHE WAS HIS LITTLE PRINCESS.
IT STARTED WHEN MOMMY WAS OUT WORKING. MOMMY WORKED NIGHTS. SHE WAS A WAITRESS.
IT STARTED AS A GAME. FIRST SHE LIKED IT. WARM AND GENTLE AND SWEET.
BUT THEN THE SECRETS CAME. UGLY, DARK SECRETS.
THE PRESSURE GOT TOO STRONG FOR HER LITTLE GIRL'S HEART. SHE STARTED WETTING THE BED, HER GRADES FELL WAY OFF IN SCHOOL. THEN THE NIGHT TERRORS CAME.
SHE TOLD A LITTLE FRIEND AT SCHOOL.
HER FRIEND TOLD HER MOTHER. AND THE EVIL CAME TO THE SURFACE.

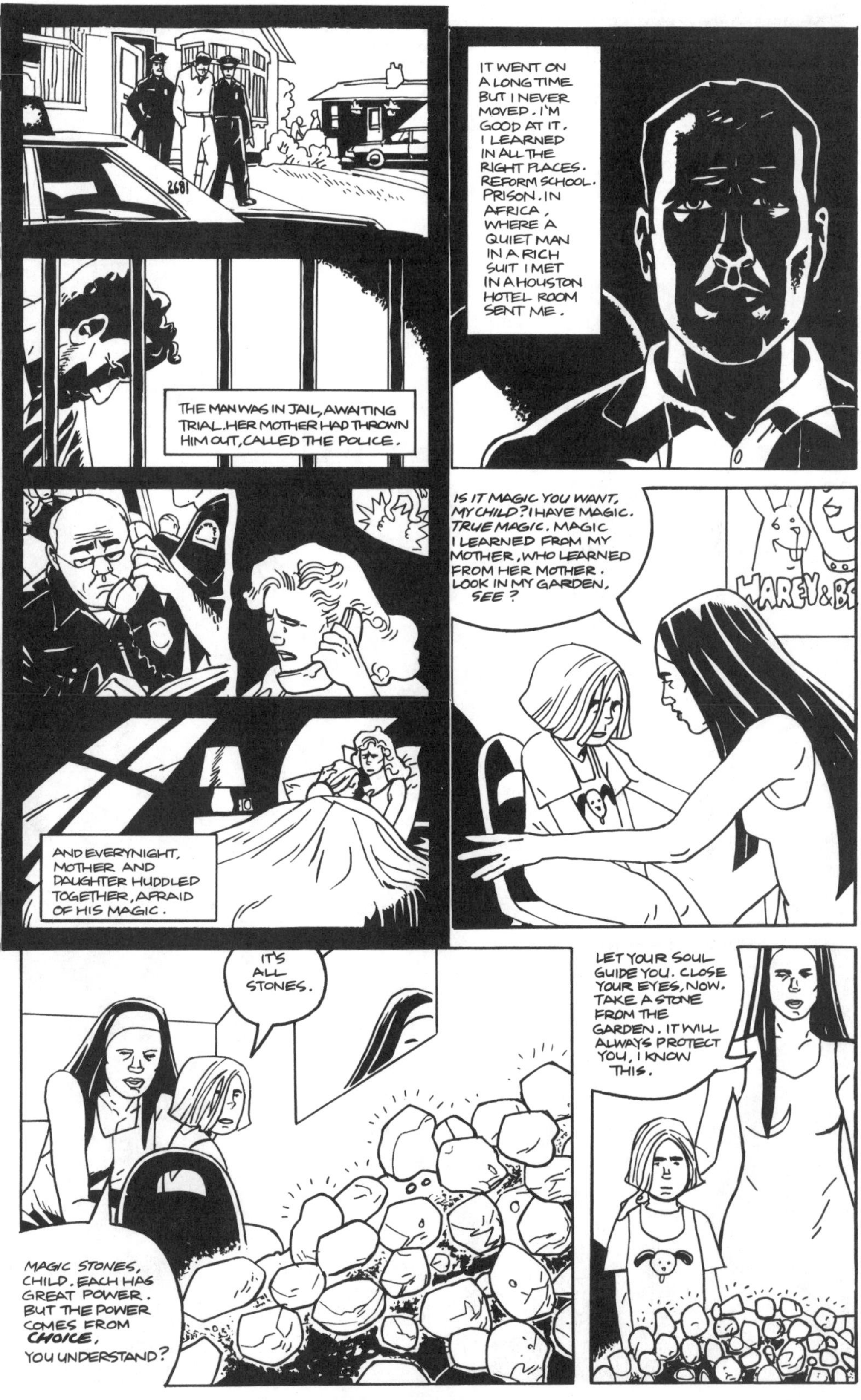
2681
THE MAN WAS IN JAIL, AWAITING TRIAL. HER MOTHER HAD THROWN HIM OUT, CALLED THE POLICE.
AND EVERYNIGHT, MOTHER AND DAUGHTER HUDDLED TOGETHER, AFRAID OF HIS MAGIC.
IT WENT ON A LONG TIME BUT I NEVER MOVED. I'M GOOD AT IT. I LEARNED IN ALL THE RIGHT PLACES. REFORM SCHOOL. PRISON. IN AFRICA, WHERE A QUIET MAN IN A RICH SUIT I MET IN A HOUSTON HOTEL ROOM SENT ME.
IS IT MAGIC YOU WANT, MY CHILD? I HAVE MAGIC. *TRUE MAGIC*. MAGIC I LEARNED FROM MY MOTHER, WHO LEARNED FROM HER MOTHER. LOOK IN MY GARDEN, SEE?
HAREY & B
IT'S ALL STONES.
MAGIC STONES, CHILD. EACH HAS GREAT POWER. BUT THE POWER COMES FROM ***CHOICE***, YOU UNDERSTAND?
LET YOUR SOUL GUIDE YOU. CLOSE YOUR EYES, NOW. TAKE A STONE FROM THE GARDEN. IT WILL ALWAYS PROTECT YOU, I KNOW THIS.

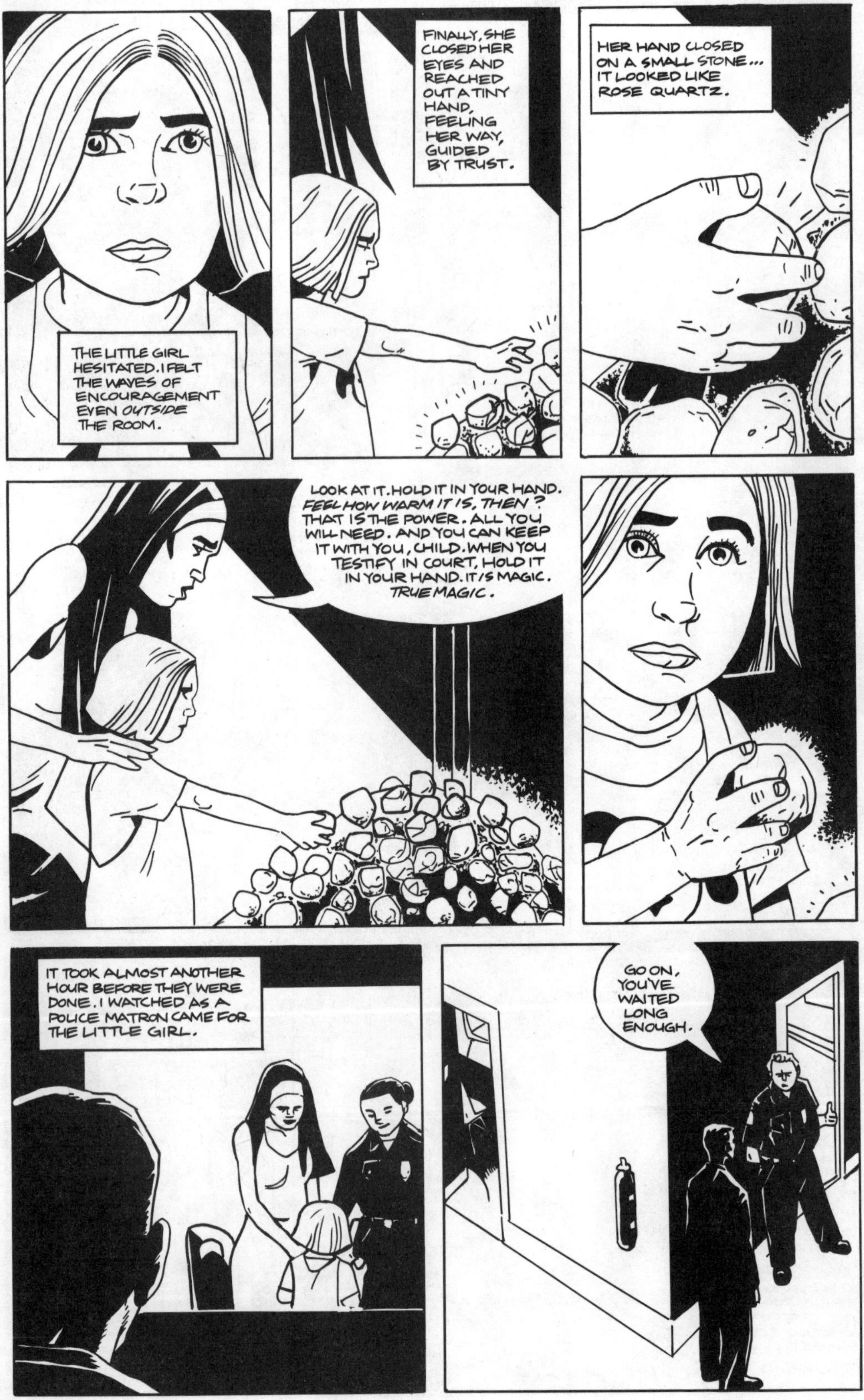
THE LITTLE GIRL HESITATED. I FELT THE WAVES OF ENCOURAGEMENT EVEN *OUTSIDE* THE ROOM.
FINALLY, SHE CLOSED HER EYES AND REACHED OUT A TINY HAND, FEELING HER WAY, GUIDED BY TRUST.
HER HAND CLOSED ON A SMALL STONE... IT LOOKED LIKE ROSE QUARTZ.
LOOK AT IT. HOLD IT IN YOUR HAND. *FEEL HOW WARM IT IS, THEN?* THAT IS THE POWER. ALL YOU WILL NEED. AND YOU CAN KEEP IT WITH YOU, CHILD. WHEN YOU TESTIFY IN COURT, HOLD IT IN YOUR HAND. IT'S MAGIC. *TRUE MAGIC*.
IT TOOK ALMOST ANOTHER HOUR BEFORE THEY WERE DONE. I WATCHED AS A POLICE MATRON CAME FOR THE LITTLE GIRL.
GO ON, YOU'VE WAITED LONG ENOUGH.

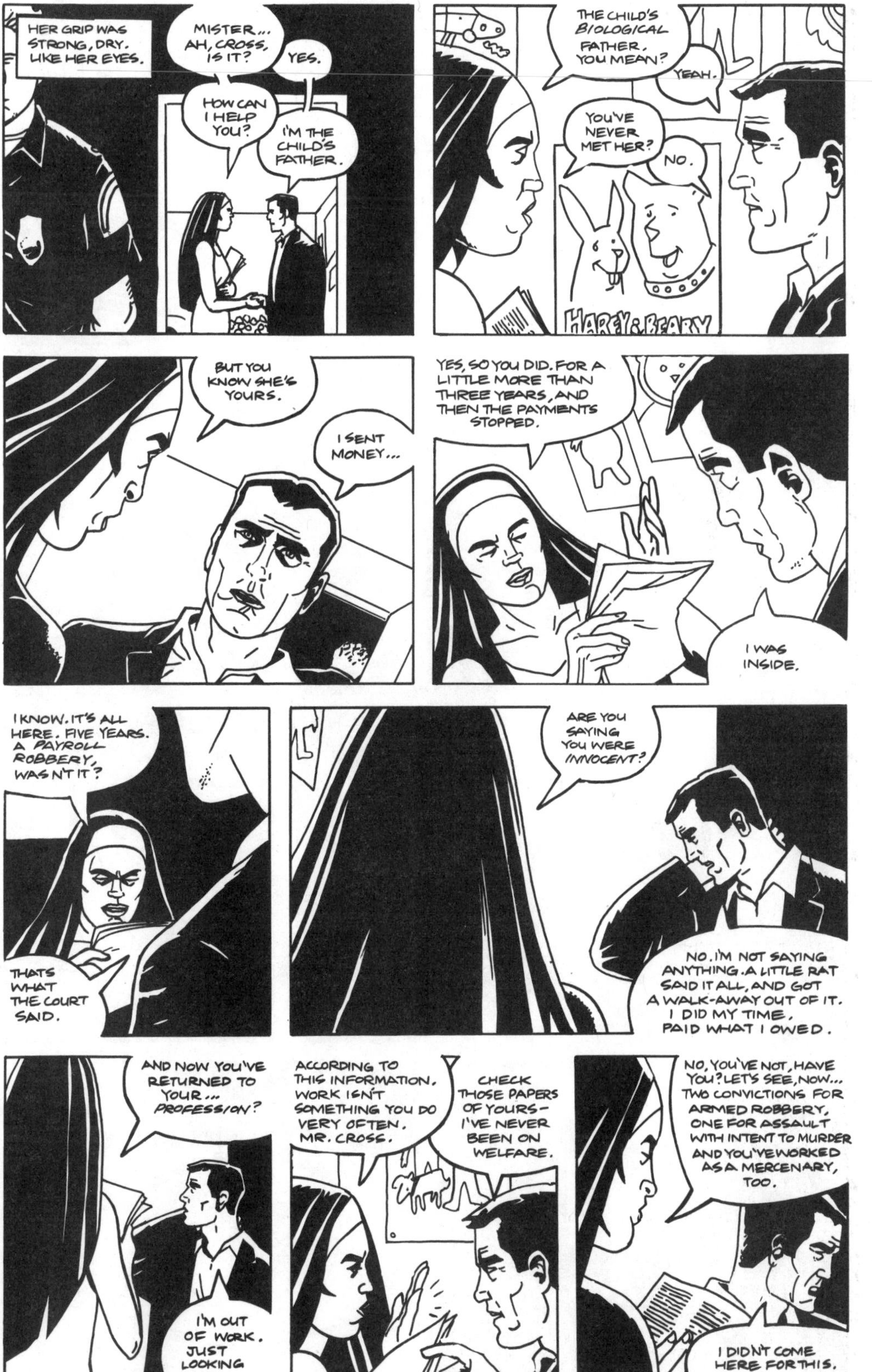
HER GRIP WAS STRONG, DRY. LIKE HER EYES.
MISTER... AH, CROSS, IS IT?
YES.
HOW CAN I HELP YOU?
I'M THE CHILD'S FATHER.
THE CHILD'S BIOLOGICAL FATHER, YOU MEAN?
YEAH.
YOU'VE NEVER MET HER?
NO.
HAREY & BEARY
BUT YOU KNOW SHE'S YOURS.
I SENT MONEY...
YES, SO YOU DID. FOR A LITTLE MORE THAN THREE YEARS, AND THEN THE PAYMENTS STOPPED.
I WAS INSIDE.
I KNOW. IT'S ALL HERE. FIVE YEARS. A PAYROLL ROBBERY, WASN'T IT?
THATS WHAT THE COURT SAID.
ARE YOU SAYING YOU WERE INNOCENT?
NO. I'M NOT SAYING ANYTHING. A LITTLE RAT SAID IT ALL, AND GOT A WALK-AWAY OUT OF IT. I DID MY TIME, PAID WHAT I OWED.
AND NOW YOU'VE RETURNED TO YOUR... PROFESSION?
I'M OUT OF WORK. JUST LOOKING AROUND.
ACCORDING TO THIS INFORMATION, WORK ISN'T SOMETHING YOU DO VERY OFTEN, MR. CROSS.
CHECK THOSE PAPERS OF YOURS– I'VE NEVER BEEN ON WELFARE.
NO, YOU'VE NOT, HAVE YOU? LET'S SEE, NOW... TWO CONVICTIONS FOR ARMED ROBBERY, ONE FOR ASSAULT WITH INTENT TO MURDER AND YOU'VE WORKED AS A MERCENARY, TOO.
I DIDN'T COME HERE FOR THIS.

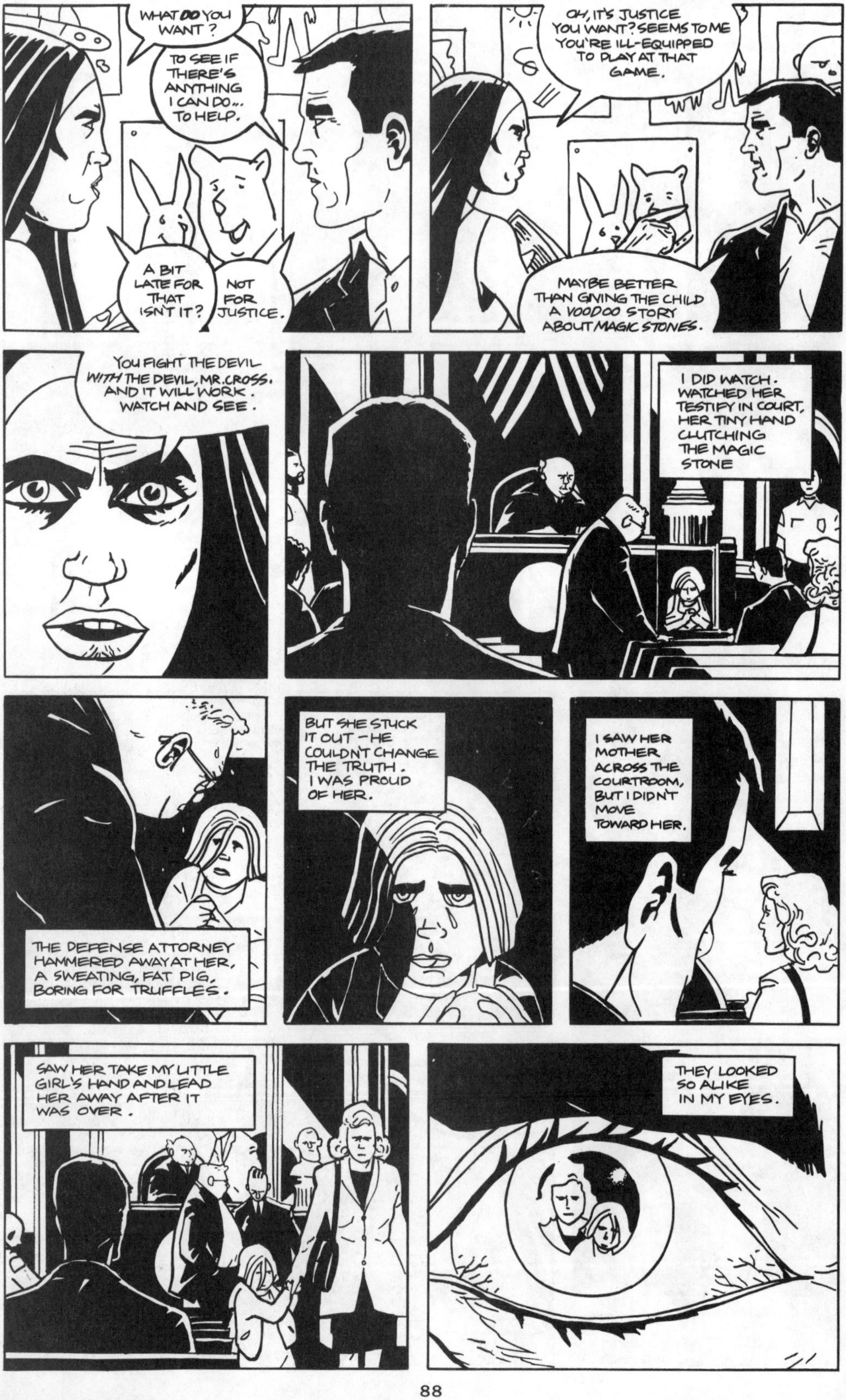
WHAT DO YOU WANT?
TO SEE IF THERE'S ANYTHING I CAN DO... TO HELP.
A BIT LATE FOR THAT ISN'T IT?
NOT FOR JUSTICE.
OH, IT'S JUSTICE YOU WANT? SEEMS TO ME YOU'RE ILL-EQUIPPED TO PLAY AT THAT GAME.
MAYBE BETTER THAN GIVING THE CHILD A VOODOO STORY ABOUT MAGIC STONES.
YOU FIGHT THE DEVIL WITH THE DEVIL, MR. CROSS. AND IT WILL WORK. WATCH AND SEE.
I DID WATCH. WATCHED HER TESTIFY IN COURT, HER TINY HAND CLUTCHING THE MAGIC STONE
THE DEFENSE ATTORNEY HAMMERED AWAY AT HER, A SWEATING, FAT PIG, BORING FOR TRUFFLES.
BUT SHE STUCK IT OUT - HE COULDN'T CHANGE THE TRUTH. I WAS PROUD OF HER.
I SAW HER MOTHER ACROSS THE COURTROOM, BUT I DIDN'T MOVE TOWARD HER.
SAW HER TAKE MY LITTLE GIRL'S HAND AND LEAD HER AWAY AFTER IT WAS OVER.
THEY LOOKED SO ALIKE IN MY EYES.

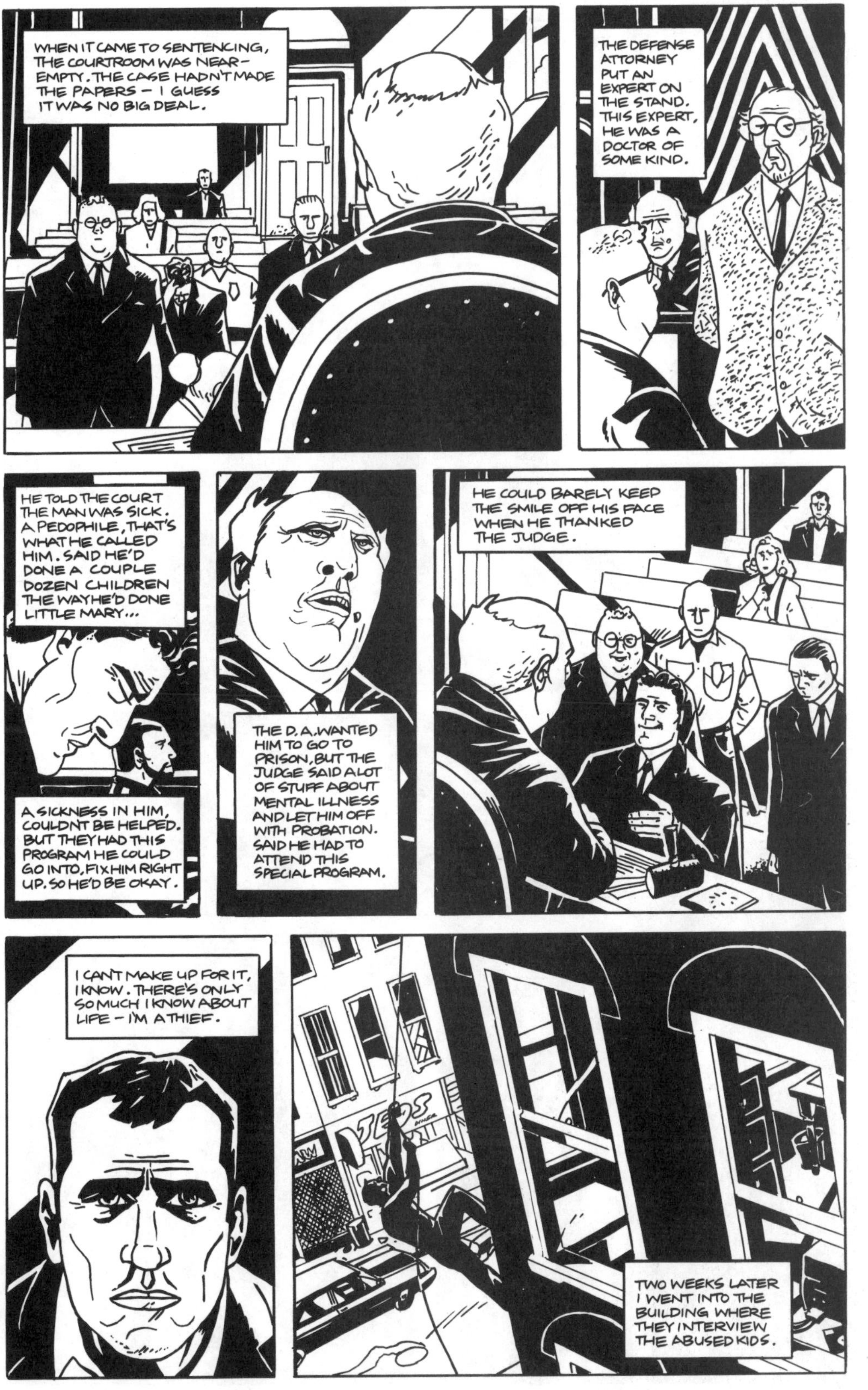
WHEN IT CAME TO SENTENCING, THE COURTROOM WAS NEAR-EMPTY. THE CASE HADN'T MADE THE PAPERS — I GUESS IT WAS NO BIG DEAL.
THE DEFENSE ATTORNEY PUT AN EXPERT ON THE STAND. THIS EXPERT, HE WAS A DOCTOR OF SOME KIND.
HE TOLD THE COURT THE MAN WAS SICK. A PEDOPHILE, THAT'S WHAT HE CALLED HIM. SAID HE'D DONE A COUPLE DOZEN CHILDREN THE WAY HE'D DONE LITTLE MARY...
A SICKNESS IN HIM, COULDN'T BE HELPED. BUT THEY HAD THIS PROGRAM HE COULD GO INTO, FIX HIM RIGHT UP. SO HE'D BE OKAY.
THE D.A. WANTED HIM TO GO TO PRISON, BUT THE JUDGE SAID ALOT OF STUFF ABOUT MENTAL ILLNESS AND LET HIM OFF WITH PROBATION. SAID HE HAD TO ATTEND THIS SPECIAL PROGRAM.
HE COULD BARELY KEEP THE SMILE OFF HIS FACE WHEN HE THANKED THE JUDGE.
I CAN'T MAKE UP FOR IT, I KNOW. THERE'S ONLY SO MUCH I KNOW ABOUT LIFE — I'M A THIEF.
TED'S DINER
TWO WEEKS LATER I WENT INTO THE BUILDING WHERE THEY INTERVIEW THE ABUSED KIDS.

I FOUND THE JAMAICAN WOMAN'S PLAYROOM WITH MY PENCIL FLASH. THE LOCK YIELDED IN AN EYE-BLINK.

I FILLED MY POCKET WITH MAGIC STONES FROM HER GARDEN.

IT TOOK ME ANOTHER FEW DAYS TO FIND THE MAN'S ADDRESS, WATCH HIS MOVEMENTS, GET THE TIMING RIGHT.

IT'S ALMOST MIDNIGHT NOW. DARK INSIDE HIS APARTMENT BUILDING TOO— I UNSCREWED THE LIGHT BULBS IN THE HALLWAY.

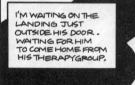

I'M WAITING ON THE LANDING JUST OUTSIDE HIS DOOR. WAITING FOR HIM TO COME HOME FROM HIS THERAPY GROUP.

WAITING WITH A SOCK FULL OF MAGIC STONES.

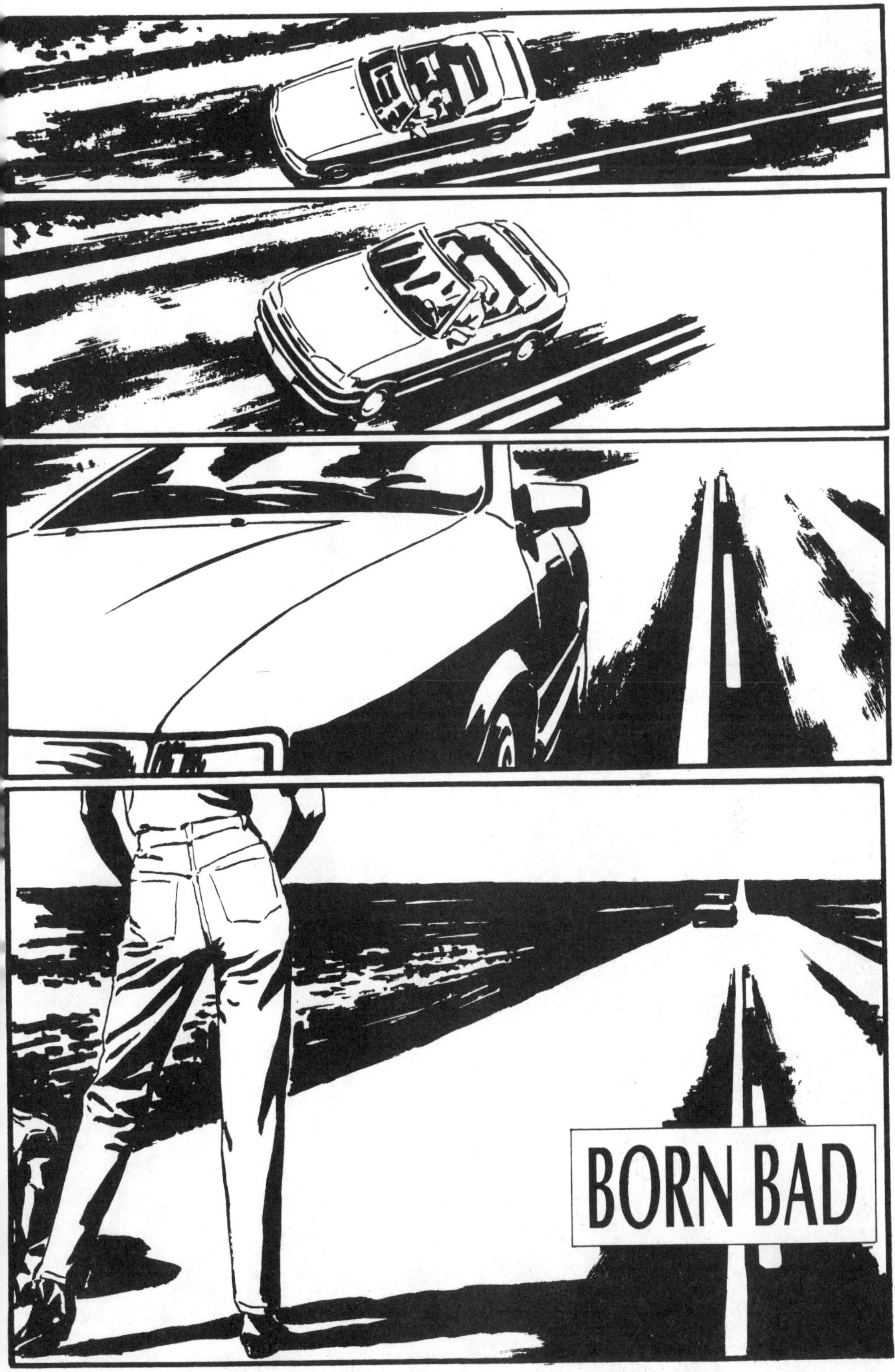
BORN BAD

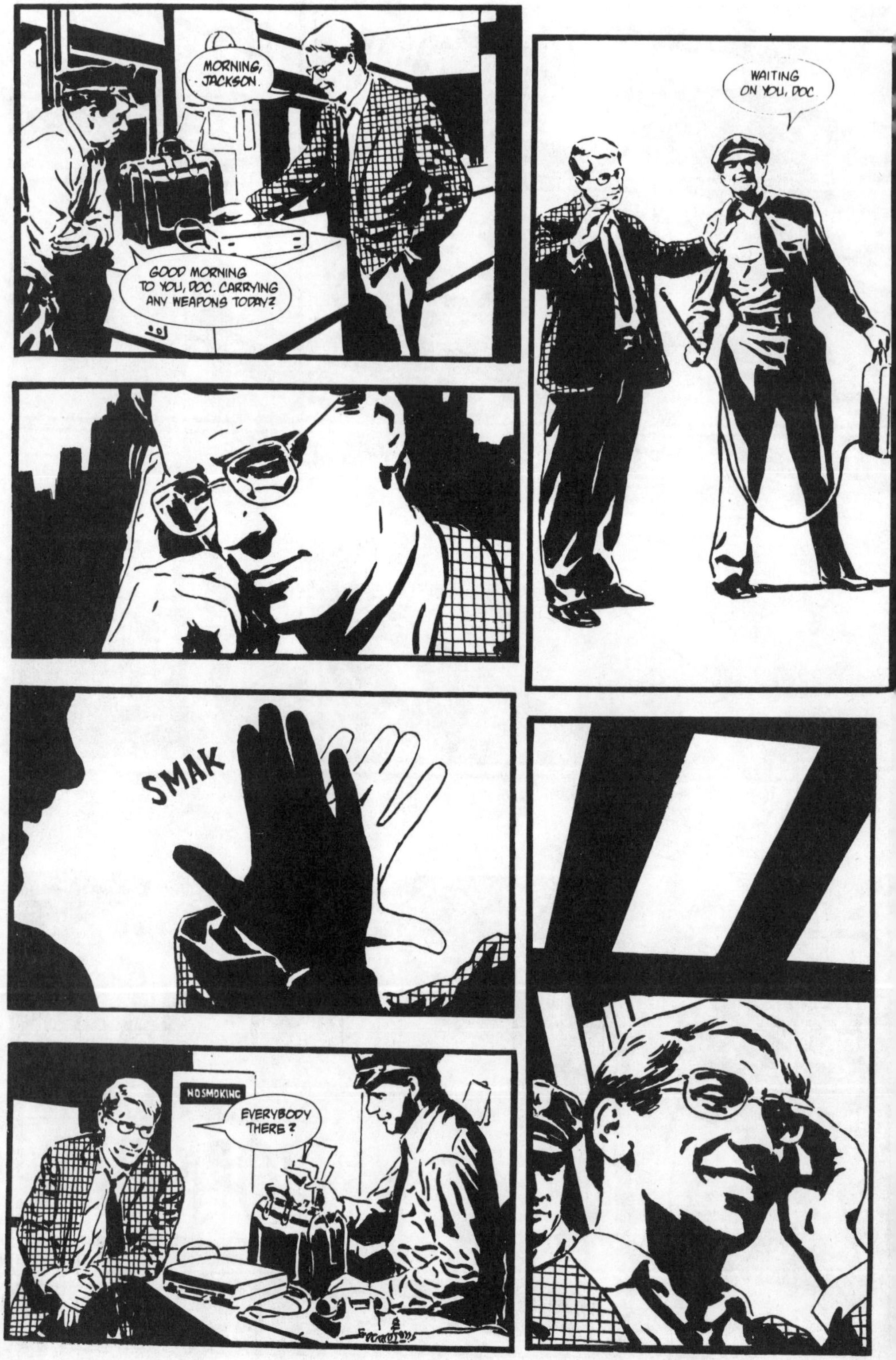
MORNING, JACKSON.
GOOD MORNING TO YOU, DOC. CARRYING ANY WEAPONS TODAY?
WAITING ON YOU, DOC.
SMAK
NO SMOKING
EVERYBODY THERE?

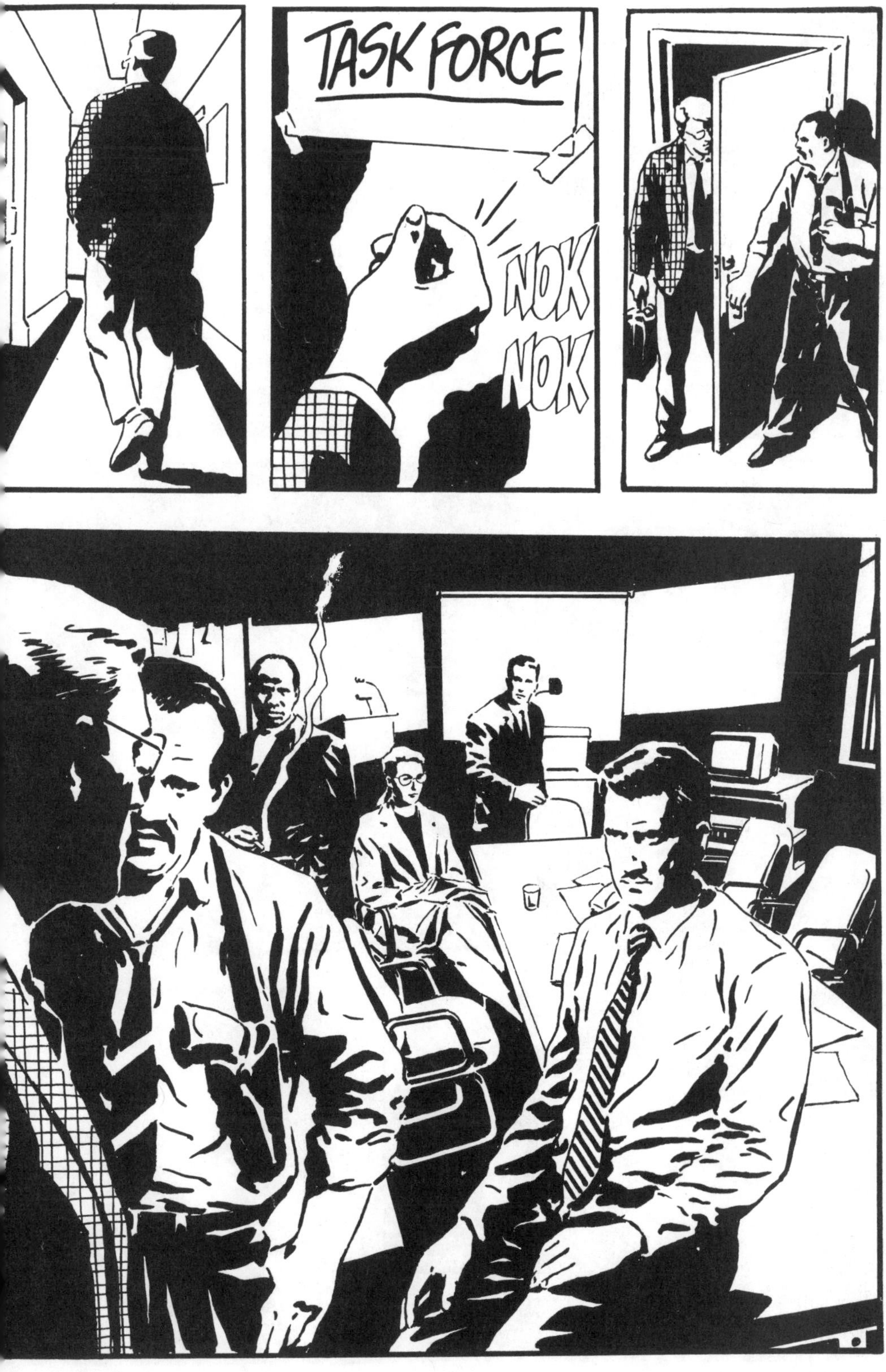
TASK FORCE
NOK
NOK

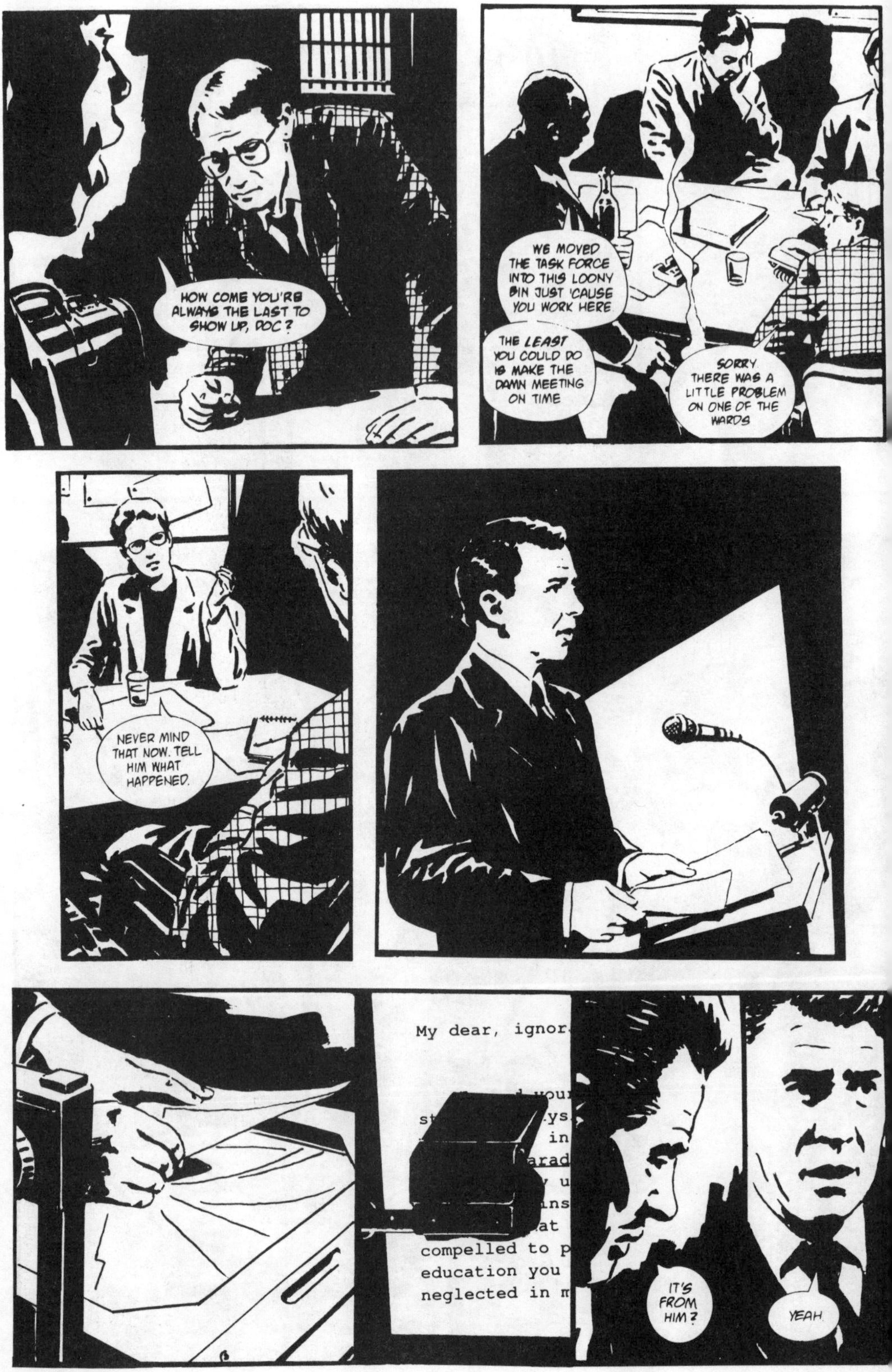
HOW COME YOU'RE ALWAYS THE LAST TO SHOW UP, DOC?
WE MOVED THE TASK FORCE INTO THIS LOONY BIN JUST 'CAUSE YOU WORK HERE.
THE LEAST YOU COULD DO IS MAKE THE DAMN MEETING ON TIME
SORRY. THERE WAS A LITTLE PROBLEM ON ONE OF THE WARDS.
NEVER MIND THAT NOW. TELL HIM WHAT HAPPENED.
My dear, ignor
compelled to p
education you
neglected in m
IT'S FROM HIM?
YEAH.

WE XEROXED THE WHOLE THING. SEVEN PAGES. THE LAB BOYS WENT OVER IT WITH AN ELECTRON MICROSCOPE.

My dear, ignorant Dr. Ru$

I read your fascinati
stupid "analysis" of my
motivations in the June

"TYPED ON A COMPUTER, PROBABLY THAT LAPTOP HE CARRIES AROUND. IT WAS PRINTED OUT ON A LASER PRINTER."

rade. It was

"GENERIC PAPER, STANDARD #10 BUSINESS ENVELOPE UNTRACEABLE."

insight, so

of logic that I felt

BUT WE KNOW IT'S HIM--HE LEFT US A PERFECT THUMBPRINT BELOW THE SIGNATURE.

DAMN!

POSTMARK?

TUCSON, ARIZONA. FOUR DAYS AGO.

CENTRAL POST OFFICE. HE WON'T BE THERE NOW.

HE'S ALWAYS SO NEAT, SO PRECISE.

YEAH.

LOOKS LIKE YOUR IDEA WORKED, DOC.

WHEN YOU WROTE THAT ARTICLE ABOUT THE SURGEON ...THE ONE WHERE YOU SAID HE HAD TO HAVE BEEN AN ABUSED CHILD...IT MADE HIM MAD. SMOKED HIM OUT.

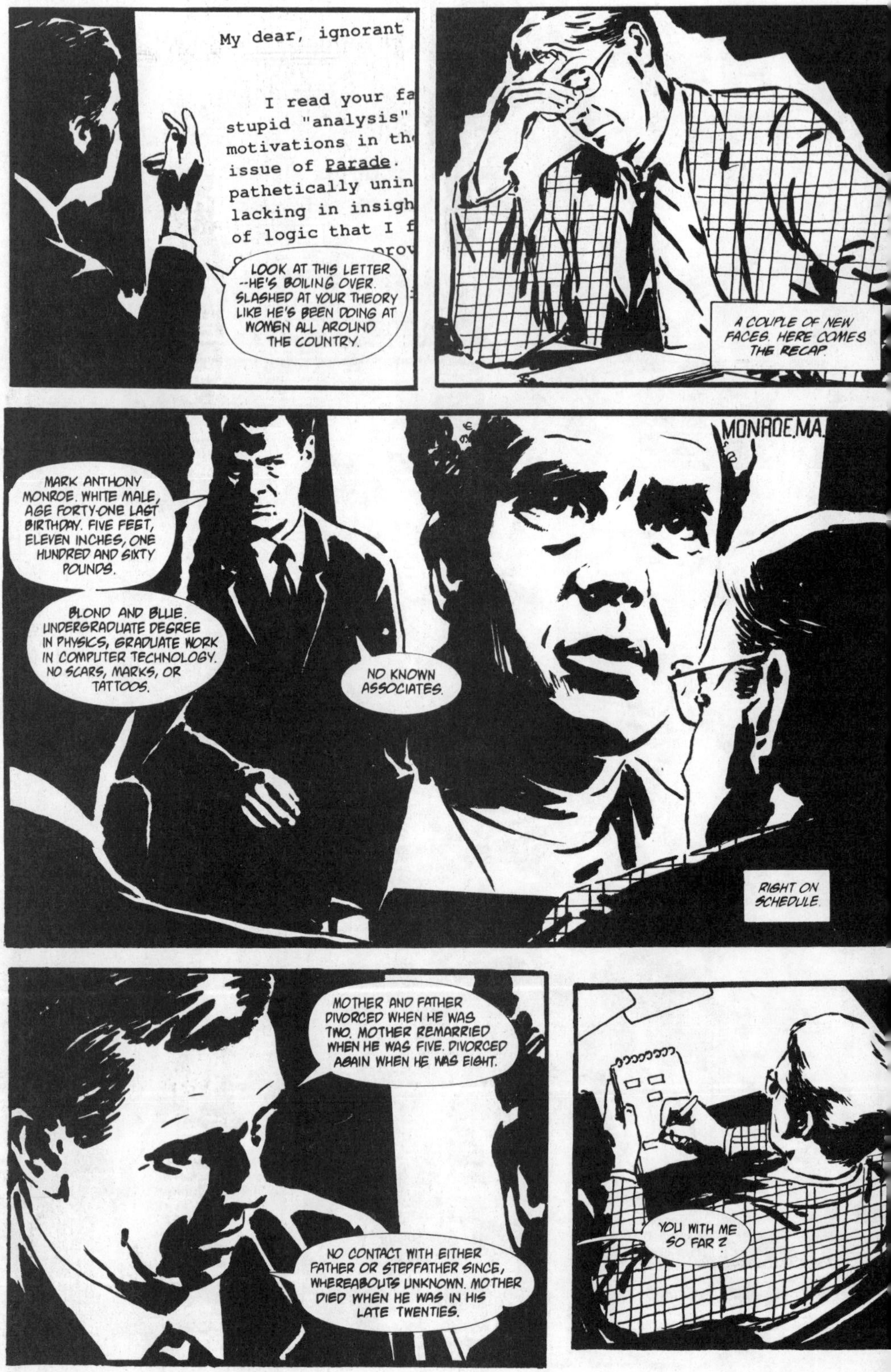
My dear, ignorant
I read your fa
stupid "analysis"
motivations in th
issue of Parade.
pathetically unin
lacking in insigh
of logic that I f
LOOK AT THIS LETTER --HE'S BOILING OVER. SLASHED AT YOUR THEORY LIKE HE'S BEEN DOING AT WOMEN ALL AROUND THE COUNTRY.
A COUPLE OF NEW FACES. HERE COMES THE RECAP.
MONROE, MA.
MARK ANTHONY MONROE. WHITE MALE, AGE FORTY-ONE LAST BIRTHDAY. FIVE FEET, ELEVEN INCHES, ONE HUNDRED AND SIXTY POUNDS.
BLOND AND BLUE. UNDERGRADUATE DEGREE IN PHYSICS, GRADUATE WORK IN COMPUTER TECHNOLOGY. NO SCARS, MARKS, OR TATTOOS.
NO KNOWN ASSOCIATES.
RIGHT ON SCHEDULE.
MOTHER AND FATHER DIVORCED WHEN HE WAS TWO. MOTHER REMARRIED WHEN HE WAS FIVE. DIVORCED AGAIN WHEN HE WAS EIGHT.
NO CONTACT WITH EITHER FATHER OR STEPFATHER SINCE, WHEREABOUTS UNKNOWN. MOTHER DIED WHEN HE WAS IN HIS LATE TWENTIES.
YOU WITH ME SO FAR ?

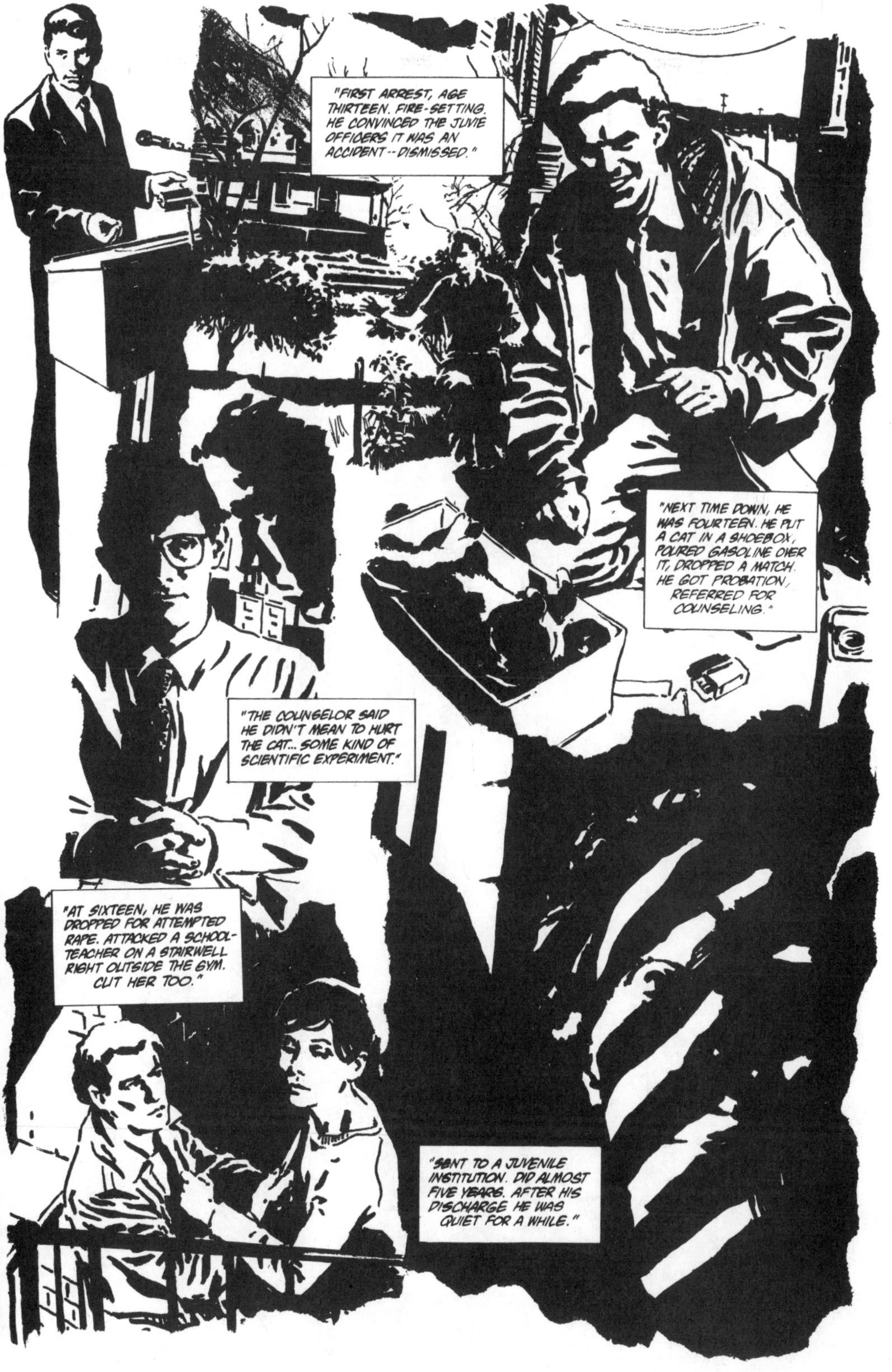
"FIRST ARREST, AGE THIRTEEN. FIRE-SETTING. HE CONVINCED THE JUVIE OFFICERS IT WAS AN ACCIDENT--DISMISSED."
"NEXT TIME DOWN, HE WAS FOURTEEN. HE PUT A CAT IN A SHOEBOX, POURED GASOLINE OVER IT, DROPPED A MATCH. HE GOT PROBATION, REFERRED FOR COUNSELING."
"THE COUNSELOR SAID HE DIDN'T MEAN TO HURT THE CAT... SOME KIND OF SCIENTIFIC EXPERIMENT."
"AT SIXTEEN, HE WAS DROPPED FOR ATTEMPTED RAPE. ATTACKED A SCHOOL-TEACHER ON A STAIRWELL RIGHT OUTSIDE THE GYM. CUT HER TOO."
"SENT TO A JUVENILE INSTITUTION. DID ALMOST FIVE YEARS. AFTER HIS DISCHARGE HE WAS QUIET FOR A WHILE."

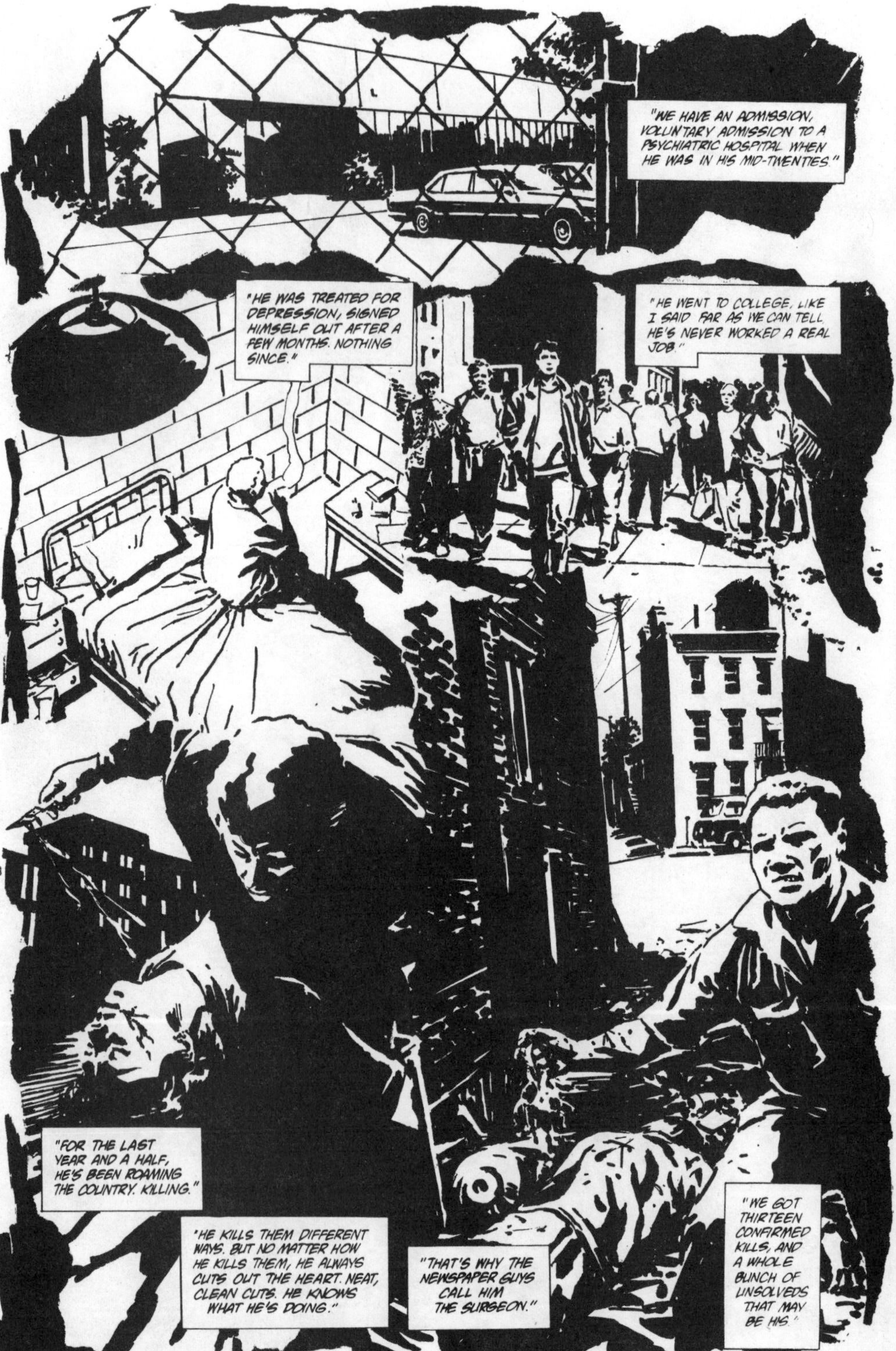
"WE HAVE AN ADMISSION, VOLUNTARY ADMISSION TO A PSYCHIATRIC HOSPITAL WHEN HE WAS IN HIS MID-TWENTIES."
"HE WAS TREATED FOR DEPRESSION, SIGNED HIMSELF OUT AFTER A FEW MONTHS. NOTHING SINCE."
"HE WENT TO COLLEGE, LIKE I SAID. FAR AS WE CAN TELL, HE'S NEVER WORKED A REAL JOB."
"FOR THE LAST YEAR AND A HALF, HE'S BEEN ROAMING THE COUNTRY. KILLING."
"HE KILLS THEM DIFFERENT WAYS. BUT NO MATTER HOW HE KILLS THEM, HE ALWAYS CUTS OUT THE HEART. NEAT, CLEAN CUTS. HE KNOWS WHAT HE'S DOING."
"THAT'S WHY THE NEWSPAPER GUYS CALL HIM THE SURGEON."
"WE GOT THIRTEEN CONFIRMED KILLS, AND A WHOLE BUNCH OF UNSOLVEDS THAT MAY BE HIS."

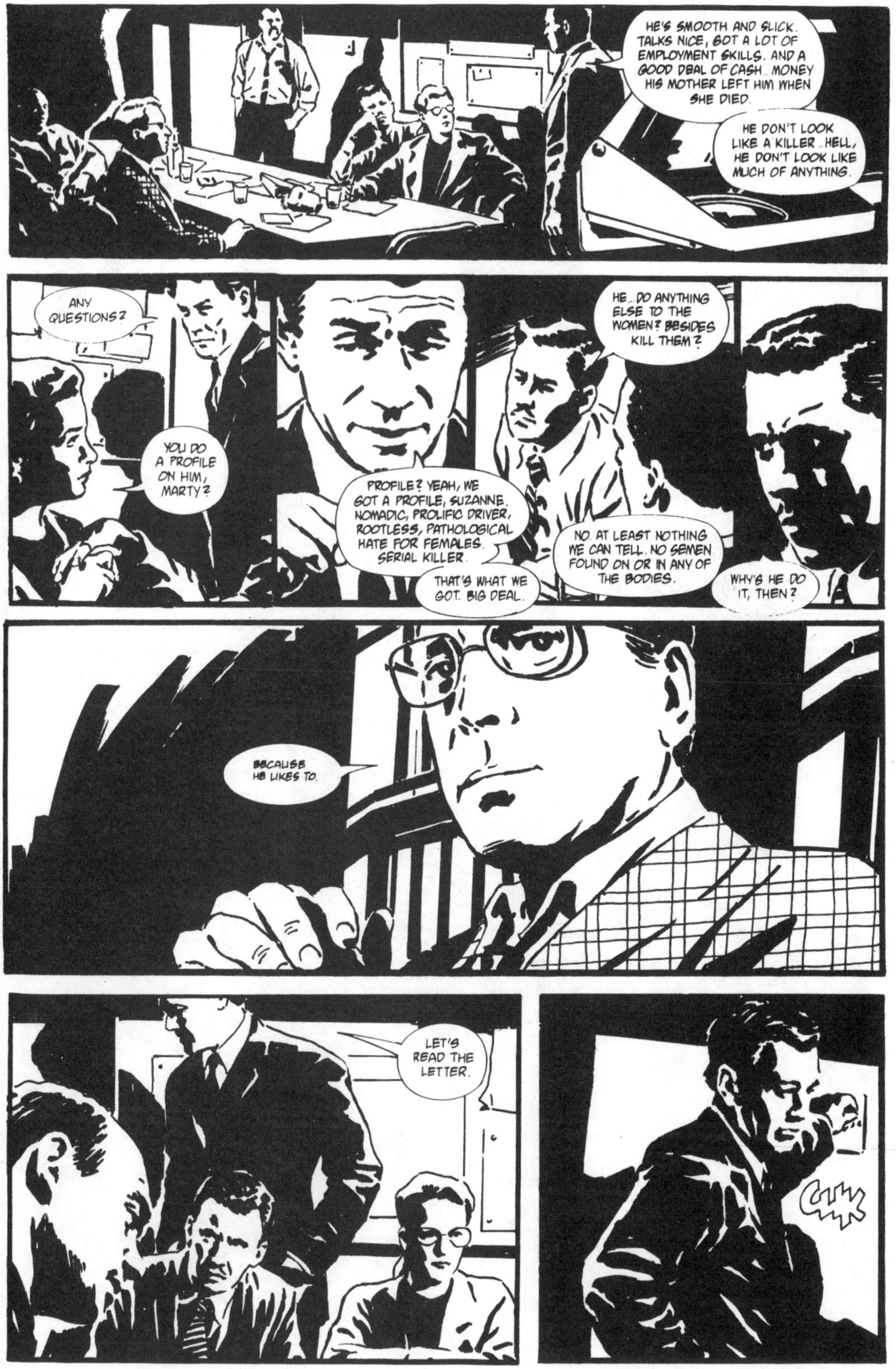
HE'S SMOOTH AND SLICK. TALKS NICE, GOT A LOT OF EMPLOYMENT SKILLS. AND A GOOD DEAL OF CASH.. MONEY HIS MOTHER LEFT HIM WHEN SHE DIED.
HE DON'T LOOK LIKE A KILLER..HELL, HE DON'T LOOK LIKE MUCH OF ANYTHING.
ANY QUESTIONS?
YOU DO A PROFILE ON HIM, MARTY?
PROFILE? YEAH, WE GOT A PROFILE, SUZANNE. NOMADIC, PROLIFIC DRIVER, ROOTLESS, PATHOLOGICAL HATE FOR FEMALES. SERIAL KILLER.
THAT'S WHAT WE GOT. BIG DEAL.
HE...DO ANYTHING ELSE TO THE WOMEN? BESIDES KILL THEM?
NO. AT LEAST NOTHING WE CAN TELL. NO SEMEN FOUND ON OR IN ANY OF THE BODIES.
WHY'S HE DO IT, THEN?
BECAUSE HE LIKES TO.
LET'S READ THE LETTER.
CLIK

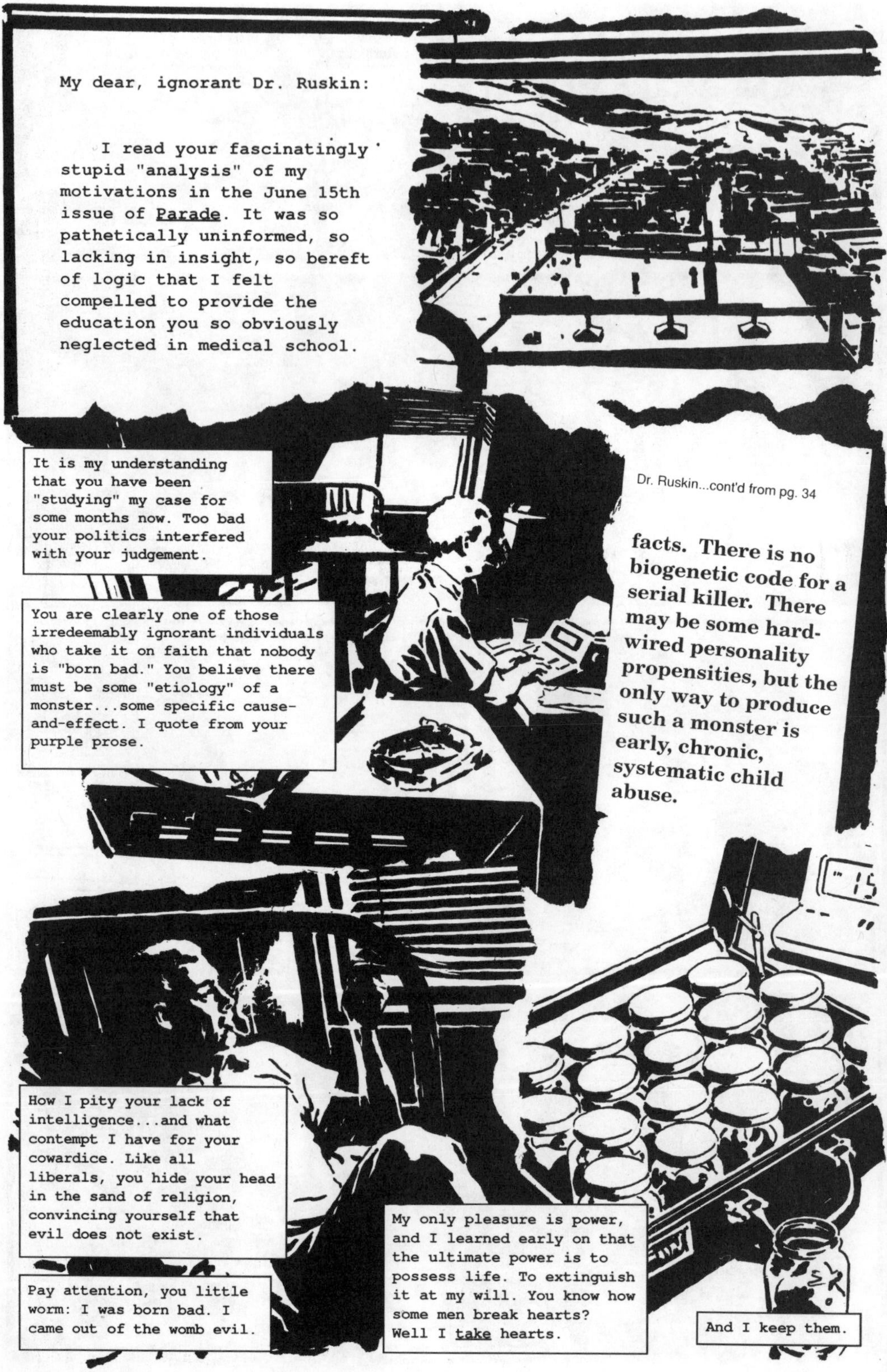
My dear, ignorant Dr. Ruskin:
I read your fascinatingly stupid "analysis" of my motivations in the June 15th issue of Parade. It was so pathetically uninformed, so lacking in insight, so bereft of logic that I felt compelled to provide the education you so obviously neglected in medical school.
It is my understanding that you have been "studying" my case for some months now. Too bad your politics interfered with your judgement.
You are clearly one of those irredeemably ignorant individuals who take it on faith that nobody is "born bad." You believe there must be some "etiology" of a monster...some specific cause-and-effect. I quote from your purple prose.
Dr. Ruskin...cont'd from pg. 34
facts. There is no biogenetic code for a serial killer. There may be some hard-wired personality propensities, but the only way to produce such a monster is early, chronic, systematic child abuse.
How I pity your lack of intelligence...and what contempt I have for your cowardice. Like all liberals, you hide your head in the sand of religion, convincing yourself that evil does not exist.
Pay attention, you little worm: I was born bad. I came out of the womb evil.
My only pleasure is power, and I learned early on that the ultimate power is to possess life. To extinguish it at my will. You know how some men break hearts? Well I take hearts.
And I keep them.

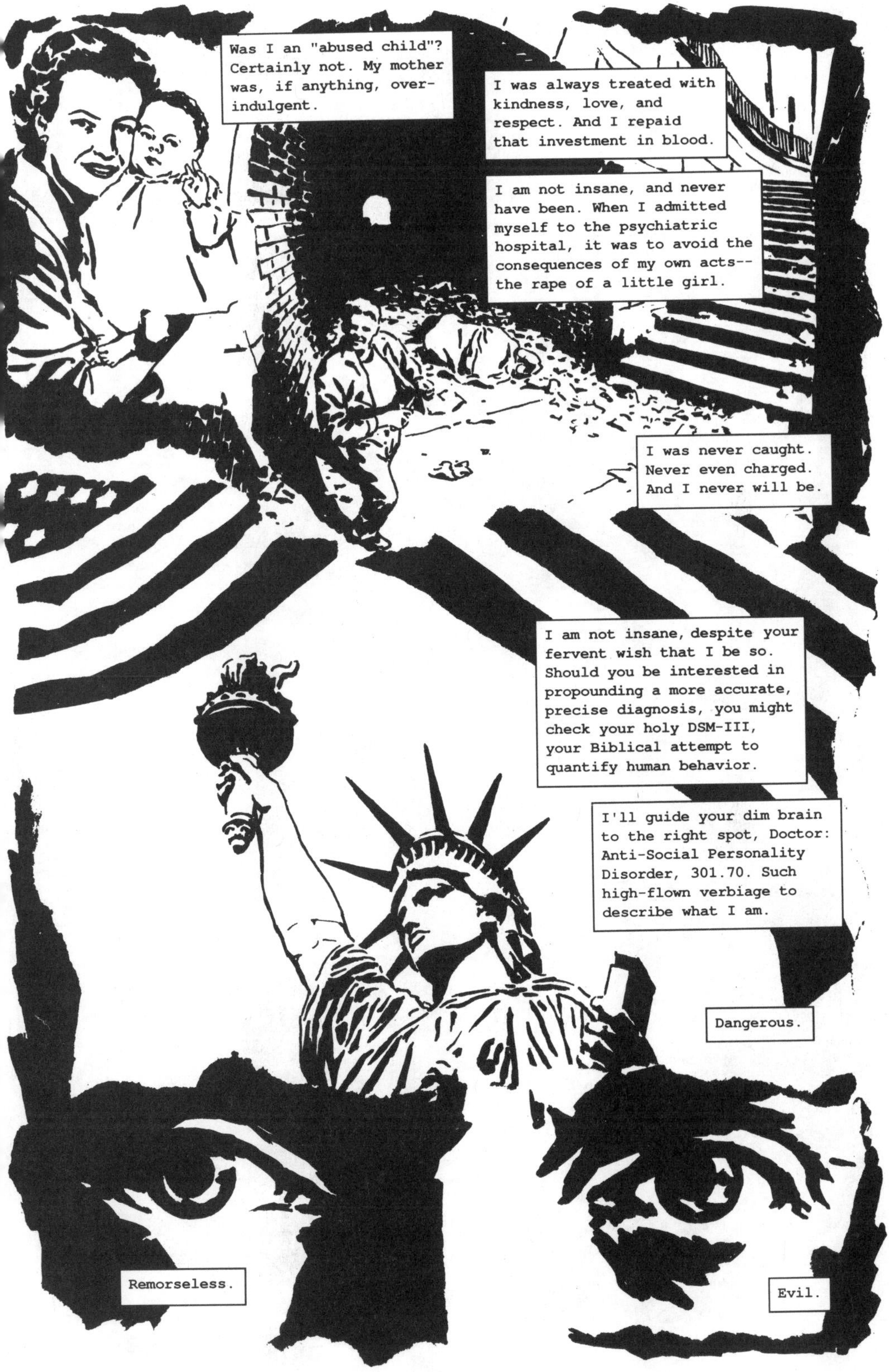

Was I an "abused child"? Certainly not. My mother was, if anything, over-indulgent.
I was always treated with kindness, love, and respect. And I repaid that investment in blood.
I am not insane, and never have been. When I admitted myself to the psychiatric hospital, it was to avoid the consequences of my own acts-- the rape of a little girl.
I was never caught. Never even charged. And I never will be.
I am not insane, despite your fervent wish that I be so. Should you be interested in propounding a more accurate, precise diagnosis, you might check your holy DSM-III, your Biblical attempt to quantify human behavior.
I'll guide your dim brain to the right spot, Doctor: Anti-Social Personality Disorder, 301.70. Such high-flown verbiage to describe what I am.
Dangerous.
Remorseless.
Evil.

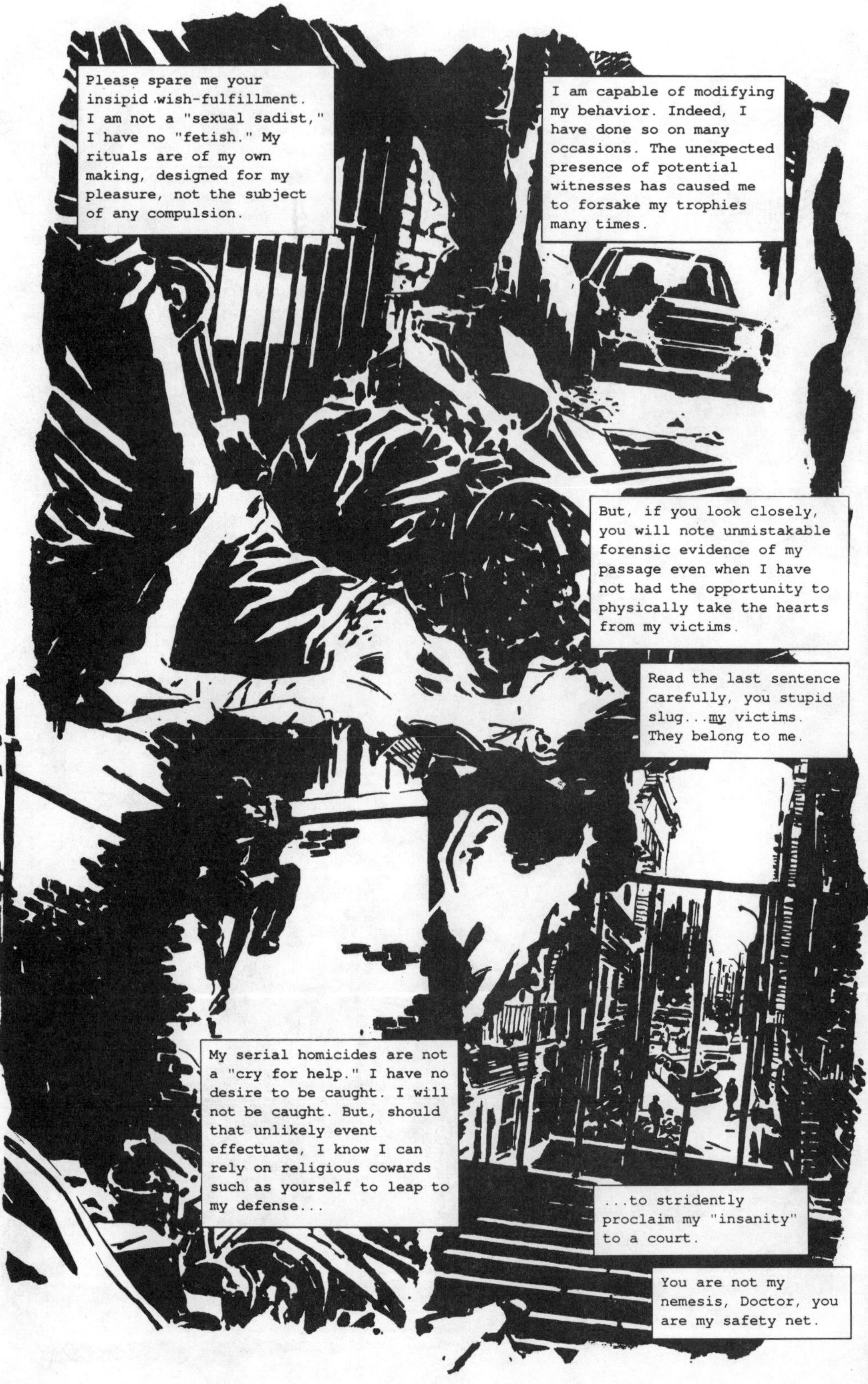
Please spare me your insipid wish-fulfillment. I am not a "sexual sadist," I have no "fetish." My rituals are of my own making, designed for my pleasure, not the subject of any compulsion.
I am capable of modifying my behavior. Indeed, I have done so on many occasions. The unexpected presence of potential witnesses has caused me to forsake my trophies many times.
But, if you look closely, you will note unmistakable forensic evidence of my passage even when I have not had the opportunity to physically take the hearts from my victims.
Read the last sentence carefully, you stupid slug...my victims. They belong to me.
My serial homicides are not a "cry for help." I have no desire to be caught. I will not be caught. But, should that unlikely event effectuate, I know I can rely on religious cowards such as yourself to leap to my defense...
...to stridently proclaim my "insanity" to a court.
You are not my nemesis, Doctor, you are my safety net.

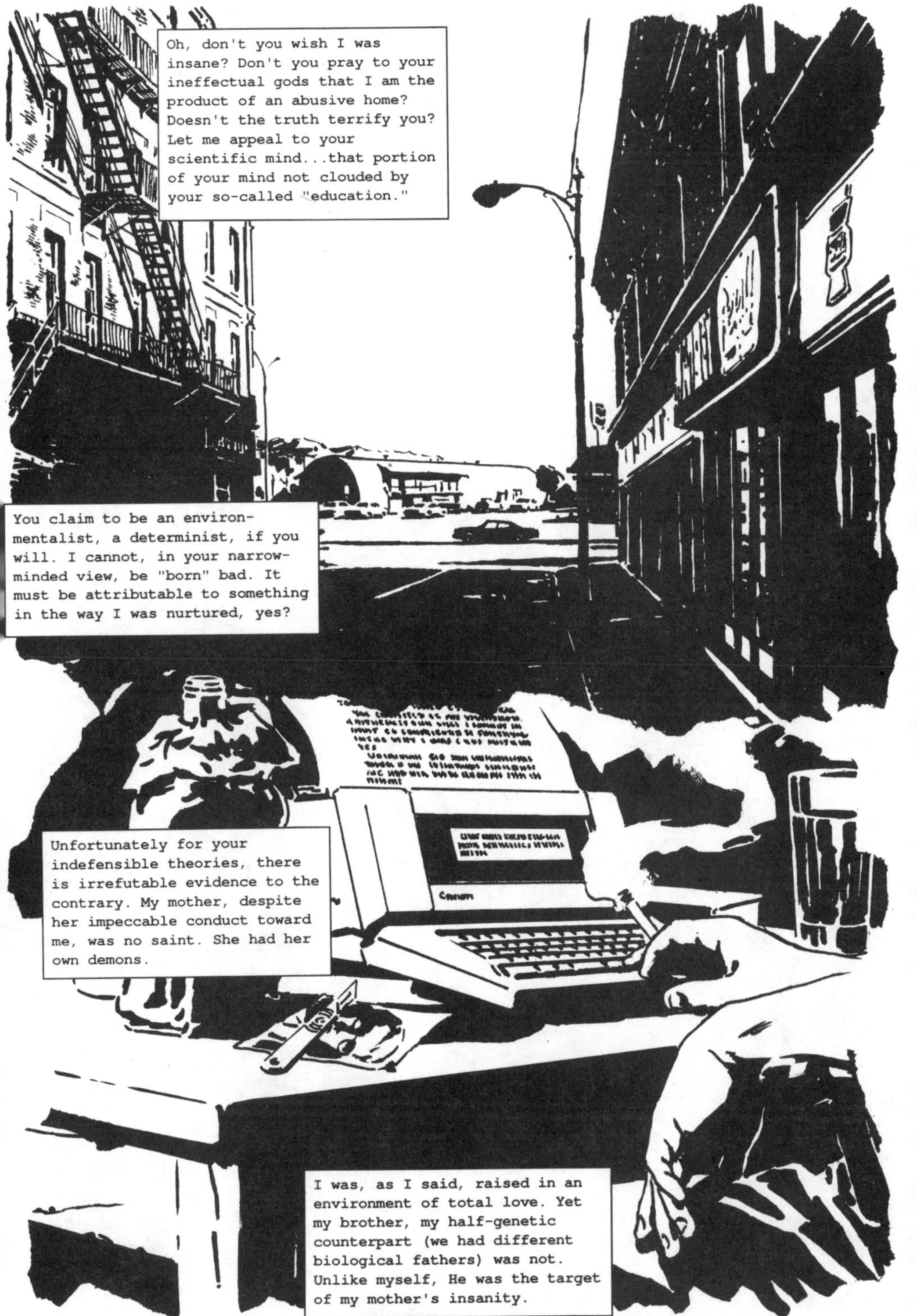
Oh, don't you wish I was insane? Don't you pray to your ineffectual gods that I am the product of an abusive home? Doesn't the truth terrify you? Let me appeal to your scientific mind...that portion of your mind not clouded by your so-called "education."
You claim to be an environmentalist, a determinist, if you will. I cannot, in your narrow-minded view, be "born" bad. It must be attributable to something in the way I was nurtured, yes?
Unfortunately for your indefensible theories, there is irrefutable evidence to the contrary. My mother, despite her impeccable conduct toward me, was no saint. She had her own demons.
I was, as I said, raised in an environment of total love. Yet my brother, my half-genetic counterpart (we had different biological fathers) was not. Unlike myself, He was the target of my mother's insanity.

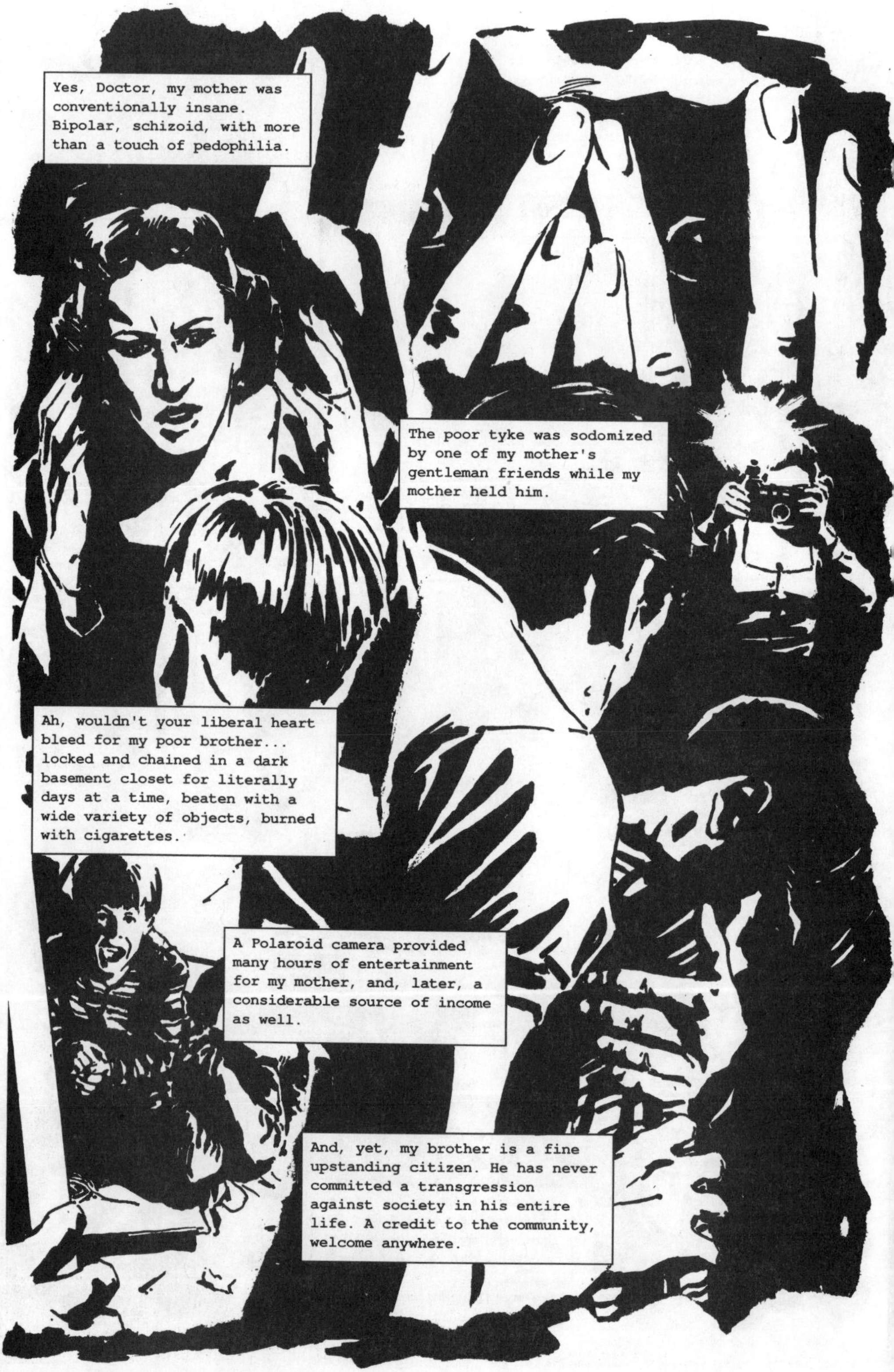
Yes, Doctor, my mother was conventionally insane. Bipolar, schizoid, with more than a touch of pedophilia.
The poor tyke was sodomized by one of my mother's gentleman friends while my mother held him.
Ah, wouldn't your liberal heart bleed for my poor brother... locked and chained in a dark basement closet for literally days at a time, beaten with a wide variety of objects, burned with cigarettes.
A Polaroid camera provided many hours of entertainment for my mother, and, later, a considerable source of income as well.
And, yet, my brother is a fine upstanding citizen. He has never committed a transgression against society in his entire life. A credit to the community, welcome anywhere.

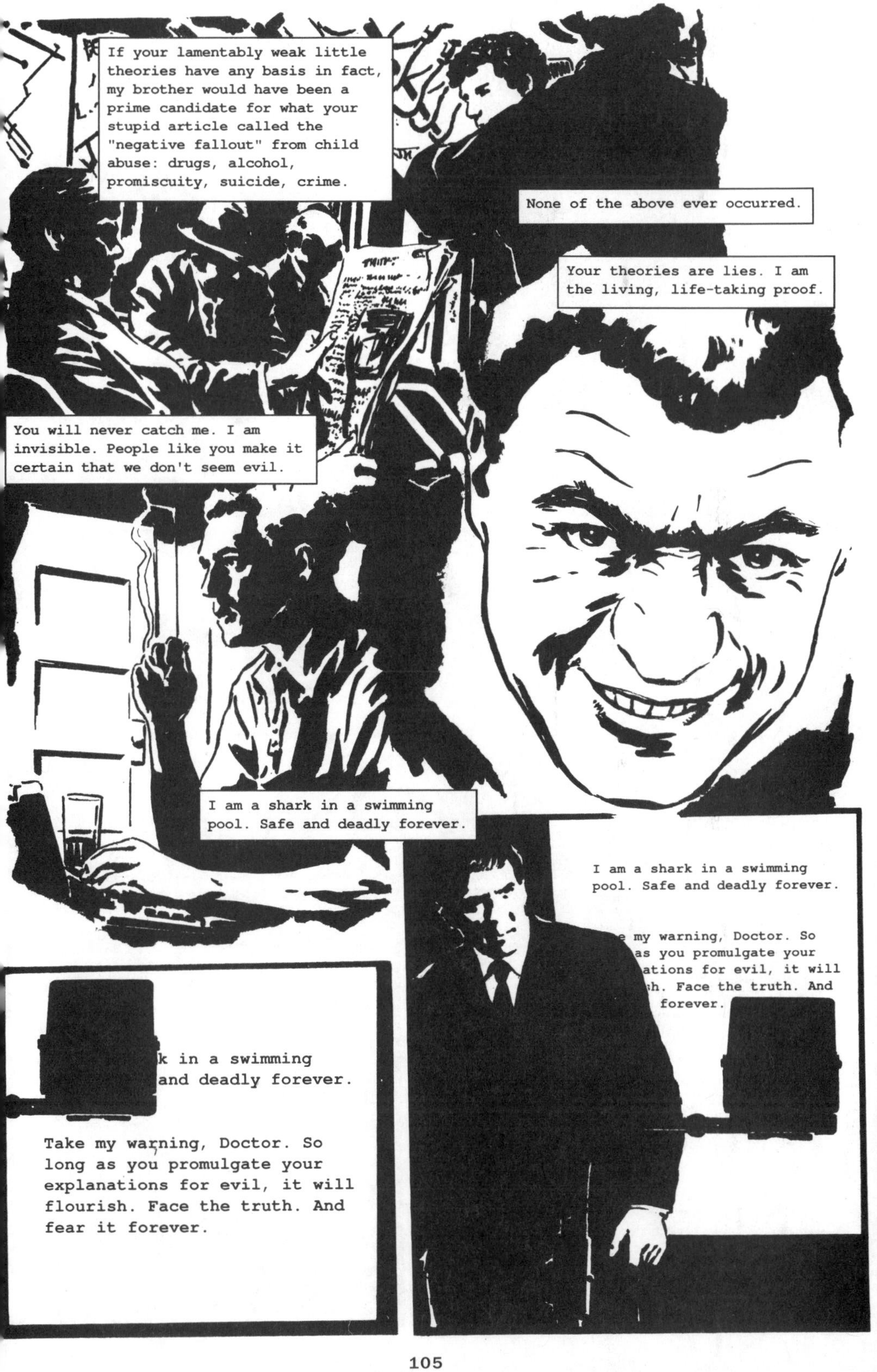
If your lamentably weak little theories have any basis in fact, my brother would have been a prime candidate for what your stupid article called the "negative fallout" from child abuse: drugs, alcohol, promiscuity, suicide, crime.
None of the above ever occurred.
Your theories are lies. I am the living, life-taking proof.
You will never catch me. I am invisible. People like you make it certain that we don't seem evil.
I am a shark in a swimming pool. Safe and deadly forever.
I am a shark in a swimming pool. Safe and deadly forever.
my warning, Doctor. So as you promulgate your ations for evil, it will h. Face the truth. And forever.
k in a swimming and deadly forever.
Take my warning, Doctor. So long as you promulgate your explanations for evil, it will flourish. Face the truth. And fear it forever.

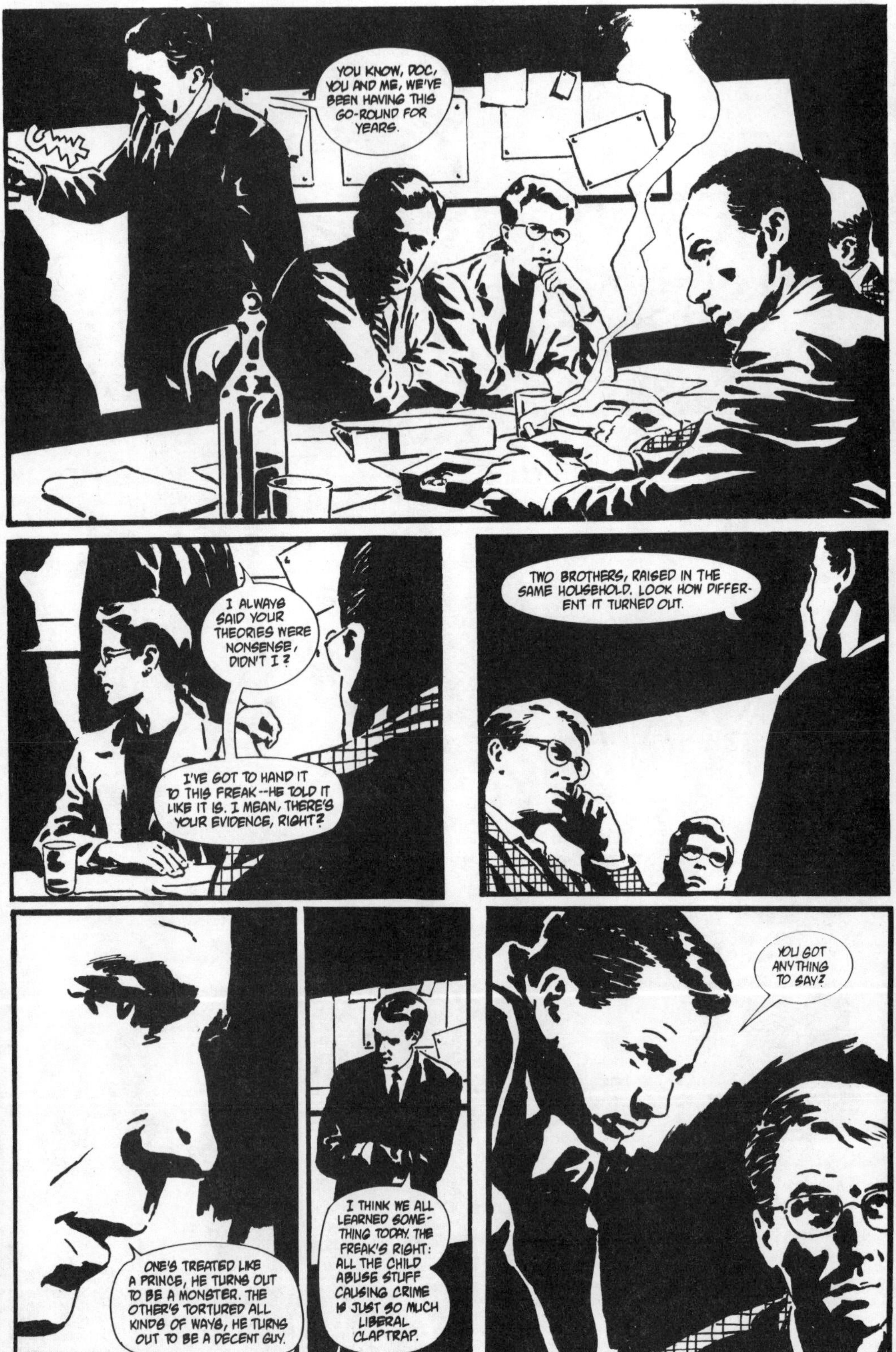
YOU KNOW, DOC, YOU AND ME, WE'VE BEEN HAVING THIS GO-ROUND FOR YEARS.
I ALWAYS SAID YOUR THEORIES WERE NONSENSE, DIDN'T I?
I'VE GOT TO HAND IT TO THIS FREAK--HE TOLD IT LIKE IT IS. I MEAN, THERE'S YOUR EVIDENCE, RIGHT?
TWO BROTHERS, RAISED IN THE SAME HOUSEHOLD. LOOK HOW DIFFERENT IT TURNED OUT.
ONE'S TREATED LIKE A PRINCE, HE TURNS OUT TO BE A MONSTER. THE OTHER'S TORTURED ALL KINDS OF WAYS, HE TURNS OUT TO BE A DECENT GUY.
I THINK WE ALL LEARNED SOMETHING TODAY. THE FREAK'S RIGHT: ALL THE CHILD ABUSE STUFF CAUSING CRIME IS JUST SO MUCH LIBERAL CLAPTRAP.
YOU GOT ANYTHING TO SAY?

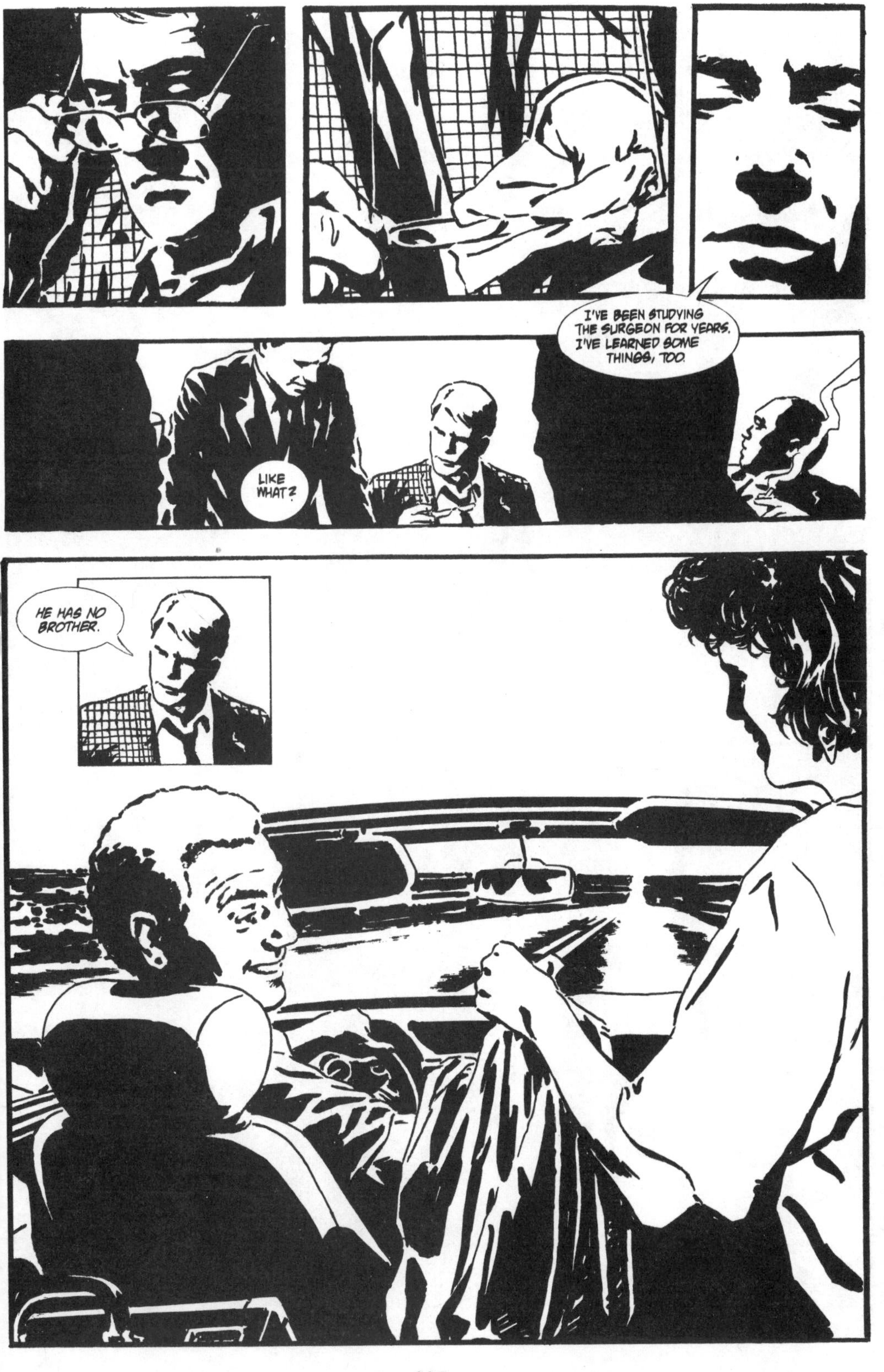
I'VE BEEN STUDYING THE SURGEON FOR YEARS. I'VE LEARNED SOME THINGS, TOO.
LIKE WHAT?
HE HAS NO BROTHER.

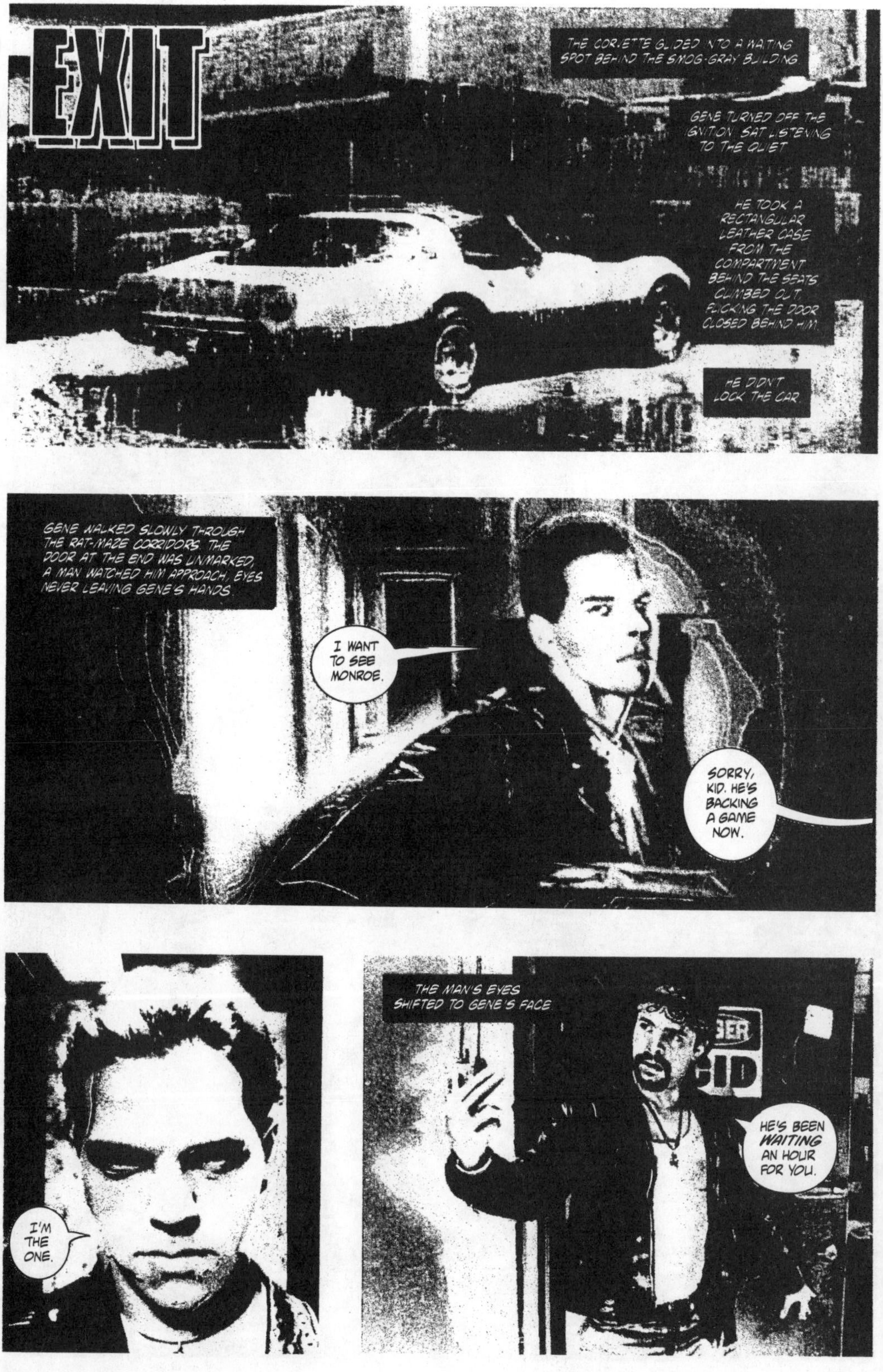
EXIT
THE CORVETTE GLIDED INTO A WAITING SPOT BEHIND THE SMOG-GRAY BUILDING.
GENE TURNED OFF THE IGNITION, SAT LISTENING TO THE QUIET.
HE TOOK A RECTANGULAR LEATHER CASE FROM THE COMPARTMENT BEHIND THE SEATS, CLIMBED OUT, FLICKING THE DOOR CLOSED BEHIND HIM.
HE DIDN'T LOCK THE CAR.
GENE WALKED SLOWLY THROUGH THE RAT-MAZE CORRIDORS. THE DOOR AT THE END WAS UNMARKED. A MAN WATCHED HIM APPROACH, EYES NEVER LEAVING GENE'S HANDS.
I WANT TO SEE MONROE.
SORRY, KID. HE'S BACKING A GAME NOW.
I'M THE ONE.
THE MAN'S EYES SHIFTED TO GENE'S FACE.
HE'S BEEN WAITING AN HOUR FOR YOU.

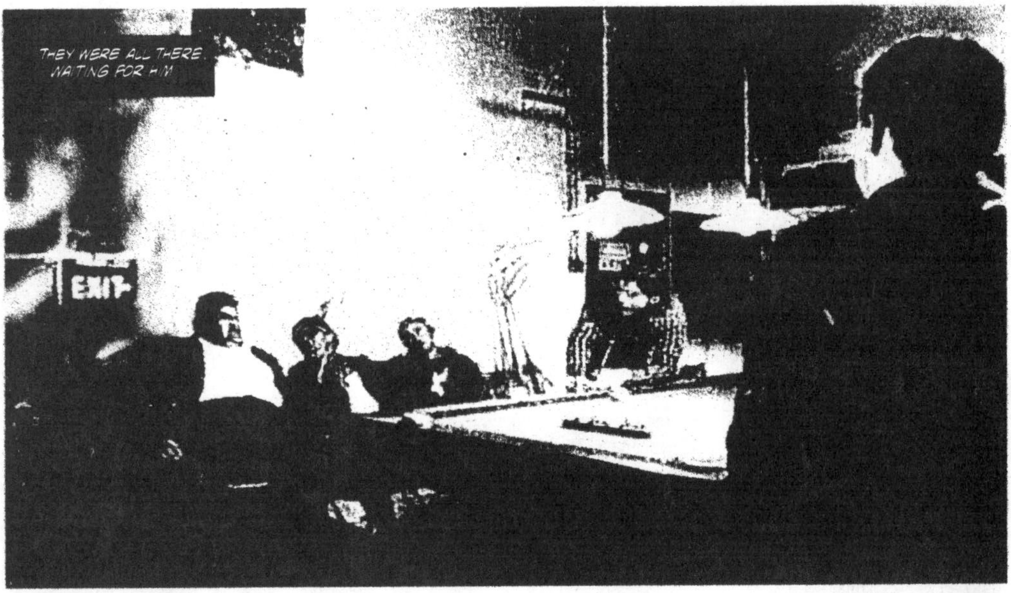
THEY WERE ALL THERE. WAITING FOR HIM.

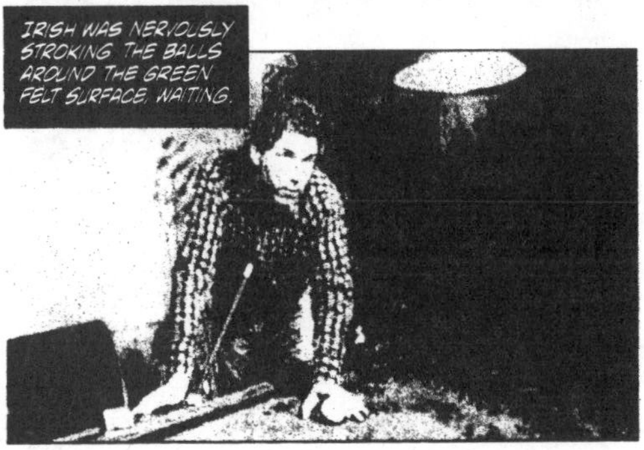
IRISH WAS NERVOUSLY STROKING THE BALLS AROUND THE GREEN FELT SURFACE. WAITING.

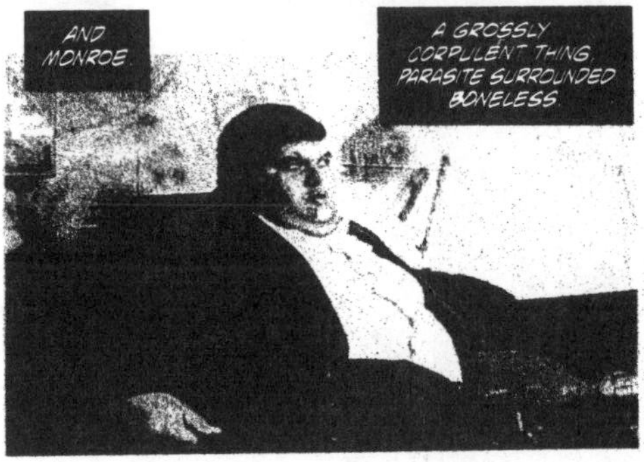
AND MONROE.
A GROSSLY CORPULENT THING. PARASITE SURROUNDED BONELESS.

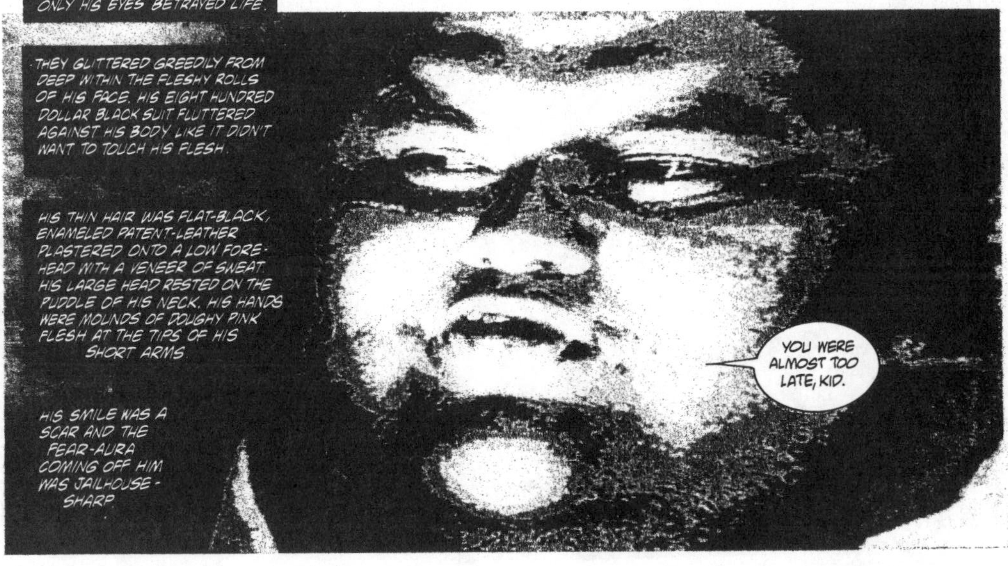
ONLY HIS EYES BETRAYED LIFE.
THEY GLITTERED GREEDILY FROM DEEP WITHIN THE FLESHY ROLLS OF HIS FACE. HIS EIGHT HUNDRED DOLLAR BLACK SUIT FLUTTERED AGAINST HIS BODY LIKE IT DIDN'T WANT TO TOUCH HIS FLESH.
HIS THIN HAIR WAS FLAT-BLACK, ENAMELED PATENT-LEATHER PLASTERED ONTO A LOW FORE-HEAD WITH A VENEER OF SWEAT. HIS LARGE HEAD RESTED ON THE PUDDLE OF HIS NECK. HIS HANDS WERE MOUNDS OF DOUGHY PINK FLESH AT THE TIPS OF HIS SHORT ARMS.
YOU WERE ALMOST TOO LATE, KID.
HIS SMILE WAS A SCAR AND THE FEAR-AURA COMING OFF HIM WAS JAILHOUSE-SHARP.

I'M HERE NOW.

I'LL LET IT GO, GENE. YOU DON'T GET A CUT THIS TIME.

THE WATCHERS GRINNED, TAKING THEIR CUE.

THREE LARGE WHEN YOU WIN.

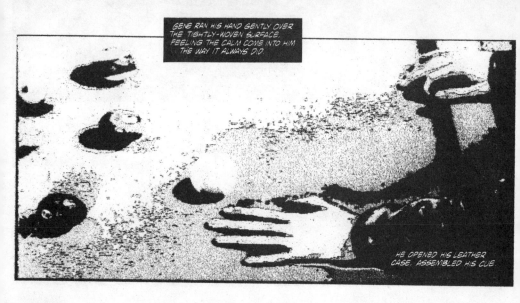

GENE RAN HIS HAND GENTLY OVER THE TIGHTLY-WOVEN SURFACE, FEELING THE CALM COME INTO HIM THE WAY IT ALWAYS DID.

HE OPENED HIS LEATHER CASE, ASSEMBLED HIS CUE.

IRISH WON THE LAG.

GENE CAREFULLY ROUGHENED THE TIP OF HIS CUE, APPLIED THE BLUE CHALK, STEPPED TO THE TABLE, HOLDING THE WHITE CUE BALL IN HIS LEFT HAND, BOUNCING IT SOFTLY, WAITING.

DON'T EVEN THINK ABOUT LOSING.

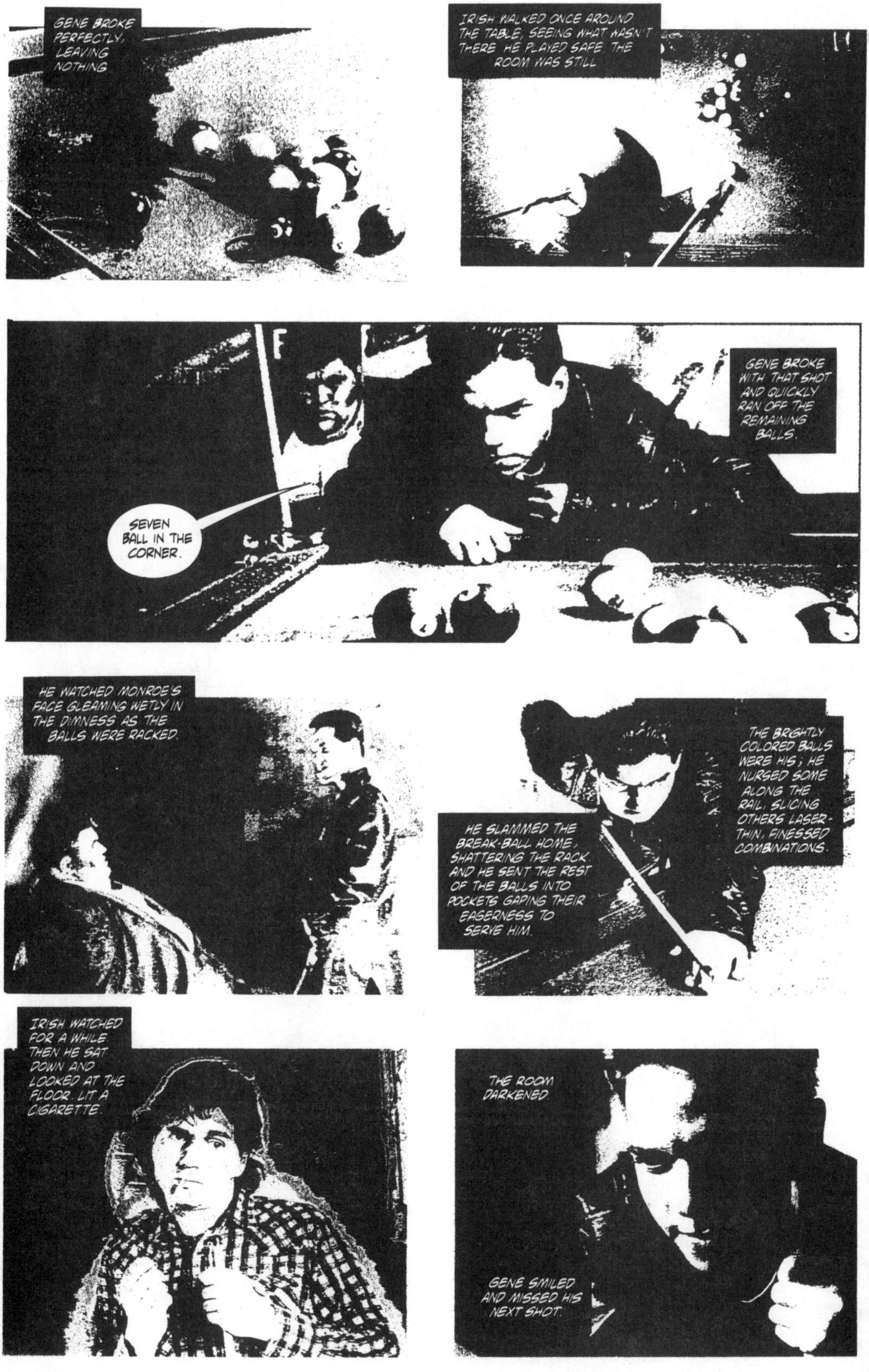
GENE BROKE PERFECTLY, LEAVING NOTHING.
IRISH WALKED ONCE AROUND THE TABLE, SEEING WHAT WASN'T THERE. HE PLAYED SAFE. THE ROOM WAS STILL.
GENE BROKE WITH THAT SHOT AND QUICKLY RAN OFF THE REMAINING BALLS.
SEVEN BALL IN THE CORNER.
HE WATCHED MONROE'S FACE GLEAMING WETLY IN THE DIMNESS AS THE BALLS WERE RACKED.
HE SLAMMED THE BREAK-BALL HOME, SHATTERING THE RACK. AND HE SENT THE REST OF THE BALLS INTO POCKETS GAPING THEIR EAGERNESS TO SERVE HIM.
THE BRIGHTLY COLORED BALLS WERE HIS; HE NURSED SOME ALONG THE RAIL, SLICING OTHERS LASER-THIN, FINESSED COMBINATIONS.
IRISH WATCHED FOR A WHILE. THEN HE SAT DOWN AND LOOKED AT THE FLOOR. LIT A CIGARETTE.
THE ROOM DARKENED.
GENE SMILED AND MISSED HIS NEXT SHOT.

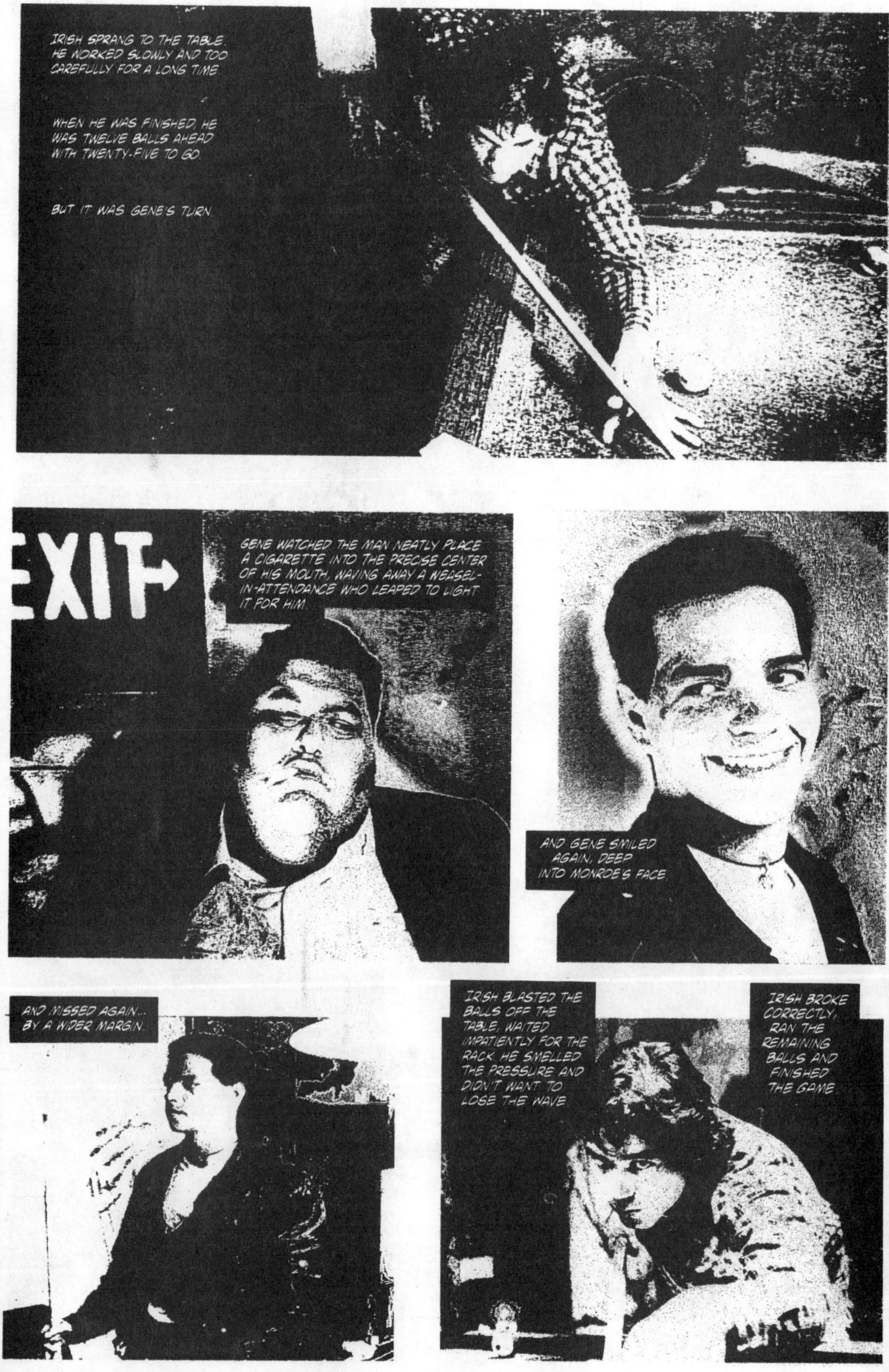
IRISH SPRANG TO THE TABLE. HE WORKED SLOWLY AND TOO CAREFULLY FOR A LONG TIME.
WHEN HE WAS FINISHED, HE WAS TWELVE BALLS AHEAD WITH TWENTY-FIVE TO GO.
BUT IT WAS GENE'S TURN.
EXIT
GENE WATCHED THE MAN NEATLY PLACE A CIGARETTE INTO THE PRECISE CENTER OF HIS MOUTH, WAVING AWAY A WEASEL-IN-ATTENDANCE WHO LEAPED TO LIGHT IT FOR HIM.
AND GENE SMILED AGAIN, DEEP INTO MONROE'S FACE.
AND MISSED AGAIN... BY A WIDER MARGIN.
IRISH BLASTED THE BALLS OFF THE TABLE, WAITED IMPATIENTLY FOR THE RACK. HE SMELLED THE PRESSURE AND DIDN'T WANT TO LOSE THE WAVE.
IRISH BROKE CORRECTLY, RAN THE REMAINING BALLS AND FINISHED THE GAME.

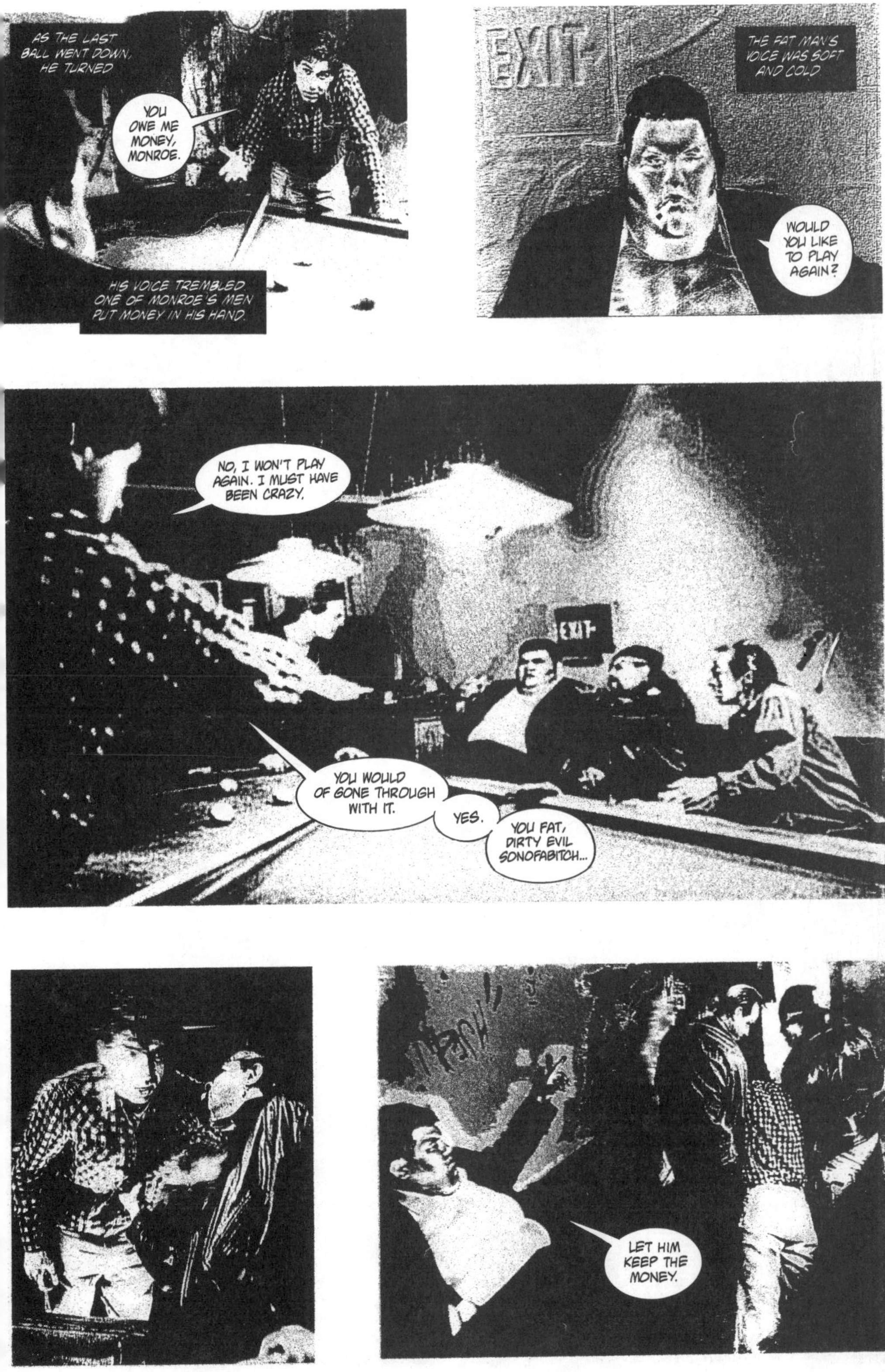
AS THE LAST BALL WENT DOWN, HE TURNED
YOU OWE ME MONEY, MONROE.
HIS VOICE TREMBLED. ONE OF MONROE'S MEN PUT MONEY IN HIS HAND.
THE FAT MAN'S VOICE WAS SOFT AND COLD.
EXIT
WOULD YOU LIKE TO PLAY AGAIN?
NO, I WON'T PLAY AGAIN. I MUST HAVE BEEN CRAZY.
EXIT
YOU WOULD OF GONE THROUGH WITH IT.
YES.
YOU FAT, DIRTY EVIL SONOFABITCH...
LET HIM KEEP THE MONEY.

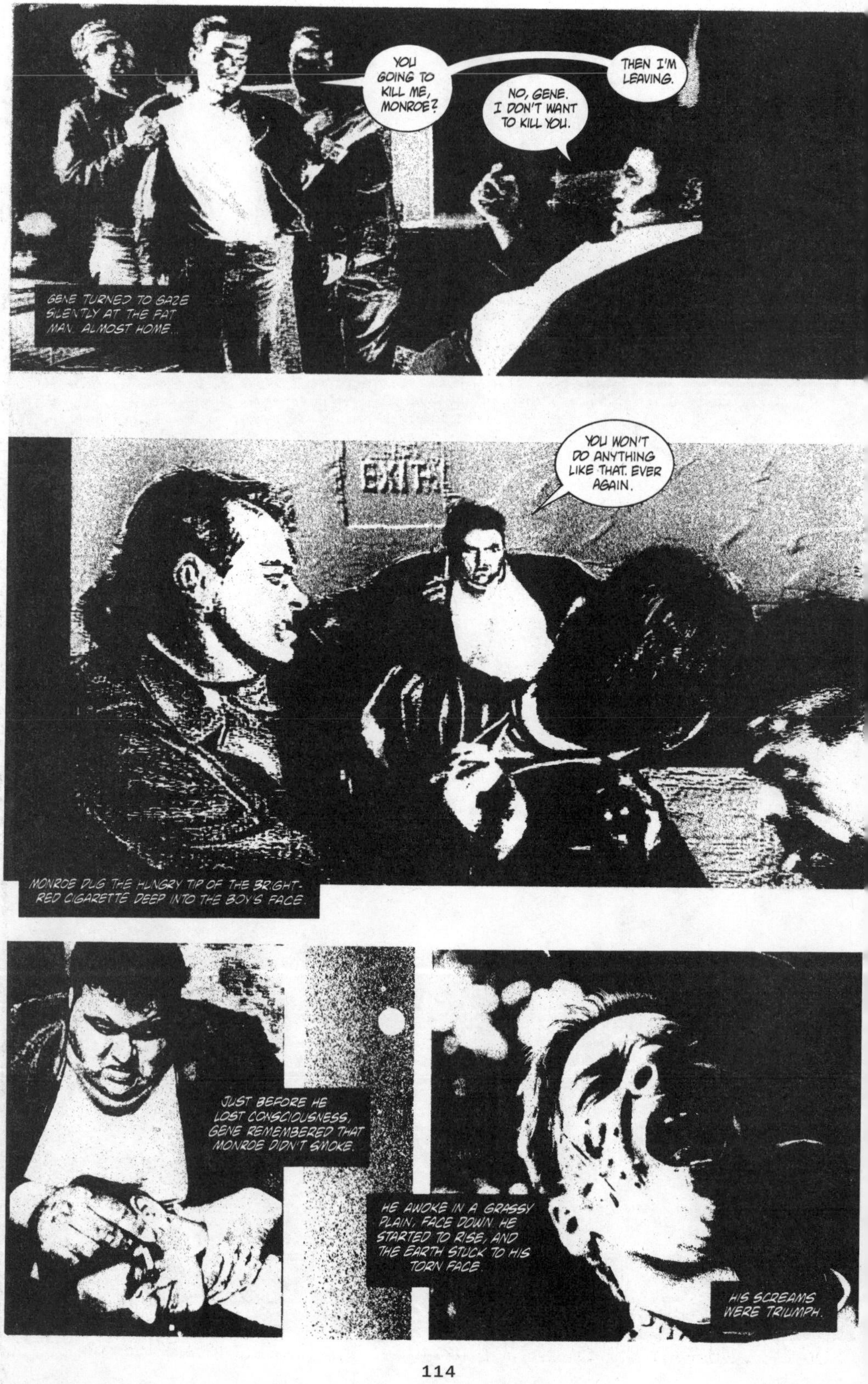
YOU GOING TO KILL ME, MONROE?
NO, GENE. I DON'T WANT TO KILL YOU.
THEN I'M LEAVING.
GENE TURNED TO GAZE SILENTLY AT THE FAT MAN. ALMOST HOME...
YOU WON'T DO ANYTHING LIKE THAT. EVER AGAIN.
MONROE DUG THE HUNGRY TIP OF THE BRIGHT-RED CIGARETTE DEEP INTO THE BOY'S FACE.
JUST BEFORE HE LOST CONSCIOUSNESS, GENE REMEMBERED THAT MONROE DIDN'T SMOKE.
HE AWOKE IN A GRASSY PLAIN, FACE DOWN. HE STARTED TO RISE, AND THE EARTH STUCK TO HIS TORN FACE.
HIS SCREAMS WERE TRIUMPH.

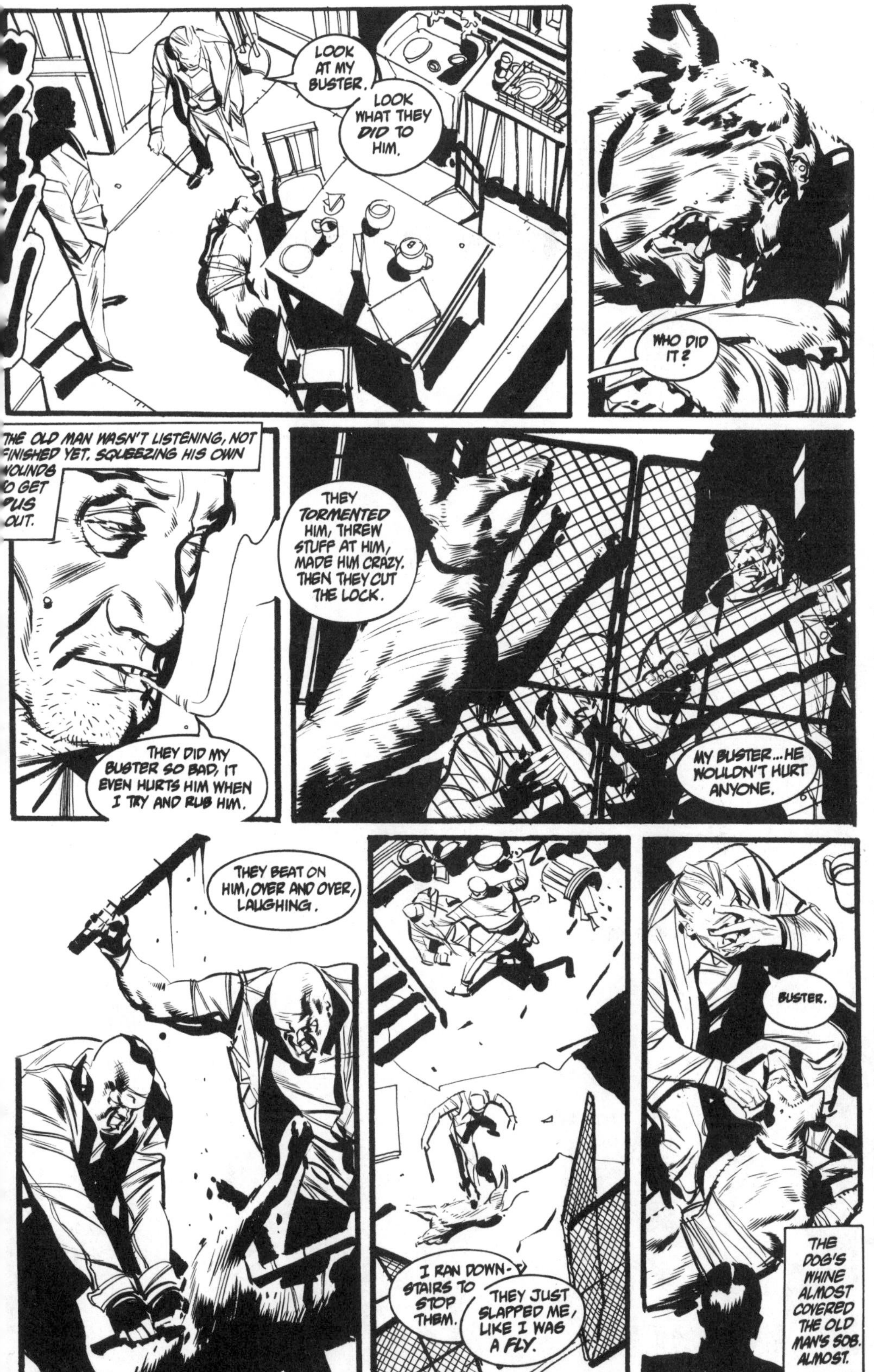
LOOK AT MY BUSTER.
LOOK WHAT THEY DID TO HIM.
WHO DID IT?
THE OLD MAN WASN'T LISTENING, NOT FINISHED YET. SQUEEZING HIS OWN WOUNDS TO GET PUS OUT.
THEY DID MY BUSTER SO BAD, IT EVEN HURTS HIM WHEN I TRY AND RUB HIM.
THEY TORMENTED HIM, THREW STUFF AT HIM, MADE HIM CRAZY. THEN THEY CUT THE LOCK.
MY BUSTER...HE WOULDN'T HURT ANYONE.
THEY BEAT ON HIM, OVER AND OVER, LAUGHING.
I RAN DOWN-STAIRS TO STOP THEM.
THEY JUST SLAPPED ME, LIKE I WAS A FLY.
BUSTER.
THE DOG'S WHINE ALMOST COVERED THE OLD MAN'S SOB. ALMOST.

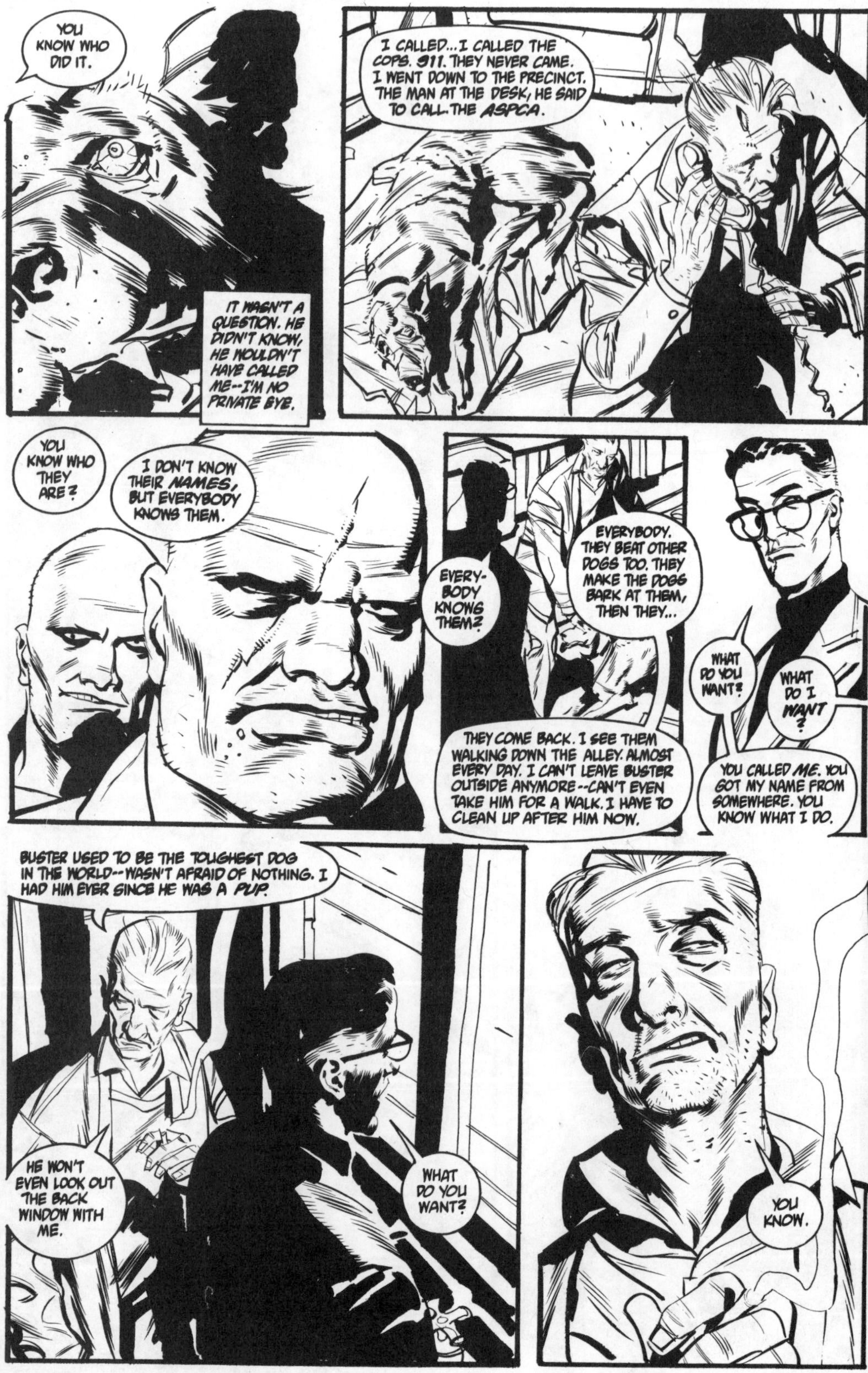

YOU KNOW WHO DID IT.
IT WASN'T A QUESTION. HE DIDN'T KNOW, HE WOULDN'T HAVE CALLED ME--I'M NO PRIVATE EYE.
I CALLED... I CALLED THE COPS. 911. THEY NEVER CAME. I WENT DOWN TO THE PRECINCT. THE MAN AT THE DESK, HE SAID TO CALL THE ASPCA.
YOU KNOW WHO THEY ARE?
I DON'T KNOW THEIR NAMES, BUT EVERYBODY KNOWS THEM.
EVERY-BODY KNOWS THEM?
EVERYBODY. THEY BEAT OTHER DOGS TOO. THEY MAKE THE DOGS BARK AT THEM, THEN THEY...
THEY COME BACK. I SEE THEM WALKING DOWN THE ALLEY. ALMOST EVERY DAY. I CAN'T LEAVE BUSTER OUTSIDE ANYMORE--CAN'T EVEN TAKE HIM FOR A WALK. I HAVE TO CLEAN UP AFTER HIM NOW.
WHAT DO YOU WANT?
WHAT DO I WANT?
YOU CALLED ME. YOU GOT MY NAME FROM SOMEWHERE. YOU KNOW WHAT I DO.
BUSTER USED TO BE THE TOUGHEST DOG IN THE WORLD--WASN'T AFRAID OF NOTHING. I HAD HIM EVER SINCE HE WAS A PUP.
HE WON'T EVEN LOOK OUT THE BACK WINDOW WITH ME.
WHAT DO YOU WANT?
YOU KNOW.

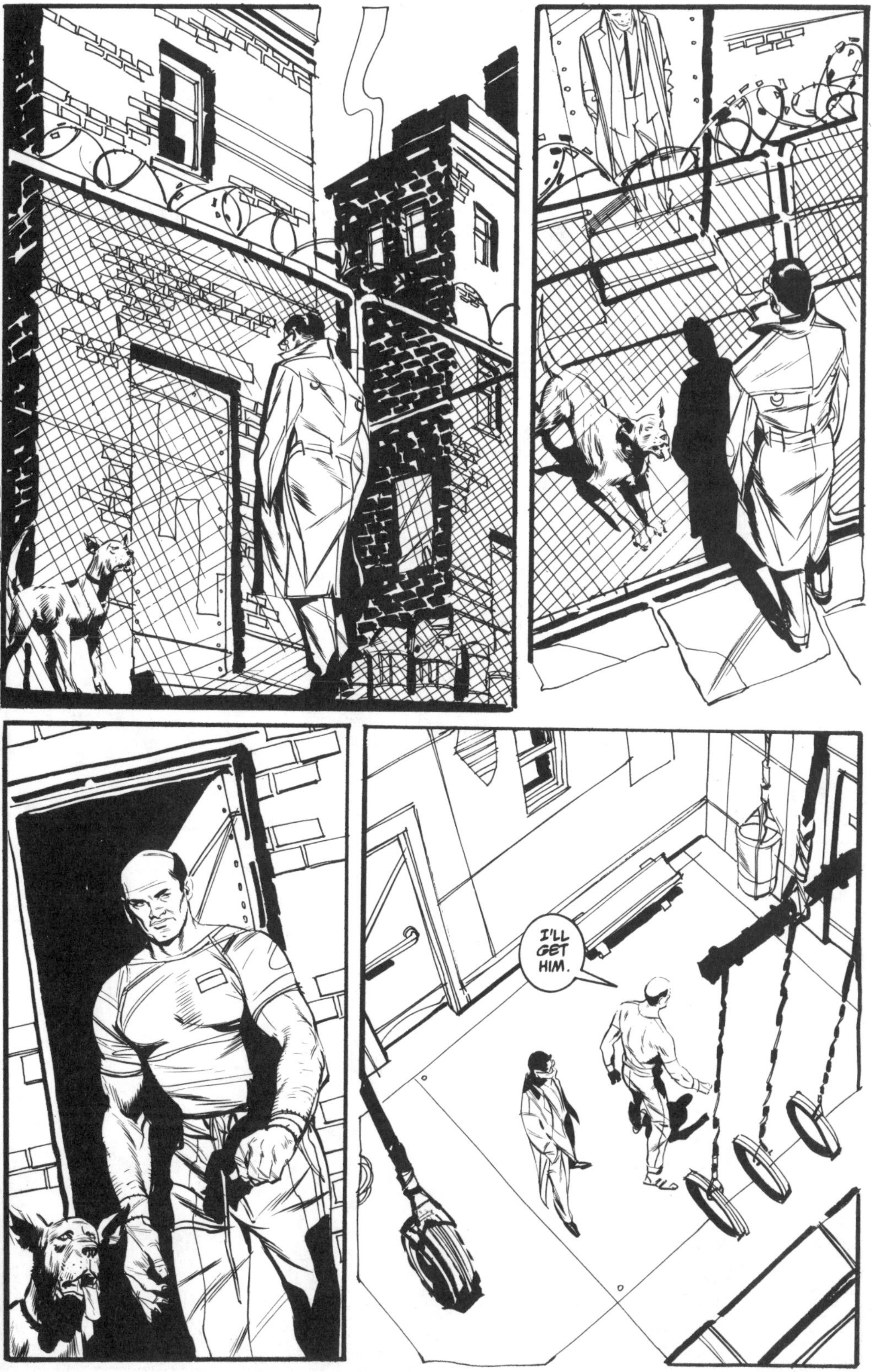
I'LL GET HIM.

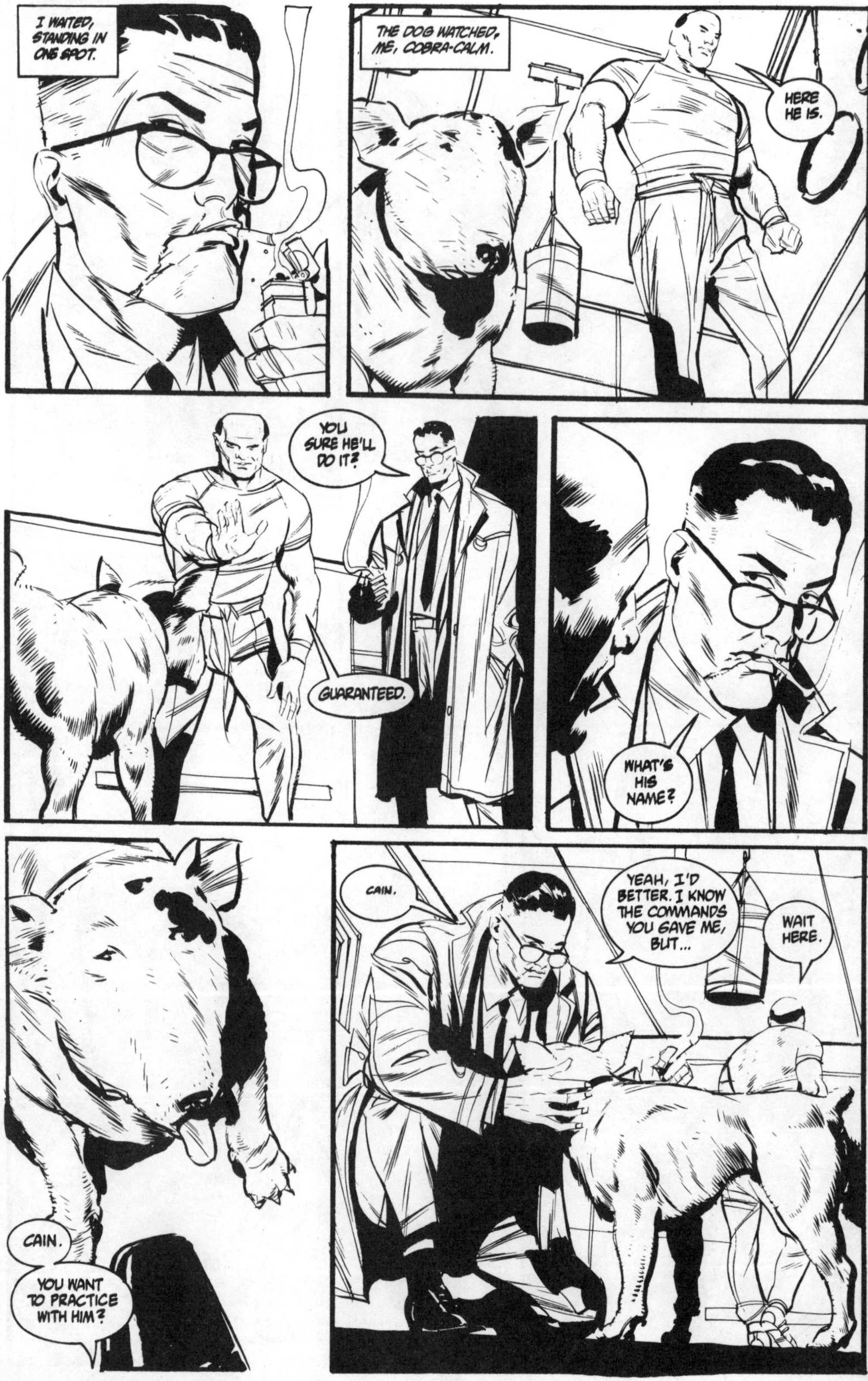
I WAITED, STANDING IN ONE SPOT.
THE DOG WATCHED, ME, COBRA-CALM.
HERE HE IS.
YOU SURE HE'LL DO IT?
GUARANTEED.
WHAT'S HIS NAME?
CAIN.
YOU WANT TO PRACTICE WITH HIM?
CAIN.
YEAH, I'D BETTER. I KNOW THE COMMANDS YOU GAVE ME, BUT...
WAIT HERE.

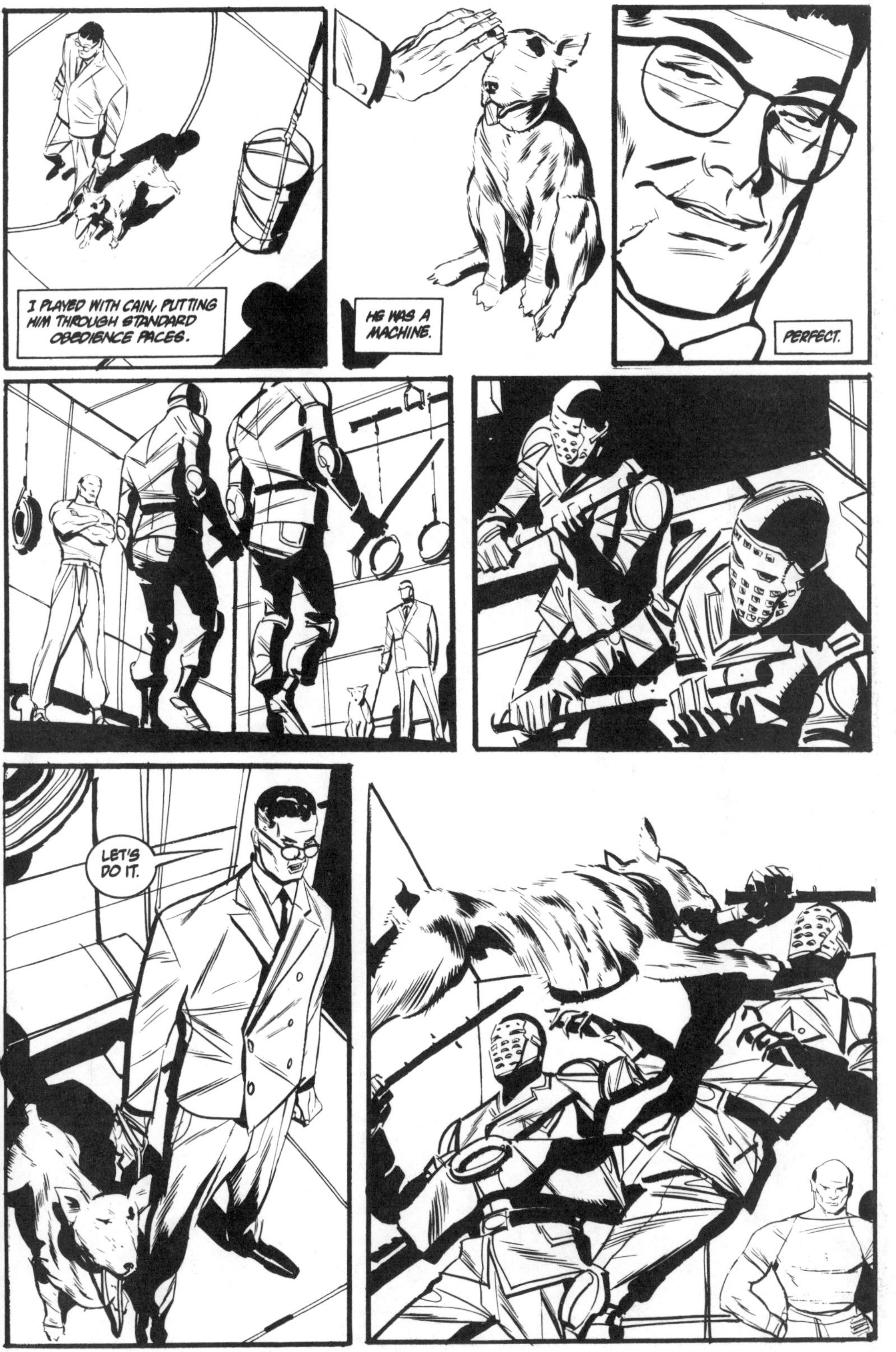
I PLAYED WITH CAIN, PUTTING HIM THROUGH STANDARD OBEDIENCE PACES.
HE WAS A MACHINE.
PERFECT.
LET'S DO IT.

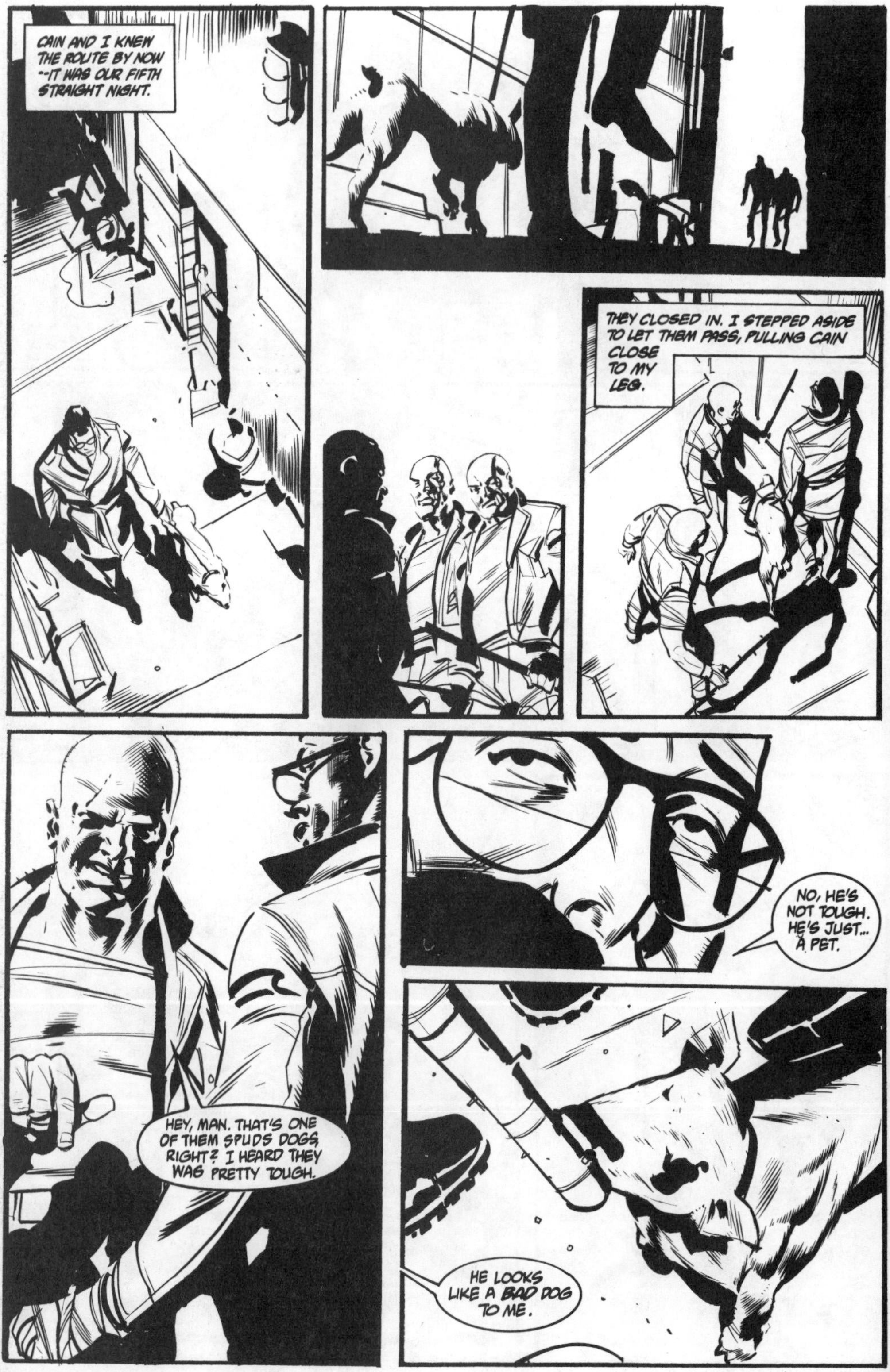
CAIN AND I KNEW THE ROUTE BY NOW --IT WAS OUR FIFTH STRAIGHT NIGHT.
THEY CLOSED IN. I STEPPED ASIDE TO LET THEM PASS, PULLING CAIN CLOSE TO MY LEG.
HEY, MAN. THAT'S ONE OF THEM SPUDS DOGS, RIGHT? I HEARD THEY WAS PRETTY TOUGH.
NO, HE'S NOT TOUGH. HE'S JUST... A PET.
HE LOOKS LIKE A BAD DOG TO ME.

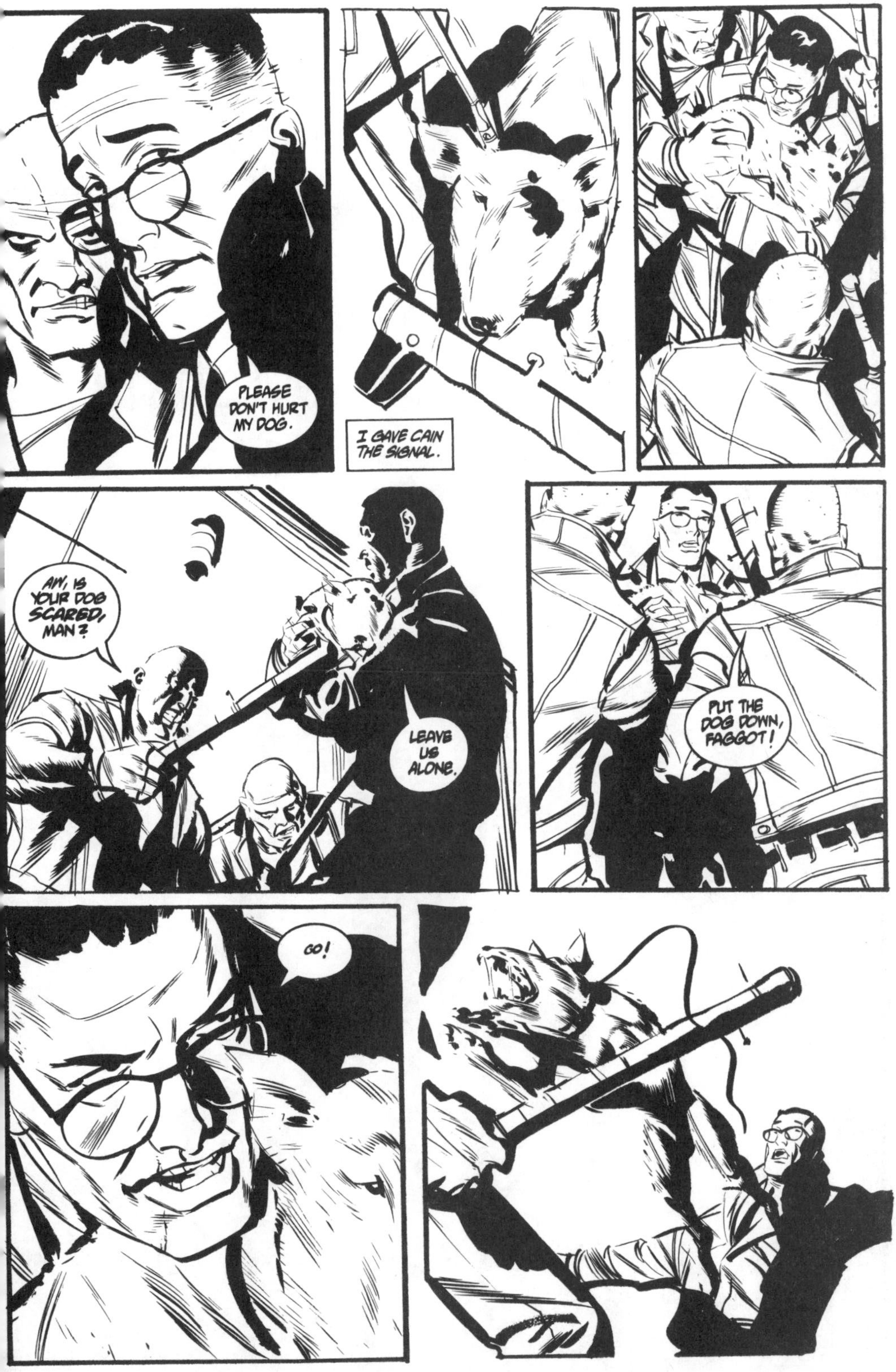
PLEASE DON'T HURT MY DOG.
I GAVE CAIN THE SIGNAL.
AW, IS YOUR DOG SCARED, MAN?
LEAVE US ALONE.
PUT THE DOG DOWN, FAGGOT!
GO!

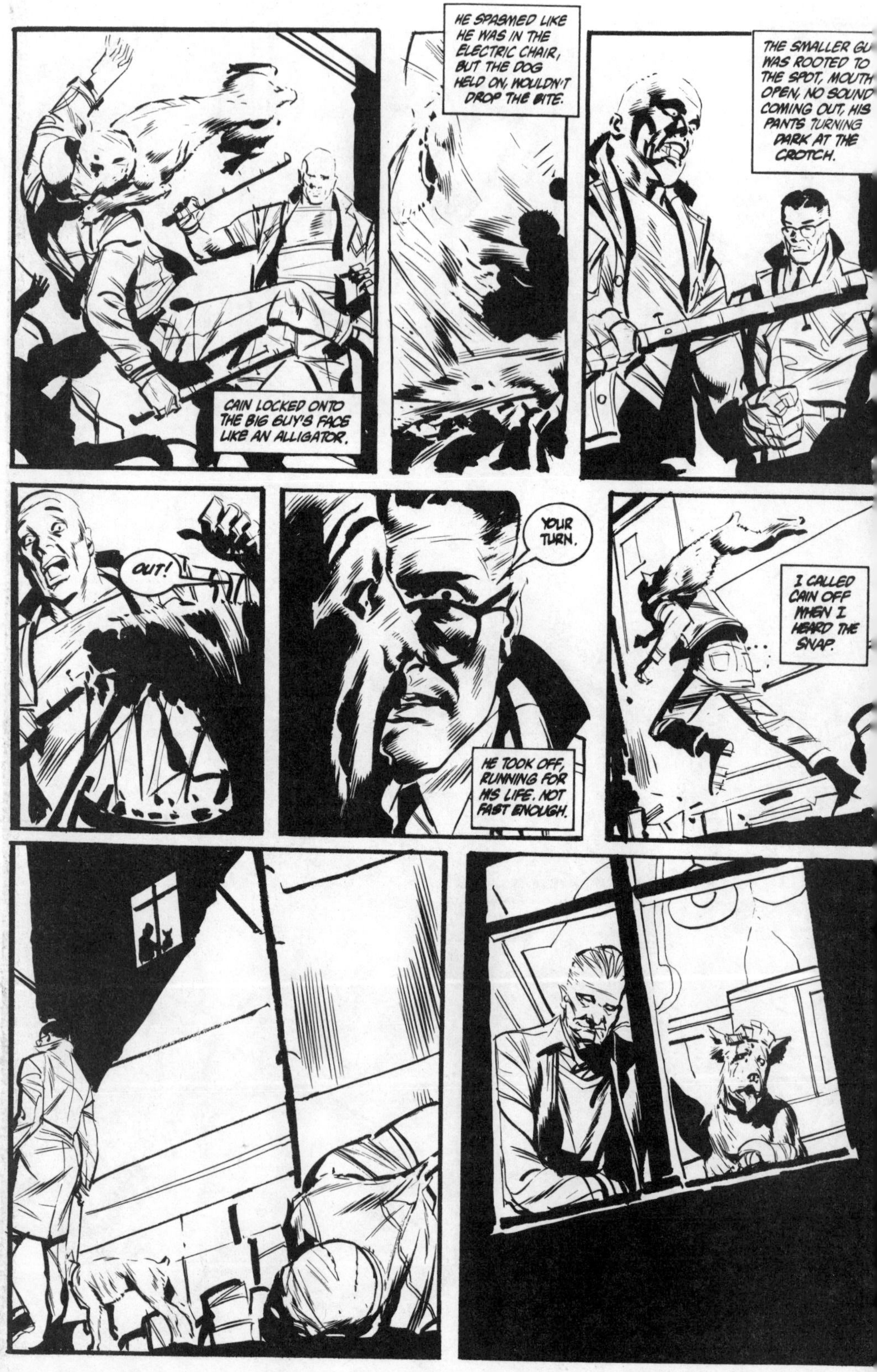
CAIN LOCKED ONTO THE BIG GUY'S FACE LIKE AN ALLIGATOR.
HE SPASMED LIKE HE WAS IN THE ELECTRIC CHAIR, BUT THE DOG HELD ON, WOULDN'T DROP THE BITE.
THE SMALLER GU WAS ROOTED TO THE SPOT, MOUTH OPEN, NO SOUND COMING OUT, HIS PANTS TURNING DARK AT THE CROTCH.
OUT!
YOUR TURN.
HE TOOK OFF, RUNNING FOR HIS LIFE. NOT FAST ENOUGH.
I CALLED CAIN OFF WHEN I HEARD THE SNAP.

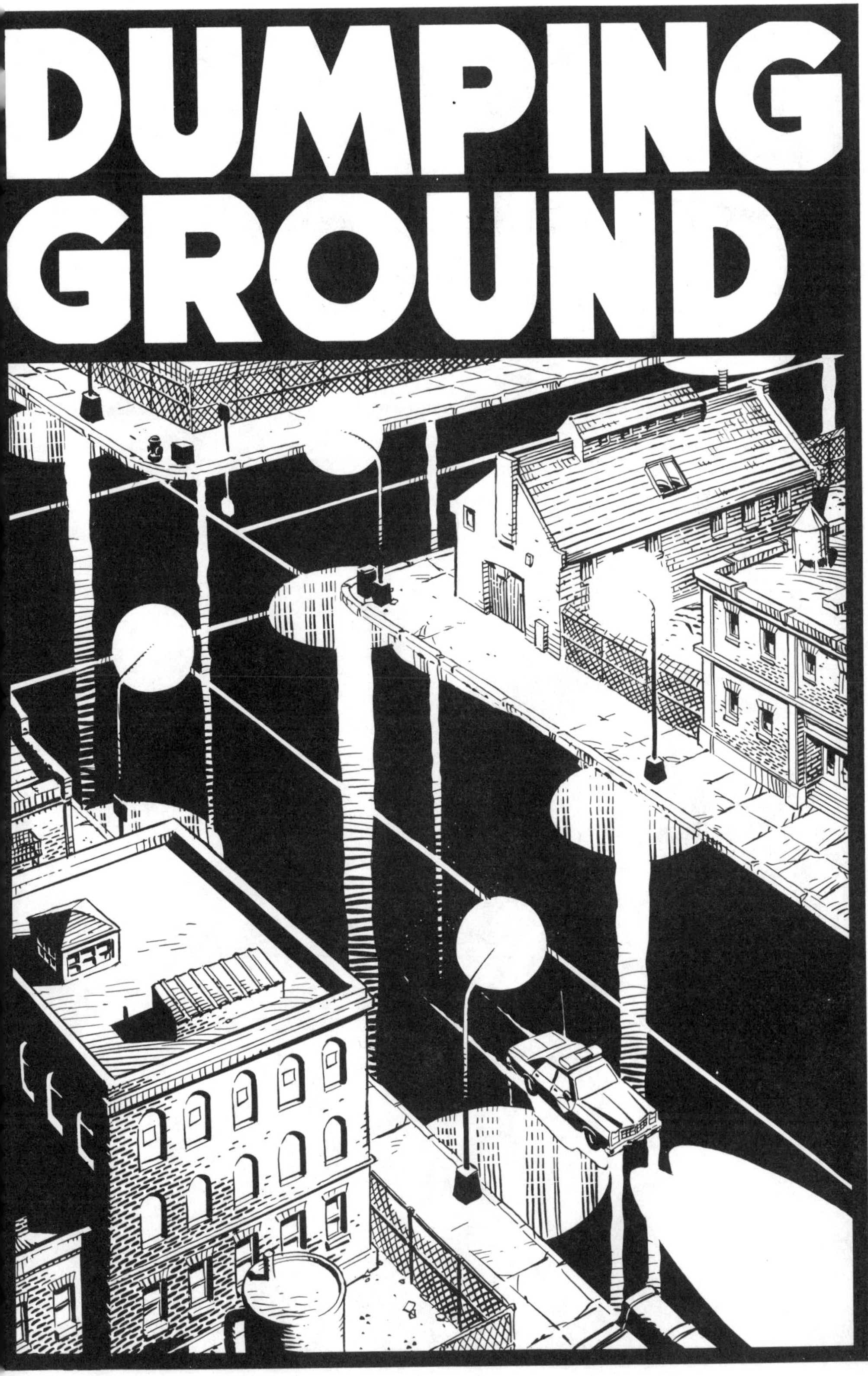
DUMPING
GROUND

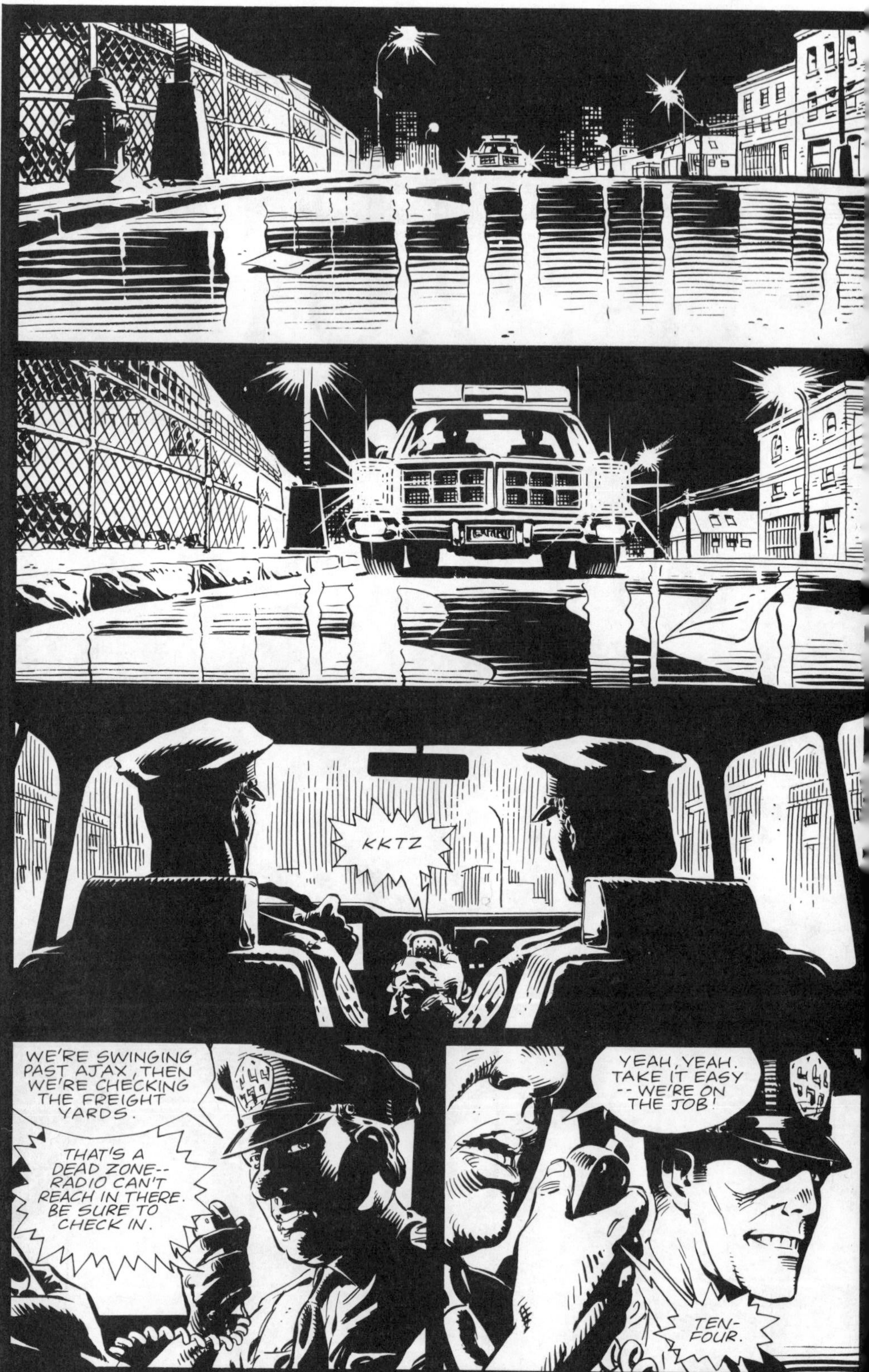
KKTZ
WE'RE SWINGING PAST AJAX, THEN WE'RE CHECKING THE FREIGHT YARDS.
THAT'S A DEAD ZONE-- RADIO CAN'T REACH IN THERE. BE SURE TO CHECK IN.
YEAH, YEAH. TAKE IT EASY -- WE'RE ON THE JOB!
TEN-FOUR.

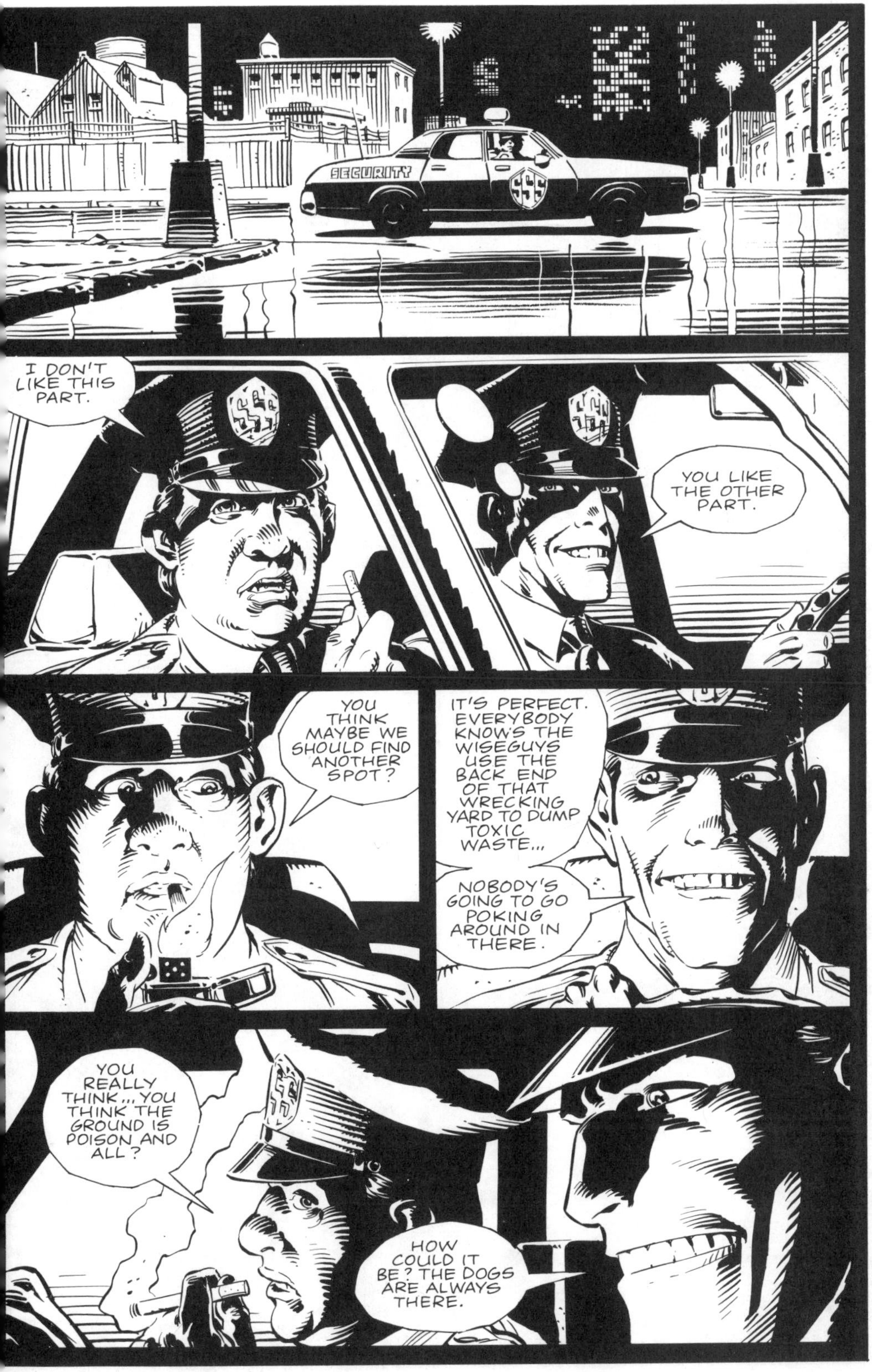
SECURITY
I DON'T LIKE THIS PART.
YOU LIKE THE OTHER PART.
YOU THINK MAYBE WE SHOULD FIND ANOTHER SPOT?
IT'S PERFECT. EVERYBODY KNOW'S THE WISEGUYS USE THE BACK END OF THAT WRECKING YARD TO DUMP TOXIC WASTE...
NOBODY'S GOING TO GO POKING AROUND IN THERE.
YOU REALLY THINK... YOU THINK THE GROUND IS POISON AND ALL?
HOW COULD IT BE? THE DOGS ARE ALWAYS THERE.

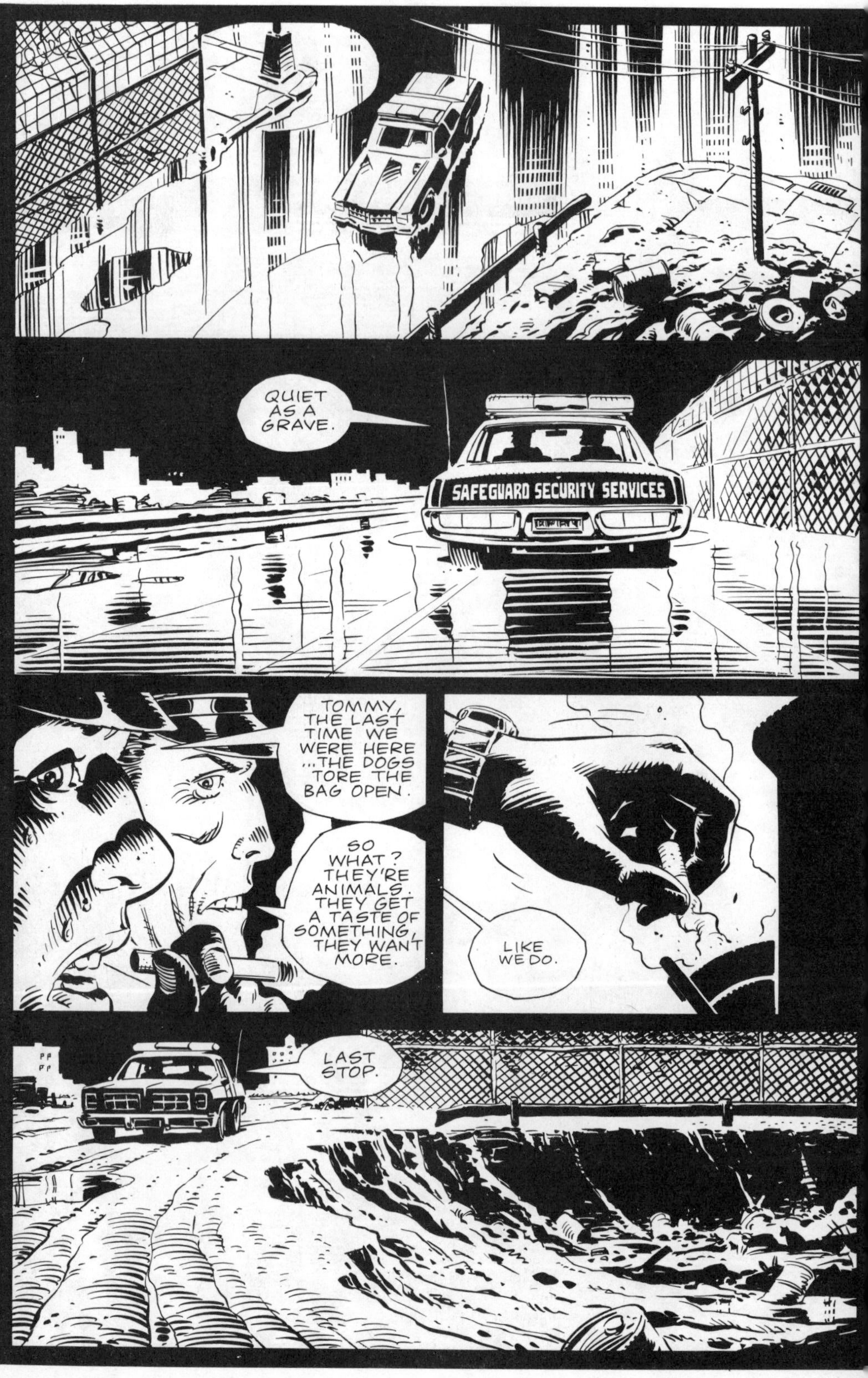
QUIET AS A GRAVE.
SAFEGUARD SECURITY SERVICES
TOMMY, THE LAST TIME WE WERE HERE ...THE DOGS TORE THE BAG OPEN.
SO WHAT? THEY'RE ANIMALS. THEY GET A TASTE OF SOMETHING, THEY WAN'T MORE.
LIKE WE DO.
LAST STOP.

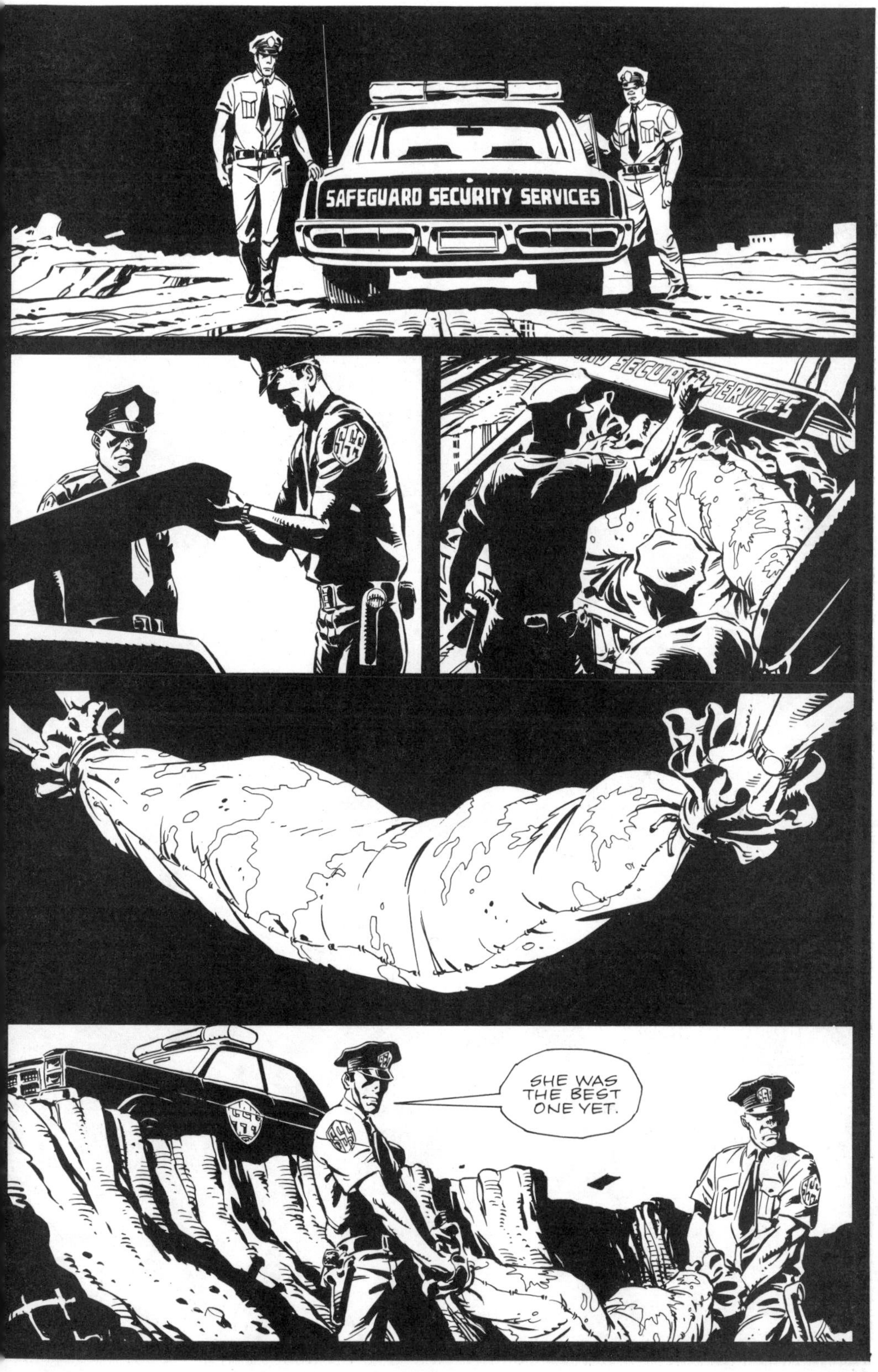
SAFEGUARD SECURITY SERVICES
SHE WAS THE BEST ONE YET.

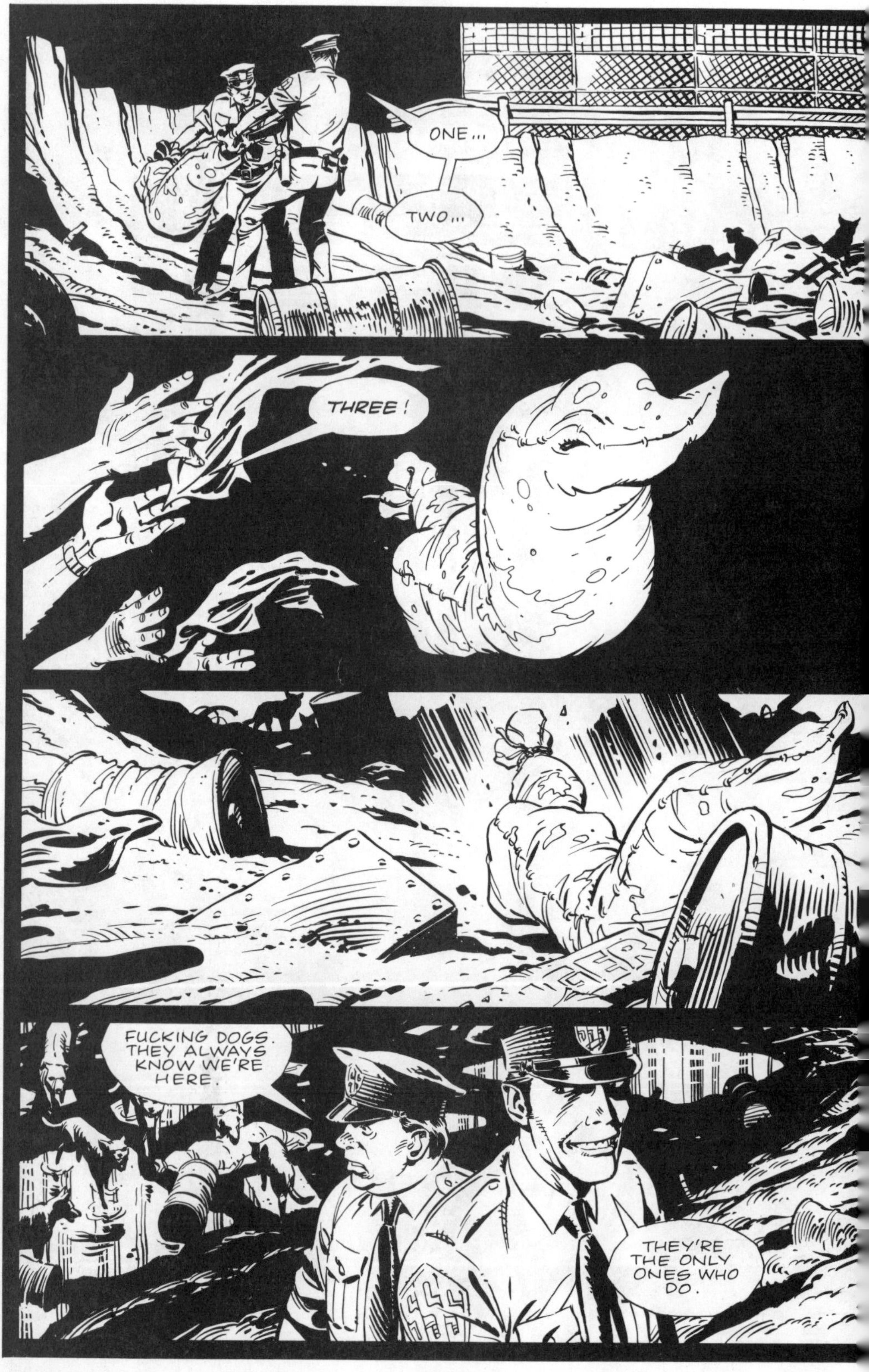
ONE...
TWO...
THREE!
FUCKING DOGS. THEY ALWAYS KNOW WE'RE HERE.
THEY'RE THE ONLY ONES WHO DO.

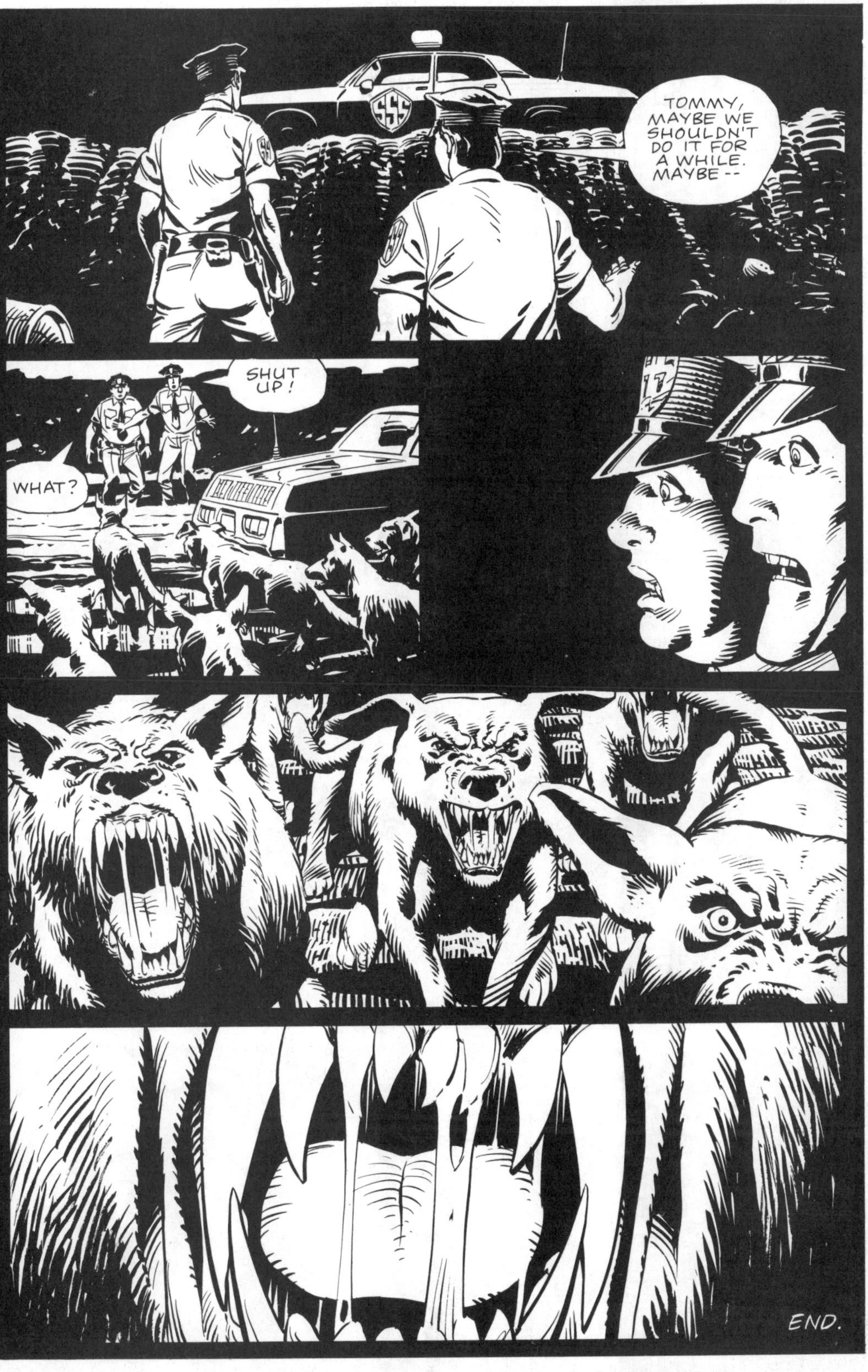
TOMMY, MAYBE WE SHOULDN'T DO IT FOR A WHILE. MAYBE --
SHUT UP!
WHAT?
END.

LYNCH LAW

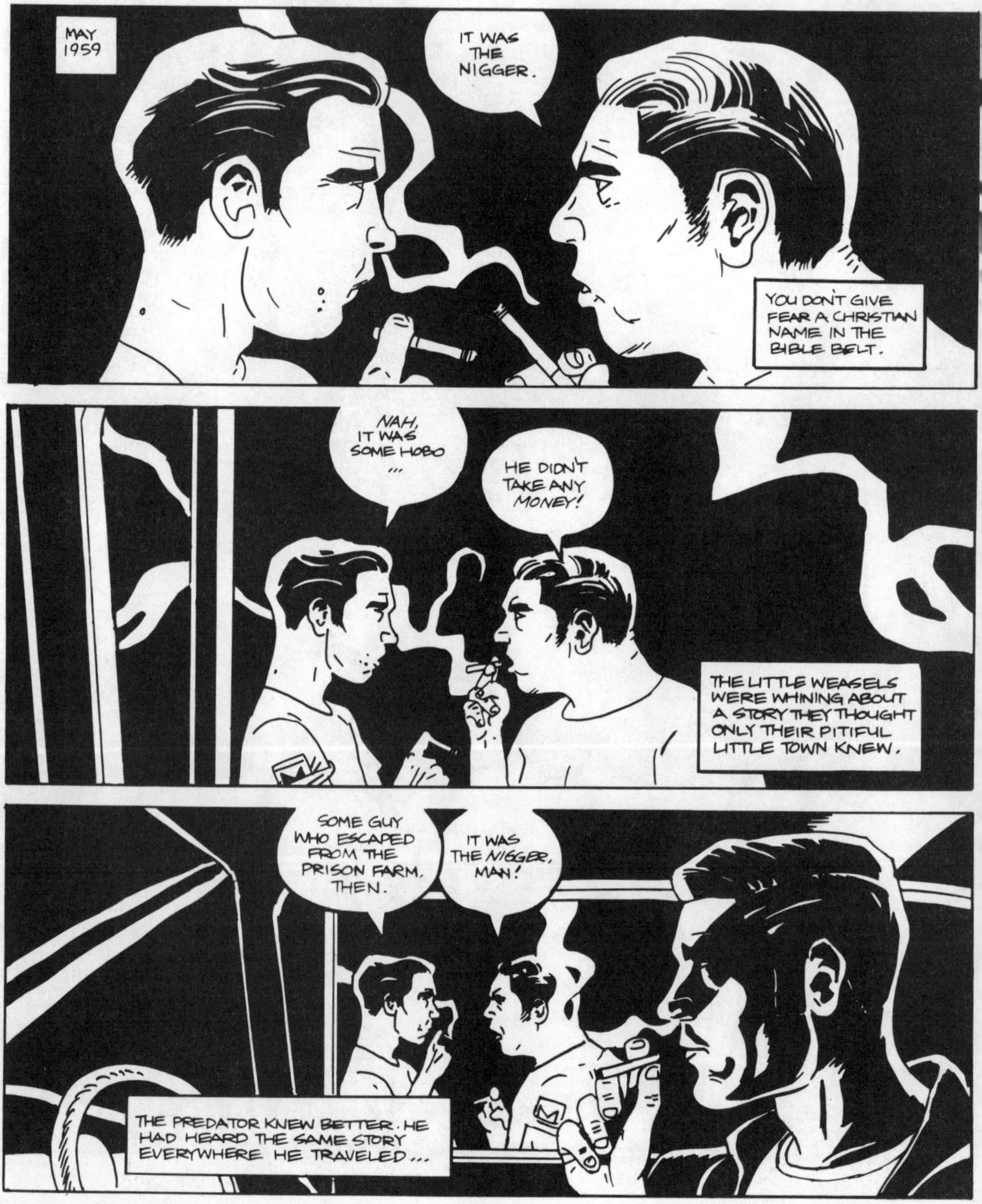
MAY 1959
IT WAS THE NIGGER.
YOU DON'T GIVE FEAR A CHRISTIAN NAME IN THE BIBLE BELT.
NAH, IT WAS SOME HOBO ...
HE DIDN'T TAKE ANY MONEY!
THE LITTLE WEASELS WERE WHINING ABOUT A STORY THEY THOUGHT ONLY THEIR PITIFUL LITTLE TOWN KNEW.
SOME GUY WHO ESCAPED FROM THE PRISON FARM, THEN.
IT WAS THE NIGGER, MAN!
THE PREDATOR KNEW BETTER. HE HAD HEARD THE SAME STORY EVERYWHERE HE TRAVELED...

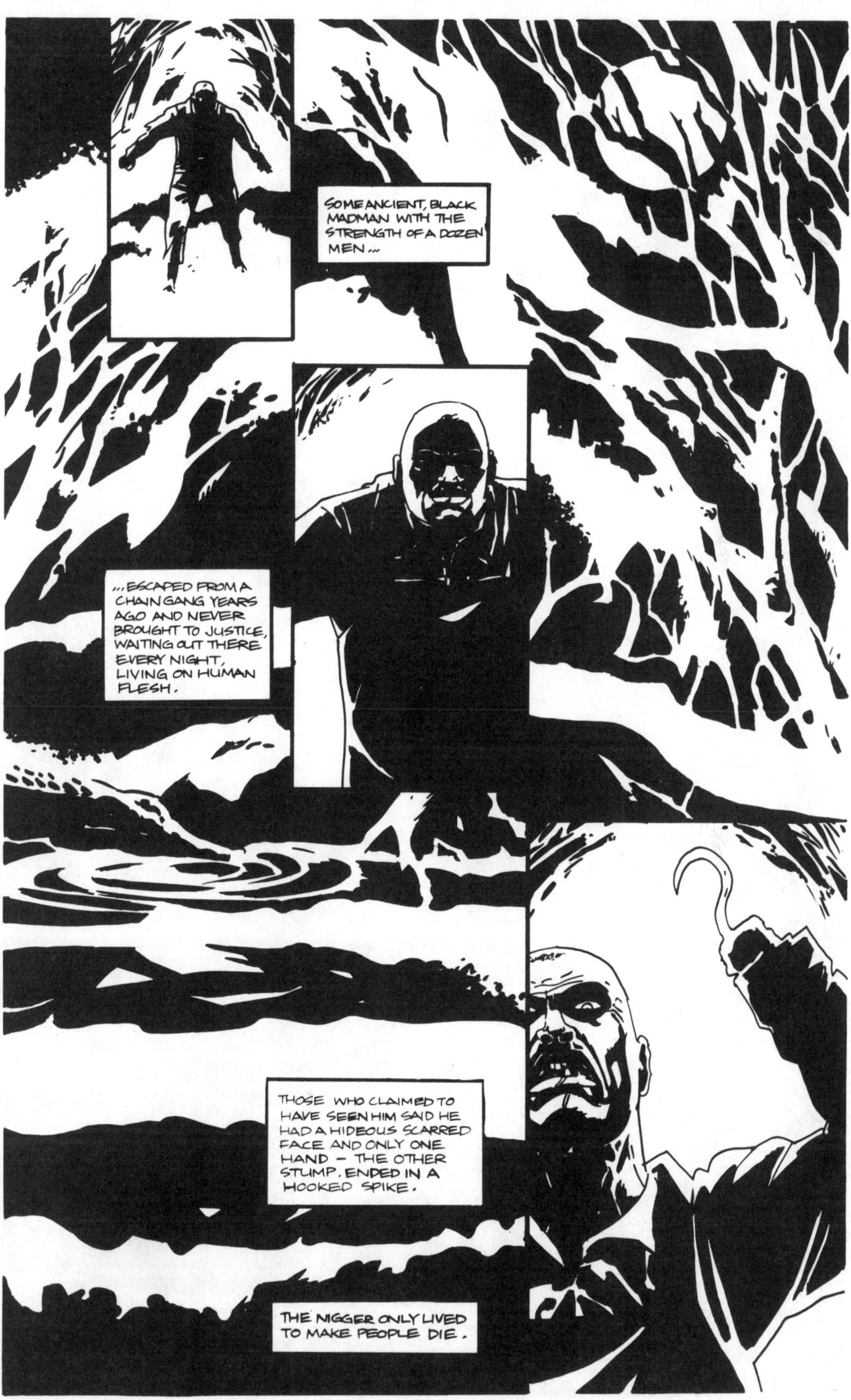
SOME ANCIENT, BLACK MADMAN WITH THE STRENGTH OF A DOZEN MEN...
...ESCAPED FROM A CHAIN GANG YEARS AGO AND NEVER BROUGHT TO JUSTICE, WAITING OUT THERE EVERY NIGHT, LIVING ON HUMAN FLESH.
THOSE WHO CLAIMED TO HAVE SEEN HIM SAID HE HAD A HIDEOUS SCARRED FACE AND ONLY ONE HAND - THE OTHER STUMP. ENDED IN A HOOKED SPIKE.
THE NIGGER ONLY LIVED TO MAKE PEOPLE DIE.

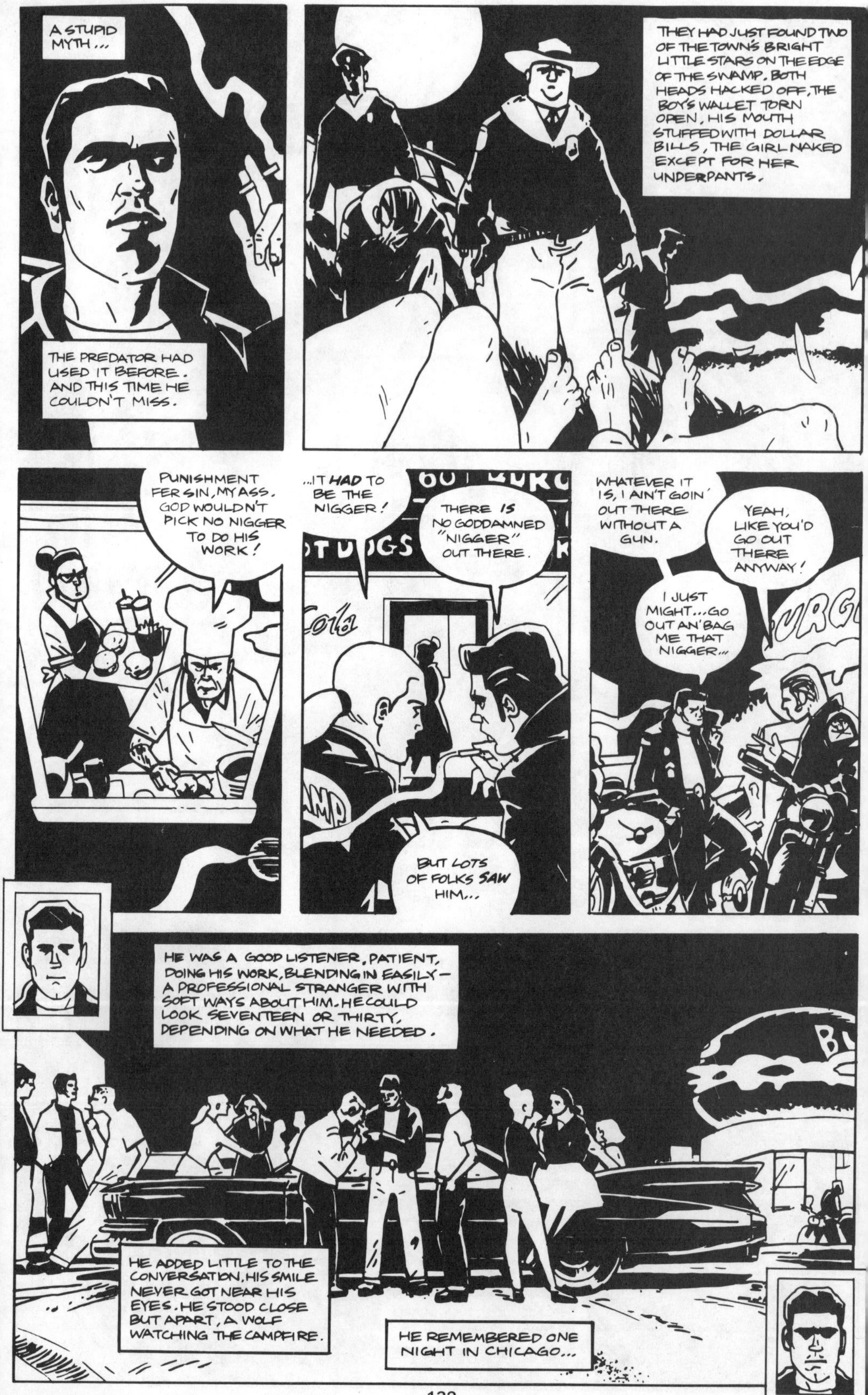
A STUPID MYTH...
THE PREDATOR HAD USED IT BEFORE. AND THIS TIME HE COULDN'T MISS.
THEY HAD JUST FOUND TWO OF THE TOWN'S BRIGHT LITTLE STARS ON THE EDGE OF THE SWAMP. BOTH HEADS HACKED OFF, THE BOY'S WALLET TORN OPEN, HIS MOUTH STUFFED WITH DOLLAR BILLS, THE GIRL NAKED EXCEPT FOR HER UNDERPANTS.
PUNISHMENT FER SIN, MY ASS. GOD WOULDN'T PICK NO NIGGER TO DO HIS WORK!
...IT HAD TO BE THE NIGGER!
THERE IS NO GODDAMNED "NIGGER" OUT THERE.
BUT LOTS OF FOLKS SAW HIM...
WHATEVER IT IS, I AIN'T GOIN' OUT THERE WITHOUT A GUN.
YEAH, LIKE YOU'D GO OUT THERE ANYWAY!
I JUST MIGHT... GO OUT AN' BAG ME THAT NIGGER...
HE WAS A GOOD LISTENER, PATIENT, DOING HIS WORK, BLENDING IN EASILY—A PROFESSIONAL STRANGER WITH SOFT WAYS ABOUT HIM. HE COULD LOOK SEVENTEEN OR THIRTY, DEPENDING ON WHAT HE NEEDED.
HE ADDED LITTLE TO THE CONVERSATION, HIS SMILE NEVER GOT NEAR HIS EYES. HE STOOD CLOSE BUT APART, A WOLF WATCHING THE CAMPFIRE.
HE REMEMBERED ONE NIGHT IN CHICAGO...

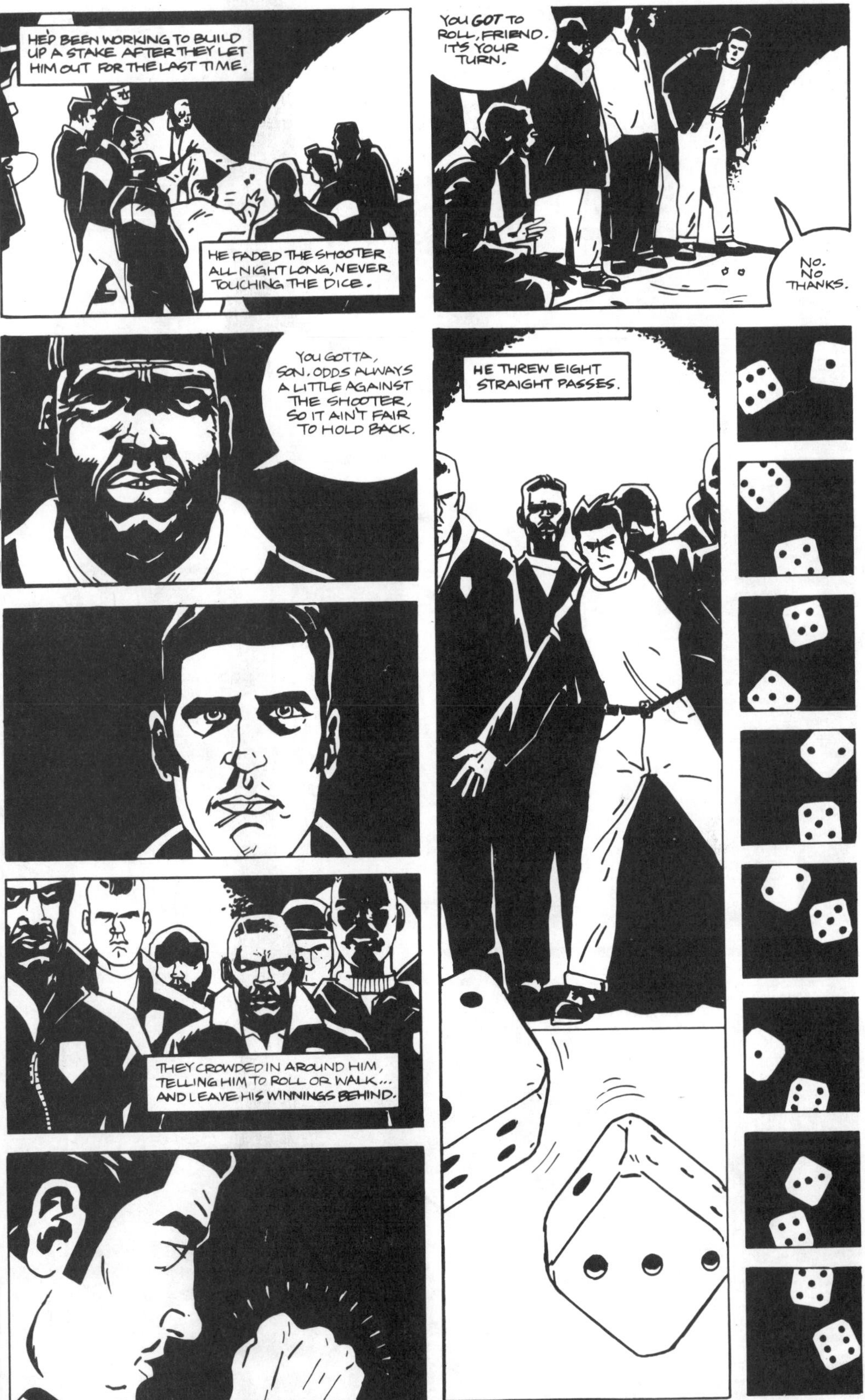
HE'D BEEN WORKING TO BUILD UP A STAKE AFTER THEY LET HIM OUT FOR THE LAST TIME.
HE FADED THE SHOOTER ALL NIGHT LONG, NEVER TOUCHING THE DICE.
YOU GOT TO ROLL, FRIEND. IT'S YOUR TURN.
NO. NO THANKS.
YOU GOTTA, SON. ODDS ALWAYS A LITTLE AGAINST THE SHOOTER, SO IT AIN'T FAIR TO HOLD BACK.
THEY CROWDED IN AROUND HIM, TELLING HIM TO ROLL OR WALK... AND LEAVE HIS WINNINGS BEHIND.
HE THREW EIGHT STRAIGHT PASSES.

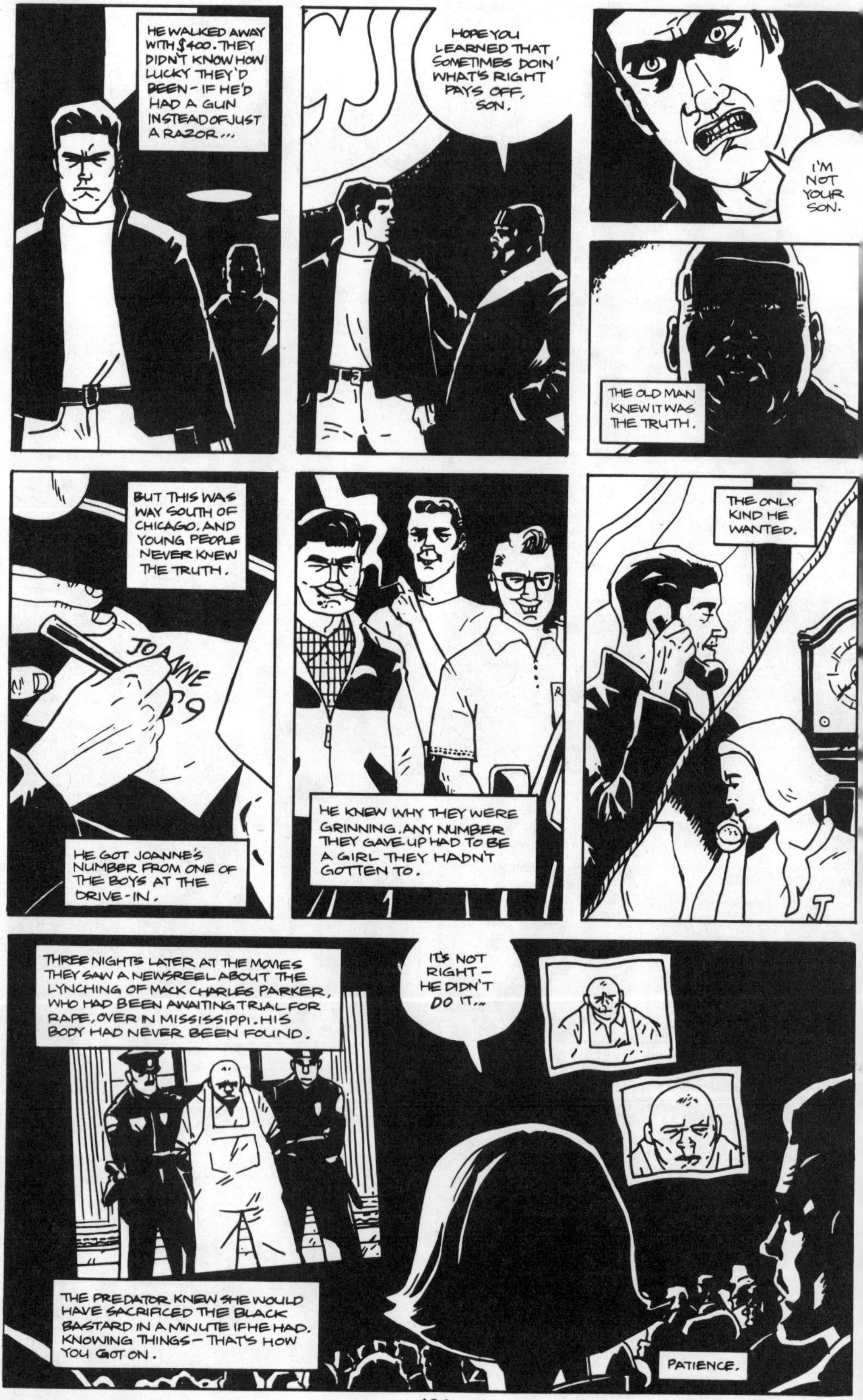
HE WALKED AWAY WITH $400. THEY DIDN'T KNOW HOW LUCKY THEY'D BEEN - IF HE'D HAD A GUN INSTEAD OF JUST A RAZOR...
HOPE YOU LEARNED THAT SOMETIMES DOIN' WHAT'S RIGHT PAYS OFF, SON.
I'M NOT YOUR SON.
THE OLD MAN KNEW IT WAS THE TRUTH.
BUT THIS WAS WAY SOUTH OF CHICAGO, AND YOUNG PEOPLE NEVER KNEW THE TRUTH.
JOANNE
HE GOT JOANNE'S NUMBER FROM ONE OF THE BOYS AT THE DRIVE-IN.
HE KNEW WHY THEY WERE GRINNING. ANY NUMBER THEY GAVE UP HAD TO BE A GIRL THEY HADN'T GOTTEN TO.
THE ONLY KIND HE WANTED.
THREE NIGHTS LATER AT THE MOVIES THEY SAW A NEWSREEL ABOUT THE LYNCHING OF MACK CHARLES PARKER, WHO HAD BEEN AWAITING TRIAL FOR RAPE, OVER IN MISSISSIPPI. HIS BODY HAD NEVER BEEN FOUND.
IT'S NOT RIGHT - HE DIDN'T DO IT...
THE PREDATOR KNEW SHE WOULD HAVE SACRIFICED THE BLACK BASTARD IN A MINUTE IF HE HAD. KNOWING THINGS - THAT'S HOW YOU GOT ON.
PATIENCE.

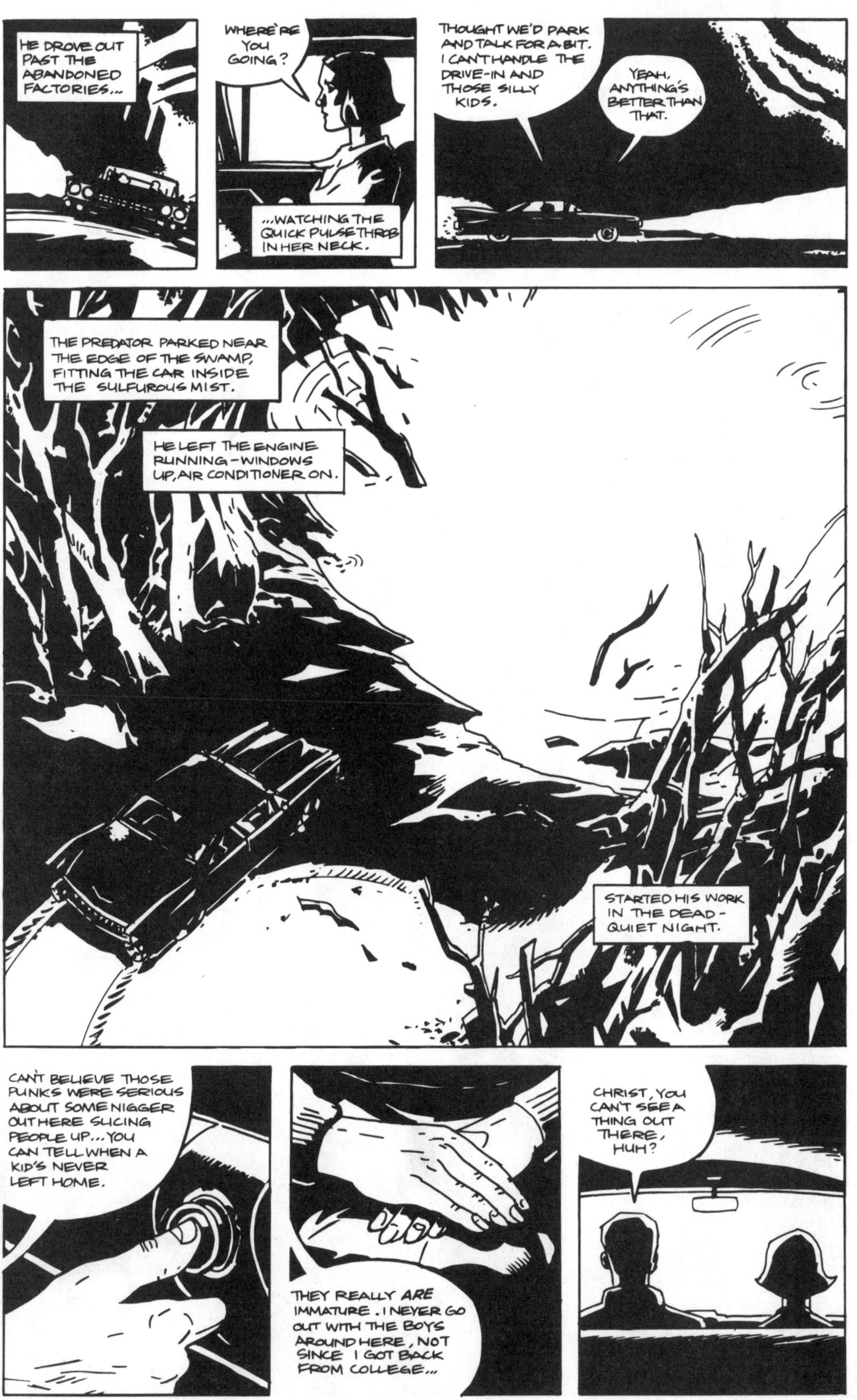

HE DROVE OUT PAST THE ABANDONED FACTORIES...
WHERE'RE YOU GOING?
...WATCHING THE QUICK PULSE THROB IN HER NECK.
THOUGHT WE'D PARK AND TALK FOR A BIT. I CAN'T HANDLE THE DRIVE-IN AND THOSE SILLY KIDS.
YEAH, ANYTHING'S BETTER THAN THAT.
THE PREDATOR PARKED NEAR THE EDGE OF THE SWAMP, FITTING THE CAR INSIDE THE SULFUROUS MIST.
HE LEFT THE ENGINE RUNNING - WINDOWS UP, AIR CONDITIONER ON.
STARTED HIS WORK IN THE DEAD-QUIET NIGHT.
CAN'T BELIEVE THOSE PUNKS WERE SERIOUS ABOUT SOME NIGGER OUT HERE SLICING PEOPLE UP... YOU CAN TELL WHEN A KID'S NEVER LEFT HOME.
THEY REALLY ARE IMMATURE. I NEVER GO OUT WITH THE BOYS AROUND HERE, NOT SINCE I GOT BACK FROM COLLEGE...
CHRIST, YOU CAN'T SEE A THING OUT THERE, HUH?

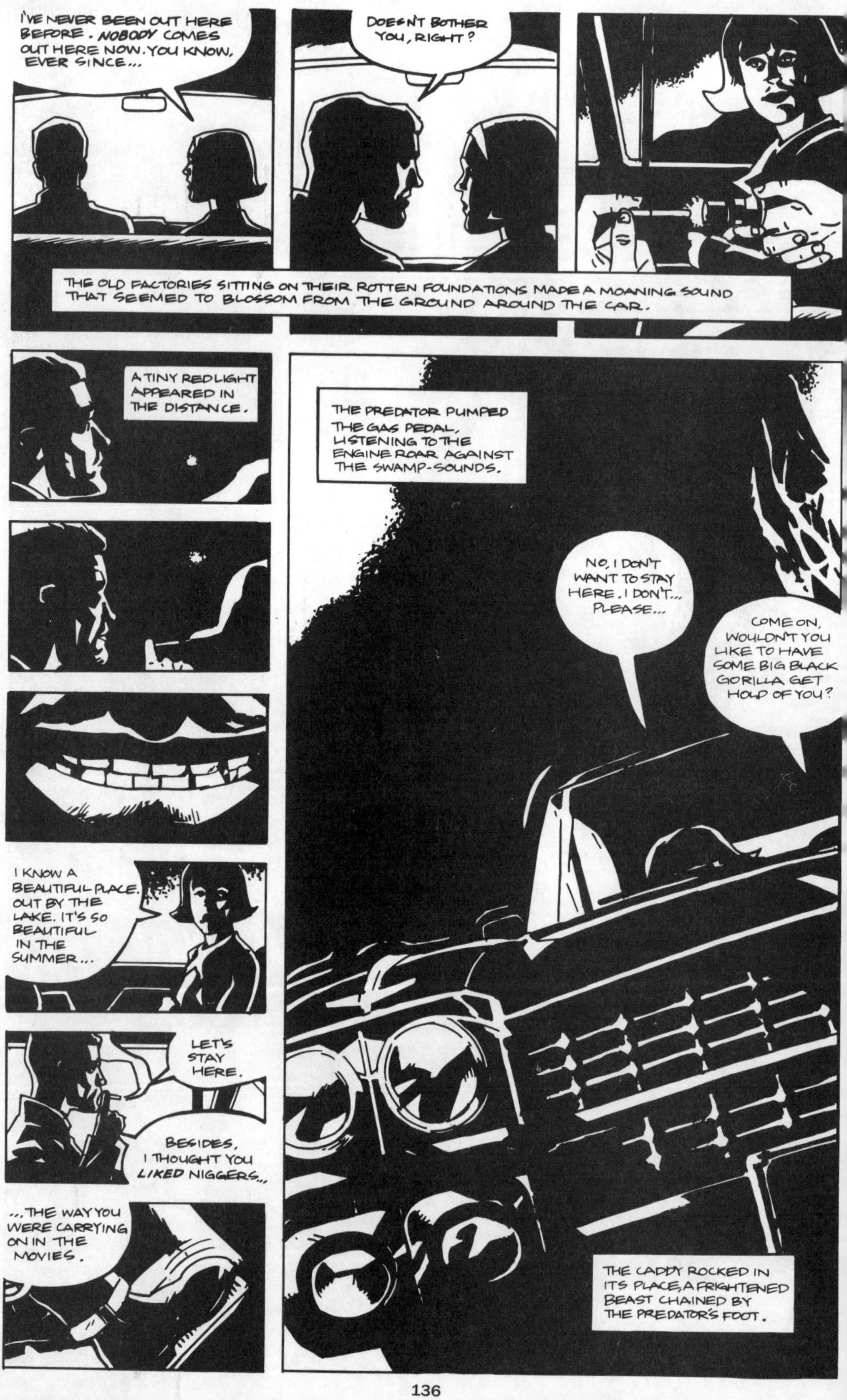

I'VE NEVER BEEN OUT HERE BEFORE. NOBODY COMES OUT HERE NOW. YOU KNOW, EVER SINCE...
DOESN'T BOTHER YOU, RIGHT?
THE OLD FACTORIES SITTING ON THEIR ROTTEN FOUNDATIONS MADE A MOANING SOUND THAT SEEMED TO BLOSSOM FROM THE GROUND AROUND THE CAR.
A TINY RED LIGHT APPEARED IN THE DISTANCE.
I KNOW A BEAUTIFUL PLACE. OUT BY THE LAKE. IT'S SO BEAUTIFUL IN THE SUMMER...
LET'S STAY HERE.
BESIDES, I THOUGHT YOU LIKED NIGGERS...
...THE WAY YOU WERE CARRYING ON IN THE MOVIES.
THE PREDATOR PUMPED THE GAS PEDAL, LISTENING TO THE ENGINE ROAR AGAINST THE SWAMP-SOUNDS.
NO, I DON'T WANT TO STAY HERE. I DON'T... PLEASE...
COME ON, WOULDN'T YOU LIKE TO HAVE SOME BIG BLACK GORILLA GET HOLD OF YOU?
THE CADDY ROCKED IN ITS PLACE, A FRIGHTENED BEAST CHAINED BY THE PREDATOR'S FOOT.

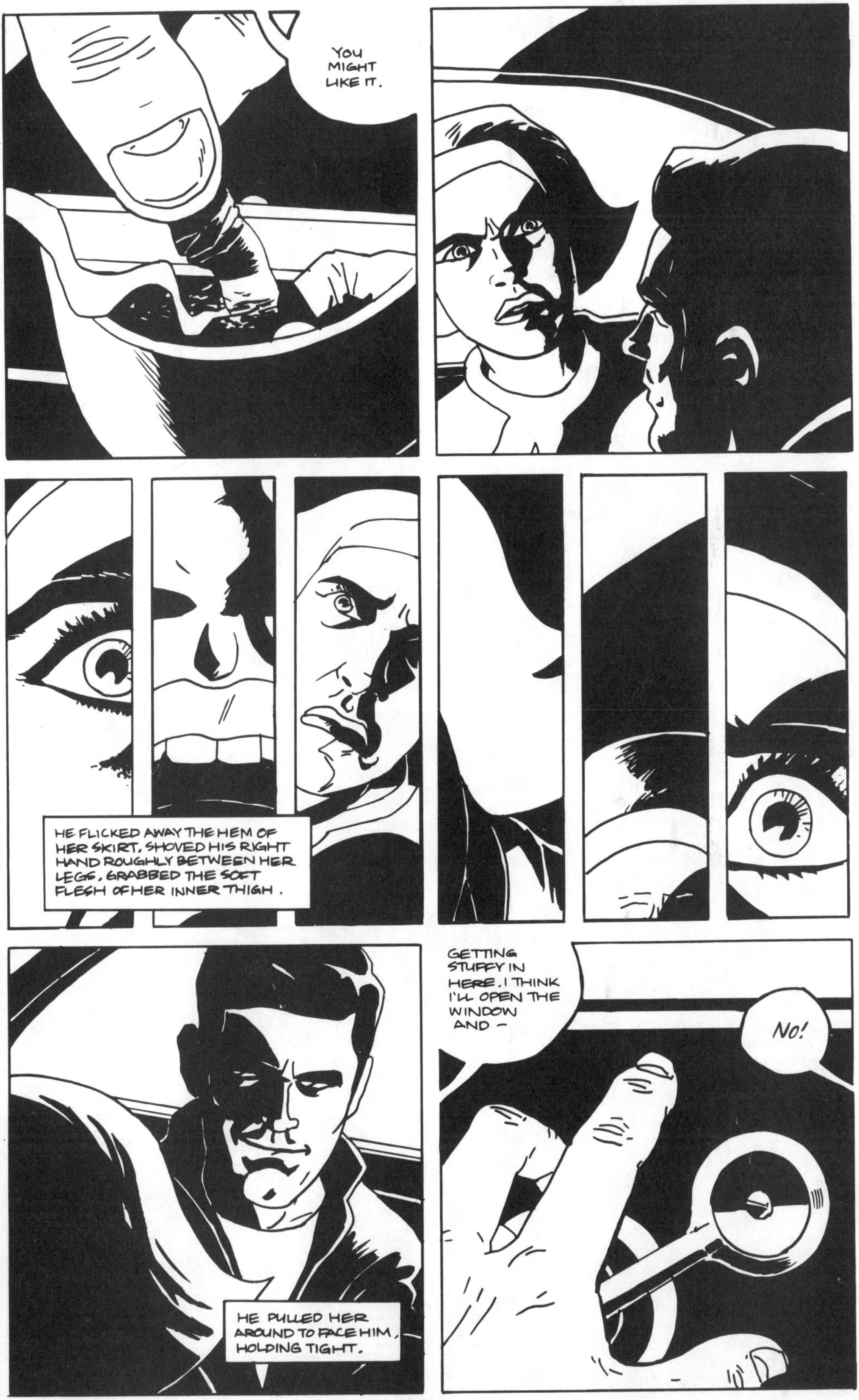
YOU MIGHT LIKE IT.
HE FLICKED AWAY THE HEM OF HER SKIRT, SHOVED HIS RIGHT HAND ROUGHLY BETWEEN HER LEGS, GRABBED THE SOFT FLESH OF HER INNER THIGH.
HE PULLED HER AROUND TO FACE HIM, HOLDING TIGHT.
GETTING STUFFY IN HERE. I THINK I'LL OPEN THE WINDOW AND -
NO!

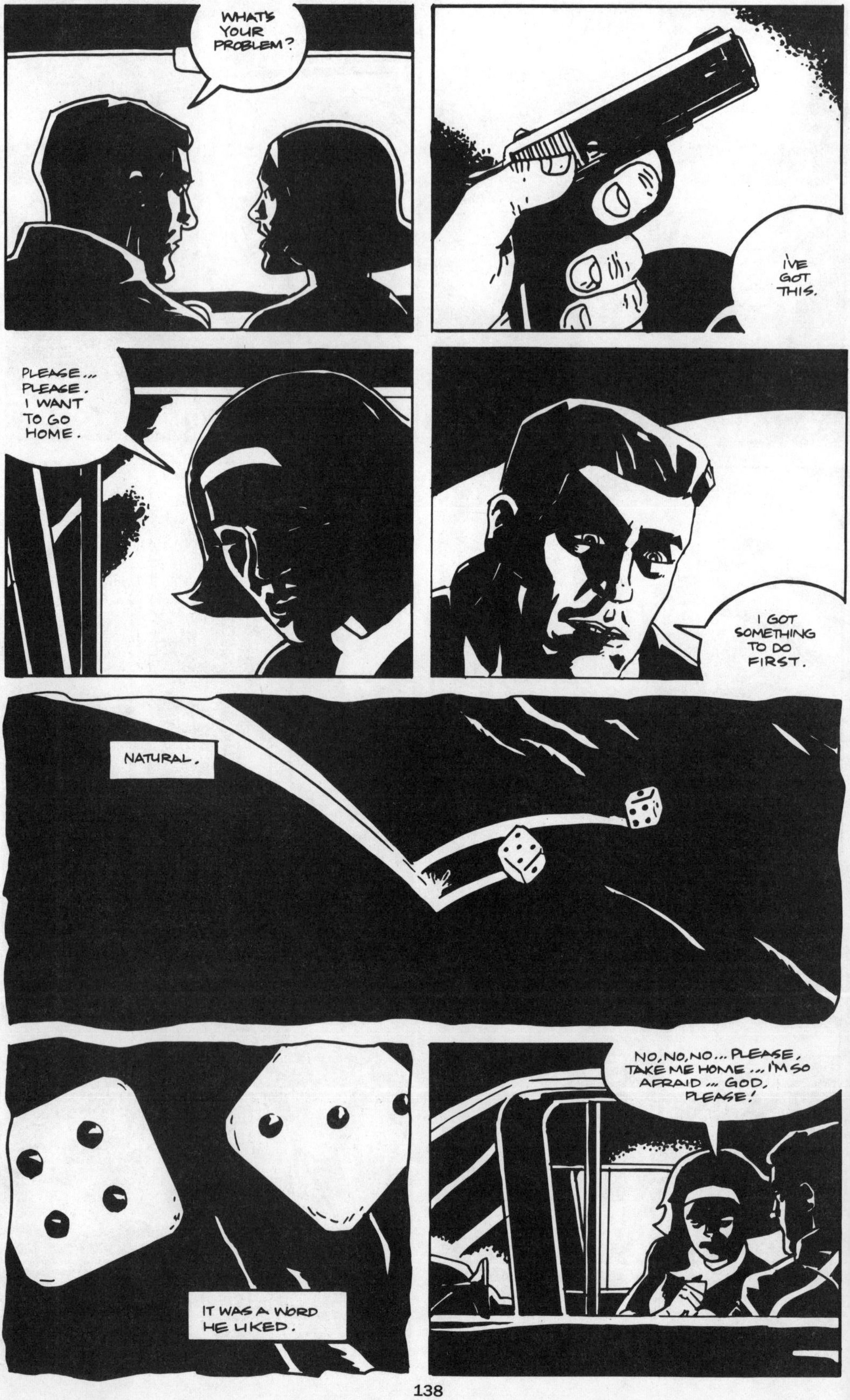
WHAT'S YOUR PROBLEM?
I'VE GOT THIS.
PLEASE... PLEASE. I WANT TO GO HOME.
I GOT SOMETHING TO DO FIRST.
NATURAL.
IT WAS A WORD HE LIKED.
NO, NO, NO... PLEASE, TAKE ME HOME... I'M SO AFRAID... GOD, PLEASE!

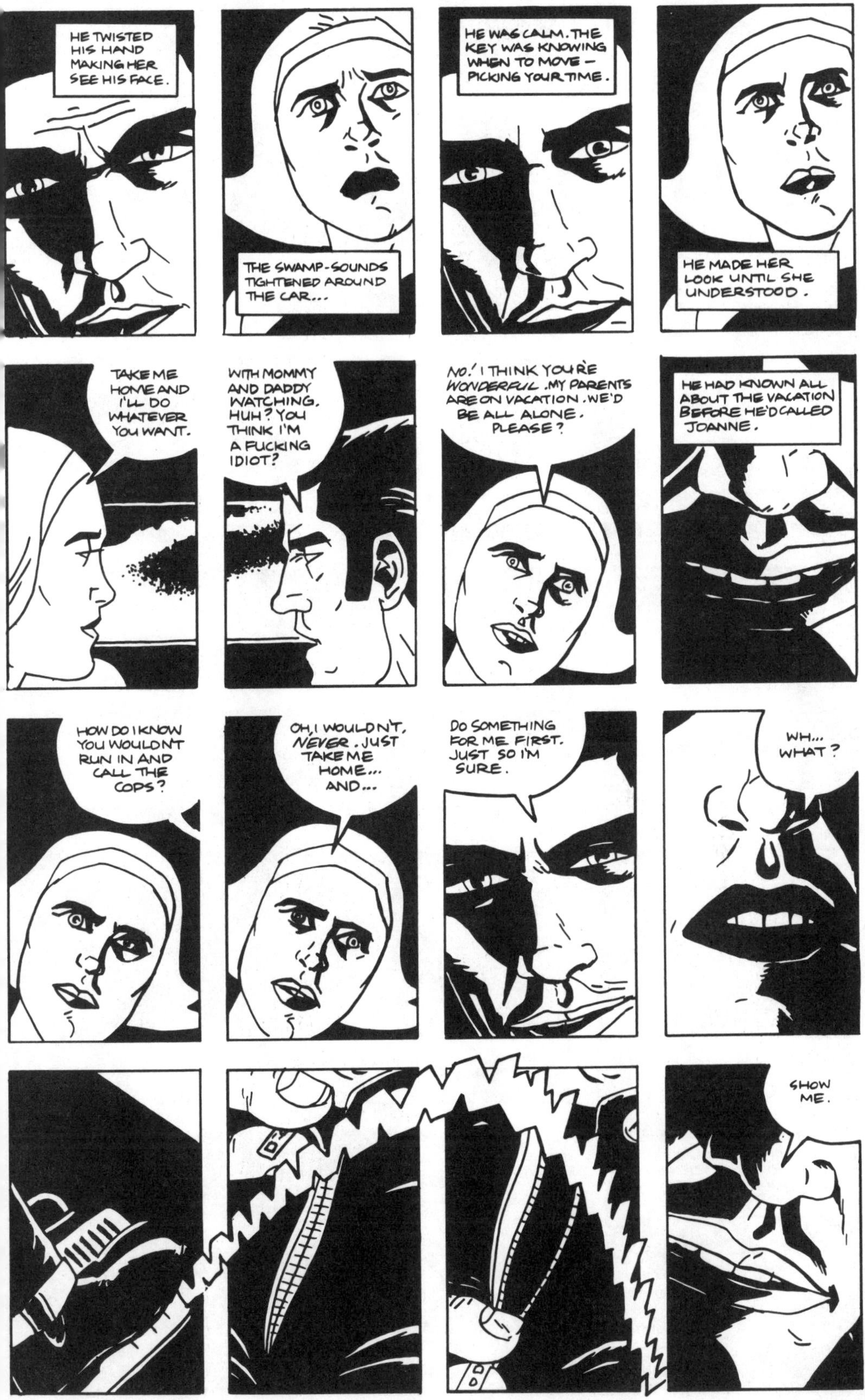
HE TWISTED HIS HAND MAKING HER SEE HIS FACE.
THE SWAMP-SOUNDS TIGHTENED AROUND THE CAR...
HE WAS CALM. THE KEY WAS KNOWING WHEN TO MOVE — PICKING YOUR TIME.
HE MADE HER LOOK UNTIL SHE UNDERSTOOD.
TAKE ME HOME AND I'LL DO WHATEVER YOU WANT.
WITH MOMMY AND DADDY WATCHING. HUH? YOU THINK I'M A FUCKING IDIOT?
NO! I THINK YOU'RE WONDERFUL. MY PARENTS ARE ON VACATION. WE'D BE ALL ALONE. PLEASE?
HE HAD KNOWN ALL ABOUT THE VACATION BEFORE HE'D CALLED JOANNE.
HOW DO I KNOW YOU WOULDN'T RUN IN AND CALL THE COPS?
OH, I WOULDN'T, NEVER. JUST TAKE ME HOME... AND...
DO SOMETHING FOR ME FIRST. JUST SO I'M SURE.
WH... WHAT?
SHOW ME.

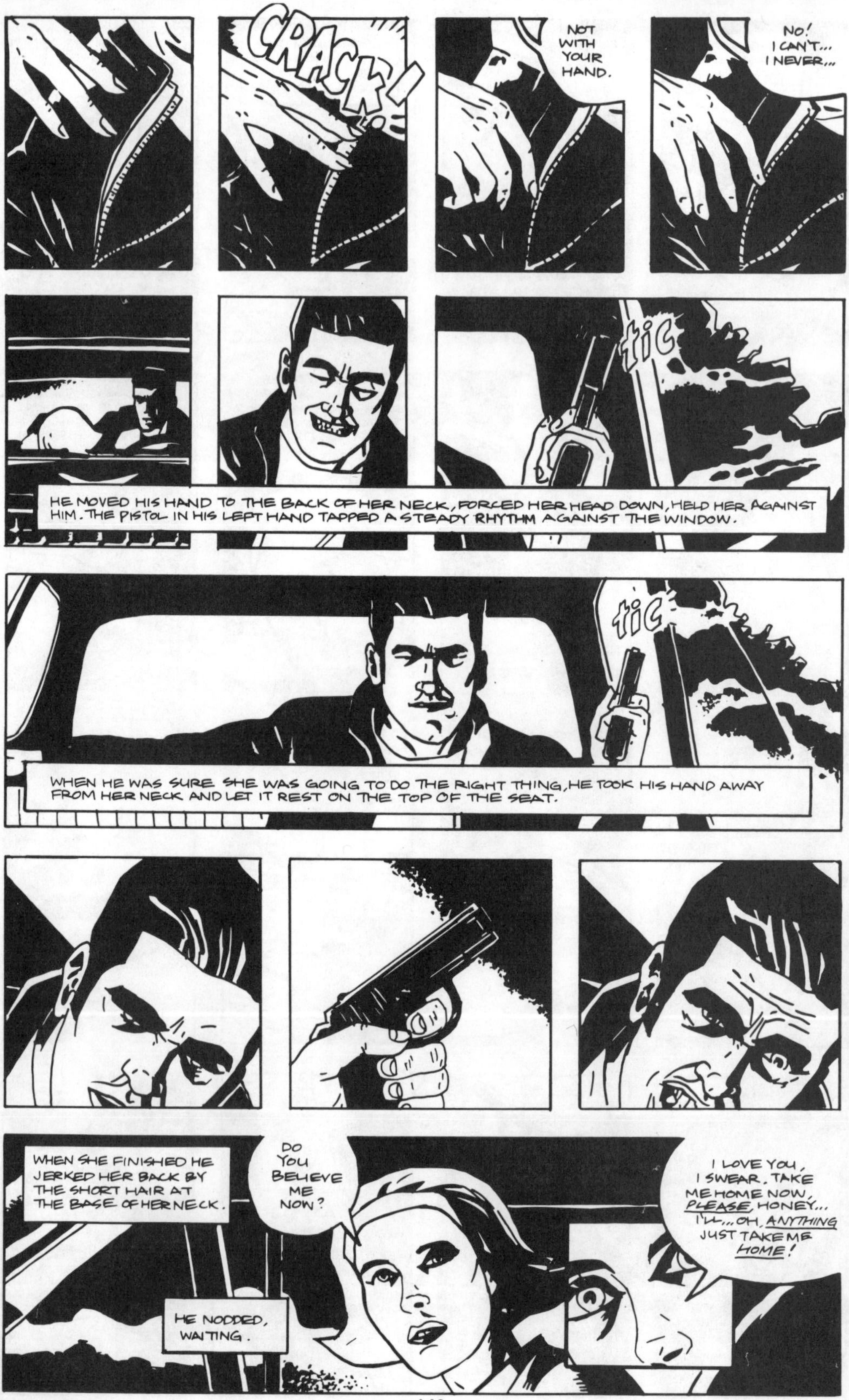
CRACK!
NOT WITH YOUR HAND.
NO! I CAN'T... I NEVER...
tic
HE MOVED HIS HAND TO THE BACK OF HER NECK, FORCED HER HEAD DOWN, HELD HER AGAINST HIM. THE PISTOL IN HIS LEFT HAND TAPPED A STEADY RHYTHM AGAINST THE WINDOW.
tic
WHEN HE WAS SURE SHE WAS GOING TO DO THE RIGHT THING, HE TOOK HIS HAND AWAY FROM HER NECK AND LET IT REST ON THE TOP OF THE SEAT.
WHEN SHE FINISHED HE JERKED HER BACK BY THE SHORT HAIR AT THE BASE OF HER NECK.
DO YOU BELIEVE ME NOW?
I LOVE YOU, I SWEAR. TAKE ME HOME NOW, PLEASE, HONEY... I'LL... OH, ANYTHING JUST TAKE ME HOME!
HE NODDED, WAITING.

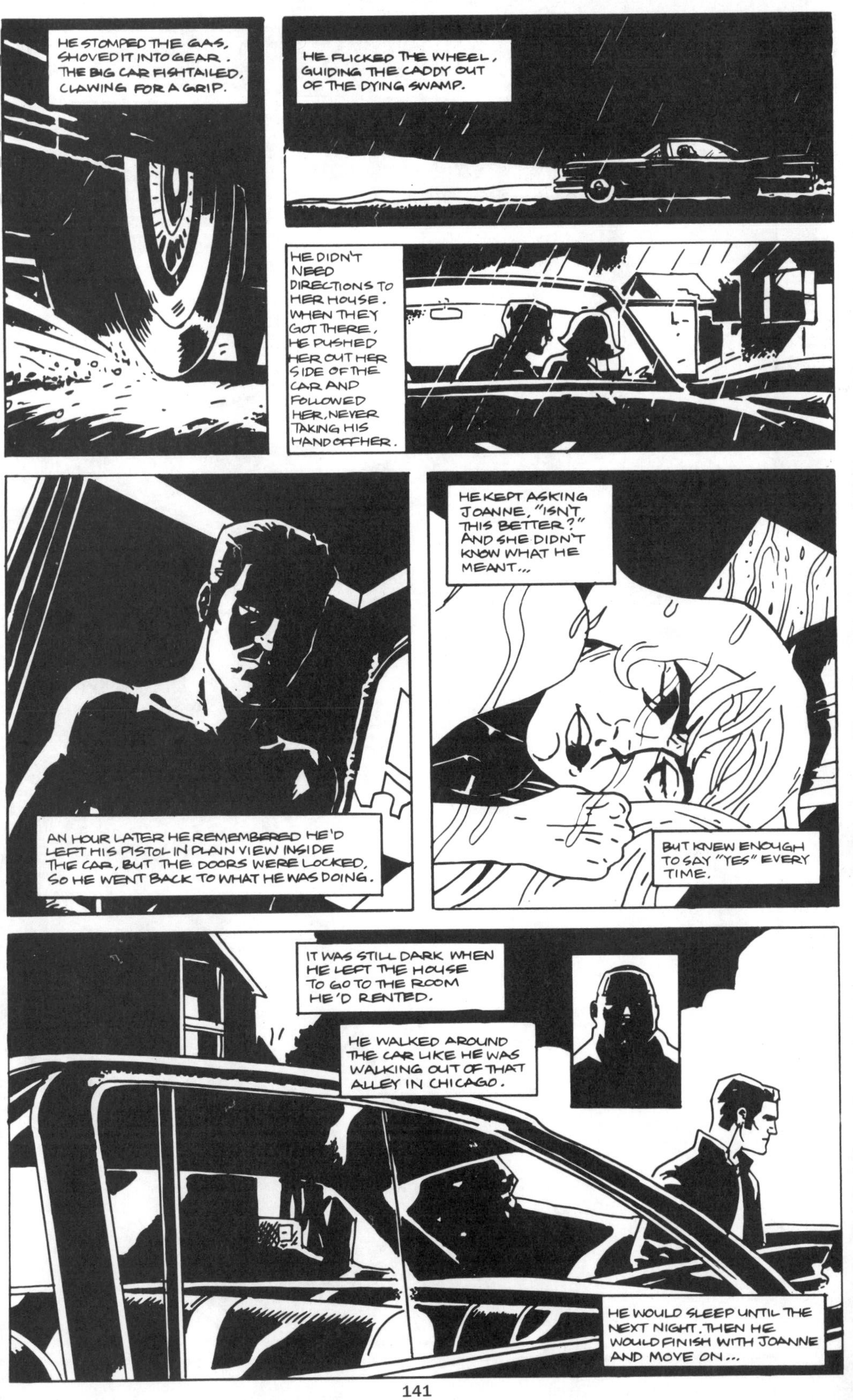
HE STOMPED THE GAS, SHOVED IT INTO GEAR. THE BIG CAR FISHTAILED, CLAWING FOR A GRIP.
HE FLICKED THE WHEEL, GUIDING THE CADDY OUT OF THE DYING SWAMP.
HE DIDN'T NEED DIRECTIONS TO HER HOUSE. WHEN THEY GOT THERE, HE PUSHED HER OUT HER SIDE OF THE CAR AND FOLLOWED HER, NEVER TAKING HIS HAND OFF HER.
AN HOUR LATER HE REMEMBERED HE'D LEFT HIS PISTOL IN PLAIN VIEW INSIDE THE CAR, BUT THE DOORS WERE LOCKED, SO HE WENT BACK TO WHAT HE WAS DOING.
HE KEPT ASKING JOANNE, "ISN'T THIS BETTER?" AND SHE DIDN'T KNOW WHAT HE MEANT...
BUT KNEW ENOUGH TO SAY "YES" EVERY TIME.
IT WAS STILL DARK WHEN HE LEFT THE HOUSE TO GO TO THE ROOM HE'D RENTED.
HE WALKED AROUND THE CAR LIKE HE WAS WALKING OUT OF THAT ALLEY IN CHICAGO.
HE WOULD SLEEP UNTIL THE NEXT NIGHT. THEN HE WOULD FINISH WITH JOANNE AND MOVE ON...

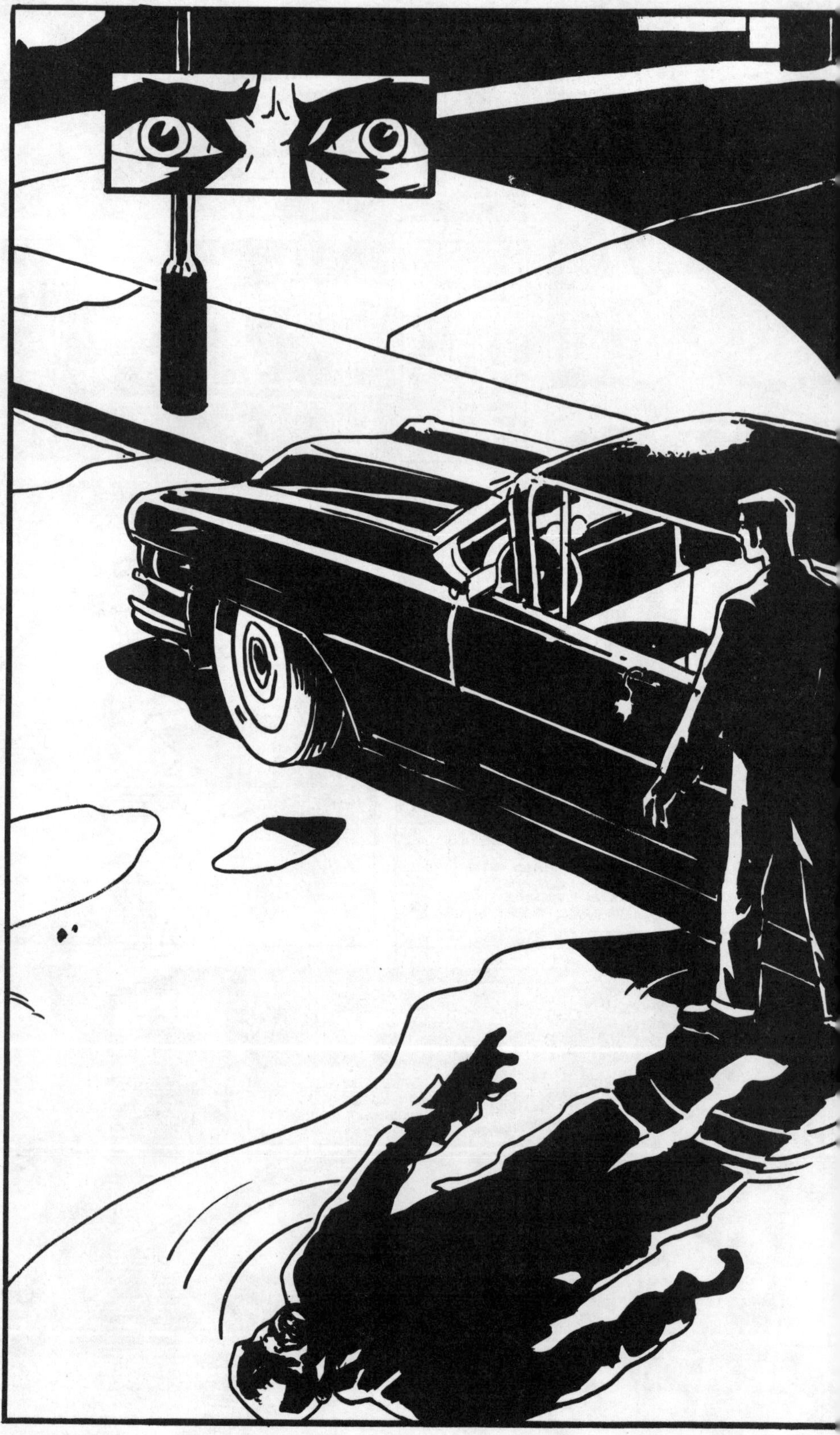

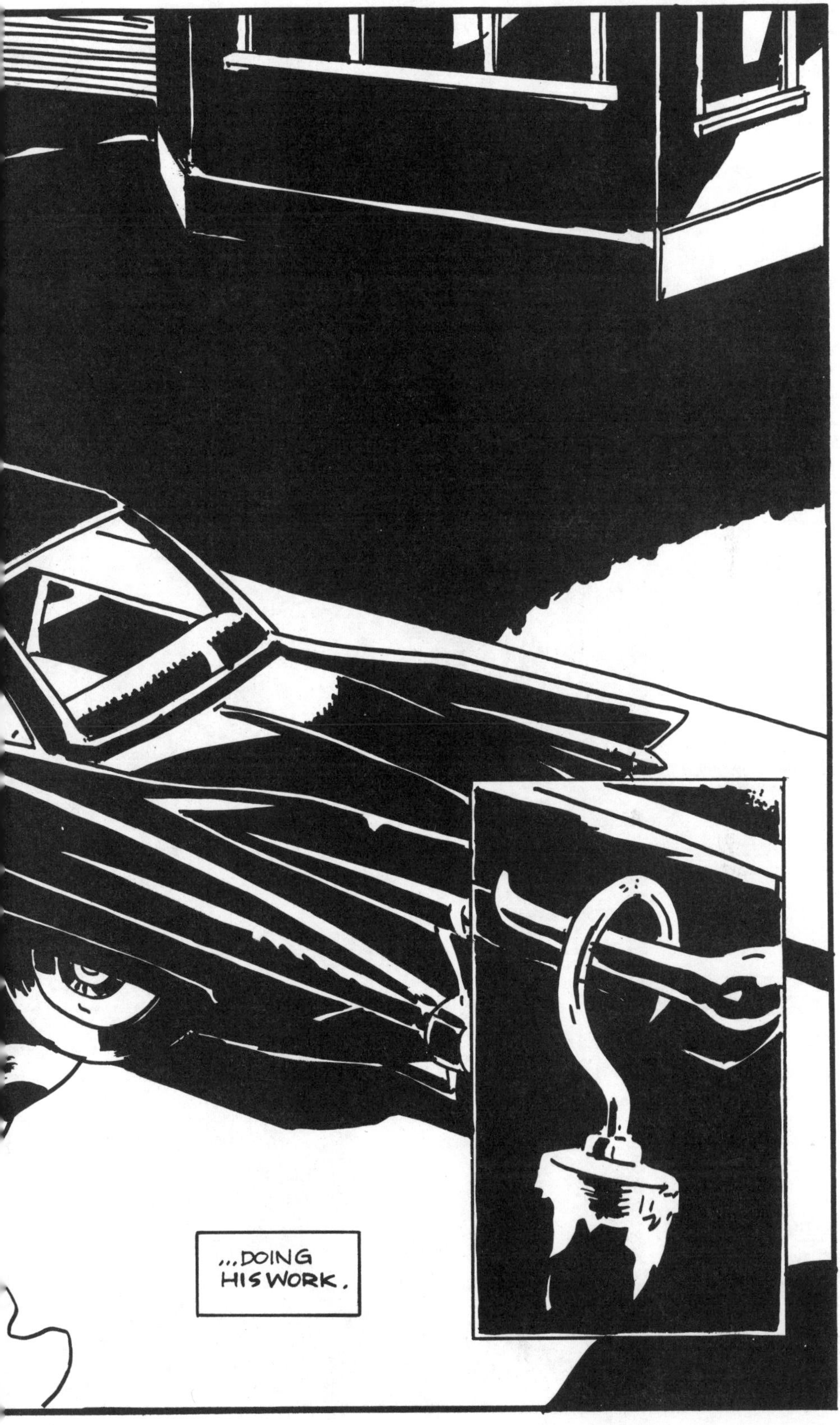
...DOING HIS WORK.

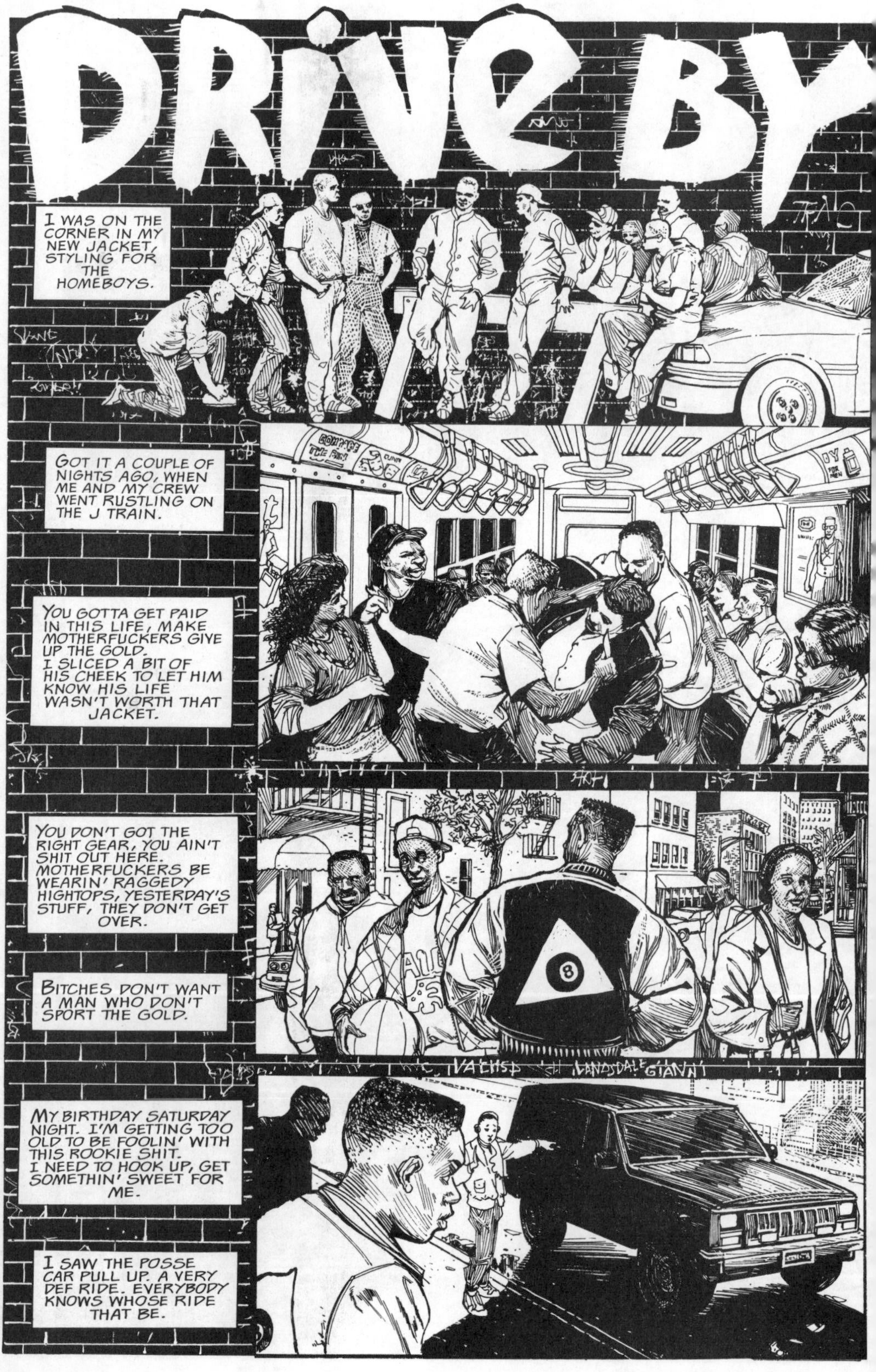
DRIVE BY
I WAS ON THE CORNER IN MY NEW JACKET, STYLING FOR THE HOMEBOYS.
GOT IT A COUPLE OF NIGHTS AGO, WHEN ME AND MY CREW WENT RUSTLING ON THE J TRAIN.
YOU GOTTA GET PAID IN THIS LIFE, MAKE MOTHERFUCKERS GIVE UP THE GOLD. I SLICED A BIT OF HIS CHEEK TO LET HIM KNOW HIS LIFE WASN'T WORTH THAT JACKET.
YOU DON'T GOT THE RIGHT GEAR, YOU AIN'T SHIT OUT HERE. MOTHERFUCKERS BE WEARIN' RAGGEDY HIGHTOPS, YESTERDAY'S STUFF, THEY DON'T GET OVER.
BITCHES DON'T WANT A MAN WHO DON'T SPORT THE GOLD.
VACHSS
LANSDALE GIANNI
MY BIRTHDAY SATURDAY NIGHT. I'M GETTING TOO OLD TO BE FOOLIN' WITH THIS ROOKIE SHIT. I NEED TO HOOK UP, GET SOMETHIN' SWEET FOR ME.
I SAW THE POSSE CAR PULL UP. A VERY DEF RIDE. EVERYBODY KNOWS WHOSE RIDE THAT BE.

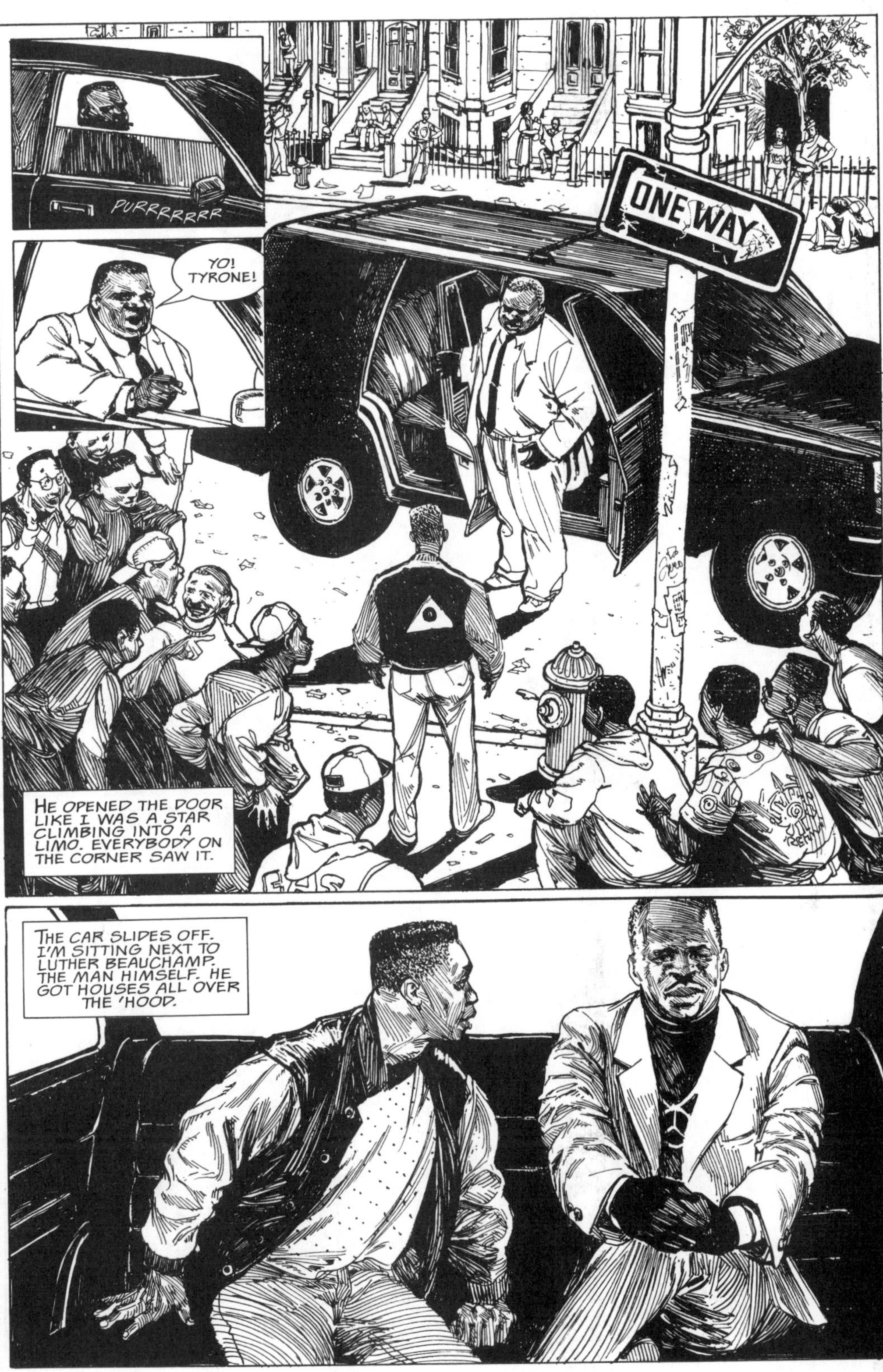
PURRRRRRRR
YO! TYRONE!
ONE WAY
HE OPENED THE DOOR LIKE I WAS A STAR CLIMBING INTO A LIMO. EVERYBODY ON THE CORNER SAW IT.
THE CAR SLIDES OFF. I'M SITTING NEXT TO LUTHER BEAUCHAMP. THE MAN HIMSELF. HE GOT HOUSES ALL OVER THE 'HOOD.

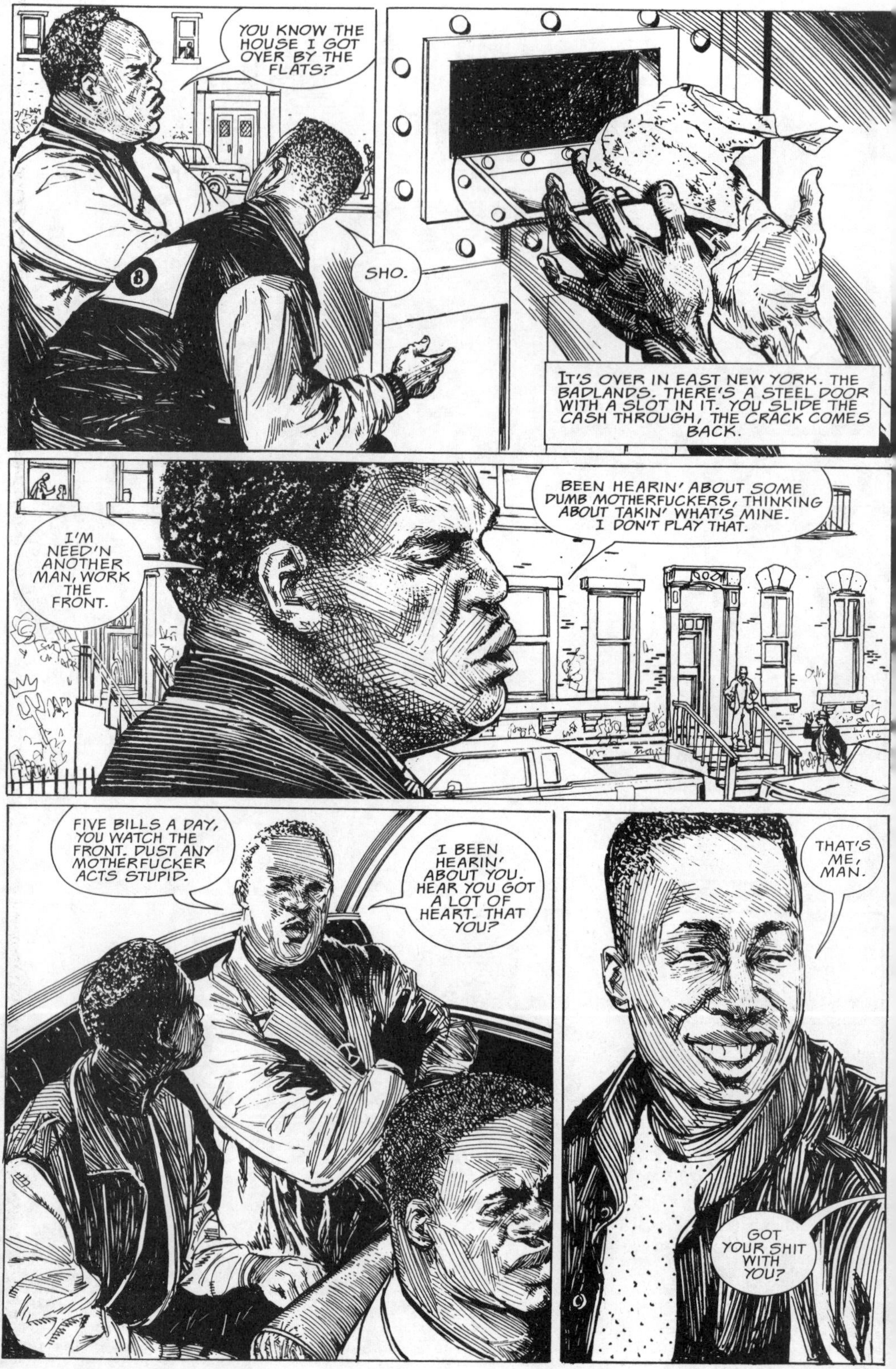
YOU KNOW THE HOUSE I GOT OVER BY THE FLATS?
SHO.
IT'S OVER IN EAST NEW YORK. THE BADLANDS. THERE'S A STEEL DOOR WITH A SLOT IN IT. YOU SLIDE THE CASH THROUGH, THE CRACK COMES BACK.
I'M NEED'N ANOTHER MAN, WORK THE FRONT.
BEEN HEARIN' ABOUT SOME DUMB MOTHERFUCKERS, THINKING ABOUT TAKIN' WHAT'S MINE. I DON'T PLAY THAT.
FIVE BILLS A DAY, YOU WATCH THE FRONT. DUST ANY MOTHERFUCKER ACTS STUPID.
I BEEN HEARIN' ABOUT YOU. HEAR YOU GOT A LOT OF HEART. THAT YOU?
THAT'S ME, MAN.
GOT YOUR SHIT WITH YOU?

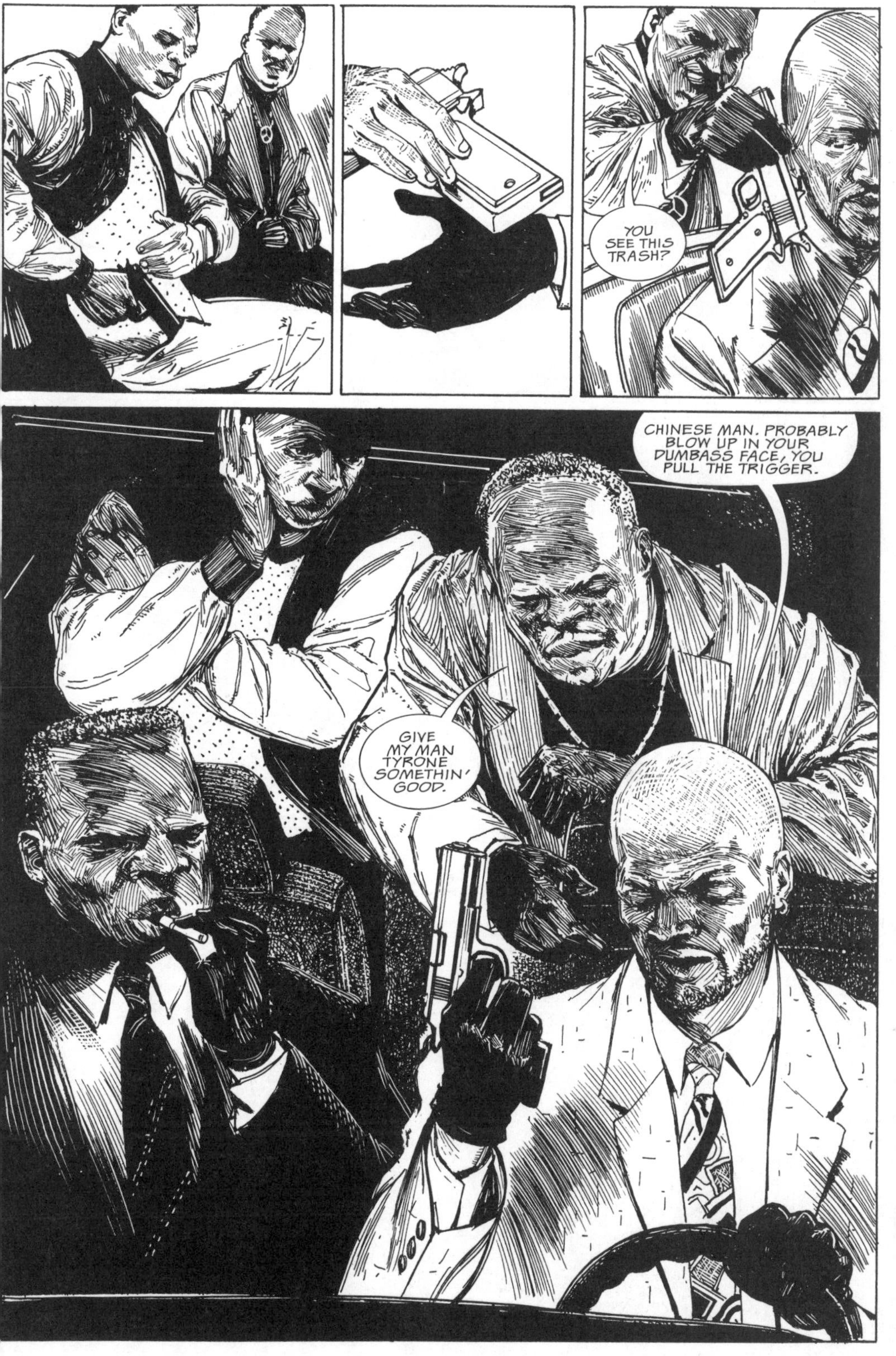
YOU SEE THIS TRASH?
CHINESE MAN. PROBABLY BLOW UP IN YOUR DUMBASS FACE, YOU PULL THE TRIGGER.
GIVE MY MAN TYRONE SOMETHIN' GOOD.

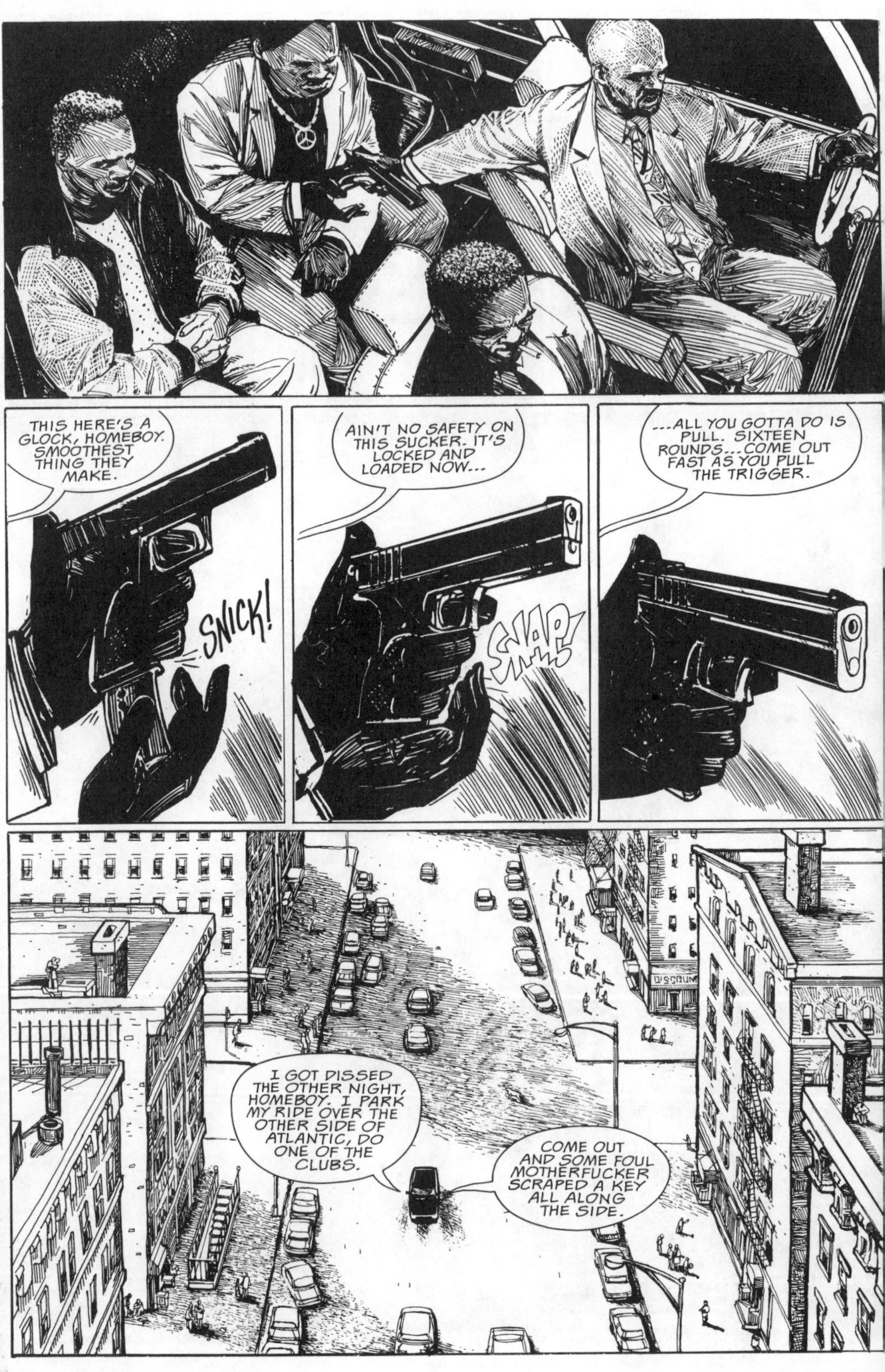
THIS HERE'S A GLOCK, HOMEBOY. SMOOTHEST THING THEY MAKE.
SNICK!
AIN'T NO SAFETY ON THIS SUCKER. IT'S LOCKED AND LOADED NOW...
SNAP!
...ALL YOU GOTTA DO IS PULL. SIXTEEN ROUNDS...COME OUT FAST AS YOU PULL THE TRIGGER.
DISCOUN
I GOT DISSED THE OTHER NIGHT, HOMEBOY. I PARK MY RIDE OVER THE OTHER SIDE OF ATLANTIC, DO ONE OF THE CLUBS.
COME OUT AND SOME FOUL MOTHERFUCKER SCRAPED A KEY ALL ALONG THE SIDE.

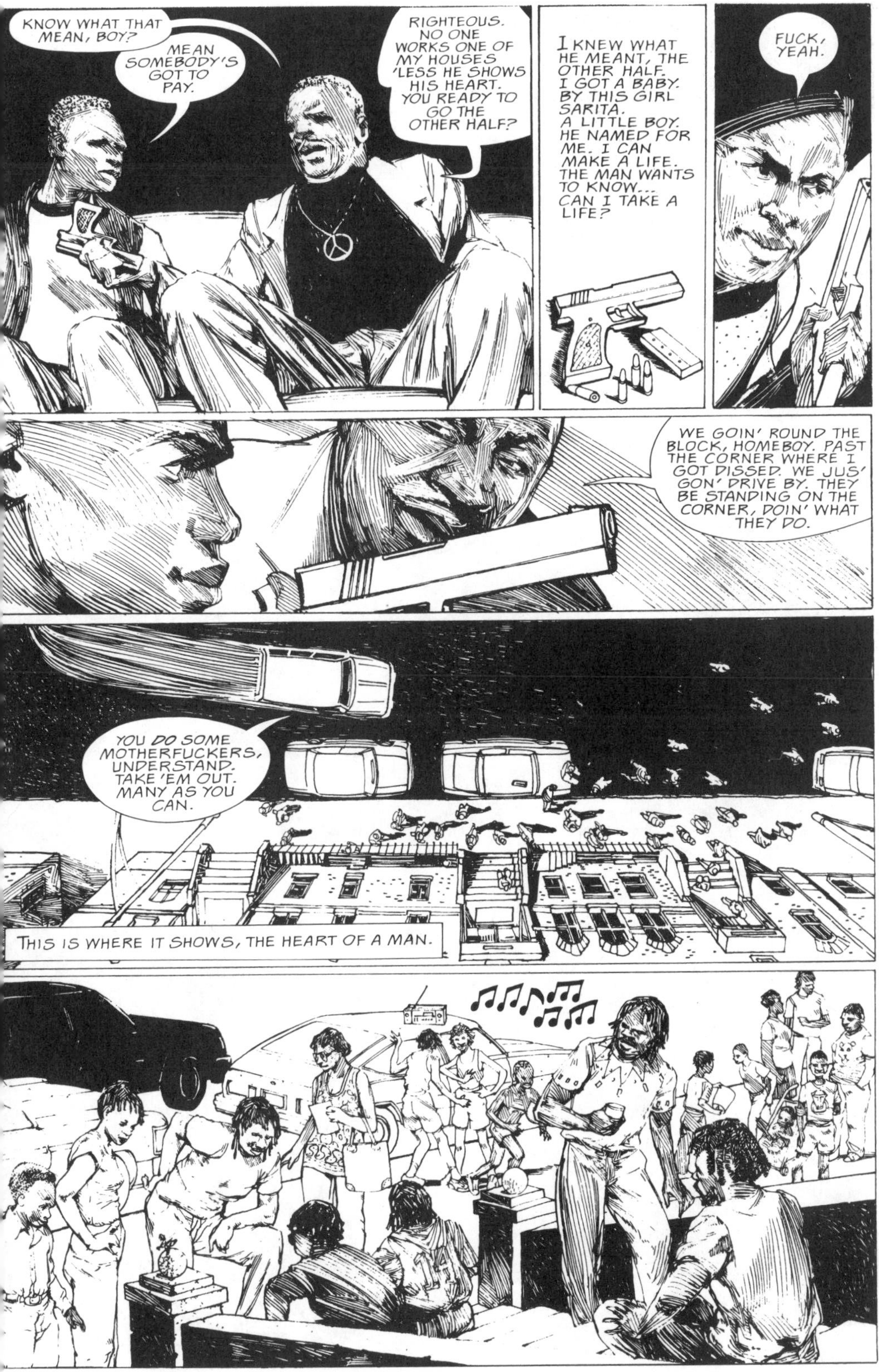
KNOW WHAT THAT MEAN, BOY?
MEAN SOMEBODY'S GOT TO PAY.
RIGHTEOUS. NO ONE WORKS ONE OF MY HOUSES 'LESS HE SHOWS HIS HEART. YOU READY TO GO THE OTHER HALF?
I KNEW WHAT HE MEANT, THE OTHER HALF. I GOT A BABY. BY THIS GIRL SARITA. A LITTLE BOY. HE NAMED FOR ME. I CAN MAKE A LIFE. THE MAN WANTS TO KNOW... CAN I TAKE A LIFE?
FUCK, YEAH.
WE GOIN' ROUND THE BLOCK, HOMEBOY. PAST THE CORNER WHERE I GOT DISSED. WE JUS' GON' DRIVE BY. THEY BE STANDING ON THE CORNER, DOIN' WHAT THEY DO.
YOU DO SOME MOTHERFUCKERS, UNDERSTAND. TAKE 'EM OUT. MANY AS YOU CAN.
THIS IS WHERE IT SHOWS, THE HEART OF A MAN.

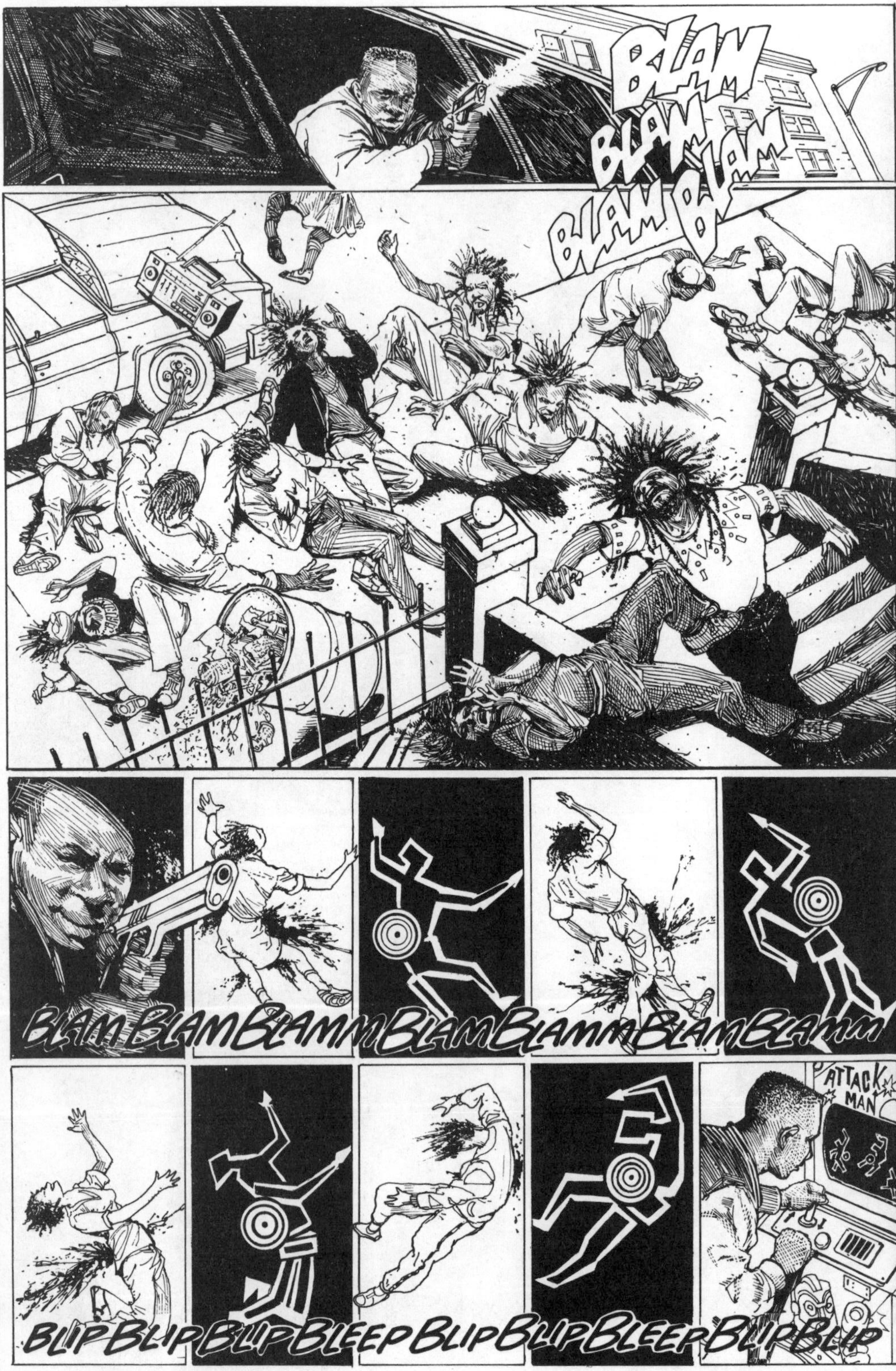
BLAM
BLAM
BLAM
BLAM
BLAM
BLAM BLAM BLAMM BLAM BLAMM BLAM BLAMM
ATTACK MAN
BLIP BLIP BLIP BLEEP BLIP BLIP BLEEP BLIP BLIP

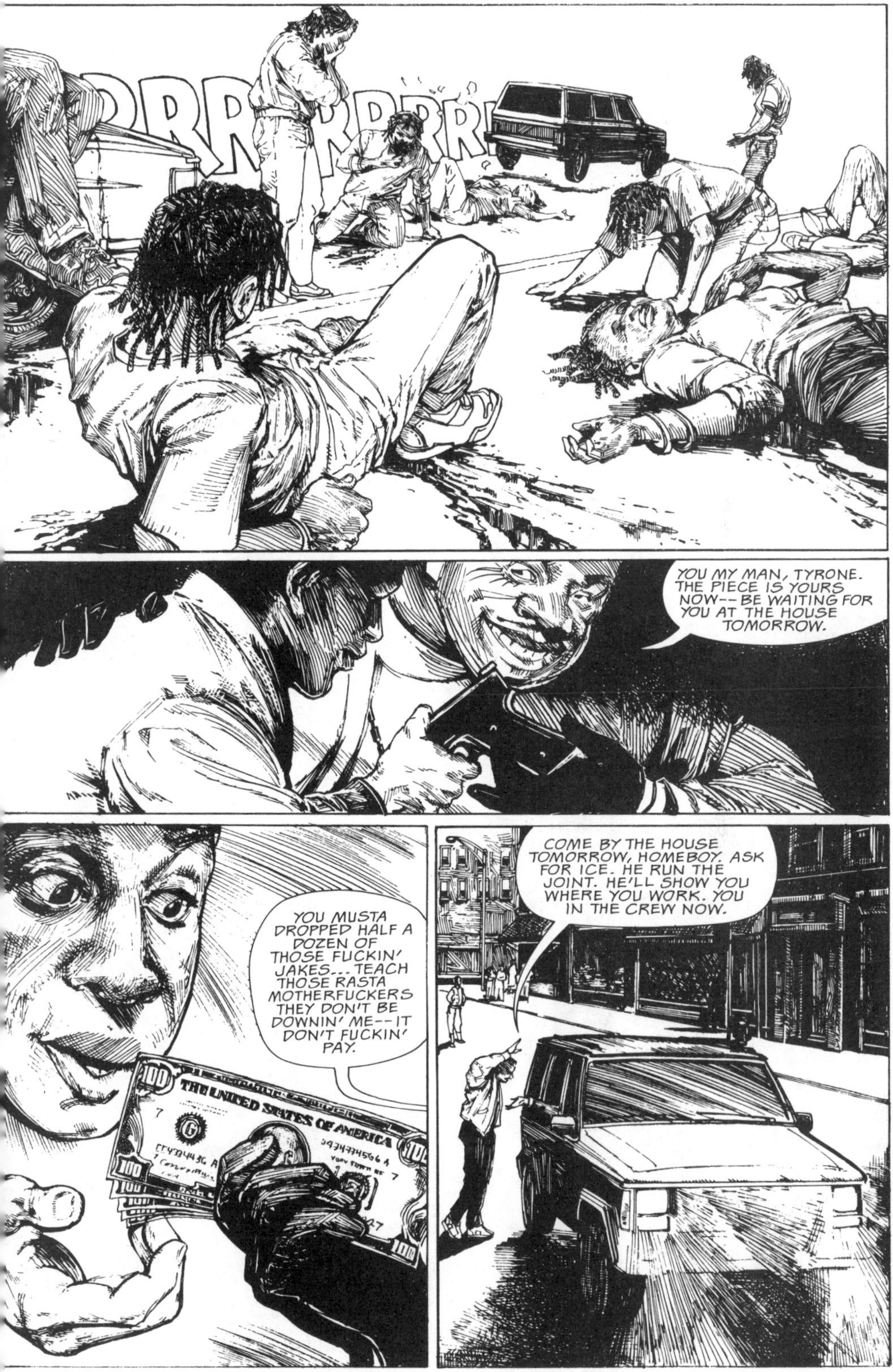
RRRRRRRR
YOU MY MAN, TYRONE. THE PIECE IS YOURS NOW--BE WAITING FOR YOU AT THE HOUSE TOMORROW.
YOU MUSTA DROPPED HALF A DOZEN OF THOSE FUCKIN' JAKES... TEACH THOSE RASTA MOTHERFUCKERS THEY DON'T BE DOWNIN' ME--IT DON'T FUCKIN' PAY.
THE UNITED STATES OF AMERICA
COME BY THE HOUSE TOMORROW, HOMEBOY. ASK FOR ICE. HE RUN THE JOINT. HE'LL SHOW YOU WHERE YOU WORK. YOU IN THE CREW NOW.

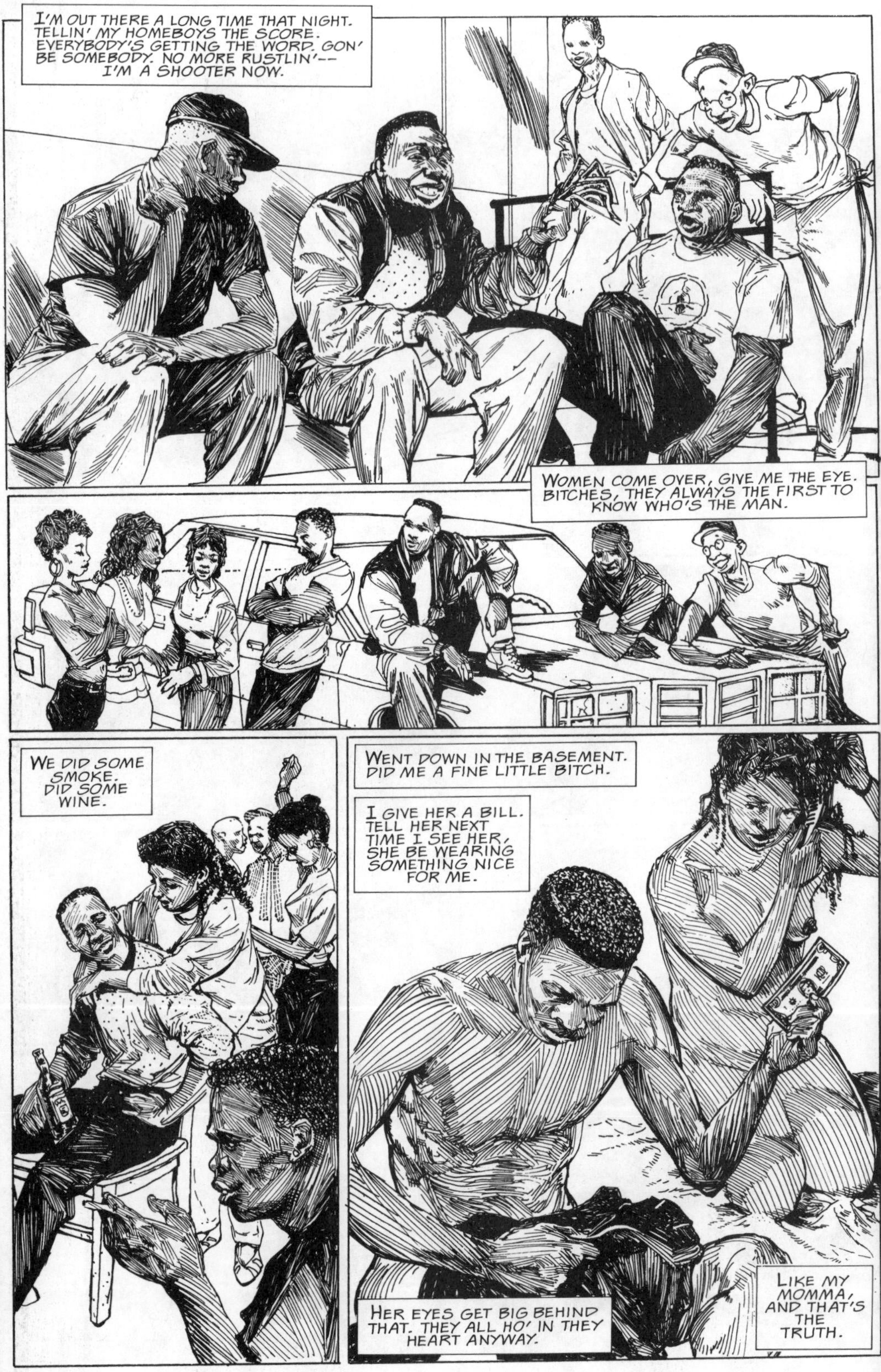
I'M OUT THERE A LONG TIME THAT NIGHT. TELLIN' MY HOMEBOYS THE SCORE. EVERYBODY'S GETTING THE WORD. GON' BE SOMEBODY. NO MORE RUSTLIN'-- I'M A SHOOTER NOW.
WOMEN COME OVER, GIVE ME THE EYE. BITCHES, THEY ALWAYS THE FIRST TO KNOW WHO'S THE MAN.
WE DID SOME SMOKE. DID SOME WINE.
WENT DOWN IN THE BASEMENT. DID ME A FINE LITTLE BITCH.
I GIVE HER A BILL. TELL HER NEXT TIME I SEE HER, SHE BE WEARING SOMETHING NICE FOR ME.
HER EYES GET BIG BEHIND THAT. THEY ALL HO' IN THEY HEART ANYWAY.
LIKE MY MOMMA, AND THAT'S THE TRUTH.

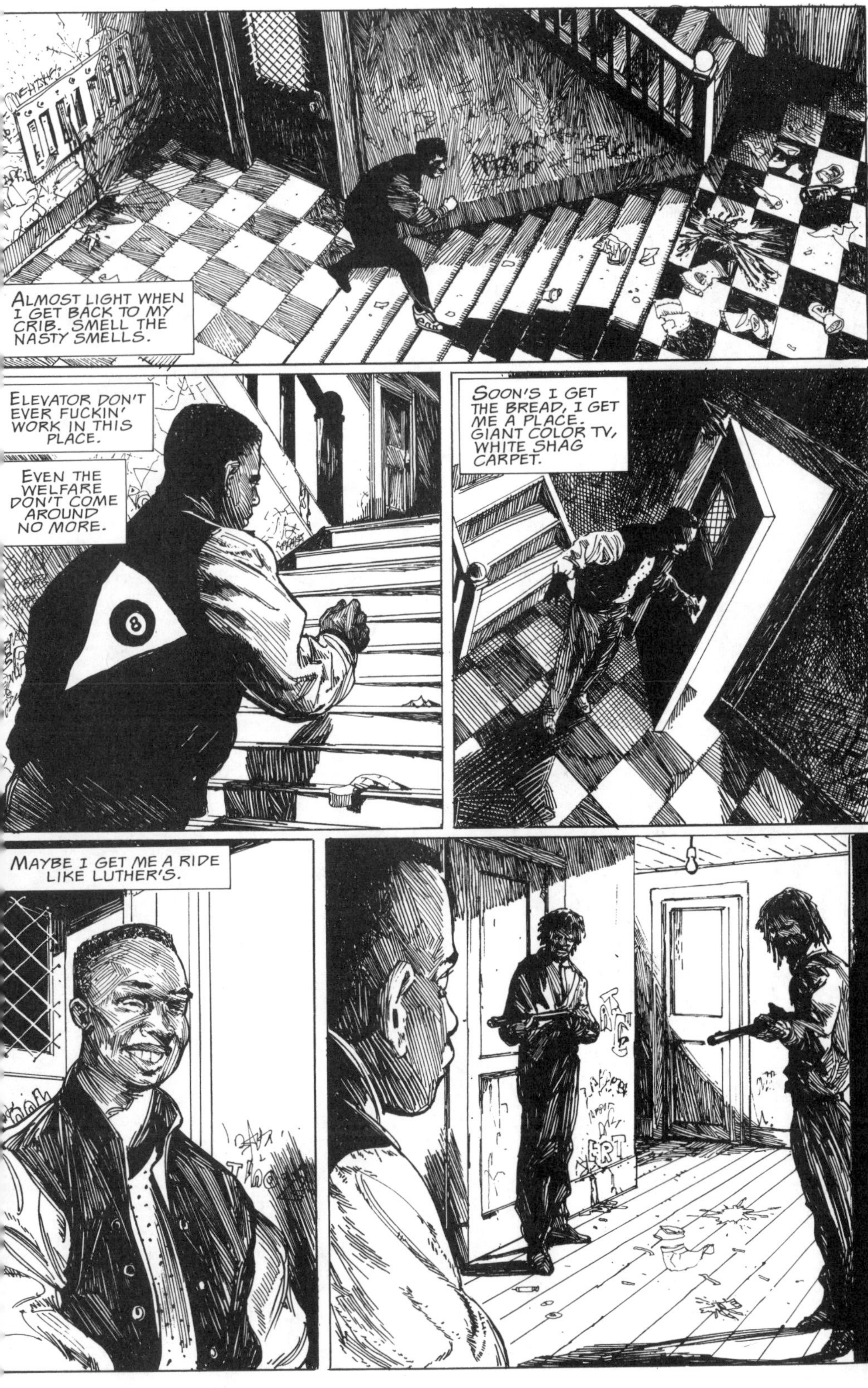
ALMOST LIGHT WHEN I GET BACK TO MY CRIB. SMELL THE NASTY SMELLS.
ELEVATOR DON'T EVER FUCKIN' WORK IN THIS PLACE.
EVEN THE WELFARE DON'T COME AROUND NO MORE.
SOON'S I GET THE BREAD, I GET ME A PLACE. GIANT COLOR TV, WHITE SHAG CARPET.
MAYBE I GET ME A RIDE LIKE LUTHER'S.

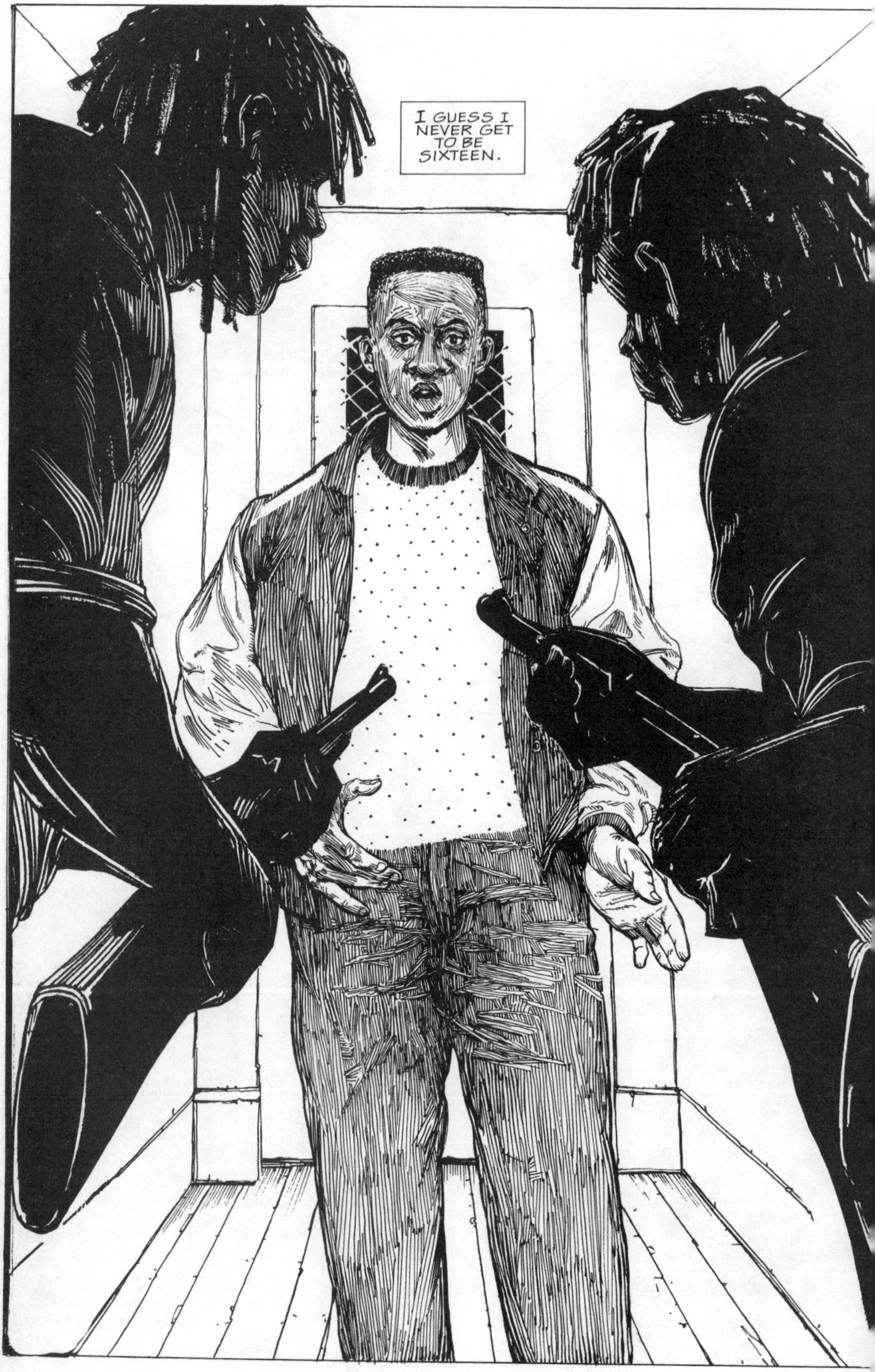
I GUESS I NEVER GET TO BE SIXTEEN.

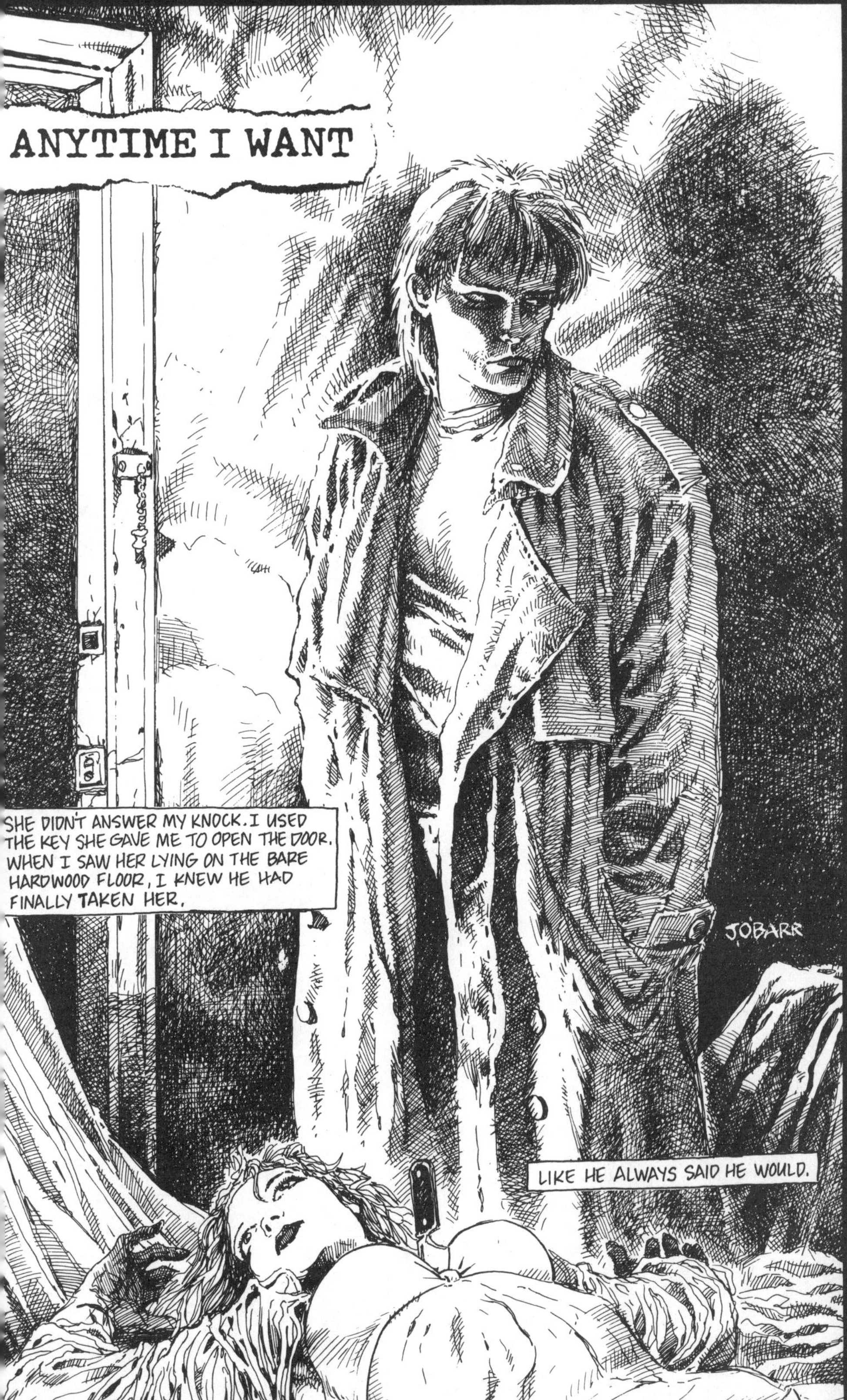
ANYTIME I WANT
SHE DIDN'T ANSWER MY KNOCK. I USED THE KEY SHE GAVE ME TO OPEN THE DOOR. WHEN I SAW HER LYING ON THE BARE HARDWOOD FLOOR, I KNEW HE HAD FINALLY TAKEN HER.
J.O'BARR
LIKE HE ALWAYS SAID HE WOULD.

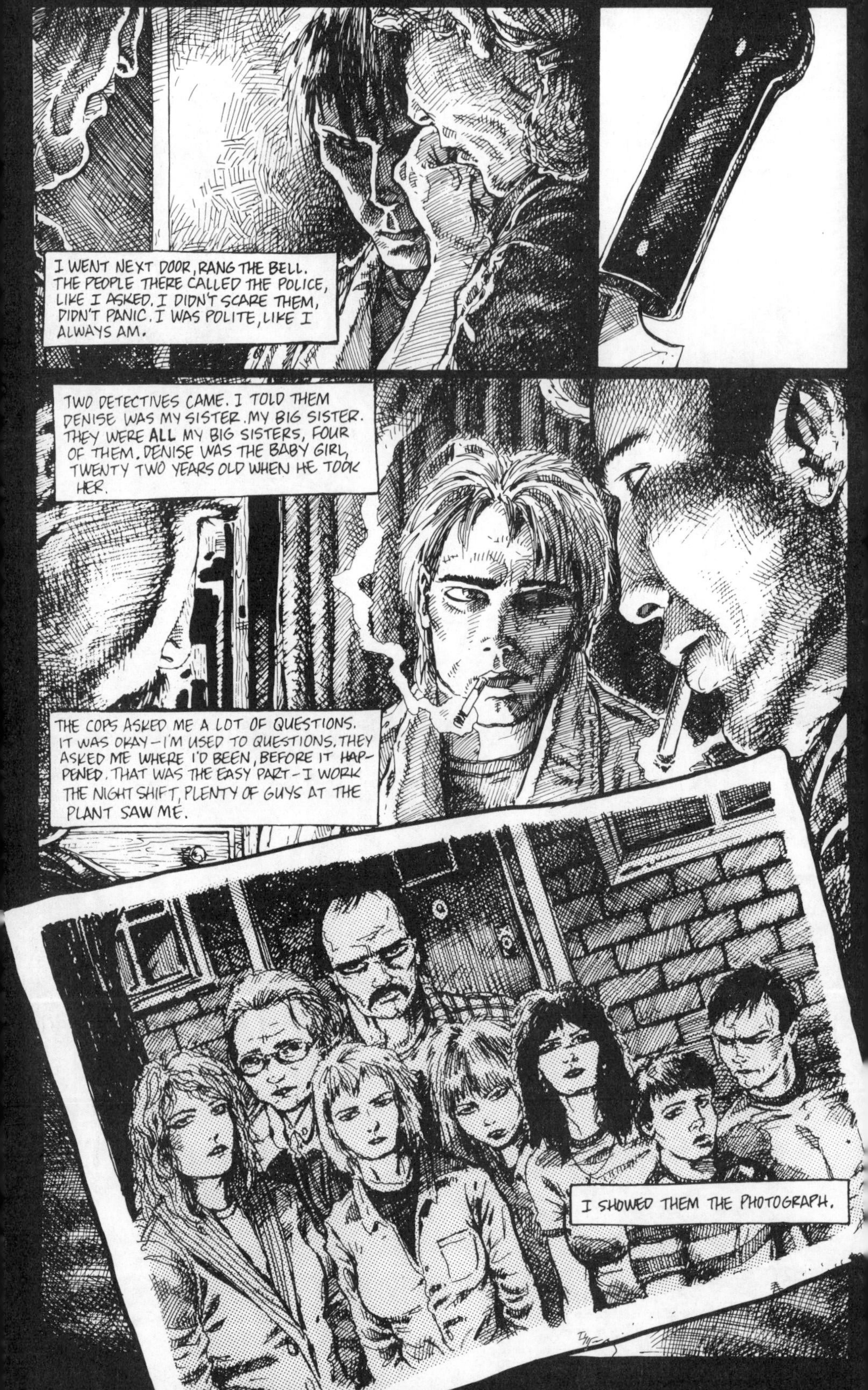
I WENT NEXT DOOR, RANG THE BELL. THE PEOPLE THERE CALLED THE POLICE, LIKE I ASKED. I DIDN'T SCARE THEM, DIDN'T PANIC. I WAS POLITE, LIKE I ALWAYS AM.
TWO DETECTIVES CAME. I TOLD THEM DENISE WAS MY SISTER. MY BIG SISTER. THEY WERE **ALL** MY BIG SISTERS, FOUR OF THEM. DENISE WAS THE BABY GIRL, TWENTY TWO YEARS OLD WHEN HE TOOK HER.
THE COPS ASKED ME A LOT OF QUESTIONS. IT WAS OKAY — I'M USED TO QUESTIONS. THEY ASKED ME WHERE I'D BEEN, BEFORE IT HAPPENED. THAT WAS THE EASY PART — I WORK THE NIGHT SHIFT, PLENTY OF GUYS AT THE PLANT SAW ME.
I SHOWED THEM THE PHOTOGRAPH.

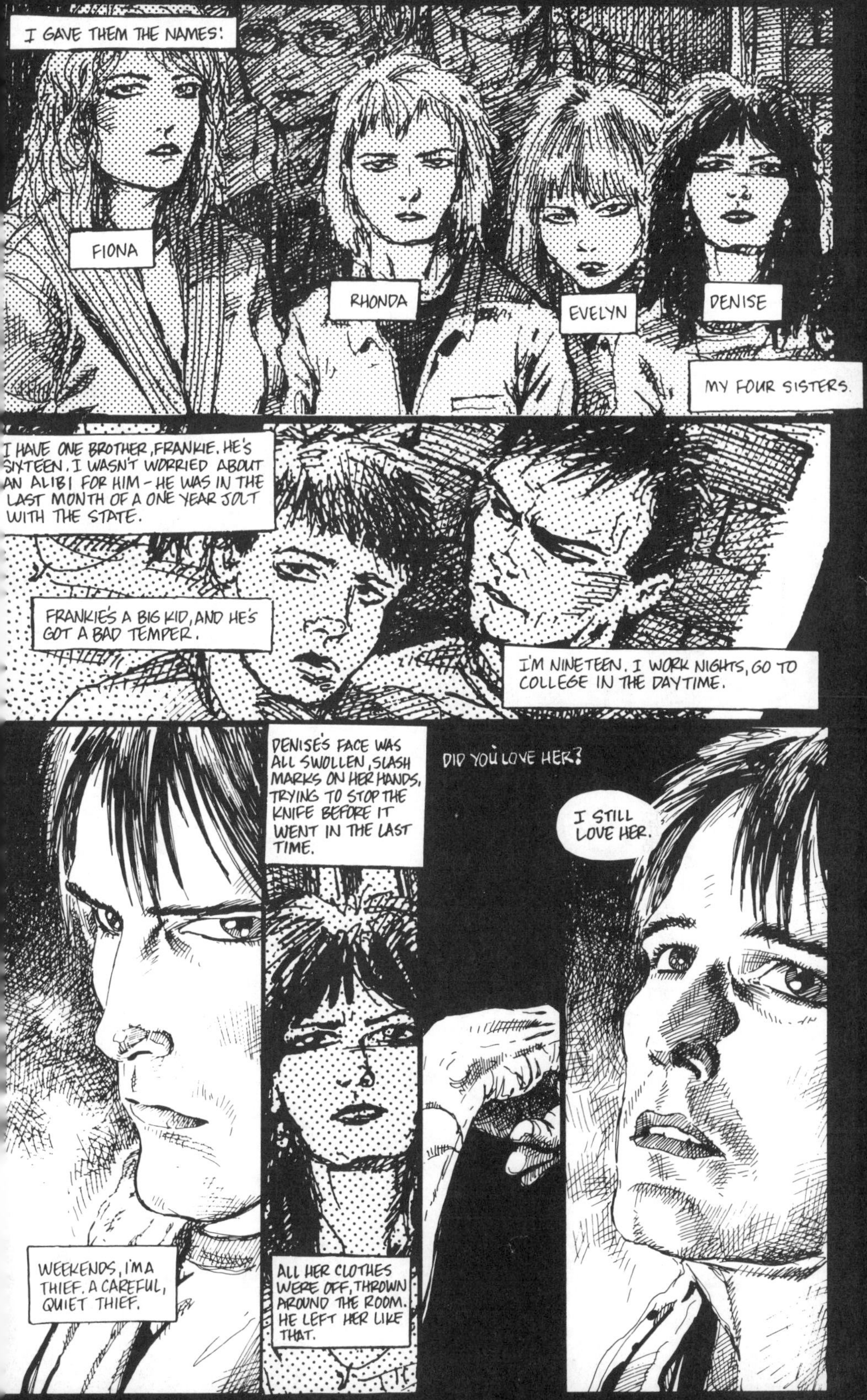
I GAVE THEM THE NAMES:
FIONA
RHONDA
EVELYN
DENISE
MY FOUR SISTERS.
I HAVE ONE BROTHER, FRANKIE. HE'S SIXTEEN. I WASN'T WORRIED ABOUT AN ALIBI FOR HIM - HE WAS IN THE LAST MONTH OF A ONE YEAR JOLT WITH THE STATE.
FRANKIE'S A BIG KID, AND HE'S GOT A BAD TEMPER.
I'M NINETEEN. I WORK NIGHTS, GO TO COLLEGE IN THE DAYTIME.
WEEKENDS, I'M A THIEF. A CAREFUL, QUIET THIEF.
DENISE'S FACE WAS ALL SWOLLEN, SLASH MARKS ON HER HANDS, TRYING TO STOP THE KNIFE BEFORE IT WENT IN THE LAST TIME.
ALL HER CLOTHES WERE OFF, THROWN AROUND THE ROOM. HE LEFT HER LIKE THAT.
DID YOU LOVE HER?
I STILL LOVE HER.

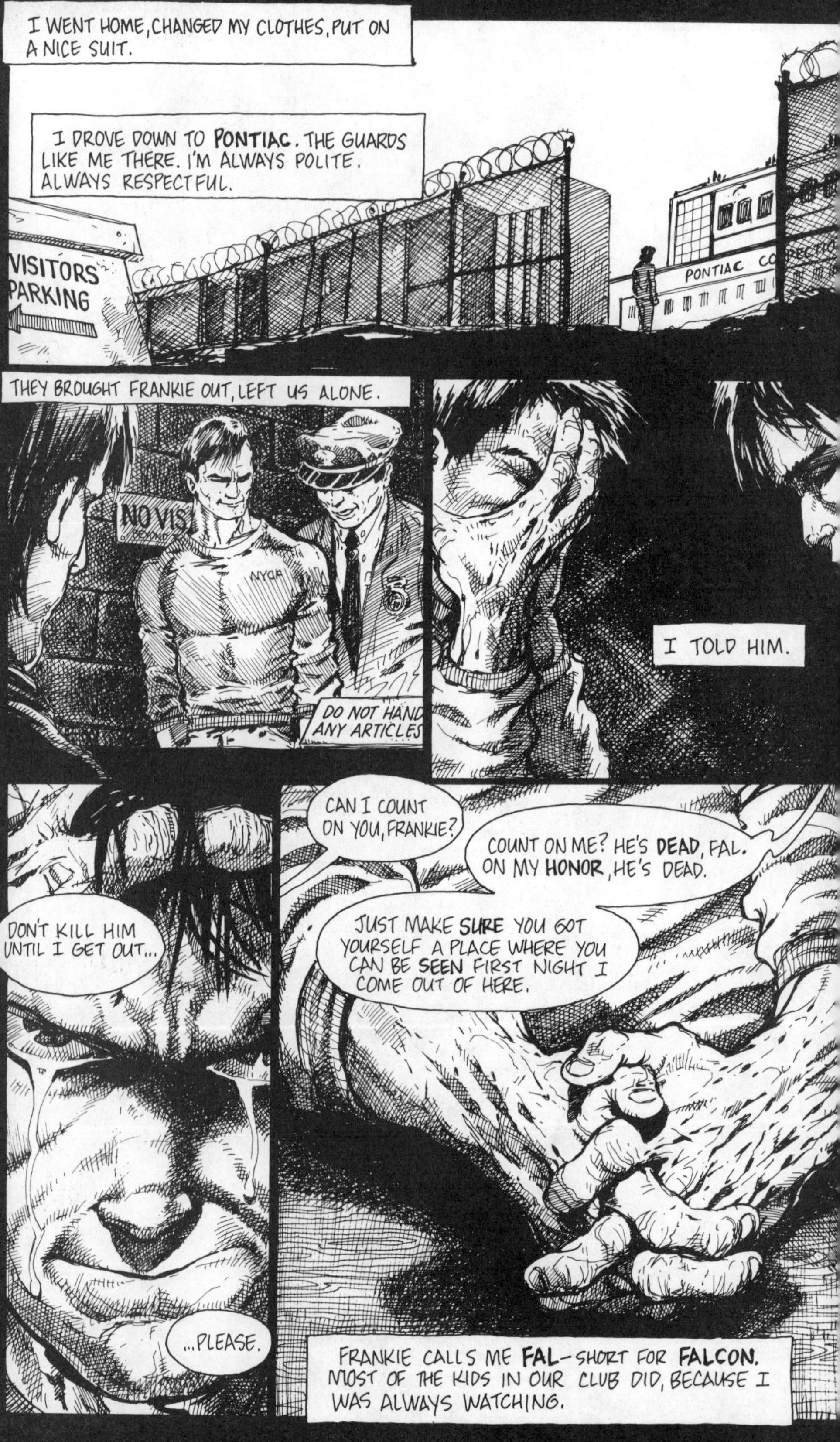

I WENT HOME, CHANGED MY CLOTHES, PUT ON A NICE SUIT.
I DROVE DOWN TO PONTIAC. THE GUARDS LIKE ME THERE. I'M ALWAYS POLITE. ALWAYS RESPECTFUL.
VISITORS PARKING
PONTIAC
THEY BROUGHT FRANKIE OUT, LEFT US ALONE.
NO VIS
NYCF
DO NOT HAND ANY ARTICLES
I TOLD HIM.
DON'T KILL HIM UNTIL I GET OUT...
...PLEASE.
CAN I COUNT ON YOU, FRANKIE?
COUNT ON ME? HE'S DEAD, FAL. ON MY HONOR, HE'S DEAD.
JUST MAKE SURE YOU GOT YOURSELF A PLACE WHERE YOU CAN BE SEEN FIRST NIGHT I COME OUT OF HERE.
FRANKIE CALLS ME FAL— SHORT FOR FALCON. MOST OF THE KIDS IN OUR CLUB DID, BECAUSE I WAS ALWAYS WATCHING.

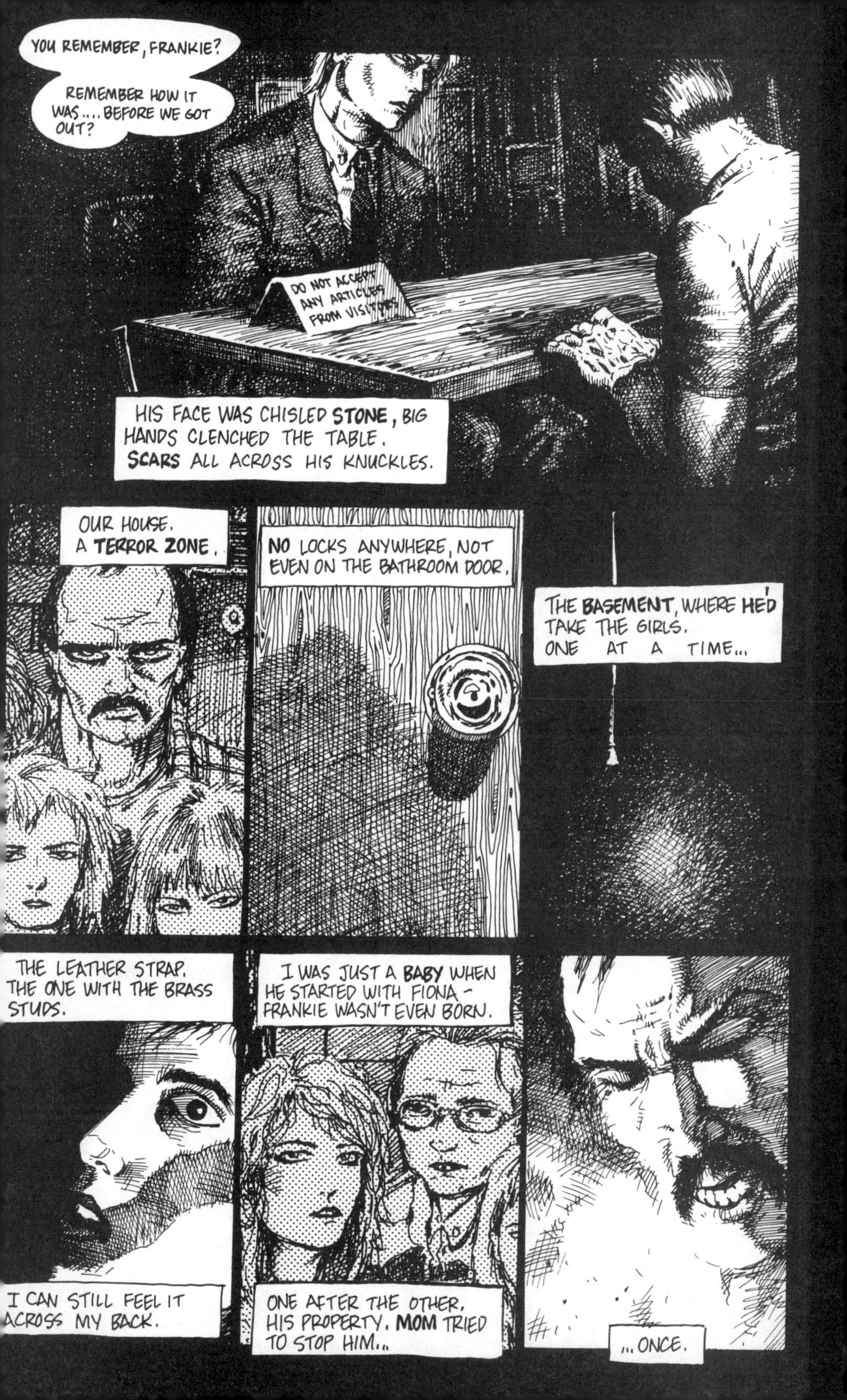
YOU REMEMBER, FRANKIE?
REMEMBER HOW IT WAS.... BEFORE WE GOT OUT?
DO NOT ACCEPT ANY ARTICLES FROM VISITORS
HIS FACE WAS CHISLED STONE, BIG HANDS CLENCHED THE TABLE. SCARS ALL ACROSS HIS KNUCKLES.
OUR HOUSE. A TERROR ZONE.
NO LOCKS ANYWHERE, NOT EVEN ON THE BATHROOM DOOR.
THE BASEMENT, WHERE HE'D TAKE THE GIRLS. ONE AT A TIME...
THE LEATHER STRAP. THE ONE WITH THE BRASS STUDS.
I CAN STILL FEEL IT ACROSS MY BACK.
I WAS JUST A BABY WHEN HE STARTED WITH FIONA - FRANKIE WASN'T EVEN BORN.
ONE AFTER THE OTHER. HIS PROPERTY. MOM TRIED TO STOP HIM..
...ONCE.

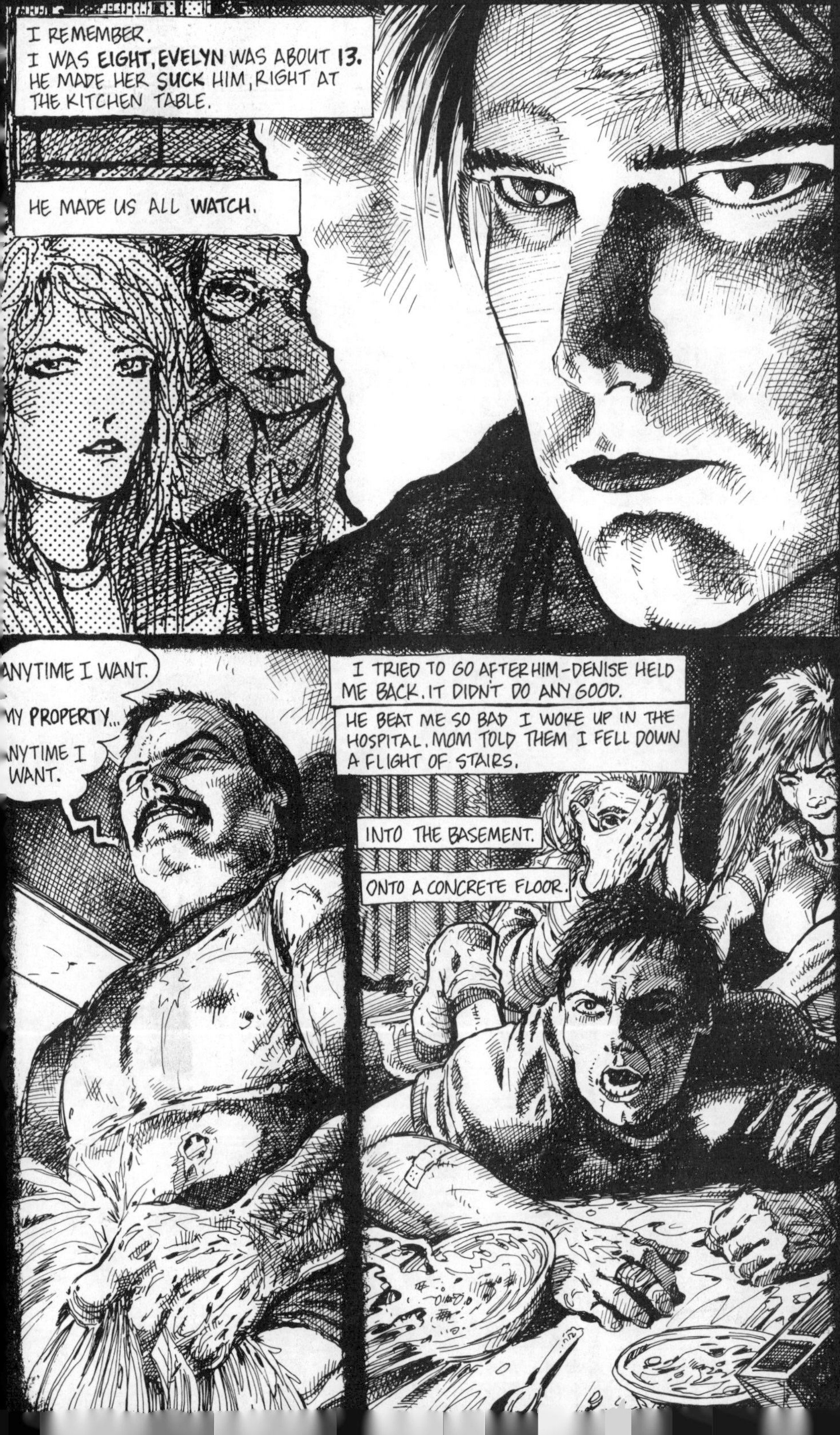
I REMEMBER.
I WAS EIGHT, EVELYN WAS ABOUT 13.
HE MADE HER SUCK HIM, RIGHT AT THE KITCHEN TABLE.
HE MADE US ALL WATCH.
ANYTIME I WANT.
MY PROPERTY...
ANYTIME I WANT.
I TRIED TO GO AFTER HIM-DENISE HELD ME BACK. IT DIDN'T DO ANY GOOD.
HE BEAT ME SO BAD I WOKE UP IN THE HOSPITAL. MOM TOLD THEM I FELL DOWN A FLIGHT OF STAIRS.
INTO THE BASEMENT.
ONTO A CONCRETE FLOOR.

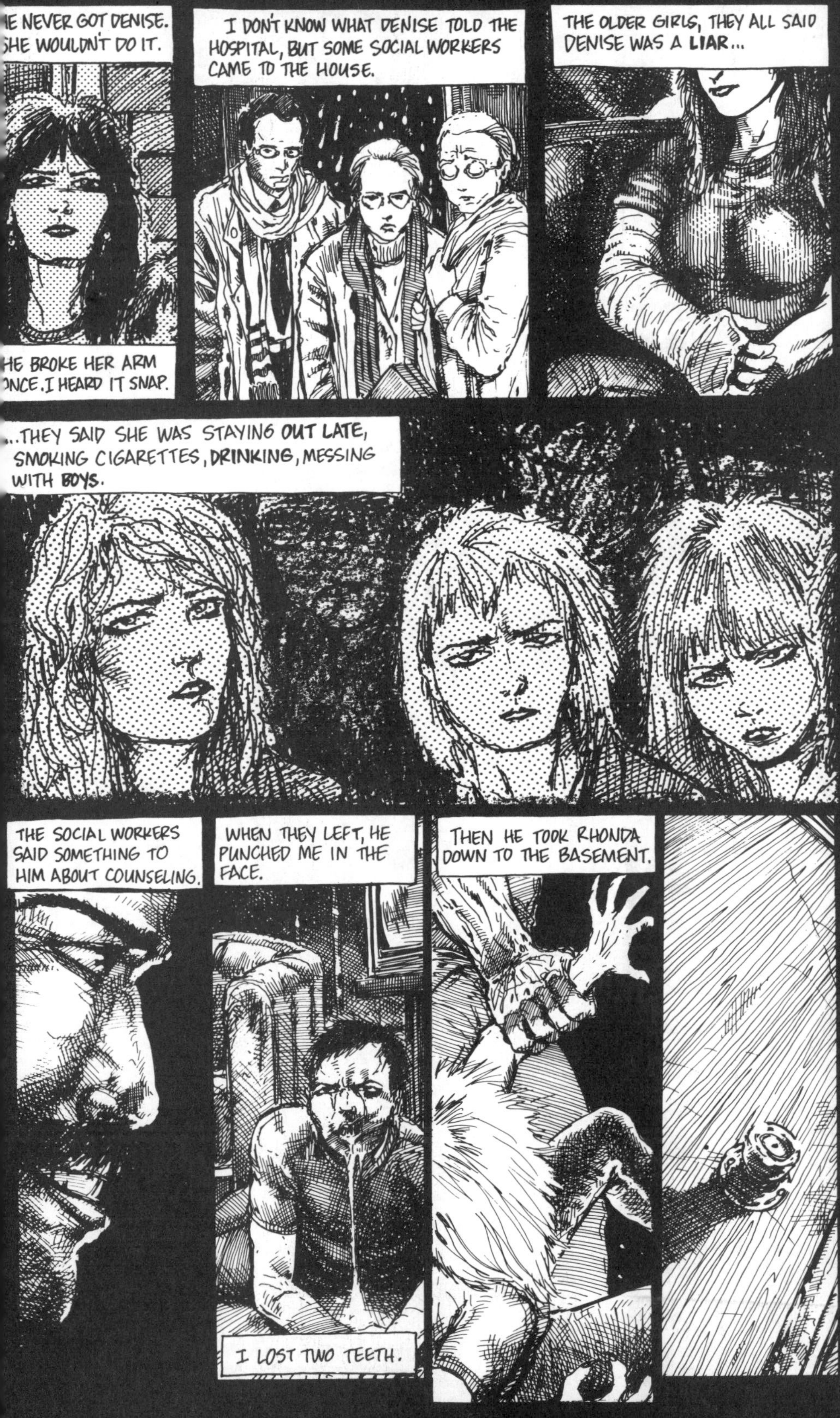

HE NEVER GOT DENISE. SHE WOULDN'T DO IT.
HE BROKE HER ARM ONCE. I HEARD IT SNAP.
I DON'T KNOW WHAT DENISE TOLD THE HOSPITAL, BUT SOME SOCIAL WORKERS CAME TO THE HOUSE.
THE OLDER GIRLS, THEY ALL SAID DENISE WAS A **LIAR**...
...THEY SAID SHE WAS STAYING **OUT LATE**, SMOKING CIGARETTES, **DRINKING**, MESSING WITH **BOYS**.
THE SOCIAL WORKERS SAID SOMETHING TO HIM ABOUT COUNSELING.
WHEN THEY LEFT, HE PUNCHED ME IN THE FACE.
I LOST TWO TEETH.
THEN HE TOOK RHONDA DOWN TO THE BASEMENT.

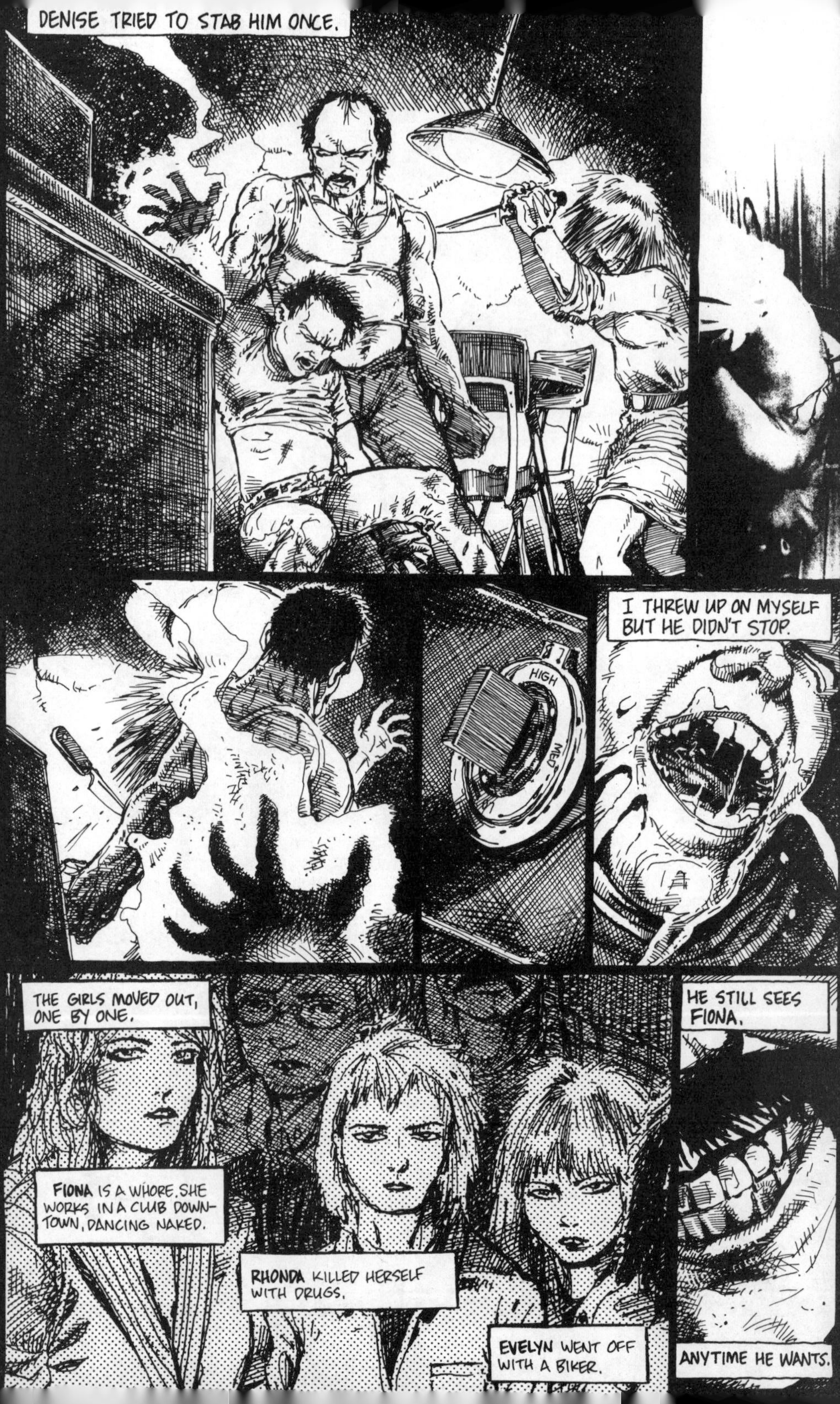
DENISE TRIED TO STAB HIM ONCE.
HIGH
MED
I THREW UP ON MYSELF BUT HE DIDN'T STOP.
THE GIRLS MOVED OUT, ONE BY ONE.
FIONA IS A WHORE. SHE WORKS IN A CLUB DOWN-TOWN, DANCING NAKED.
RHONDA KILLED HERSELF WITH DRUGS.
EVELYN WENT OFF WITH A BIKER.
HE STILL SEES FIONA.
ANYTIME HE WANTS.

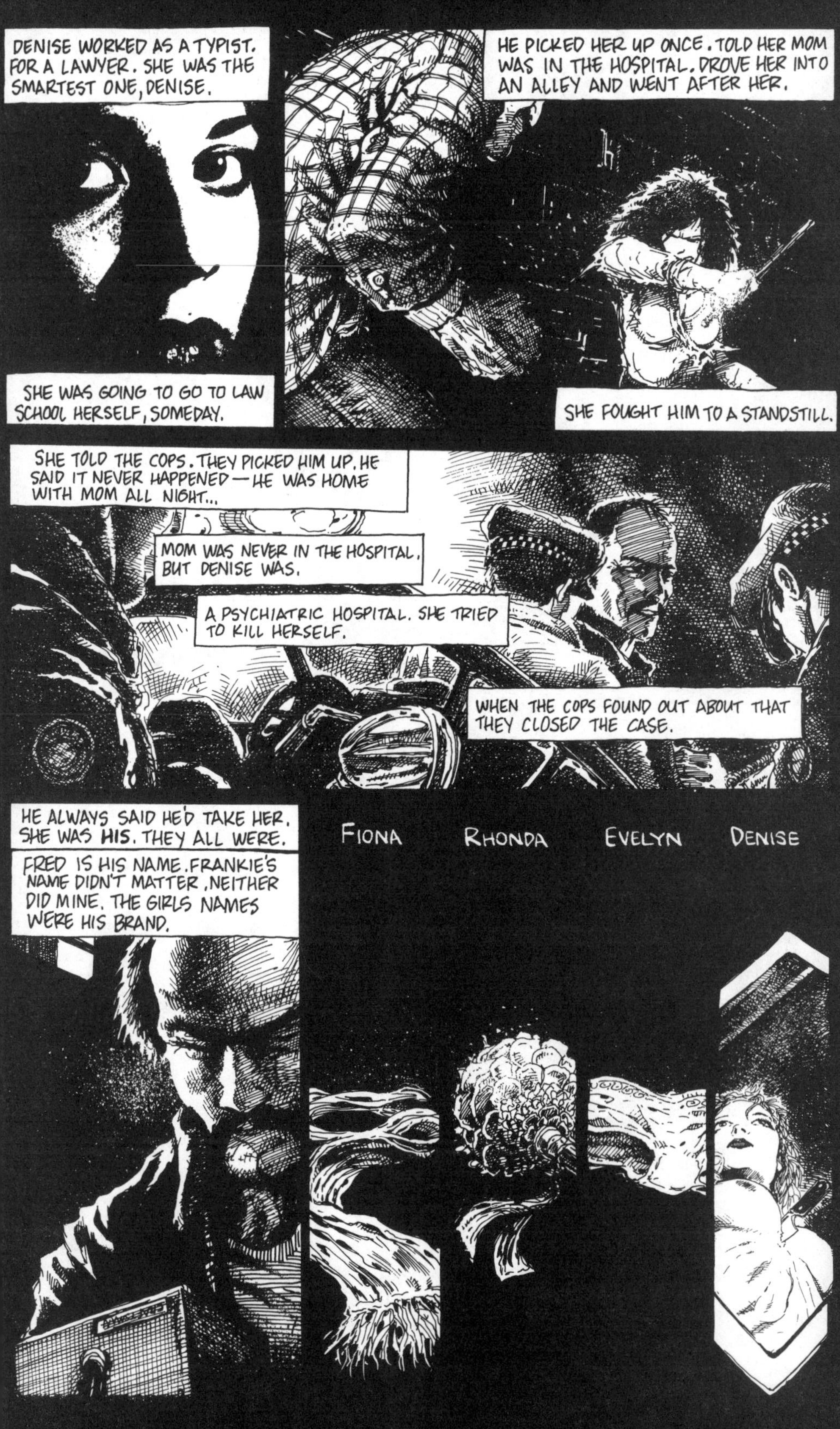
DENISE WORKED AS A TYPIST. FOR A LAWYER. SHE WAS THE SMARTEST ONE, DENISE.
SHE WAS GOING TO GO TO LAW SCHOOL HERSELF, SOMEDAY.
HE PICKED HER UP ONCE. TOLD HER MOM WAS IN THE HOSPITAL. DROVE HER INTO AN ALLEY AND WENT AFTER HER.
SHE FOUGHT HIM TO A STANDSTILL.
SHE TOLD THE COPS. THEY PICKED HIM UP. HE SAID IT NEVER HAPPENED—HE WAS HOME WITH MOM ALL NIGHT...
MOM WAS NEVER IN THE HOSPITAL, BUT DENISE WAS.
A PSYCHIATRIC HOSPITAL. SHE TRIED TO KILL HERSELF.
WHEN THE COPS FOUND OUT ABOUT THAT THEY CLOSED THE CASE.
HE ALWAYS SAID HE'D TAKE HER. SHE WAS **HIS**. THEY ALL WERE.
FRED IS HIS NAME. FRANKIE'S NAME DIDN'T MATTER, NEITHER DID MINE. THE GIRLS NAMES WERE HIS BRAND.
FIONA
RHONDA
EVELYN
DENISE

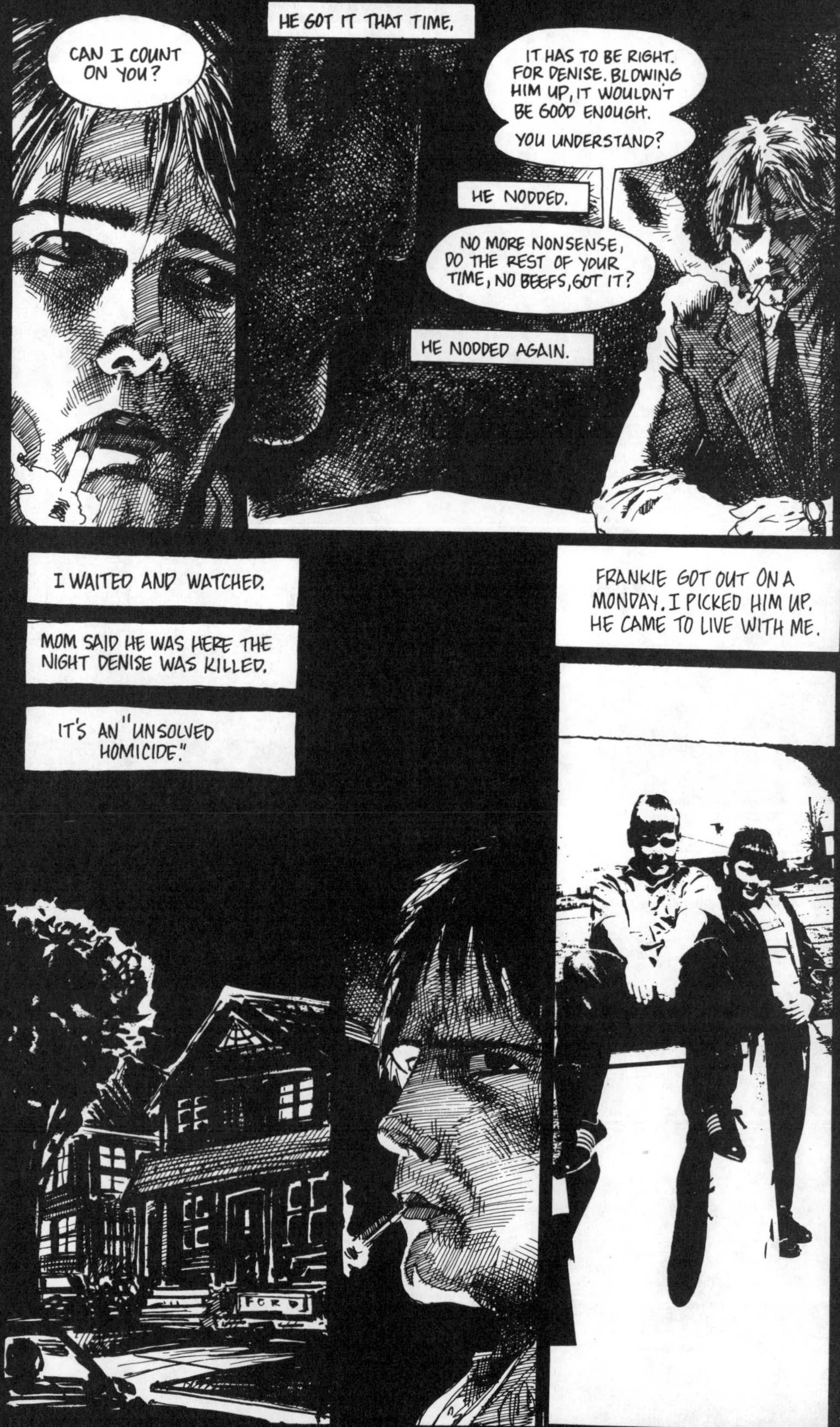
CAN I COUNT ON YOU?
HE GOT IT THAT TIME.
IT HAS TO BE RIGHT. FOR DENISE. BLOWING HIM UP, IT WOULDN'T BE GOOD ENOUGH.
YOU UNDERSTAND?
HE NODDED.
NO MORE NONSENSE, DO THE REST OF YOUR TIME, NO BEEFS, GOT IT?
HE NODDED AGAIN.
I WAITED AND WATCHED.
MOM SAID HE WAS HERE THE NIGHT DENISE WAS KILLED.
IT'S AN "UNSOLVED HOMICIDE."
FORD
FRANKIE GOT OUT ON A MONDAY. I PICKED HIM UP. HE CAME TO LIVE WITH ME.

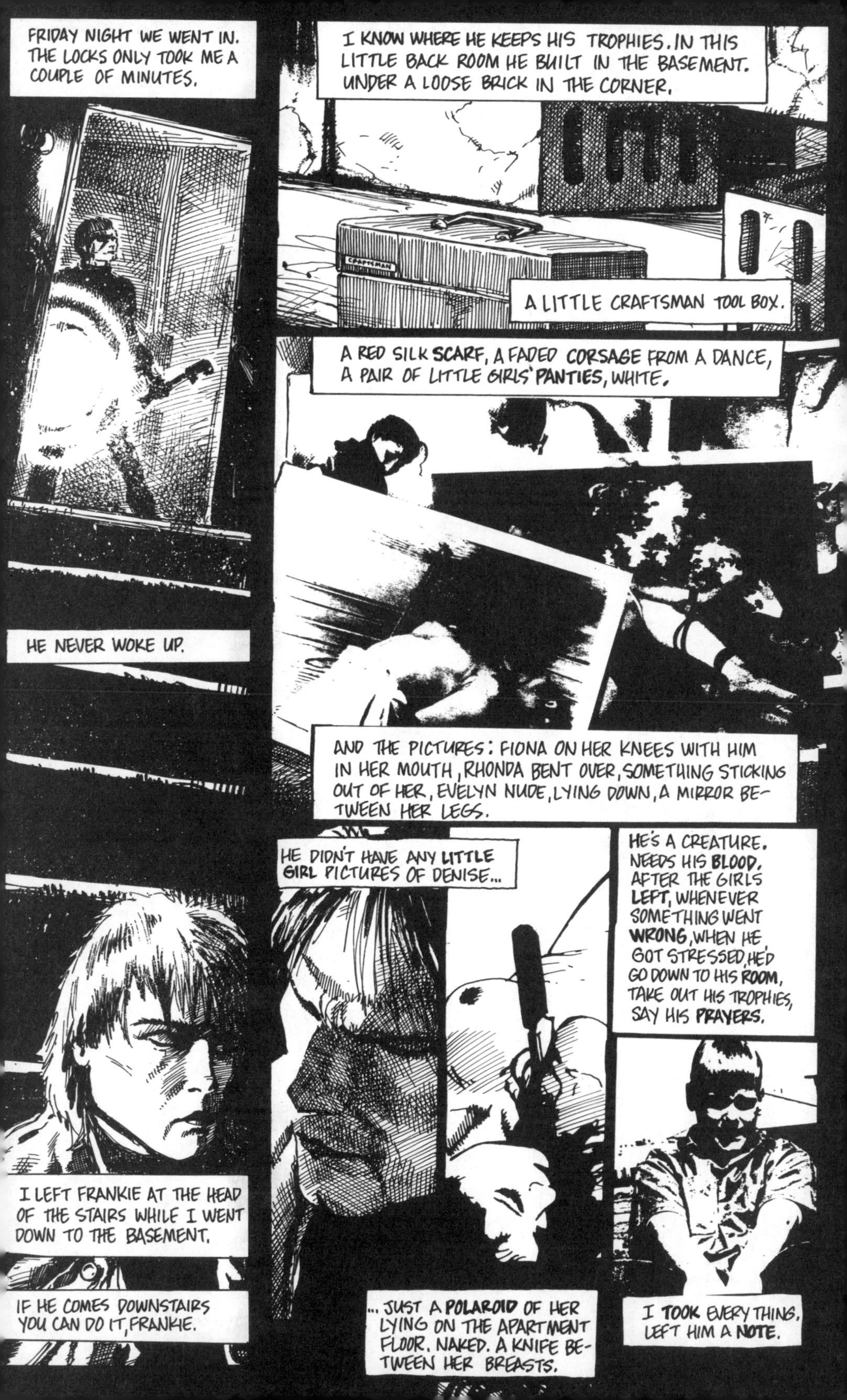
FRIDAY NIGHT WE WENT IN. THE LOCKS ONLY TOOK ME A COUPLE OF MINUTES.
HE NEVER WOKE UP.
I LEFT FRANKIE AT THE HEAD OF THE STAIRS WHILE I WENT DOWN TO THE BASEMENT.
IF HE COMES DOWNSTAIRS YOU CAN DO IT, FRANKIE.
I KNOW WHERE HE KEEPS HIS TROPHIES. IN THIS LITTLE BACK ROOM HE BUILT IN THE BASEMENT. UNDER A LOOSE BRICK IN THE CORNER.
CRAFTSMAN
A LITTLE CRAFTSMAN TOOL BOX.
A RED SILK SCARF, A FADED CORSAGE FROM A DANCE, A PAIR OF LITTLE GIRLS' PANTIES, WHITE.
AND THE PICTURES: FIONA ON HER KNEES WITH HIM IN HER MOUTH, RHONDA BENT OVER, SOMETHING STICKING OUT OF HER, EVELYN NUDE, LYING DOWN, A MIRROR BETWEEN HER LEGS.
HE DIDN'T HAVE ANY LITTLE GIRL PICTURES OF DENISE...
...JUST A POLAROID OF HER LYING ON THE APARTMENT FLOOR. NAKED. A KNIFE BETWEEN HER BREASTS.
HE'S A CREATURE. NEEDS HIS BLOOD. AFTER THE GIRLS LEFT, WHENEVER SOMETHING WENT WRONG, WHEN HE GOT STRESSED, HE'D GO DOWN TO HIS ROOM, TAKE OUT HIS TROPHIES, SAY HIS PRAYERS.
I TOOK EVERYTHING, LEFT HIM A NOTE.

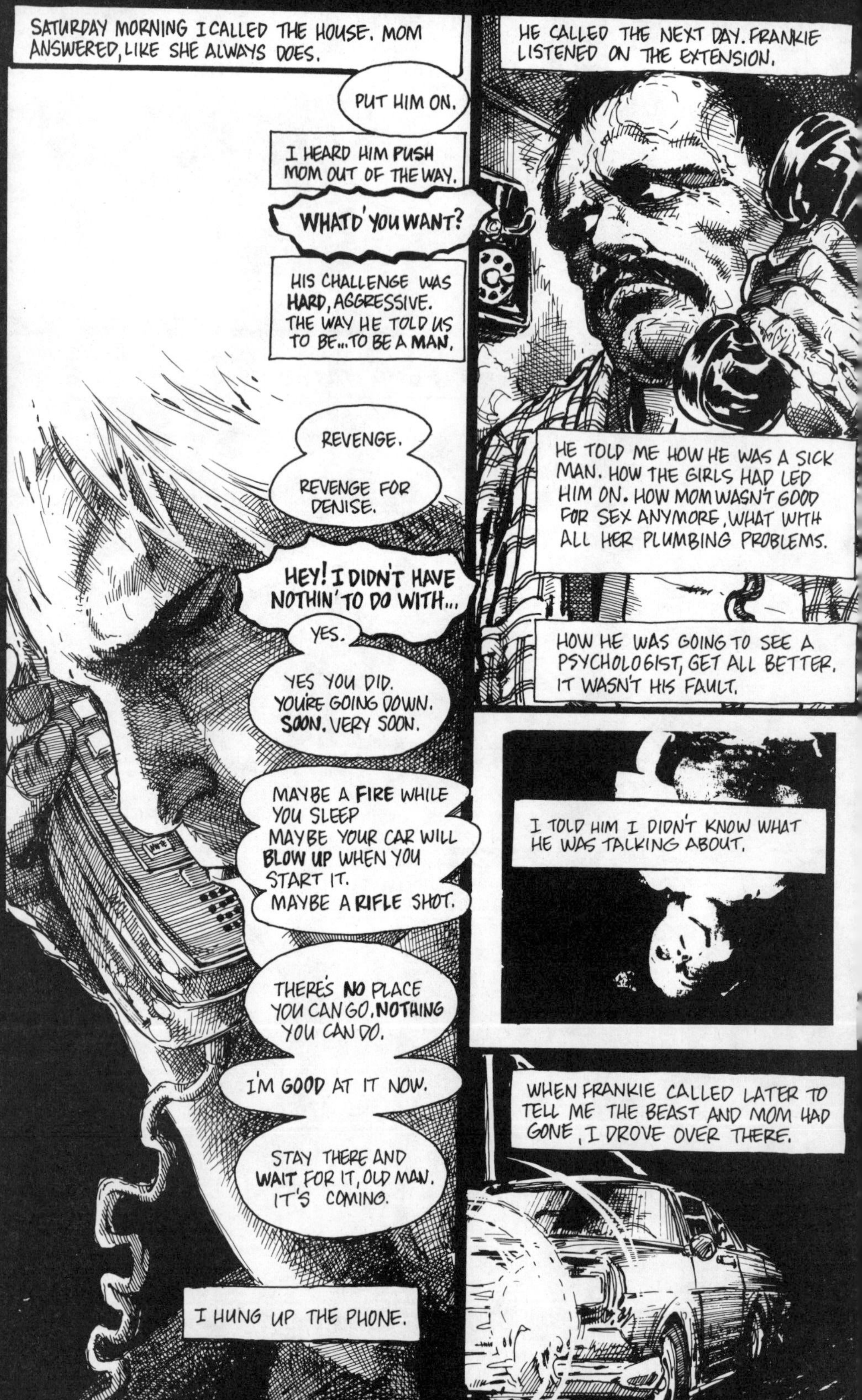
SATURDAY MORNING I CALLED THE HOUSE. MOM ANSWERED, LIKE SHE ALWAYS DOES.
PUT HIM ON.
I HEARD HIM PUSH MOM OUT OF THE WAY.
WHATD'YOU WANT?
HIS CHALLENGE WAS HARD, AGGRESSIVE. THE WAY HE TOLD US TO BE...TO BE A MAN.
REVENGE.
REVENGE FOR DENISE.
HEY! I DIDN'T HAVE NOTHIN' TO DO WITH...
YES.
YES YOU DID. YOU'RE GOING DOWN. SOON. VERY SOON.
MAYBE A FIRE WHILE YOU SLEEP
MAYBE YOUR CAR WILL BLOW UP WHEN YOU START IT.
MAYBE A RIFLE SHOT.
THERE'S NO PLACE YOU CAN GO. NOTHING YOU CAN DO.
I'M GOOD AT IT NOW.
STAY THERE AND WAIT FOR IT, OLD MAN. IT'S COMING.
I HUNG UP THE PHONE.
HE CALLED THE NEXT DAY. FRANKIE LISTENED ON THE EXTENSION.
HE TOLD ME HOW HE WAS A SICK MAN. HOW THE GIRLS HAD LED HIM ON. HOW MOM WASN'T GOOD FOR SEX ANYMORE, WHAT WITH ALL HER PLUMBING PROBLEMS.
HOW HE WAS GOING TO SEE A PSYCHOLOGIST, GET ALL BETTER. IT WASN'T HIS FAULT.
I TOLD HIM I DIDN'T KNOW WHAT HE WAS TALKING ABOUT.
WHEN FRANKIE CALLED LATER TO TELL ME THE BEAST AND MOM HAD GONE, I DROVE OVER THERE.

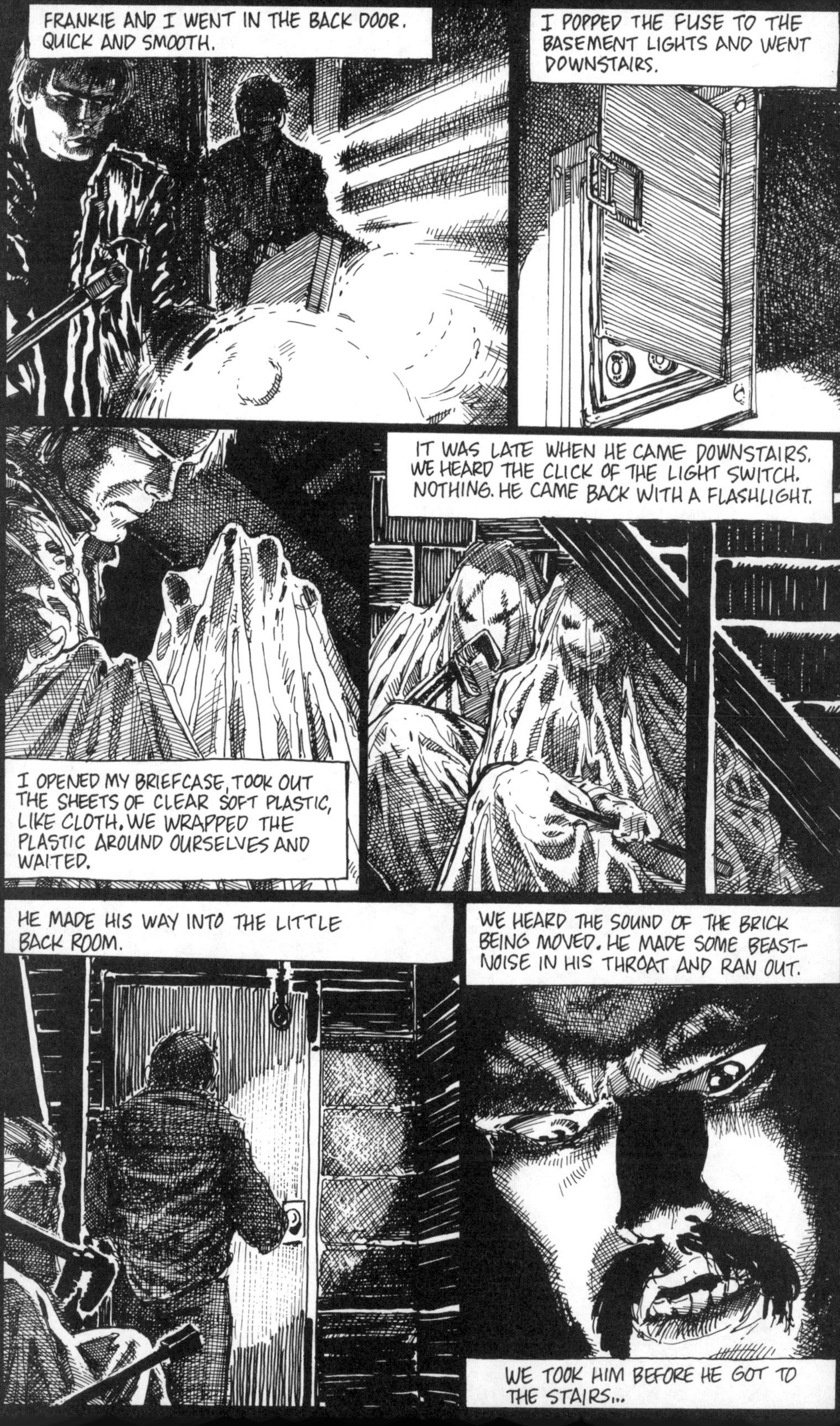
FRANKIE AND I WENT IN THE BACK DOOR. QUICK AND SMOOTH.
I POPPED THE FUSE TO THE BASEMENT LIGHTS AND WENT DOWNSTAIRS.
I OPENED MY BRIEFCASE, TOOK OUT THE SHEETS OF CLEAR SOFT PLASTIC, LIKE CLOTH. WE WRAPPED THE PLASTIC AROUND OURSELVES AND WAITED.
IT WAS LATE WHEN HE CAME DOWNSTAIRS. WE HEARD THE CLICK OF THE LIGHT SWITCH. NOTHING. HE CAME BACK WITH A FLASHLIGHT.
HE MADE HIS WAY INTO THE LITTLE BACK ROOM.
WE HEARD THE SOUND OF THE BRICK BEING MOVED. HE MADE SOME BEAST-NOISE IN HIS THROAT AND RAN OUT.
WE TOOK HIM BEFORE HE GOT TO THE STAIRS...

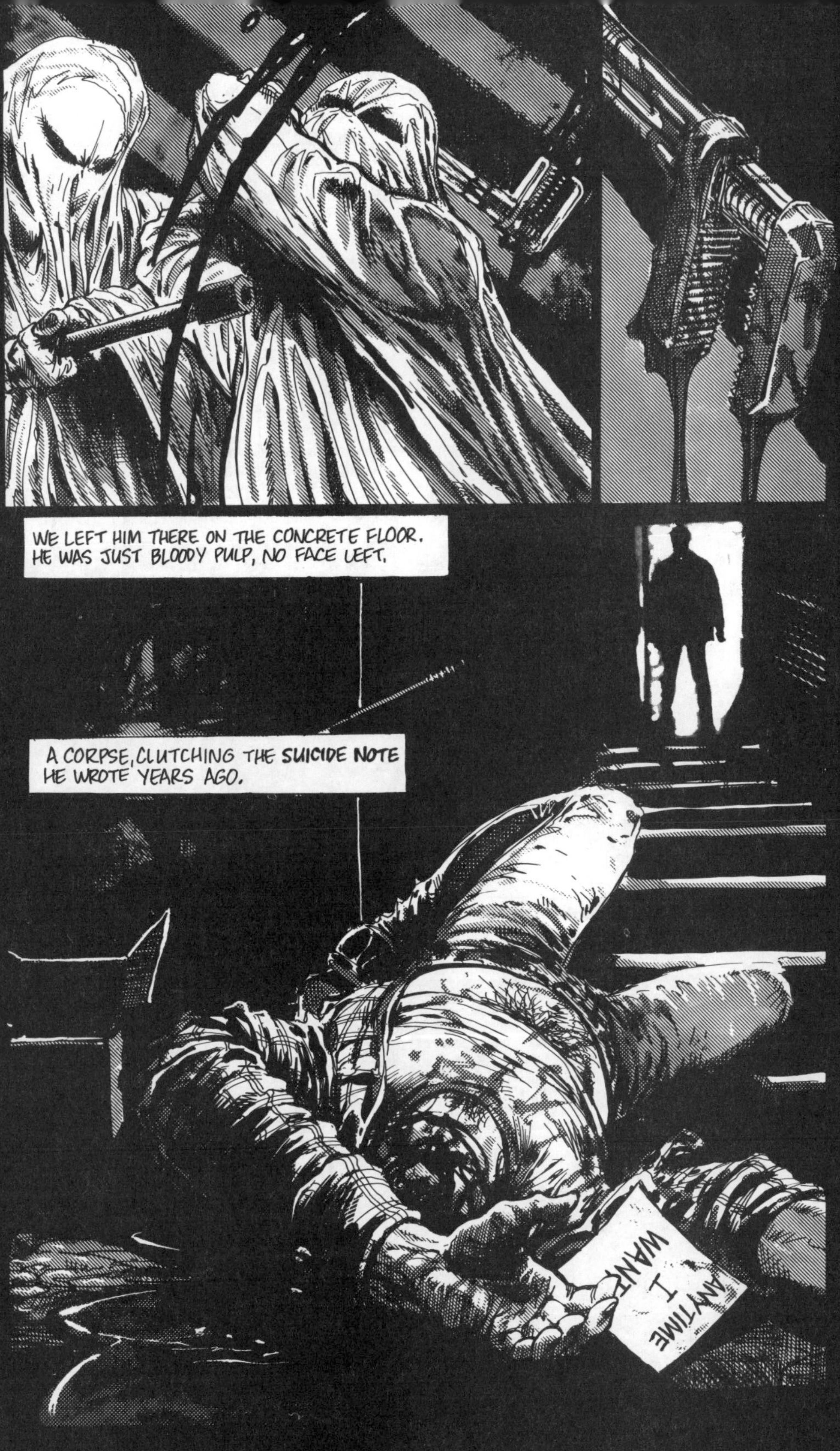
WE LEFT HIM THERE ON THE CONCRETE FLOOR. HE WAS JUST BLOODY PULP, NO FACE LEFT.
A CORPSE, CLUTCHING THE SUICIDE NOTE HE WROTE YEARS AGO.
ANYTIME
I

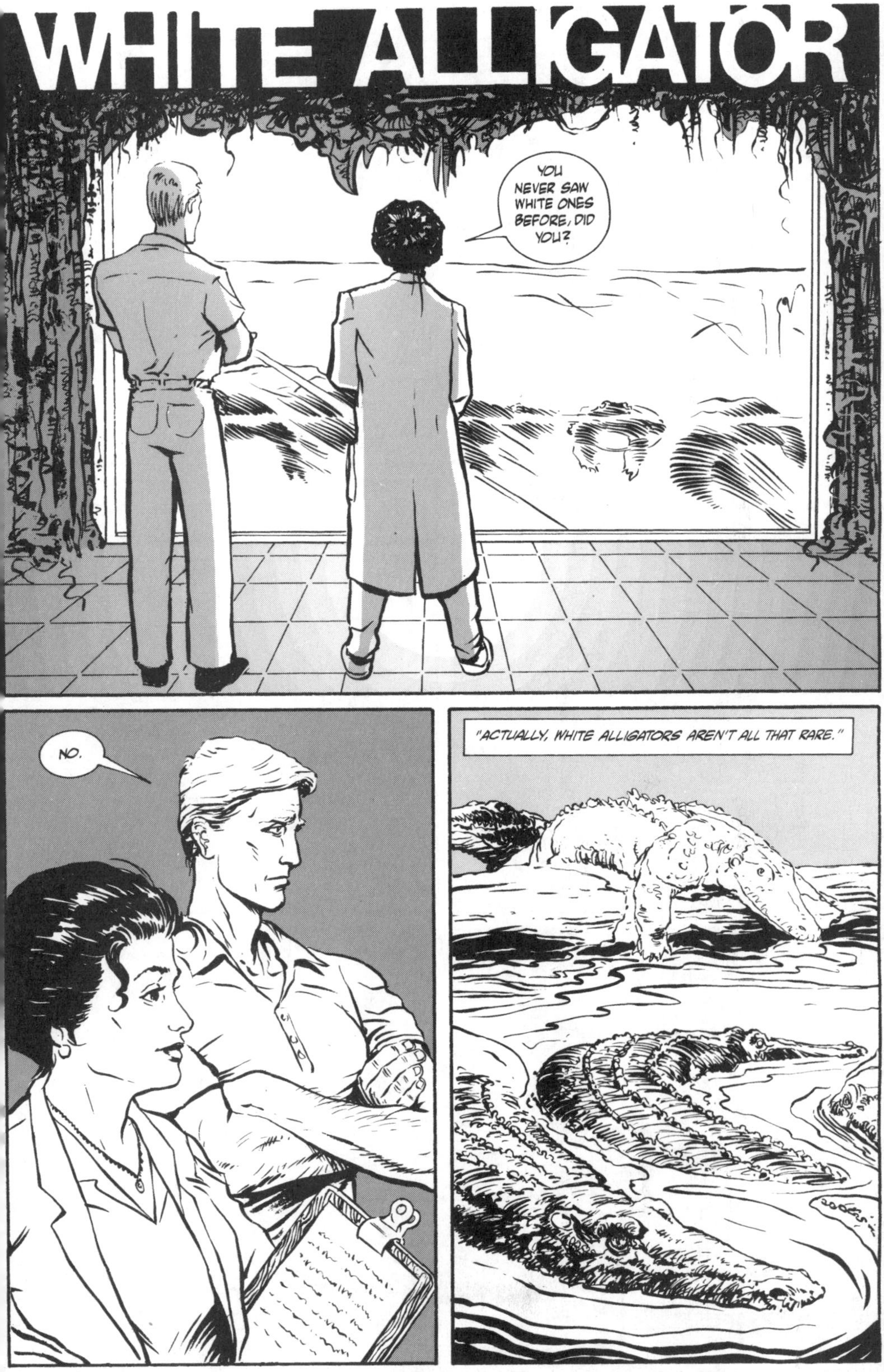
WHITE ALLIGATOR
YOU NEVER SAW WHITE ONES BEFORE, DID YOU?
NO.
"ACTUALLY, WHITE ALLIGATORS AREN'T ALL THAT RARE."

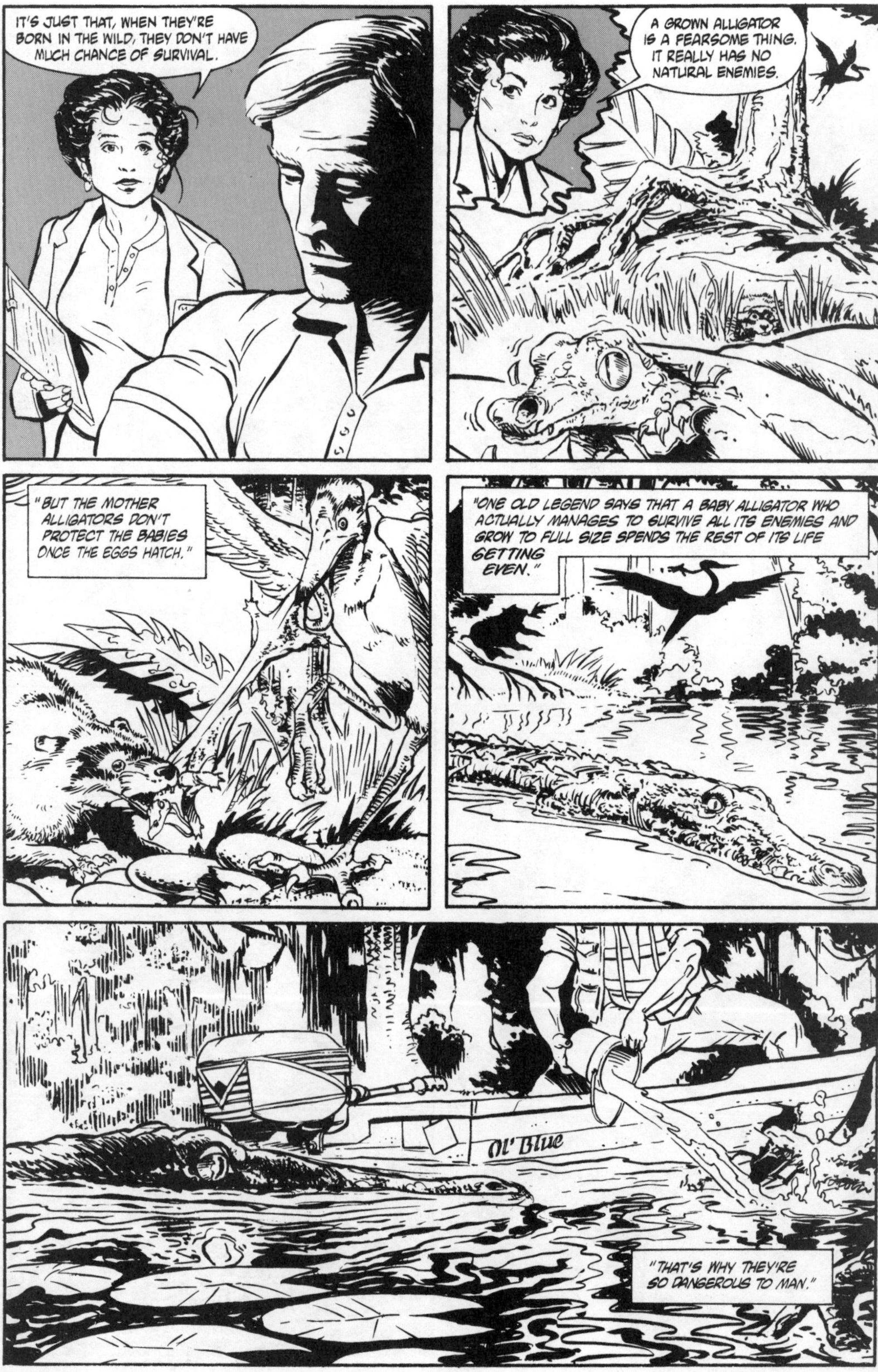
IT'S JUST THAT, WHEN THEY'RE BORN IN THE WILD, THEY DON'T HAVE MUCH CHANCE OF SURVIVAL.
A GROWN ALLIGATOR IS A FEARSOME THING. IT REALLY HAS NO NATURAL ENEMIES.
"BUT THE MOTHER ALLIGATORS DON'T PROTECT THE BABIES ONCE THE EGGS HATCH."
"ONE OLD LEGEND SAYS THAT A BABY ALLIGATOR WHO ACTUALLY MANAGES TO SURVIVE ALL ITS ENEMIES AND GROW TO FULL SIZE SPENDS THE REST OF ITS LIFE GETTING EVEN."
Ol' Blue
"THAT'S WHY THEY'RE SO DANGEROUS TO MAN."

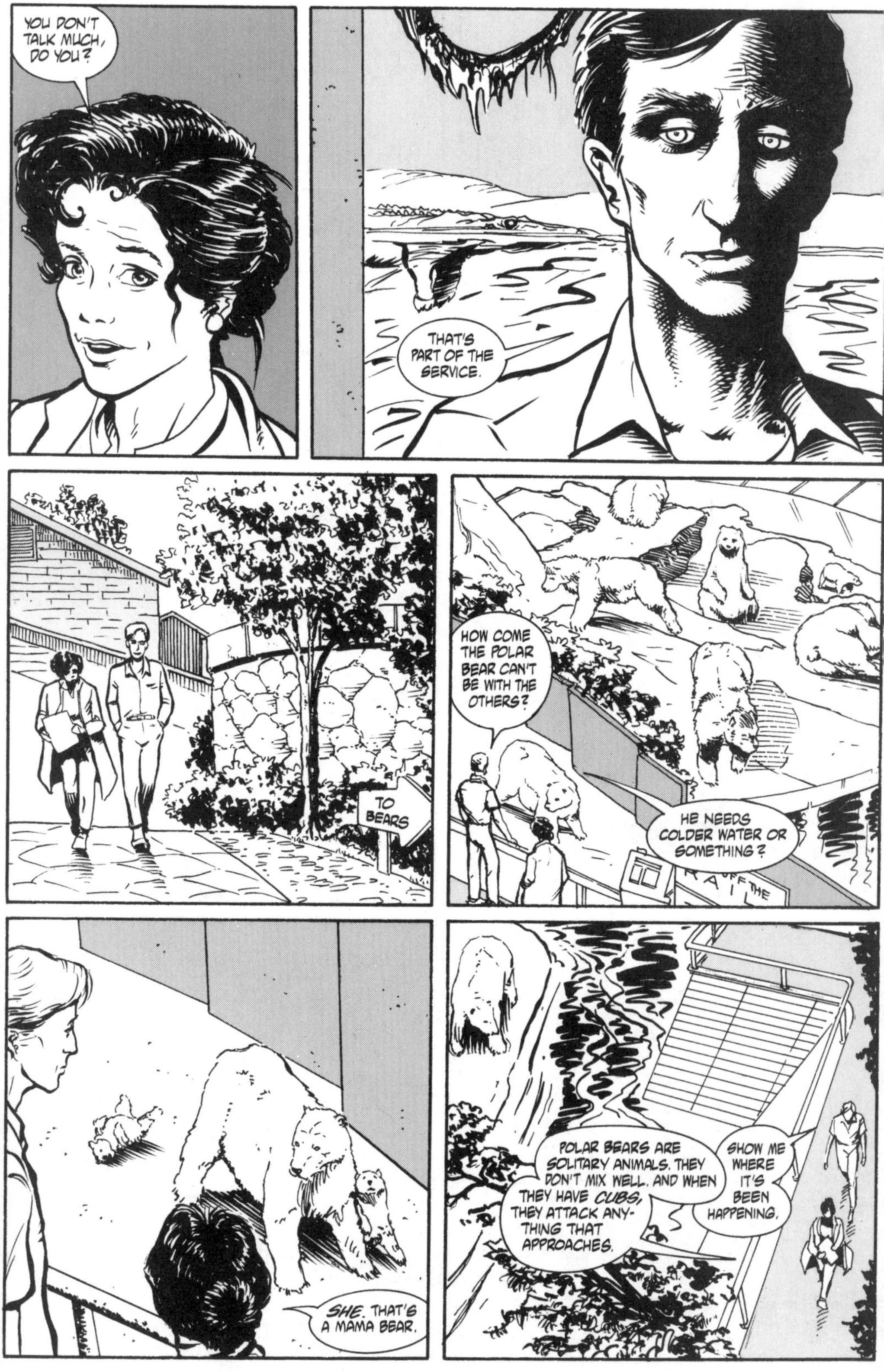
YOU DON'T TALK MUCH, DO YOU?
THAT'S PART OF THE SERVICE.
TO BEARS
HOW COME THE POLAR BEAR CAN'T BE WITH THE OTHERS?
HE NEEDS COLDER WATER OR SOMETHING?
SHE. THAT'S A MAMA BEAR.
POLAR BEARS ARE SOLITARY ANIMALS. THEY DON'T MIX WELL. AND WHEN THEY HAVE CUBS, THEY ATTACK ANYTHING THAT APPROACHES.
SHOW ME WHERE IT'S BEEN HAPPENING.

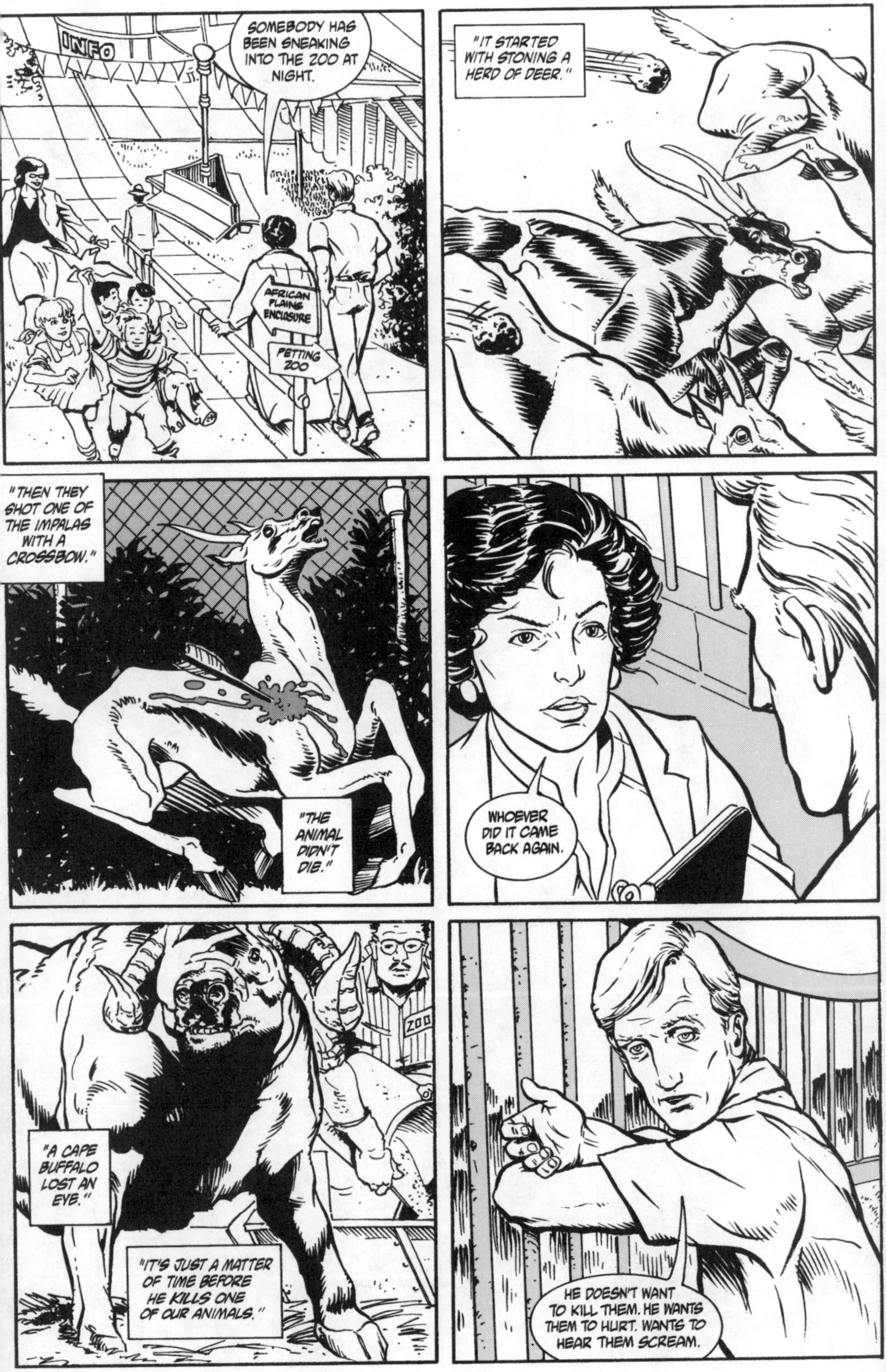
INFO
SOMEBODY HAS BEEN SNEAKING INTO THE ZOO AT NIGHT.
AFRICAN PLAINS ENCLOSURE
PETTING ZOO
"IT STARTED WITH STONING A HERD OF DEER."
"THEN THEY SHOT ONE OF THE IMPALAS WITH A CROSSBOW."
"THE ANIMAL DIDN'T DIE."
WHOEVER DID IT CAME BACK AGAIN.
ZOO
"A CAPE BUFFALO LOST AN EYE."
"IT'S JUST A MATTER OF TIME BEFORE HE KILLS ONE OF OUR ANIMALS."
HE DOESN'T WANT TO KILL THEM. HE WANTS THEM TO HURT. WANTS TO HEAR THEM SCREAM.

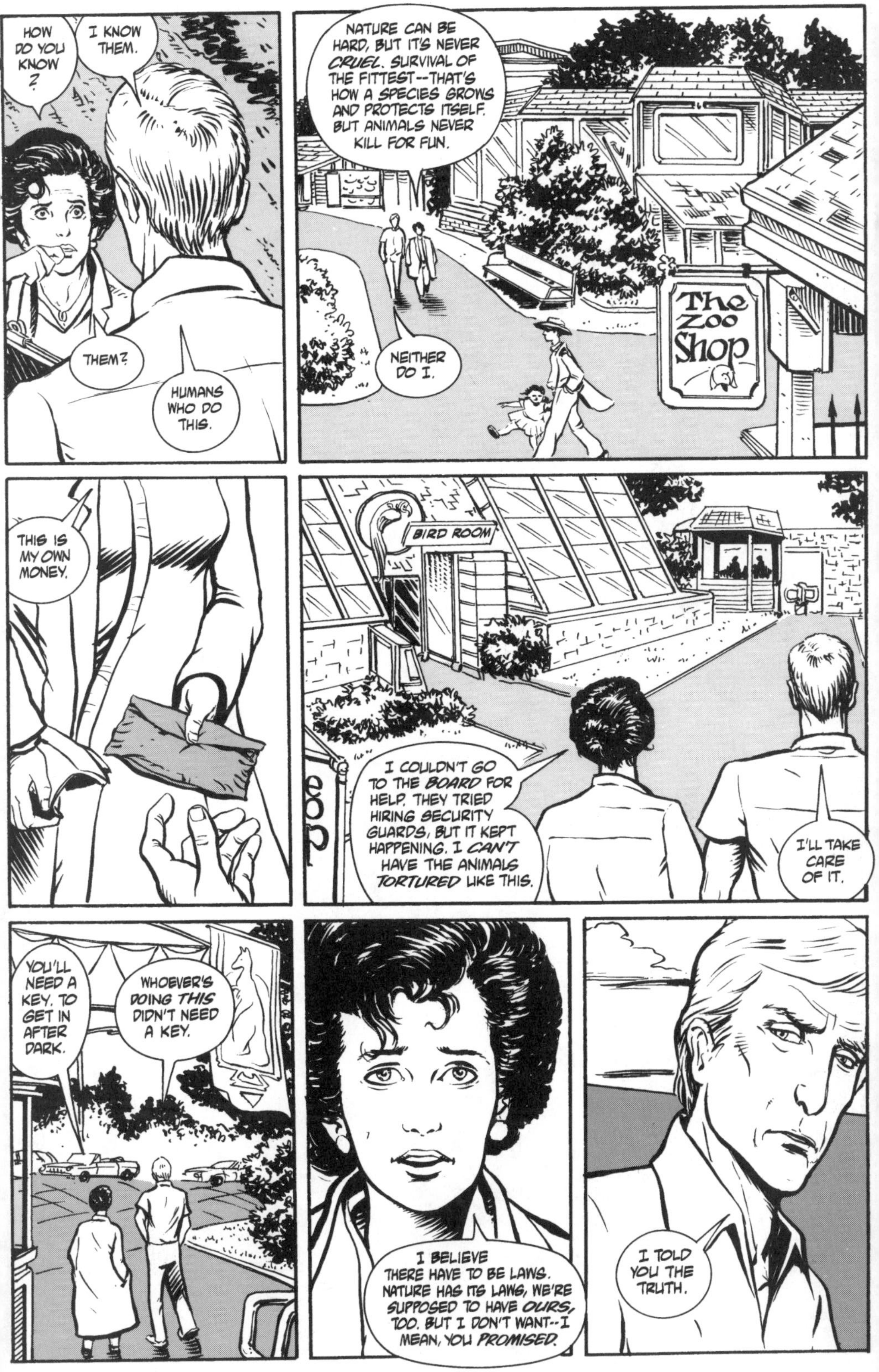

HOW DO YOU KNOW?
I KNOW THEM.
THEM?
HUMANS WHO DO THIS.
NATURE CAN BE HARD, BUT IT'S NEVER *CRUEL*. SURVIVAL OF THE FITTEST--THAT'S HOW A SPECIES GROWS AND PROTECTS ITSELF. BUT ANIMALS NEVER KILL FOR FUN.
The Zoo Shop
NEITHER DO I.
THIS IS MY OWN MONEY.
BIRD ROOM
I COULDN'T GO TO THE *BOARD* FOR HELP. THEY TRIED HIRING SECURITY GUARDS, BUT IT KEPT HAPPENING. I *CAN'T* HAVE THE ANIMALS *TORTURED* LIKE THIS.
I'LL TAKE CARE OF IT.
YOU'LL NEED A KEY. TO GET IN AFTER DARK.
WHOEVER'S DOING *THIS* DIDN'T NEED A KEY.
I BELIEVE THERE HAVE TO BE LAWS. NATURE HAS ITS LAWS, WE'RE SUPPOSED TO HAVE *OURS*, TOO. BUT I DON'T WANT--I MEAN, YOU *PROMISED*.
I TOLD YOU THE TRUTH.

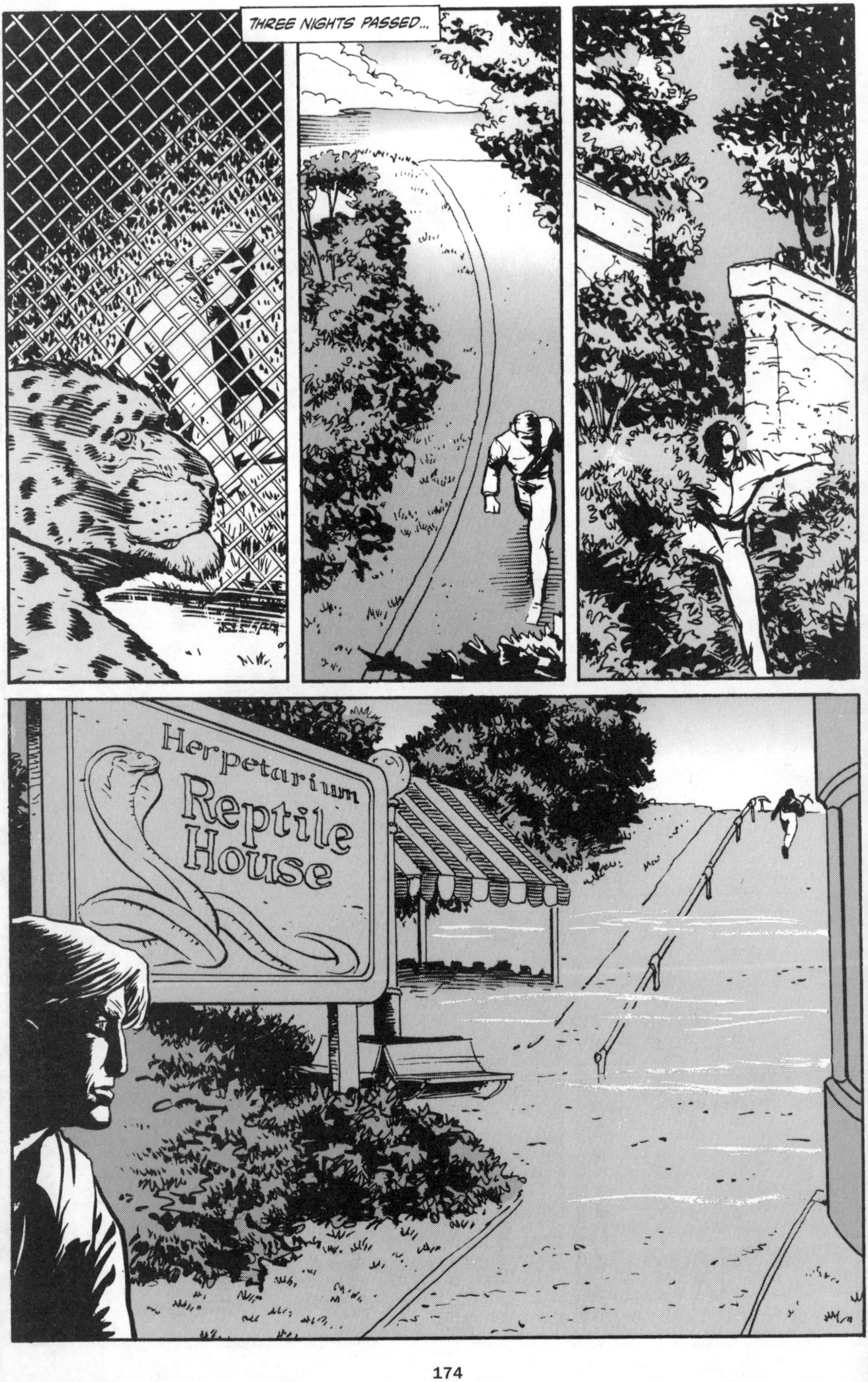
THREE NIGHTS PASSED...
Herpetarium
Reptile
House

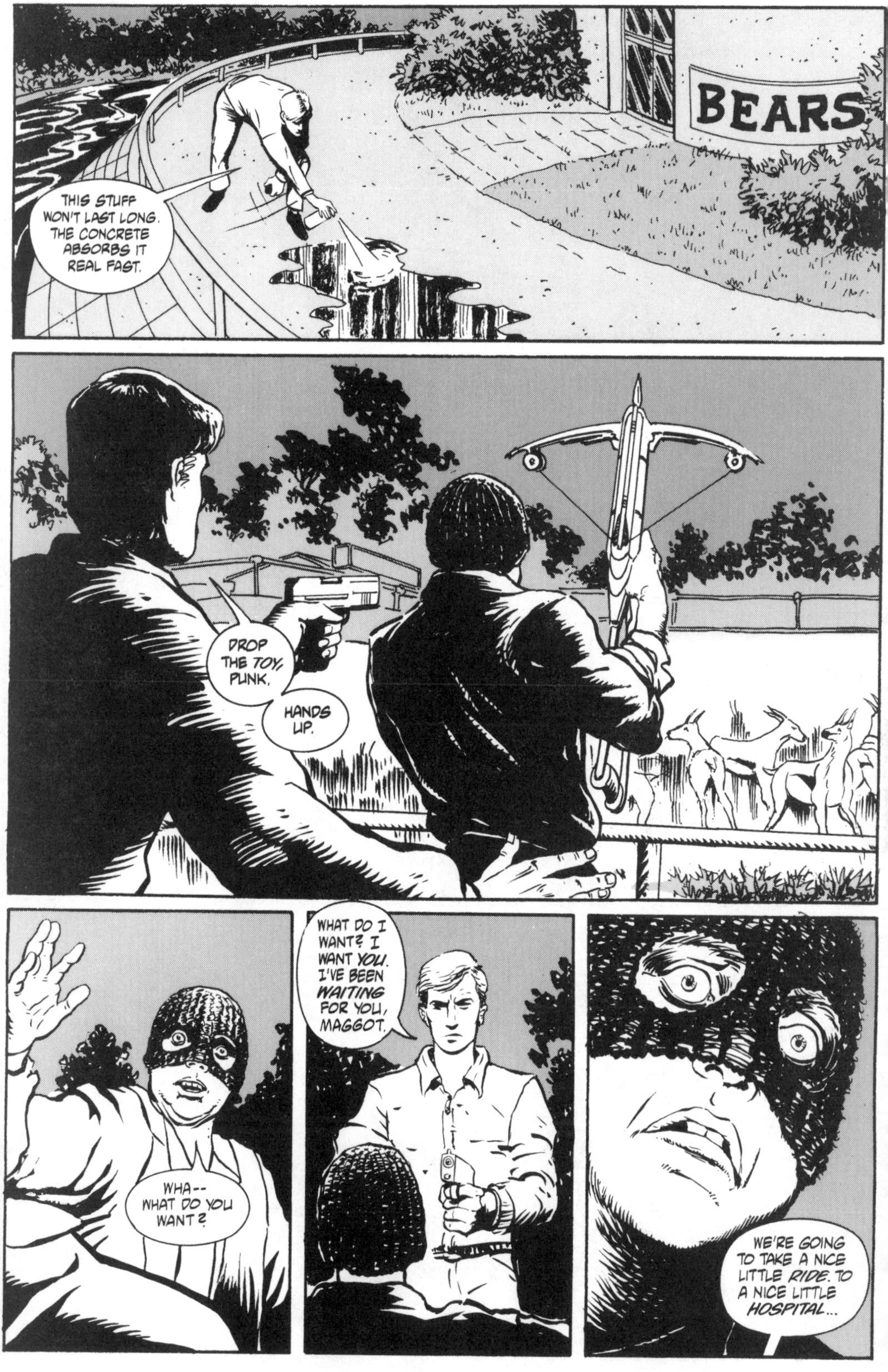
BEARS
THIS STUFF WON'T LAST LONG. THE CONCRETE ABSORBS IT REAL FAST.
DROP THE TOY, PUNK.
HANDS UP.
WHA-- WHAT DO YOU WANT?
WHAT DO I WANT? I WANT YOU. I'VE BEEN WAITING FOR YOU, MAGGOT.
WE'RE GOING TO TAKE A NICE LITTLE RIDE. TO A NICE LITTLE HOSPITAL...

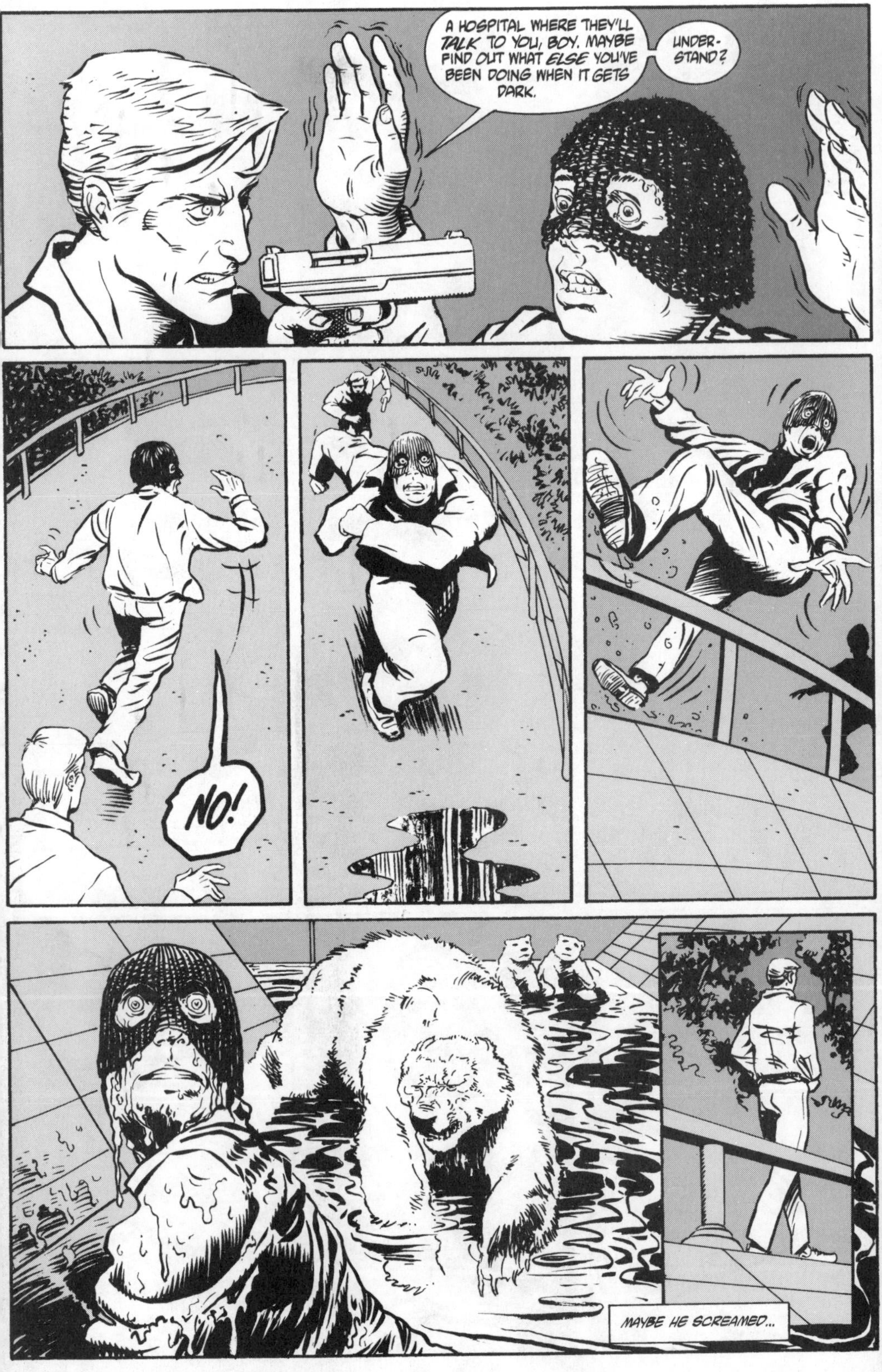
A HOSPITAL WHERE THEY'LL TALK TO YOU, BOY. MAYBE FIND OUT WHAT ELSE YOU'VE BEEN DOING WHEN IT GETS DARK.
UNDER-STAND?
NO!
MAYBE HE SCREAMED...

TREATMENT

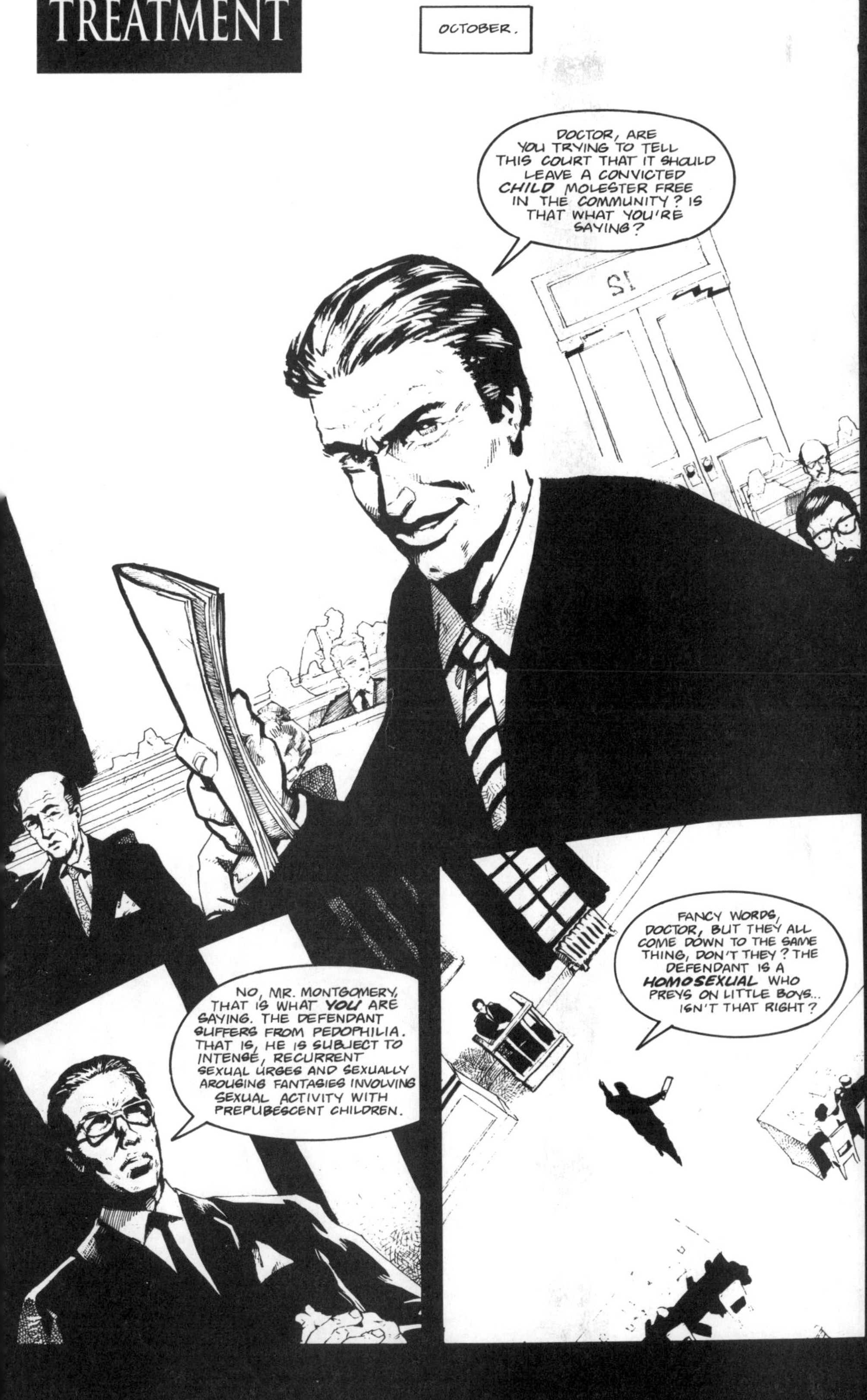

OCTOBER.
DOCTOR, ARE YOU TRYING TO TELL THIS COURT THAT IT SHOULD LEAVE A CONVICTED CHILD MOLESTER FREE IN THE COMMUNITY? IS THAT WHAT YOU'RE SAYING?
12
NO, MR. MONTGOMERY, THAT IS WHAT YOU ARE SAYING. THE DEFENDANT SUFFERS FROM PEDOPHILIA. THAT IS, HE IS SUBJECT TO INTENSE, RECURRENT SEXUAL URGES AND SEXUALLY AROUSING FANTASIES INVOLVING SEXUAL ACTIVITY WITH PREPUBESCENT CHILDREN.
FANCY WORDS, DOCTOR, BUT THEY ALL COME DOWN TO THE SAME THING, DON'T THEY? THE DEFENDANT IS A HOMOSEXUAL WHO PREYS ON LITTLE BOYS... ISN'T THAT RIGHT?

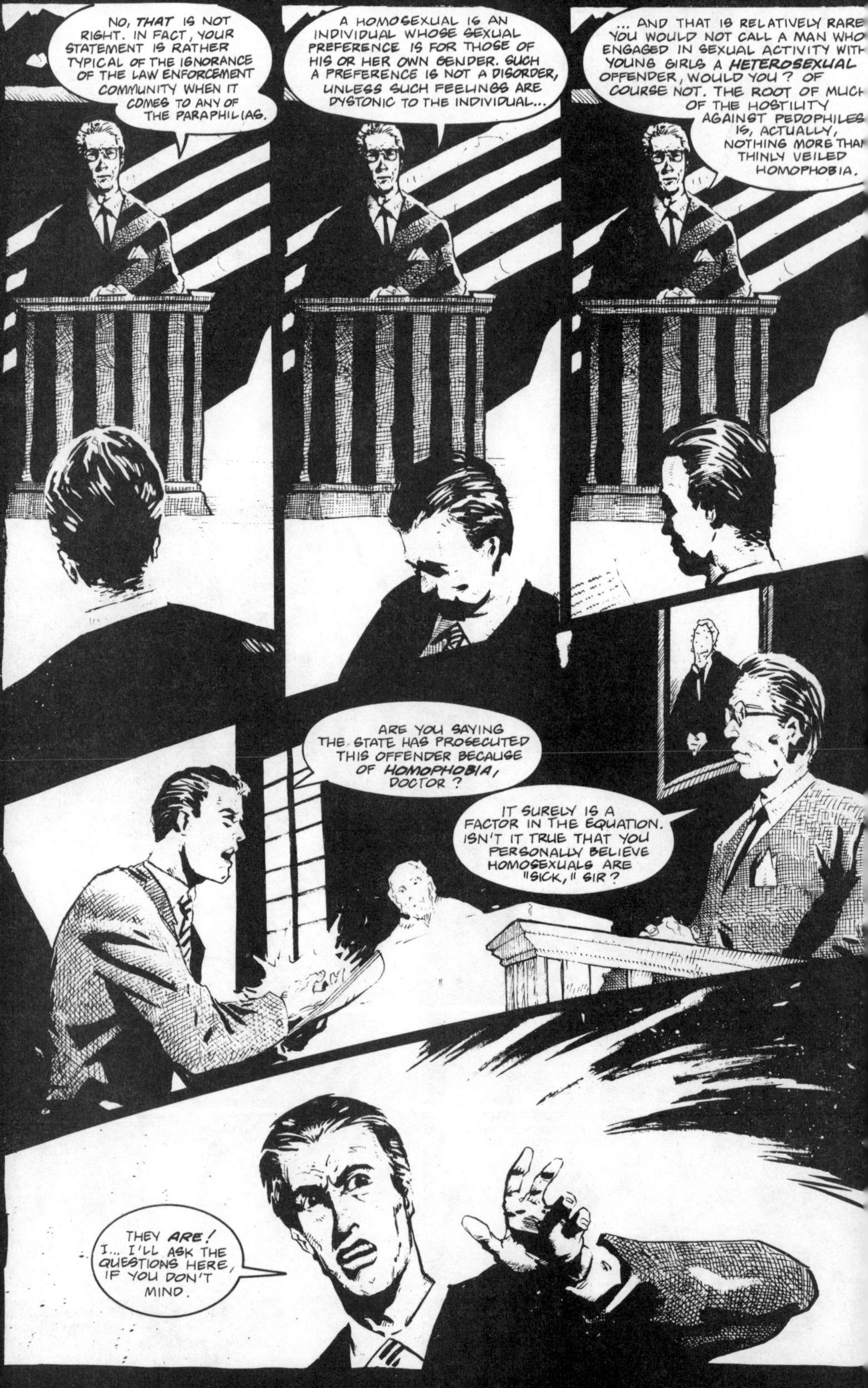

NO, THAT IS NOT RIGHT. IN FACT, YOUR STATEMENT IS RATHER TYPICAL OF THE IGNORANCE OF THE LAW ENFORCEMENT COMMUNITY WHEN IT COMES TO ANY OF THE PARAPHILIAS.
A HOMOSEXUAL IS AN INDIVIDUAL WHOSE SEXUAL PREFERENCE IS FOR THOSE OF HIS OR HER OWN GENDER. SUCH A PREFERENCE IS NOT A DISORDER, UNLESS SUCH FEELINGS ARE DYSTONIC TO THE INDIVIDUAL...
... AND THAT IS RELATIVELY RARE. YOU WOULD NOT CALL A MAN WHO ENGAGED IN SEXUAL ACTIVITY WITH YOUNG GIRLS A HETEROSEXUAL OFFENDER, WOULD YOU? OF COURSE NOT. THE ROOT OF MUCH OF THE HOSTILITY AGAINST PEDOPHILES IS, ACTUALLY, NOTHING MORE THAN THINLY VEILED HOMOPHOBIA.
ARE YOU SAYING THE STATE HAS PROSECUTED THIS OFFENDER BECAUSE OF HOMOPHOBIA, DOCTOR?
IT SURELY IS A FACTOR IN THE EQUATION. ISN'T IT TRUE THAT YOU PERSONALLY BELIEVE HOMOSEXUALS ARE "SICK," SIR?
THEY ARE! I... I'LL ASK THE QUESTIONS HERE, IF YOU DON'T MIND.

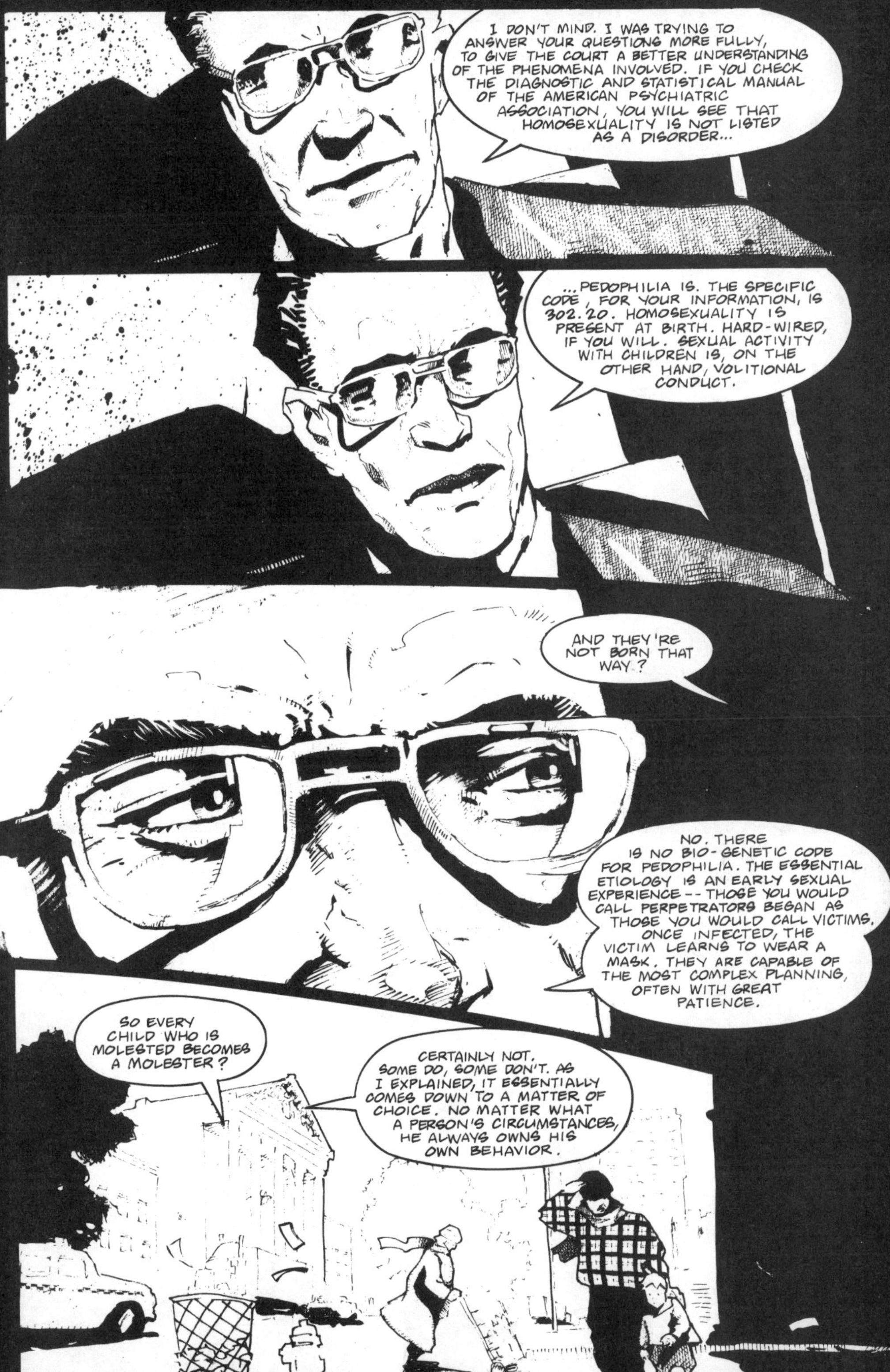
I DON'T MIND. I WAS TRYING TO ANSWER YOUR QUESTIONS MORE FULLY, TO GIVE THE COURT A BETTER UNDERSTANDING OF THE PHENOMENA INVOLVED. IF YOU CHECK THE DIAGNOSTIC AND STATISTICAL MANUAL OF THE AMERICAN PSYCHIATRIC ASSOCIATION, YOU WILL SEE THAT HOMOSEXUALITY IS NOT LISTED AS A DISORDER...
...PEDOPHILIA IS. THE SPECIFIC CODE, FOR YOUR INFORMATION, IS 302.20. HOMOSEXUALITY IS PRESENT AT BIRTH. HARD-WIRED, IF YOU WILL. SEXUAL ACTIVITY WITH CHILDREN IS, ON THE OTHER HAND, VOLITIONAL CONDUCT.
AND THEY'RE NOT BORN THAT WAY?
NO. THERE IS NO BIO-GENETIC CODE FOR PEDOPHILIA. THE ESSENTIAL ETIOLOGY IS AN EARLY SEXUAL EXPERIENCE -- THOSE YOU WOULD CALL PERPETRATORS BEGAN AS THOSE YOU WOULD CALL VICTIMS. ONCE INFECTED, THE VICTIM LEARNS TO WEAR A MASK. THEY ARE CAPABLE OF THE MOST COMPLEX PLANNING, OFTEN WITH GREAT PATIENCE.
SO EVERY CHILD WHO IS MOLESTED BECOMES A MOLESTER?
CERTAINLY NOT. SOME DO, SOME DON'T. AS I EXPLAINED, IT ESSENTIALLY COMES DOWN TO A MATTER OF CHOICE. NO MATTER WHAT A PERSON'S CIRCUMSTANCES, HE ALWAYS OWNS HIS OWN BEHAVIOR.

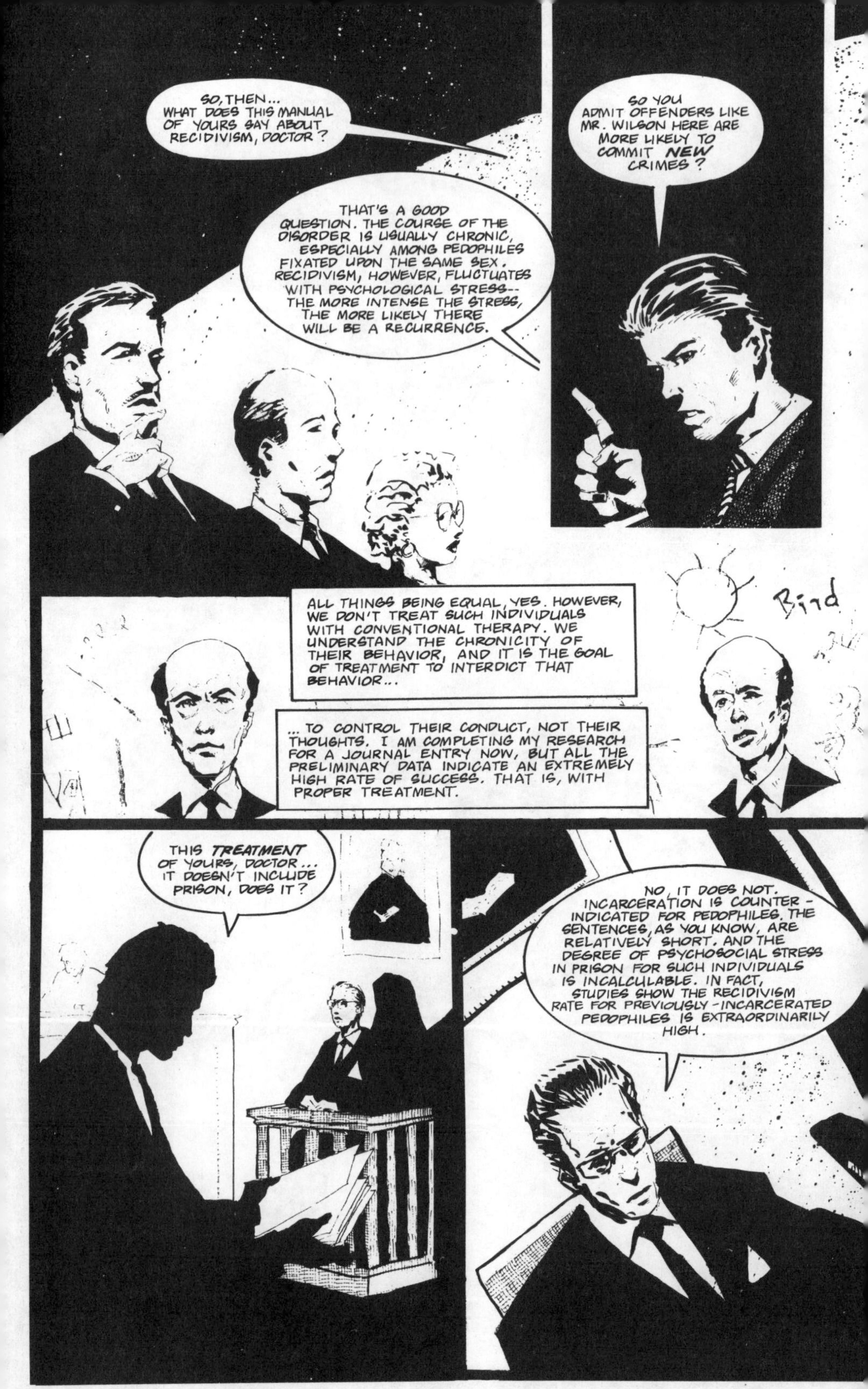

SO, THEN... WHAT DOES THIS MANUAL OF YOURS SAY ABOUT RECIDIVISM, DOCTOR?
THAT'S A GOOD QUESTION. THE COURSE OF THE DISORDER IS USUALLY CHRONIC, ESPECIALLY AMONG PEDOPHILES FIXATED UPON THE SAME SEX. RECIDIVISM, HOWEVER, FLUCTUATES WITH PSYCHOLOGICAL STRESS-- THE MORE INTENSE THE STRESS, THE MORE LIKELY THERE WILL BE A RECURRENCE.
SO YOU ADMIT OFFENDERS LIKE MR. WILSON HERE ARE MORE LIKELY TO COMMIT NEW CRIMES?
ALL THINGS BEING EQUAL, YES. HOWEVER, WE DON'T TREAT SUCH INDIVIDUALS WITH CONVENTIONAL THERAPY. WE UNDERSTAND THE CHRONICITY OF THEIR BEHAVIOR, AND IT IS THE GOAL OF TREATMENT TO INTERDICT THAT BEHAVIOR...
...TO CONTROL THEIR CONDUCT, NOT THEIR THOUGHTS. I AM COMPLETING MY RESEARCH FOR A JOURNAL ENTRY NOW, BUT ALL THE PRELIMINARY DATA INDICATE AN EXTREMELY HIGH RATE OF SUCCESS. THAT IS, WITH PROPER TREATMENT.
THIS TREATMENT OF YOURS, DOCTOR... IT DOESN'T INCLUDE PRISON, DOES IT?
NO, IT DOES NOT. INCARCERATION IS COUNTER-INDICATED FOR PEDOPHILES. THE SENTENCES, AS YOU KNOW, ARE RELATIVELY SHORT. AND THE DEGREE OF PSYCHOSOCIAL STRESS IN PRISON FOR SUCH INDIVIDUALS IS INCALCULABLE. IN FACT, STUDIES SHOW THE RECIDIVISM RATE FOR PREVIOUSLY-INCARCERATED PEDOPHILES IS EXTRAORDINARILY HIGH.

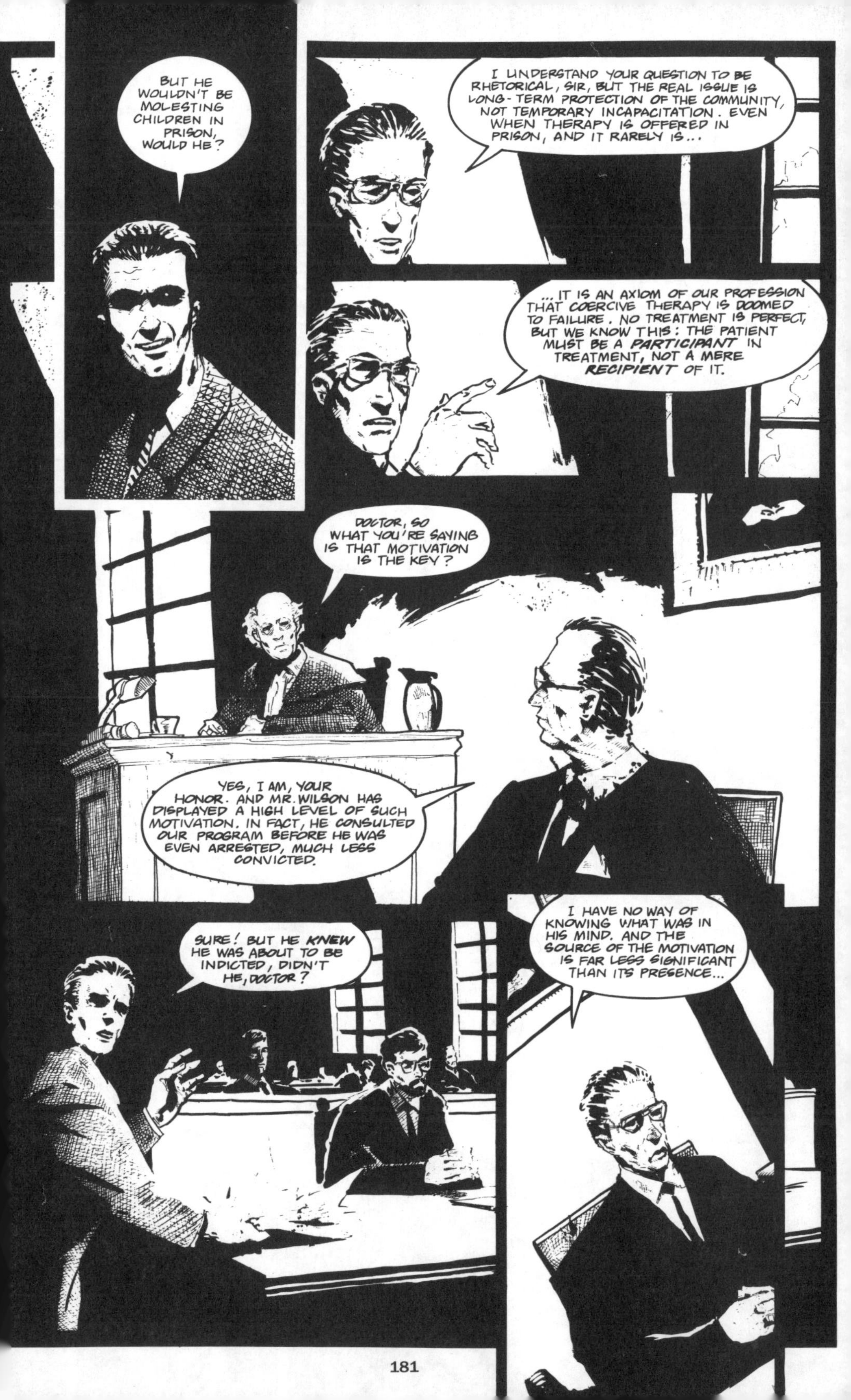
BUT HE WOULDN'T BE MOLESTING CHILDREN IN PRISON, WOULD HE?
I UNDERSTAND YOUR QUESTION TO BE RHETORICAL, SIR, BUT THE REAL ISSUE IS LONG-TERM PROTECTION OF THE COMMUNITY, NOT TEMPORARY INCAPACITATION. EVEN WHEN THERAPY IS OFFERED IN PRISON, AND IT RARELY IS...
... IT IS AN AXIOM OF OUR PROFESSION THAT COERCIVE THERAPY IS DOOMED TO FAILURE. NO TREATMENT IS PERFECT, BUT WE KNOW THIS: THE PATIENT MUST BE A PARTICIPANT IN TREATMENT, NOT A MERE RECIPIENT OF IT.
DOCTOR, SO WHAT YOU'RE SAYING IS THAT MOTIVATION IS THE KEY?
YES, I AM, YOUR HONOR. AND MR. WILSON HAS DISPLAYED A HIGH LEVEL OF SUCH MOTIVATION. IN FACT, HE CONSULTED OUR PROGRAM BEFORE HE WAS EVEN ARRESTED, MUCH LESS CONVICTED.
SURE! BUT HE KNEW HE WAS ABOUT TO BE INDICTED, DIDN'T HE, DOCTOR?
I HAVE NO WAY OF KNOWING WHAT WAS IN HIS MIND. AND THE SOURCE OF THE MOTIVATION IS FAR LESS SIGNIFICANT THAN ITS PRESENCE...

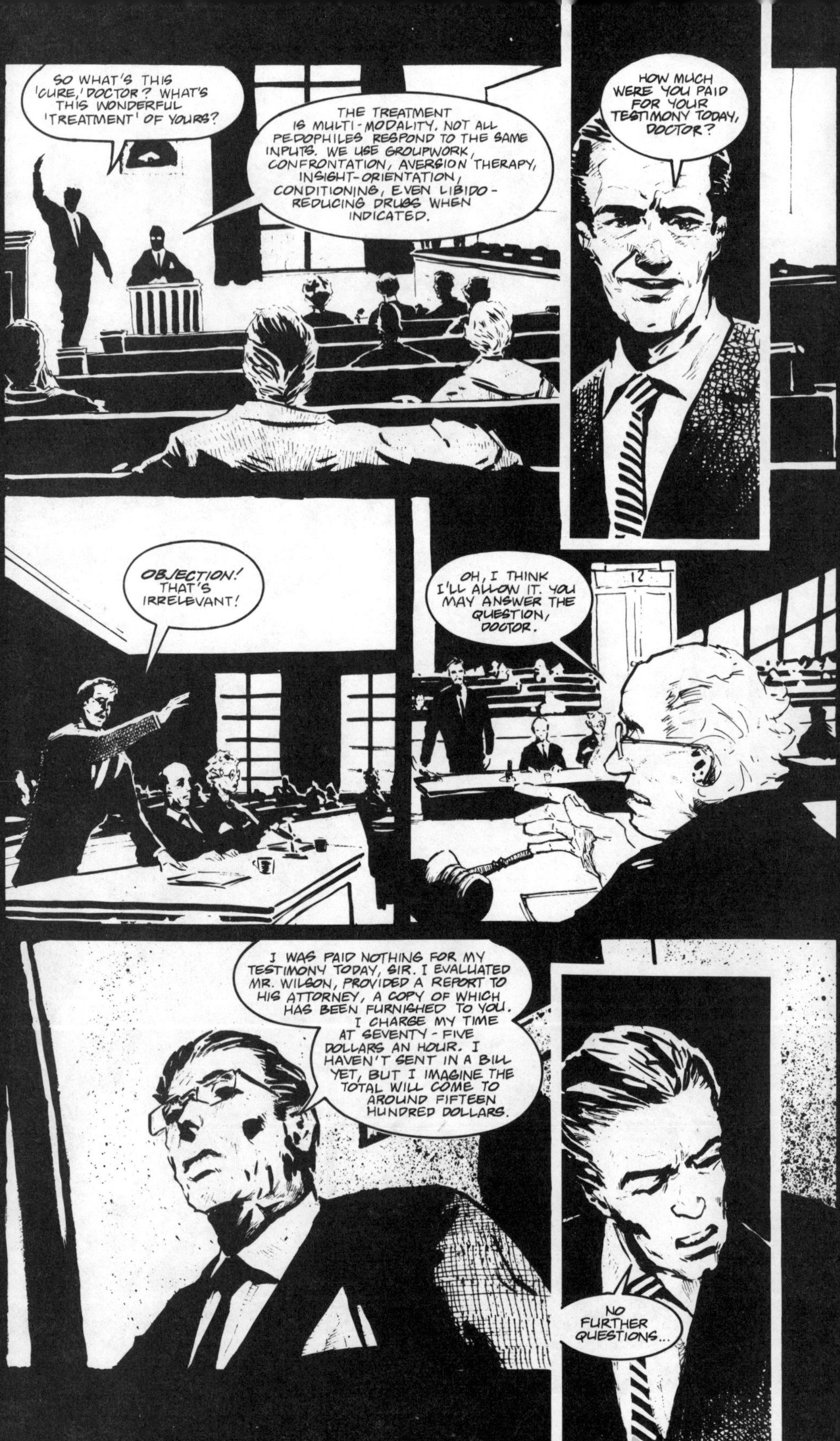
SO WHAT'S THIS 'CURE,' DOCTOR? WHAT'S THIS WONDERFUL 'TREATMENT' OF YOURS?
THE TREATMENT IS MULTI-MODALITY. NOT ALL PEDOPHILES RESPOND TO THE SAME INPUTS. WE USE GROUPWORK, CONFRONTATION, AVERSION THERAPY, INSIGHT-ORIENTATION, CONDITIONING, EVEN LIBIDO-REDUCING DRUGS WHEN INDICATED.
HOW MUCH WERE YOU PAID FOR YOUR TESTIMONY TODAY, DOCTOR?
OBJECTION! THAT'S IRRELEVANT!
OH, I THINK I'LL ALLOW IT. YOU MAY ANSWER THE QUESTION, DOCTOR.
12
I WAS PAID NOTHING FOR MY TESTIMONY TODAY, SIR. I EVALUATED MR. WILSON, PROVIDED A REPORT TO HIS ATTORNEY, A COPY OF WHICH HAS BEEN FURNISHED TO YOU. I CHARGE MY TIME AT SEVENTY-FIVE DOLLARS AN HOUR. I HAVEN'T SENT IN A BILL YET, BUT I IMAGINE THE TOTAL WILL COME TO AROUND FIFTEEN HUNDRED DOLLARS.
NO FURTHER QUESTIONS...

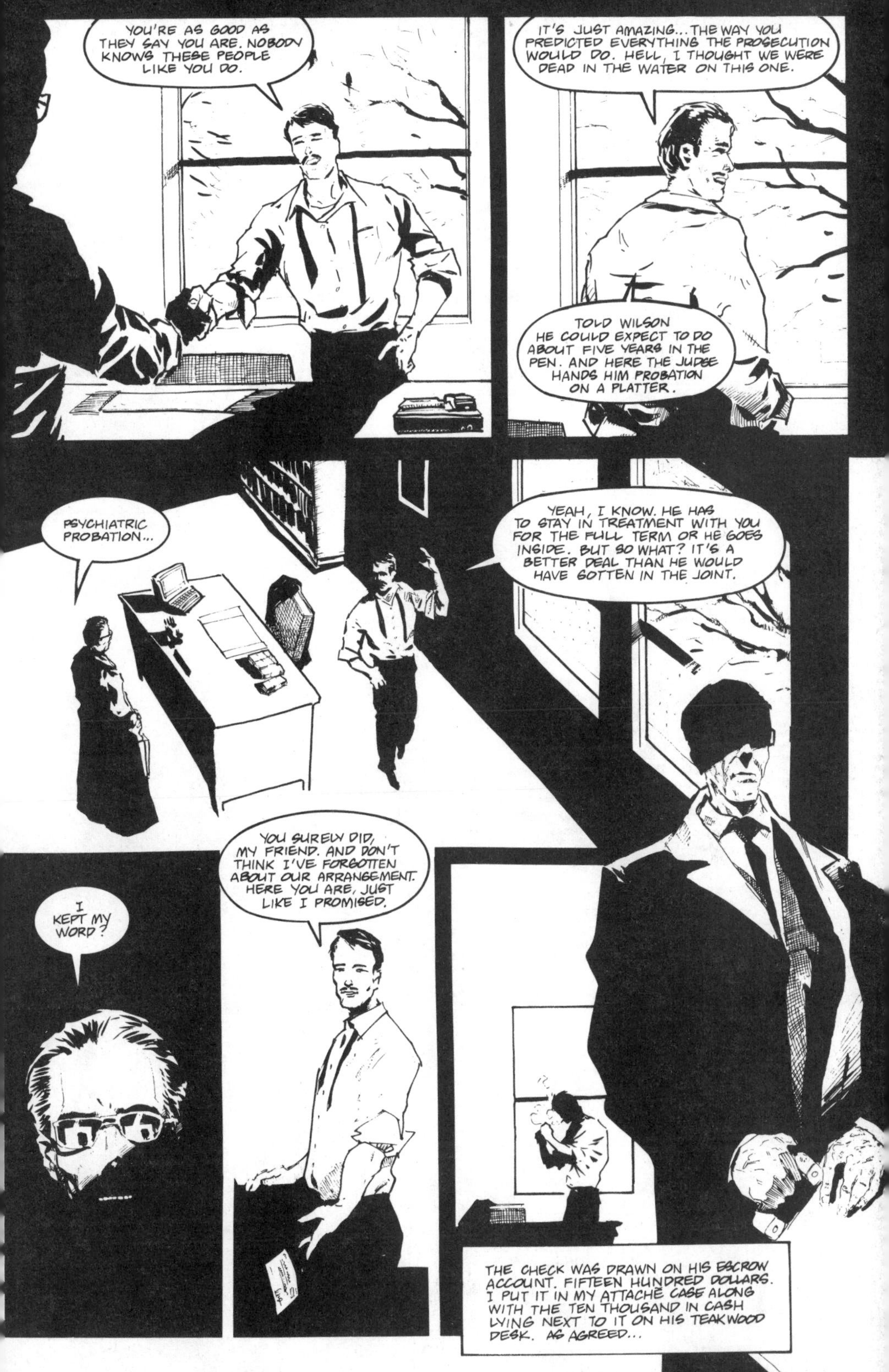
YOU'RE AS GOOD AS THEY SAY YOU ARE. NOBODY KNOWS THESE PEOPLE LIKE YOU DO.
IT'S JUST AMAZING... THE WAY YOU PREDICTED EVERYTHING THE PROSECUTION WOULD DO. HELL, I THOUGHT WE WERE DEAD IN THE WATER ON THIS ONE.
TOLD WILSON HE COULD EXPECT TO DO ABOUT FIVE YEARS IN THE PEN. AND HERE THE JUDGE HANDS HIM PROBATION ON A PLATTER.
PSYCHIATRIC PROBATION...
YEAH, I KNOW. HE HAS TO STAY IN TREATMENT WITH YOU FOR THE FULL TERM OR HE GOES INSIDE. BUT SO WHAT? IT'S A BETTER DEAL THAN HE WOULD HAVE GOTTEN IN THE JOINT.
I KEPT MY WORD?
YOU SURELY DID, MY FRIEND. AND DON'T THINK I'VE FORGOTTEN ABOUT OUR ARRANGEMENT. HERE YOU ARE, JUST LIKE I PROMISED.
THE CHECK WAS DRAWN ON HIS ESCROW ACCOUNT. FIFTEEN HUNDRED DOLLARS. I PUT IT IN MY ATTACHÉ CASE ALONG WITH THE TEN THOUSAND IN CASH LYING NEXT TO IT ON HIS TEAKWOOD DESK. AS AGREED...

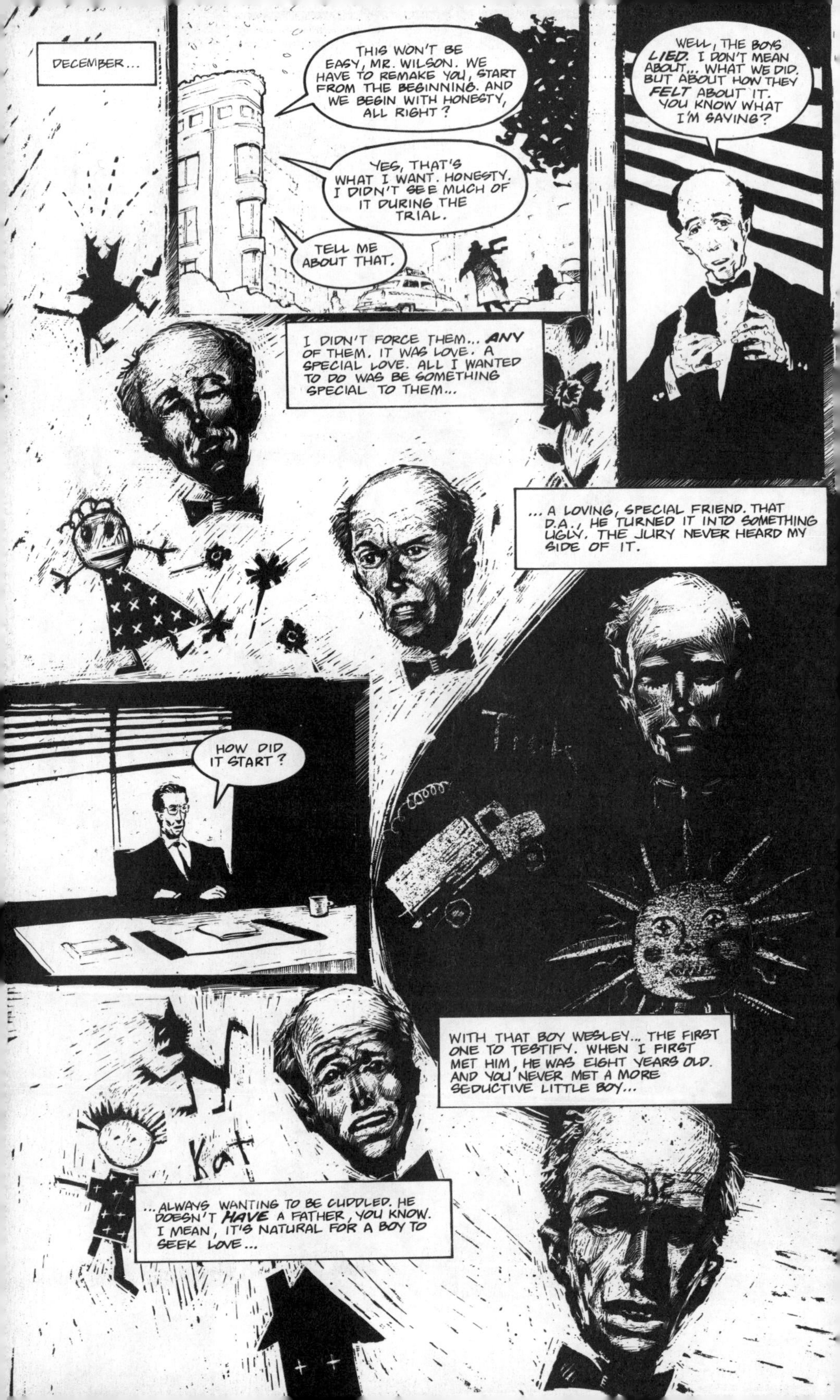

DECEMBER...
THIS WON'T BE EASY, MR. WILSON. WE HAVE TO REMAKE YOU, START FROM THE BEGINNING. AND WE BEGIN WITH HONESTY, ALL RIGHT?
YES, THAT'S WHAT I WANT. HONESTY. I DIDN'T SEE MUCH OF IT DURING THE TRIAL.
TELL ME ABOUT THAT.
WELL, THE BOYS LIED. I DON'T MEAN ABOUT... WHAT WE DID. BUT ABOUT HOW THEY FELT ABOUT IT. YOU KNOW WHAT I'M SAYING?
I DIDN'T FORCE THEM... ANY OF THEM. IT WAS LOVE. A SPECIAL LOVE. ALL I WANTED TO DO WAS BE SOMETHING SPECIAL TO THEM...
... A LOVING, SPECIAL FRIEND. THAT D.A., HE TURNED IT INTO SOMETHING UGLY. THE JURY NEVER HEARD MY SIDE OF IT.
HOW DID IT START?
WITH THAT BOY WESLEY... THE FIRST ONE TO TESTIFY. WHEN I FIRST MET HIM, HE WAS EIGHT YEARS OLD. AND YOU NEVER MET A MORE SEDUCTIVE LITTLE BOY...
Kat
...ALWAYS WANTING TO BE CUDDLED. HE DOESN'T HAVE A FATHER, YOU KNOW. I MEAN, IT'S NATURAL FOR A BOY TO SEEK LOVE...

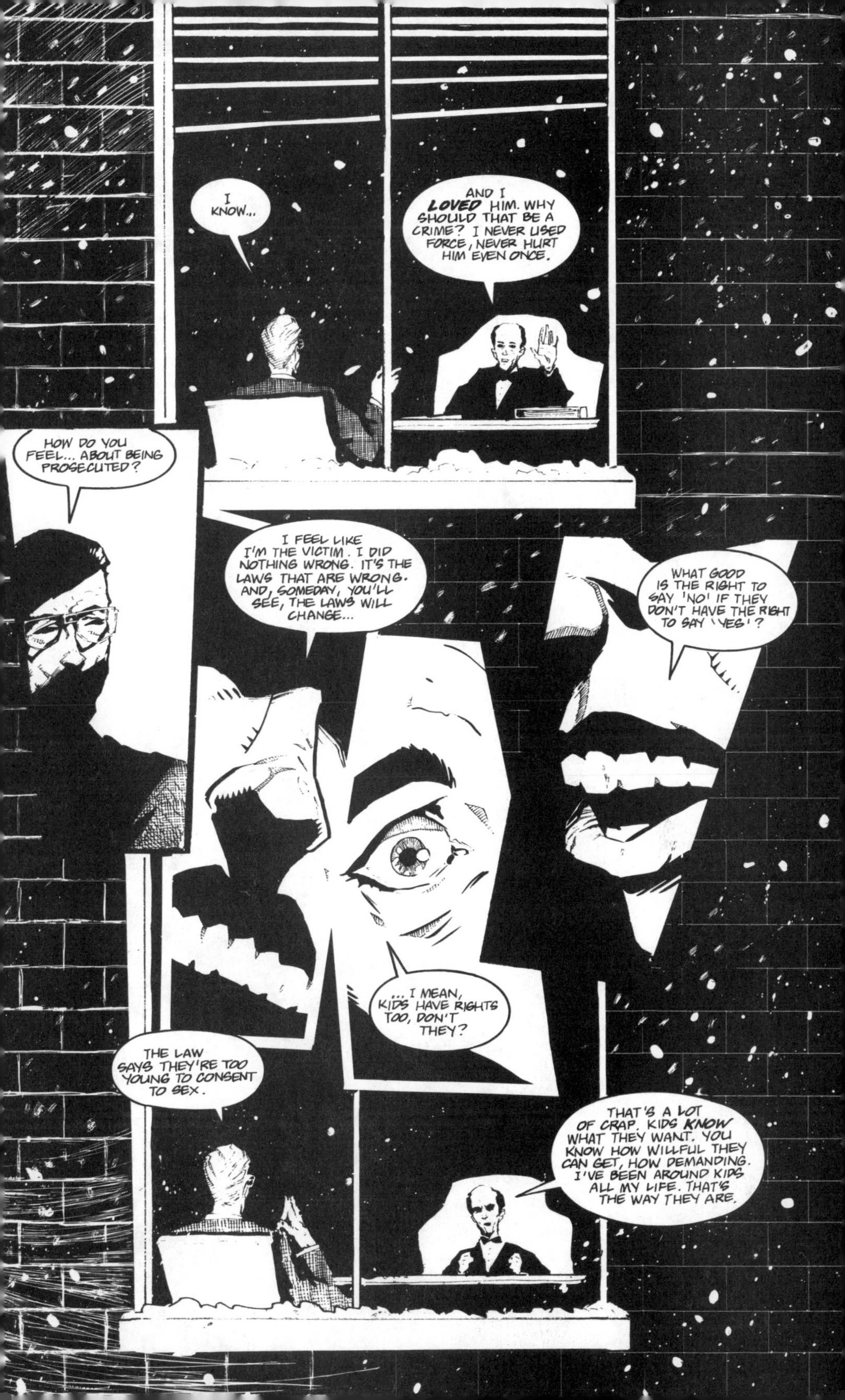

I KNOW...
AND I **LOVED** HIM. WHY SHOULD THAT BE A CRIME? I NEVER USED FORCE, NEVER HURT HIM EVEN ONCE.
HOW DO YOU FEEL... ABOUT BEING PROSECUTED?
I FEEL LIKE I'M THE VICTIM. I DID NOTHING WRONG. IT'S THE LAWS THAT ARE WRONG. AND, SOMEDAY, YOU'LL SEE, THE LAWS WILL CHANGE...
WHAT GOOD IS THE RIGHT TO SAY 'NO' IF THEY DON'T HAVE THE RIGHT TO SAY 'YES'?
...I MEAN, KIDS HAVE RIGHTS TOO, DON'T THEY?
THE LAW SAYS THEY'RE TOO YOUNG TO CONSENT TO SEX.
THAT'S A LOT OF CRAP. KIDS **KNOW** WHAT THEY WANT. YOU KNOW HOW WILLFUL THEY CAN GET, HOW DEMANDING. I'VE BEEN AROUND KIDS ALL MY LIFE. THAT'S THE WAY THEY ARE.

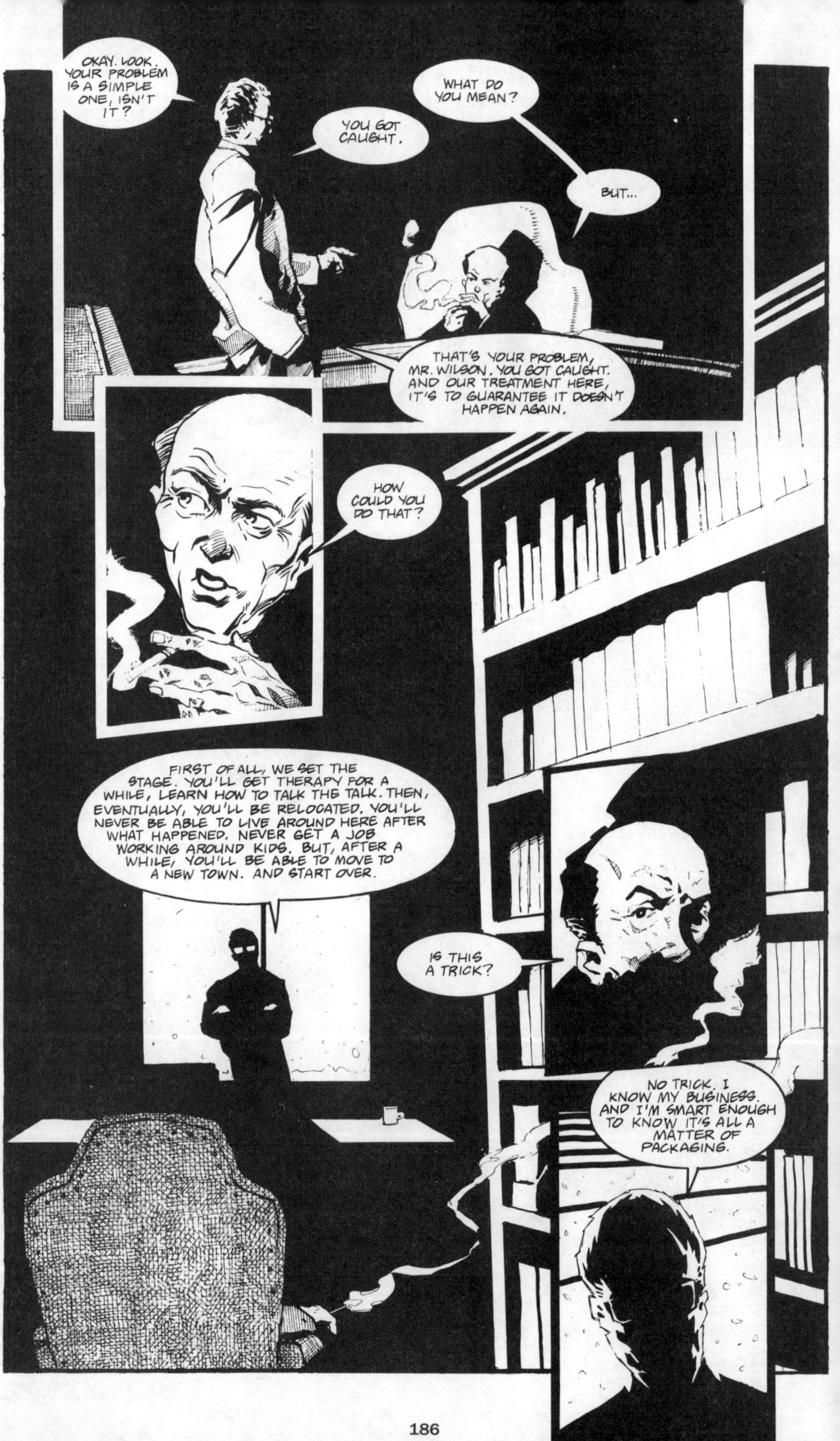
OKAY. LOOK. YOUR PROBLEM IS A SIMPLE ONE, ISN'T IT?
YOU GOT CAUGHT.
WHAT DO YOU MEAN?
BUT...
THAT'S YOUR PROBLEM, MR. WILSON. YOU GOT CAUGHT. AND OUR TREATMENT HERE, IT'S TO GUARANTEE IT DOESN'T HAPPEN AGAIN.
HOW COULD YOU DO THAT?
FIRST OF ALL, WE SET THE STAGE. YOU'LL GET THERAPY FOR A WHILE, LEARN HOW TO TALK THE TALK. THEN, EVENTUALLY, YOU'LL BE RELOCATED. YOU'LL NEVER BE ABLE TO LIVE AROUND HERE AFTER WHAT HAPPENED. NEVER GET A JOB WORKING AROUND KIDS. BUT, AFTER A WHILE, YOU'LL BE ABLE TO MOVE TO A NEW TOWN. AND START OVER.
IS THIS A TRICK?
NO TRICK. I KNOW MY BUSINESS. AND I'M SMART ENOUGH TO KNOW IT'S ALL A MATTER OF PACKAGING.

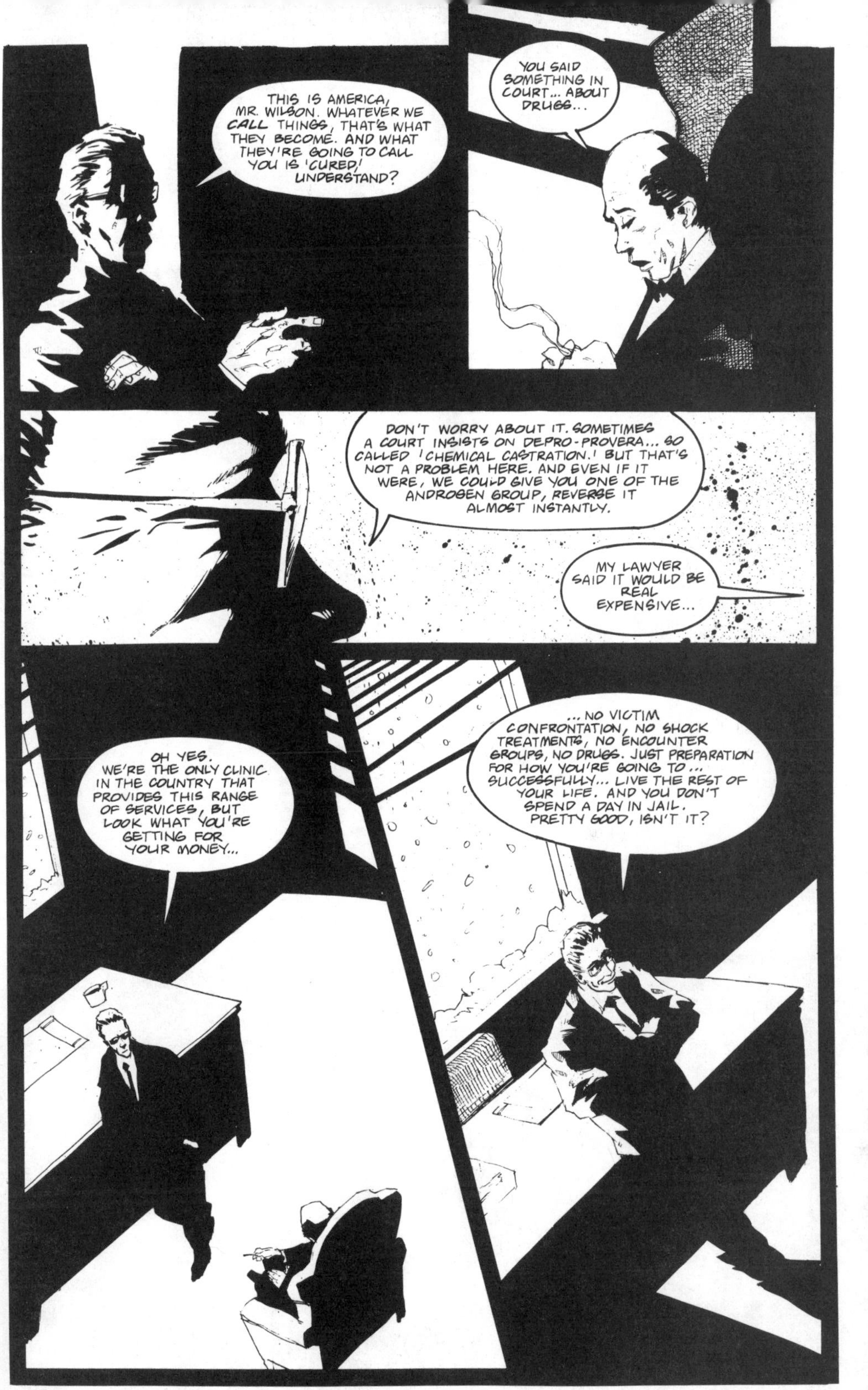
THIS IS AMERICA, MR. WILSON. WHATEVER WE CALL THINGS, THAT'S WHAT THEY BECOME. AND WHAT THEY'RE GOING TO CALL YOU IS 'CURED,' UNDERSTAND?
YOU SAID SOMETHING IN COURT... ABOUT DRUGS...
DON'T WORRY ABOUT IT. SOMETIMES A COURT INSISTS ON DEPRO-PROVERA... SO CALLED 'CHEMICAL CASTRATION.' BUT THAT'S NOT A PROBLEM HERE. AND EVEN IF IT WERE, WE COULD GIVE YOU ONE OF THE ANDROGEN GROUP, REVERSE IT ALMOST INSTANTLY.
MY LAWYER SAID IT WOULD BE REAL EXPENSIVE...
OH YES. WE'RE THE ONLY CLINIC IN THE COUNTRY THAT PROVIDES THIS RANGE OF SERVICES, BUT LOOK WHAT YOU'RE GETTING FOR YOUR MONEY...
...NO VICTIM CONFRONTATION, NO SHOCK TREATMENTS, NO ENCOUNTER GROUPS, NO DRUGS. JUST PREPARATION FOR HOW YOU'RE GOING TO... SUCCESSFULLY... LIVE THE REST OF YOUR LIFE. AND YOU DON'T SPEND A DAY IN JAIL. PRETTY GOOD, ISN'T IT?

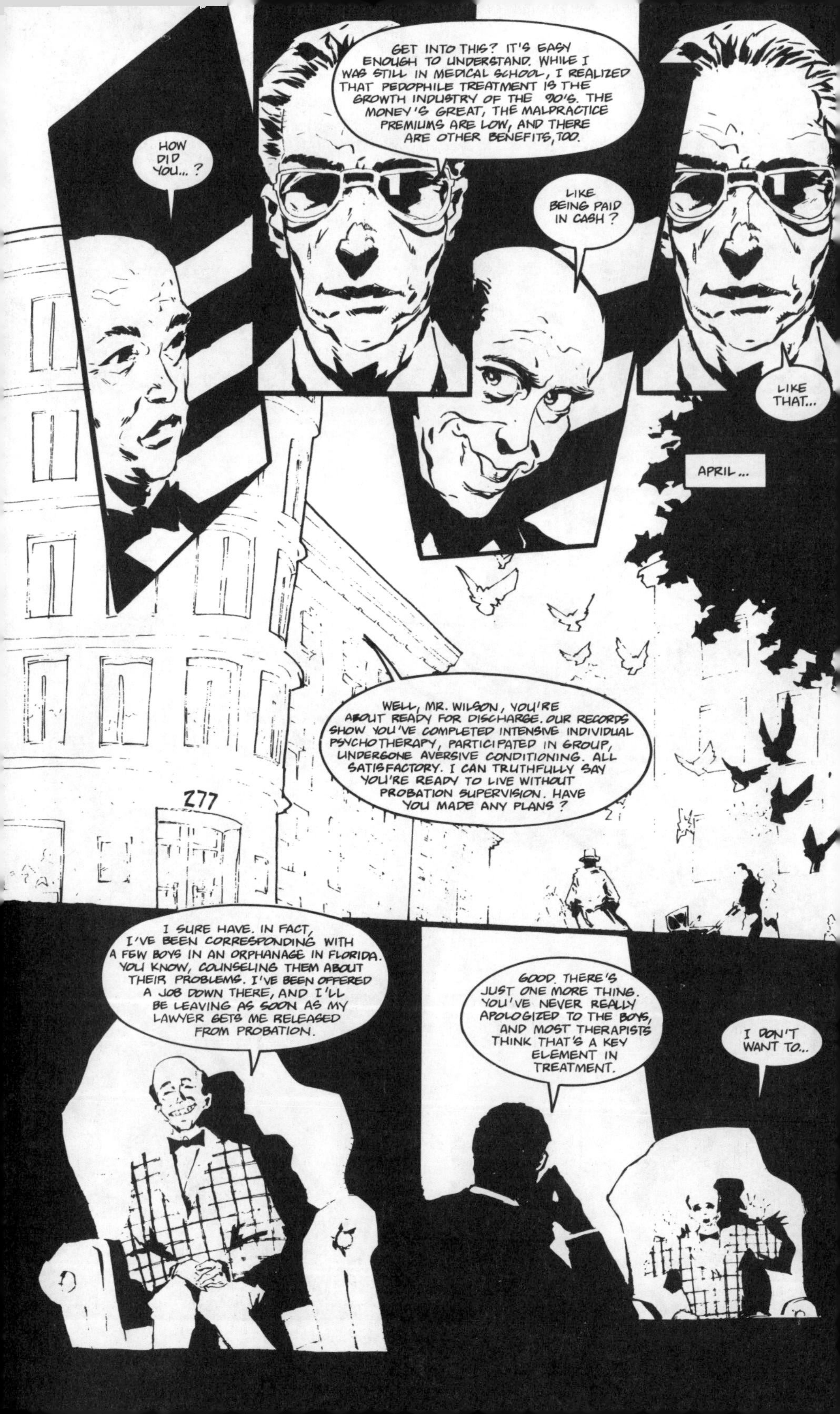
HOW DID YOU...?
GET INTO THIS? IT'S EASY ENOUGH TO UNDERSTAND. WHILE I WAS STILL IN MEDICAL SCHOOL, I REALIZED THAT PEDOPHILE TREATMENT IS THE GROWTH INDUSTRY OF THE '90'S. THE MONEY'S GREAT, THE MALPRACTICE PREMIUMS ARE LOW, AND THERE ARE OTHER BENEFITS, TOO.
LIKE BEING PAID IN CASH?
LIKE THAT...
APRIL...
WELL, MR. WILSON, YOU'RE ABOUT READY FOR DISCHARGE. OUR RECORDS SHOW YOU'VE COMPLETED INTENSIVE INDIVIDUAL PSYCHOTHERAPY, PARTICIPATED IN GROUP, UNDERGONE AVERSIVE CONDITIONING. ALL SATISFACTORY. I CAN TRUTHFULLY SAY YOU'RE READY TO LIVE WITHOUT PROBATION SUPERVISION. HAVE YOU MADE ANY PLANS?
277
I SURE HAVE. IN FACT, I'VE BEEN CORRESPONDING WITH A FEW BOYS IN AN ORPHANAGE IN FLORIDA. YOU KNOW, COUNSELING THEM ABOUT THEIR PROBLEMS. I'VE BEEN OFFERED A JOB DOWN THERE, AND I'LL BE LEAVING AS SOON AS MY LAWYER GETS ME RELEASED FROM PROBATION.
GOOD. THERE'S JUST ONE MORE THING. YOU'VE NEVER REALLY APOLOGIZED TO THE BOYS, AND MOST THERAPISTS THINK THAT'S A KEY ELEMENT IN TREATMENT.
I DON'T WANT TO...

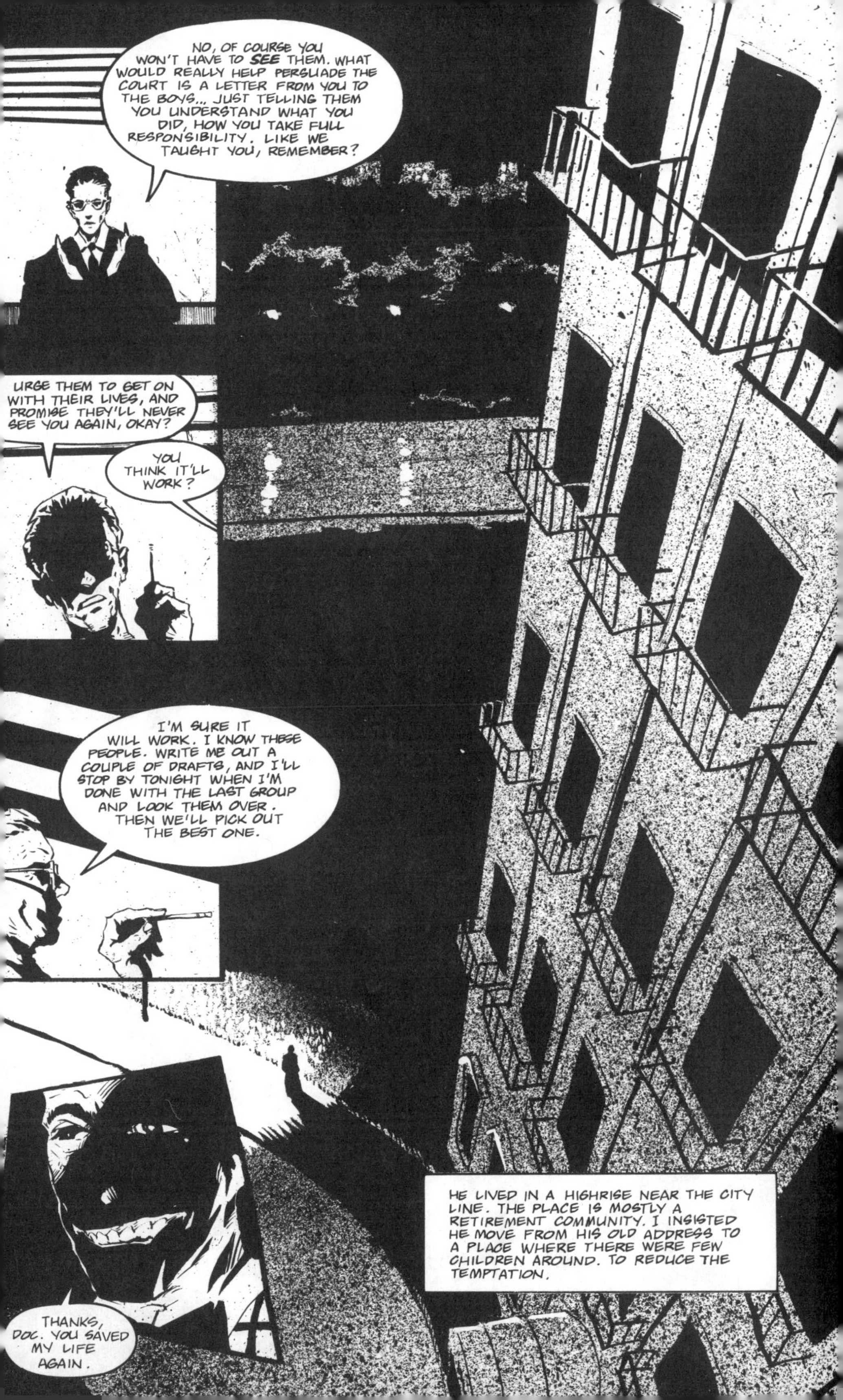
NO, OF COURSE YOU WON'T HAVE TO SEE THEM. WHAT WOULD REALLY HELP PERSUADE THE COURT IS A LETTER FROM YOU TO THE BOYS... JUST TELLING THEM YOU UNDERSTAND WHAT YOU DID, HOW YOU TAKE FULL RESPONSIBILITY. LIKE WE TAUGHT YOU, REMEMBER?
URGE THEM TO GET ON WITH THEIR LIVES, AND PROMISE THEY'LL NEVER SEE YOU AGAIN, OKAY?
YOU THINK IT'LL WORK?
I'M SURE IT WILL WORK. I KNOW THESE PEOPLE. WRITE ME OUT A COUPLE OF DRAFTS, AND I'LL STOP BY TONIGHT WHEN I'M DONE WITH THE LAST GROUP AND LOOK THEM OVER. THEN WE'LL PICK OUT THE BEST ONE.
THANKS, DOC. YOU SAVED MY LIFE AGAIN.
HE LIVED IN A HIGHRISE NEAR THE CITY LINE. THE PLACE IS MOSTLY A RETIREMENT COMMUNITY. I INSISTED HE MOVE FROM HIS OLD ADDRESS TO A PLACE WHERE THERE WERE FEW CHILDREN AROUND. TO REDUCE THE TEMPTATION.

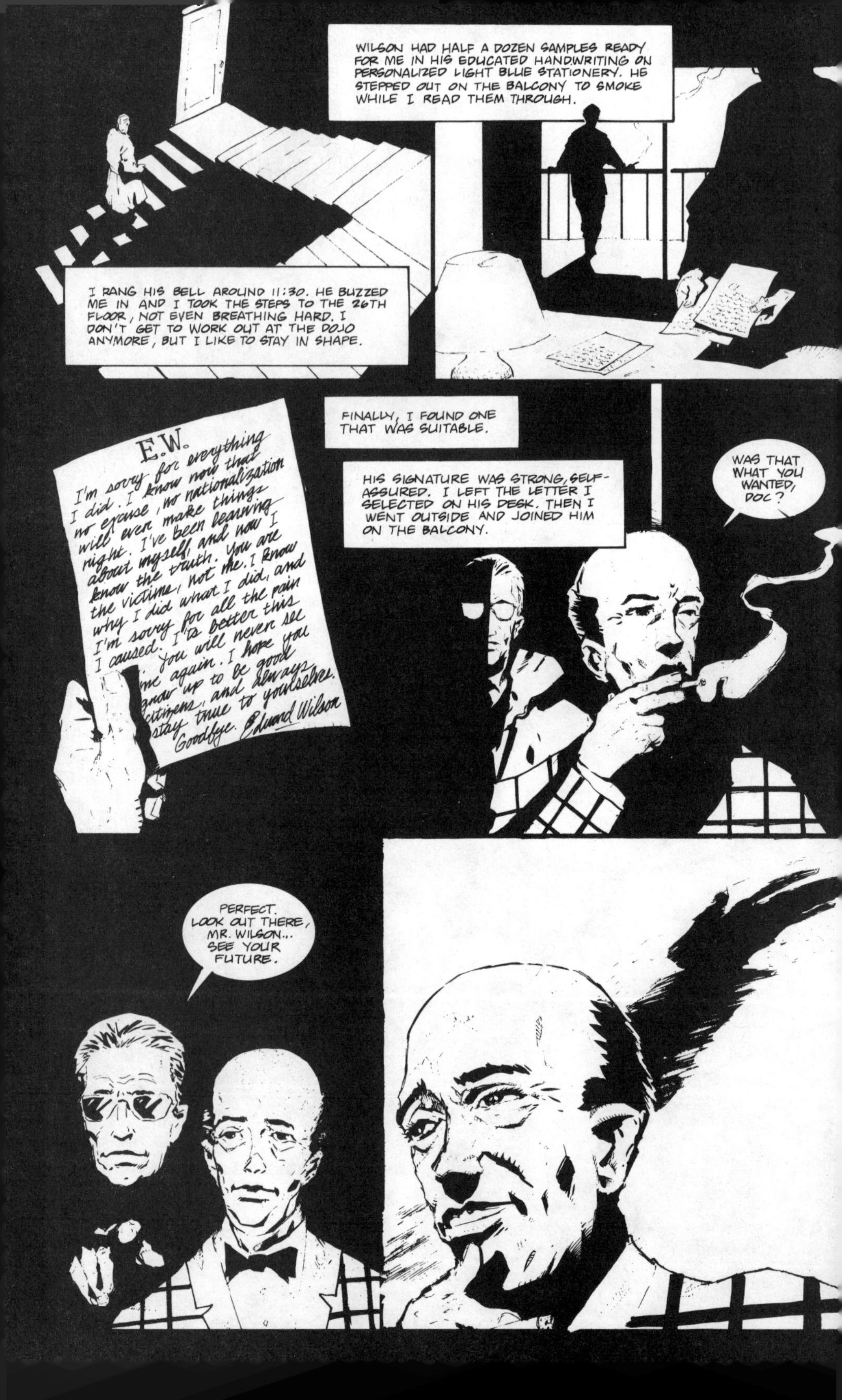

WILSON HAD HALF A DOZEN SAMPLES READY FOR ME IN HIS EDUCATED HANDWRITING ON PERSONALIZED LIGHT BLUE STATIONERY. HE STEPPED OUT ON THE BALCONY TO SMOKE WHILE I READ THEM THROUGH.
I RANG HIS BELL AROUND 11:30. HE BUZZED ME IN AND I TOOK THE STEPS TO THE 26TH FLOOR, NOT EVEN BREATHING HARD. I DON'T GET TO WORK OUT AT THE DOJO ANYMORE, BUT I LIKE TO STAY IN SHAPE.
E.W.
I'm sorry for everything
I did. I know now that
no excuse, no nationalization
will ever make things
right. I've been learning
about myself, and now I
know the truth. You are
the victims, not me. I know
why I did what I did, and
I'm sorry for all the pain
I caused. It's better this
You will never see
me again. I hope you
grow up to be good
citizens, and always
stay true to yourselves.
Goodbye. Edward Wilson
FINALLY, I FOUND ONE THAT WAS SUITABLE.
HIS SIGNATURE WAS STRONG, SELF-ASSURED. I LEFT THE LETTER I SELECTED ON HIS DESK. THEN I WENT OUTSIDE AND JOINED HIM ON THE BALCONY.
WAS THAT WHAT YOU WANTED, DOC?
PERFECT. LOOK OUT THERE, MR. WILSON... SEE YOUR FUTURE.

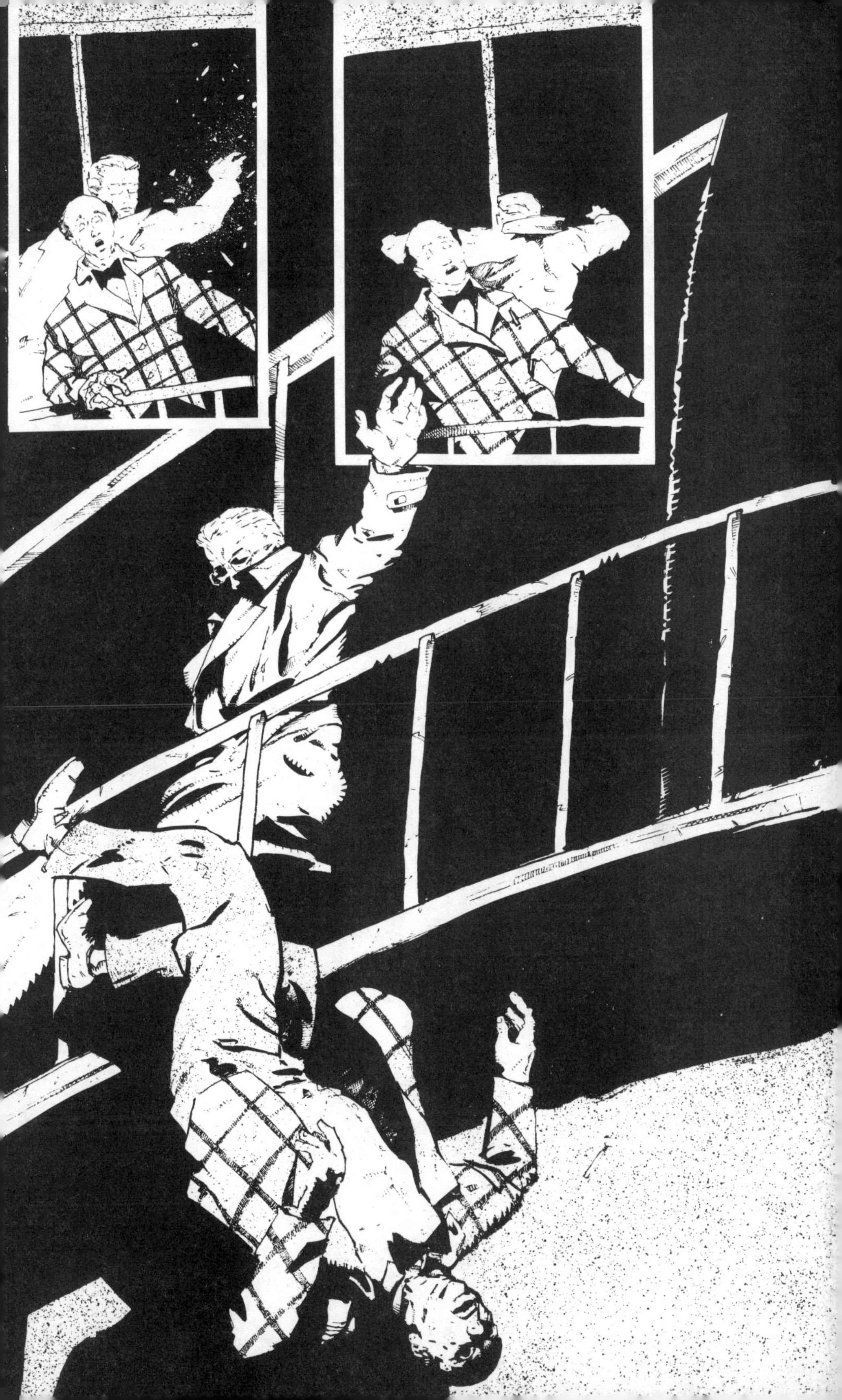

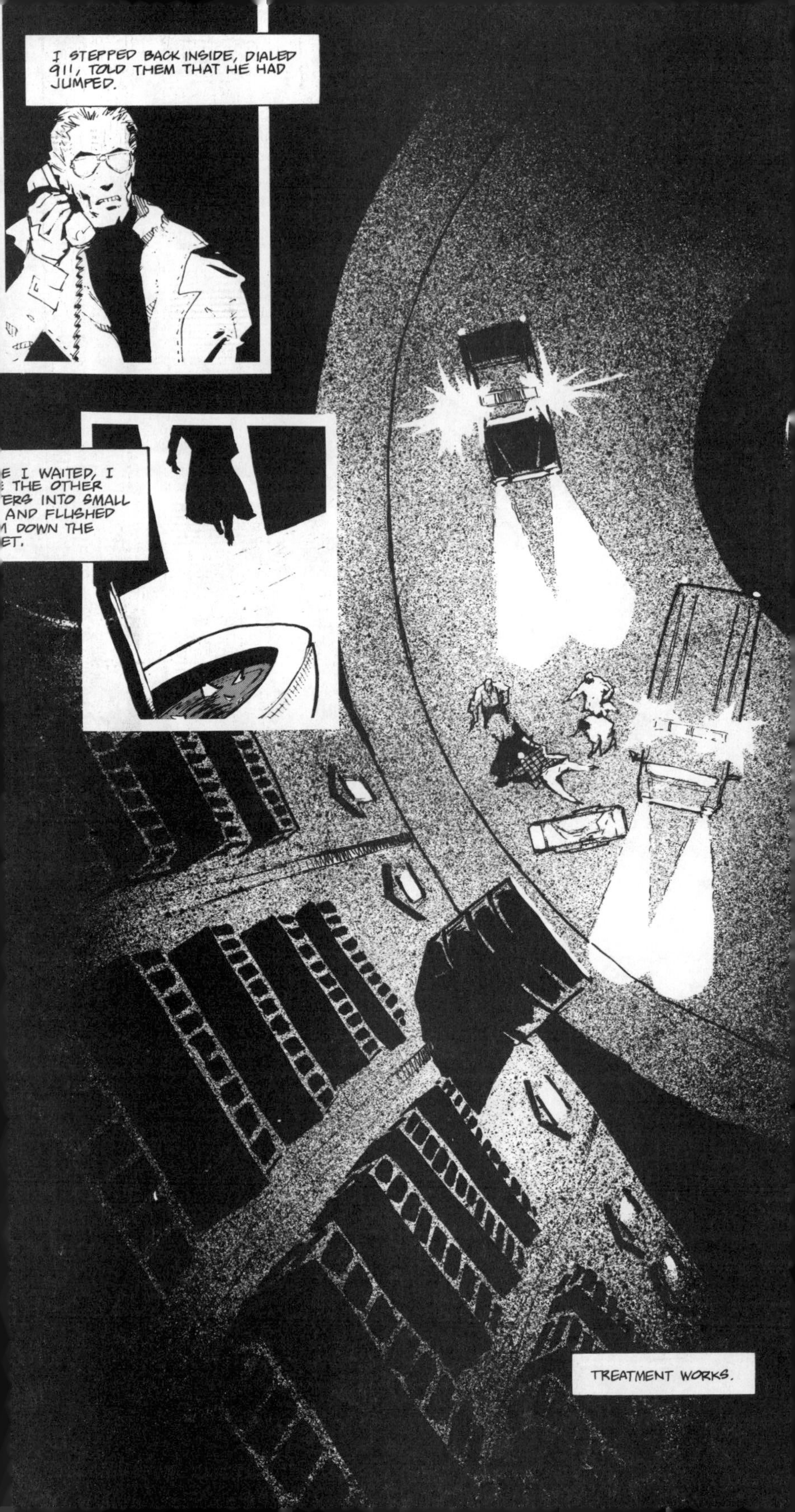

I STEPPED BACK INSIDE, DIALED 911, TOLD THEM THAT HE HAD JUMPED.
E I WAITED, I E THE OTHER ERS INTO SMALL AND FLUSHED M DOWN THE ET.
TREATMENT WORKS.

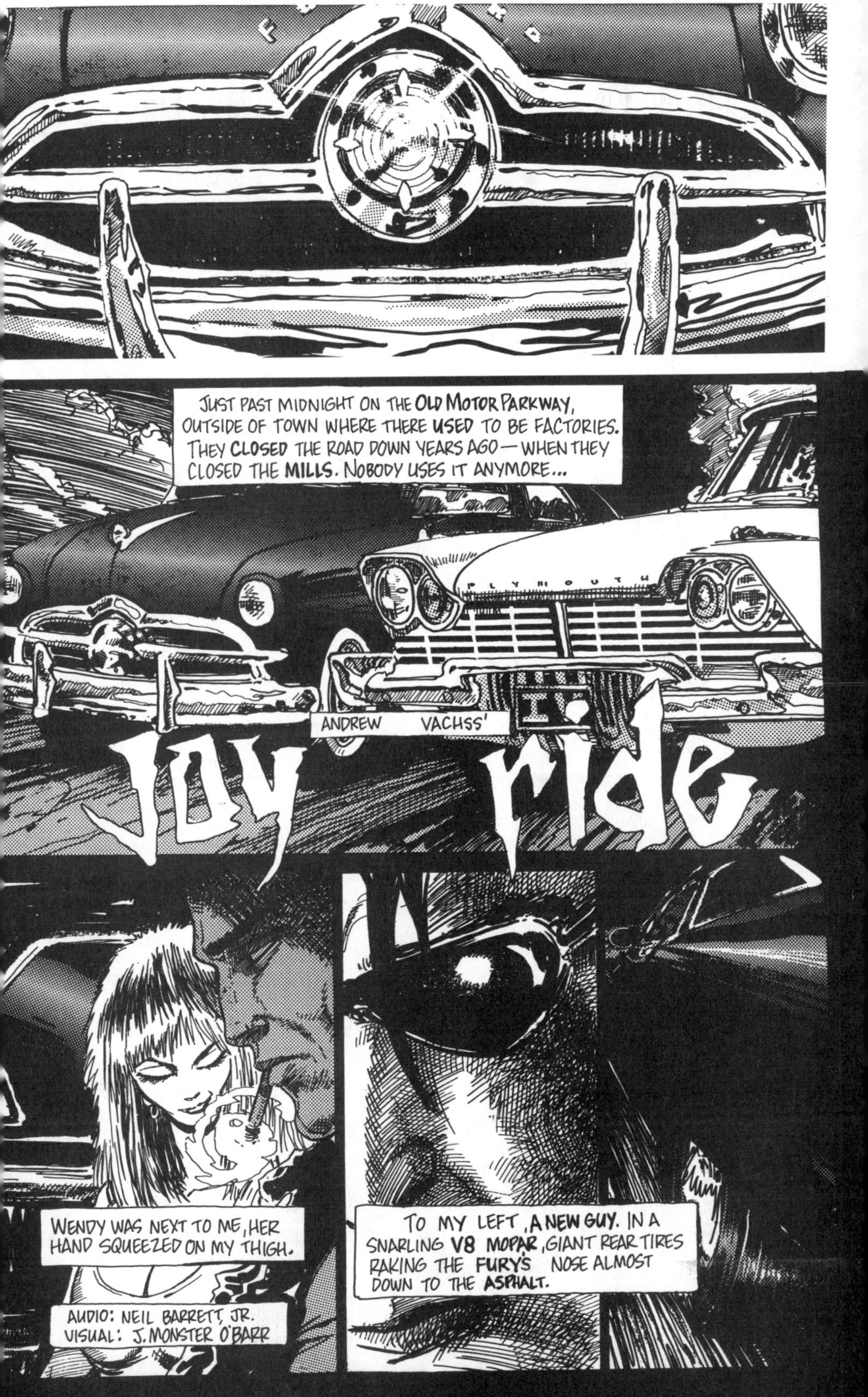
JUST PAST MIDNIGHT ON THE OLD MOTOR PARKWAY, OUTSIDE OF TOWN WHERE THERE USED TO BE FACTORIES. THEY CLOSED THE ROAD DOWN YEARS AGO— WHEN THEY CLOSED THE MILLS. NOBODY USES IT ANYMORE...
PLYMOUTH
ANDREW VACHSS'
JOY RIDE
WENDY WAS NEXT TO ME, HER HAND SQUEEZED ON MY THIGH.
AUDIO: NEIL BARRETT, JR.
VISUAL: J. MONSTER O'BARR
TO MY LEFT, A NEW GUY. IN A SNARLING V8 MOPAR, GIANT REAR TIRES RAKING THE FURY'S NOSE ALMOST DOWN TO THE ASPHALT.

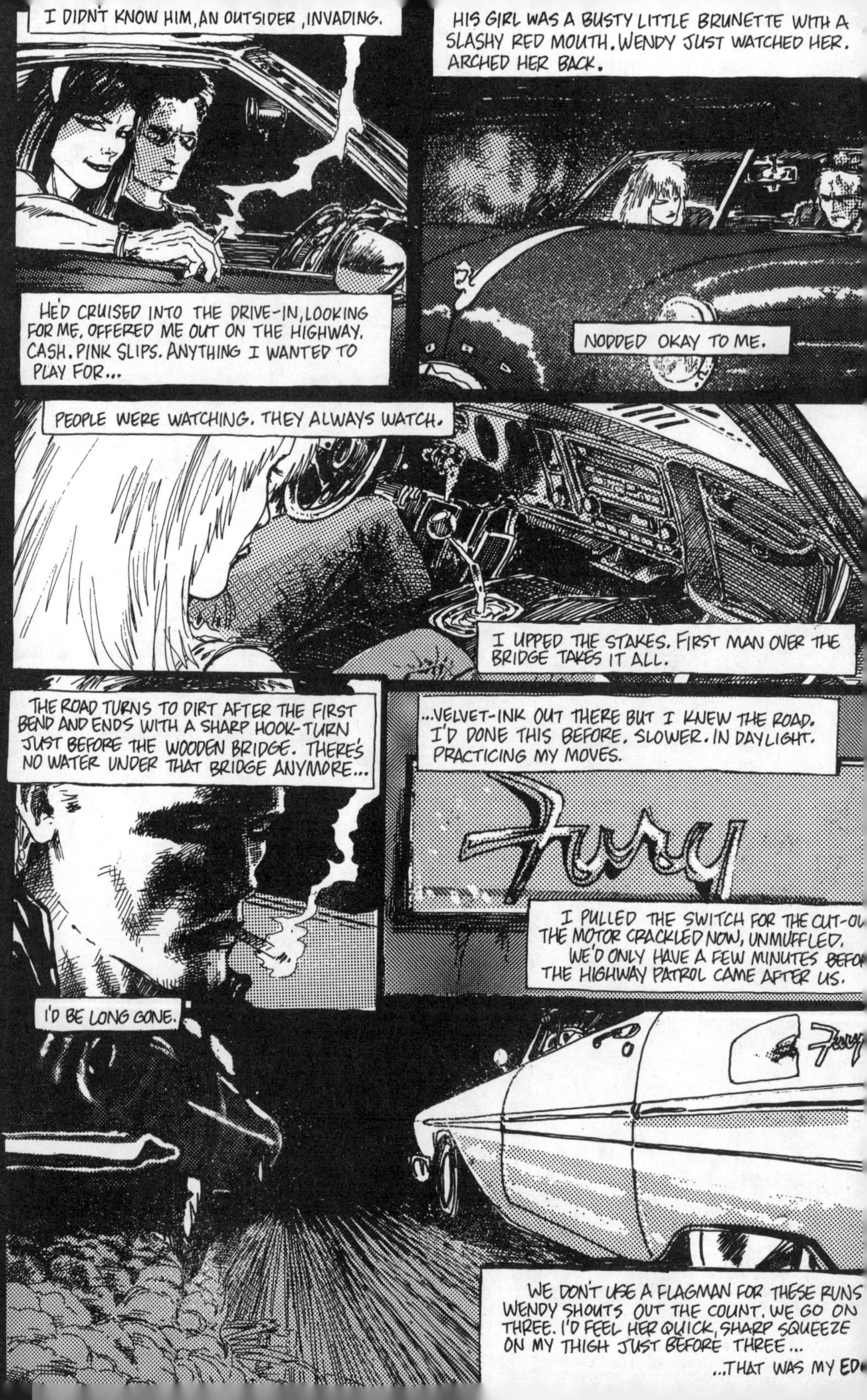
I DIDN'T KNOW HIM, AN OUTSIDER, INVADING.
HIS GIRL WAS A BUSTY LITTLE BRUNETTE WITH A SLASHY RED MOUTH. WENDY JUST WATCHED HER. ARCHED HER BACK.
HE'D CRUISED INTO THE DRIVE-IN, LOOKING FOR ME. OFFERED ME OUT ON THE HIGHWAY. CASH. PINK SLIPS. ANYTHING I WANTED TO PLAY FOR...
NODDED OKAY TO ME.
PEOPLE WERE WATCHING. THEY ALWAYS WATCH.
I UPPED THE STAKES. FIRST MAN OVER THE BRIDGE TAKES IT ALL.
THE ROAD TURNS TO DIRT AFTER THE FIRST BEND AND ENDS WITH A SHARP HOOK-TURN JUST BEFORE THE WOODEN BRIDGE. THERE'S NO WATER UNDER THAT BRIDGE ANYMORE...
...VELVET-INK OUT THERE BUT I KNEW THE ROAD. I'D DONE THIS BEFORE. SLOWER. IN DAYLIGHT. PRACTICING MY MOVES.
Fury
I PULLED THE SWITCH FOR THE CUT-OU THE MOTOR CRACKLED NOW, UNMUFFLED. WE'D ONLY HAVE A FEW MINUTES BEFO THE HIGHWAY PATROL CAME AFTER US.
I'D BE LONG GONE.
WE DON'T USE A FLAGMAN FOR THESE RUNS WENDY SHOUTS OUT THE COUNT. WE GO ON THREE. I'D FEEL HER QUICK, SHARP SQUEEZE ON MY THIGH JUST BEFORE THREE...
...THAT WAS MY ED

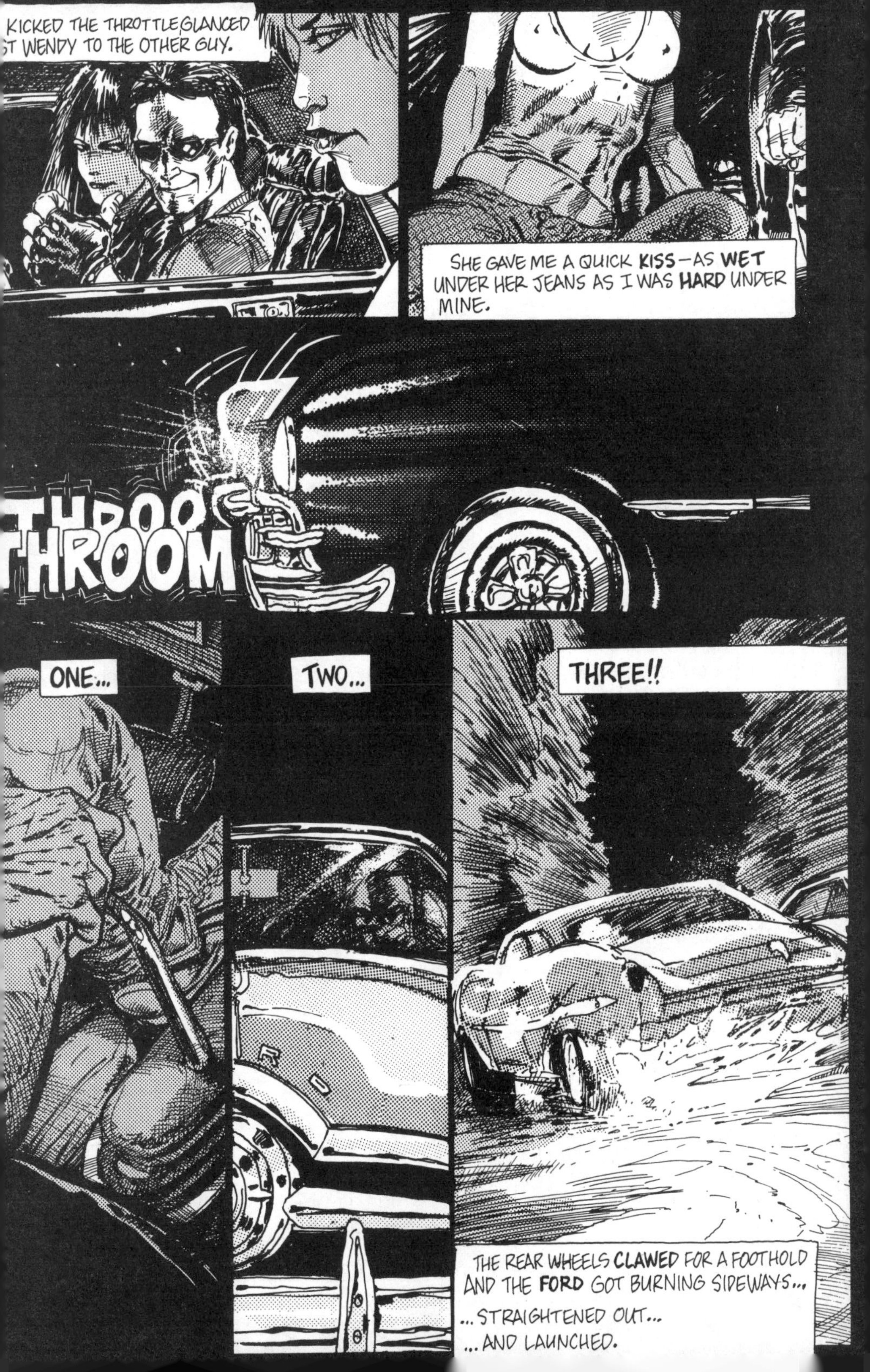

KICKED THE THROTTLE, GLANCED
T WENDY TO THE OTHER GUY.
SHE GAVE ME A QUICK KISS—AS WET UNDER HER JEANS AS I WAS HARD UNDER MINE.
THROOM THROOM
ONE...
TWO...
THREE!!
THE REAR WHEELS CLAWED FOR A FOOTHOLD AND THE FORD GOT BURNING SIDEWAYS...
...STRAIGHTENED OUT...
...AND LAUNCHED.

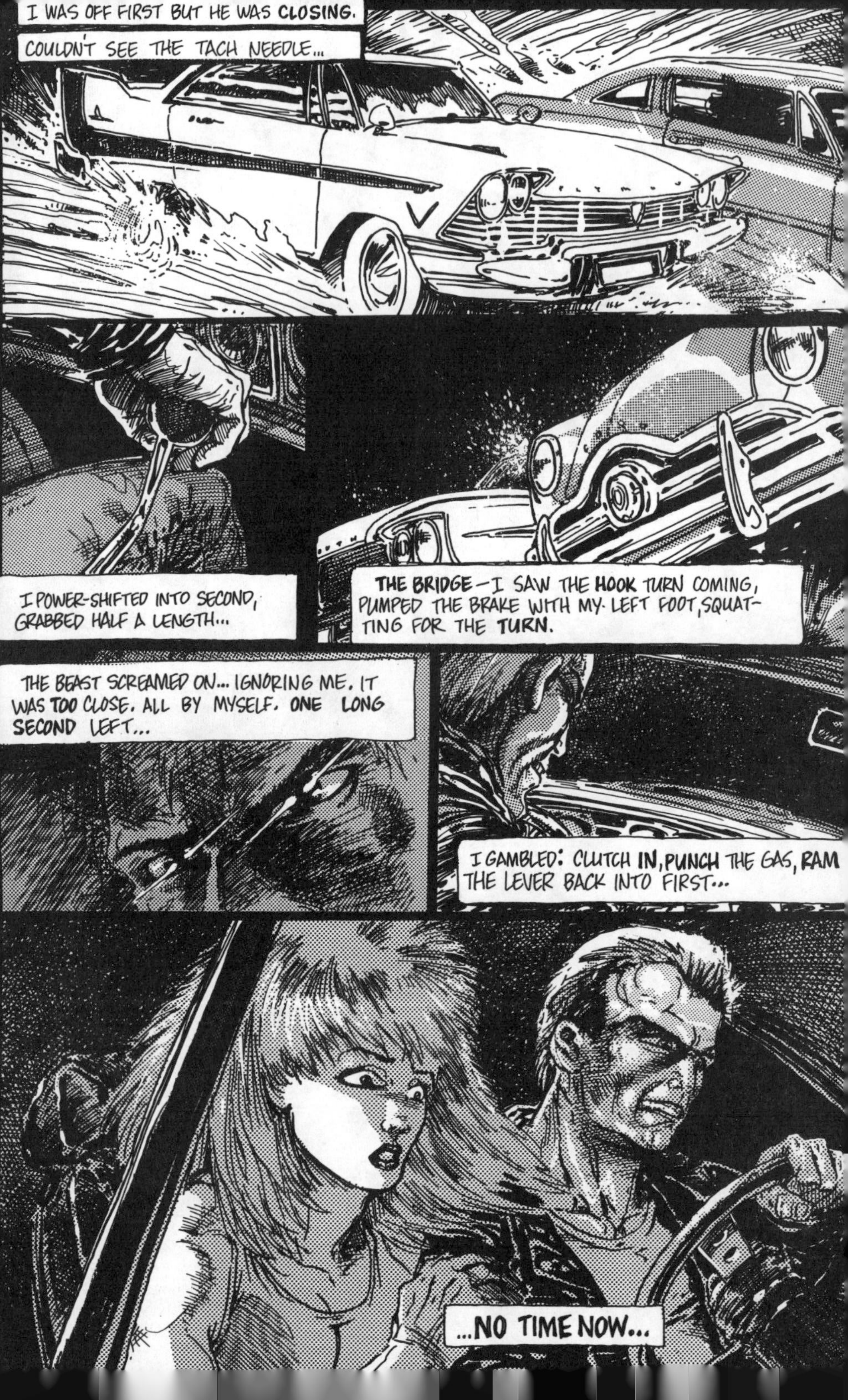
I WAS OFF FIRST BUT HE WAS CLOSING.
COULDN'T SEE THE TACH NEEDLE...
I POWER-SHIFTED INTO SECOND, GRABBED HALF A LENGTH...
THE BRIDGE—I SAW THE HOOK TURN COMING, PUMPED THE BRAKE WITH MY LEFT FOOT, SQUATTING FOR THE TURN.
THE BEAST SCREAMED ON... IGNORING ME. IT WAS TOO CLOSE. ALL BY MYSELF. ONE LONG SECOND LEFT...
I GAMBLED: CLUTCH IN, PUNCH THE GAS, RAM THE LEVER BACK INTO FIRST...
...NO TIME NOW...

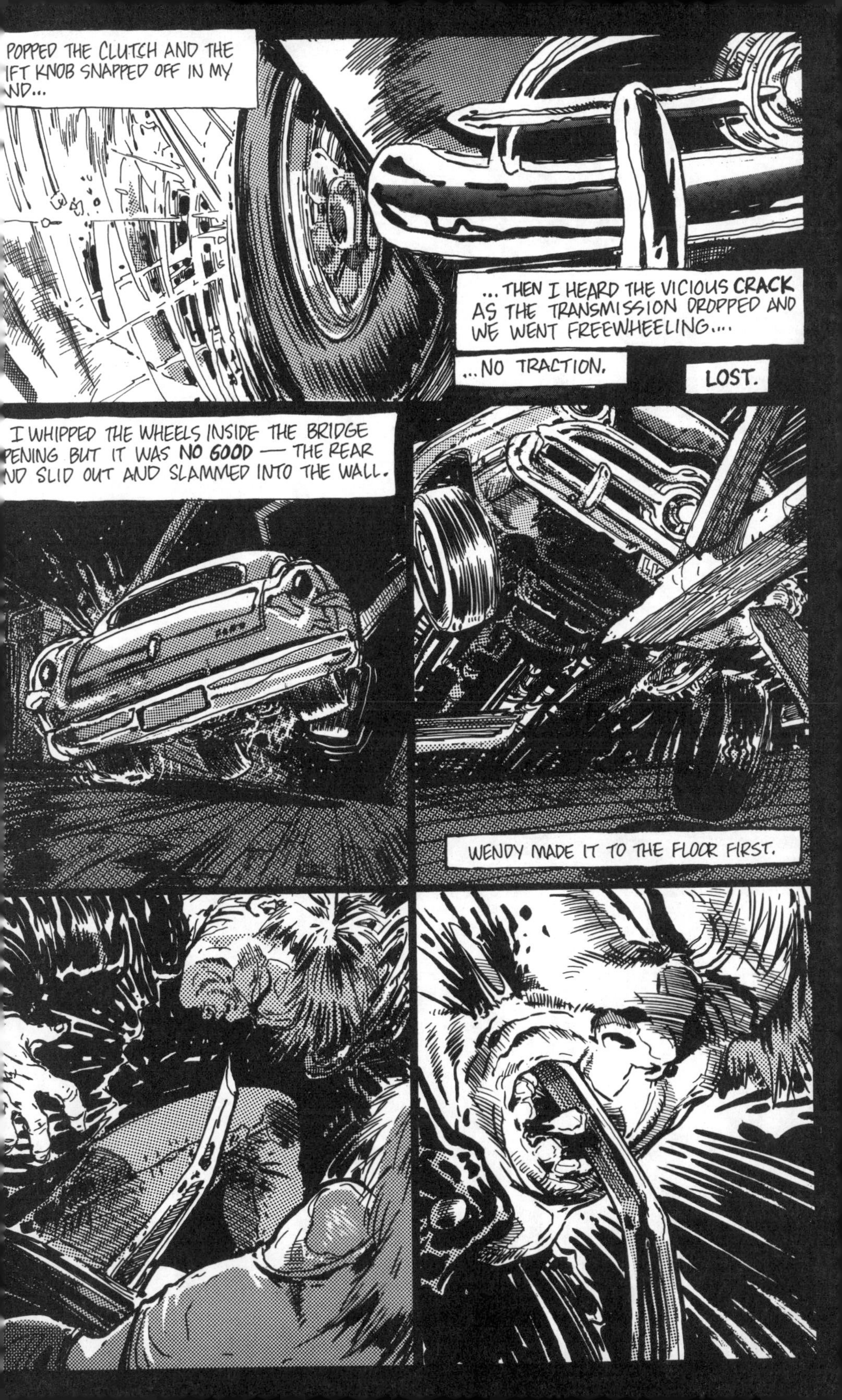
POPPED THE CLUTCH AND THE
IFT KNOB SNAPPED OFF IN MY
ND...
... THEN I HEARD THE VICIOUS CRACK
AS THE TRANSMISSION DROPPED AND
WE WENT FREEWHEELING....
...NO TRACTION.
LOST.
I WHIPPED THE WHEELS INSIDE THE BRIDGE
PENING BUT IT WAS NO GOOD — THE REAR
ND SLID OUT AND SLAMMED INTO THE WALL.
WENDY MADE IT TO THE FLOOR FIRST.

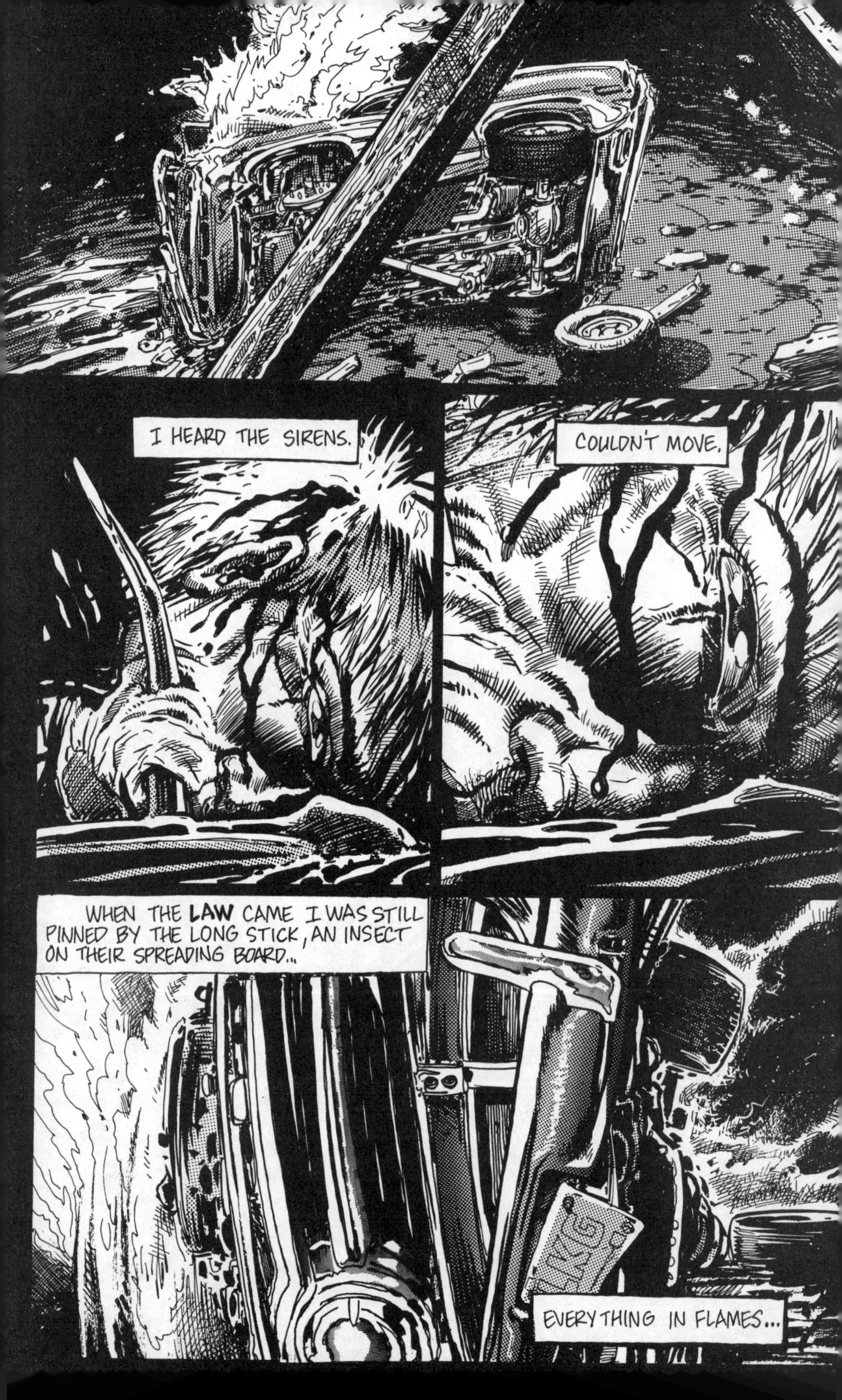
I HEARD THE SIRENS.
COULDN'T MOVE.
WHEN THE LAW CAME I WAS STILL PINNED BY THE LONG STICK, AN INSECT ON THEIR SPREADING BOARD...
EVERYTHING IN FLAMES...

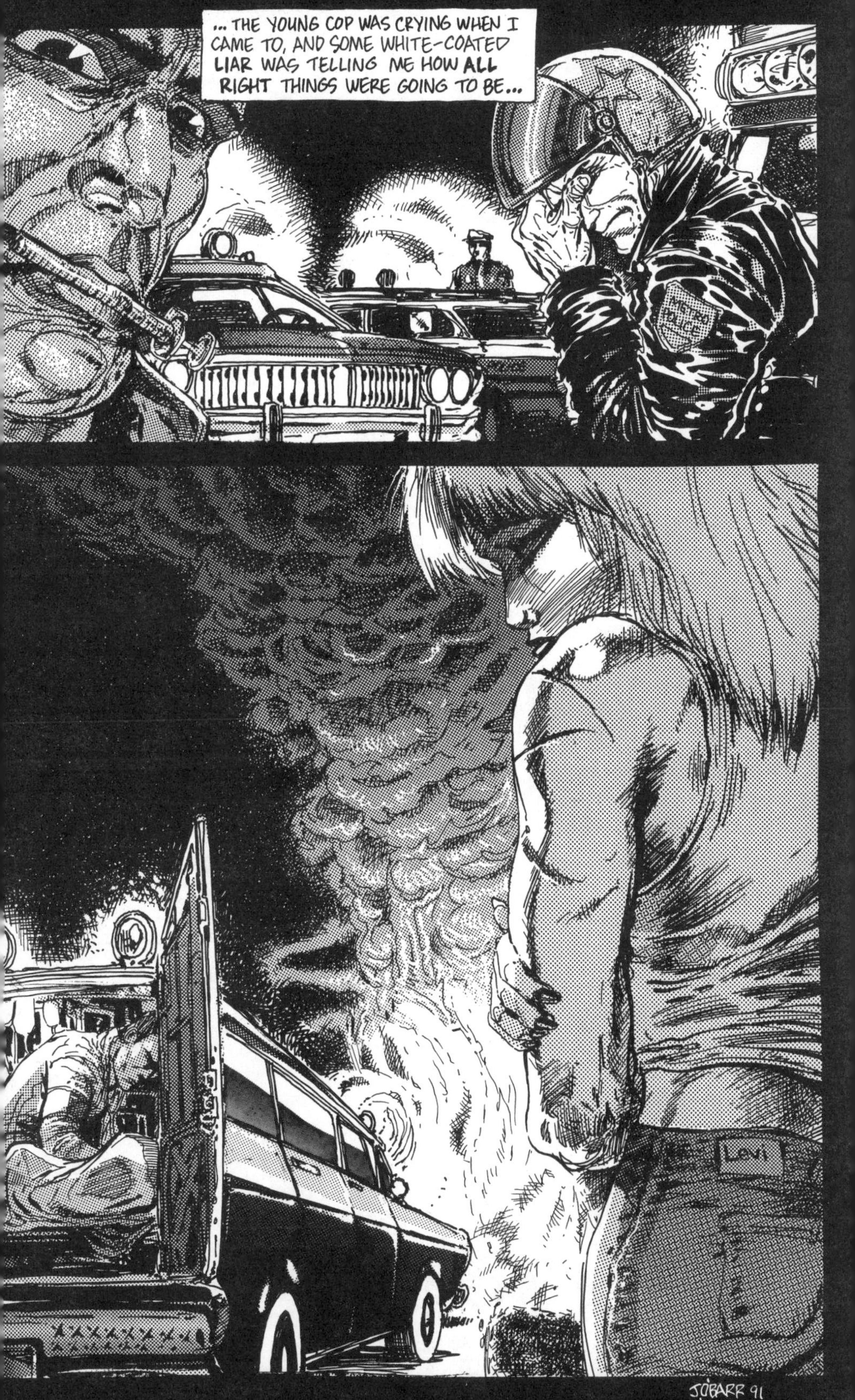
... THE YOUNG COP WAS CRYING WHEN I CAME TO, AND SOME WHITE-COATED LIAR WAS TELLING ME HOW ALL RIGHT THINGS WERE GOING TO BE...
LEVI
J. O'BARR 91

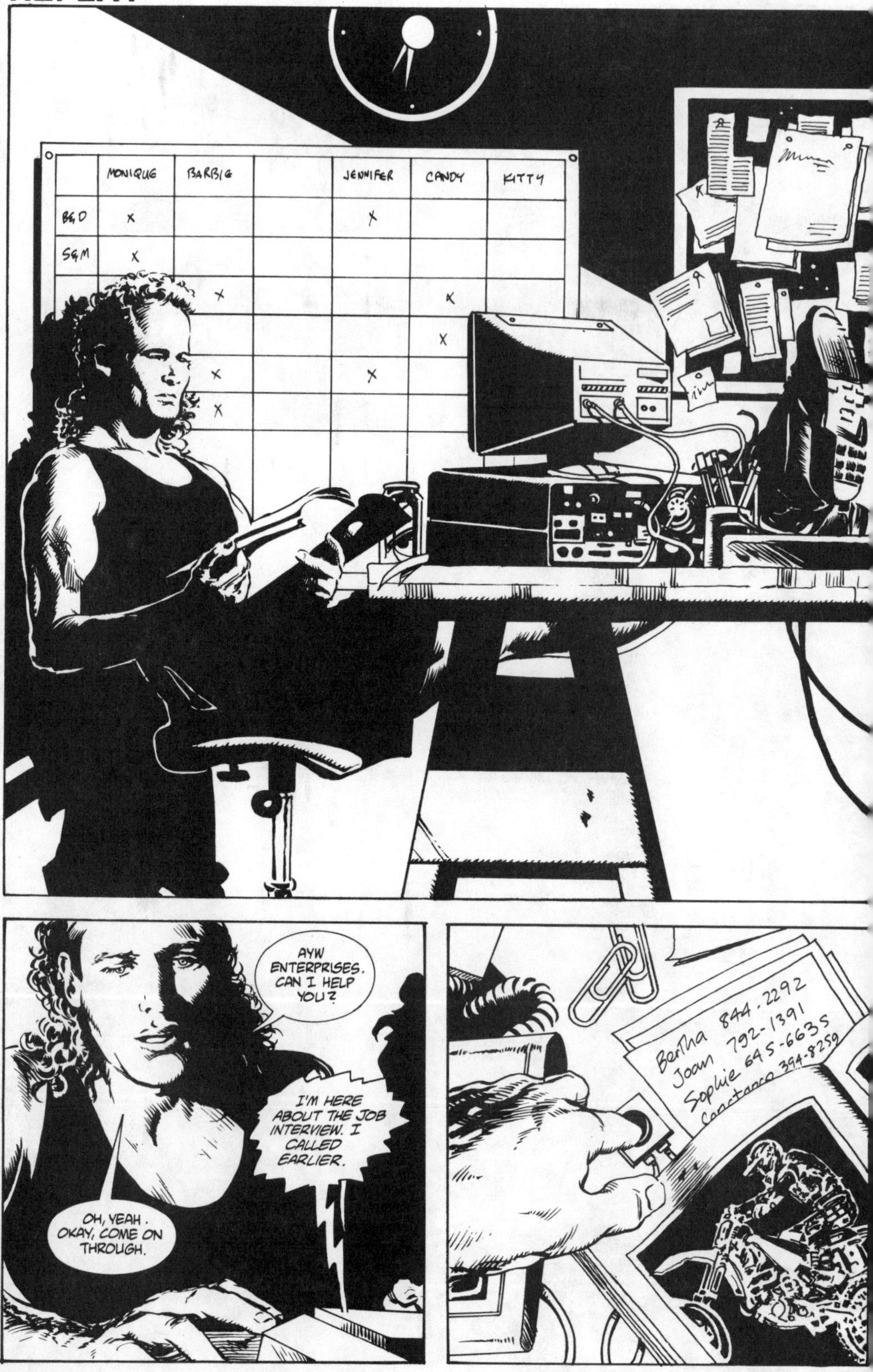
MONIQUE
BARBIE
JENNIFER
CANDY
KITTY
B&D
S&M
AYW ENTERPRISES. CAN I HELP YOU?
I'M HERE ABOUT THE JOB INTERVIEW. I CALLED EARLIER.
OH, YEAH. OKAY, COME ON THROUGH.
Bertha 844.2292
Joan 792-1391
Sophie 645-6635

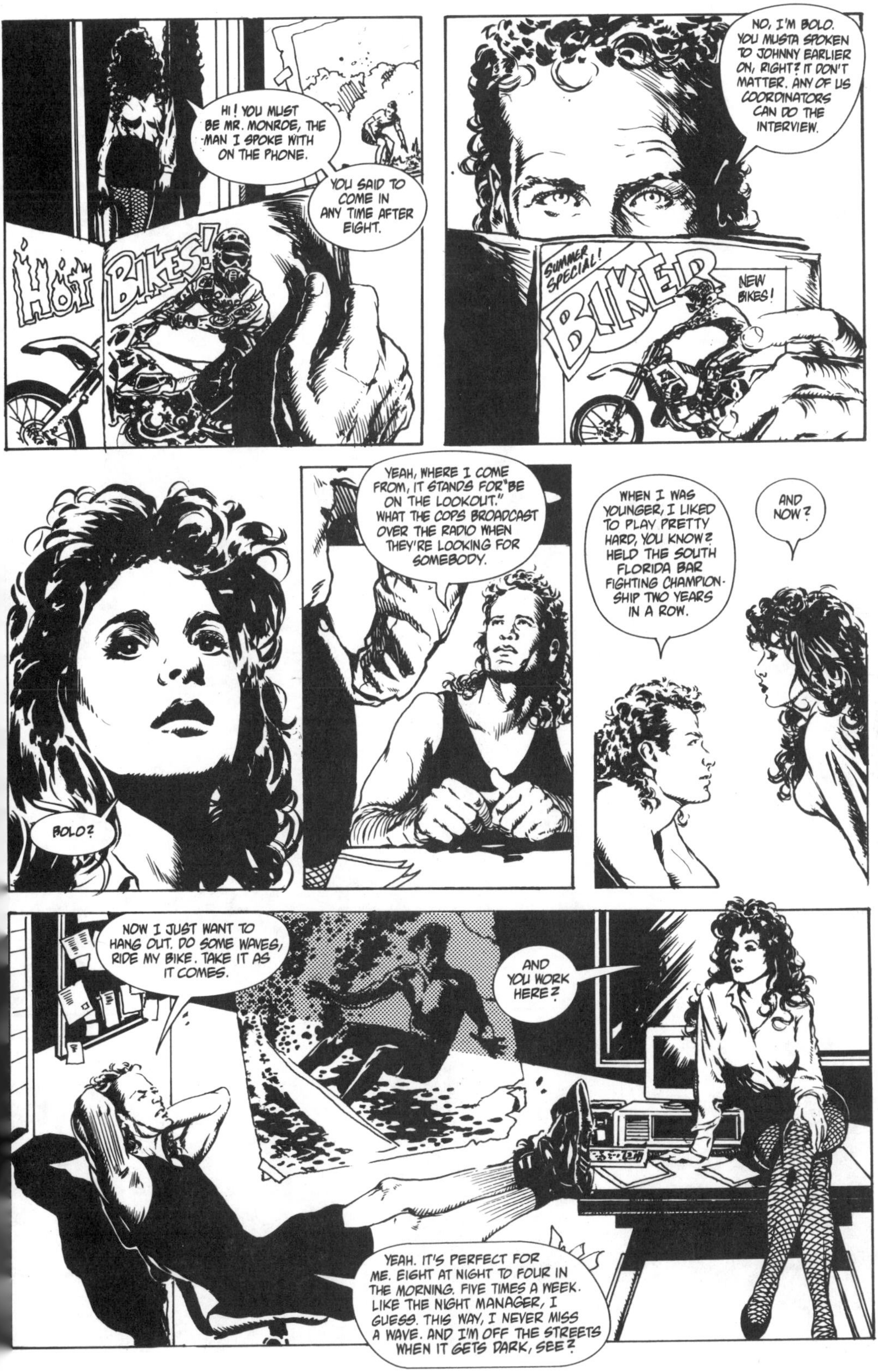
HI! YOU MUST BE MR. MONROE, THE MAN I SPOKE WITH ON THE PHONE.
YOU SAID TO COME IN ANY TIME AFTER EIGHT.
HOT BIKES!
NO, I'M BOLO. YOU MUSTA SPOKEN TO JOHNNY EARLIER ON, RIGHT? IT DON'T MATTER. ANY OF US COORDINATORS CAN DO THE INTERVIEW.
SUMMER SPECIAL!
BIKER
NEW BIKES!
BOLO?
YEAH, WHERE I COME FROM, IT STANDS FOR "BE ON THE LOOKOUT." WHAT THE COPS BROADCAST OVER THE RADIO WHEN THEY'RE LOOKING FOR SOMEBODY.
WHEN I WAS YOUNGER, I LIKED TO PLAY PRETTY HARD, YOU KNOW? HELD THE SOUTH FLORIDA BAR FIGHTING CHAMPIONSHIP TWO YEARS IN A ROW.
AND NOW?
NOW I JUST WANT TO HANG OUT. DO SOME WAVES, RIDE MY BIKE. TAKE IT AS IT COMES.
AND YOU WORK HERE?
YEAH. IT'S PERFECT FOR ME. EIGHT AT NIGHT TO FOUR IN THE MORNING. FIVE TIMES A WEEK. LIKE THE NIGHT MANAGER, I GUESS. THIS WAY, I NEVER MISS A WAVE. AND I'M OFF THE STREETS WHEN IT GETS DARK, SEE?

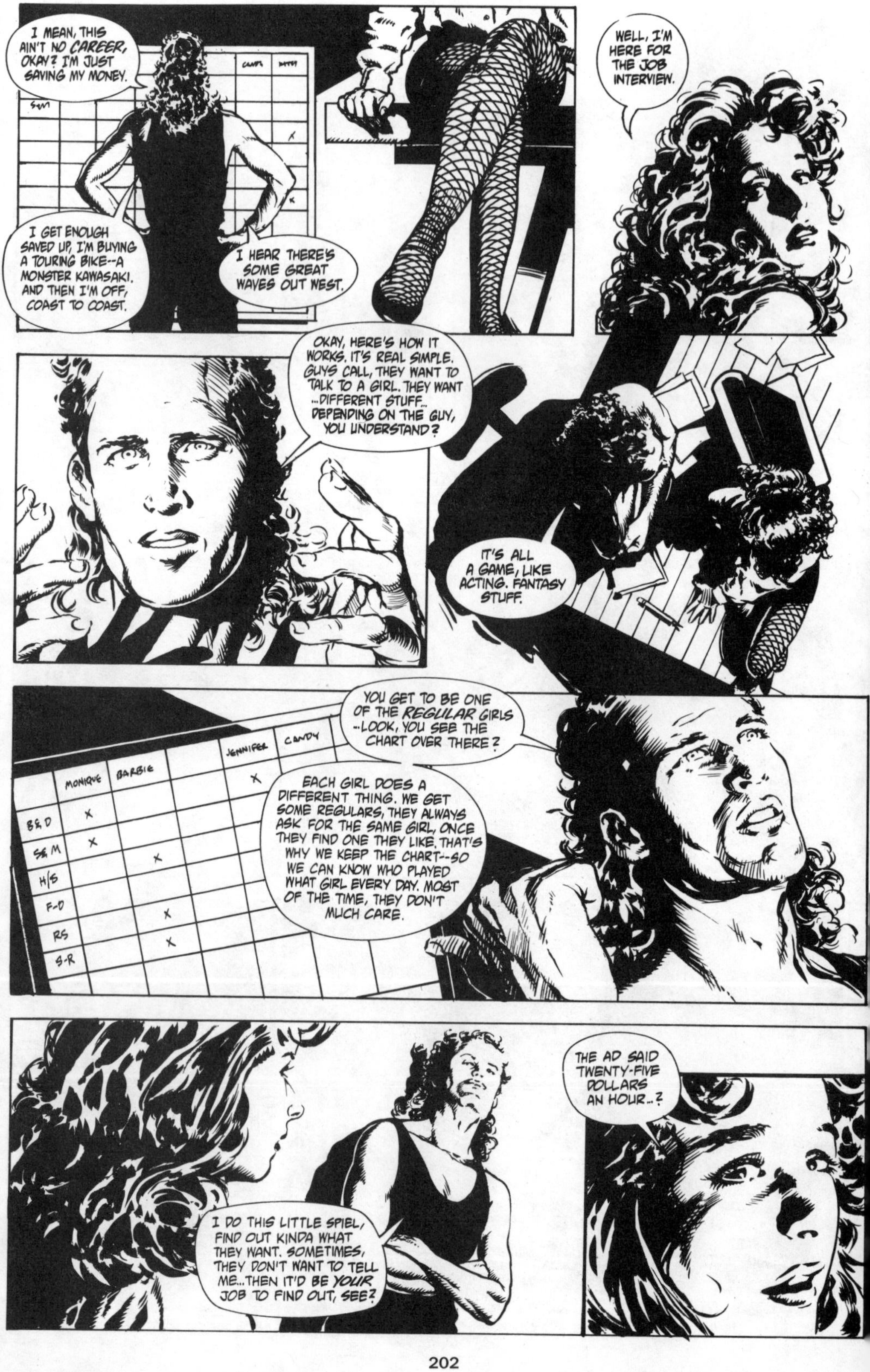
I MEAN, THIS AIN'T NO CAREER, OKAY? I'M JUST SAVING MY MONEY.
I GET ENOUGH SAVED UP, I'M BUYING A TOURING BIKE--A MONSTER KAWASAKI. AND THEN I'M OFF, COAST TO COAST.
I HEAR THERE'S SOME GREAT WAVES OUT WEST.
WELL, I'M HERE FOR THE JOB INTERVIEW.
OKAY, HERE'S HOW IT WORKS. IT'S REAL SIMPLE. GUYS CALL, THEY WANT TO TALK TO A GIRL. THEY WANT ...DIFFERENT STUFF... DEPENDING ON THE GUY, YOU UNDERSTAND?
IT'S ALL A GAME, LIKE ACTING. FANTASY STUFF.
YOU GET TO BE ONE OF THE REGULAR GIRLS --LOOK, YOU SEE THE CHART OVER THERE?
JENNIFER
CANDY
MONIQUE
BARBIE
B&D
S&M
H/S
F-D
RS
S-R
EACH GIRL DOES A DIFFERENT THING. WE GET SOME REGULARS, THEY ALWAYS ASK FOR THE SAME GIRL, ONCE THEY FIND ONE THEY LIKE, THAT'S WHY WE KEEP THE CHART--SO WE CAN KNOW WHO PLAYED WHAT GIRL EVERY DAY. MOST OF THE TIME, THEY DON'T MUCH CARE.
I DO THIS LITTLE SPIEL, FIND OUT KINDA WHAT THEY WANT. SOMETIMES, THEY DON'T WANT TO TELL ME...THEN IT'D BE YOUR JOB TO FIND OUT, SEE?
THE AD SAID TWENTY-FIVE DOLLARS AN HOUR...?

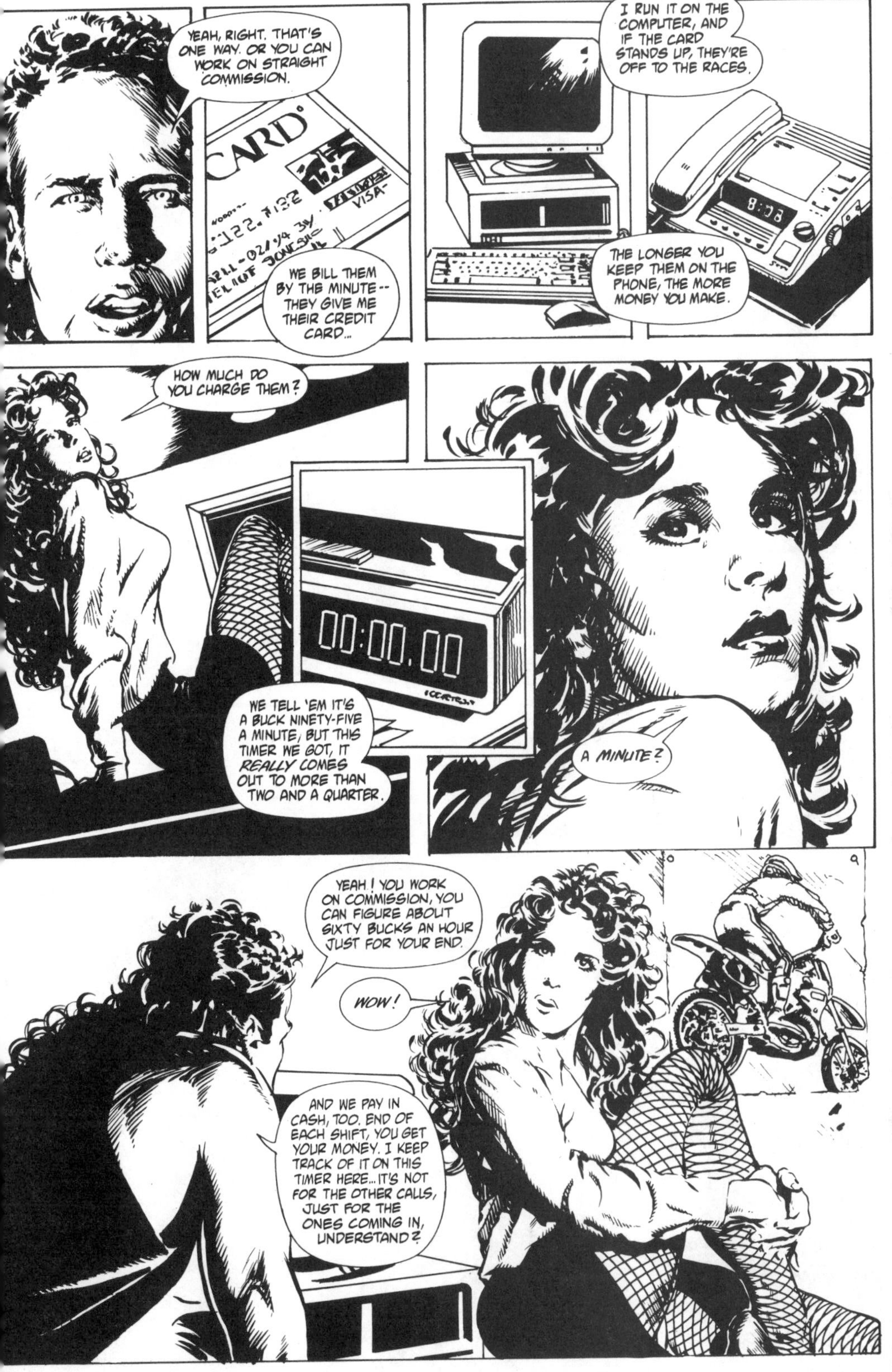
YEAH, RIGHT. THAT'S ONE WAY. OR YOU CAN WORK ON STRAIGHT COMMISSION.
WE BILL THEM BY THE MINUTE-- THEY GIVE ME THEIR CREDIT CARD...
I RUN IT ON THE COMPUTER, AND IF THE CARD STANDS UP, THEY'RE OFF TO THE RACES.
THE LONGER YOU KEEP THEM ON THE PHONE, THE MORE MONEY YOU MAKE.
HOW MUCH DO YOU CHARGE THEM?
00:00.00
WE TELL 'EM IT'S A BUCK NINETY-FIVE A MINUTE, BUT THIS TIMER WE GOT, IT *REALLY* COMES OUT TO MORE THAN TWO AND A QUARTER.
A *MINUTE*?
YEAH! YOU WORK ON COMMISSION, YOU CAN FIGURE ABOUT SIXTY BUCKS AN HOUR JUST FOR YOUR END.
WOW!
AND WE PAY IN CASH, TOO. END OF EACH SHIFT, YOU GET YOUR MONEY. I KEEP TRACK OF IT ON THIS TIMER HERE... IT'S NOT FOR THE OTHER CALLS, JUST FOR THE ONES COMING IN, UNDERSTAND?

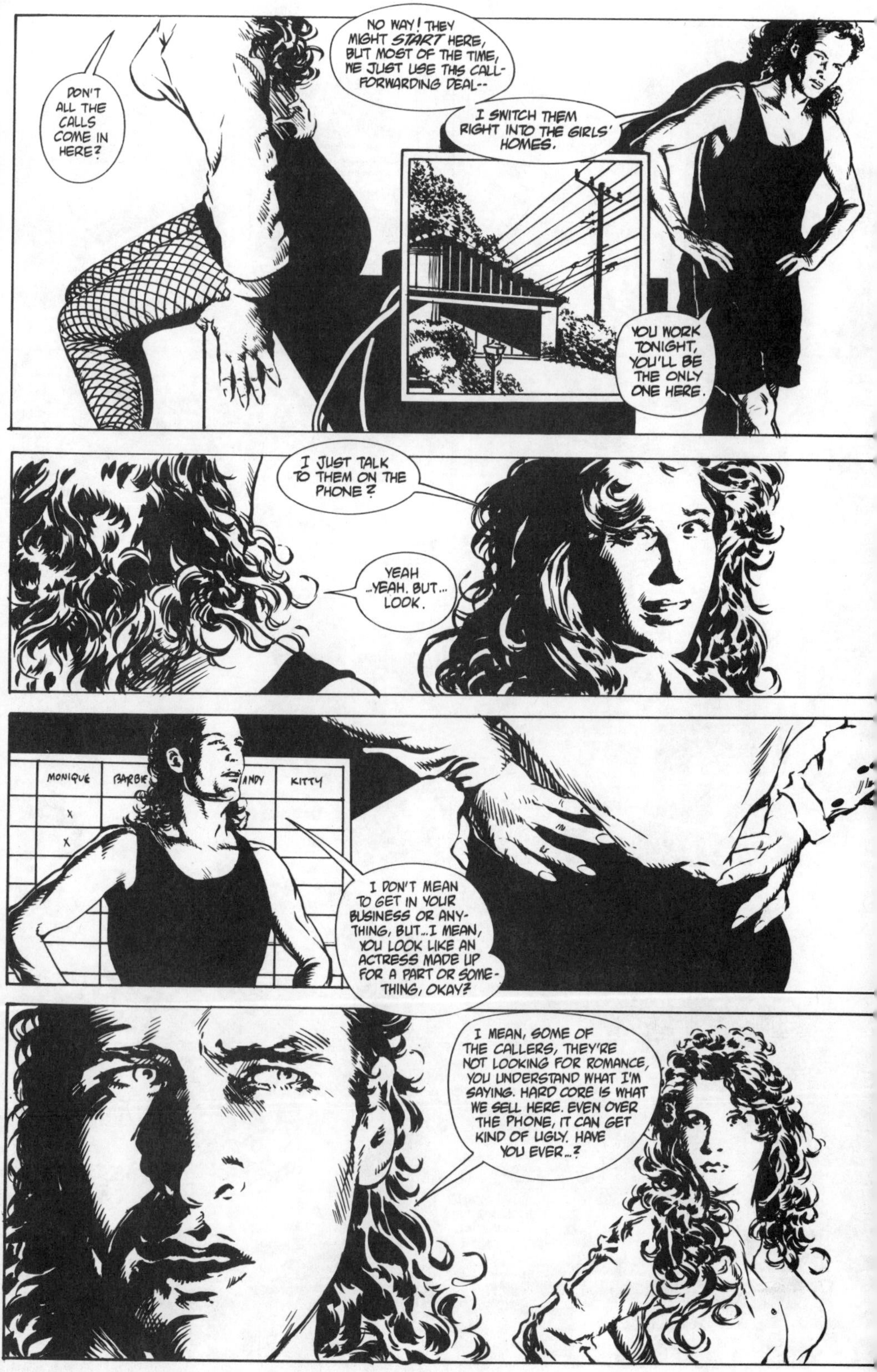
DON'T ALL THE CALLS COME IN HERE?
NO WAY! THEY MIGHT START HERE, BUT MOST OF THE TIME, WE JUST USE THIS CALL-FORWARDING DEAL--
I SWITCH THEM RIGHT INTO THE GIRLS' HOMES.
YOU WORK TONIGHT, YOU'LL BE THE ONLY ONE HERE.
I JUST TALK TO THEM ON THE PHONE?
YEAH ...YEAH. BUT... LOOK.
MONIQUE
BARBIE
KITTY
I DON'T MEAN TO GET IN YOUR BUSINESS OR ANY-THING, BUT...I MEAN, YOU LOOK LIKE AN ACTRESS MADE UP FOR A PART OR SOME-THING, OKAY?
I MEAN, SOME OF THE CALLERS, THEY'RE NOT LOOKING FOR ROMANCE, YOU UNDERSTAND WHAT I'M SAYING. HARD CORE IS WHAT WE SELL HERE. EVEN OVER THE PHONE, IT CAN GET KIND OF UGLY. HAVE YOU EVER...?

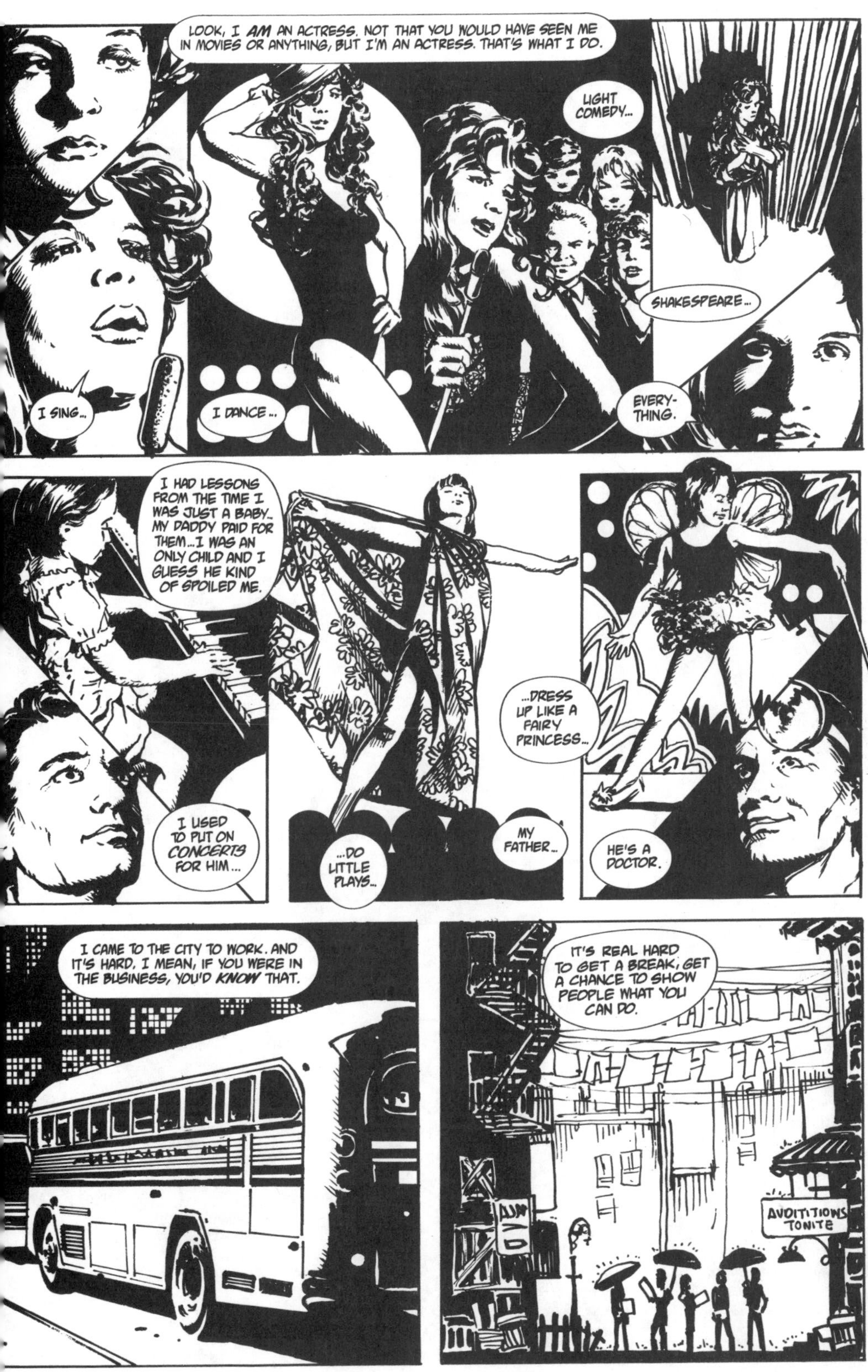
LOOK, I AM AN ACTRESS. NOT THAT YOU WOULD HAVE SEEN ME IN MOVIES OR ANYTHING, BUT I'M AN ACTRESS. THAT'S WHAT I DO.
I SING...
I DANCE...
LIGHT COMEDY...
SHAKESPEARE...
EVERY-THING.
I HAD LESSONS FROM THE TIME I WAS JUST A BABY.. MY DADDY PAID FOR THEM...I WAS AN ONLY CHILD AND I GUESS HE KIND OF SPOILED ME.
I USED TO PUT ON CONCERTS FOR HIM...
...DO LITTLE PLAYS...
...DRESS UP LIKE A FAIRY PRINCESS...
MY FATHER...
HE'S A DOCTOR.
I CAME TO THE CITY TO WORK. AND IT'S HARD. I MEAN, IF YOU WERE IN THE BUSINESS, YOU'D KNOW THAT.
IT'S REAL HARD TO GET A BREAK, GET A CHANCE TO SHOW PEOPLE WHAT YOU CAN DO.
AUDITITIONS TONITE

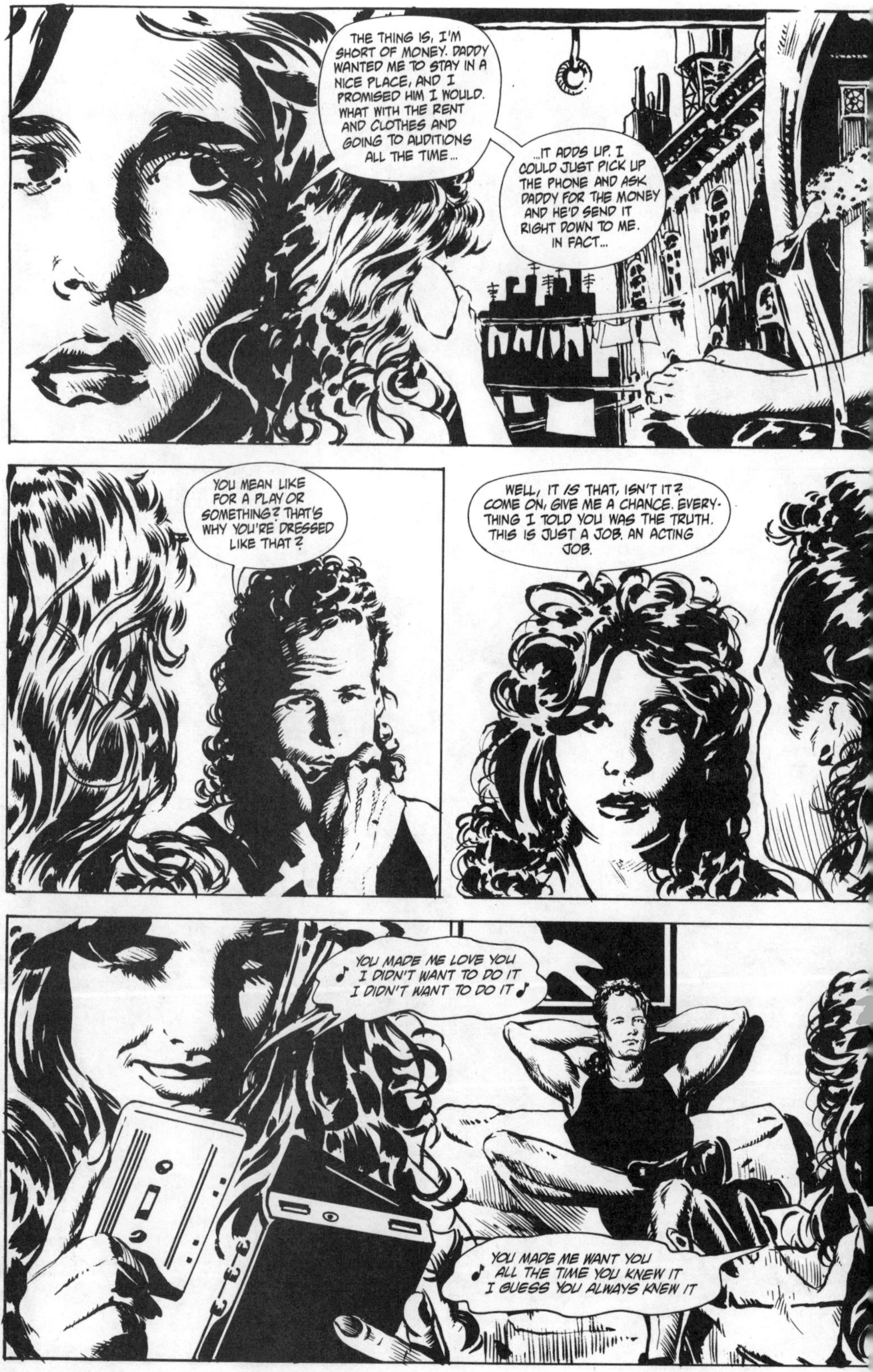
THE THING IS, I'M SHORT OF MONEY. DADDY WANTED ME TO STAY IN A NICE PLACE, AND I PROMISED HIM I WOULD. WHAT WITH THE RENT AND CLOTHES AND GOING TO AUDITIONS ALL THE TIME...
...IT ADDS UP. I COULD JUST PICK UP THE PHONE AND ASK DADDY FOR THE MONEY AND HE'D SEND IT RIGHT DOWN TO ME. IN FACT...
YOU MEAN LIKE FOR A PLAY OR SOMETHING? THAT'S WHY YOU'RE DRESSED LIKE THAT?
WELL, IT *IS* THAT, ISN'T IT? COME ON, GIVE ME A CHANCE. EVERYTHING I TOLD YOU WAS THE TRUTH. THIS IS JUST A JOB. AN ACTING JOB.
♪ YOU MADE ME LOVE YOU I DIDN'T WANT TO DO IT I DIDN'T WANT TO DO IT ♪
♪ YOU MADE ME WANT YOU ALL THE TIME YOU KNEW IT I GUESS YOU ALWAYS KNEW IT

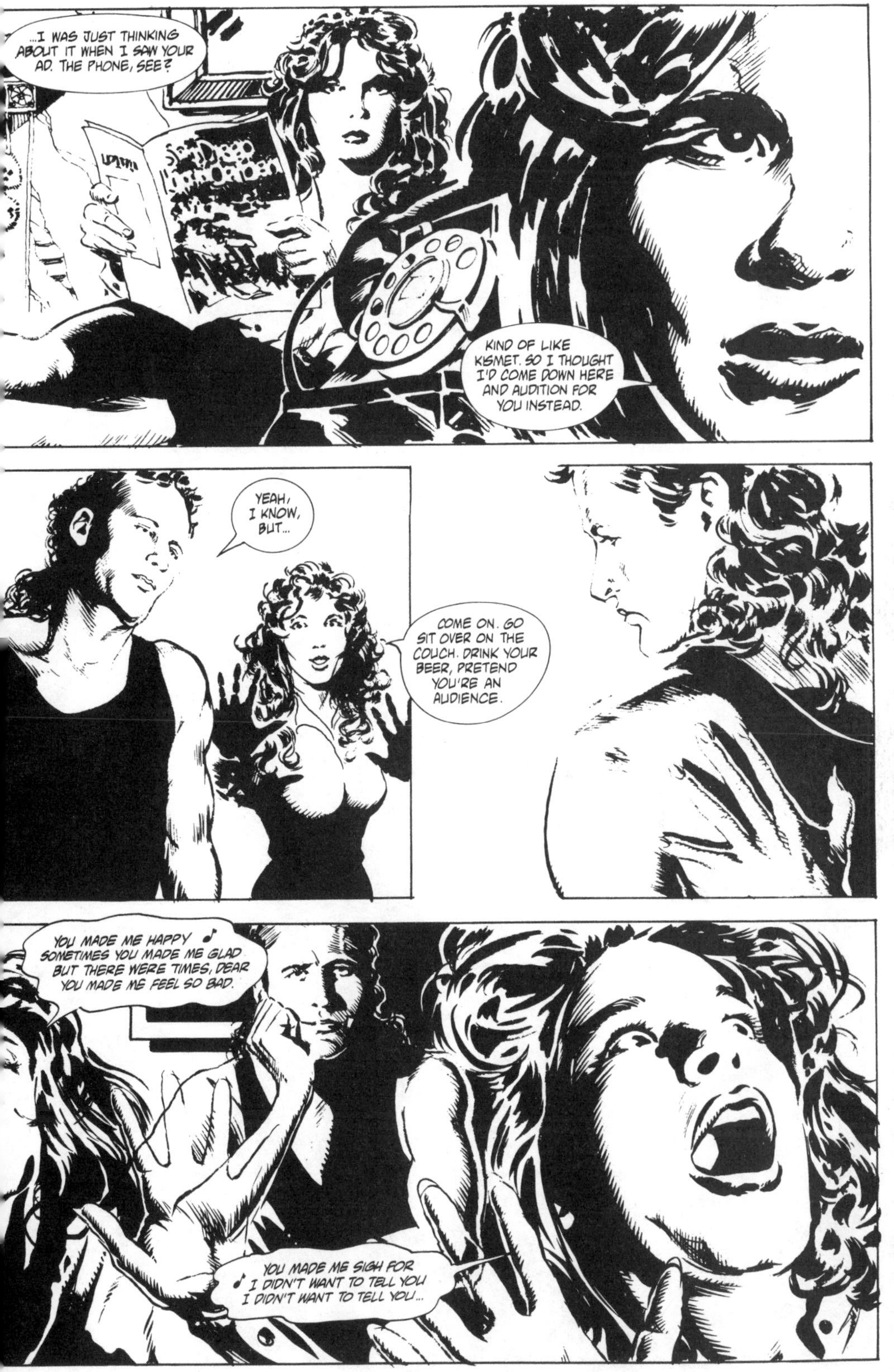
...I WAS JUST THINKING ABOUT IT WHEN I SAW YOUR AD. THE PHONE, SEE?
KIND OF LIKE KISMET. SO I THOUGHT I'D COME DOWN HERE AND AUDITION FOR YOU INSTEAD.
YEAH, I KNOW, BUT...
COME ON. GO SIT OVER ON THE COUCH. DRINK YOUR BEER, PRETEND YOU'RE AN AUDIENCE.
YOU MADE ME HAPPY ♪ SOMETIMES YOU MADE ME GLAD BUT THERE WERE TIMES, DEAR YOU MADE ME FEEL SO BAD.
YOU MADE ME SIGH FOR ♪ I DIDN'T WANT TO TELL YOU I DIDN'T WANT TO TELL YOU...

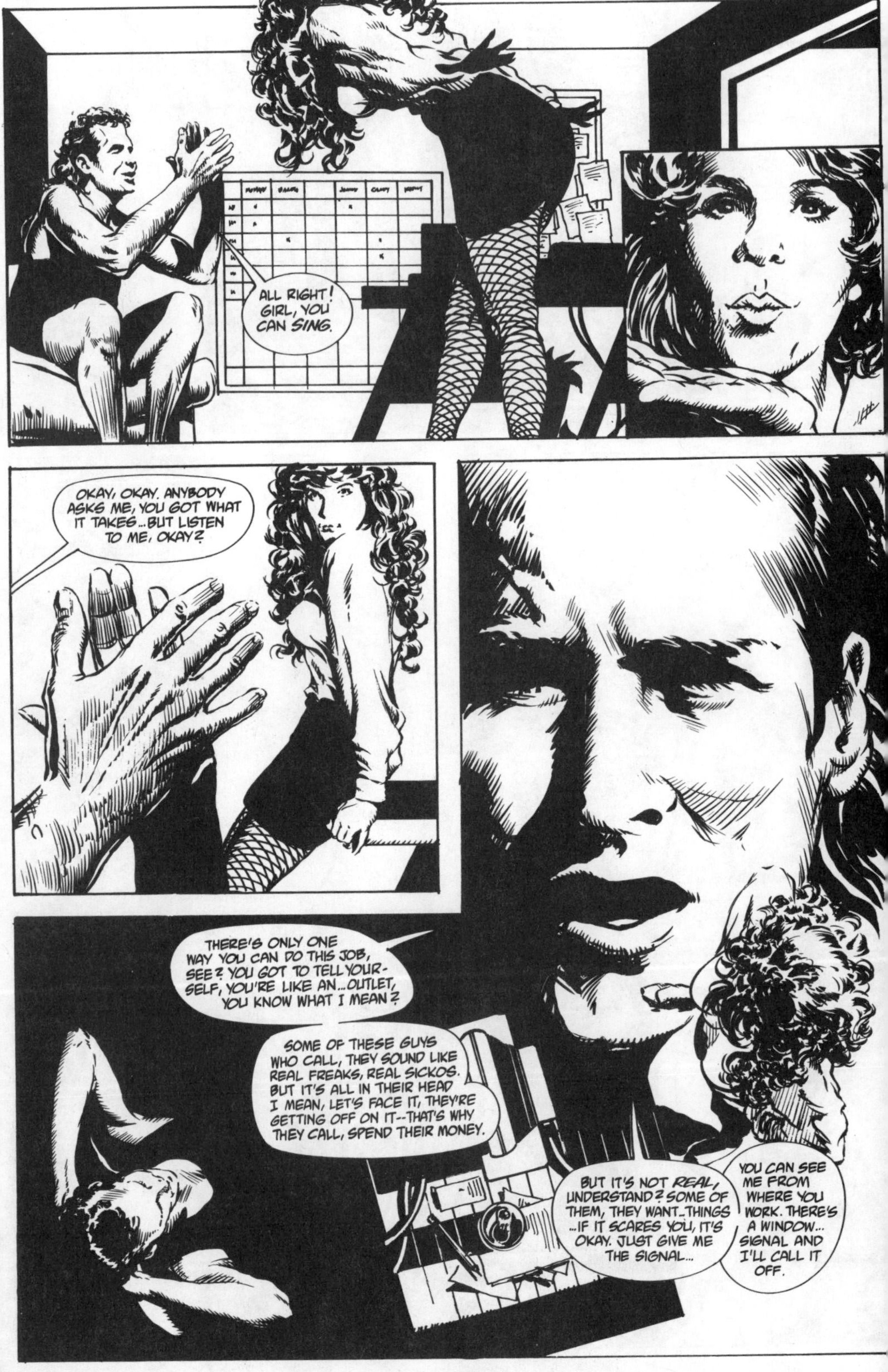
ALL RIGHT! GIRL, YOU CAN SING.
OKAY, OKAY. ANYBODY ASKS ME, YOU GOT WHAT IT TAKES...BUT LISTEN TO ME, OKAY?
THERE'S ONLY ONE WAY YOU CAN DO THIS JOB, SEE? YOU GOT TO TELL YOURSELF, YOU'RE LIKE AN...OUTLET, YOU KNOW WHAT I MEAN?
SOME OF THESE GUYS WHO CALL, THEY SOUND LIKE REAL FREAKS, REAL SICKOS. BUT IT'S ALL IN THEIR HEAD I MEAN, LET'S FACE IT, THEY'RE GETTING OFF ON IT--THAT'S WHY THEY CALL, SPEND THEIR MONEY.
BUT IT'S NOT REAL, UNDERSTAND? SOME OF THEM, THEY WANT...THINGS ...IF IT SCARES YOU, IT'S OKAY. JUST GIVE ME THE SIGNAL...
YOU CAN SEE ME FROM WHERE YOU WORK. THERE'S A WINDOW... SIGNAL AND I'LL CALL IT OFF.

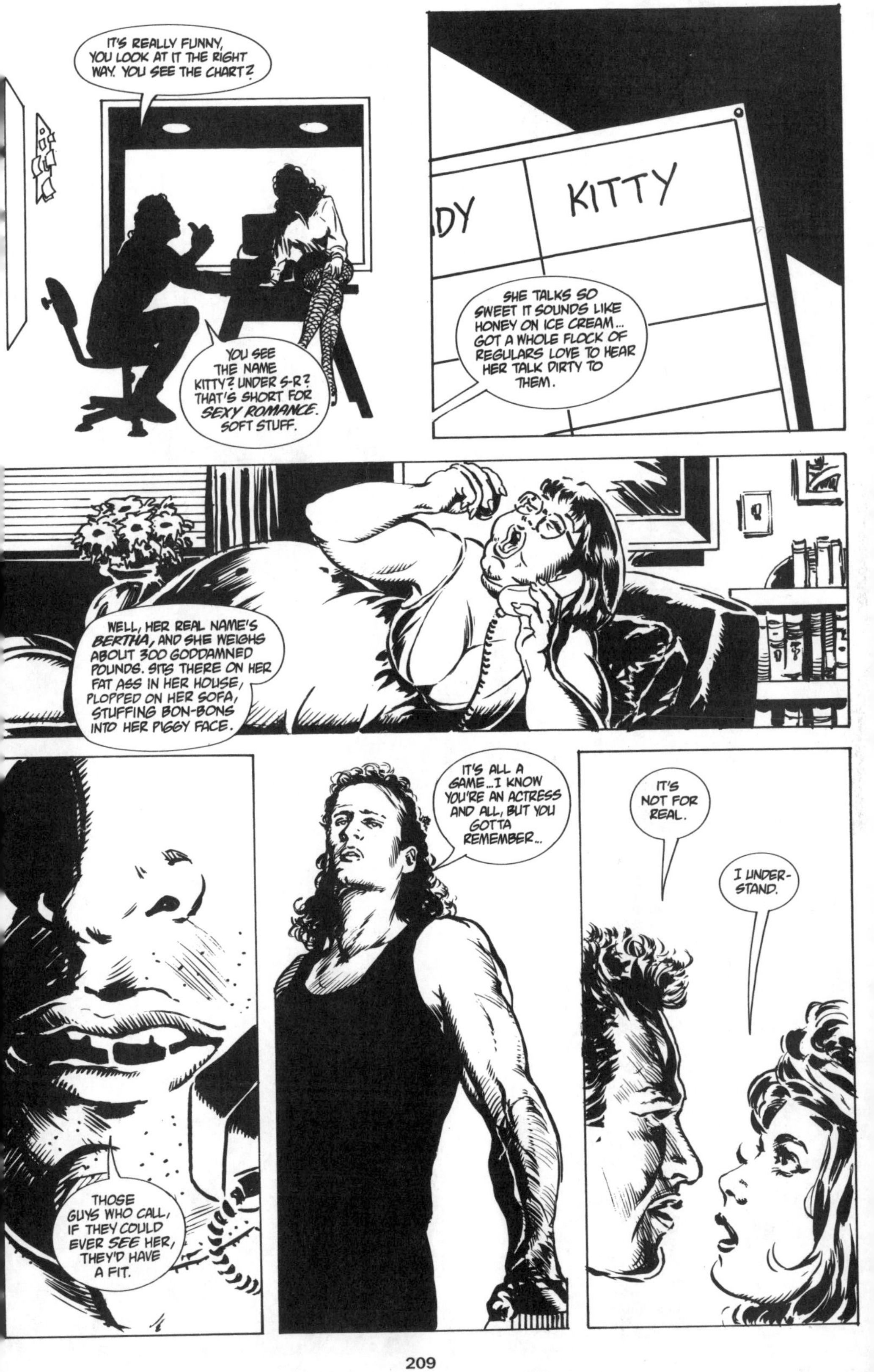
IT'S REALLY FUNNY, YOU LOOK AT IT THE RIGHT WAY. YOU SEE THE CHART?
YOU SEE THE NAME KITTY? UNDER S-R? THAT'S SHORT FOR SEXY ROMANCE. SOFT STUFF.
DY
KITTY
SHE TALKS SO SWEET IT SOUNDS LIKE HONEY ON ICE CREAM... GOT A WHOLE FLOCK OF REGULARS LOVE TO HEAR HER TALK DIRTY TO THEM.
WELL, HER REAL NAME'S BERTHA, AND SHE WEIGHS ABOUT 300 GODDAMNED POUNDS. SITS THERE ON HER FAT ASS IN HER HOUSE, PLOPPED ON HER SOFA, STUFFING BON-BONS INTO HER PIGGY FACE.
THOSE GUYS WHO CALL, IF THEY COULD EVER SEE HER, THEY'D HAVE A FIT.
IT'S ALL A GAME... I KNOW YOU'RE AN ACTRESS AND ALL, BUT YOU GOTTA REMEMBER...
IT'S NOT FOR REAL.
I UNDERSTAND.

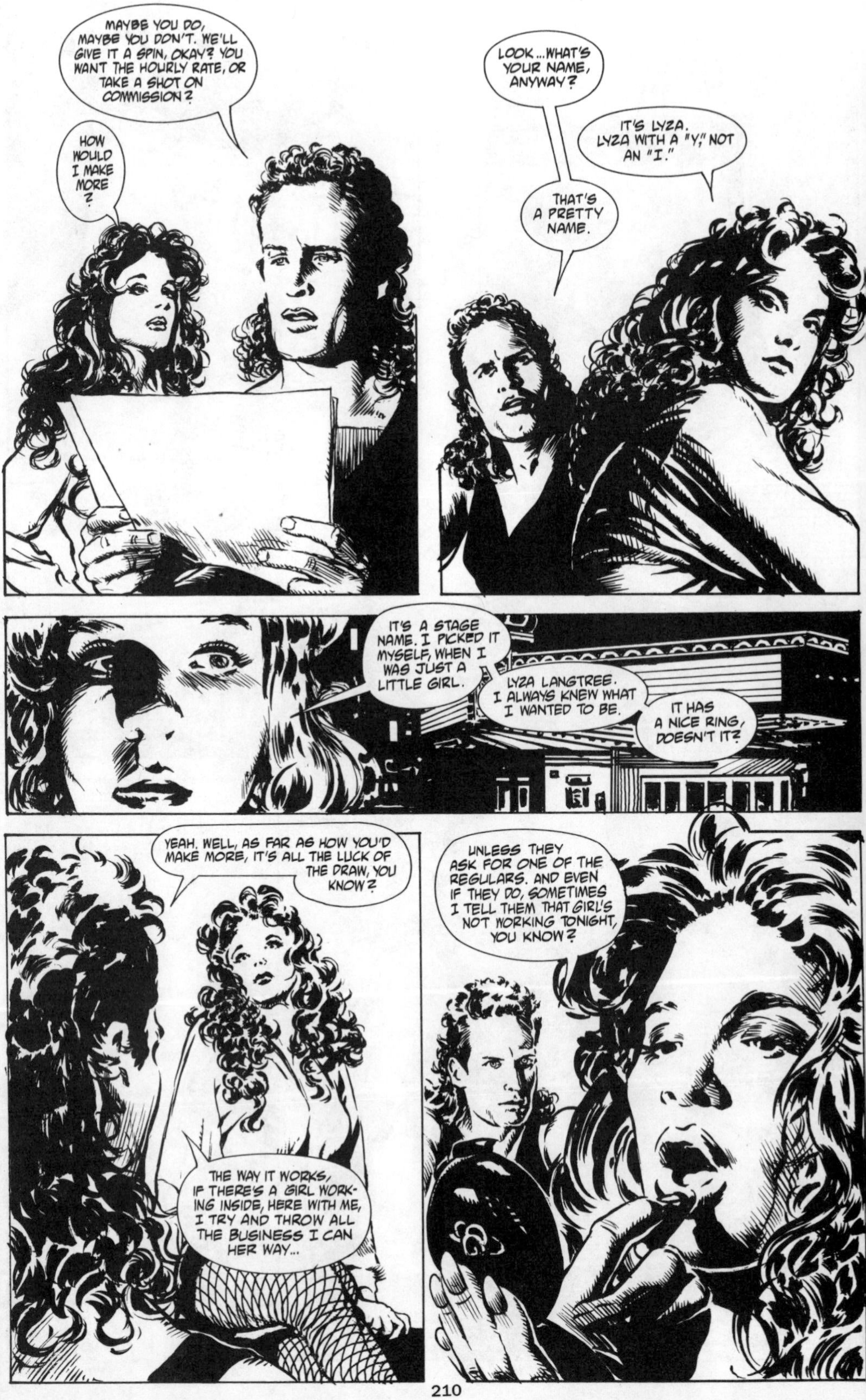
MAYBE YOU DO, MAYBE YOU DON'T. WE'LL GIVE IT A SPIN, OKAY? YOU WANT THE HOURLY RATE, OR TAKE A SHOT ON COMMISSION?
HOW WOULD I MAKE MORE?
LOOK...WHAT'S YOUR NAME, ANYWAY?
IT'S LYZA. LYZA WITH A "Y," NOT AN "I."
THAT'S A PRETTY NAME.
IT'S A STAGE NAME. I PICKED IT MYSELF, WHEN I WAS JUST A LITTLE GIRL.
LYZA LANGTREE. I ALWAYS KNEW WHAT I WANTED TO BE.
IT HAS A NICE RING, DOESN'T IT?
YEAH. WELL, AS FAR AS HOW YOU'D MAKE MORE, IT'S ALL THE LUCK OF THE DRAW, YOU KNOW?
THE WAY IT WORKS, IF THERE'S A GIRL WORKING INSIDE, HERE WITH ME, I TRY AND THROW ALL THE BUSINESS I CAN HER WAY...
UNLESS THEY ASK FOR ONE OF THE REGULARS. AND EVEN IF THEY DO, SOMETIMES I TELL THEM THAT GIRL'S NOT WORKING TONIGHT, YOU KNOW?

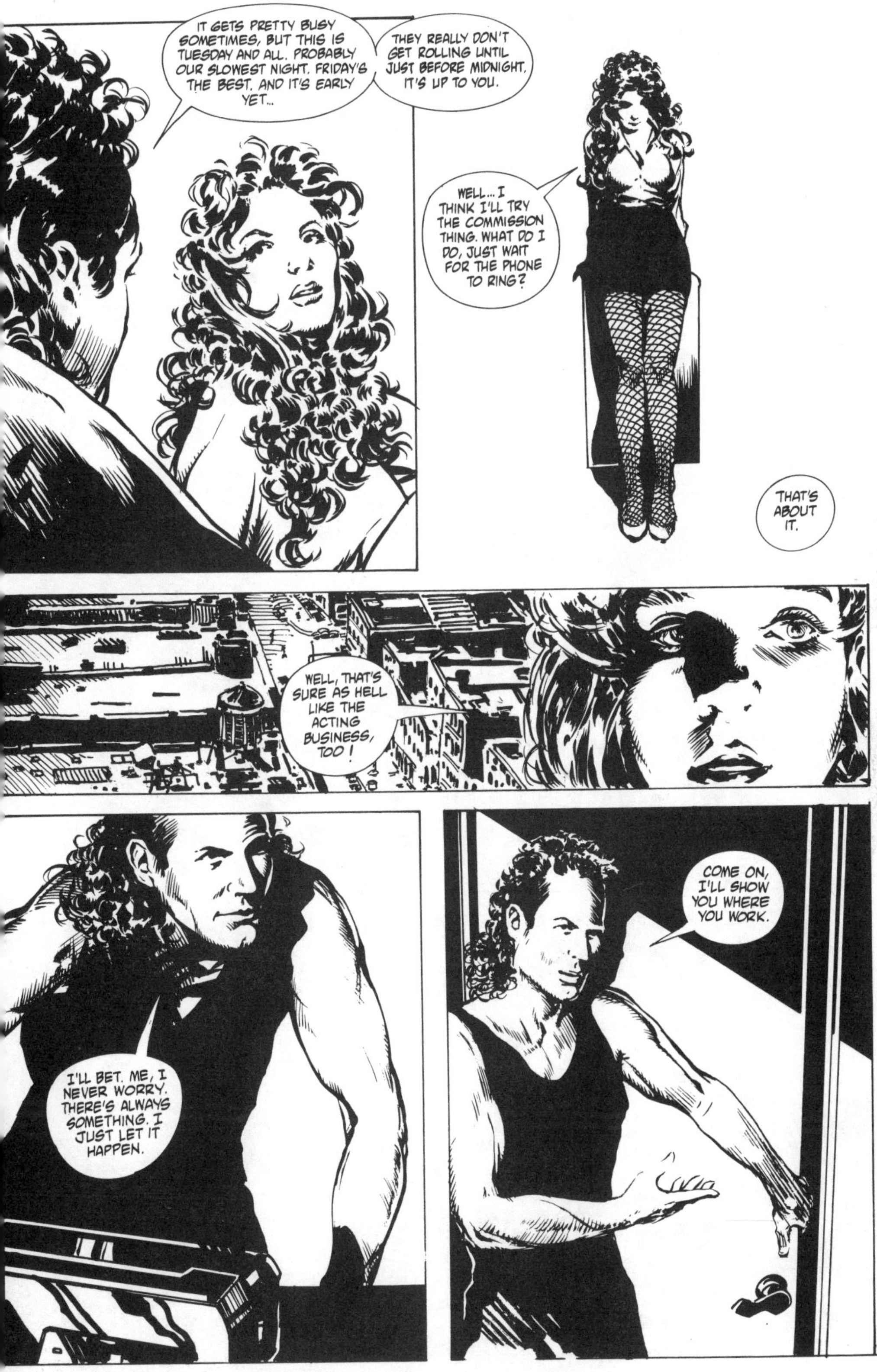
IT GETS PRETTY BUSY SOMETIMES, BUT THIS IS TUESDAY AND ALL. PROBABLY OUR SLOWEST NIGHT. FRIDAY'S THE BEST. AND IT'S EARLY YET...
THEY REALLY DON'T GET ROLLING UNTIL JUST BEFORE MIDNIGHT. IT'S UP TO YOU.
WELL... I THINK I'LL TRY THE COMMISSION THING. WHAT DO I DO, JUST WAIT FOR THE PHONE TO RING?
THAT'S ABOUT IT.
WELL, THAT'S SURE AS HELL LIKE THE ACTING BUSINESS, TOO!
I'LL BET. ME, I NEVER WORRY. THERE'S ALWAYS SOMETHING. I JUST LET IT HAPPEN.
COME ON, I'LL SHOW YOU WHERE YOU WORK.

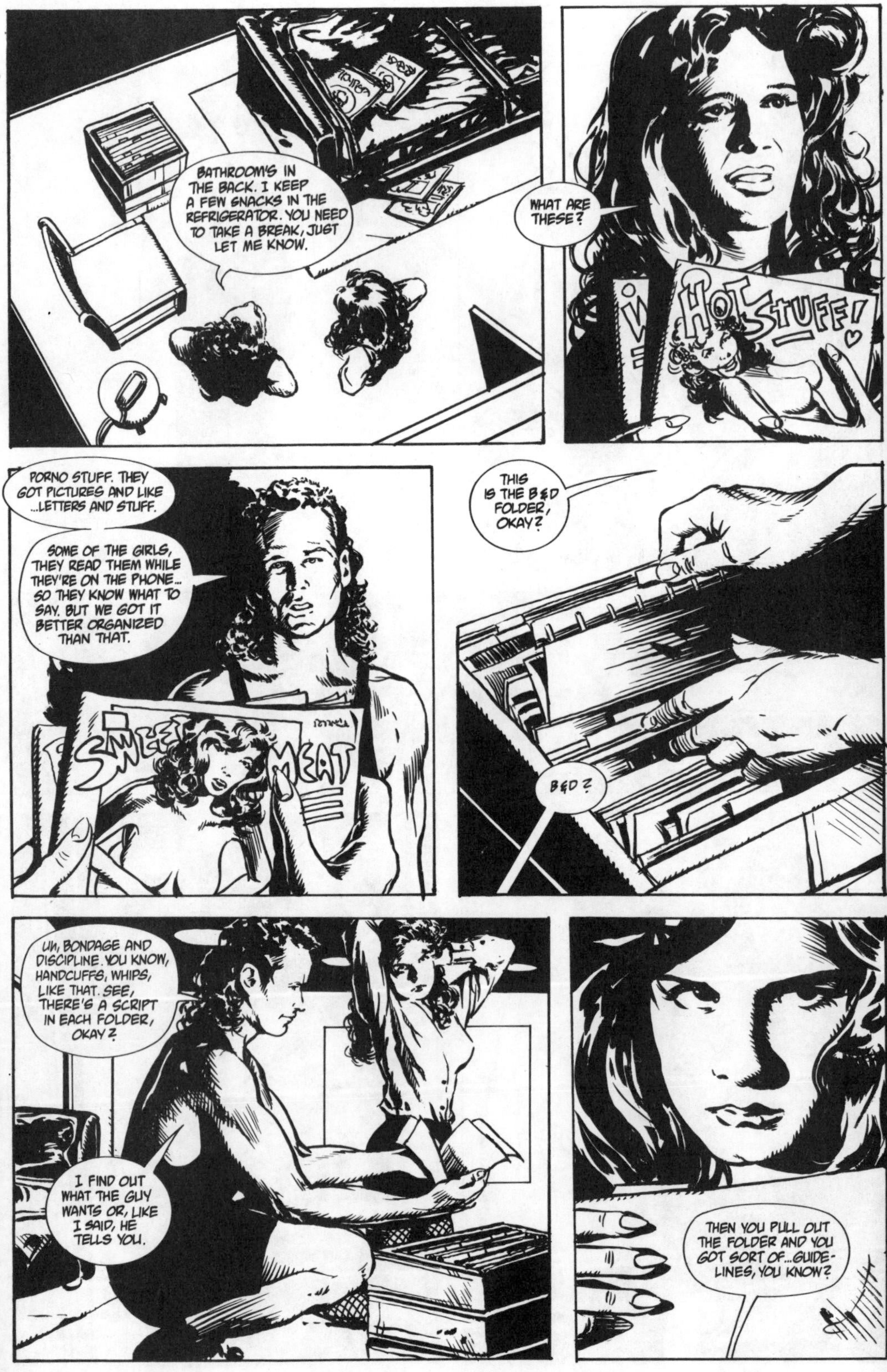

BATHROOM'S IN THE BACK. I KEEP A FEW SNACKS IN THE REFRIGERATOR. YOU NEED TO TAKE A BREAK, JUST LET ME KNOW.
WHAT ARE THESE?
HOT STUFF!
PORNO STUFF. THEY GOT PICTURES AND LIKE ...LETTERS AND STUFF.
SOME OF THE GIRLS, THEY READ THEM WHILE THEY'RE ON THE PHONE... SO THEY KNOW WHAT TO SAY. BUT WE GOT IT BETTER ORGANIZED THAN THAT.
SWEET MEAT
THIS IS THE B&D FOLDER, OKAY?
B&D?
UH, BONDAGE AND DISCIPLINE. YOU KNOW, HANDCUFFS, WHIPS, LIKE THAT. SEE, THERE'S A SCRIPT IN EACH FOLDER, OKAY?
I FIND OUT WHAT THE GUY WANTS OR, LIKE I SAID, HE TELLS YOU.
THEN YOU PULL OUT THE FOLDER AND YOU GOT SORT OF...GUIDE-LINES, YOU KNOW?

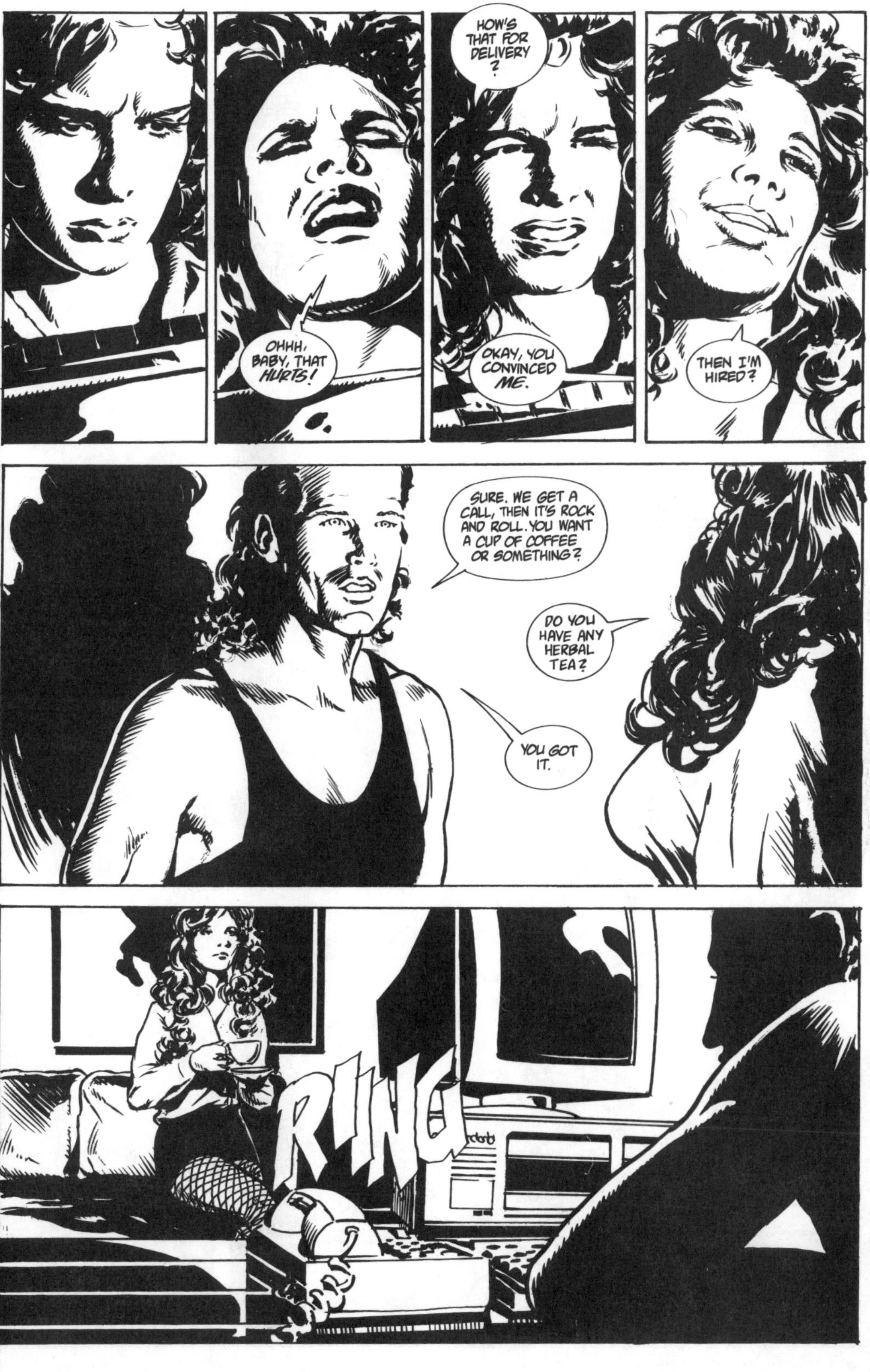
OHHH, BABY, THAT HURTS!
HOW'S THAT FOR DELIVERY?
OKAY, YOU CONVINCED ME.
THEN I'M HIRED?
SURE. WE GET A CALL, THEN IT'S ROCK AND ROLL. YOU WANT A CUP OF COFFEE OR SOMETHING?
DO YOU HAVE ANY HERBAL TEA?
YOU GOT IT.
RING

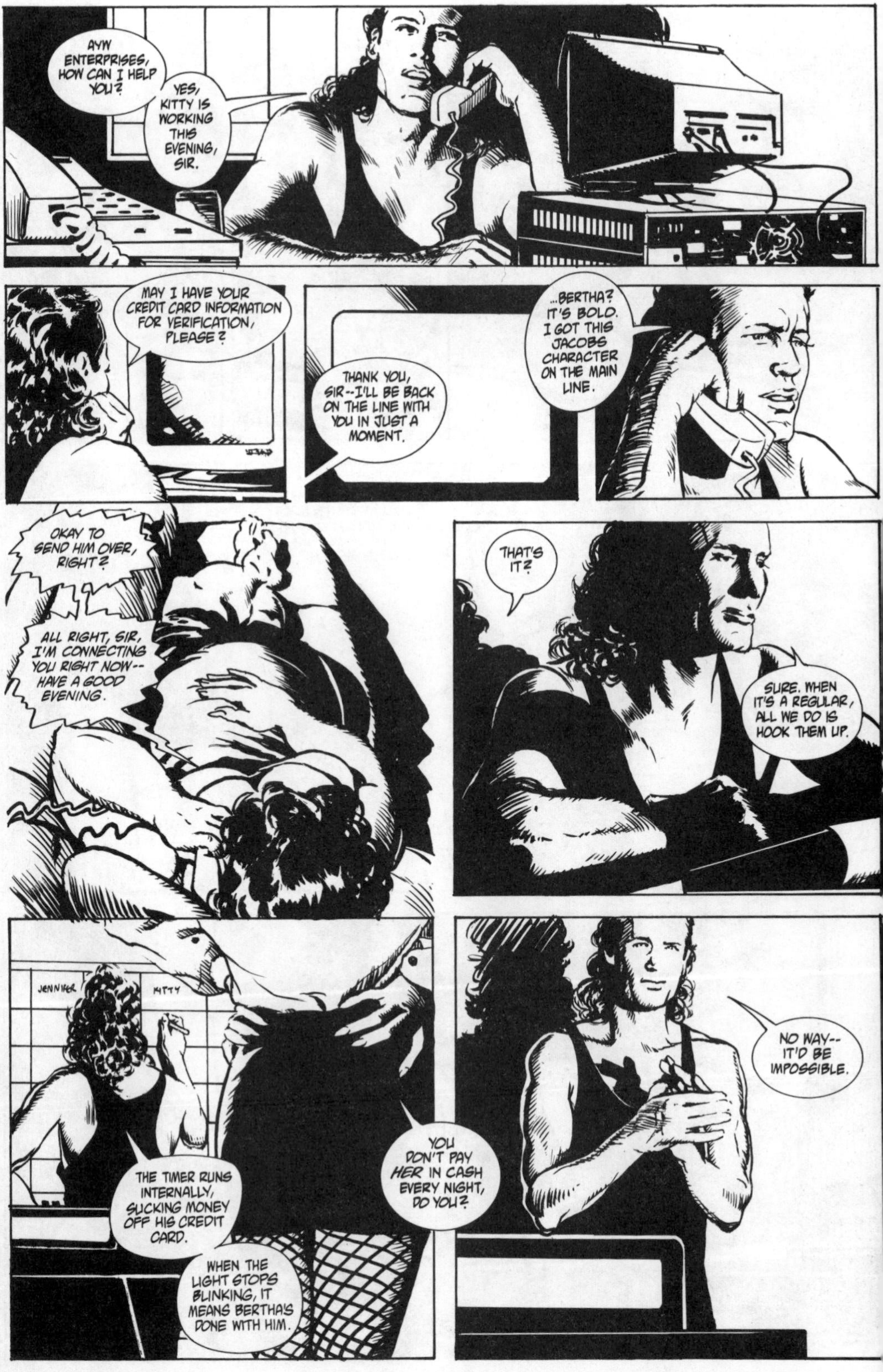
AYW ENTERPRISES, HOW CAN I HELP YOU?
YES, KITTY IS WORKING THIS EVENING, SIR.
MAY I HAVE YOUR CREDIT CARD INFORMATION FOR VERIFICATION, PLEASE?
THANK YOU, SIR--I'LL BE BACK ON THE LINE WITH YOU IN JUST A MOMENT.
...BERTHA? IT'S BOLO. I GOT THIS JACOBS CHARACTER ON THE MAIN LINE.
OKAY TO SEND HIM OVER, RIGHT?
ALL RIGHT, SIR, I'M CONNECTING YOU RIGHT NOW-- HAVE A GOOD EVENING.
THAT'S IT?
SURE. WHEN IT'S A REGULAR, ALL WE DO IS HOOK THEM UP.
JENNIFER
KITTY
THE TIMER RUNS INTERNALLY, SUCKING MONEY OFF HIS CREDIT CARD.
WHEN THE LIGHT STOPS BLINKING, IT MEANS BERTHA'S DONE WITH HIM.
YOU DON'T PAY HER IN CASH EVERY NIGHT, DO YOU?
NO WAY-- IT'D BE IMPOSSIBLE.

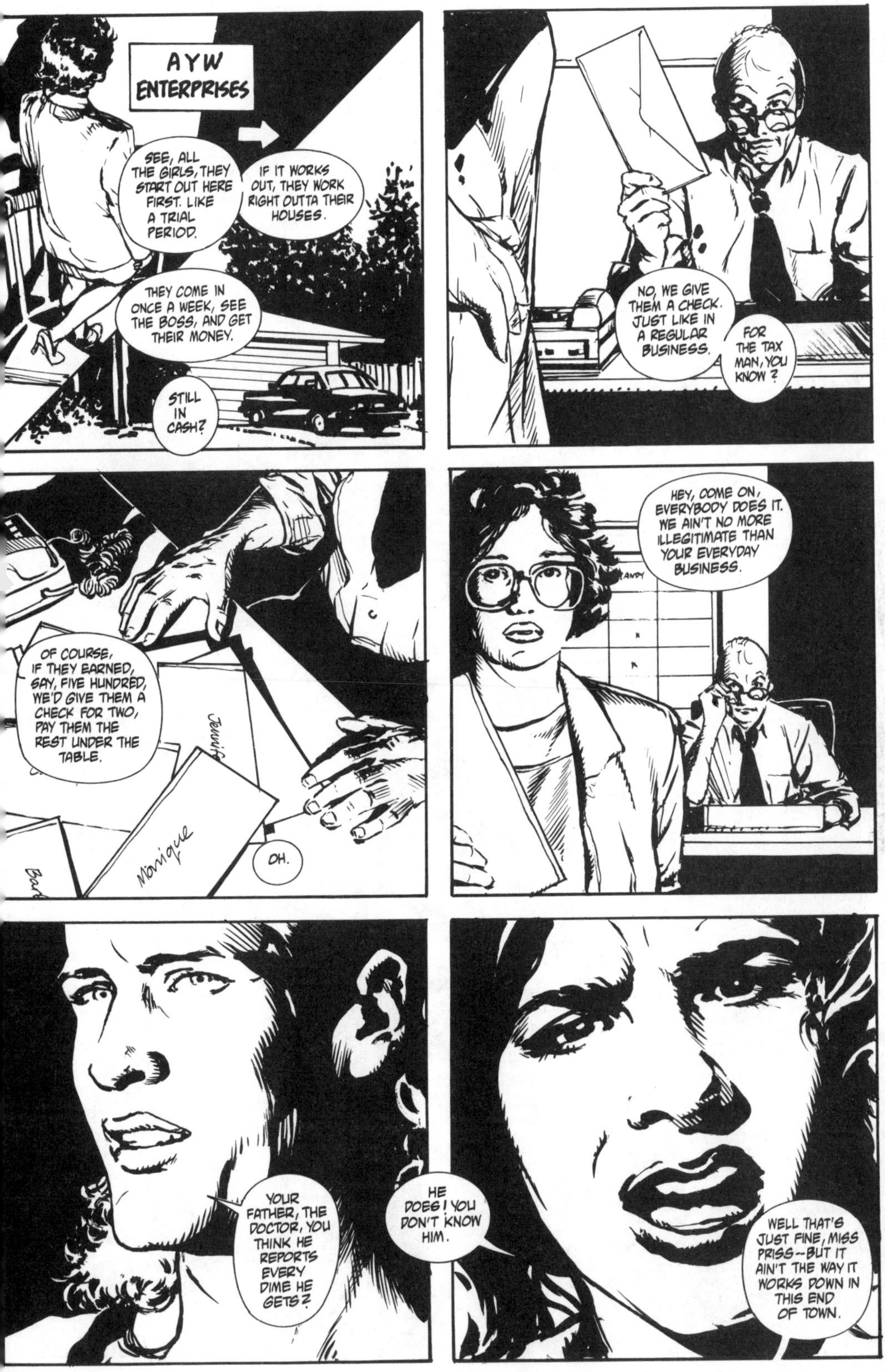

AYW ENTERPRISES
SEE, ALL THE GIRLS, THEY START OUT HERE FIRST. LIKE A TRIAL PERIOD.
IF IT WORKS OUT, THEY WORK RIGHT OUTTA THEIR HOUSES.
THEY COME IN ONCE A WEEK, SEE THE BOSS, AND GET THEIR MONEY.
STILL IN CASH?
NO, WE GIVE THEM A CHECK. JUST LIKE IN A REGULAR BUSINESS.
FOR THE TAX MAN, YOU KNOW?
OF COURSE, IF THEY EARNED, SAY, FIVE HUNDRED, WE'D GIVE THEM A CHECK FOR TWO, PAY THEM THE REST UNDER THE TABLE.
Monique
OH.
HEY, COME ON, EVERYBODY DOES IT. WE AIN'T NO MORE ILLEGITIMATE THAN YOUR EVERYDAY BUSINESS.
YOUR FATHER, THE DOCTOR, YOU THINK HE REPORTS EVERY DIME HE GETS?
HE DOES! YOU DON'T KNOW HIM.
WELL THAT'S JUST FINE, MISS PRISS--BUT IT AIN'T THE WAY IT WORKS DOWN IN THIS END OF TOWN.

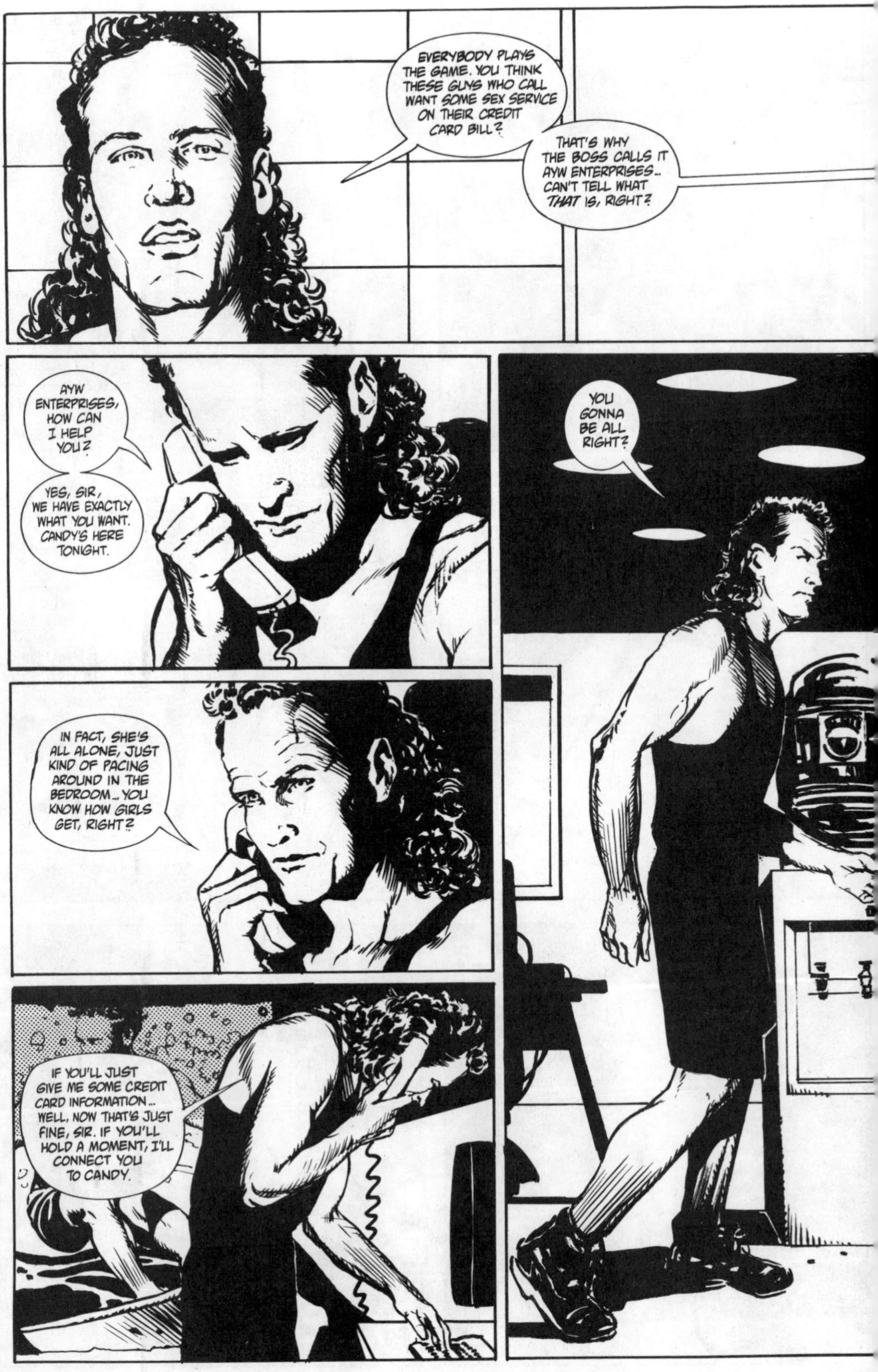
EVERYBODY PLAYS THE GAME. YOU THINK THESE GUYS WHO CALL WANT SOME SEX SERVICE ON THEIR CREDIT CARD BILL?
THAT'S WHY THE BOSS CALLS IT AYW ENTERPRISES... CAN'T TELL WHAT *THAT* IS, RIGHT?
AYW ENTERPRISES, HOW CAN I HELP YOU?
YES, SIR, WE HAVE EXACTLY WHAT YOU WANT. CANDY'S HERE TONIGHT.
IN FACT, SHE'S ALL ALONE, JUST KIND OF PACING AROUND IN THE BEDROOM... YOU KNOW HOW GIRLS GET, RIGHT?
IF YOU'LL JUST GIVE ME SOME CREDIT CARD INFORMATION... WELL, NOW THAT'S JUST FINE, SIR. IF YOU'LL HOLD A MOMENT, I'LL CONNECT YOU TO CANDY.
YOU GONNA BE ALL RIGHT?

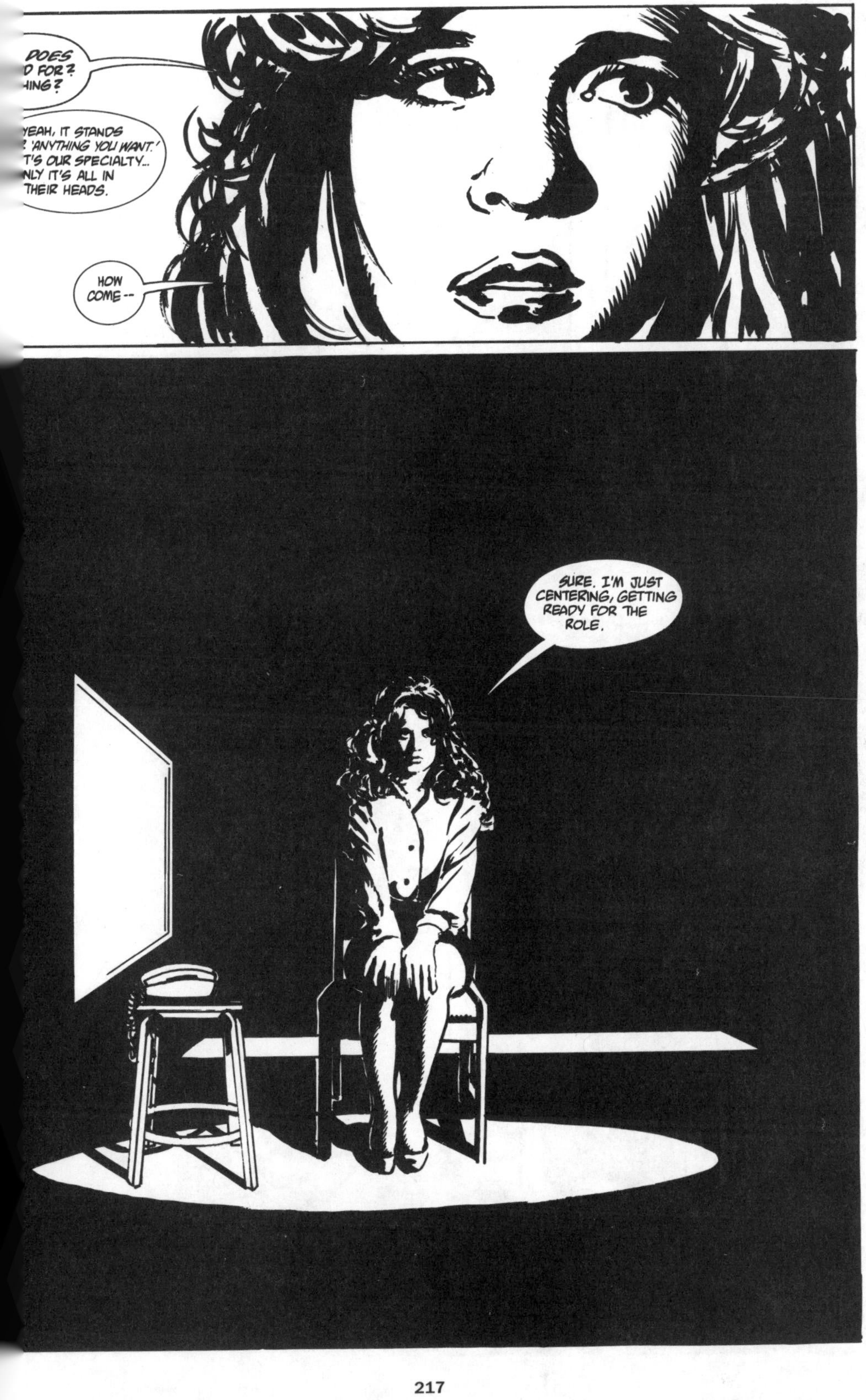

DOES
D FOR?
HING?
YEAH, IT STANDS
'ANYTHING YOU WANT.'
T'S OUR SPECIALTY...
NLY IT'S ALL IN
THEIR HEADS.
HOW COME--
SURE. I'M JUST CENTERING, GETTING READY FOR THE ROLE.

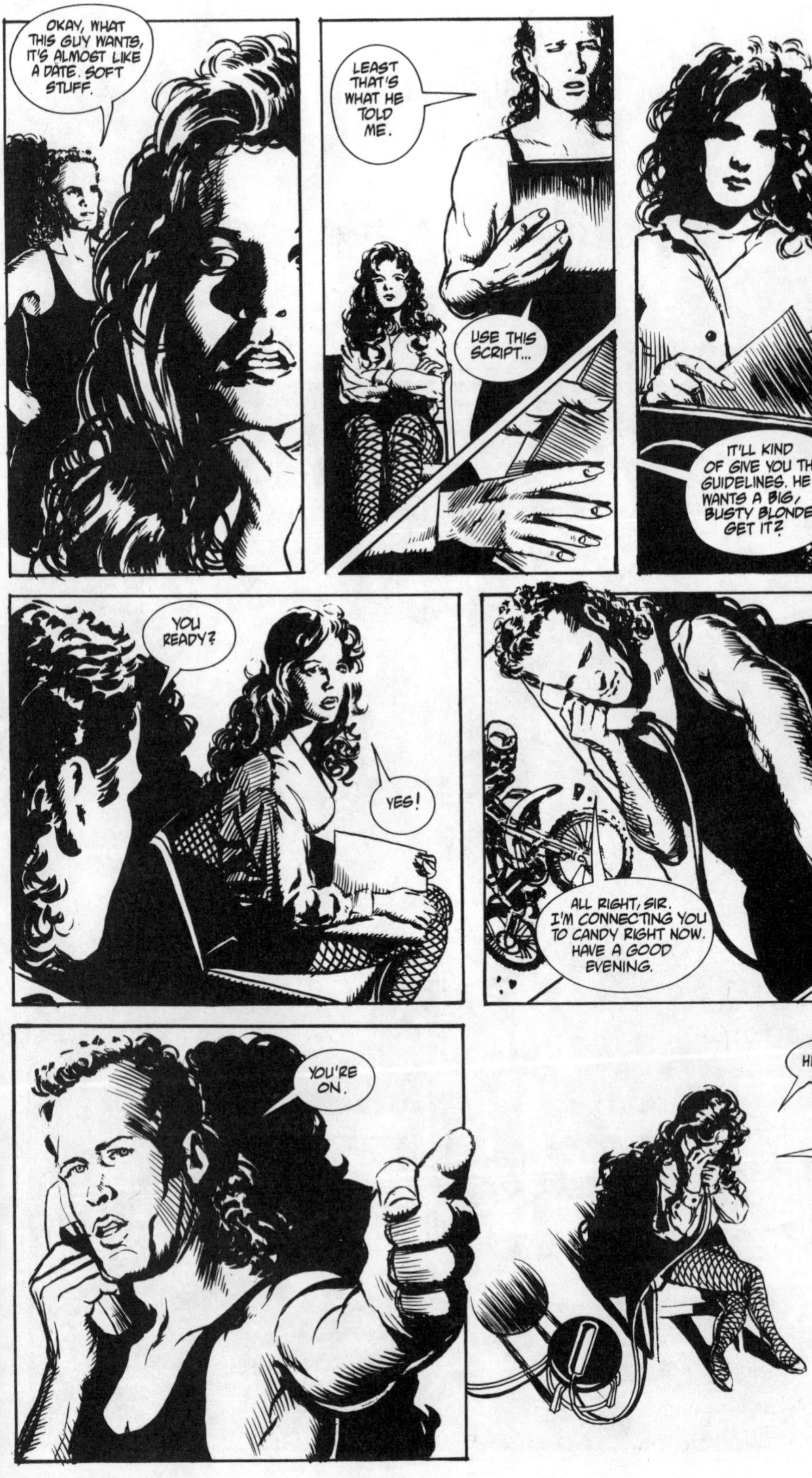
OKAY, WHAT THIS GUY WANTS, IT'S ALMOST LIKE A DATE. SOFT STUFF.
LEAST THAT'S WHAT HE TOLD ME.
USE THIS SCRIPT...
IT'LL KIND OF GIVE YOU THE GUIDELINES. HE WANTS A BIG, BUSTY BLONDE, GET IT?
YOU READY?
YES!
ALL RIGHT, SIR. I'M CONNECTING YOU TO CANDY RIGHT NOW. HAVE A GOOD EVENING.
YOU'RE ON.
HEL-LO.
WHO IS THIS?

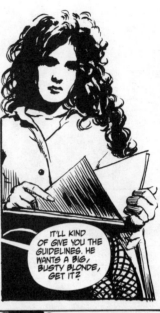

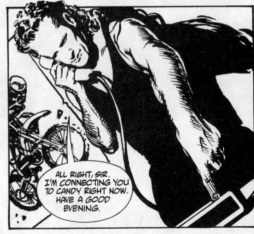

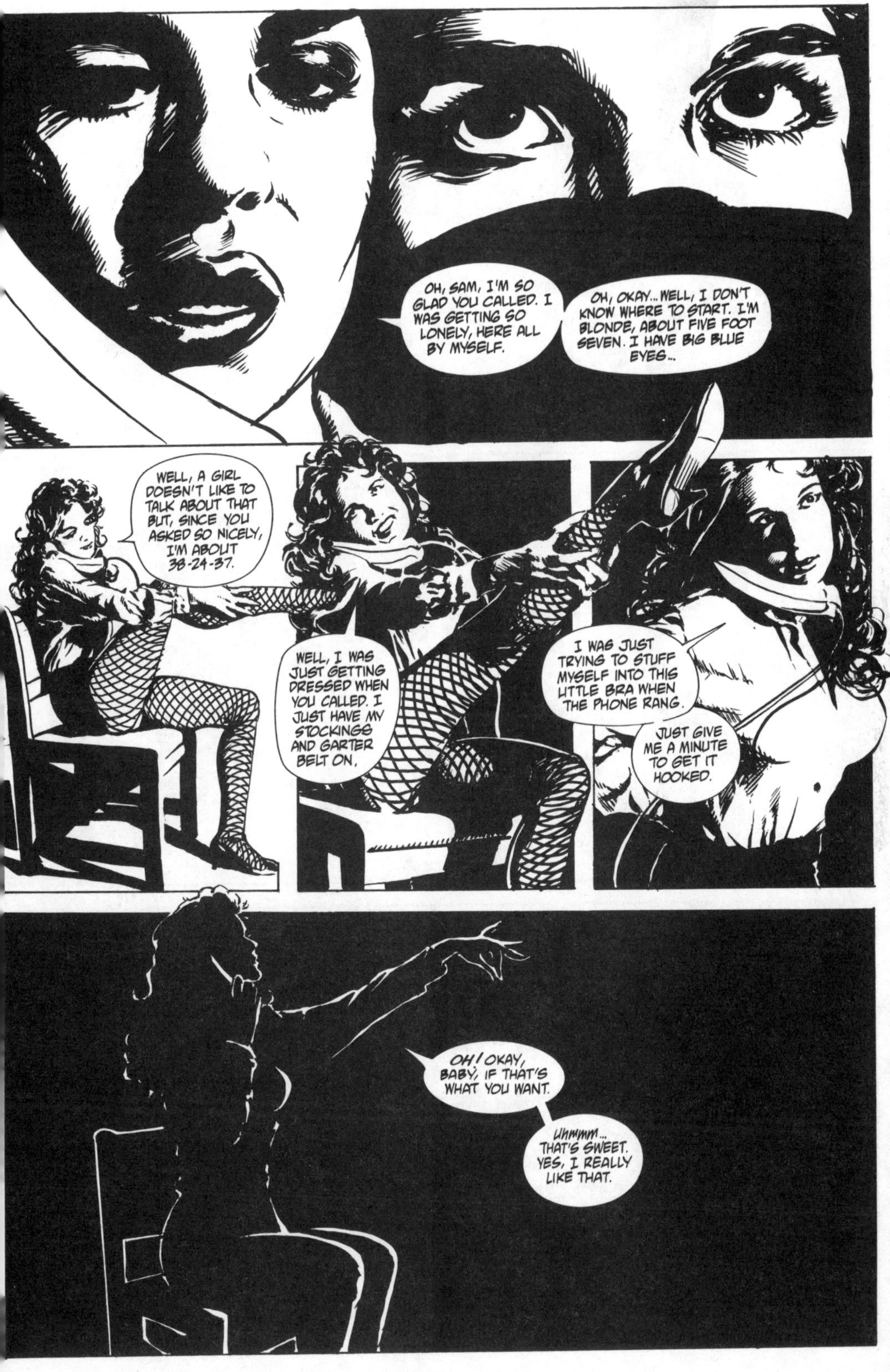

OH, SAM, I'M SO GLAD YOU CALLED. I WAS GETTING SO LONELY, HERE ALL BY MYSELF.
OH, OKAY... WELL, I DON'T KNOW WHERE TO START. I'M BLONDE, ABOUT FIVE FOOT SEVEN. I HAVE BIG BLUE EYES...
WELL, A GIRL DOESN'T LIKE TO TALK ABOUT THAT BUT, SINCE YOU ASKED SO NICELY, I'M ABOUT 38-24-37.
WELL, I WAS JUST GETTING DRESSED WHEN YOU CALLED. I JUST HAVE MY STOCKINGS AND GARTER BELT ON.
I WAS JUST TRYING TO STUFF MYSELF INTO THIS LITTLE BRA WHEN THE PHONE RANG.
JUST GIVE ME A MINUTE TO GET IT HOOKED.
OH! OKAY, BABY, IF THAT'S WHAT YOU WANT.
Uhmmm... THAT'S SWEET. YES, I REALLY LIKE THAT.

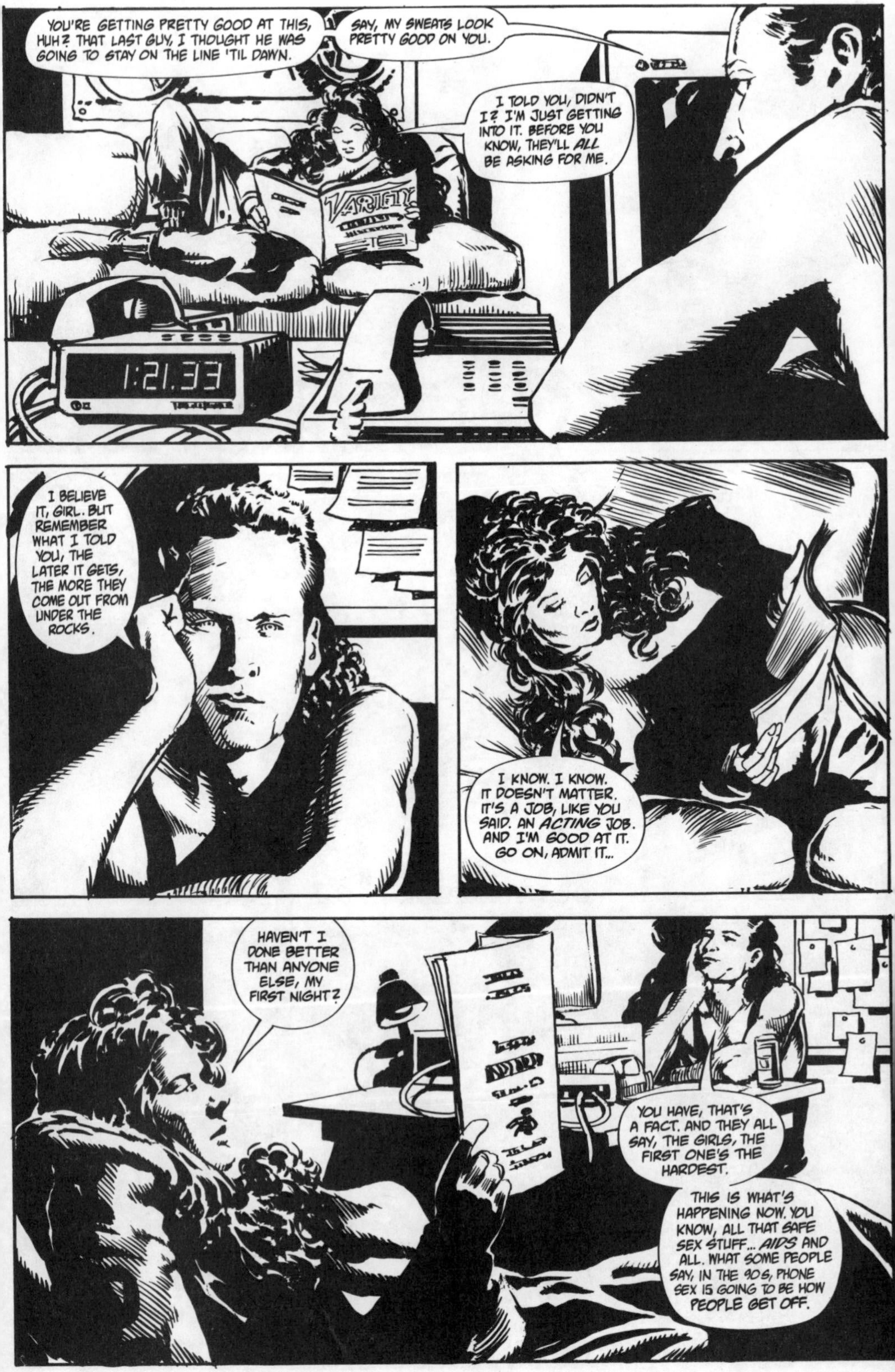

YOU'RE GETTING PRETTY GOOD AT THIS, HUH? THAT LAST GUY, I THOUGHT HE WAS GOING TO STAY ON THE LINE 'TIL DAWN.
SAY, MY SWEATS LOOK PRETTY GOOD ON YOU.
I TOLD YOU, DIDN'T I? I'M JUST GETTING INTO IT. BEFORE YOU KNOW, THEY'LL *ALL* BE ASKING FOR ME.
1:21.33
I BELIEVE IT, GIRL. BUT REMEMBER WHAT I TOLD YOU, THE LATER IT GETS, THE MORE THEY COME OUT FROM UNDER THE ROCKS.
I KNOW. I KNOW. IT DOESN'T MATTER. IT'S A JOB, LIKE YOU SAID. AN *ACTING* JOB. AND I'M GOOD AT IT. GO ON, ADMIT IT...
HAVEN'T I DONE BETTER THAN ANYONE ELSE, MY FIRST NIGHT?
YOU HAVE, THAT'S A FACT. AND THEY ALL SAY, THE GIRLS, THE FIRST ONE'S THE HARDEST.
THIS IS WHAT'S HAPPENING NOW. YOU KNOW, ALL THAT SAFE SEX STUFF... *AIDS* AND ALL. WHAT SOME PEOPLE SAY, IN THE 90s, PHONE SEX IS GOING TO BE HOW PEOPLE GET OFF.

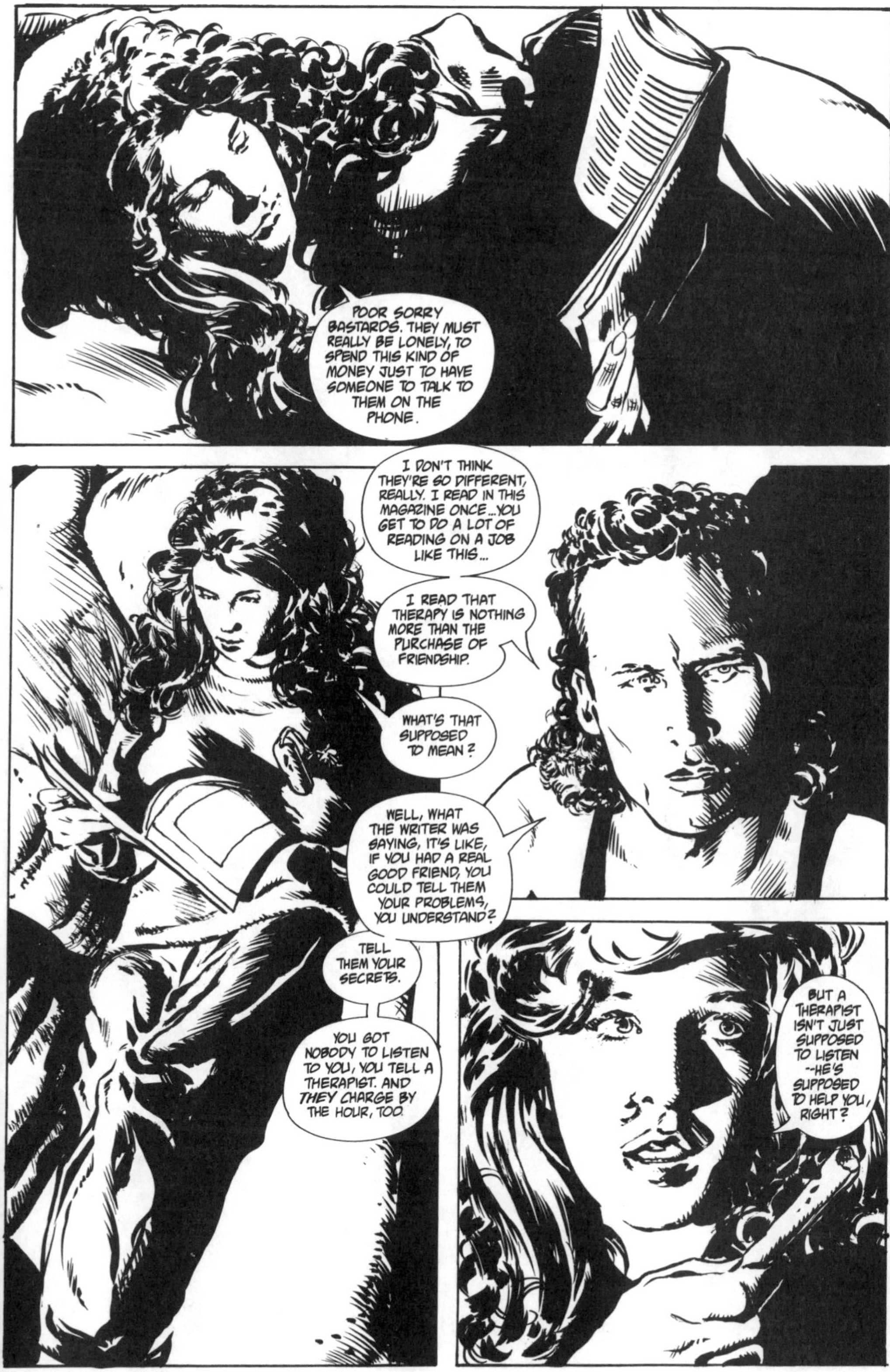
POOR SORRY BASTARDS. THEY MUST REALLY BE LONELY, TO SPEND THIS KIND OF MONEY JUST TO HAVE SOMEONE TO TALK TO THEM ON THE PHONE.
I DON'T THINK THEY'RE SO DIFFERENT, REALLY. I READ IN THIS MAGAZINE ONCE...YOU GET TO DO A LOT OF READING ON A JOB LIKE THIS...
I READ THAT THERAPY IS NOTHING MORE THAN THE PURCHASE OF FRIENDSHIP.
WHAT'S THAT SUPPOSED TO MEAN?
WELL, WHAT THE WRITER WAS SAYING, IT'S LIKE, IF YOU HAD A REAL GOOD FRIEND, YOU COULD TELL THEM YOUR PROBLEMS, YOU UNDERSTAND?
TELL THEM YOUR SECRETS.
YOU GOT NOBODY TO LISTEN TO YOU, YOU TELL A THERAPIST. AND THEY CHARGE BY THE HOUR, TOO.
BUT A THERAPIST ISN'T JUST SUPPOSED TO LISTEN --HE'S SUPPOSED TO HELP YOU, RIGHT?

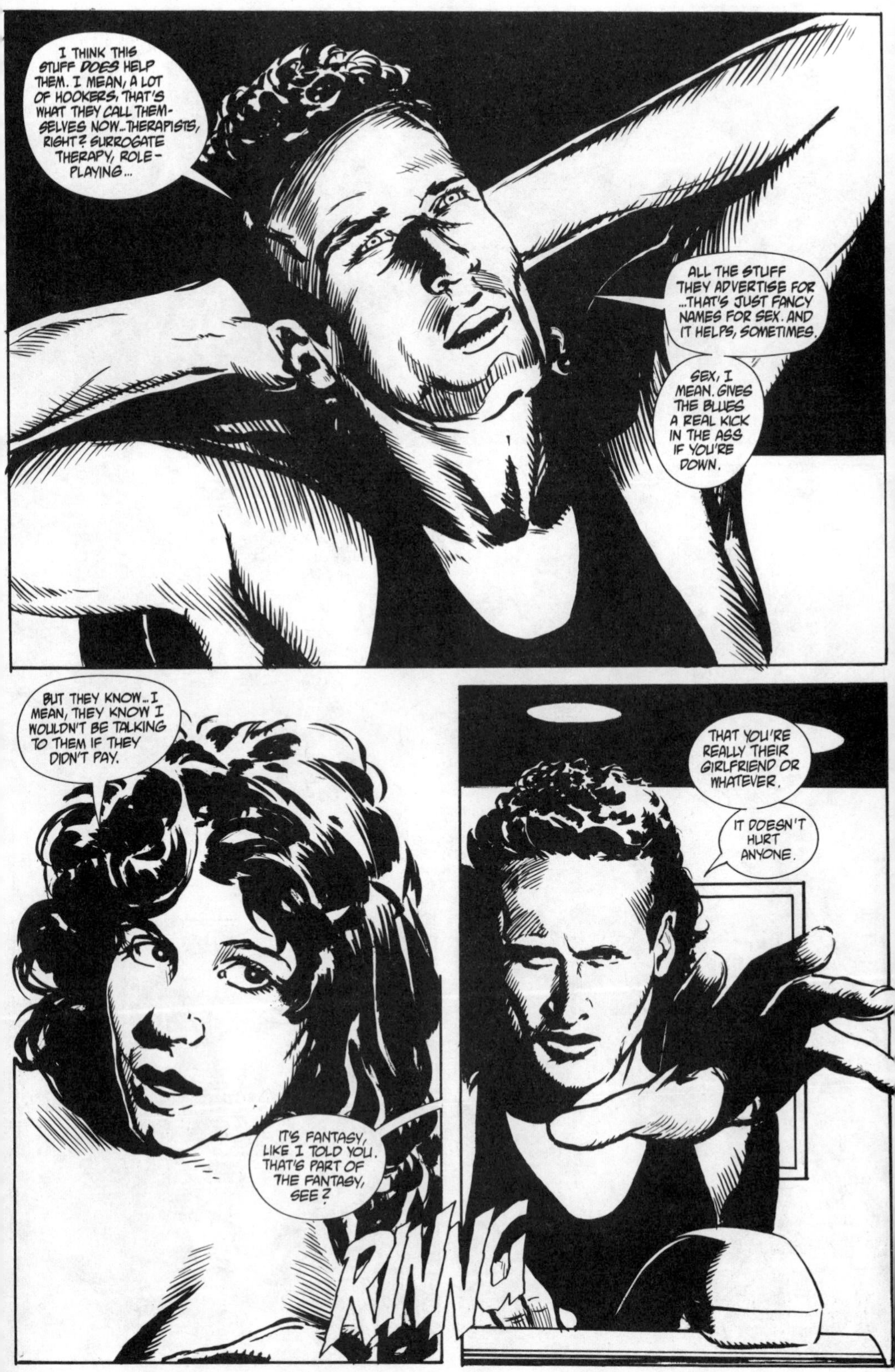
I THINK THIS STUFF DOES HELP THEM. I MEAN, A LOT OF HOOKERS, THAT'S WHAT THEY CALL THEMSELVES NOW...THERAPISTS, RIGHT? SURROGATE THERAPY, ROLE-PLAYING...
ALL THE STUFF THEY ADVERTISE FOR ...THAT'S JUST FANCY NAMES FOR SEX. AND IT HELPS, SOMETIMES.
SEX, I MEAN. GIVES THE BLUES A REAL KICK IN THE ASS IF YOU'RE DOWN.
BUT THEY KNOW...I MEAN, THEY KNOW I WOULDN'T BE TALKING TO THEM IF THEY DIDN'T PAY.
THAT YOU'RE REALLY THEIR GIRLFRIEND OR WHATEVER.
IT DOESN'T HURT ANYONE.
IT'S FANTASY, LIKE I TOLD YOU. THAT'S PART OF THE FANTASY, SEE?
RINNG

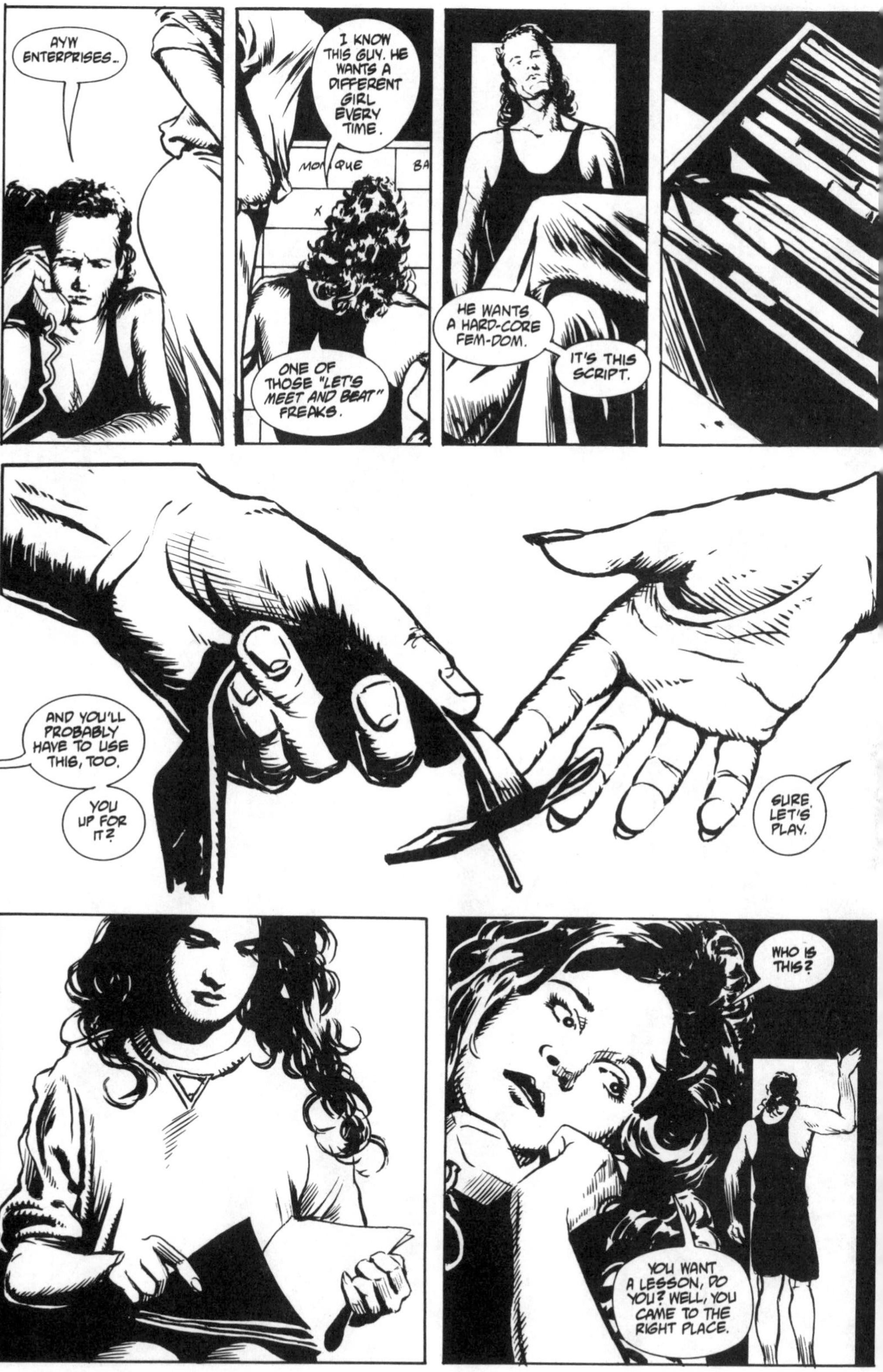

AYW ENTERPRISES..
I KNOW THIS GUY. HE WANTS A DIFFERENT GIRL EVERY TIME.
MON QUE
BA
ONE OF THOSE "LET'S MEET AND BEAT" FREAKS.
HE WANTS A HARD-CORE FEM-DOM.
IT'S THIS SCRIPT.
AND YOU'LL PROBABLY HAVE TO USE THIS, TOO.
YOU UP FOR IT?
SURE. LET'S PLAY.
WHO IS THIS?
YOU WANT A LESSON, DO YOU? WELL, YOU CAME TO THE RIGHT PLACE.

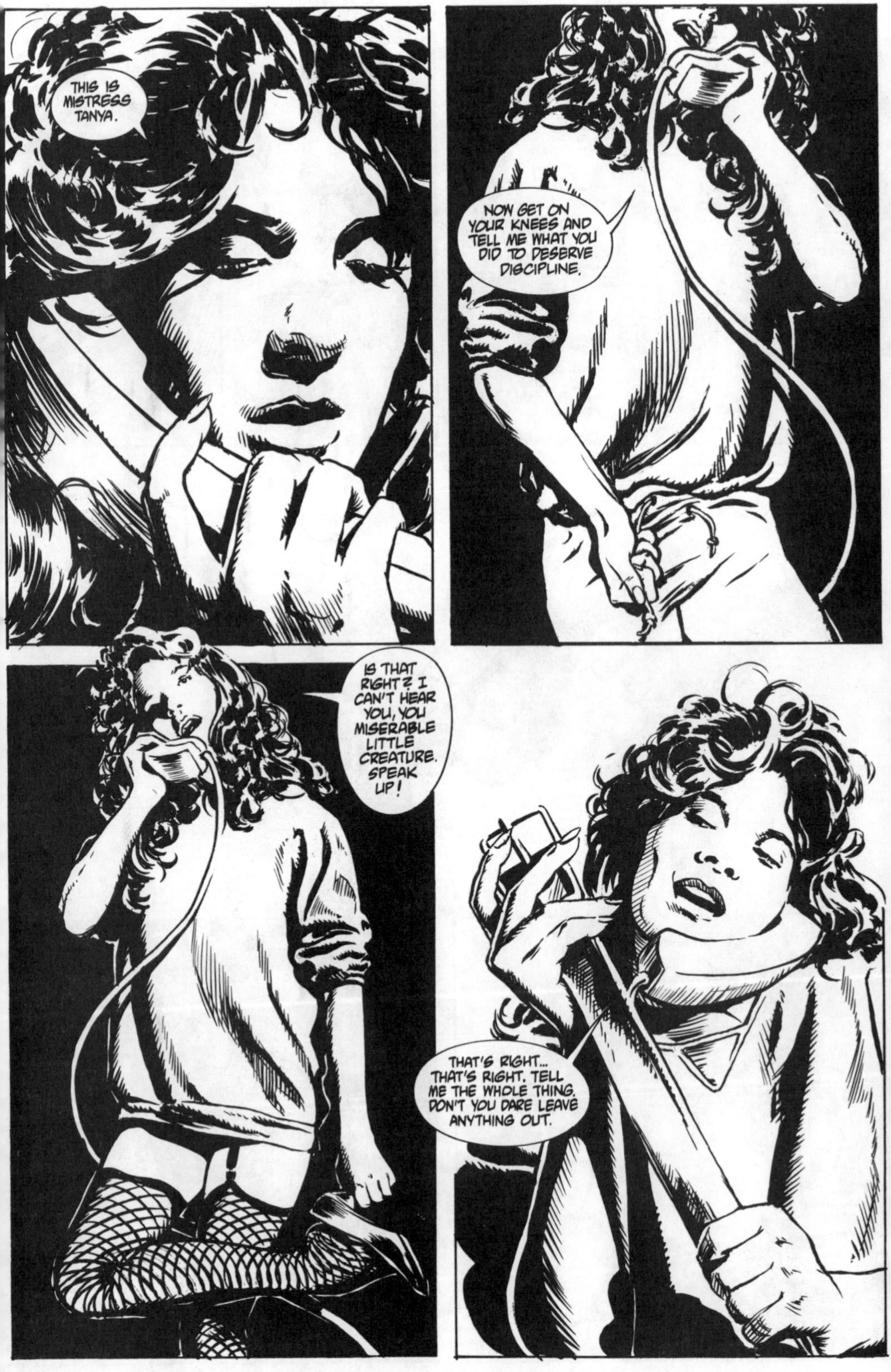
THIS IS MISTRESS TANYA.
NOW GET ON YOUR KNEES AND TELL ME WHAT YOU DID TO DESERVE DISCIPLINE.
IS THAT RIGHT? I CAN'T HEAR YOU, YOU MISERABLE LITTLE CREATURE. SPEAK UP!
THAT'S RIGHT... THAT'S RIGHT. TELL ME THE WHOLE THING. DON'T YOU DARE LEAVE ANYTHING OUT.

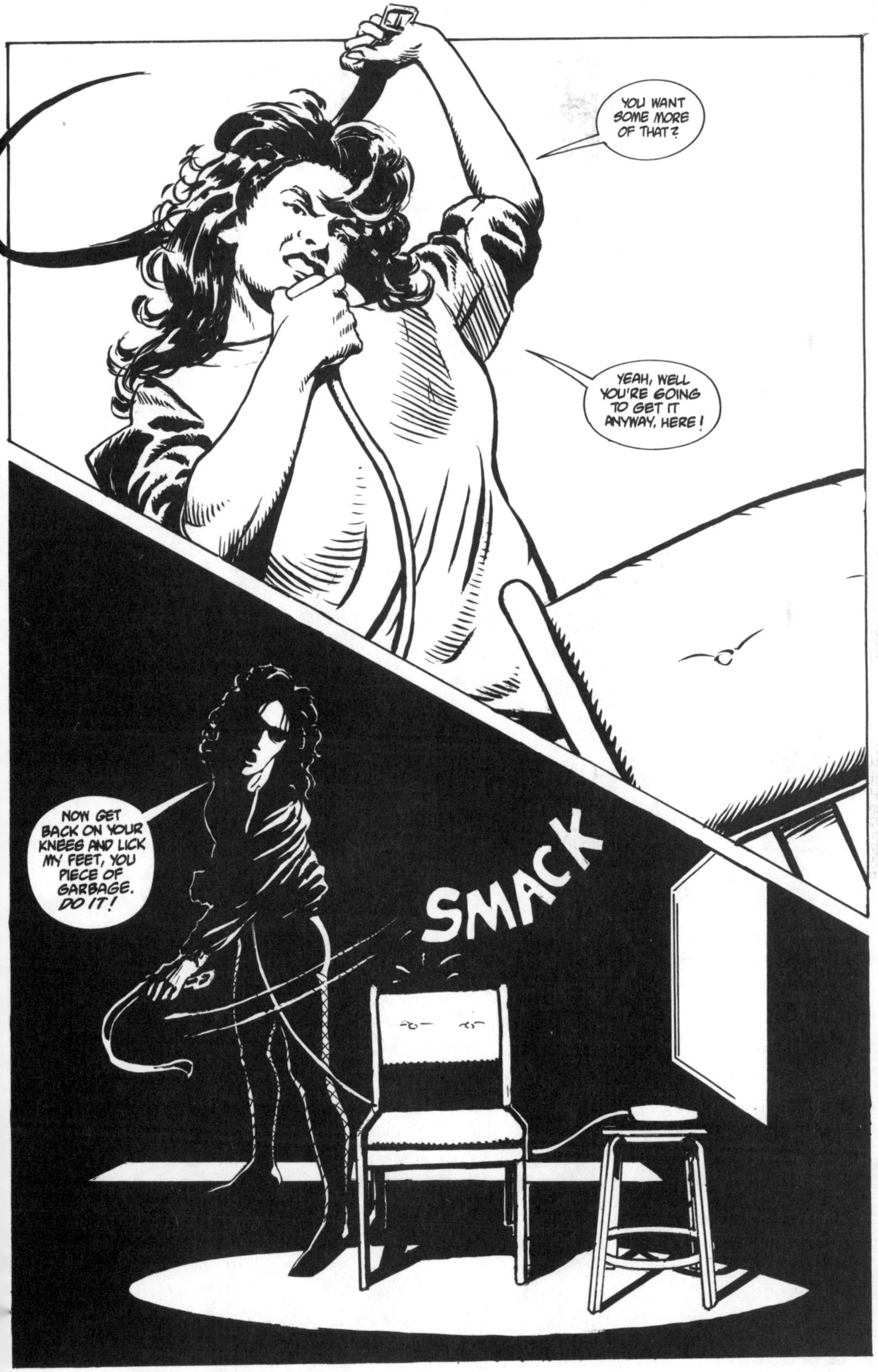
YOU WANT SOME MORE OF THAT?
YEAH, WELL YOU'RE GOING TO GET IT ANYWAY, HERE!
SMACK
NOW GET BACK ON YOUR KNEES AND LICK MY FEET, YOU PIECE OF GARBAGE. DO IT!

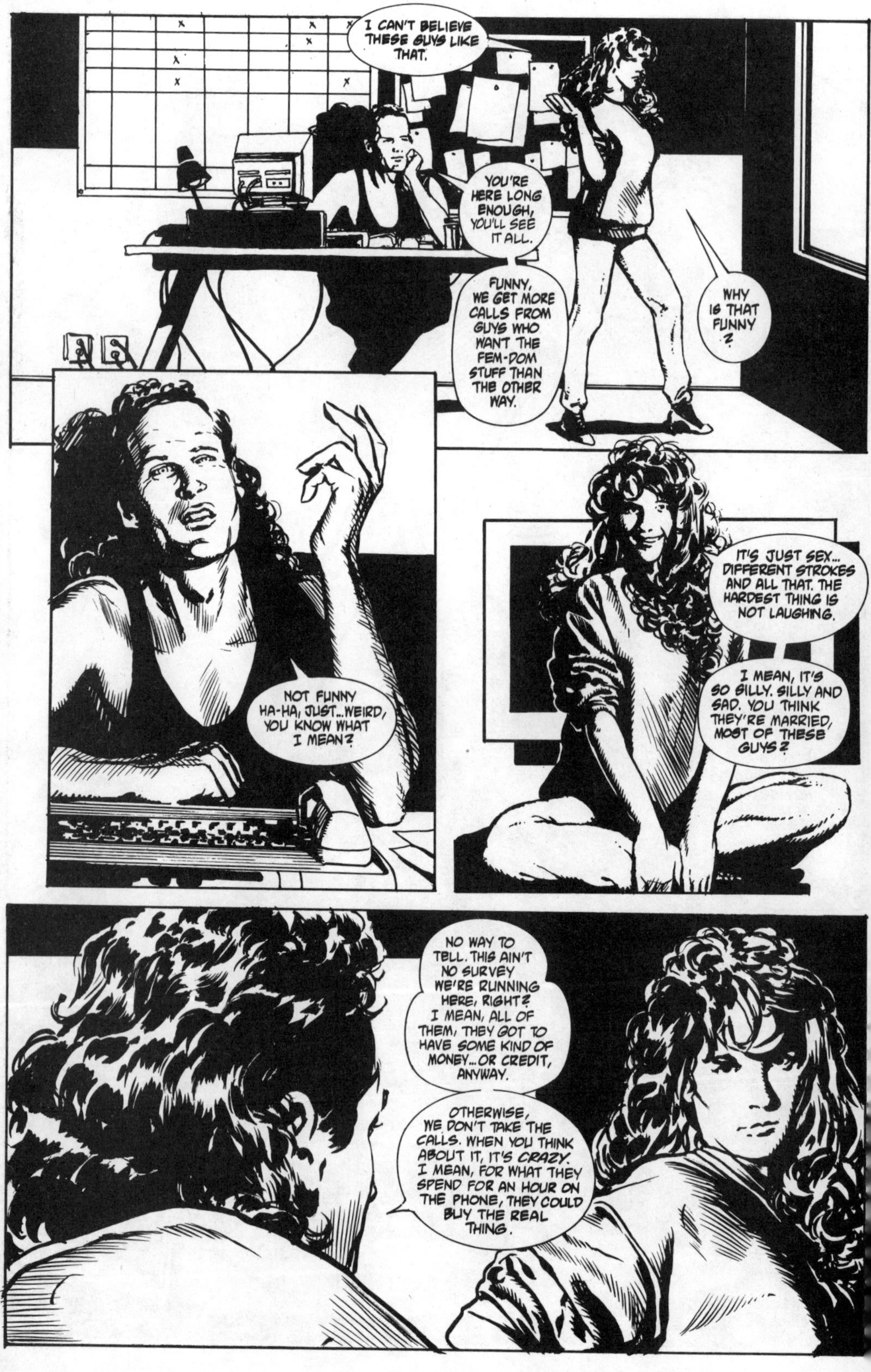

I CAN'T BELIEVE THESE GUYS LIKE THAT.
YOU'RE HERE LONG ENOUGH, YOU'LL SEE IT ALL.
FUNNY, WE GET MORE CALLS FROM GUYS WHO WANT THE FEM-DOM STUFF THAN THE OTHER WAY.
WHY IS THAT FUNNY?
NOT FUNNY HA-HA, JUST...WEIRD, YOU KNOW WHAT I MEAN?
IT'S JUST SEX... DIFFERENT STROKES AND ALL THAT. THE HARDEST THING IS NOT LAUGHING.
I MEAN, IT'S SO SILLY. SILLY AND SAD. YOU THINK THEY'RE MARRIED, MOST OF THESE GUYS?
NO WAY TO TELL. THIS AIN'T NO SURVEY WE'RE RUNNING HERE, RIGHT? I MEAN, ALL OF THEM, THEY GOT TO HAVE SOME KIND OF MONEY...OR CREDIT, ANYWAY.
OTHERWISE, WE DON'T TAKE THE CALLS. WHEN YOU THINK ABOUT IT, IT'S *CRAZY*. I MEAN, FOR WHAT THEY SPEND FOR AN HOUR ON THE PHONE, THEY COULD BUY THE REAL THING.

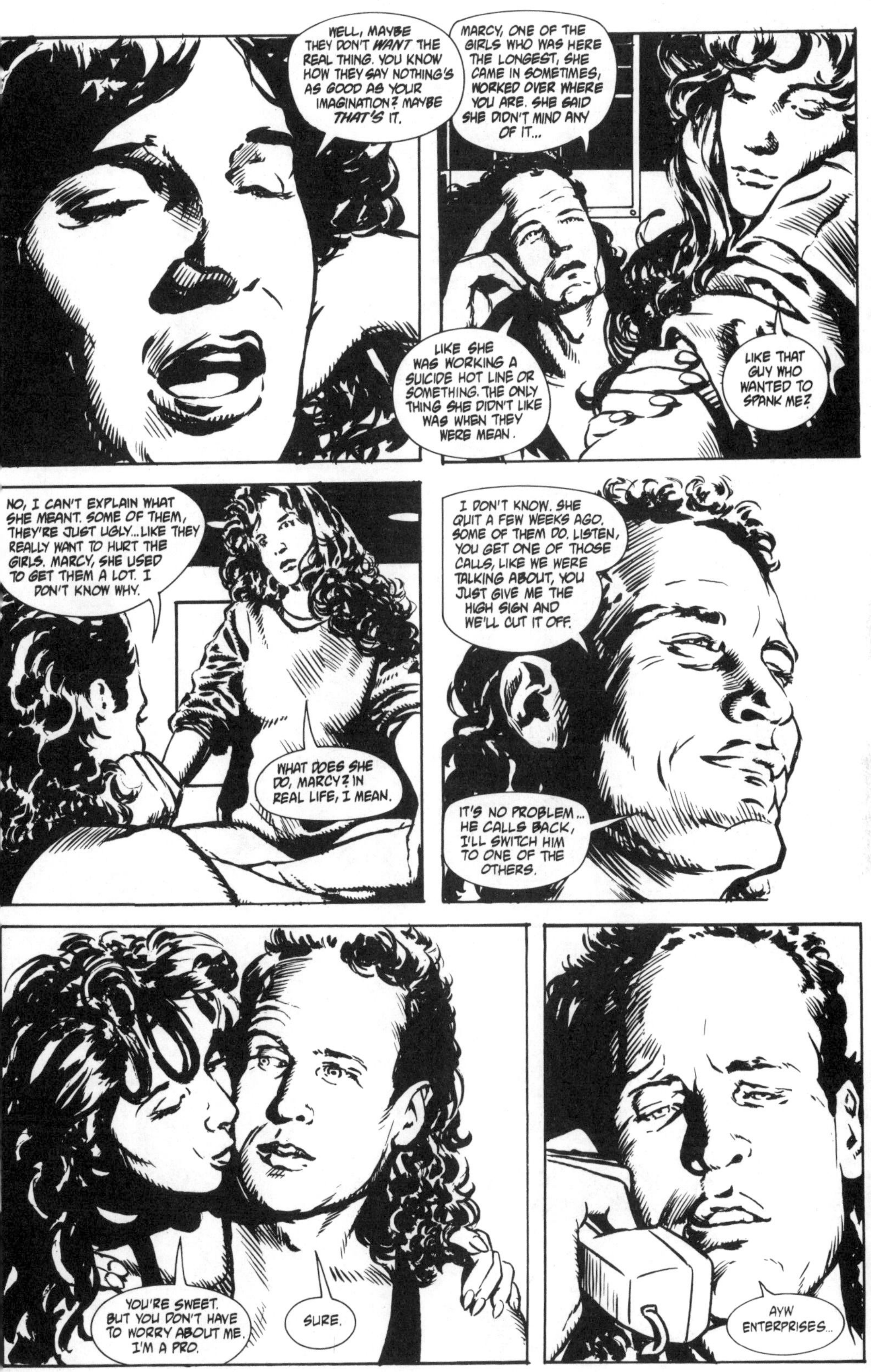
WELL, MAYBE THEY DON'T *WANT* THE REAL THING. YOU KNOW HOW THEY SAY NOTHING'S AS GOOD AS YOUR IMAGINATION? MAYBE *THAT'S* IT.
MARCY, ONE OF THE GIRLS WHO WAS HERE THE LONGEST, SHE CAME IN SOMETIMES, WORKED OVER WHERE YOU ARE. SHE SAID SHE DIDN'T MIND ANY OF IT...
LIKE SHE WAS WORKING A SUICIDE HOT LINE OR SOMETHING. THE ONLY THING SHE DIDN'T LIKE WAS WHEN THEY WERE MEAN.
LIKE THAT GUY WHO WANTED TO SPANK ME?
NO, I CAN'T EXPLAIN WHAT SHE MEANT. SOME OF THEM, THEY'RE JUST UGLY...LIKE THEY REALLY WANT TO HURT THE GIRLS. MARCY, SHE USED TO GET THEM A LOT. I DON'T KNOW WHY.
WHAT DOES SHE DO, MARCY? IN REAL LIFE, I MEAN.
I DON'T KNOW. SHE QUIT A FEW WEEKS AGO. SOME OF THEM DO. LISTEN, YOU GET ONE OF THOSE CALLS, LIKE WE WERE TALKING ABOUT, YOU JUST GIVE ME THE HIGH SIGN AND WE'LL CUT IT OFF.
IT'S NO PROBLEM... HE CALLS BACK, I'LL SWITCH HIM TO ONE OF THE OTHERS.
YOU'RE SWEET. BUT YOU DON'T HAVE TO WORRY ABOUT ME. I'M A PRO.
SURE.
AYW ENTERPRISES...

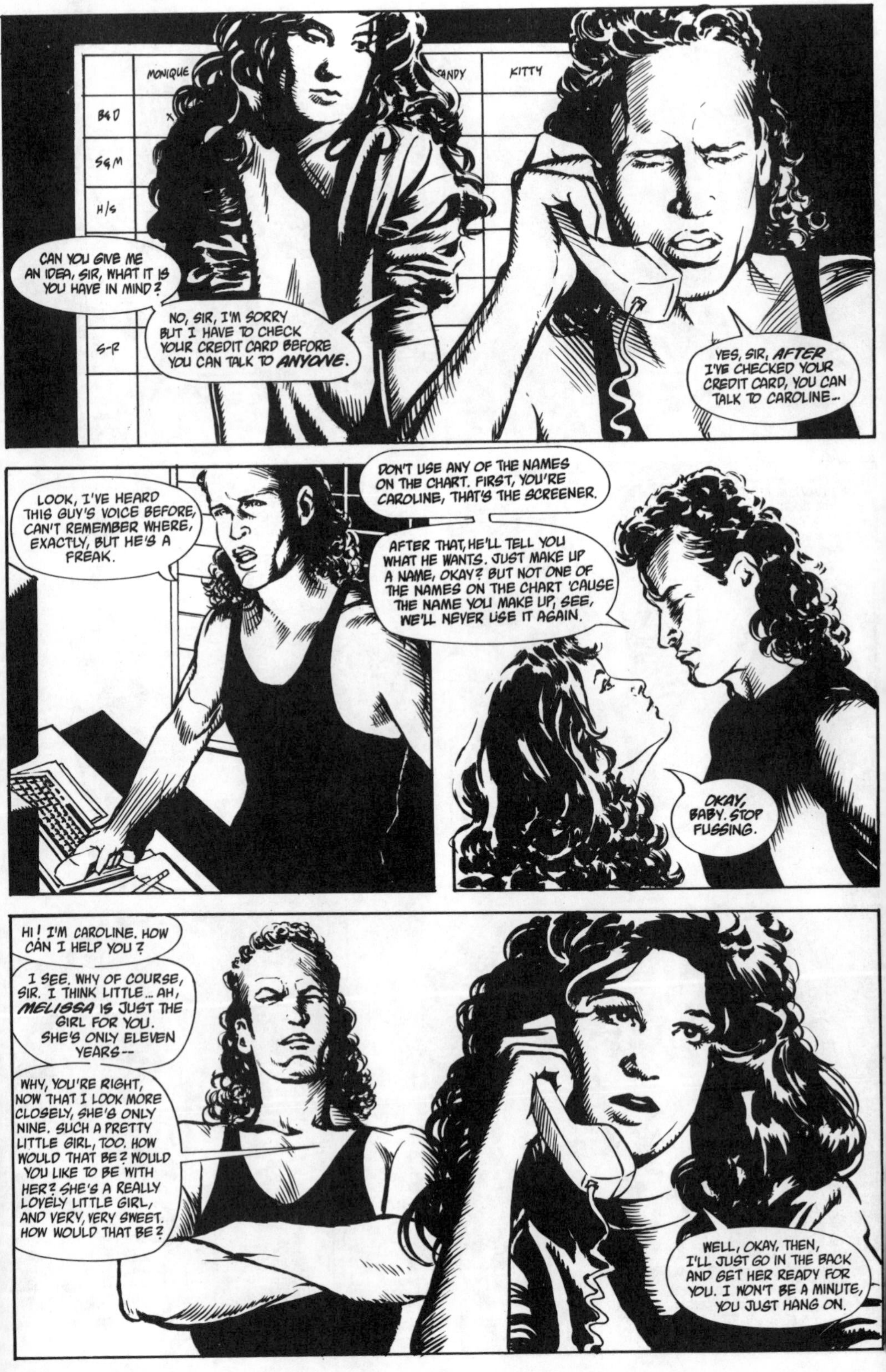
MONIQUE
CANDY
KITTY
B&D
S&M
H/S
S-R
CAN YOU GIVE ME AN IDEA, SIR, WHAT IT IS YOU HAVE IN MIND?
NO, SIR, I'M SORRY BUT I HAVE TO CHECK YOUR CREDIT CARD BEFORE YOU CAN TALK TO ANYONE.
YES, SIR, AFTER I'VE CHECKED YOUR CREDIT CARD, YOU CAN TALK TO CAROLINE...
LOOK, I'VE HEARD THIS GUY'S VOICE BEFORE, CAN'T REMEMBER WHERE, EXACTLY, BUT HE'S A FREAK.
DON'T USE ANY OF THE NAMES ON THE CHART. FIRST, YOU'RE CAROLINE, THAT'S THE SCREENER.
AFTER THAT, HE'LL TELL YOU WHAT HE WANTS. JUST MAKE UP A NAME, OKAY? BUT NOT ONE OF THE NAMES ON THE CHART 'CAUSE THE NAME YOU MAKE UP, SEE, WE'LL NEVER USE IT AGAIN.
OKAY, BABY. STOP FUSSING.
HI! I'M CAROLINE. HOW CAN I HELP YOU?
I SEE. WHY OF COURSE, SIR. I THINK LITTLE... AH, MELISSA IS JUST THE GIRL FOR YOU. SHE'S ONLY ELEVEN YEARS--
WHY, YOU'RE RIGHT, NOW THAT I LOOK MORE CLOSELY, SHE'S ONLY NINE. SUCH A PRETTY LITTLE GIRL, TOO. HOW WOULD THAT BE? WOULD YOU LIKE TO BE WITH HER? SHE'S A REALLY LOVELY LITTLE GIRL, AND VERY, VERY SWEET. HOW WOULD THAT BE?
WELL, OKAY, THEN, I'LL JUST GO IN THE BACK AND GET HER READY FOR YOU. I WON'T BE A MINUTE, YOU JUST HANG ON.

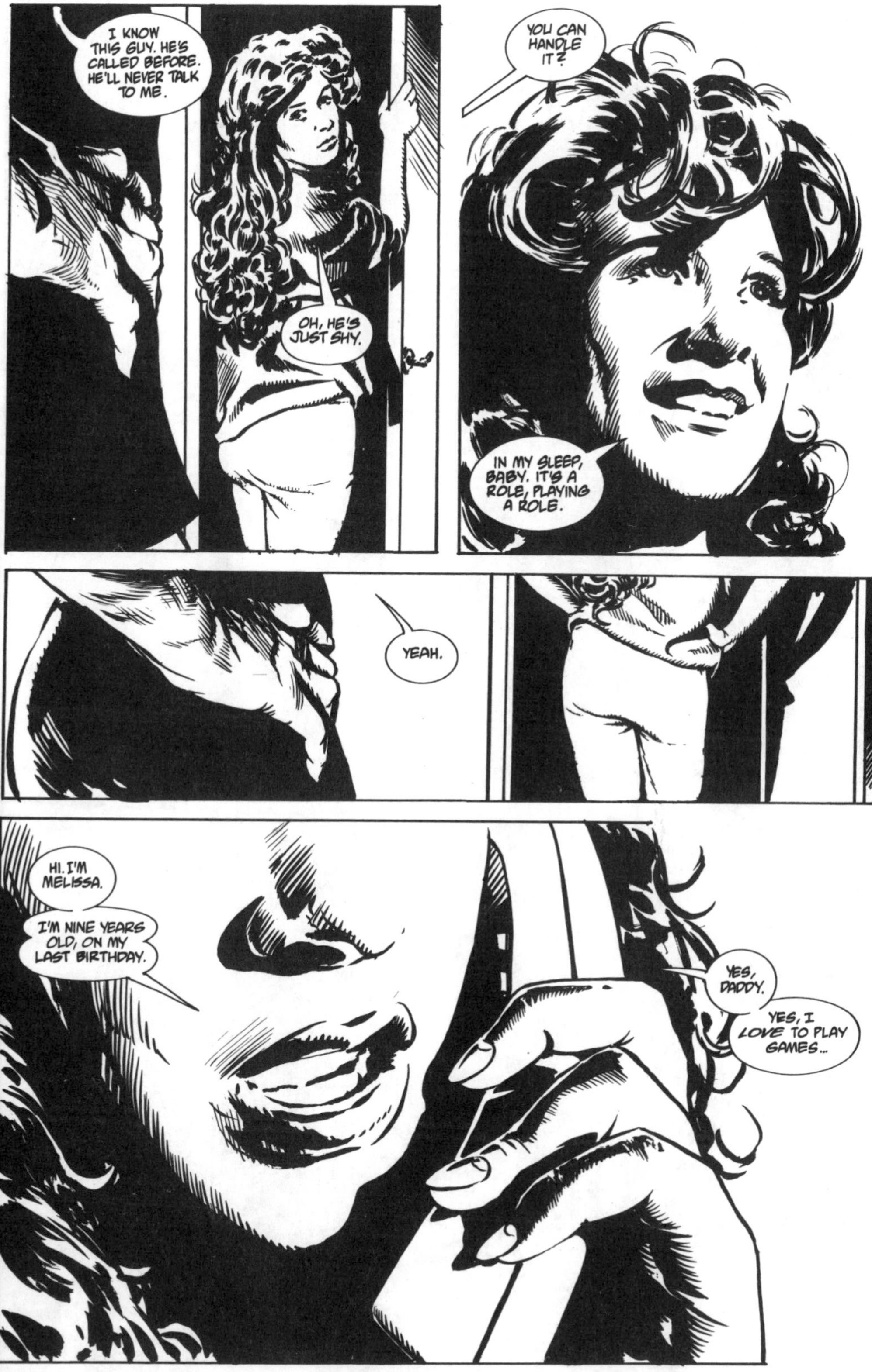
I KNOW THIS GUY. HE'S CALLED BEFORE. HE'LL NEVER TALK TO ME.
OH, HE'S JUST SHY.
YOU CAN HANDLE IT?
IN MY SLEEP, BABY. IT'S A ROLE, PLAYING A ROLE.
YEAH.
HI. I'M MELISSA.
I'M NINE YEARS OLD, ON MY LAST BIRTHDAY.
YES, DADDY.
YES, I *LOVE* TO PLAY GAMES...

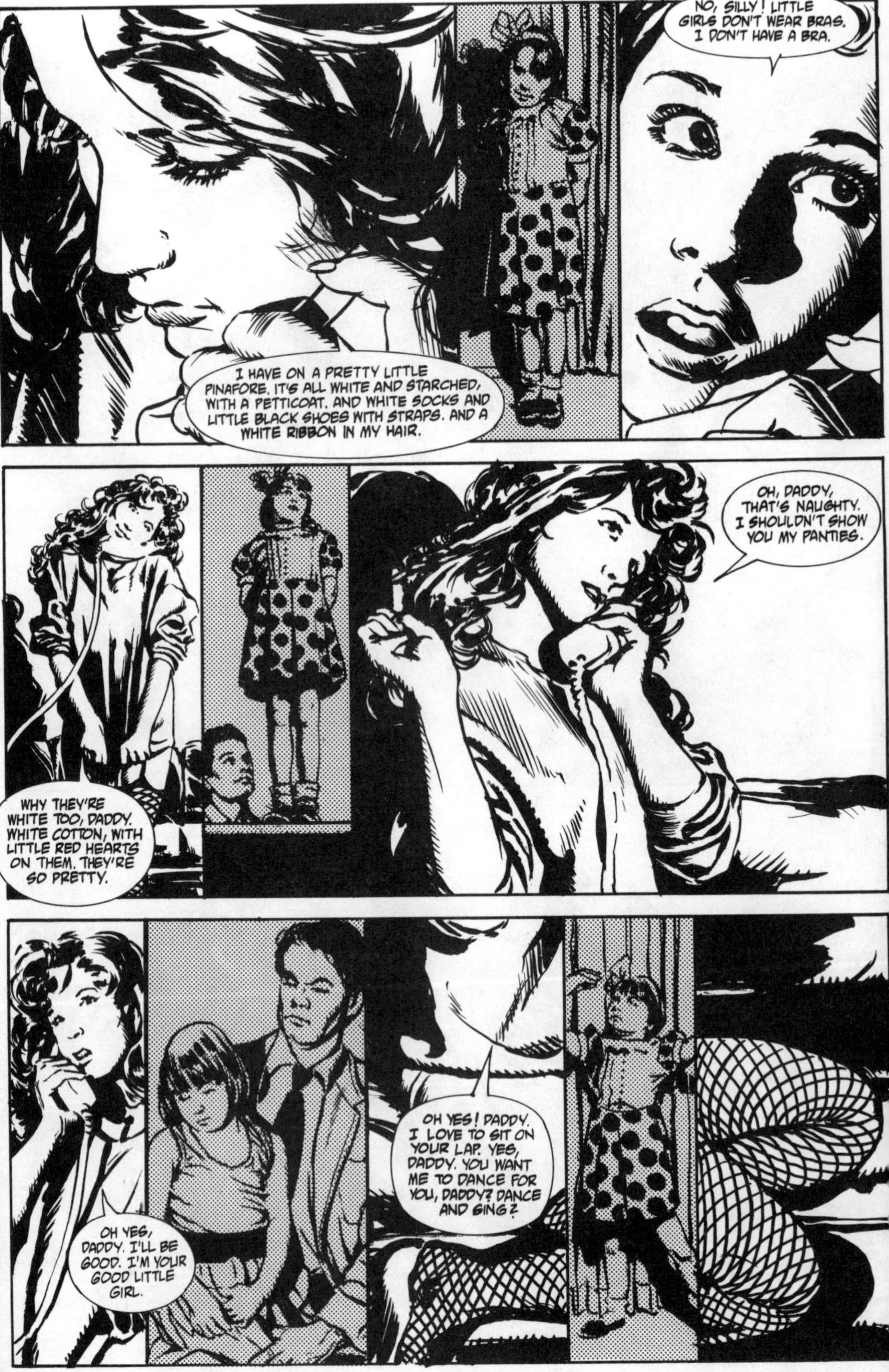
I HAVE ON A PRETTY LITTLE PINAFORE. IT'S ALL WHITE AND STARCHED, WITH A PETTICOAT. AND WHITE SOCKS AND LITTLE BLACK SHOES WITH STRAPS. AND A WHITE RIBBON IN MY HAIR.
NO, SILLY! LITTLE GIRLS DON'T WEAR BRAS. I DON'T HAVE A BRA.
OH, DADDY, THAT'S NAUGHTY. I SHOULDN'T SHOW YOU MY PANTIES.
WHY THEY'RE WHITE TOO, DADDY. WHITE COTTON, WITH LITTLE RED HEARTS ON THEM. THEY'RE SO PRETTY.
OH YES, DADDY. I'LL BE GOOD. I'M YOUR GOOD LITTLE GIRL.
OH YES! DADDY. I LOVE TO SIT ON YOUR LAP. YES, DADDY. YOU WANT ME TO DANCE FOR YOU, DADDY? DANCE AND SING?

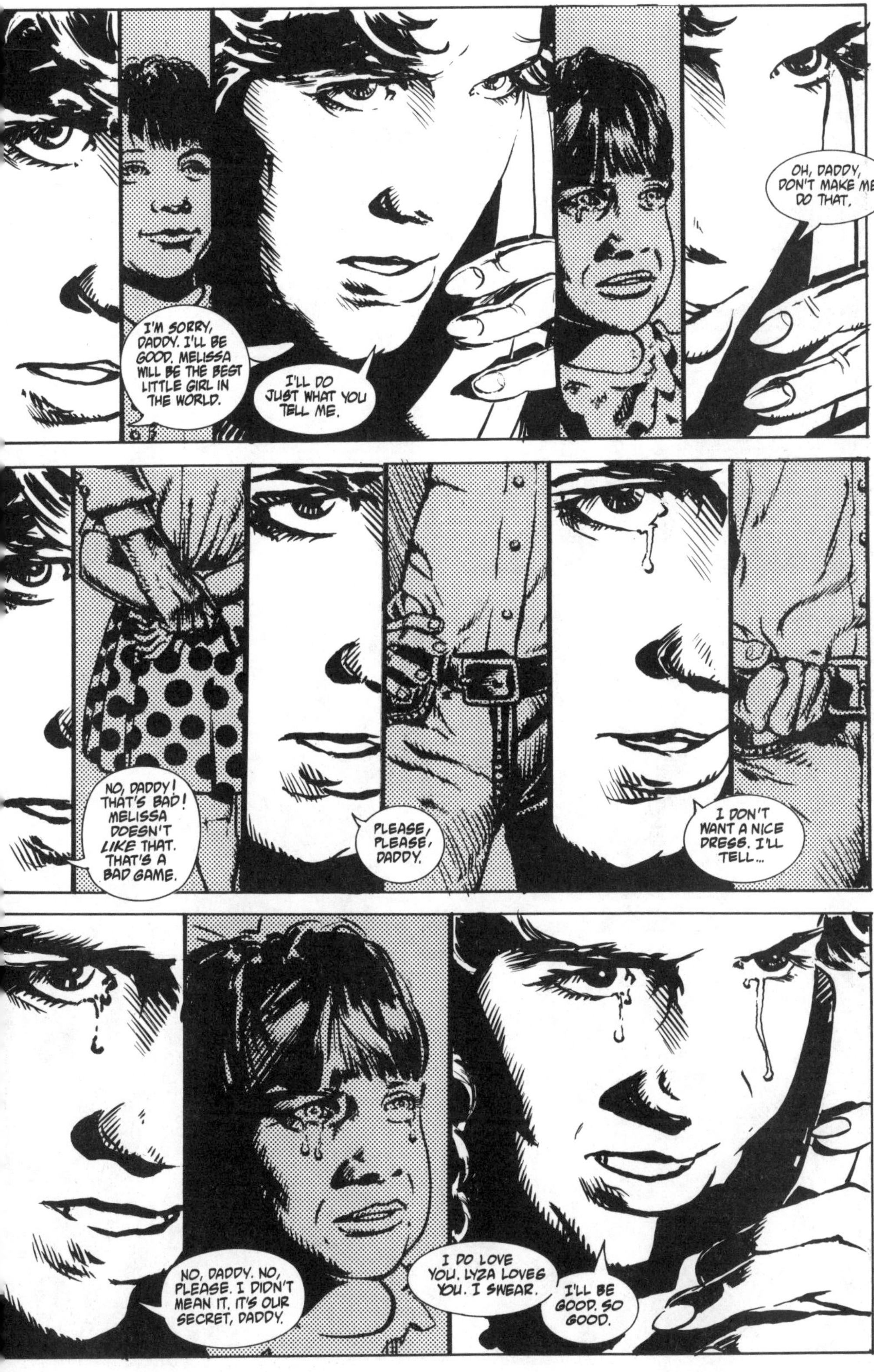

I'M SORRY, DADDY. I'LL BE GOOD. MELISSA WILL BE THE BEST LITTLE GIRL IN THE WORLD.
I'LL DO JUST WHAT YOU TELL ME.
OH, DADDY, DON'T MAKE ME DO THAT.
NO, DADDY! THAT'S BAD! MELISSA DOESN'T LIKE THAT. THAT'S A BAD GAME.
PLEASE, PLEASE, DADDY.
I DON'T WANT A NICE DRESS. I'LL TELL...
NO, DADDY. NO, PLEASE. I DIDN'T MEAN IT. IT'S OUR SECRET, DADDY.
I DO LOVE YOU. LYZA LOVES YOU. I SWEAR.
I'LL BE GOOD. SO GOOD.

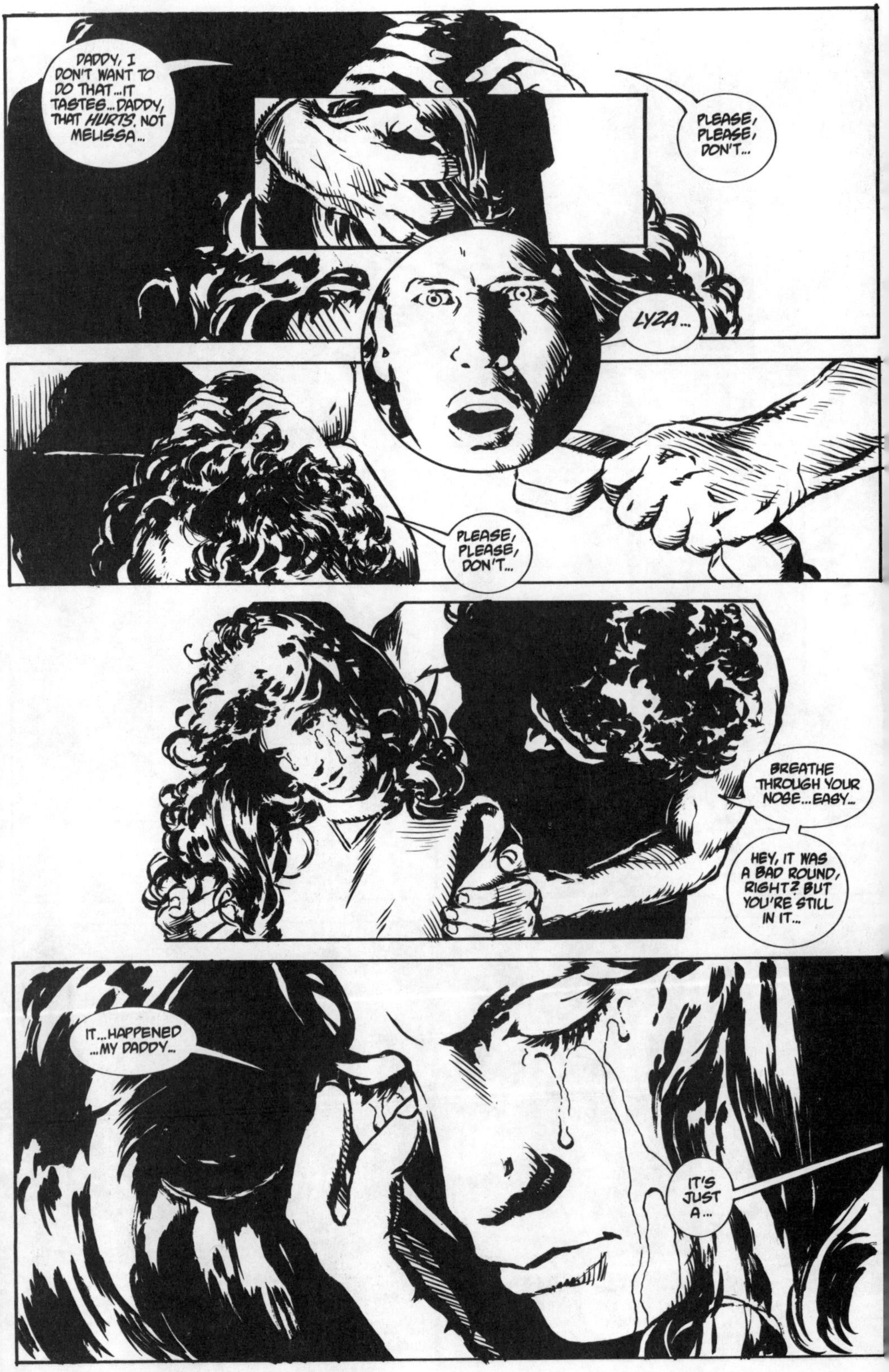
DADDY, I DON'T WANT TO DO THAT...IT TASTES...DADDY, THAT *HURTS*. NOT MELISSA...
PLEASE, PLEASE, DON'T...
LYZA...
PLEASE, PLEASE, DON'T...
BREATHE THROUGH YOUR NOSE...EASY...
HEY, IT WAS A BAD ROUND, RIGHT? BUT YOU'RE STILL IN IT...
IT...HAPPENED ...MY DADDY...
IT'S JUST A...

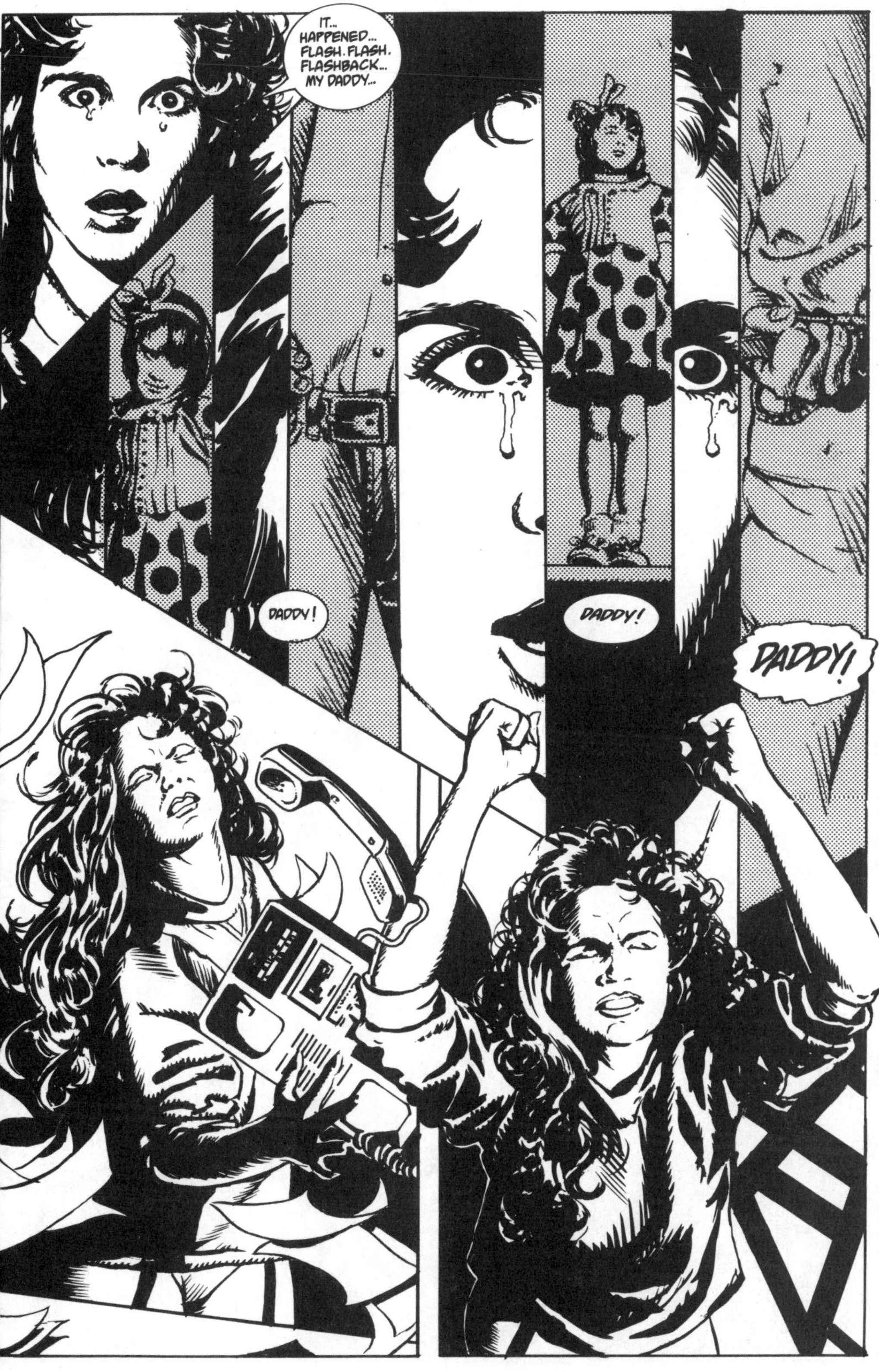

IT.. HAPPENED... FLASH. FLASH. FLASHBACK... MY DADDY...
DADDY!
DADDY!
DADDY!

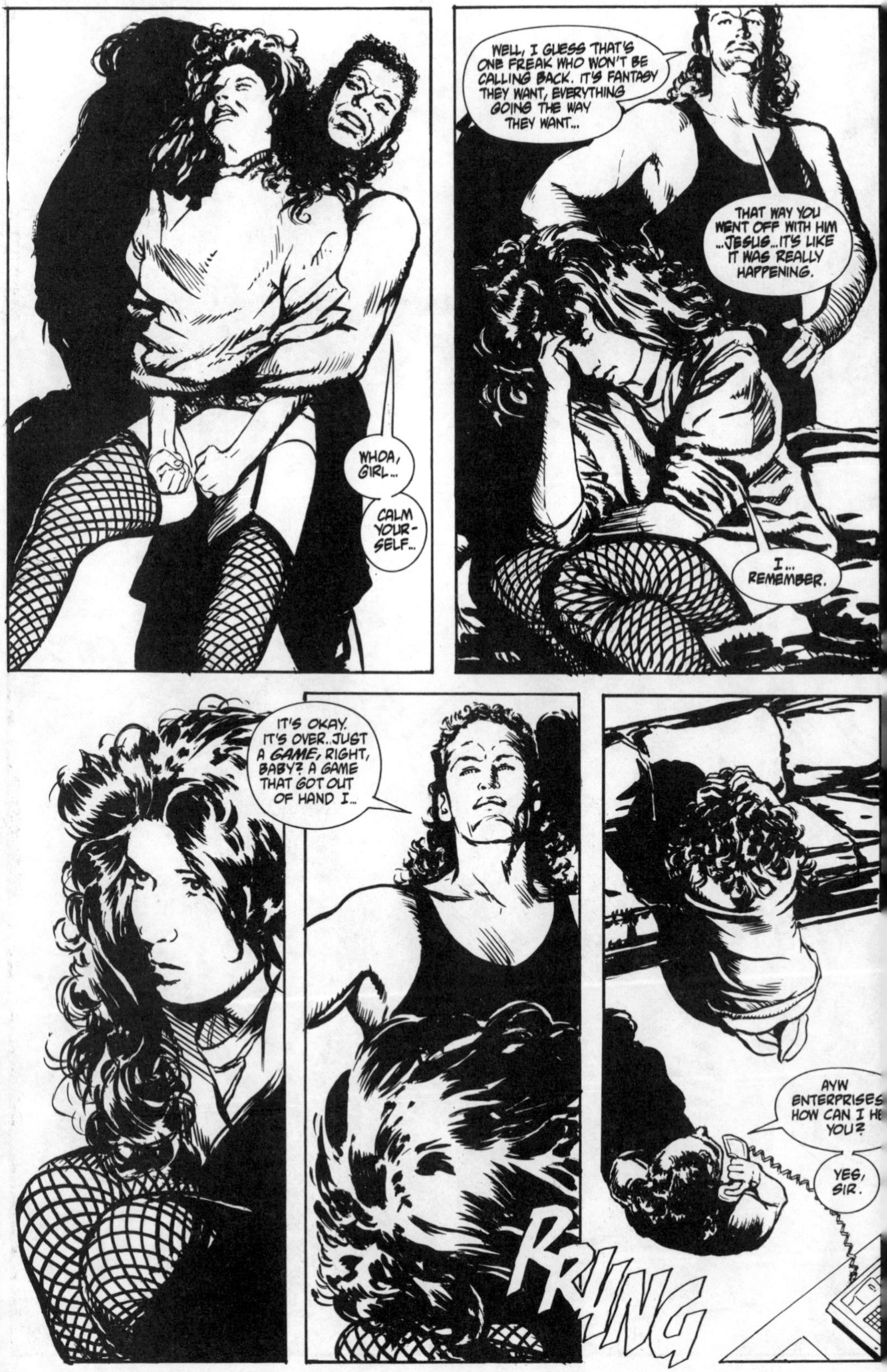
WHOA, GIRL...
CALM YOURSELF...
WELL, I GUESS THAT'S ONE FREAK WHO WON'T BE CALLING BACK. IT'S FANTASY THEY WANT, EVERYTHING GOING THE WAY THEY WANT...
THAT WAY YOU WENT OFF WITH HIM ...JESUS...IT'S LIKE IT WAS REALLY HAPPENING.
I... REMEMBER.
IT'S OKAY. IT'S OVER..JUST A *GAME*, RIGHT, BABY? A GAME THAT GOT OUT OF HAND I...
RRING
AYW ENTERPRISES HOW CAN I HE YOU?
YES, SIR.

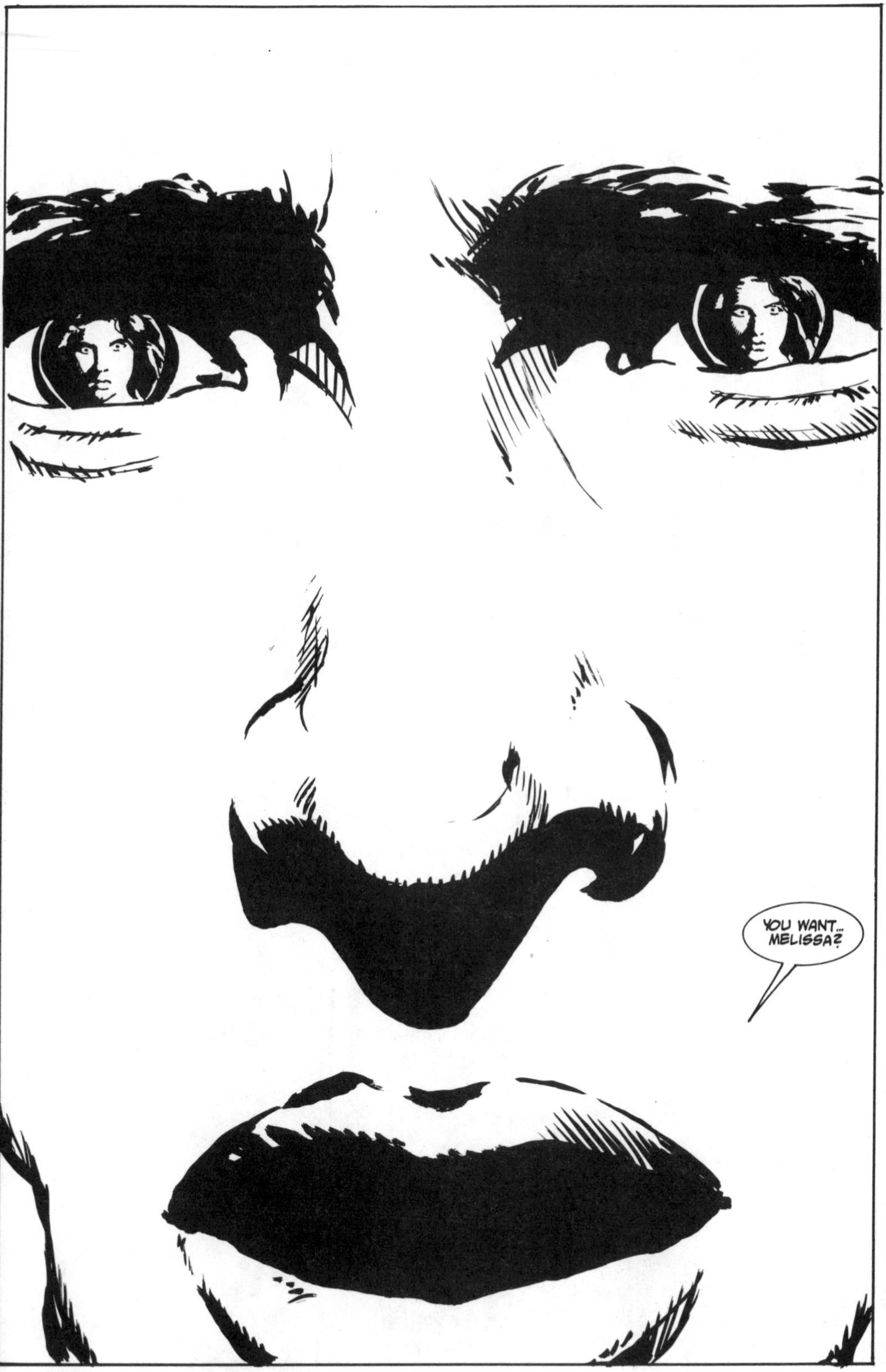
YOU WANT...
MELISSA?

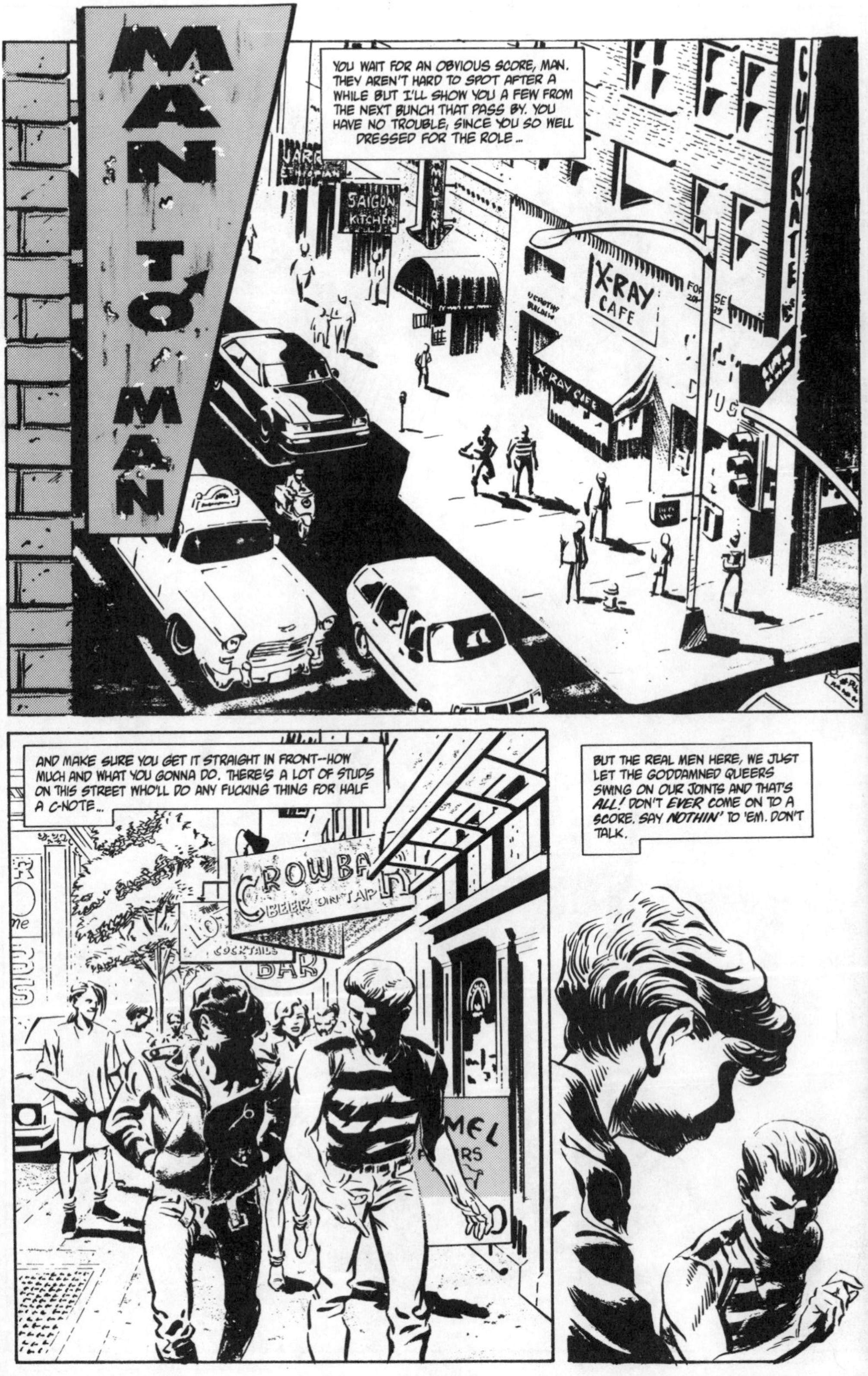
MAN TO MAN
YOU WAIT FOR AN OBVIOUS SCORE, MAN. THEY AREN'T HARD TO SPOT AFTER A WHILE BUT I'LL SHOW YOU A FEW FROM THE NEXT BUNCH THAT PASS BY. YOU HAVE NO TROUBLE, SINCE YOU SO WELL DRESSED FOR THE ROLE...
SAIGON KITCHEN
X-RAY CAFE
CUT RATE
AND MAKE SURE YOU GET IT STRAIGHT IN FRONT--HOW MUCH AND WHAT YOU GONNA DO. THERE'S A LOT OF STUDS ON THIS STREET WHO'LL DO ANY FUCKING THING FOR HALF A C-NOTE...
BEER ON TAP
COCKTAILS
BAR
BUT THE REAL MEN HERE, WE JUST LET THE GODDAMNED QUEERS SWING ON OUR JOINTS AND THAT'S ALL! DON'T EVER COME ON TO A SCORE. SAY NOTHIN' TO 'EM. DON'T TALK.

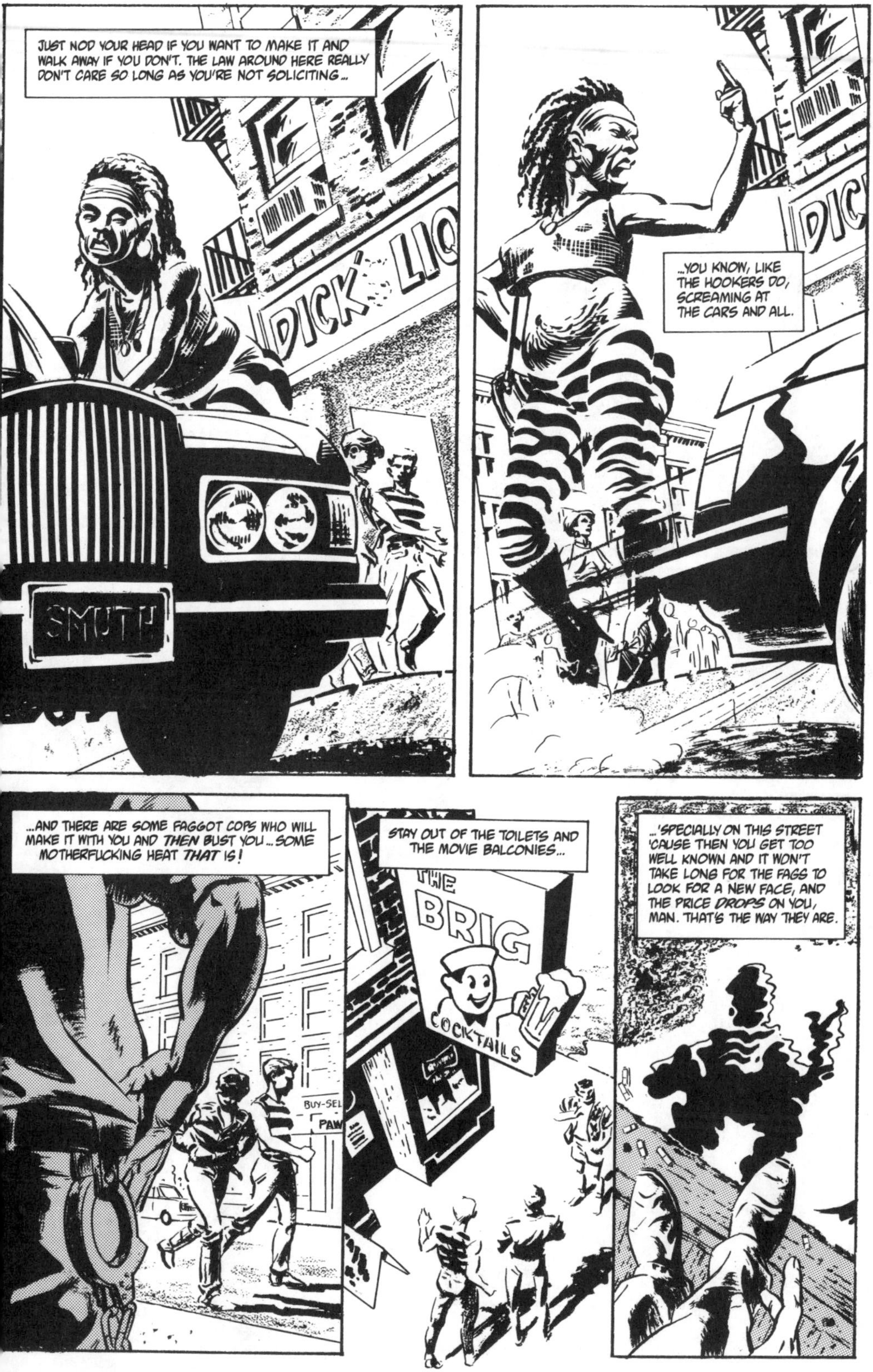
JUST NOD YOUR HEAD IF YOU WANT TO MAKE IT AND WALK AWAY IF YOU DON'T. THE LAW AROUND HERE REALLY DON'T CARE SO LONG AS YOU'RE NOT SOLICITING...
DICK'S LIQ
SMUTH
...YOU KNOW, LIKE THE HOOKERS DO, SCREAMING AT THE CARS AND ALL.
DIC
...AND THERE ARE SOME FAGGOT COPS WHO WILL MAKE IT WITH YOU AND *THEN* BUST YOU... SOME MOTHERFUCKING HEAT *THAT* IS!
STAY OUT OF THE TOILETS AND THE MOVIE BALCONIES...
THE BRIG
COCKTAILS
BUY-SEL
PAW
...'SPECIALLY ON THIS STREET 'CAUSE THEN YOU GET TOO WELL KNOWN AND IT WON'T TAKE LONG FOR THE FAGS TO LOOK FOR A NEW FACE, AND THE PRICE *DROPS* ON YOU, MAN. THAT'S THE WAY THEY ARE.

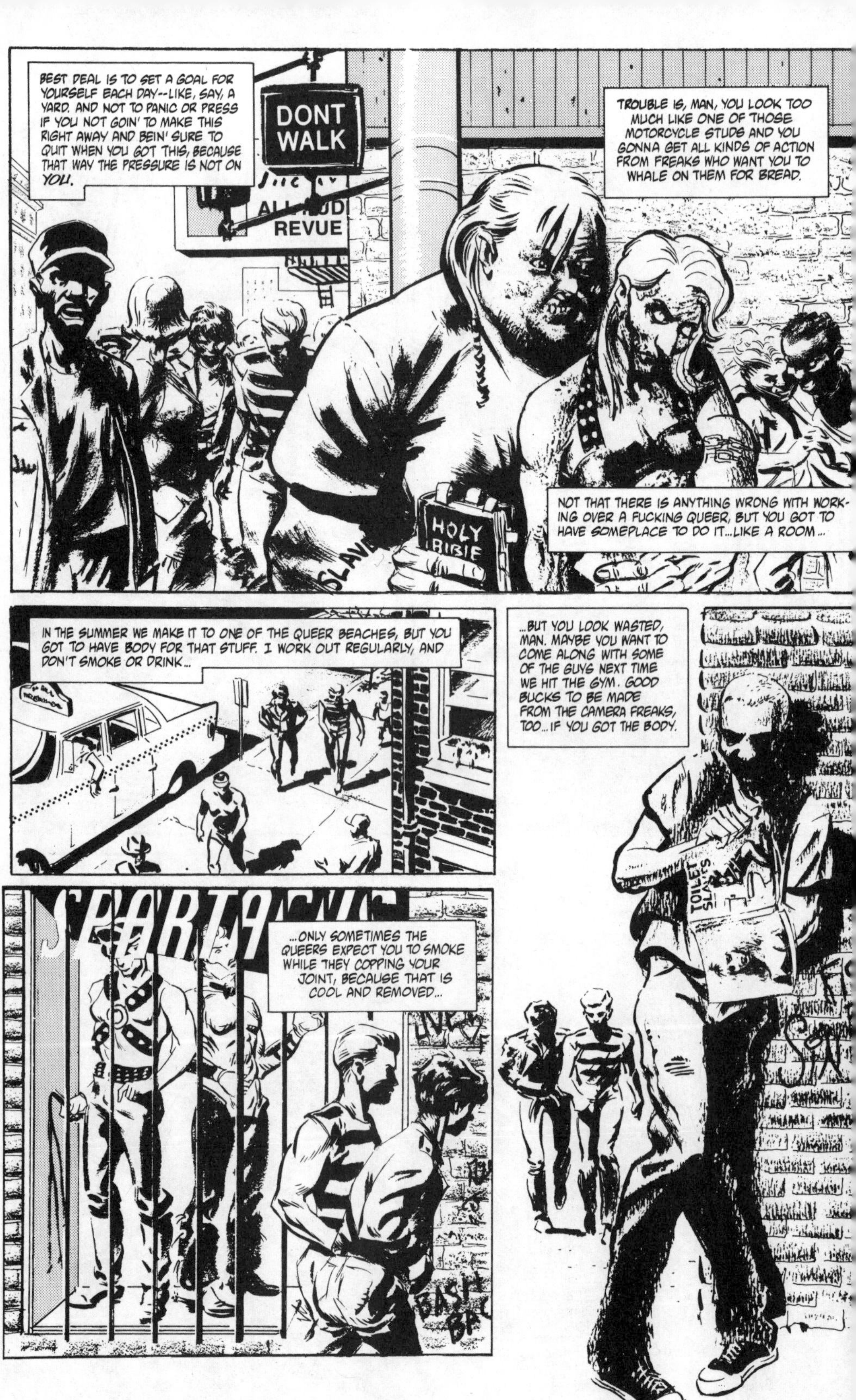
BEST DEAL IS TO SET A GOAL FOR YOURSELF EACH DAY--LIKE, SAY, A YARD. AND NOT TO PANIC OR PRESS IF YOU NOT GOIN' TO MAKE THIS RIGHT AWAY AND BEIN' SURE TO QUIT WHEN YOU GOT THIS, BECAUSE THAT WAY THE PRESSURE IS NOT ON YOU.
DONT WALK
REVUE
TROUBLE IS, MAN, YOU LOOK TOO MUCH LIKE ONE OF THOSE MOTORCYCLE STUDS AND YOU GONNA GET ALL KINDS OF ACTION FROM FREAKS WHO WANT YOU TO WHALE ON THEM FOR BREAD.
HOLY BIBLE
NOT THAT THERE IS ANYTHING WRONG WITH WORKING OVER A FUCKING QUEER, BUT YOU GOT TO HAVE SOMEPLACE TO DO IT...LIKE A ROOM...
IN THE SUMMER WE MAKE IT TO ONE OF THE QUEER BEACHES, BUT YOU GOT TO HAVE BODY FOR THAT STUFF. I WORK OUT REGULARLY, AND DON'T SMOKE OR DRINK...
...BUT YOU LOOK WASTED, MAN. MAYBE YOU WANT TO COME ALONG WITH SOME OF THE GUYS NEXT TIME WE HIT THE GYM. GOOD BUCKS TO BE MADE FROM THE CAMERA FREAKS, TOO...IF YOU GOT THE BODY.
...ONLY SOMETIMES THE QUEERS EXPECT YOU TO SMOKE WHILE THEY COPPING YOUR JOINT, BECAUSE THAT IS COOL AND REMOVED...
TOILET SLAVES